Frommer's®

ICELAND

3rd Edition

P9-CQB-807

By Nicholas Gill

FrommerMedia LLC

Previous page: Icelandic horses.
This page: Lupine flowers on the Stokksnes headland.

FROMMER'S STAR RATINGS SYSTEM

Every hotel, restaurant, and attraction listed in this guide has been ranked for quality and value. Here's what the stars mean:

★	Recommended
★★	Highly Recommended
★★★	A must! Don't miss!

AN IMPORTANT NOTE

The world is a dynamic place. Hotels change ownership, restaurants hike their prices, museums alter their opening hours, and buses and trains change their routings. And all of this can occur in the several months after our authors have visited, inspected, and written about these hotels, restaurants, museums, and transportation services. Though we have made valiant efforts to keep all our information fresh and up-to-date, some few changes can inevitably occur in the periods before a revised edition of this guidebook is published. So please bear with us if a tiny number of the details in this book have changed. Please also note that we have no responsibility or liability for any inaccuracy or errors or omissions, or for inconvenience, loss, damage, or expenses suffered by anyone as a result of assertions in this guide.

CONTENTS

Stykkishólmur

A LOOK AT ICELAND

One of the last bastions of raw beauty on Earth, Iceland is a surreal place to be. In a land that seems magnificently stark and unyielding, everything is mutable, from the sultry geothermal pools bubbling up from the earth's interior to the mystical, shape-shifting skies. It's a singular ecosytem of mossy tundra, jagged mountains, glacial valleys, and icy sea, where storybook animals like puffins, reindeer, and whales leap out of the monochromatic tableau. Iceland was a Viking settlement, and its Nordic bonafides are evident in its architecture, food, and bloodlines. For adventurers, Iceland has glaciers to hike, sea cliffs to mount, and ancient lava tubes to explore. Natural geothermal pools are the social hot spots, literally—that the steamy soaks often are surrounded by stunning icy landscapes only adds to the wonder of being there. In Iceland you can clamber over volcanic gorges, sail among icebergs, and feel the hot whisper of the fires down below in a geothermal spring. Afterward, head indoors to a cozy fire, sip Icelandic craft beers, and imagine yourself a hero in an ancient Icelandic saga, home at last.

Natural hot springs known as Grjótagjá in North Iceland near Myvatn Lake. See p. 201.

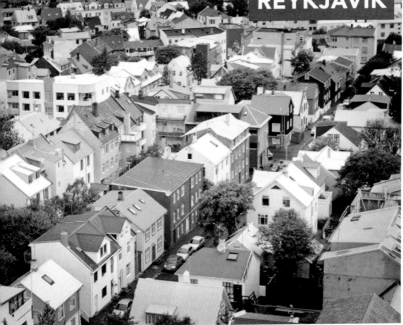

The colorful rooftops of Reykjavík.

Visible from everywhere in the city, the magnificent Lutheran church, Hallgrímskirkja, is Iceland's tallest, photographed here against a night sky aglow with Northern Lights. See p. 89.

The distinctive orange beaks, tuxedoed bodies, and clown eyes make Atlantic puffins irresistible photo ops. Most puffins breed in Iceland and are known to mate for life.

A guide in period dress in the open-air Árbær Museum, 15 minutes east of Reykjavík, demonstrates how housework was done in a traditional farmhouse kitchen in 19th-century Iceland. See p. 61.

The glittering interior of the Harpa concert hall, an architectural landmark built in 2011 and boasting state-of-the-art acoustics and a distinctive honeycomb glass ceiling. See p. 54.

New Icelandic cuisine on a plate: This dill-bilberry cream and dulse sorbet, topped with whey-marinated dulse, is from Reykjavík's innovative Dill restaurant. See p. 76.

The lava-tube cave, Raufarhólshellir, about 30 miles southeast of Reykjavík, is essentially an empty riverbed of lava formed some 3,700 years ago. See p. 117.

NORTH ICELAND

Explorer on an Icelandic tour.

Boiling mudpot in a geothermal area around Hverir.

Colorful Northern Lights, *aurora borealis*, shimmering above the Arctic Henge, a modern sundial structure inspired by Stonehenge. See p. 221.

A woman pauses before the crater of Hverfell Volcano near Mývatn Lake. See p. 204.

The wooden Húsavíkurkirkja church, circa 1907, the most famous landmark in Húsavík. See p. 212.

Two troll "dolls" with a polar bear. Trolls are legendary figures in Iceland mythology.

Mývatn Lake, a popular attraction in the geo-thermal valley of Leirhnjúkur. See p. 202.

The sparse sub-Arctic landscape along Road 87, near Húsavík.

Dogsledding on frozen Mývatn Lake in early spring.

Family of blue morph Arctic fox cubs playing near Hornstrandir.

Visitors admiring the Reykholt geyser eruption in 2010.

Set back against the sea cliffs in Arnarstapi, this stone troll sculpture represents Bárður Snæfellsás, a half-man, half-giant guardian spirit from the Icelandic sagas. See p. 40.

A young girl swimming in a thermal pool against the background of icy sea.

The picturesque harbor of Stykkishólmur. See p. 139.

The popular Hraunfossar waterfall in winter. See p. 125.

The rocky fjords of Stykkishólmur at sunset. See p. 139.

A traditional hut in the Westfjords. Because of the scarcity of wood, early Iceland settlers built dwellings out of sod and turf. Few remain today.

SOUTH ICELAND

Small, hardy, and good-natured, Icelandic horses are ideal for horseback-rider beginners.

Sunrise on Seljalandfoss waterfall on the Seljalandsa river. See p. 246.

A tour group takes a walk on a glacier in Skaftafell National Park. See p. 257.

A U.S. Navy DC-3 airplane crashed on the Sólheimasandur beach in 1973 (the crew survived), and since then the abandoned wreck has become a tourist attraction.

Vik Rock formation against night sky peppered with stars. See p. 248.

Vikurkirkja Church in Vík í Mýrdal village, with flowers blooming in foreground. See p. 250.

Couple viewing the panorama at Landmannal-
auger on the Laugavegurinn Trail, the famous
trek to Thorsmork, Skógar. See p. 237.

The Gljúfurárfoss Falls, hidden in an enclosed
canyon. See p. 246.

Two hikers amid the sweeping volcanic landscape of Lakagígar, the Laki craters. See p. 256.

THE BEST OF ICELAND

S traddling the rift between the Eurasian and North American continental plates, Iceland's one-of-a-kind geography leaves little to the imagination. In summer the country is moss-covered lava fields, steep rocky mountainsides dotted with free-roaming sheep, pockets of green forest in an otherwise treeless expanse, and bright nights of song and dance in the crisp polar air. By winter, shimmering lights dart across the sky like restless ghosts, people bathe in hot springs with snow melting in the rising steam, and fairy lights glow in all the windows.

This is the essence of Iceland: endless variations of magnificent scenery and adventure. Iceland's astonishing beauty often has an austere, primitive, even surreal cast that arouses reverence, wonderment, mystery, and awe. Lasting impressions could include a lone tuft of blue wildflowers against a bleak desert moonscape or a fantastical promenade of icebergs calved into a lake from a magisterial glacier.

Iceland's people are freedom-loving, egalitarian, self-reliant, and worldly. The country established a parliamentary democracy more than a millennium ago, and today its people write, publish, and read more books per capita than any other people on earth. Iceland remains one of the world's best countries to live in, based on life expectancy, education levels, medical care, income, and other U.N. criteria. **Reykjavík** has become one of the world's most fashionable urban hot spots.

For such a small place, Iceland has made more than its fair share of global news. In 2008, the booming economy overstretched itself wildly and went into meltdown, leading to the collapse of the country's three main banks and leaving the nation with a massive debt load. It has since bounced back, and effects on the tourist industry have been minimal—one of the main reasons being a better exchange rate for most tourists. Then there was the 2010 volcanic eruption in South Iceland, which produced an ash cloud big enough to ground planes across Europe, divert flights from North America, and irrevocably change the surrounding landscape. Yet even at the height of the eruption, it was business as usual in most places across Iceland. When some areas near the volcano became temporarily inaccessible,

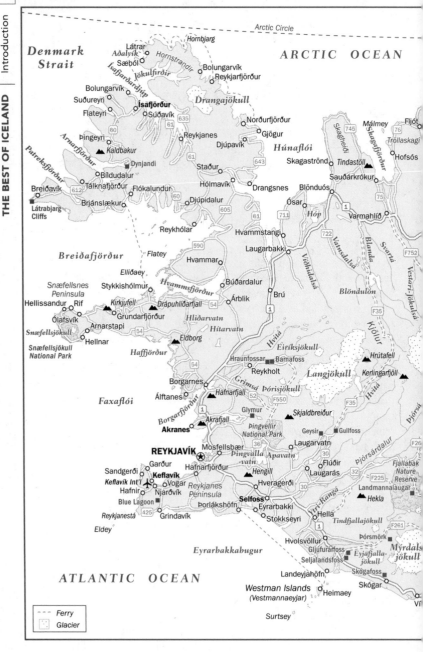

tourists were presented with once-in-a-lifetime alternatives, such as lava sightseeing by helicopter.

Throughout this book, we inform you about Iceland's top places to visit, dine, and sleep, and in this chapter, we give you a taste of the very best. Some are classics, such as the Blue Lagoon, while others are less well-known. We hope you'll benefit from the inside information—and that you'll go see for yourself and create your own list of "bests."

ICELAND'S best AUTHENTIC EXPERIENCES

o **Getting a Massage at the Blue Lagoon:** While you float on your back in womblike weightlessness, enveloped between a blanket and a floating mat, the masseuse's hands work their magic. Afterward, you can resume the central activity at this spa: bathing in an opaque, blue-green lagoon in the middle of a jet-black lava field and smearing white silica mud all over yourself. If you want to take it to the next level, the more exclusive **Retreat Spa** is tucked away in a private section of the lagoon. See p. 104.

o **Gazing at the Northern Lights from a Hot Tub:** You'll have to visit off-peak to be treated to this jaw-droppingly magic display of light dancing across the sky, seen only on clear, cold nights and best enjoyed from the luxurious warmth and comfort of one of Iceland's countless hot tubs. See p. 63.

o **Soak in a Local Hot Pot:** While no one doubts the awesomeness of the Blue Lagoon or the Mývatn Nature Baths, it's unlikely you will see an Icelander at either. They're getting their fix at simple local pools and hot pots, which serve as the social hub of nearly every community in the country, even on the beachfront in tiny Krossnes in the north of the Westfjords. See **Fosshotel Reykholt,** p. 127.

o **See a Performance at Harpa:** This remarkable, glass-covered concert hall and conference center on Reykjavík's waterfront is one of the world's great cultural spaces. It's home to the Icelandic Opera and the Iceland Symphony Orchestra, but don't be surprised if a rock concert or jazz show fills the storied halls. See p. 54.

o **Whale-Watching:** Whether you sail from the whale-watching homeland of Húsavík, nearby Dalvík, or even right from Reykjavík, your chances of seeing at least some of the more than 20 species of cetaceans that visit Icelandic waters are quite good. Depending on the time of year, you might even spot puffins, seals, and other marine species on the way. See p. 65.

ICELAND'S best HOTELS

o **Hótel Djúpavík** (Strandir Coast; www.djupavik.com; ✆ **451-4037**): Beautifully situated on the wild and remote Strandir Coast, this former boardinghouse for seasonal herring workers is so warmly and authentically connected to its past that any luxury deficits are irrelevant. See p. 163.

- **The Retreat** (Grindavík; www.bluelagoon.com; ✆ **420-8800**): Unlike the rest of the Blue Lagoon, the Retreat is ultra-exclusive. Hidden behind high lava walls from the rest of the Blue Lagoon is a world-class spa, a private lagoon section, and topnotch dining. See p. 104.
- **101 Hótel** (Reykjavík; www.101hotel.is; ✆ **580-0101**): This chic design hotel has a lock on Iceland's fashion set. The place is cool to the bone, right down to the zebra-striped lounge chairs and the contemporary art collection lining the halls. See p. 67.
- **Hótel Egilsen** (Stykkishólmur; www.egilsen.is; ✆ **554-7700**): This beautifully restored, circa-1867 red house is the most charming building in one of Iceland's most charming harbors. Small and intimate, it's a place to mingle with guests over a glass of wine and cookies in the lounge. See p. 142.
- **Hótel Búðir** (Snæfellsnes Peninsula; www.budir.is; ✆ **435-6700**): This country-hip boutique pad with an estimable restaurant is surrounded by nothing but ocean, broad sandbanks, sprawling lava, stone ruins of fishermen's huts, and a restored 19th-century church, with Snæfellsjökull glacier loftily presiding over the scene. See p. 137.
- **Hótel Ranga** (Hella; www.hotelranga.is; ✆ **487-5700**): Awake to a Northern Lights alert from South Iceland's premier resort, a posh, wood-lined lodge with quirky themed suites. Relax in the hot pots fronting one of the country's great trout rivers. See p. 243.
- **Hótel Tindastóll** (Sauðárkrókur; www.hoteltindastoll.com; ✆ **453-5002**): Each large, handsome room in this lovingly restored 1884 Norwegian kit home is an ideal synthesis of luxury and provincial charm. The natural-stone hot tub is the finishing touch. See p. 182.
- **ION Luxury Adventure Hotel** (Selfoss; www.ioniceland.is; ✆ **482-3415**): Iceland's first cushy design hotel to set up in a remote area, the ION has a surprising past as an inn for workers at a nearby geothermal plant. Jutting out on pillars off the slopes of Mount Hengill, it's home to a spa, a modern Icelandic restaurant, and enough edgy artwork to fill a museum. See p. 115.
- **Kex Hostel** (Reykjavík; www.kexhostel.is; ✆ **561-6060**): Housed in an old biscuit factory just off the downtown waterfront, this hostel is as good as they come. From the barber's chair near the lobby and jazz nights in the restaurant to found-object decorations and a heated outdoor patio, this is roughing it without the roughing part. See p. 73.

ICELAND'S best RESTAURANTS

- **Dill** (Reykjavík; ✆ **552-1522**): With elegant tasting menus that explore native products and techniques, Iceland's first Michelin-starred restaurant has taken modern Icelandic cuisine to levels far beyond anything the country has ever seen. See p. 76.
- **Fjöruborðið** (Stokkseyri; ✆ **483-1550**): Icelanders drive long distances—and sometimes come by helicopter from Reykjavík—to butter their bibs at this famed lobster house on Iceland's southwestern coast. See p. 120.

o **Humarhöfnin** (Höfn; ✆ **478-1200**): With Höfn the lobster capital of Iceland, it's no surprise that this restaurant's name translates to "lobster harbor." The special, of course, is the Icelandic lobster (actually a langoustine), and it's served every which way you can imagine. See p. 270.

o **Narfeyrarstofa** (Stykkishólmur; ✆ **438-1119**): Just off the Stykkish harbor, this old-fashioned dining room serves some of Iceland's best seafood. The blue mussels, harvested just offshore, are the specialty, though you won't go wrong with the lamb, either. See p. 143.

o **Moss Restaurant** (Grindavík; ✆ **420-8700**): The luxe tasting menus change with the seasons at this refined restaurant tucked away in a corner of the Blue Lagoon's Retreat hotel. Check out the wine cellar, several floors below and carved out of lava. See p. 104.

o **Sægreifinn** (Reykjavík; ✆ **553-1500**): Often called simply "the lobster soup place," Reykjavík's ultimate low-budget dining experience offers a spicy, creamy lobster soup along with other local seafood treats in a tiny seafront warehouse. See p. 80.

o **Slippurinn** (Vestmannaeyjabær; ✆ **481-1515**): The Westman Islands are probably the last place you would expect to find one of the country's best restaurants, but believe it. The chef of this family-run operation incorporates native wild herbs into dishes and cocktails, and he experiments with all sorts of traditional techniques like salting, pickling, and smoking. See p. 232.

o **Tjöruhúsið** (Ísafjörður; ✆ **456-4419**): This no-nonsense Westfjords restaurant serves up generous portions of amazingly fresh and tasty pan-fried fish without the slightest fuss. Ask the cook if the fish is frozen, and you'll get a look of utter horror. See p. 158.

o **Vogafjós Cowshed Cafe** (Lake Mývatn; ✆ **464-4303**): Looking directly into the milking shed, this restaurant redefines the term "farm to table." Sample the lamb, raised right outside, or the Arctic char, smoked out back. See p. 209.

ICELAND'S best OUTDOOR EXPERIENCES

o **Askja:** This staggering whorl of volcanic mountains, circling an 8km-wide (5-mile) bowl formed by collapsed magma chambers, is one of Earth's grandest pockmarks and the most sought-out destination in Iceland's desolate interior. Visitors can swim in a warm, opaque blue-green pond at the bottom of a steep crater—a real "if my friends could see me now" moment. See p. 308.

o **Fjaðrárgljúfur:** Iceland has several dramatic gorges, but this one's spiky crags and vertiginous ledges virtually summon the mystics and landscape painters. Fjaðrárgljúfur is close to the Ring Road in South Iceland, and the trail along the rim is a breeze. See p. 255.

o **Hverfell:** Of all the monuments to Iceland's volcanism, this tephra explosion crater near Mývatn is the most monolithic. A jet-black bowl of humbling proportions, it has a stark, elemental authority. See p. 204.

o **Laki Craters:** This monstrous row of more than a hundred craters, lined up along a 25km (16-mile) fissure, is scar tissue from the most catastrophic volcanic eruption in Iceland's history. Velvety coatings of gray-green moss soften Laki's terrible, bleak beauty. See p. 254.

o **Langjökull Glacier:** Take a modified glacier vehicle with giant tires into the ice caves of Langjökull, Iceland's second largest glacier. Strap on crampons and hike through the manmade caves and admire the different shades of ice and formations. There's even a small chapel built within the ice if marriage is on the table! See p. 126.

o **Látrabjarg:** These colossal sea cliffs mark the dizzying, dramatic outer limit of Europe's westernmost reach. Fourteen kilometers (8.7 miles) long and up to 441m (1,447 ft.) high, this is one of the world's most densely populated bird colonies. The sheer volume of birds is unbelievable, and the puffins are particularly willing to have their picture taken. See p. 146.

o **Leirhnjúkur:** In a country with no shortage of primordial, surreal landscapes, this lava field in the Krafla caldera of northeast Iceland out-weirds them all. An easy trail wends its way among steaming clefts, each revealing a prismatic netherworld of mosses and minerals. See p. 206.

ICELAND'S best WATERFALLS

o **Dettifoss:** Europe's mightiest waterfall, abruptly marking the southern limit of northeast Iceland's Jökulsárgljúfur Canyon, is a massive curtain of milky-gray glacial water thundering over a 44m (144-ft.) precipice. To stand next to it is as hypnotic as it is bone-rattling. See p. 218.

o **Dynjandi:** As you approach the six waterfalls of Dynjandi in the Westfjords, it seems as if a white blanket has been draped across steep giant steps leading up the rocky cliff. The main waterfall, Fjallfoss, tumbles almost 100m (328 ft.), but its majesty also lies in its breadth: 60m (197 ft.) at the bottom, 30m (98 ft.) at the top. It's an easy walk up to the base of the main falls, and worth it for the view of the fjord and the boom of the water. See p. 151.

o **Glymur:** Iceland's tallest waterfall is nimble and graceful: Streamlets descend like ribbons of a maypole into a fathomless canyon mantled in bird nests and lush mosses. The hike there is somewhat treacherous, but those who brave it are rewarded with enchanting scenery—and possibly total solitude—all within easy range of Reykjavík. See p. 96.

o **Gullfoss:** Here, the Hvitá River hurtles over a low tier, turns 90 degrees, plunges into a cloud of spray, and shimmies offstage through a picturesque gorge. This astounding waterfall is the climax to the "Golden Circle," Iceland's most popular day tour from the capital. See p. 96.

o **Svartifoss:** In southeast Iceland's Skaftafell area, these falls provide a dramatic white contrast to the surrounding dark columnar basalt gorge. The water begins its descent at a rocky overhang, making it easy to walk behind the falling water below, though raincoats are still recommended. See p. 259.

THE best OF SECRET ICELAND

o **Heimaey (Home Island):** As the only town in the gorgeous Westman Islands, Heimaey—surrounded by magnificent sea cliffs and two ominous volcanic cones—would have made this list for its setting (and cute puffin population) alone. Its distinctive local identity and heroic resilience in the aftermath of a devastating 1973 eruption only add to its luster. See p. 226.

o **Ísafjörður:** Westfjords is almost a country unto itself, and its honorary capital has real vibrancy despite its remoteness and small population. Credit the phenomenal setting, thriving dockside, first-rate dining, hip cafes, and festivals ranging from alternative music to "swamp soccer." See p. 153.

o **Seyðisfjörður:** The arrival point for the European ferry and a fashionable summer retreat for Icelandic artists, this dramatically situated Eastfjords village has a cosmopolitan pulse that squares perfectly with its tiny scale and pristine surroundings. Chalet-style wooden kit homes from the 19th and early 20th centuries provide a rare architectural historicity. See p. 288.

o **Siglufjörður:** This isolated, untouristy fjord town has a picture-perfect setting and an endearing nostalgia for its herring-boom glory days (case in point, the ambitious Herring Era Museum) and fabulous hiking. See p. 179.

o **Vík:** The southernmost village in Iceland wears its fine setting lightly, but the landscape stays vividly etched in the mind: the lovely beaches of black volcanic sand, the spiky sea stacks offshore, and, on the Reynisfjall cliffs, the most scenic walk on Iceland's south coast. See p. 248.

ICELAND'S best WALKS

o **Borgarfjörður Eystri:** This well-rounded coastal region combines many geological marvels found in the interior—particularly rhyolite mountainsides and their marbled patterns—with an abundance of flowering plants and the romantic melancholy of its formerly inhabited fjords and inlets. Locals have put great effort into designing maps, marking trails, and setting up 4WD tours of the area. See p. 293.

o **Hornstrandir Nature Reserve:** The northernmost extremity of the Westfjords is for those whose eyes always roam to the farthest corners of the map. Protected since 1975, this sawtoothed peninsula has no roads, no airstrips, no year-round residents—only the beguiling coastline, flowering meadows, and cavorting birds and Arctic foxes the Vikings first encountered more than a millennium ago. See p. 164.

o **Kerlingarfjöll:** A short detour from the relatively accessible Kjölur Route through the interior, this mountain cluster in the shadow of Hofsjökull has an astonishing range of scenery: lofty mountains, chiseled ravines, exotic geothermal fields, glimmering icecaps. The clinchers are the hot springs that form enormous natural Jacuzzis. See p. 304.

o **Kverkfjöll:** Deep within Iceland's highland desert interior, this geothermally restless mountain spur protrudes from Vatnajökull amid charred expanses of red, brown, and black rock dusted with lichen and moss. Best-known for a wondrous glacial ice cave, Kverkfjöll is anything but a one-hit natural wonder and merits 2 or 3 days to appreciate its austere gravitas. See p. 308.

o **Landmannalaugar:** This area's undulating, multi-hued rhyolite slopes—with marbled streaks of yellow, red, green, white, and purple scree—make it one of the most photogenic landscapes on the planet and the most celebrated hiking area in Iceland. See p. 236.

o **Laugavegurinn:** A world-renowned 4-day trek between Landmannalaugar and Þórsmörk through a cavalcade of inland scenery. Mossy lava fields, hot spring baths, glacial valleys, and desert expanses combine to make this a hiker's paradise. See p. 237.

o **Skaftafell:** Close to the Ring Road (Route 1) on the southern edge of Vatnajökull, and within the Vatnajökull National Park, Skaftafell is the most accessible of Iceland's major hiking destinations, with startling panoramas of serrated peaks, shimmering icecaps, and barren floodplains stretching toward the sea. See p. 257.

o **Sveinstindur–Skælingar:** Landmannalaugar unjustly steals the limelight from many nearby interior regions, most notably this amazing stretch of mountains and sediment-filled river valleys between Landmannalaugar and Vatnajökull. Views from the peak of Sveinstindur over the glacier-gouged Lake Langisjór are among the most sublime in all of Iceland. See p. 238.

o **Þakgil:** This idyllic campsite is in a perfectly sheltered, stream-fed gully near the southeast edge of Mýrdalsjökull. The surrounding Tuff mountains have been elaborately sculpted by wind and water erosion; trails lead right to the moraines of the receding glacier. See p. 251.

o **Þórsmörk:** This verdant alpine oasis, encircled by monumental glaciers and river-braided valleys of silt, has the aura of an enchanted refuge—a nice counterpoint to the distinctly Martian appeal of most interior regions. See p. 245.

ICELAND'S best MUSEUMS

o **National Museum of Iceland** (Reykjavík; www.natmus.is; ✆ 530-2200): This museum's permanent but innovative and ever-evolving exhibit, "The Making of a Nation," covers the entire span of Icelandic history and culture. You might anticipate a numbing encyclopedic survey, but the curators' selective restraint manages to say more with less. See p. 56.

o **Einar Jónsson Museum** (Reykjavík; www.lej.is; ✆ 551-3797): The work of Iceland's most revered sculptor draws heavily on classical mythology and traditional folklore, with a virtuoso command of gesture and ingenious meshings of human and beastly forms. His romantic symbolism carries deep emotional and spiritual resonance. See p. 57.

- **Glaumbær** (Varmahlíð; www.glaumbaer.is; ✆ **453-6173**): If you visit just one of Iceland's museums housed inside preserved 19th- and early-20th-century turf-roofed farm buildings, make it Glaumbær in the northwest. The most affecting moments are when you imagine the smell of burning peat and the sounds of the family clan puttering about these dark, damp, snug rooms through the long winters. See p. 174.

- **Harbor House Museum** (Reykjavík; www.artmuseum.is; ✆ **590-1200**): Erró—the most prominent Icelandic artist of the late 20th century—has donated most of his life's work to this contemporary art branch of the Reykjavík Art Museum. The exhibit spaces are inside a 1930s-era warehouse, perfectly suited to Erró's vast, cartoon-style montages. See p. 53.

- **Icelandic Museum of Rock 'n' Roll** (Keflavík; www.rokksafn.is; ✆ **420-1030**): Opened in 2014, this beautiful ode to Icelandic rock tells the history of the island's vibrant music scene, from the first radio signal at the neighboring air base. The highly interactive exhibits allow visitors to tap the bass, play drums, and even step up to the turntables. See p. 106.

- **Settlement Center** (Borgarnes; www.landnam.is; ✆ **437-1600**): With state-of-the-art multimedia exhibits dedicated to *Egils Saga* and the first 60 years of Icelandic settlement, this engaging museum tries almost too hard to turn learning into a kind of amusement-park fun-house—but we're not complaining. See p. 124.

- **Eldheimar** (Heimaey; http://eldheimar.is; ✆ **488-2700**): Most of the hundreds of houses buried during the 1973 eruption were never dug out. Like the ruins of Pompeii, this one house was excavated, and its remains are like a time capsule of that dramatic moment. See p. 228.

- **Skógar Folk Museum** (Skógar; www.skogasafn.is; ✆ **487-8845**): This is without a doubt the greatest of Iceland's many folk museums, with an enormous artifact collection ranging from fishing boats to carved headboards and makeshift mousetraps. One of the quirkiest relics is a hollow fishbone used as a straw to feed milk to young boys so that they would not be prone to seasickness. See p. 249.

ICELAND IN CONTEXT

Tell friends you're going to Iceland, and some may wonder whether they'd even be able to place the little country on a map. Most people know only that it's somewhere west of Europe—and close enough to clog the continent's skies with ash should a volcano or two decide to awaken, as did Eyjafjallajökull in 2010 and Bárðarbunga in 2015.

Iceland, dangling from the Arctic Circle between Greenland and Norway like a prickly Christmas decoration, is indeed a land of volcanoes. Eruptions are rare (on a tourist scale if not on a planetary one), but evidence of the country's volcanic history abounds in the landscape—from moss-covered lava fields stretching as far as the eye can see to geysers and hot springs, black beaches and basalt-lined bays, and the craters and volcanic mountains themselves (often teasingly hidden away under glaciers).

In some places, houses half-swallowed by lava have been preserved for show. The Westman Islands showcase a port extension created during a 1973 eruption (p. 226), when some quick-thinking locals decided to tame the lava stream, hosing it down from boats on one side so that it would flow into the sea to improve the shape of the existing harbor.

Amid Iceland's rocky landscape are grassy meadows, multicolored mountains, torpid glacial tongues, waterfalls cascading from impossibly high cliffs into lush valleys, picturesque towns bordering the fjords, and one of the trendiest capitals in Europe. The towns boast roofs in rainbow shades, and almost every house has its own swimming pool and hot tubs.

The meadows and mountainsides are home to thousands of sheep—legally entitled to roam free during summer—and crisscrossed with all manner of stream, brook, spring, river, and lake. You see turf-roofed houses and stone-walled sheep-sorting pens, tiny churches, and, if you look carefully enough, even tinier elf houses embedded in hillocks, with brightly painted doors.

In this northern, tree-scarce land, the openness of the view is surprising and refreshing, and returning visitors immediately breathe in the crisp, invigorating polar air. It is no illusion—the eye really can see farther, the grass really is greener, the summer days

Misnomer #1: Iceland Is Much Greener than Icy Greenland

With a couple dozen glaciers and a white winter landscape that is further enhanced by the lack of trees, Iceland has no shortage of ice. But for the rest of the year Iceland is greener than green, literally: The lack of sunshine over the winter months means that grasses and mosses need to be super-photosynthesizers to survive here, so consequentially, they are greener than similar vegetation farther south of the Arctic. According to the saga of Erik the Red, when Erik set out exploring and came across the southeast tip of Greenland, it looked fertile enough to set up shop (climate scientists today theorize that it really was much more fertile then). So, Erik sent a ship back with word of the new settlement, hoping to attract enough people to make the venture worthwhile. But what to call this new land? Greenland had a more promising ring than Iceland, so that's what he settled on. Incidentally, the settlement ultimately failed, though experts haven't yet agreed as to what went wrong.

are longer, and the spring water coming from your tap is cleaner. In winter, the darkness is celebrated with lights in every window and often in the sky, too, when the magical *aurora borealis,* or the northern lights, appear like ghosts dancing among the stars. Small children are pulled to school on tobog-gans, and people head to the ski areas on the weekend.

In addition to all its natural wonders, Iceland is also a modern nation with a rich culture and sense of history. Consistent with the diverse surroundings, the typical Icelander is a fisherman, a singer, a banker, a sheep farmer, and anything in between—even, quite often, two or three of these at once. You probably saw the 2010 volcanic eruption on TV, and you've probably listened to Björk's music, but we hope you get the chance to see for yourself some of the rest of what this amazing island and its people have to offer.

ICELAND TODAY

Iceland's 103,000 square kilometers (39,756 sq. miles), with 4,970km (3,088 miles) of coastline, make it the 16th-largest island in the world. Only Madagascar, Britain, and Cuba are larger single independent island states. Hvannadalshnjúkur, Iceland's highest peak, rises 2,110m (6,922 ft.). Roughly 10% of the country is covered in glaciers, and the land is a hotbed of geothermal activity. Natural hot water piped into Icelandic homes means that most of the population has inexpensive, non-polluting heating. Icelanders boast one of the highest life expectancy rates in the world, perhaps because of the clean air, clean water, and plentiful fish.

Only about 4% of Iceland's population of just over 338,000 people live in rural areas, with roughly three-quarters living in Reykjavík, the capital. If you think the streets are looking more crowded than these figures suggest, keep in mind that around 2 million tourists each year are out and about, too, especially during the summer.

The country's Alþing (parliament) sits in Reykjavík, and its current prime minister is Katrín Jakobsdóttir (since 2017). Guðni Thorlacius Jóhannesson (2016) is serving his first term as president.

Most of the tiny amount of Iceland's arable land is used for grazing, and just 1% to 2% of Icelanders are engaged in agriculture. Iceland imports much of its foodstuffs, but also produces vegetables, meat, fish, and dairy. The Icelandic economy has traditionally been driven by fishing and fisheries products, but the other main export today is aluminum.

In 2007, when Iceland was surfing the economic boom, the U.N. named it the world's best country to live in: It had the best life expectancy, best education levels, and best medical care, and personal income was at an all-time high. When the economy crashed starting in October 2008, the country suffered great financial losses, and many Icelanders were left floundering in an ocean of debt. For months, the people of Iceland protested their outrage on a daily basis outside the houses of parliament, banging on pots and pans and pelting the vehicles of politicians with eggs and *skyr* (an Icelandic milk

ELVES IN THE ICELANDIC psyche

Of all the species of Iceland's hidden people, elves are by far the most numerous and prominent. In fact, many 19th-century folk tales use "elves" and "hidden people" interchangeably. Generally, elves are said to be good-looking, and they dress in rustic styles prevalent in the early 20th century, sometimes with pointy hats. Male elves are skilled craftsmen and often work as farmers and smiths.

Elves are fiercely protective of their homes, which are usually inside rocks, hills, and cliffs, and even in underground wells or springs. Occasionally roads are diverted or building plans altered so as not to disturb them (p. 296), as tales often tell of the bad luck that follows those who don't respect their terrain. People have been lured into elf homes, never to return from the hidden world. Though elves are quite dangerous, especially if their homes are disturbed, they often help humans and are true to their word. Elf women have suddenly appeared to help women with difficult childbirths. On the other hand, elves have also been said to steal human

babies in the night, replacing them with one of their own. To prevent this, Icelandic mothers would make a sign of the cross both above and below their babies after laying them in the cradle.

The term **"Hidden People"** *(huldufólk)* applies collectively to various humanoid creatures living in Iceland, including elves, dwarves, gnomes, trolls, and so on. When Viking ships first arrived in Iceland, dragon heads were removed from the prows so as not to disturb the guardian spirits of the land. These spirits are ancestral to the hidden people, who have always been strongly identified with features of the landscape. Hidden people are widely mentioned in sagas written during the first centuries of settlement. For the most part they have remained a folkloric phenomenon parallel to Christian belief, but sometimes they have been incorporated into Christian frameworks. In one accounting, Eve was washing her children to prepare them to meet God. God arrived sooner than expected, so she kept the unwashed children hidden, and God saw fit to keep them hidden forever.

product similar to yogurt). The government was finally driven out of office by what is now known as the "kitchenware revolution."

The relatively small size of the country and its economy was one of the reasons it was hit so hard and so early by the global financial crisis. But this has also enabled Iceland to bounce back on its feet relatively quickly. Unlike the rest of the world in the years that followed, Iceland let its banks fail and jailed those convicted of crimes. Within a few years it was already hard to see any outward signs of an economy in trouble, and the government continues to offer tax incentives to people willing to keep constructing buildings or expanding businesses, in order to keep the wheels of commerce turning.

Although some Icelanders went so far as to migrate (mostly to Norway) during the height of the slump, migration to Iceland has steadily continued (almost 13% of the population is foreign), and on the whole people still have an excellent standard of living.

ART & ARCHITECTURE
Art

Art plays a significant role in Icelandic culture, with several dozen registered galleries in the Reykjavík area alone. Exhibitions aren't just limited to galleries; many artists exhibit their work in other public places including shopping malls, restaurants, cafes, and abandoned herring factories. Sometimes buildings are turned into works of art, such as the illumination of Icelandic lighthouses by artist Arna Valsdóttir in 2004. Some of the more prominent contemporary artists in Iceland include the postmodern artist **Erró, Kristján Guðmundsson** (the Carnegie Art Award winner of 2010), **Ólafur Elíasson** (the Danish/Icelandic artist famous for the installation *The Weather Project* at London's Tate Modern), and **Ragnar Kjartansson** (also of the Icelandic band

ICELAND'S THOUSAND YEARS DATELINE

800–1050 The age of the Vikings, when Norsemen brought terror to the coasts of Europe.

871+/–2 The age of settlement. According to the Íslendingabók (The Book of Icelanders), the settlement of Iceland began around 870, with the arrival of Ingólfur Arnarson in Reykjavík. In the 4th century B.C., long before the land was ever settled, it was described by the Greek explorer Pytheas of Marseille, who referred to it as "Thule."

930 The need for a common law in Iceland leads to the creation of the Alþing, an annual political assembly of some 40 local chieftains. A Law Speaker is elected who has to commit the laws to memory and recite them. The first Alþing takes place in Lögberg (Law Hill) at Thingvellir and continues for more than 300 years until the Norwegian crown takes over.

982 After being exiled from Iceland, Erik the Red heads for Greenland

"Trabant"), whose recent exhibition *The End—Venice* won critical acclaim. For more on art in Iceland, **www.sim.is** has good listings for galleries and exhibitions. The **Reykjavík Art Museum** at Tryggvagata 17 (© **590-1201**) also has good online resources at **www.artmuseum.is**.

Architecture

Traditional architecture in Iceland was very basic, suffering from the lack of wood. Icelanders built their homes out of sod and turf, with supporting structures often made from driftwood. Some of the later turf houses have been preserved, such as **Skógar** (p. 248), **Glaumbær** (p. 174), and **Keldur** (p. 242). During the medieval period, many wooden-framed churches were built, followed by a number of stone constructions in the 18th century. The **church** in **Hólar** (p. 177) is the largest stone-built church from this period.

The first notable influences on Icelandic architecture were Danish and appeared during the expansion of Reykjavík, when merchants set up trading posts in Iceland. These houses were typically wood-framed with pitched roofs. The Swiss chalet style (a Norwegian import) was another strong influence, here modified with corrugated-iron surfacing in place of cladding and painted in a variety of hues.

MODERN ARCHITECTURE

Some believe that one of the greatest tragedies for Icelandic architecture was the arrival of **functionalism.** The Reykjavík cityscape is dotted with buildings that look like stacks of Legos (though some are nicely painted) and concrete apartment blocks. The lack of any decent town planning has resulted in a mish-mash of vastly different styles that only clash with every new building project. During the boom period before the economic crash, skyscrapers were raised next to traditional wooden houses without any consideration for creating an aesthetically pleasing complementary style. As a result, the smaller

and establishes a settlement of around 300 houses with 3,000 inhabitants. His son, Leifur the Lucky, hearing about a land west of Greenland, sails off and discovers Vineland in North America. The explorers try to settle on the coast of present-day Newfoundland, but are forced our after 3 years by hostile Indians.

1000　Christianity is brought to Iceland when missionaries from Norway convert a southern chieftain (a relative of the King of Norway). For a while Iceland remains both pagan and Christian, until a compromise is made by the Law

Speaker Þorgeir who, after spending a day thinking and reflecting in silence (with a cloak spread over him to discourage people from interrupting), proclaims that Iceland will be Christian, as long as people are still free to worship the old gods.

1120　The sagas of Iceland constitute the first extensive body of prose composed in a European language and largely recount events between 870 and 1350. The fact that most Icelanders are still able to read and understand them is remarkable. Written in a narrative

continues

buildings simply look out of place. Some beautiful buildings do exist, however, including the **Alþingishús,** the current parliament building in the heart of the city, which is hewn out of Icelandic stone, and **Háteigskirkja,** a snow-white church crowned with four elegant black turrets in the 105 area of Reykjavík. The $150-million **Harpa concert hall** and conference center on Reykjavík's waterfront is built around a steel framework covered with geometric-shaped glass panels of different colors resembling the scales of a fish (p. 54).

FIRE, ICE & BONSAI FORESTS

If someone added up every tourist's wildest dream and designed a country, the result would be Iceland. Iceland is not only spectacularly beautiful, but it's also incredibly diverse, and nature at its most stunning is easily accessible to visitors. There are few places on the planet where you can walk behind a waterfall, climb onto a glacier, explore a lava cave, marvel at an erupting volcano (or at the blackened hills still steaming months afterward), sail among icebergs on a glacial lake, watch water erupting into the air from a geyser, and scuba-dive along the rift between two continental plates—all in one weekend. Not just that, but visitors can spend their evenings eating at the finest restaurants and partying in some of the world's trendiest bars. If it's not summer, you may even be lucky enough to observe some magical northern lights as you wander back to your hotel.

The only thing Icelandic nature does lack is trees. You will not get lost in a forest. (The advice in Iceland if you do manage this unlikely feat: "Stand up!") It is widely believed that Iceland was once much more forested, but that the first settlers, mostly from Norway, didn't understand that trees on Iceland would not grow back as quickly as demand required. Later, when building materials were scarce, driftwood coming from places as far away as Russia

similar to the modern novel, the first manuscripts, the *Íslendingabók* (Book of Icelanders) and *Landnámabók* (Book of Settlements), were written by Ari the Wise. The most famous writer of the sagas is Snorri Sturlasson, who wrote *Heimskringla* (Orb of the World), a history of the kings of Norway. The greatest manuscript of the sagas is the *Möðruvallabók* (the Möðruvellir Book), which includes 11 of the Icelandic family sagas.

1262–1380 Norwegian rule. Plans by the Norwegian crown to take over Iceland are first recorded in the year 1220, when Snorri Sturlasson unsuccessfully tried to win Iceland over to the king of Norway. A period of conflict ensues, culminating in the Battle of Örlygsstaðir in North Iceland. Conflict continues until 1262, when Gissur (the first earl of Iceland) induces the chieftain of the lands to swear allegiance to the king. Iceland remains in the realm of the Kings of Norway until 1376, when the crowns of Norway and Denmark are inherited by King Ólaf. Iceland then becomes subject to the Danish throne and remains so until 1944.

became extremely valuable, and laws were devised to govern a person's right to claim driftwood based on where it washed ashore.

Today there are many reforestation efforts in Iceland, particularly in the east, but the landscape as a whole is still very bare. All the better to see those lovely undulating hills, many would argue. One might expect the land to seem barren as a result, but that would be forgetting the endless fields of green, green grass and the multifarious moss. It's not just your average garden variety of moss—it's moss in abundance, moss of dozens of species, moss that has grown across lava fields for centuries and centuries, so thick in places that you can't be sure anymore if there are rocks underneath. It reminds you that the soil here is rich, the earth is warm beneath the snow, and the land itself seems vibrant and alive. The landscape takes on a different character, and it feels liberating to be able to see so far with so few obstructions. If you live in a wooded area, you may even feel a little claustrophobic at first when you return home.

ICELAND IN POPULAR CULTURE
Music

It's quite amazing that a country with only 338,000 people can produce so many talented musicians, with such a diversity of styles and genres. The rise of Iceland as a producer of popular music came with **Björk**'s arrival on the scene in 1993, and it has since developed into an important international music hub with annual festivals that attract people from all over the world. Artists such as: **Mínus, Gus Gus, Emiliana Torrini, Sigur Rós, Ólafur Arnalds,** and **Of**

1300 Fish exports from Iceland to England are recorded in English import records. The industry expands over the next 100 years as demand increases from Europe, probably because fish is allowed on religious fasts.	around Easter 1404. The second epidemic occurs in 1494–95 and also claims a significant proportion of the population, but does not reach the Westfjords.
1402–1495 The plague sweeps through Iceland a little later than it does in Europe, arriving in the 15th century with two major epidemics. The first arrives around 1402 and spreads rapidly from Hvalfjörður in the west, to the north and south, finally reaching the east by 1403. The plague claims around 50% of the population before dying out	**1536** Religious reformation. The introduction of Lutheranism in Iceland is not as peaceful as the transition to Christianity, bringing violence and murder. The Danish government in Iceland is wiped out twice as it tries to convert the Icelanders to Protestantism. In 1552, another royal Danish government is established and completes the reformation of Iceland.

continues

Monsters and Men have all made the crossover into global music markets. One of the most notable music festivals in Iceland, **Airwaves** (p. 30) attracts lots of international media attention. For 5 days in mid-October, Reykjavík buzzes with talent scouts and journalists from around the world, there to check out the plethora of local and international bands showcased on the stages of all available music venues. The festival is affiliated with the national airline, Icelandair, which offers package tours to Iceland during Airwaves.

New bands to be on the lookout for include: **Agent Fresco, Bloodgroup, the Esoteric Gender, Mammút, Sin Fang Bous, Sudden Weather Change,** and **Worm is Green.** Also check out Keflavík's **Icelandic Museum of Rock 'n' Roll** (p. 106), which details the history of the nation's pop music scene, from the first radio signals from the American military base to current artists. Another good resource for Icelandic music is **www.icelandmusic.is**, the online music portal from Iceland Music Export that promotes native acts and lists tour dates. For listings, check out "The Reykjavík Grapevine," a free monthly circular, also available online at **www.grapevine.is**.

Apart from pop music, Iceland also has a vibrant classical, opera, and jazz scene, with some dedicated venues in Reykjavík. The annual **Jazz Festival**

1600–1785 The Dark Ages was a particularly pious period for Icelanders as they lived under the repressive thumb of the orthodox Lutheran church. At least 25 people accused of witchcraft were burned at the stake.	**1830–1904** Fight for autonomy. During this period Iceland struggles with the Danish rulers for more power, and in 1874 is awarded its own constitution and legislative power, limited to internal affairs. Icelanders have to wait 30 more years to win complete control.
1751–1806 During this period, Reykjavík emerges as the capital of Iceland. First comes the opening of a wool industry workshop by a team of Icelandic entrepreneurs, then the abolition of monopoly, which leads to the establishment of more trading hubs, and finally the relocation of Iceland's main administration offices.	**1873–1914** Emigration. Around 50 million people head to America from Europe, including 15,000 Icelanders (20% of the population at the time). Most leave from the north and east of Iceland.
	1916 Workers' movement. This year sees the establishment of a national federation of trade unions.

(https://reykjavikjazz.is) in September (p. 29) is held at venues around town, ranging from concert halls to a brewery, and features many Icelandic jazz musicians alongside international names. The newest opera celebrity in Iceland is **Garðar Thór Cortes,** who can be heard (among a wealth of other Icelandic talent) at the **Icelandic Opera** (www.opera.is; p. 90). The **Iceland Symphony Orchestra** (https://en.sinfonia.is) performs regularly in the 1,800-seat concert hall in the **Harpa** (Reykjavík Concert and Conference Center).

Books

With one of the most literate populations in the world, Iceland produces more novels per capita than any other country, so don't be surprised if every second Icelander you meet has published his or her own book. Icelanders are prolific writers and won't hesitate to self-publish. The country's most revered 20th-century writer is Nobel Prize–winner **Halldór Laxness,** whose work is widely available in English and countless other languages. Among other popular modern authors whose books you'll find in English are **Yrsa Sigurðardóttir,** author and musician **Sjón,** and crime writer **Arnaldur Indriðason.**

Sagas

Among the great literary works of medieval Europe, the Icelandic sagas retain the most importance and immediacy to the nation that produced them. Many consider the sagas Iceland's greatest national treasure, and their status is consistent with the Icelandic people's love of literature. Iceland's people trace their ancestry back to the Vikings, and the Icelandic language has changed relatively little in the last thousand years. Today's Icelanders can quite clearly comprehend the original texts of the sagas—even better than most English speakers do in deciphering the works of Shakespeare, penned several centuries later. The sagas are still best-sellers in Iceland, and all students are required to read them.

1944 Sovereignty. On June 17, 1944, independence is established and the Republic of Iceland is formed, with a ceremony in Þingvellir (where the first Alþing was established in 930).

1955 Halldór Laxness wins the Nobel Prize for literature with his book *Independent People.*

1958 Fish Fight #1. After World War II, Iceland expanded its fishing boundaries, and in this year sets them at 12 nautical miles from the coast. British trawlers under protection of British warships oppose the boundary. This first Cod War is eventually resolved through diplomacy.

1972 Fish Fight #2. In 1972, after an economic slump, Iceland extends its fishing boundary to 50 nautical miles. The British answer with a second Cod War.

1975 Fish Fight #3. When Iceland further extends its fishing boundary to 200 nautical miles, the Cod War becomes more destructive. Diplomatic ties are severed, and the British orders their warships to ram Icelandic fishing vessels. Iceland fights back with a secret weapon: a sharp hook dragged

continues

Most of the sagas originate in the 12th to 14th centuries but recount events of the 10th and 11th centuries, when Icelanders were experimenting with self-government and transitioning to Christianity. The sagas do not neatly correspond to any modern literary genre, but might be called historical novels. The storylines follow a general pattern, in which conflicts escalate into multi-generational blood feuds and personal codes must be reconciled with the maintenance of the social fabric. (Readers expecting stories of handsome knights rescuing fair-haired maidens locked in castles tend to be disappointed.) The narrative style is terse and action-oriented, with infrequent dialogue and not much introspective probing. Yet the sagas seem remarkably contemporary in their depth of character, intimacy of domestic scenes, well-developed sense of irony, and profound grasp of psychological motivation.

About 40 Icelandic sagas have survived, most written anonymously. The two most widely available collections are *The Sagas of Icelanders* (Penguin, 2001) and *Eirik the Red and Other Icelandic Sagas* (Oxford, 1999). As wonderful as these collections are, both are highly selective. Of the six most revered sagas—*Egil's Saga, Eyrbyggja Saga, Grettis Saga, Hrafnkel's Saga, Laxdæla Saga,* and *Njál's Saga*—the Penguin collection includes *Egil's Saga, Hrafnkel's Saga,* and *Laxdæla Saga,* while the Oxford collection has only *Hrafnkel's Saga.*

All the major sagas are in print as individual volumes. Which one you choose could depend on which region you plan to visit: *Egil's Saga, Eyrbyggja Saga,* and *Laxdæla Saga* are set in the west; *Njál's Saga* in the south; and *Hrafnkel's Saga* in the east. Grettir the Strong, the hero of *Grettis Saga,* spends his final years on Drangey (p. 176) in the northwest. *Egils Saga* is the subject of a fine exhibit at the new Settlement Center (p. 124) in Borgarnes. *Njál's Saga* is often considered the greatest literary achievement of all the sagas; see p. 124.

underwater in the path of British ships. In the end Britain is forced to back down and Iceland regains power of its primary natural resource, a symbolic win for tiny nations around the world.

1970–1980 Girl power and red stockings. In the 1970s, a radical women's movement forms called Rauðsokkahreyfingin (the Red Stockings) to campaign for the rights of women in Iceland. The movement gathers strength, and in 1975 a rally is attended by 20% of the population of Reykjavík. Women all over the country take a mass day off from work and domestic duties.

1973 On January 23, 1973, a crack appears in the long-inactive volcano Helgafell on Heimaey (Home Island). Fortunately, because of a recent storm, the entire fishing fleet is at hand to assist in the evacuation of the island during the massive eruption. The resulting mountain, named Eldfell, adds an extra 233m (764 ft.) to the island's height.

1980 The much-admired Vigdís Finnbogadóttir becomes the world's first democratically elected female president.

1986 Iceland hosts the famous meeting between Ronald Reagan and

Modern Fiction

The dominant figure of modern Icelandic literature is **Halldór Laxness** (p. 24), winner of the 1955 Nobel Prize for Literature. His most renowned work is the 1946 novel *Independent People,* a compassionate and often comic story of a poor sheep farmer determined to live unbeholden to anyone. English translations of several other Laxness novels remain in print. *World Light* (1937) is the life tale of a marginal, starry-eyed poet, a foil for Laxness to work out the conflicting imperatives of art and political engagement. *Iceland's Bell* (1943) explores Danish colonial oppression of Iceland in the late 17th century, with most characters based on actual historical figures. *The Atom Station* (1948) is a more outright political satire dealing with issues stirred up by the American-run NATO base in Iceland. *The Fish Can Sing* (1957) is a particularly gentle coming-of-age story about a boy's pursuit of a mysterious male operatic star. *Paradise Reclaimed* (1960) concerns a late-19th-century farmer who abandons his family, emigrates to Mormon Utah, and later returns to Iceland as a missionary.

Currently Iceland's most popular writer—both at home and abroad—is **Arnaldur Indriðason,** whose crime novels feature inspector Erlendur Sveinsson, a rather gloomy divorced man who spends his evenings reading Icelandic sagas. Seven of Arnaldur's works have been translated into English, and in 2005 his *Silence of the Grave* won Britain's coveted Golden Dagger Award. The film version of his novel *Jar City* was Iceland's candidate for the 2008 Academy Award for Best Foreign Language Film. We cannot also forget **Sigurjón Birgir Sigurðsson,** aka **Sjón,** the Icelandic author and Oscar-nominated songwriter, whose *CoDex 1962: A Trilogy,* set in 3 different decades and jumping from one genre to the next, is already being hailed as one of the century's great works of literary art.

Mikhail Gorbachev during the Reykjavík summit, where both leaders take important diplomatic steps toward ending the Cold War.

1993 Björk releases her first solo album, *Debut,* which goes on to receive global critical acclaim and propels her to international stardom, making her Iceland's biggest star.

2003–2008 Kárahnjúkar hydropower project. A massive dam project created in order to provide power for an aluminum smelter in the east of Iceland outrages environmentalists and causes much controversy. The project goes ahead anyway and floods large areas of Iceland's natural wilderness.

2006 The U.S. pullout. On September 30, American forces based in the Keflavík NATO base pulls out of Iceland after a 55-year post–World War II presence in Iceland. The area, which was home to more than 1,200 servicemen and women, has since been turned into student housing.

2007 The U.N. names Iceland the world's best country to live in, based on life expectancy, education levels, medical care, income, and other criteria.

continues

Nonfiction

Iceland was widely venerated in Victorian England, and **William Morris**'s translations of sagas were household reading. Several Victorians wrote Icelandic studies and travelogues, some of which have been reprinted. *Letters from High Latitudes* (Hard Press, 2006), by the prominent statesman and diplomat **Lord Dufferin** (1826–1902), is an often wild account of his 1856 travels in Iceland, Norway, and Spitzbergen. (**Tim Moore**'s *Frost on My Moustache: The Arctic Exploits of a Lord and a Loafer,* published in 2000 by Abacus, is a hilarious account of Moore's misadventures while retracing Dufferin's route.) *Iceland: Its Scenes and Sagas* (Signal Books, 2007), by the eclectic scholar, novelist, and folk-song collector **Sabine Baring-Gould** (1834–1924), is a magnificent account of his 1862 journey across Iceland on horseback, interlaced with learned musings on the sagas. *Ultima Thule, Or, A Summer in Iceland* (Kessinger Publishing, 2007), written in 1875 by explorer and ethnologist **Richard Francis Burton** (1821–1890), is an equally penetrating and erudite portrait of Icelandic society.

Ring of Seasons: Iceland, Its Culture and History (University of Michigan Press, 2000)—by **Terry G. Lacy,** an American sociologist who has lived in Iceland since the 1970s—is highly engaging and insightful.

History of Iceland: From the Settlement to the Present Day, by **Jón R. Hjálmarsson** (Iceland Review Press, 1993), is a tidy, 200-page primer on Icelandic history. *Iceland's 1100 Years: History of a Marginal Society,* by **Gunnar Karlsson** (Hurst & Company, 2000; reprinted in the U.S. as *The History of Iceland* by University of Minnesota Press), is twice as long and has a bit more intellectual heft. Readers particularly interested in the historical context of the Icelandic sagas should pick up **Jesse Byock**'s authoritative study *Viking Age Iceland* (Penguin, 2001).

2008 Rise and fall. What goes up must come down. After years of thriving, October 2008 sees the global recession take hold, leaving Iceland in debt so severe that within 3 weeks the major banks of Iceland are declared insolvent, the króna plummets, and suddenly the interest rates for cheap car and house loans—pinned to foreign currency—doubles. Many Icelandic families find themselves unable to make ends meet. The government comes under heavy criticism and is ultimately forced to resign after a mass protest. After a general election in 2009, the Social Democrats are elected to lead the country out of recession.

2010 On March 20, a vent fissure eruption opens in Fimmvörðuháls in the south of Iceland, followed shortly by a larger volcanic eruption in Eyjafjallajökull, directly to the west of the first. The ash cloud from the second volcano brings European air traffic to a halt for more than a week, creating the biggest-ever shutdown of passenger traffic.

2010 In May, the Best Party (Besti Flokkurinn), led by comedian Jon Gnarr, wins control of Reykjavík, with more than a third of the vote in the city elections. Pledges

Iceland: Land of the Sagas (Villard, 1990) is a coffee-table paperback, with 150 pages split evenly between **Jon Krakauer**'s evocative photographs and **David Roberts'** essayistic reflections on Iceland's landscape and literary heritage. *Iceland Saga* (The Bodley Head, 1987) also takes the reader on a kind of literary tour, but from a more informed perspective; author **Magnús Magnússon** translated many sagas himself.

Film

Iceland is perhaps better know for its fantastic film locations used in big-budget films and television (such as *Game of Thrones, Batman Begins,* or *Journey to the Center of the Earth*) than its home-produced creations. Icelanders may not have the money to make similar films, but they do make films and have been doing so for nearly a century. They even have their own national film award, the "Edda Award." Though smaller individual films have been made since the 1920s, bigger productions weren't carried out until 1980, when the Icelandic Film Fund was founded at Kvikmyndamiðstöð. Since then, dozens of Icelandic films have been produced, with some critically acclaimed films like *Englar Alheimsins* (Angels of the Universe) and *Reykjavík 101.* You can keep up with Iceland's film industry at **www.icelandicfilmcentre.is**.

EATING & DRINKING IN ICELAND

Icelandic cuisine is much improved from 20 years ago, when leaden Scandinavian comfort food was the standard. Several imaginative and exciting restaurants are leading the charge in Reykjavík. The enthusiasm is palpable—sometimes waiters can hardly wait to explain everything happening on your plate. Outside Reykjavík and major towns, however, good food choices can be

include "sustainable transparency," free towels at swimming pools, and a new polar bear for the city zoo.

2011 Iceland is honored as special guest at the Frankfurt International Book Fair, the world's leading book marketplace, in recognition of its rich literary heritage.

2013 Keflavík-formed band Of Monsters and Men, which began after winning a local battle of the bands contest a few years earlier, appears on *Saturday Night Live*.

2015 Although it did not receive as much international attention as the Eyjafjallajökull eruption, the

Bárðarbunga eruption in central Iceland lasts 6 months and is the largest continuous eruption in Iceland in the past several hundred years.

2016 The smallest nation to ever appear in the Euro 2016 futbol championship, Iceland ties Portugal, then famously beats Austria and England. They eventually lose in the quarterfinals to France, a game that an estimated one-tenth of the country's population travels to Paris to see.

HALLDÓR LAXNESS: champion of the common man

Halldór Kiljan Laxness (1902–1998), author of 62 books in a span of 68 years, is the undisputed giant of modern Icelandic literature. (For suggested titles, see p. 21.) Born Halldór Guðjónsson in Reykjavík, he left Iceland after World War I to travel. In France he converted to Catholicism, adopting the last name Laxness and middle name Kiljan, after the Irish saint. In 1927 he published *The Great Weaver from Kashmir,* his first major novel. Three years later, after an ill-fated attempt to break into the Hollywood film industry, he returned to Iceland and became immersed in socialism, which greatly informed his novels: Lead characters are typically impoverished and exploited by a corrupt establishment. But his most overriding, lifelong subject was simply the common man; Catholicism, socialism, absurdism, and Taoism all framed this concern at different stages in his life. After winning the Nobel Prize for Literature in 1955, he was overjoyed that among his many congratulatory notes was one from a local Icelandic society of pipe layers; it was the only card to which he responded.

more restricted, aside from a few creative eateries. Village restaurants usually conform to a basic model: meat soup and catch of the day (both of which can be a joy), plus an ever-present array of burgers, pizzas, pasta, and fries. But the reality is, if you like fish you can't really go wrong here. Whether it's cod, salt cod, local lobster, or mussels, or other fish such as herring, there's a sea-loving element similar to that of the eastern U.S.

Icelanders like their food saucy, salty, and well-seasoned. In good restaurants, this only complements the natural ingredients. Icelandic ingredients are remarkably free of contaminants. Antibiotics, added hormones, and pesticides are rare. The meat could even be described as aromatic, reflecting the healthy outdoor lifestyle of the livestock (and even poultry). Lamb is what you'd expect it to taste like after the lambs have spent the summer roaming the mountains, nibbling on mosses and wild blueberry leaves. Fish is so fresh that it's difficult to prepare badly, and so abundant that it's still somewhat reasonably priced. Restaurant service is almost always friendly and helpful, if not ingratiating. In general, waiters like being asked for advice when you're ordering. As in much of Europe, you may have to tackle someone to get your bill.

Typical dining hours are a little on the late side. On weekends it can be difficult to find anyplace open before 10am, except in hotels. Icelanders usually eat dinner around 8pm or later.

Restaurants
VALUE-CONSCIOUS DINERS

Food in Iceland can become a major expense, especially if you're dining in hotel restaurants, which tend to serve some pretty average food for astronomical prices. If you want to save money on food, then the best way is to **cook for yourself.** Icelandic hoteliers are well aware of high food prices, and many budget lodgings offer access to guest kitchens. Another way to save money is to **focus on lunch as your main meal,** because dinner prices are often higher. If you do want a three-course meal, try the **"chef's menu;"** it might look expensive, but the price is almost always cheaper than buying the three, or even two, courses separately. On the other hand, many Icelanders get by on just soup, bread, and salad for lunch. Many convenience stores have relatively inexpensive salad bars. Look out for the **daily specials,** or the two-person menus, which are often cheaper than other items on the menu. **Fast food** is often necessary to keep you solvent, or when nothing else is available. Thankfully, Iceland has some of Scandinavia's best hot dogs (see "Hot Dog Utopia," p. 79), available at almost every filling station. Burgers are everywhere, often served with a kind of cocktail sauce reminiscent of Russian dressing.

FISH & LAMB
Menu advice can be crudely edited down to two words: *fish* and *lamb.*

Sheep imports are banned, and the lamb stock is exactly what the Vikings brought over. Icelandic lambs roam so freely that they can almost be described as game. Many Icelanders claim they can taste the wild berries, moss, and herbs that the lambs feed on. Slaughtering starts in mid-August, peaks in September, and continues into November, so late-season visitors may get the freshest cuts.

Most of Iceland's export income comes from fish. Simply put: Iceland serves up the freshest fish in the world. The most common local species are cod, haddock, catfish, monkfish, halibut, plaice, trout, Arctic char, and salmon.

Of course, fish and lamb are hardly the whole story. **Icelandic beef** is raised in equally healthy circumstances. Delicious **wild reindeer** from eastern Iceland appears on some menus, as is the once endangered **Icelandic goat** (ordering actually encourages farms to produce it). Icelanders also have centuries of experience cooking **seabirds,** especially puffins and guillemots.

PRODUCE
Iceland's freshest produce comes from geothermally heated greenhouses. Locally grown vegetables are specially marked in supermarkets; top products are tomatoes, cucumbers, and bell peppers. An Icelandic salad still has some catching up to do; it's often just iceberg lettuce with a few vegetable shavings.

DAIRY
Iceland's dairy products are just as wholesome and exceptional as the fish and lamb, but far less widely known. Icelanders consume lots of whole milk; reduced-fat milk is available in markets but is slow to catch on. Iceland also produces great cheese, especially Camembert and blue cheese.

But Iceland's greatest food invention is a yogurt-like product called *skyr,* which is gaining popularity abroad, too. *Skyr* is a kind of high-protein whipped whey that tastes like a cross between plain yogurt, cream cheese, and soft-serve ice cream, yet somehow, it's nonfat. Icelanders usually eat it thinned with milk (and sometimes cream). You'll find all sorts of varieties (blueberry, melon, pear, vanilla…) in markets and convenience stores, as well as infused into desserts at restaurants.

CRAZY THINGS TO taste IN ICELAND

Icelanders have faced severe hardship and learned not to let any digestible species or spare parts go to waste—hence the following guide to some of the more peculiar Icelandic specialties you may find on your menu:

o **Hákarl** This is Iceland's most notorious food: Greenlandic shark, uncooked and putrefied. Sharks have no kidneys, so urea collects in their blood, and the meat has high concentrates of acid and ammonia. If you eat it raw, you might die. So, it's cut up and placed in an outdoor kiln for 3 months while the toxins drain out. Then it's hung to dry and cured for another 3 months. The shark is served in small cubes that have the look and texture of mozzarella cheese. The taste is indescribable. According to Icelanders, eating *hákari* gives you stamina. Traditionally it's washed down with *brennivín* (wine that burns), an 80-proof clear drink made from angelica root or caraway seeds, and known affectionately as "Black Death." Even more intense is the fermented skate, or *skata*, which is traditionally served on December 23. The smell is so horrid that restaurants put signs on their doors warning patrons, and many can be seen walking around in old clothes so their new ones don't catch the stink.

o **Horse (hestur)** The pagan practice of eating horsemeat was banned by Christian authorities in the 11th century, but they relented in the 18th century during a famine. Whatever your personal feelings for these magisterial animals, they're perfectly healthy to eat and don't taste bad either. Traditionally the meat is eaten in stews, but unless you're staying at a farm, you're more likely to find it served very rare, even raw.

o **Cod tongues (gellur)** These walnut-size delicacies, extracted from Iceland's most bounteous fish species, are surrounded by a thick, fatty membrane from under the tongue that doesn't lift cleanly from the tender, savory meat inside. You'll just have to get it all down. They're best ordered in spring or fall when the cod are leaner, though some say that's missing the point.

o **Dried haddock (harðfiskur)** This has been a staple in Iceland for centuries, and is available in every convenience store. It's best eaten as the locals do, with a little butter, but can also be treated as a healthier alternative to crisps. It has become trendy among body builders for its high levels of protein.

o **Whale (hvalur)** The only species served up is minke whale, not an

TRADITIONAL FOODS

For more on Iceland's often terrifying traditional foods, see the nearby sidebar.

DRINK

Coffee in Iceland is simply excellent. Most baristas know exactly how to heat the milk without burning it and apply just the right amount of pressure to the coffee press. An average latte or cappuccino costs around 700kr ($5.70).

Alcoholic drinks in Iceland are very expensive. Beer is served in ½-liter (1-pint) glasses and costs around 1,000kr ($8). Cocktails are around 1,850kr ($15) and an average glass of wine is around 1,500kr ($12). Icelanders normally endangered species, though Iceland's decision to hunt them again is hardly uncontroversial, especially after the one company that still hunts killed a highly endangered blue whale in 2018. Consumption has risen thanks to tourists using the "I'll just try it once and see what its all about" argument. As sashimi it looks more disturbing than it tastes; the raw meat is a deep red, even purplish. Even cooked whale steaks are served very red in the middle. And the taste? It's said to be a sort of cross between tuna and beef, though it can be tough and rank when not prepared properly.

○ **Svið** This is half of a boiled sheep's head, cut down the middle and laid on its side, all the better for eye contact with your meal. If you're sharing, go for the cheeks and lips. Svið is also served cold if you like, and can be found at **Fjárhúsið** restaurant in Reykjavík's Grandi Mathöll, a food hall in the fishpacking district.

○ **Slátur** Leftover lamb parts, including the liver and blood, are minced, mixed, then sewn up and cooked inside the lamb's stomach lining.

○ **Hrútspungar** These are ram's testicles pickled in whey, often mixed with garlic and pressed into a kind

of cake or spread, which tastes like pâté way past its due date. Some Americans call these "Rocky Mountain oysters."

○ **Puffin (lundi)** From May to mid-August, you'll likely have an opportunity to eat Iceland's unbearably cute unofficial mascot. Puffin can be smoked, pickled, or eaten raw. Traditionally it's overcooked, but in restaurants it's almost always served rare. Like whale, eating puffin is becoming more controversial as their population numbers become increasingly threatened.

○ **Cormorant (skarfur)** This seabird tastes similar to puffin, only greasier and less fishy.

○ **Guillemot (langvía)** This coastal bird's meat looks and feels like beef but tastes like duck, with odd overtones of liver and seaweed.

○ **Fulmar eggs (fillsegg)** These oily seabird eggs make a good start to a meal.

○ **Reindeer (hreindýr)** Santa introduced reindeer to eastern Iceland from Norway in the 18th century. All are wild, and only about 1,200 are culled each year, so prices are high, although reindeer burger patties are often available cheaply from the frozen-meats section at markets. Hunting season is late fall, so most tourists eat vacuum-packed meat.

buy all their booze from the state-run store **Vínbúðinn** (www.vinbudin.is; ☏ **560-7700**), with more than a dozen branches in the Reykjavík area alone; one of the main stores is on Austurstræti 10a in downtown. Nights normally kick off at home-based parties, with partygoers not venturing out until around 11pm. Unless there's a special promotion (or money is no object for you) don't offer to buy a round! *Tip:* Liquor at the duty-free store by baggage at Keflavík airport is considerably cheaper than elsewhere in the country. It's the reason you'll see so many Icelanders loading up on wine and liquor as soon as they get off the plane.

Iceland Calendar of Events

JANUARY

New Year's Day. This is really a 2-day holiday, as nothing reopens until January 3. January 1.

Þrettándinn. This day marks the end of the Christmas season. Icelanders celebrate with a kind of New Year's Eve reprise, including bonfires, fireworks, and traditional songs, while children throw snowballs at cars. January 6.

Þorrablót. This ancient Viking midwinter tradition—named for Þorri, a month in the old Icelandic calendar—was originally a feast of sacrifice involving the blood of oxen and goats. Contemporary celebrations involve dancing, singing, drinking, and eating traditional Norse dishes, including singed sheep's head, pickled rams' testicles, and putrefied shark. Þorrablót dinners can be found in some Reykjavík restaurants; in smaller towns, visitors are often invited to join the locals. From the Friday that falls within January 19 to January 25 through most of February.

FEBRUARY

Food and Fun (www.foodandfun.is). For 4 days, Reykjavík's best restaurants create discounted set menus. In a televised competition, top international chefs are challenged to create dishes on the spot from purely Icelandic ingredients. Late February.

Winter Lights Festival (http://winterlights festival.is). Reykjavík is dramatically lit up for this cornucopia of cultural events: anything from fashion shows to figure skating to outdoor choral performances to belly-dancing troupes. Late February.

Bolludagur. "Bun Day" is celebrated by eating cream puffs (bollur) in multiple varieties. In the morning, children aim to catch their parents still in bed, and then beat them with decorated "bun wands" (bolluvondur). Parents are then obligated to give their children one cream puff for each blow received. Monday before Ash Wednesday.

Sónar (www.sonarreykjavik.com). This annual winter music festival brings dozens of major international musical acts and DJs to the Harpa for 3 days of performances. Many restaurants participate. Mid-February.

Sprengidagur. The name of this holiday translates into "bursting day" and is celebrated by eating salted meat and peas to the point of popping. Many restaurants participate. Day before Ash Wednesday.

Ash Wednesday (Öskudagur). Children dress in costume and traipse around town singing for candy. It's much like Halloween, and also a day for pranks. Seventh Wednesday before Easter.

MARCH/APRIL

Beer Day. This unofficial holiday marks the anniversary of the legendary day in 1989 when beer with an alcohol content above 2.2% was made legal. Guess how it's celebrated. March 1.

Easter Sunday. Easter holds special meaning in Iceland, as it marks the end of the long, dark winter. Most workers get a full 5 days off, from Holy Thursday to Easter Monday, and closures cause difficulties for tourists. Families gather and celebrate with smoked lamb and huge chocolate eggs. Easter weekend is especially lively in Ísafjörður, the cultural heart of the Westfjords, with skiing competitions and the "I Never Went South" rock music festival (p. 156). March or April.

First Day of Summer. Summer starts early in the old Icelandic calendar. The end of long winter nights is celebrated with gift-giving, parades, street entertainment, and sporting events. The Thursday that falls within April 19 to April 25.

Reykjavík Fashion Festival. The main platform for promoting Icelandic fashion designers, this 4-day festival takes place at venues around the capital. Mid-March.

MAY

Labor Day. Coinciding with International Workers' Day, Labor Day in Iceland is celebrated with parades and speeches in towns and cities across the country. Many businesses close, but some stores may stay open. May 1.

Reykjavík Arts Festival (www.artfest.is). For two to three weeks, Reykjavík is swept up in this government-sponsored event. Many international artists and performers are included. Mid-May.

Ascension Day. The Christian holiday commemorating Christ's ascension to heaven. Schools and most workplaces are closed. Forty days after Easter. Icelanders also celebrate a public holiday on **Whit Monday,** the day after Pentecost (7 weeks after Easter).

JUNE/JULY

Seafarer's Day & Festival of the Sea. This holiday salutes those who make their living by the sea, and is celebrated across the country with parades, cultural events, great seafood, and rowdy parties. Fishermen partake in rescue demonstrations, swimming and rowing races, and various strongman competitions. "Festival of the Sea" is the local celebration in Reykjavík, which may take place the following weekend. First weekend of June.

National Day. This public holiday marks Iceland's full independence from Denmark in 1944. The day starts off on a solemn and patriotic note, but by afternoon crowds have flocked to the streets to watch parades, traditional dancing, street performers, and theatrical entertainment. (One of the most meaningful gatherings is at Þingvellir National Park, where the Icelandic parliament first assembled in 930.) Each town celebrates in its own way, so check locally for details. June 17.

Summer Solstice (www.fi.is). On the longest day of the year, many Icelanders gather late at night to watch the sun dip below the horizon and scoop back up again shortly afterward. Formal events are rare, but visitors are usually welcome to join local celebrations. Each year, the Ferðafélag Íslands host an all-night climb up to the Snæfellsnes glacier. June 21.

Arctic Open (www.arcticopen.is). This 4-day championship golf tournament in Akureyri, open to professionals and amateurs, continues into the morning hours under the midnight sun. Late June.

Viking Festival (www.fjorukrain.is). For 10 days, modern-day Viking hordes descend on Hafnarfjörður, a town near Reykjavík, for traditional crafts, merrymaking in period costume, and staged battles with Christian forces. Although some participants are Scandinavians, more are Britons and Germans—the Vikings' historic victims. The festival began in 1995 and is run by Hafnarfjörður's Viking Village hotel and restaurant. Between weekends it moves to Sauðárkrókur on the north coast. Mid-June.

Akureyri Summer Arts Festival (www.akureyri.is). For 10 weeks in summer, Iceland's "northern capital" hosts an assortment of concerts and exhibitions in venues across town. Late June to August.

LungA Festival (www.lunga.is; © 861-5859). This festival is fast becoming one of Iceland's prominent music festivals. It invites young people ages 16 to 25 to join workshops led by artists involved in everything from visual art to circus performance to fashion design. Non-Icelanders are welcome, and the week culminates with live concerts by prominent Icelandic bands. Third weekend of July.

AUGUST

Verslunarmannahelgi (August Long Weekend or **Bank Holiday Weekend).** On this party weekend, Icelanders often leave town and camp out en masse. The most well-known destination is the Westman Islands, where locals join thousands of visitors at the campgrounds to hear live bands and gather round the bonfire into the morning hours. Plenty of events also take place in towns. First weekend in August.

Gay Pride (www.hinsegindagar.is/en). The biggest Pride event in Iceland includes a parade, concerts, and all-night parties. Second weekend in August.

Reykjavík Marathon and Culture Night (www.marathon.is). Surely the 3,500 participants in Reykjavík's annual marathon appreciate the purity of the air. Runners can choose between the full marathon, a half-marathon, a 10km (6-mile) run, or 7km (4-mile) and 3km (2-mile) "fun runs." The rest of the day and night are loaded with free concerts and cultural events, and once it's reasonably dark, a fireworks display kicks off. Third weekend in August.

Reykjavík Jazz Festival (www.reykjavikjazz.is). Icelandic and international groups in a variety of styles play clubs and other venues across town. Late August.

Reykjavík Dance Festival (www.reykjavik dancefestival.com). Contemporary choreographers from around the world are invited to participate in this 4-day event. End of August/early September.

SEPTEMBER

Reykjavík International Film Festival (www. riff.is). This 10-day event includes film classics, premieres, retrospectives, seminars, and workshops. Late September or early October.

NOVEMBER

Iceland Airwaves (www.icelandairwaves. com). This 5-day showcase of Iceland's alternative/indie music talent (with many international bands thrown in) attracts more visitors to Iceland than any other event. Crowds are thick with journalists and talent scouts; when the bands are through, top DJs spin until dawn. Icelandair sponsors Airwaves and arranges special packages from Europe and America. Early November.

DECEMBER

Christmas season. In late December, Icelanders only get 4 or 5 hours of daylight, which could explain their enthusiasm for Christmas and its lights. Icelandic children count the 13 days leading up to the holiday with a group of "yuletide lads," all offspring of a grotesque troll named Grýla. (In traditional lore, Grýla ate naughty children, but in the 18th century, threatening them with Grýla was outlawed.) Each day from December 12 to December 24, a different lad descends from the mountains into human homes. Each lad is named for the mischief he gets into: Sausage Snatcher, Door Slammer, Bowl Licker, and so on. At bedtime children leave a shoe in the window, and wake up to find a small present from the nighttime visitor. From Christmas Day through January 6 they come in succession all over again. Both Christmas Eve and Christmas Day are public holidays (Dec 24 and 25).

New Year's Eve. Private use of fireworks is legal on this one night only, and the entire citizenry sets the skies ablaze in celebration. (Reykjavík is a particularly chaotic sight.) Oceanside bonfires are another New Year's ritual. For a more refined experience in Reykjavík, try the trumpet and organ recital in Hallgrímskirkja.

SUGGESTED ITINERARIES

Advance planning can save you a lot of grief in Iceland. From early June until the end of August, places to stay and tours often fill up, and knowing some things in advance, such as if and when you'll need a rental car—and whether it will have 4WD—will affect your itinerary.

We also suggest allowing for some free time in your itinerary. In Iceland, the factors most likely to derail an overbooked itinerary are the weather and weather-based cancellations of domestic flights. Free time is also useful for when you find a place you'd like to explore more thoroughly or for when a local fisherman suddenly offers you a boat trip around a nearby island, as has happened in our experience.

To jumpstart your planning, a few itineraries are suggested below. Others are found throughout the book, just waiting for you to string them together. We've even known people to flag all the swimming pools and hot springs for an itinerary, treating this pool-crazed country as a giant (albeit non-tropical) resort.

THE BEST OF ICELAND IN 4 DAYS

Word is getting around that Iceland is great for casual 3- or 4-day escapes. The basic components of an Iceland long weekend are Reykjavík and excursions from Reykjavík, often including the Blue Lagoon spa. Every night of this itinerary is spent in Reykjavík. In high season, make sure to call a few days ahead for dinner reservations (and for in-water massages at the Blue Lagoon).

Day 1: Reykjavík

If you're out and about before 9am, head to **Grái Kötturinn** (p. 81) for pancakes, bacon, and strong Icelandic coffee. Begin the sightseeing stage at the **Tourist Information Office** (p. 45) inside the **City Hall (Ráðhús)** (p. 56), where you can pick up maps and brochures, and arrange tours and car rental if necessary, not to mention gaze at the enormous 3D map of Iceland. Stroll over to **Tjörnin Pond** (p. 55) and then take a short walk to three compelling sites—the **871±2 Settlement Museum** (p. 53), the **City Cathedral (Dómkirkjan)** (p. 51) in

The Best of Iceland in 4 Days

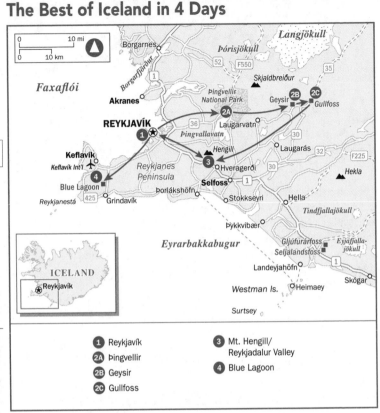

1 Reykjavík

2A Þingvellir

2B Geysir

2C Gullfoss

3 Mt. Hengill/
Reykjadalur Valley

4 Blue Lagoon

Austurvöllur Square, and the **Harbor House Museum (Hafnarhús)** (p. 53), dedicated to contemporary art. All three open at 10am.

For a casual lunch, visit **Sægreifinn** (p. 80) for lobster soup and a seafood kebab. After lunch, head to the eastern half of the city and survey Reykjavík's two main shopping streets, **Laugavegur** and **Skólavörðustígur.** Nearby is the **Culture House** (p. 52), with a wonderful exhibit of medieval manuscripts. To recharge, drop into the city's oldest cafe, **Mokka Kaffi** (p. 81) and try its famous waffles.

Skólavörðustígur leads uphill to Reykjavík's most iconic landmark, **Hallgrímskirkja** (p. 57), where you can ascend the elevator for a panoramic view. Don't miss the **Einar Jónsson Museum** (p. 57) next door, dedicated to Iceland's most renowned sculptor; weekend hours are 2 to 5pm. From here it's a half-hour stroll down Njarðargata and across the park to the **National Museum** (p. 56) south of Tjörnin Pond. Alternatively, skip the museum and catch bus 14 to **Laugardalslaug** (p. 63) for a rejuvenating taste of Iceland's geothermal bathing culture, and ply your hot tub companions for travel advice. (Be prepared for the ubiquitous question, "How do you like Iceland?")

Enjoy an unforgettable dinner at **Skal!** (p. 79), followed by nightclub-hopping into the wee hours—but keep in mind that Reykjavík's night scene hardly *begins* until the wee hours—and a 2am hotdog with "the lot" at **Bæjarins Bestu** (p. 79).

Day 2: The Golden Circle

An enormous wealth of day excursions depart from Reykjavík, but the most popular is the **"Golden Circle" tour** (p. 108) to Þingvellir (p. 109), the historic rift valley where the Icelandic parliament first convened in 930; **Geysir** (p. 113), the geothermal hotspot that lent its name to all geysers; and the majestic **Gullfoss waterfall** (p. 114). Sign up for an 8-hour bus tour (p. 108) or, for more flexibility, rent a car.

Day 3: Hot Springs Tour

The geothermal hot springs of **Reykjadalur Valley** (p. 118), tucked inside the scenic **Mt. Hengill hiking area,** near Hveragerði, are a bather's delight. The most memorable way to reach Reyjkadalur is on horseback; **Eldhestar** (p. 117) offers a 9-hour tour from Reykjavík, with 5 or 6 hours in the saddle. (The small, manageable, good-natured Icelandic horse is great for beginners.) Alternatively, rent a car for the day and hike the route, or sign up for a group hike. The drive is less than an hour one-way, and the hike can be accomplished in as little as 2½ hours round-trip. Don't forget your swimsuit.

Day 4: The Blue Lagoon

The **Blue Lagoon spa** (p. 102)—built around a blue geothermal lake within a jet-black expanse of lava—is Iceland's most popular visitor destination. Sign up with tour company **Reykjavík Excursions** (p. 103) for transportation to the lagoon on the way to the airport, then bathe and exfoliate to your heart's content until it's time to catch your flight home. Allow 2 hours at the lagoon, more if you plan on spa treatments or eating at one of the restaurants.

THE BEST OF SOUTH ICELAND IN 1 WEEK

A driving tour through south Iceland's natural wonders—capped off by a journey to the magnificent Westman Islands—is hard to beat. This itinerary is designed for summer; for off-season travel, see "Off Season," in chapter 11, p. 316.

Day 1: Reykjavík

See p. 31 for our recommended Reykjavík itinerary, which includes a full day's worth of activity and an overnight stay.

Day 2: Höfn & Vatnajökull

Take the morning flight (weekdays only) to Iceland's southeast hub, **Höfn** (p. 265). For lunch, head to one of the restaurants near the harbor to sample langoustine (this is the Icelandic capital for the shellfish), then rent a car and drive to the intersection of Route F985 and the Ring Road to catch the 2pm **snowmobiling** tour (p. 263) on Europe's largest glacier, **Vatnajökull** (p. 263). (Alternatively, try cross-country skiing on Vatnajökull with outfitter **From Coast to Mountains.**) Spend the night in Höfn or any farmstay close by.

Day 3: Höfn to Vík

Drive west along the southern coast from Höfn to **Vík** (p. 248), along what is probably the most mind-boggling stretch of the Ring Road. The first stop is the bizarre yet majestic **Jökulsárlón glacial lagoon,** full of parading icebergs. The next stop is **Skaftafell**, within the **Vatnajökull National Park,** for a 2-hour hike to the striking basalt formations of **Svartifoss** (p. 259). After a coffee break at **Systrakaffi** in the hamlet of **Kirkjubæjarklaustur** (p. 254), take an hour to peruse the rim of the **Fjaðrárgljúfur gorge** (p. 254). Spend the night in Iceland's southernmost village, Vík.

Day 4: Vík to Hella-Hvolsvöllur

The day starts with the best walk on Iceland's south coastline: a 3-hour jaunt along the **Reynisfjall sea cliffs** (p. 250). (If this is too much hiking, take a casual stroll on the black sand beach next to Vík.) After resuming your trip westward on the Ring Road, detour on Route 215 south to the **Reynisfjara beach** (p. 251), just west of Reynisfjall, and witness the awe-inspiring sea cave **Hálsanefshellir.** The next stop is **Dyrhólaey** (p. 249), a promontory and nature reserve with bustling bird cliffs and an iconic rock archway over the sea. In the village of **Skógar,** investigate the towering **Skógafoss waterfall** (p. 249) and the prolific collection at Iceland's best **folk museum.** You are now very close to the site of the 2010 **Eyjafjallajökull** eruption, and you can experience an eruption simulation and watch a 4D documentary at the **Lava Centre.** Notice the features in the landscape caused by the eruption, such as lava formations and fissures. Head south at **Hvolsvöllur** (p. 239) to reach the port of **Landeyjahöfn** (p. 228) for the 6:30pm or 9:30pm ferry (7:30pm/10:30pm weekends) to the spectacular **Westman Islands** (p. 226), where you'll spend 2 nights in the village of **Heimaey** (p. 228).

Day 5: Westman Islands

Take a boat trip into the sea caves, play a round of golf inside a volcano crater, stroll the coastline spotting puffins, and investigate the aftereffects of a devastating 1973 volcanic eruption, including at **Eldheimar** (p. 228), the museum of remembrance. Street signs have been erected in the lava above where the corresponding streets once were, and a few houses, hauntingly half-swallowed by lava, are preserved. Take at least one meal at **Slippurinn** (p. 232), a restaurant in an old machine workshop in the shipyard whose chef forages for wild herbs and works with the local farmers and fishermen.

Day 6: Westman Islands to Hekla

After another walk along the Westmans' dramatic coastline, take a morning or early afternoon ferry back to **Landeyjahöfn** and continue west. From the Ring Road west of Hella, take Route 26 northeast into **Þjórsárdalur valley** (p. 232) for views of Iceland's other notorious volcano, **Hekla** (p. 234). Head for the **Hekla Center** and check on the volcano's seismometer readings, then stay the night at **Leirubakki** hotel on the same property.

Day 7: Gullfoss & Geysir to Reykjavík

Turn on to Route 32, then walk or drive to the lithe and beautiful **Háifoss** (p. 234), Iceland's second tallest waterfall. After visiting **Þjóðveldisbærinn** (p. 234), a reconstruction of a Viking longhouse from the settlement era, drive to **Stöng** (p. 233) to see the ruins that Þjóðveldisbærinn was based on. From Stöng, a short walk extends to **Gjáin gorge** (p. 233), a lush and bewitching enclave. Turn right on Route 30 and proceed north to the majestic **Gullfoss** (p. 114). Ten minutes away is **Geysir** (p. 113), where you can witness eruptions of the **Strokkur** geyser. Return to Reykjavík for a final evening in the capital.

ICELAND'S RING ROAD IN 10 DAYS

With 2 weeks at your disposal, consider this epic driving tour around the whole country, with plenty of opportunities to leave the car behind and experience Iceland's great outdoors directly underfoot. This whirlwind itinerary circles the country clockwise, with Reykjavík as the start and finish point. Technically, Iceland's Ring Road can be "done" in 3 days, but a week is a sensible minimum, and 2 weeks if you're adding the Westfjords. As with most driving tours of Iceland, this itinerary is possible in spring or fall, but is best experienced from early June until mid-September. A conventional rental car can easily handle the route, though a 4WD vehicle expands your options considerably, particularly for excursions into the interior. *Note:* Some museums and other sightseeing stops may be closed outside of summer.

Day 1: Reykjavík

The first day and night is spent in the Iceland's thriving first city; see p. 31 for our recommended full-day itinerary.

Day 2: Reykjavík to Sauðárkrókur

Set off from Reykjavík around 9am and drive 132 km (82 miles) north of Reykjavík to **Húsafell** (p. 126), the launch spot for a midday tour into the manmade ice tunnels carved inside the **Langjökull glacier.** Continue on to **Blönduós** (p. 172) and make a slight detour on Route 74 to the **Icelandic Seal Center** (p. 170), your first stop on the Vatnsnes peninsula. Here you will catch great views of the Strandir coast and hopefully spot a few seals. Cross the peninsula on Route 744 to **Sauðárkrókur** (p. 176), in the **Skagafjörður region.** Before checking in to your hotel, visit **Gestastofa Sútarans** (p. 176), Europe's only fish-leather tannery.

Day 3: Sauðárkrókur to Skagafjörður

On your way out of Sauðárkrókur, stop by the **Glaumbær folk museum** (p. 174), the best of Iceland's many museums dedicated to preserving 19th-century turf-roofed farmhouses, vital repositories of Icelandic cultural memory (closing time 6pm). Spend the rest of the day exploring **Skagafjörður,** stopping in **Hofsós** (p. 178), 34 km (21 miles) away, halfway up the fjord's eastern shore, to visit the **Icelandic Emigration Center** (p. 178), which recounts the stories of the many Icelandic emigrants who sailed to North America from the village. Drive 55km (35 miles) to the northeast until you reach **Siglufjörður** (p. 179), set inside a short, steep-sided fjord less than 40km (25 miles) from the Arctic Circle. Explore the town's maritime past at the **Herring Era museum** and have a beer at the Seagull 67 brewery, before checking into your hotel.

Day 4: Akureyri

Continue to **Akureyri** (p. 185), 76.4 km (47½ miles) away, then visit the **Akureyri Art Museum,** the **Akureyri Church**—with its distinctive and appealingly grandiose Art Deco twin spires—and Einar Jónsson's poignant 1901 sculpture *The Outlaw* (Útlaginn). Head 10km (6¼ miles) south of Akureyri on Route 821 to visit the **Christmas House** (p. 199) for some summer Christmas cheer and cinnamon-coated almonds. Visit the outdoor restroom here; it's hilarious. Back in Akureyri, wind down with the massaging water jets at the **Akureyri Swimming Pool.** Dine at **Strikið,** where you can enjoy views of the city and the mountains across the fjord.

Day 5: Akureyri to Mývatn

On your way out of Akureyri, stop at **Safnasafnið,** an innovative art museum seeking to transcend the divide between contemporary and folk art (opens at 10am). The next road stop, 50km (31 miles) from Akureyri, is the elegant **Goðafoss waterfall** (p. 201). Backtrack 4km (2¼ miles), and turn right on Route 85 north to **Húsavík** (p. 210), Iceland's **whale-watching** mecca. (Call ahead if the weather is iffy.) Buy your boat tickets, then bone up before the tour at the **Whale Museum.**

After the 3-hour excursion, head for the **Húsavík Museum.** Stock up on groceries before dining at one of Húsavík's two best restaurants, **Gamli Baukur** and **Salka.** Head back south on Route 85, then take Route 87 to **Reykjahlíð village** (p. 203) on **Lake Mývatn,** where you'll spend the next 2 nights.

Day 6: Mývatn–Krafla

Today is devoted to sampling the geological marvels of **Mývatn** (p. 201) and **Krafla** (p. 205). Drive first to **Grjótagjá,** an eerie fissure and geothermal vent, then take an hour to climb to the rim of **Hverfell,** a tephra explosion crater. Drive on to **Dimmuborgir lava field**—or, if you feel like tackling a more challenging hike, descend the south side of Hverfell down to Dimmuborgir. Don't miss **Kirkjan** ("The Church") lava archway—the clearly marked Kirkjuvegur trail will take you right through it. Continue circling Mývatn, until you reach the **Skútustaðagígar** pseudocraters for another 30-minute ramble. Tireless visitors can add the 2-hour round-trip hike up **Vindbelgjarfjall** to survey the day's triumphs thus far.

Drive east of Mývatn to **Hverir** (p. 205), pinch yourself to make sure this hellish geothermal hotspot is not a bizarre Martian dream, then head into Krafla and spend an hour exploring the strange and beautiful **Leirhnjúkur lava field** (p. 206). On your way back to Mývatn, enjoy a rejuvenating swim in the mineral-rich waters of **Mývatn Nature Baths** (p. 206). At 6pm, drop into **Vogafjós Cowshed Cafe** (p. 209) and enjoy a homemade smoked trout treat, while cows are milked on the other side of a plate-glass window. For dinner, reserve at **Mylla** in the **Hotel Mývatn** (p. 208) or the more casual **Gamli Bærinn** (p. 209).

Day 7: Mývatn to Seyðisfjörður

The next fuel stop is a long way off, so fill the tank before setting out and confirm with staff that road conditions to Dettifoss are suitable. About 36km (22 miles) east of Reykjahlíð, exit the Ring Road on to Route 864 and proceed 32km (20 miles) to **Dettifoss** (p. 218), Europe's mightiest waterfall. From Dettifoss, hike 1.5km (1 mile) to the more understated **Selfoss falls** (p. 218).

Return to the Ring Road and continue east. In clear weather, you should have fantastic views south to **Herðubreið,** voted Iceland's most-loved mountain in a national poll. Sixteen kilometers (10 miles) east of the Route 864 junction, turn right on Route 901 and proceed 8km (5 miles) to **Möðrudalur** for lunch at the **Fjallakaffi** (p. 300). Ask about road conditions farther ahead on Route 901, to help choose the best route to **Sænautasel** (p. 299), a reconstructed turf farm serving coffee and pancakes in the middle of nowheresville. Keep this place in mind on the final day of the trip as you pass through farmland that endured the most ash fall during the 2010 Eyjafjallajökull eruption—Sænautasel fared much worse and was abandoned in 1875 after the Askja eruption fouled the area with ash.

From Sænautasel, return to the Ring Road and continue to **Egilsstaðir** (p. 299), the commercial hub of east Iceland. From here it's a 28km (17-mile) detour to the lovely coastal village of **Seyðisfjörður** (p. 288), with a breathtaking descent into the fjord. Dinner is at **Skaftfell** cafe/gallery, followed by a stroll along the waterfront.

Day 8: Seyðisfjörður to Höfn

Linger in Seyðisfjörður, walking among the 19th- and early-20th-century chalet-style kit homes. Devotees of outmoded technology should visit the old telegraph station at the **Technical Museum of East Iceland** (p. 290). After returning to Egilsstaðir, decide on a route to **Höfn** (p. 265), the regional hub of southeast Iceland. The Ring Road is the most direct. The longer route—which affords more Eastfjords coastal scenery—follows Route 92 to Reyðarfjörður, then Route 96 through a tunnel to Fáskrúðs-fjörður and along the coast before it rejoins the Ring Road. Stops along Route 96 include **Steinasafn Petru** (p. 275), a magnificent rock collection in **Stöðvarfjörður** (p. 275) begun by a local woman in 1946. Both routes pass **Djúpivogur** (p. 272), a charming fishing village and the launch point for 4-hour boat trips to **Papey Island** (p. 274). Before dinner at Höfn's inviting **Kaffi Hornið** (p. 270), visit the supermarket on Vesturbraut to pick up lunch for tomorrow.

Day 9: Höfn to Vík

The 272km (169-mile) stretch of Ring Road from Höfn to Vík is a nonstop procession of stunning scenery. The first requisite stop is **Jökulsárlón** (p. 262), an otherworldly lake full of icebergs calved from **Vatnajökull,** Europe's largest glacier. After another 55km (34 miles), turn into **Vatna-jökull National Park** at **Skaftafell** (p. 259) and bring your lunch along for a 2- to 3-hour hike to **Svartifoss waterfall,** the turf-roofed **Sel farm-house,** and **Sjónarsker viewpoint,** overlooking an incredible panorama of majestic peaks, looming glaciers, and barren floodplains. In the tiny, isolated village of **Kirkjubæjarklaustur** (p. 254), recharge with after-noon tea or a taste of Iceland's infamous fermented shark at **Systrakaffi** (p. 257). Shortly west of Kirkjubæjarklaustur, exit on Route 206 and proceed 3km (2 miles) to the lovely, contemplative **Fjaðrárgljúfur gorge** (p. 255) for an hour-long walk along the rim. For dinner in Vík, set out for the casual **Halldórskaffi** (p. 254).

Day 10: Vík to Reykjavík

The morning is devoted to Vík's magnificent coastal environs. Allow 3 hours for the round-trip walk along the **Reynisfjall sea cliffs** (p. 250) to the viewpoint looking west toward **Mýrdalsjökull** and the **Dyrhólaey promontory** (p. 249), identified by its enormous, natural arch of rock. (If this is too much hiking, just stroll on Vík's black sand beach and gaze at the iconic **Reynisdrangar** sea stacks.) Back behind the wheel, take Route 215 from the Ring Road to the pebbly **Reynisfjara beach** (p. 251) on the western side of Reynisfjall, and peer into the spellbinding sea cave **Hálsanefshellir.** If you have time, Dyrhólaey is another enticing side trip, especially for birders. West of Vík, you're in the area most affected by the 2010 **Eyjafjallajökull** eruption, though it's easy to pass by with-out noticing the new features in the landscape if you're not familiar with the way it was before (see p. 240). Thirty-three kilometers (21 miles) from Vík is the **Skógar Folk Museum** (p. 249), Iceland's most glorious and affecting collection of folk artifacts. One kilometer (¾ mile) away is the hypnotic **Skógafoss waterfall** (p. 249). Now hightail it back to Reykjavík, just in time for dinner at **Nostra** (p. 77) for a valedictory feast.

HOME-BASE REYKJAVÍK: 5 DAYS WITH THE FAMILY

This itinerary is designed for a family staying in Reykjavík for 5 days, exploring the city and going on a few day-trip adventures farther afield. Depending on the ages of your children, the itinerary can easily be modified for overnight stays, especially if you want to go around the Ring Road, which could be an unforgettable family road trip. But sometimes basing the family in one place and taking day trips makes for a much more relaxed holiday. The order of days can also be switched around based on everyone's mood and the latest weather report. Consider booking less central—hence less expensive—accommodation for this sort of trip, especially if you're hiring a car for the whole period.

Day 1: Árbær Museum & Reykjavík Zoo

Get your bearings in the city with a morning stroll along Reykjavík's two main shopping streets, **Laugavegur** and **Skólavörðustígur.** At the top of Skólavörðustígur, ascend the Hallgrímskirkja (p. 57) elevator for a panoramic view. From here you could walk down **Njarðargata** and across the park to the **National Museum** (p. 56)—which has multimedia exhibits and a dress-up room for children—but we recommend catching a bus to the Árbær **Open Air Museum** (p. 61) instead. People in period costume explain how to weave wool or smoke meat, and Icelandic history is put in context without the yawn factor as children explore the turf-roofed houses. (If you're reading this as you head down Njarðargata to the more convenient National Museum, note the modern residential rendition of a turf roof at the corner of Fjólugata so that you won't miss out entirely!)

Bus 19 will take you from Árbær Museum to the **Reykjavík Zoo** (p. 59)—ask the driver to let you know when to get off. Have lunch at the nearby botanical garden's **greenhouse cafe,** then meet the animals of Iceland, from domestic chickens and sheep to wild reindeer and Arctic foxes. Check the daily animal petting schedule. There's also a family park and "science world" for any tireless children, before calling it a day.

Day 2: Laxnes, Esja & Borgarnes

Rent a car for 2 days. Set off from Reykjavík on the Ring Road heading north to drive 74km (46 miles) to Borgarnes, but take a short detour at Route 36 to sign up for a 9:30am horse ride at **Laxnes Horse Farm** (p. 66). Next stop is **Esja,** Reykjavík's "home mountain" (p. 95), where you can stretch your legs while exploring the small wooded areas at the mountain's base. Head up the mountain until you're happy with the view or overcome by thoughts of lunch. Continue on to Borgarnes, heading for the **Settlement Center** (p. 124), an interactive museum dedicated to the stories of the first 60 years of Icelandic settlement. Younger children may want to stick to the exhibit on *Njál's Saga—Egil's Saga* can get a bit gruesome at points, though some brave kids might appreciate Egil's life-size witches and gory scenes. Back in Reykjavík, enjoy a quick dip in the closest pool before dinner.

Day 3: Geysir & Stokkseyri

Gullfoss is a mighty and beautiful waterfall, but if that's not enough to impress children, **Geysir** is sure to get their attention. To follow the typical **"Golden Circle"** route (p. 108), take Route 1 north of Mosfellsbær, then turn right on Route 36. From Þingvellir, continue east on Route 36, turn left on Route 365, and turn left again on Route 37 in Laugarvatn; when Route 37 ends, turn left on Route 35. From there it's a short way to Geysir, where you can all marvel at the enormous jets of water suddenly shooting into the air, and another 10 minutes to Gullfoss. Watch your footing at both places and keep children close—the unimposing rope barriers belie the dangers of Geysir's multiple hot springs and the steep, deep gorge at Gullfoss. Jump in the car and head back to Reykjavík.

Day 4: Sagas, Seaside & Shopping

Pack swimming gear and towels, but begin with a trip to the **Pearl** (p. 197). Go upstairs and outside to admire a 360-degree view of the capital, and then make a quick stop at the Christmas store, saving time for lunch at the cafe. From here, walk down through the wooded Öskjuhlíð hill and across to **Nauthólsvík** beach (p. 59). Watch the children play on the white sand (imported!) from the comfort of the long hot tub. Who said Iceland wasn't a beach holiday destination? For a spot of shopping, catch a bus to **Kringlan** shopping mall (p. 85), where you can choose to leave your children (ages 3–9) at the **Adventure Land** child-minding area for an hour or two. From Kringlan, you can take a longish but leisurely walk back to the heart of town via **Miklatún Park,** popping into **Kjarvalsstaðir Art Museum** (p. 58) for a peek at the works of Jóhannes Kjarval, one of Iceland's most admired artists (free for children under 18).

Day 5: The Pond to the Blue Lagoon

On your final day, begin by strolling over to **Tjörnin Pond** (p. 55), where you can feed the ducks and gaze at the enormous 3D map of Iceland inside the **City Hall (Ráðhús)** (p. 56). See if the children can work out where they've been, and show them (if you can find it!) where the big Eyjafjallajökull eruption happened in 2010. Sign up with tour company **Reykjavík Excursions** (p. 62) for transportation to the **Blue Lagoon spa**

(p. 102) on the way to the airport, then bathe and exfoliate to your heart's content until it's time to catch your flight home. The children will especially enjoy covering each other in the white silica mud without knowing they're getting a health treatment. It's hard to omit this unique send-off from any itinerary in Iceland.

FOODIE ICELAND

Historically Icelandic food was oriented toward survival rather than pleasure, but that is no longer the case. A 6-day drive along the west coast will bring you in touch with many of the country's culinary highlights, from Reykjavík's finest farm-to-table bistros to unchartered farming and fishing villages, home to some of the island's best seafood. Iceland's foodie route can be done year-round, though be sure to reserve hotels and tables early during the summer.

Day 1: Reykjavík

Spend your first day eating around the capital. After tasting your first *skyr,* Iceland's high-protein yogurt, during your hotel breakfast, walk over to **Reykjavík Roasters** (p. 81), the city's premier specialty coffee shop and roaster, for a quick pick-me-up. For lunch, head over to **Matur og Drykkur** (p. 76), a stylish Icelandic bistro that aims to rescue long-lost recipes like halibut soup. Rest up because you will be having dinner at **Dill** (p. 76), one of the top restaurants in all of Scandinavia, for a seven-course tasting menu sourced from local fishermen and farmers that's paired with natural wines. For a nightcap, head upstairs to **Mikkeller & Friends** (p. 88), the local branch of cult Danish brewer Mikkeller.

Day 2: Reykjavík to Búðir

Set off from Reykjavík around 9am and drive 74km (46 miles) north of Reykjavík to the **Háafell goat farm** outside Borgarnes, to see how this once endangered breed is being saved through culinary means. Pick up samples of goat cheese and other products at the farm, then make the short drive to **Krauma** where you can sample their Icelandic goat platter after a dip in the geothermal baths. Then it's time to begin your exploration of the beautiful **Snæfellsnes Peninsula.** Start your journey along the south coast, stopping only for a short horseback riding excursion before reaching **Hótel Búðir** (p. 137), where you will spend the night, enjoying a meal of local fish or game in the elegant dining room and a glass of wine or craft beer overlooking the ocean in the lounge.

Day 3: Búðir to Stykkishólmur

In the morning, continue to the village of **Arnarstapi** (p. 132), signing up for a snowmobile tour of **Snæfellsjökull glacier** (p. 132), then take a 2-hour walk along the sculpted lava coastline between Arnarstapi and **Hellnar,** where you can stop for fish and chips from the food trucks near the lava archway. Stroll through **Djúpalónssandur,** a picturesque beach tucked inside a rocky cove, and drive through the gnarled lava field **Berserkjahraun** (p. 135). Spend the night in **Stykkishólmur,** where you'll sample the local seafood delicacies, such as mussels or scallops, from **Narfeyrarstofa** (p. 143).

Day 4: Stykkishólmur to Suðureyri

Witness the uncountable islands and shallow marine habitat of **Breiðafjörður**—while eating shellfish straight from the shell—on the 11am **Unique Adventure boat tour** (p. 155) from **Stykkishólmur.** Then board the 3:30pm car ferry to **Brjánslækur** on the Westfjords' south coast. Forming the convoluted claw shape in Iceland's northwest corner, the **Westfjords** (p. 144) have been criminally overlooked by the tourist industry. Drive to **Suðureyri** (p. 152), Iceland's (if not all of Europe's) most sustainable fishing village.

Day 5: Suðureyri to Ísafjörður

Sign up for a **Fisherman Culture tour** (p. 152), which will visit the country's oldest fishing station in Bolungarvík, an eco-friendly fish processing plant, and a local food trail to sample regional delicacies. Take your dinner in **Ísafjörður** (p. 153), the Westfjords' appealing capital, where you can enjoy a generous dish of pan-fried fish at **Tjöruhúsið** restaurant (p. 158) next to the Heritage Museum.

Day 6: Ísafjörður to Reykjavík

Drive along the winding coastline of **Ísafjarðardjúp Bay** to the **Heydalur Country Hotel** (p. 160), and chat up the resident parrot over lunch in a converted barn. Choose among Heydalur's recreational activities—sea kayaking, horseback riding, fishing, and hiking—relaxing afterward in the natural geothermal pool. Cross the "neck" of the Westfjords to Hólmavík, where you can grab an afternoon snack at **Galdrasýning á Ströndum** (p. 161), better known as the Museum of Icelandic Sorcery and Witchcraft, which has a restaurant that surprisingly serves some of the best blue mussels around. Then drive back to Reykjavík to end the night with pork belly and a local craft beer at gastropub **Sæmundur í Sparifötunum** (p. 78).

HIKING ICELAND

Iceland's most world-renowned trek—a 4-day route blessed with astonishing scenery—is the hike known as **Laugavegurinn** (p. 237), connecting the interior wonderland of **Landmannalaugar** (p. 236) to the alpine oasis of **Þórsmörk** (p. 245). Facilities along the route are hardly luxurious, but you can hire a tour company to transport your bags from mountain hut to mountain hut. The Laugavegurinn is passable from roughly the beginning of July to early September. Book the mountain huts well in advance.

Day 1: Reykjavík

See p. 31 for our full-day Reykjavík itinerary. You'll also need this day to stock up on **groceries** (and perhaps some last-minute supplies), because provisions are generally unavailable on the trail. If you are going with a tour group, check with the operator to see if food is provided.

Days 2 & 3: Landmannalaugar

Board the morning bus from Reykjavík to **Landmannalaugar,** whose rhyolite landscape is a photographer's dream. This wondrous hiking zone within **Fjallabak Nature Reserve** (p. 236) is one of the best in the country. Plan to spend 2 nights at the mountain hut run by Ferðafélag Íslands to allow yourself a leisurely day and a half for exploring the region. Bathing in the natural hot springs near where you're staying is a perfect nightcap.

Days 4 to 7: The Laugavegurinn

Four days is the ideal amount of time to hike through this fabulous procession of interior scenery. The entire route is 55km (34 miles), with **mountain huts** spaced at roughly 14km (9-mile) intervals. You may be hankering for privacy by the time you reach Þórsmörk, so consider booking a private room at the **Húsadalur Volcano Huts** (p. 246) for your last night in the region.

Day 8: Back to Reykjavík

Enjoy another day hike (p. 245) in Þórsmörk before catching the 3pm bus back to Reykjavík for your final evening in the capital. Round out the evening with a hearty meal at **Þrír Frakkar** (p. 77)—welcome back to the real world indeed—and prepare for your next-day departure home.

REYKJAVÍK

R eykjavík, the world's northernmost capital, is more cosmopolitan than you can shake a martini at, yet the city also clings affectionately to its parochialism. Greater Reykjavík is home to more than half the country's population, and almost all visitors to Iceland pass through the city, many venturing no farther than the city limits before heading back to the airport. Reykjavík has become a destination in itself. Whether you're packing hiking boots, fishing rods, or zoom lenses, it's easy to fill a long weekend or a whole fortnight in Reykjavík.

4

For most of its history, Reykjavík suffered a backward reputation among European cities, but this has only intensified its heady sensation of newfound wealth and authority. Thirty years ago, no one even dreamed Reykjavík would become an international arbiter of hipness, especially in music and nightlife.

Despite its reputation for wild nights, Reykjavík by day is the most subdued of European capitals. Its cosmopolitan edge seems at odds with its squat, boxy architecture. It almost feels wrong to leave the world's problems so far behind: Iceland's urban life is virtually free of crime (aside from some artful graffiti), homelessness, and pollution. Reykjavík is committed to sustainable development, with aggressive tree planting, home heating and electrical systems powered by underground hot springs—that faint egg smell in bathrooms is a natural by-product—and a few buses running on hydrogen fuel (look for steam emissions from the roof). One night a year, since 2006, the entire city turns off all lights for 30 minutes simultaneously. Sleepy children stand outside gazing up at the night sky alongside their parents: Reykjavíkians paying tribute to the romance of their town's original, natural state.

Reykjavík hosts a multitude of festivals. Most events take place outside of summer, belying the widespread perception of Iceland as a one-season destination. See chapter 2, p. 28, for a schedule of annual events.

ORIENTATION
Getting There

BY PLANE   International flights arrive at **Keflavík International Airport** (www.isavia.is/en/keflavik-airport), about 50km (31 miles) southwest of Reykjavík. Taxis into the city cost around 16,000kr for up to four people, so most visitors come to town on the **Flybus** (www.re.is; ⓒ **580-5400**). Tickets are 5,500kr for adults, 2,750kr for children 12 to 15, and free for children 11 and under. Taxis and the Flybus are clearly positioned outside the arrival hall; both accept credit cards. The Flybus stops at the BSÍ bus terminal, almost all hotels and guesthouses, and the City Hostel. If your accommodation isn't on the list of Flybus stops, it may offer a free transfer from the BSÍ terminal, or there might be a stop within easy walking distance. If that fails, you could still save money by taking the Flybus to the BSÍ terminal and catching a taxi from there. Flybus departures from Reykjavík to the airport are timed to coincide with departing international flights.

Domestic flights (and flights from Greenland and the Faeroe Islands) arrive at **Reykjavík Airport** (www.isavia.is/en/reykjavik-airport), just south of the city. For more on domestic air travel, see "Getting Around," in chapter 11, p. 318.

BY FERRY   No scheduled international ferries arrive in Reykjavík; ferries from Europe arrive at **Seyðisfjörður** on the east coast. For information on cruise ships, see "Getting There," in chapter 11, p. 317.

Visitor Information

INFORMATION OFFICES
The main **Tourist Information Office** (Aðalstræti 2; ⓒ **411-6040;** www.visit reykjavik.is; daily 8am–8pm) is in the City Hall, beside Tjörnin pond. On the premises is a stunning scale model of Iceland, a fee-free **tour office,** which can book places to stay, car rentals, and tours. The office has an extensive selection of brochures, guides, maps, and other information about Iceland, arranged by region.

ONLINE
Run by the city's tourist office, **www.visitreykjavik.is** has thorough, well-mapped listings of hotels, restaurants, museums, and sights, as well as a schedule of events. *What's On in Iceland* (**www.whatson.is**) covers dining, places to stay, and city activities and events. *The Reykjavík Grapevine* (**www.grapevine. is**), a free English-language circular, is a useful guide to current happenings.

Getting Around

BY BICYCLE   Reykjavík is easily explored by bicycle and has a good network of bike paths. Riding on sidewalks and footpaths is widely tolerated, and most trails are illuminated in fall and winter. A free biking map is available at the Tourist Information Office (p. 50). We recommend the popular route that takes you around the coastline and into the peaceful Elliðaár Valley.

There are several **bike rental** businesses in town, including **Reykjavík Bike Tours,** Ægisgarður 7 (https://icelandbike.com; ⓒ **694-8956;** daily 9am–5pm), which carries high-quality Trek bicycles and provides studded tires in winter. Rates are 4,900kr per day with discounts for 4-hour segments, half-days, or longer rentals. They also run frequent bike and Segway tours around town. Reykjavík's citywide bikeshare program, **WOW citybike** (https://wowcitybike.com), lets you rent bikes from 15 stations scattered around town. The price is 350kr per trip (max 30 min.) or 3,900kr per monthly pass.

BY BUS   Reykjavík's bus service **Strætó** (www.bus.is; ℂ **540-2700**) is very reliable. The major bus hubs are Lækjartorg (in the city, at the north end of Lækjargata), Hlemmur (on the eastern end of Laugavegur), and the **BSÍ bus terminal** (www.bsi.is; Vatnsmýrarvegur 10) south of downtown. Free bus maps are available at www.bus.is (check out the impressive "Journey Planner" feature), the Tourist Information Office, and bus hubs. Most travelers use buses only to reach outlying hotels or sights such as the Pearl, Laugardalur Park, and the Árbær Museum. Local routes venture as far as the suburbs of Hafnarfjörður, Mosfellsbær, and Akranes (see chapter 5). Most long-distance routes leave from the BSÍ terminal.

Buses operate Monday to Saturday from 6:35am to midnight and Sunday from 9:30am to midnight, with set departure times usually every 20 minutes, or every 30 minutes evenings, weekends, and on some routes during summer. The flat fare of 460kr for adults or 220kr for children 6 to 18 (exact change only or purchased through the Strætó smartphone app) is collected on the bus. Transfers *(skiptimiði)* are free within a certain time frame (normally 45 min.) and must be requested from your first driver. The **Reykjavík City Card** (p. 50) includes free unlimited bus travel for 1, 2, or 3 days.

BY CAR   Reykjavík's narrow one-way streets and parking regulations discourage many drivers, but by international standards the city is quite negotiable. Public parking—marked on most tourist maps—usually requires buying a ticket at a kiosk and placing it on the dashboard. Meters vary in cost by zone but start at around 100kr per hour; fees must be paid from 10am to 6pm weekdays and from 10am to 2pm Saturday. Parking is free Sundays and evenings. One parking strategy is to simply park just outside the city's heart, where there are no meters. For information on car rentals and driving in Iceland, see "Getting Around," in chapter 11.

BY FOOT   Reykjavík is a good walking town, easily navigable on foot, with most of the tourist sites, restaurants, and shops concentrated along the central streets.

BY TAXI   Taxis are expensive: Meters start at 550kr, and a short ride across town is routinely 1,500kr. Sharing helps, as taxis charge per ride, not per passenger. The best taxi companies are **BSR Taxis** (www.taxireykjavik.is; ℂ **561-0000**) and **Hreyfill** (www.hreyfill.is; ℂ **588-5522**). Both accept credit cards inside the taxi. There is no need to tip.

[FastFACTS] REYKJAVÍK

Banks/Currency Exchange   Banks are usually open Monday to Friday 9:15am to 4pm, or until 6:30pm in Kringlan Mall (p. 85). All banks change foreign currency, and many have 24-hour ATMs.

Drugstores   Drugstores *(Apótek)* are usually open Monday through Friday 9am to 6 or 7pm, and Saturday to 4pm. Drugstores that stay open late include **Lyf og heilsa** (Háaleitisbraut 68 at

Austurver, close to Kringlan Mall; ✆ **581-2101;** daily 8am–10pm) and **Lyfja Apótek** (Lágmúli 5, near Laugardalur Park; ✆ **533-2300;** daily 8am–midnight).
Emergencies Dial ✆ **112** for ambulance, fire, or police. See also "Medical Help," below.

Grocery Stores/ Supermarkets Bónus (Laugavegur 59, ✆ **562-8200;** and Hallveigarstígur 1, ✆ **517-0425;** Mon–Thurs midday–6:30pm; Fri 10am–7:30pm; Sat 10am–6pm; Sun midday–6pm) is the best market in the city center. **10–11** markets are open 24 hours; a small branch is on Austurstræti 17 (✆ **552-1011)** and a larger one is at Barónsstígur 4 (corner of Hverfisgata; ✆ **511-5311).** At Kringlan Mall is **Hagkaup** (✆ **563-5200;** Mon–Wed 10am–8pm; Thurs 10am–9pm; Fri–Sat 10am–8pm; Sun midday–8pm).

Internet Access Many hotels offer free Wi-Fi or have guest terminals, and most cafes have free Wi-Fi. Access is also available at the City Library (Tryggvagata 15; www.borgarbokasafn.is; ✆ **411-6100;** Mon–Thurs 10am–7pm; Fri 11am–6pm; Sat–Sun 1–5pm).

Laundromat Reykjavík has no self-service laundromats. If you're near Laugardalur Park, you can use the machines in the City Hostel (p. 74).

Lost & Found Call the **police hotline** at ✆ **444-1000** to see if someone has turned in your item. They even occasionally post lost items on their Instagram feed.

Luggage Storage Hotels can usually store luggage; otherwise, use the **BSÍ bus terminal** (Vatnsmýrarvegur 10; ✆ **580-5400;** daily 4:30am–midnight). The charge is 500kr per item for the first 24 hours, 300kr each additional 24 hours.

Medical Help For emergencies, dial ✆ **112.** The main 24-hour emergency room is at **National University Hospital,** Fossvogur (✆ **543-2000;** bus: 11, 13, or 18). For non-emergencies, **standard hours** are 9am to 5pm Monday to Friday; doctors are on duty 24 hours at the National University Hospital (✆ **525-1000)** and during nonworking hours in Kópavogur at the **Læknavaktin Medical Center,** Smáratorg 1 (✆ **1770;** Mon–Fri 5–11:30pm, Sat–Sun 9am–11:30pm; bus: 2, 24, or 28). After 11:30pm, or on weekends and holidays, you can call for a telephone consultation, or possibly a "home visit." Standard appointment fees are around 8,000kr, but phone consultations are free. For **dental emergencies,** call ✆ **575-0505.**

Police For emergencies, call ✆ **112.** The main station (✆ **444-1000)** is at Hverfisgata 113–115, opposite the Hlemmur bus station.

Post Offices Post offices are open 9am to 6pm weekdays. The central branch is at Pósthússtræti 5, at the corner of Austursræti (✆ **580-1200).** You can also buy stamps at some bookstores and tourist shops.

Restrooms Public coin-operated restrooms (50kr) are in a few downtown locations, indicated by "WC" icons on tourist maps. City Hall (p. 56) has free restrooms, and most cafes are tolerant of walk-ins.

Telephone Public phones are sparse in Reykjavík, but you can find them at post offices, on the southwest corner of Austurvöllur Square, and on Lækjargata. They accept coins or phone cards, which are available at post offices, filling stations, kiosks, and convenience stores.

Tipping Tipping is not expected.

EXPLORING REYKJAVÍK

In many ways, comparisons between Reykjavík and other European cities are best left alone. It boasts no castles, skyscrapers, grand squares, or monuments; the oldest house dates from 1764. Reykjavík's grandeur resides in its people, landscape, and culture: the museums, the music, the burgeoning restaurant and bistro culture, the geothermal pools, the style and attitude, the bustle and nightlife, and the cultivation of civic space.

Exploring Reykjavík

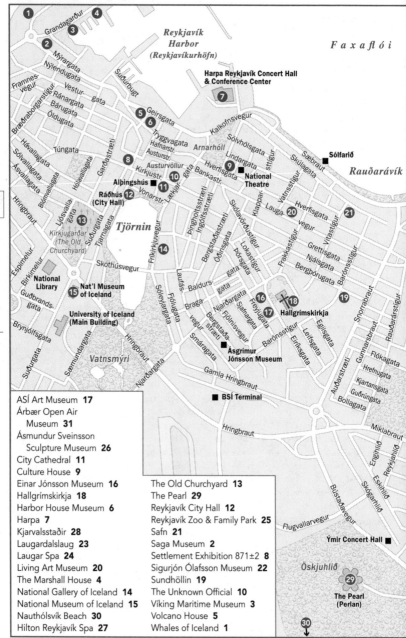

Reykjavík Harbor
(Reykjavíkurhöfn)

Faxaflói

Harpa Reykjavík Concert Hall
& Conference Center

Rauðarávík

Sólfarið

National Theatre

Alþingishús
Ráðhús (City Hall)

Tjörnin

Kirkjugarðar
(The Old Churchyard)

National Library

Nat'l Museum of Iceland

University of Iceland (Main Building)

Vatnsmýri

Ásgrímur Jónsson Museum

Hallgrímskirkja

BSÍ Terminal

Öskjuhlíð

The Pearl (Perlan)

Ymir Concert Hall

4

REYKJAVÍK | Exploring Reykjavík

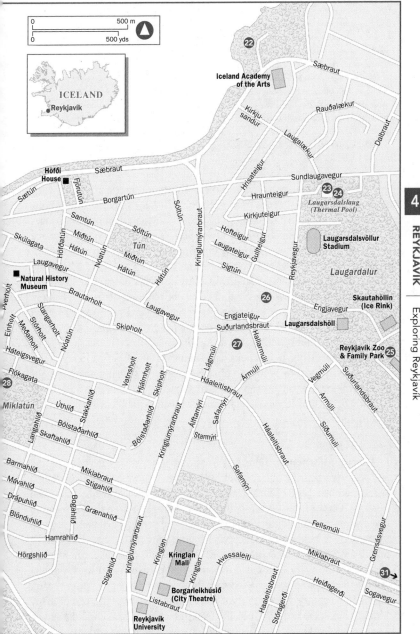

ICELAND
• Reykjavík

0   500 m
0   500 yds

Iceland Academy
of the Arts

Sæbraut

Kirkju-
sandur

Rauðalækur

Dalbraut

Laugalækur

Höfði
House

Sæbraut

Fjörutún

Borgartún

Sætún

Sóltún

Hrísateigur

Sundlaugavegur

Hraunteigur

Laugarsdalslaug
(Thermal Pool)

Kirkjuteigur

Samtún

Sóltún

Hofteigur

Kringlumýrarbraut

Laugateigur

Miðtún

Tún

Skúlagata

Höfðatún

Hátún

Miðtún

Gullteigur

Sigtún

Laugarsdalsvöllur
Stadium

Laugavegur

Nóatún

Hátún

Laugardalur

Reykjavegur

Natural History
Museum

Brautarholt

Þverholt

Laugavegur

Stangarholt

Skautahöllin
(Ice Rink)

Skiphólt

Engjavegur

Einholt

Stórholt

Nóatún

Medalholt

Engjateigur

Laugarsdalshöll

Háteigsvegur

Suðurlandsbraut

Hallarmúli

Flókagata

Vatnsholt

Lágmúli

Reykjavík Zoo
& Family Park

Miklatún

Úthlíð

Hjálmholt

Háaleitisbraut

Ármúli

Vegmúli

Suðurlandsbraut

Langahlíð

Bólstaðarhlíð

Skiphólt

Álftamýri

Ármúli

Skaftahlíð

Bólstaðarhlíð

Kringlumýrarbraut

Safamýri

Síðumúli

Barmahlíð

Miklabraut

Starmýri

Háaleitisbraut

Mávahlíð

Stigahlíð

Dráphlíð

Bogahlíð

Grænahlíð

Safamýri

Blönduhlíð

Fellsmúli

Hamrahlíð

Miklabraut

Grensásvegur

Hörgshlíð

Stigahlíð

Kringlumýrarbraut

Kringlan

Kringlan Mall

Hvassaleiti

Miklabraut

Heiðargerði

Sogavegur

Kringlan

Háaleitisbraut

Borgarleikhúsið
(City Theatre)

Listabraut

Stóragerði

Reykjavík
University

The Reykjavík City Card

This little gem can save you a bundle. The card includes admission to most major museums and galleries, along with access to public transport and all of the city's pools (p. 63). Cards come in three varieties: 24-hour (3,800kr), 48-hour (5,400kr), and 72-hour (6,500kr), activated the first time you use it. To calculate how soon you'll break even, consider that museums are routinely 1,400kr, pools 600kr, and buses 350kr.

Most museums are free 1 day of the week, so patient and flexible schedulers can do without the card. Cards are available at the Tourist Information Office (below), BSÍ bus terminals (p. 46), the City Hostel (p. 74), and the three branches of the Reykjavík Art Museum (p. 66, 58, and 58), but not online. (Check www.visitreykjavik.is/travel/reykjavik-city-card for the full list.)

As you survey the sights, keep some architectural notes in mind. Many Reykjavík buildings—largely from 1910 to 1930 but extending to the present—have corrugated iron siding, a distinctly Icelandic architectural trademark. Whatever its aesthetic merit, it was born of necessity: Wood is scarce and rots in the driving wind and rain, and iron is more stable in earthquakes. Since World War II, residents have brightened the cityscape with sidings and trims in cheerful reds, blues, and greens. Almost no traditional turf structures (see box p. 175) survive within city limits, but the tradition survives in modern Icelandic architecture; strolling around the residential areas off the main street downtown, you will stumble across the occasional turf-roofed house or garage (such as at the corner of Fjólugata and Njarðargata).

Other Icelandic style innovations date from the Nationalist period of architecture, roughly 1920 to 1950, and often have to do with using native materials and invoking native landscapes. Look for interior and exterior walls made from solid or crushed Icelandic rock varieties, such as gabbro, rhyolite, basalt, and sometimes lava.

Old City

The **Tourist Information Office** at Aðalstræti 2 (p. 45) is a good starting point. **Aðalstræti** is the oldest street in Reykjavík, and the point from which all street numbers begin: The higher the number, the greater the distance from Aðalstræti. On the footpath across the road (Vesturgata) from the information office, the official hub of Reykjavík is marked, the perfect (if clichéd) place to stand a moment before you launch your journey around the city. **Ingólfstorg** ("Ingólfur's Square") takes up most of Aðalstræti's eastern edge. Ingólfur Arnarson, traditionally regarded as Iceland's first permanent settler, is thought to have settled here around 870—though Reykjavík didn't have a proper street until the 18th century. For most of its history, Reykjavík was just one of many hereditary coastal estates. In 1613 the Danish monarch, who had imposed an oppressive trade monopoly on its Iceland colony, bought the settlement under threat of force. Reykjavík then grew into a kind of shantytown for seasonal workers assisting Danish merchants, mostly associated with the fishing trade.

The **oldest house** in Reykjavík, from 1764, is at Aðalstræti 10; plans are afoot to open the house for tours. (The **871±2 Settlement Museum,** at Aðalstræti 16, is listed on p. 53.)

A block east of Aðalstræti is **Austurvöllur Square,** an important outdoor gathering place and potent national symbol to every Icelander. During the early days of the financial crisis in 2008 (p. 13), this is where people gathered to protest. In December, a Christmas tree arrives here, a gift from the people of Oslo, as Iceland produces no adequately tall specimens. By European standards the square has little architectural distinction, but Austurvöllur has only been a public green since 1930. In the middle is a **statue of Jón Sigurðsson** (1811–1879), the hero of Iceland's independence movement from Denmark. His birthday, June 17, was designated "National Day" after Icelandic independence in 1944. On the pedestal is a relief called "The Pioneer," depicting an early settler, amid cliffs and basalt columns, forging a trail for later generations, who are lined up waiting to follow. Both the statue and relief are by Iceland's best-known sculptor, Einar Jónsson (p. 57).

Jón Sigurðsson looks approvingly at **Alþingishús (Parliament House),** an 1880 stone building with a glass and stone annex added in 2002. From October to May you can watch parliamentary proceedings from the visitors' gallery (Mon 3pm; Tues–Wed 1:30pm; Thurs 10:30am). The Alþingishús (or Alþingi) and City Cathedral next door represent Icelandic independence and Reykjavík's coming of age in the late 18th century. In 1797, the Danish king consolidated Iceland's northern and southern bishoprics into a single diocese in Reykjavík, just as the cathedral was being completed. The following year, the Icelandic parliament (Alþing) was moved here from Þingvellir, only to be abolished 2 years later. It was reinstated in 1845 in an advisory role to the Danish authorities. Behind the Alþingi is the **Parliament House Garden,** the country's oldest park maintaining its original design: a traditional, formal layout with paths emanating from a circular lawn.

The elegant, understated **City Cathedral (Dómkirkjan)** ★ (© **520-9700;** Mon–Fri 10am–4:30pm unless in use for services; Sat–Sun often busy for weddings, but open before or after; high mass Sunday 11am; various masses Sun evenings; prayer mass Tues 12:10–12:30pm) is a good counterweight to the grandiosity of Hallgrímskirkja. National independence received its first religious blessing here, and annual sessions of parliament start here with a prayer service. Completed in 1796, the cathedral was enlarged in 1848 by Copenhagen's royal architect, L. A. Winstrup, using a conventional blend of neoclassical and baroque features. The loft was the original site of the National Museum and Archives, and still has an interesting photo exhibit. Check the information box outside the church for concerts and events, listed in Icelandic but often discernible anyway.

Also in Austurvöllur Square is the **Hótel Borg,** Iceland's first luxury hotel, built in 1930 to accommodate foreign guests for the millennial celebration of Iceland's first parliamentary assembly at Þingvellir. It's been an important cultural landmark ever since: Public dances for Allied soldiers were held here

4

during World War II; foreign visitors suffering under prohibition laws found refuge at the bar; and Iceland's punk rockers performed here in the 1980s. Come in the morning to breakfast among parliament members, or visit for a drink in the small, wildly decorated lounge.

One long block east of Austurvöllur is **Lækjargata,** a broad avenue dividing the western and eastern halves of the city. Originally there was a brook here, and underneath the pavement, Tjörnin pond still drains to the sea.

In the courtyard behind Lækjargata 6 is the **Unknown Official ★**. Several countries have monuments to the Unknown Soldier, but perhaps only Iceland has a sculpture paying tribute to—in lighthearted manner—the thankless, anonymous job of the bureaucrat. The 1994 sculpture by Magnús Tómasson depicts a man in a suit holding a briefcase, with his head and shoulders subsumed in a slab of unsculpted stone.

Reykjavík's geographical heart, **Lækjartorg Square,** has an important history of public meetings. From the square, look northeast to the **statue of Ingólfur Arnarson** holding his spear aloft, and the grassy slope of **Arnarhóll,** which was named for him. According to the Icelandic sagas, Ingólfur became Iceland's first permanent settler in 874. After his exile from Norway on murder charges, he wintered for 3 years on the south coast of Iceland. Arnarson decided on Reykjavík after following a pagan ritual that involved throwing his high-seat pillars (carved wooden columns set at the corner of a chieftain's chair) into the sea and trusting the gods to guide him to the right spot. Ingólfur's slaves, so the story goes, found the pillars 3 years later right at Arnarhóll. The statue by Einar Jónsson (p. 57) was unveiled in 1924.

Austurstræti leads from Ingólfstorg to Lækjargata, then changes name to **Bankastræti,** which proceeds east from Lækjartorg Square, and after 3 small blocks divides into two busy commercial streets, **Laugavegur** and **Skólavörðustígur.** Austurstræti, Bankastræti, and Laugavegur form a fairly straight line, and many assume Laugavegur covers this whole stretch. A block north of Laugavegur is **Hverfisgata,** another good street for strolling and people-watching.

Laugavegur (Hot Spring Path), Iceland's busiest and most prestigious commercial street, was originally built as a trail for maids walking to Laugardalur to wash laundry in the natural springs. The street's odd jumble of buildings reflects the emergent needs of commerce and benign neglect of architectural planners.

Culture House (Þjóðmenningarhúsið) ★ MUSEUM Designed by

the Danish architect Johannes Magdahl Nielse, the Culture House opened in 1909 to house the National Library and the National Archives of Iceland. Several other institutions occupied the space over the next century, and in 2013 it merged with the National Museum. A renovation completed in 2013 added a cafe and a museum shop, as well as a series of temporary exhibitions that reflect Iceland's visual art history and cultural heritage.

Hverfisgata 15, east of Ingólfsstræti ("Landsbókasafn" is etched over the door). www.culturehouse.is. ✆ **530-2210.** Admission 2,000kr adults; 1,000kr seniors/students; free for children 17 and under. Daily 10am–5pm May–Sept 15; Tues–Sun 10am–5pm Sept 16–April. Free guided tours in English Mon and Fri 3pm, group tours by request.

The Marshall House ★★ MUSEUM   An important destination for contemporary art from both established and emerging artists, this four-floor museum opened in a former fish-meal factory in 2017. Inside are three separate independent galleries: The **Living Art Museum (Nýlistasafnið, or Nýló)** (☏ **551-4350**); **Gallery Kling & Bang** (☏ **554-2003**); and **Studio Ólafur Elíasson** (☏ **551-3666**), Elíasson's only studio in his home country. The space has quickly become a hub for Reykjavík's art community.

Grandagarður 20. https://marshallhusid.is. Free admission. Tues–Sun noon–6pm; Thurs noon–9pm. Guided tours available.

Settlement Exhibition 871±2 ★ MUSEUM   The oldest known evidence of human habitation in Reykjavík was found in 2001 on the southern end of Aðalstræti by workers excavating an underground parking garage. They discovered a wall fragment that dated to 871, plus or minus a couple of years—hence the name of the museum. The remains of a Viking longhouse was found soon after. These artifacts have been preserved in their original location and are now surrounded by high-tech panoramic displays that tackle the larger questions of why the Vikings came to Reykjavík, how they adapted to its conditions, and what the landscape originally looked like. The ruin itself is basically just a wall foundation, and the museum's greatest feat is bringing the longhouse back to life using digital projectors.

Aðalstræti 16. www.reykjavikmuseum.is. ☏ **411-6370.** Admission 1,650kr adults; 1,000kr students; free for seniors/children 17 and under. Daily 9am–6pm.

Old Port (Hafn)

The port north and west of the old city, built from 1913 to 1917, was the largest construction project to that point in Icelandic history. (Before then, most ships had to drop anchor well out to sea and transport goods in by rowboat.) Dredged rocks were hauled away by a locomotive, which is still on display along the shoreline east of the harbor. Today, most boat traffic has moved east to Sundahöfn port, but the old port isn't a museum yet.

Traditionally, the area most visited by tourists has been the eastern pier, where Reykjavík's puffin and whale-watching tours (p. 65) depart. The western piers have seen a considerable amount of development in recent years, including trendy shopping boutiques, a chocolate factory, a food hall, and museums. This is where you will also find the most fishing vessels, as well as the *Óðinn,* a grey Coast Guard vessel with a vertical stripe in blue, white, and red. The Coast Guard is the closest thing Iceland has to a military, and it defends the country's territorial fishing waters. The Coast Guard were sent out to slice British fishing nets in the so-called "Cod Wars," which date back to 1432 but culminated in the 1970s, when Britain broke off diplomatic relations. (Icelanders like to say this was the only war the British Navy ever lost.)

Harbor House Museum (Hafnarhús) ★★ MUSEUM   One of three branches that make up the Reykjavík Art Museum, this renovated 1930s warehouse has a permanent collection of native works, including those of Erró, an Icelandic-born artist who was based in Paris and best known for his large-scale comic-book-style dreamscapes and montages. There are usually two or three temporary exhibitions of Icelandic or international contemporary art on display as well. The second floor has a wonderful reading room with hundreds of art books, children's toys, and a view over the waterfront.

Tryggvagata 17. www.artmuseum.is. ✆ **590-1200.** Admission 1,650kr adults; 1,100kr students; seniors/children 17 and under free. Daily 10am–5pm; Thurs 10am–10pm.

Harpa ★★★ CONCERT HALL   On the easternmost point of the harbor is Reykjavík's concert hall and conference center, which opened in 2011. The building became an instant city landmark with its dramatic honeycomb glass casing—designed by renowned Icelandic-Danish artist Ólafur Elíasson—which was constructed piece by piece and reflects both the sky and the ocean. With state-of-the-art acoustics, Harpa encompasses a variety of halls and is the country's premier music and event venue (see p. 90), with films, concerts, and performances occurring here every night of the week. Additionally, the space contains half a dozen stores, two restaurants, and a long-distance bus stop. Purchase tickets at the box office for **guided tours** (1,500kr per person; 30 min.) that take you behind the scenes of each performance space and explain the design features at great length. Multiple tours are offered daily during the summer, with fewer in the winter.

Austurbakki 2. www.harpa.is. ✆ **528-5000.** Daily 8am–midnight.

Saga Museum ★ MUSEUM   Now in the harbor area rather than one of the hot water tanks at the Pearl, this privately run museum conveys many of the legends from the Icelandic sagas in 17 exhibits. While listening to an audio device, visitors move among installations enlivened by eerily lifelike wax historical figures like Snorri Sturlusson, Ingolfur Arnarson, and Leifur Eiriksson. There's gore aplenty too: feuding Vikings, witches burned at the stake, the beheading of Iceland's last Catholic bishop. At the end of the tour, your family can dress up in Viking outfits for a photo op (additional fee).

Grandagardi 2. www.sagamuseum.is. ✆ **511-1517.** Admission 2,200kr adults; 1,700kr children; 800kr seniors/students. Daily 10am–6pm. Bus 14.

Víking Maritime Museum ★★ MUSEUM   Opened in 2005 in a converted fish-freezing plant, this museum is helping to revive the once-fading western harbor area. The permanent exhibit delves into the country's 20th-century seafaring heritage via well-crafted ship models and dioramas with life-size fishermen. It holds an impressive amount of nautical artifacts and memorabilia, such as buoy lights and engine controls. The re-created captain's room and claustrophobic sleeping quarters are standouts, while permanent-exhibition rooms feature a series devoted to 150 years of fisheries in Iceland. Guided tours are available at 1, 2, and 3pm.

Grandagarður 8. www.maritimemuseum.is. ✆ **517-9400.** Admission 1,850kr adults; 1,100kr students 24 and under; free for seniors/children 17 and under. June–Sept 11am–5pm. Bus 14.

Whales of Iceland ★ MUSEUM   The largest whale exhibition in Europe, this museum opened on the western harbor area in 2014. With counsel from

Children in Iceland are noticeably well integrated into adult life, and you'll feel welcome bringing them almost anywhere. They are often seen feeding the voracious waterfowl in **Tjörnin pond** (below) by City Hall. The **Volcano Show** at the Volcano House (p. 90) has enough geological violence and destruction to be entertaining, even if the film quality is outdated. **Whale-watching** (p. 65), **puffin-watching** (p. 65), and the **Reykjavík Zoo & Family Park** ★ (p. 59) are all pretty foolproof.

Horseback riding and other activities are outlined on p. 65. The most engaging museums are the open-air **Árbær Museum** ★ (p. 61) and **Whales of Iceland.** Perhaps best of all are the **outdoor thermal pools,** a family institution throughout the country (see "Pool Guide" box, p. 63). The deluxe **Laugar Spa** ★ (p. 64) can entertain your children while you pamper yourself, and the **Kringlan Mall** offers a child-minding service while you shop.

4

marine biologist Edda Elísabet Magnúsdóttir, who helped gather information and illustrative material, they have created a warehouse filled with 23 life-size models made of foam and steel and hung from the walls and ceiling. The models include a variety of species such as the beluga whale and the orca, plus baleen varieties like bowhead, humpback, and blue whales, all backlit by a chilling blue glow.

Fiskislóð 23. www.whalesoficeland.is. ⓒ **571-0077.** Admission 2,900kr adults; 1,500kr seniors; 1,500kr children 7–15; free for children 6 and under. Daily 9am–7pm. Bus 14.

Around The Pond

Tjörnin, the city's central pond, makes for a great circular walk. Several early-20th-century timber houses, built for the newly emergent middle class, are clustered along Tjarnargata on the western shore. It's worth strolling by to appreciate their gingerbread-house flourishes.

National Gallery of Iceland (Listasafn Íslands) ★ GALLERY This
landmark gallery was founded in 1884 in Copenhagen before being moved to Reykjavík. It has no permanent exhibit, but instead pulls from its own collection, the largest and probably most important repository of Icelandic art. Among the 19th- and 20th-century works on display are Iceland's endless variations of light and natural formations, a window into the country's history. The museum has a pleasant **cafe** on the top floor.

Fríkirkjuvegur 7. www.listasafn.is. ⓒ **515-9600.** Admission 1,500kr adults; 750kr seniors/ disabled/children 17 and under. Tues–Sun 11am–5pm. Free guided tours Tues and Fri 12:10pm.

The Old Churchyard (Suðurgata or Hólavallagarður Cemetery) ★
CEMETERY One block west of the pond, in a leafy area between Ljosvallagata and Suðurgata, this cemetery was consecrated in 1838 and is the burial ground for several of the city's luminaries. Jón Sigurðsson, the most important leader of Iceland's independence movement, is found here: Walk from the

REYKJAVÍK | Exploring Reykjavík

main entrance on Ljosvallagata straight down the center, past the old chapel bell, and it's the beige obelisk on the left, a few plots before you reach the outer wall. Its lack of ostentation speaks volumes about Iceland's egalitarian ideals.

Main entrance on Ljosvallagata. ✆ **562-2510.** Cemetery open 24 hr.; office weekdays 9am–1pm.

Reykjavík City Hall (Ráðhús) ★ CITY HALL   On the northern shore of Lake Tjörnin, this gray concrete, metal, and glass building boldly stands out with its dripping, moss-covered walls and seemingly floating base. The usual pomposity and self-importance of city halls is absent, replaced by democratic symbolism: The ground floor looks almost like a natural extension of the public street. The exhibition hall contains an enormous 3D relief map of Iceland, which took four men 4 years to construct. This is also the home of the tourist information center, which has extensive information for tourists, as well as a tour booking desk.

North end of Lake Tjörnin. ✆ **411-1111.** Free admission. Mon–Fri 8am–7pm; Sat–Sun noon–6pm. Cafe daily weekdays 11am–6pm; Sat–Sun noon–6pm.

South of the Pond

National Museum of Iceland ★★ MUSEUM   This sizable museum condenses Iceland's entire history and culture into one digestible bite. More than 2,000 artifacts from various parts of the country are on display, including the Valþjófsstaður door, a Romanesque-style church door featuring elaborate medieval engravings depicting scenes from the legendary 12th-century knight's tale *Le Chevalier au Lion.* The permanent "Making of a Nation" exhibit selects specific figures, objects, and vignettes to represent stages and themes of Icelandic history: A charming, old instant-photo booth, for example, signals the onset of modernity. The exhibit begins with a pagan burial site and ends with a traditional Icelandic dress refashioned by contemporary artist Ásdís Elva Pétursdóttir in transparent plastic.

The ground floor houses the free **National Gallery of Photography** ★, which, in keeping with the exhibit upstairs, features the Iceland of yore. The cafe on the ground floor is best for morning or afternoon tea, with little for lunch. The museum shop has more interesting souvenirs than many of the bigger tourist shops.

Suðurgata 41. www.natmus.is. ✆ **530-2200.** National Museum admission 2,000kr adults; 1,000kr senior/students; free for children 17 and under. Museum and Gallery daily 10am–5pm. Bus: 1, 3, 4, 5, 6, 11, 12, or 14.

East of the Old City

ASÍ Art Museum (Ásmundarsalur) ★ MUSEUM   Set in a villa that dates to the 1930s, which was used as an artist residence and workshop, this small, selective contemporary art museum is run by the Icelandic workers' union. In summer it exhibits works from its collection of 20th-century Icelandic art, which includes renowned paintings by Old Icelandic masters like Jóhannes S. Kjarval og Jón Stefánsson, whose *Fjallamjölk* (Mountain Milk) was inspired by the landscape of Þingvellir, as well as some masterpieces of the "Cobra" painter Svavar Guðnason.

Freyjugata 41. www.listasafnasi.is. ☏ **553-2155.** Free admission. May–Sept daily 10am–4pm; Oct–Apr weekends 1–4pm.

Einar Jónsson Museum ★★ MUSEUM   Iceland's best-known sculptor, Einar Jónsson (1874–1954), designed the plans for this museum, which was built after he donated his works to the Icelandic people. Some say it is his biggest sculpture. It served as his studio, as a gallery for his works, and even as his home. Often inspired by Icelandic folklore, Jónsson's sculptures depict classical human and mythological figures in wildly imaginative and unorthodox poses. He identified with the romantic symbolists, and his sculptures speak in allegories, personifications, and ciphers. In the 1930s, W. H. Auden mockingly summed up his work as "Time pulling off the boots of Eternity with one hand while keeping the wolf from the door with the other." Outside is a small park with 26 bronze castings of his work, well worth a look even if the rest of the museum is closed.

Eiríksgata. www.lej.is. ☏ **551-3797.** Admission 1,000kr adults; 300kr senior/students; free for children 17 and under. Free admission to sculpture park. June–Sept 15 Tues–Sun 1–5pm; Sept 16–Nov and Feb–May Sat–Sun 2–5pm. Closed Dec–Jan.

Hallgrímskirkja (Hallgríms Church) ★ CHURCH   Visible from everywhere in the city, Hallgrímskirkja, the tallest and largest church in Iceland, is perhaps the most photographed building in Reykjavík. It was designed by state architect Guðjón Samúelsson (1887–1950), who never saw it completed: Work began in 1945 and continued for 49 years. The church is named for Reverend Hallgrímur Pétursson (1614–1674), Iceland's foremost hymn writer and an ecclesiastical scholar and poet. His best-known work, *Hymns of the Passion,* is still sung and recited as verse in homes throughout Iceland (an English translation is available in the gift shop). For a fee you can ascend the 75m (246 ft.) steeple by elevator for great views over the city. At the top are three bells representing Hallgrímur, his wife, and his daughter, who died young.

   The distinctive exterior, with its prominent steeple, is often described in terms both primordial and futuristic—as if the church were some kind of volcano or glacier transformed into a rocket ship. Guðjón was indeed inspired by the Icelandic landscape, and the frontal columns are meant to resemble the hexagonal basalt formed by cooling lava. In contrast, the interior is quite traditional, with Gothic high-pointed vaults and tall, narrow windows. The uniform, textured-concrete surfaces can seem pedestrian, even to those accustomed to Lutheran principles of simplicity, and the altar is so ordinary as to resemble a hotel lobby. It could have been very different: a photograph hung in the entry hall depicts Einar Jónsson's proposed alternative design, a fantastical creation to rival Gaudí's cathedral in Barcelona. An Art Deco spire supports human figures in relief trudging upward amid Middle Eastern–inspired domes. In 2010, a new bronze and blue-glass door for the church was unveiled. Designed by Leifur Breiðfjörð, the door draws a connection with the windows, especially when lit up by the late evening sun.

Concerts here often involve the church's most popular interior feature: a gigantic organ built in Germany in 1992. It's about 15m (50ft.) tall, with 72 stops, 5,275 pipes, and remarkable sound projection. The church also hosts drama, art exhibitions, and even public debates. Especially recommended are choral performances, a form in which Icelanders have always excelled.

A **statue of Leifur (Leif) Eiriksson** is aligned directly in front of the church, as if he's about to lead it down the hill. The statue was a gift from the U.S. to commemorate the 1,000th anniversary of the founding of Iceland's parliament. It was also a tacit acknowledgment that Leifur beat Christopher Columbus to North America by almost 500 years. (Excavations in Newfoundland have settled this question beyond a doubt.)

Skólavörðuholt, at SE end of Skólavörðustígur. www.hallgrimskirkja.is. ✆ **510-1000.** Daily 9am–8pm. Suggested donation 100kr. Elevator to tower 1,000kr adults; 100kr children. Holy Communion sung Sun 11am and Wed 8am. Prayers Tues 10:30am. Meditation with organ music Thurs at noon. Anglican service in English usually last Sun of each month at 2pm. Organ concerts mid-June to mid-Aug at noon on Thurs and Sat; longer performances Sun 8pm.

Kjarvalsstaðir ★ GALLERY   The '60s-era modernist building holds three galleries: two with temporary exhibits and one drawing from the museum's large collection of paintings and sculptures by well-established Icelandic and international artists. A branch of the Reykjavík Art Museum, it offers a permanent exhibition of key works by one of Iceland's most beloved landscape painters, Jóhannes Sveinsson Kjarval (1885–1972), the most highly regarded painter in Icelandic history, for whom the museum is named. Deeply inspired by native landscapes and folklore, his work is too varied to pigeonhole stylistically, but "expressionist" approximates the thick, paint-laden brushstrokes and abstract arrangements of tone and shape.

Flókagata. www.artmuseum.is. ✆ **517-1290.** Admission free. Daily 10am–5pm. Bus: 1, 3, 4, 5, 6, or 13.

Laugardalur

According to legend, Ingólfur Arnarson chose the name Reykjavík, or "Smokey Bay," when he saw distant steam rising from what is now Laugardalur (Hot Spring Valley), thinking it to be smoke. Those hot springs still heat the Laugardalslaug pool, and Icelandic families are also drawn by the zoo, family park, botanical garden, sports stadiums, and luxury Laugar Spa (see also "Outdoor Activities," p. 63).

Ásmundur Sveinsson Sculpture Museum (Ásmundarsafn) ★★ MUSEUM   Opened in 1983, this branch of the Reykjavík Art Museum is dedicated to the works of modernist sculptor Ásmundur Sveinsson (1893–1982). Sveinsson designed and built this futuristic home and studio, inspired by Turkish and Egyptian models, which he thought fitting for Iceland's treeless environment. The museum focuses almost entirely on his work, influenced by Henry Moore and the cubists. Often drawing from Icelandic folklore, his pieces range from recognizable human forms to pure abstract shapes. More of Ásmundur's work can be found in the small outdoor sculpture park.

Sigtún, near the sports complex in Laugardalur Park. www.artmuseum.is. © **553-2155.** Admission free. May–Sept daily 10am–5pm; Oct–Apr 1–5pm. Bus: 2, 14, 15, 17, or 19.

Reykjavík Zoo & Family Park ★ ZOO   Reykjavík's odd little zoo, which opened in 1990, is one of the few in the world that concentrates on domestic animals. It's kind of like one big petting zoo, with sheep, horses, cattle, pigs, goats, reindeer, and mink. An animal petting schedule is posted each day— foxes at midday—and pony rides begin at 2pm. There are also enclosures with wild native species, such as the Arctic fox, the only indigenous land mammal. The aquarium, opened in 2004, holds seals and fish native to the North Atlantic. The **Family Park** is surefire children's entertainment, with boats, a go-cart driving school complete with traffic lights, and a "science world," where little ones can measure their screams in big decibels.

Hafrafell (at Engjaveg, Laugardalur Park, behind sports complex). www.mu.is. © **411-5900.** Admission Mon–Fri 880kr adults; 660kr children 5–12; free for kids 4 and under. Rides cost extra. May 15 to mid-Aug daily 10am–6pm; mid-Aug to May 14 daily 10am–5pm. Bus: S2, 14, 15, 17, or 19.

Sigurjón Ólafsson Museum ★ MUSEUM   This museum, a division of the National Gallery, was founded in 1984 by the widow of Icelandic sculptor Sigurjón Ólafsson (1908–1982) in tribute to her late husband. Set inside his former oceanside studio, it is devoted exclusively to his work, ranging from formal busts to primitivist metal totems to wood pieces haphazardly stuck together. Additionally, there are sketches, drawings, and biographical material, as well as a pleasant cafe with homemade pies and cakes and peaceful waterfront views. A summer concert series brings in musical acts every Tuesday night at 8:30pm (2,500kr admission).

Laugarnestangi 70. www.lso.is. © **553-2906.** Admission 1,000kr adults; 500kr seniors; free for children 17 and under. June–Aug Tues–Sun 2–5pm; Sept–May Sat–Sun 2–5pm, but closed intermittently for long periods, check website. Bus: 12 or 15.

Öskjuhlíð Hill

This wooded area to the south of the city is a perfectly nice walking, jogging, or biking retreat.

Nauthólsvík Beach ★ BEACH   If Icelanders going to the beach sounded odd when you first heard it, don't worry, it is odd. At Nauthólsvík, runoff hot water from the city's geothermal heating system is pumped into the ocean through a beach of imported yellow sand. The ocean temperature is brought to about 18°C (64.4°F), and Icelandic families flock here on warm days to sunbathe and splash around. A hot water pool and hot pots give it the air of a more formal facility. You can rent towels or store valuables for 350kr. Afterward, swing by **Bragginn Bistro** (www.bragginnbistro.is; © **419-1200;** main courses 2,890kr–6,990kr) next door in an old Army barracks for a full meal or drink.

Nauthólsvegur, directly south of the Pearl. © **511-6630.** May 15–Aug daily 10am–7pm. Bus: 16.

The Pearl (Perlan) ★ TOWER   Other than maybe Hallgrímskirkja, there is no other dominant architectural feature more present in the Reykjavík skyline than this futuristic glass dome. In the 1930s, master artist Johannes Kjarval had dreams for a structure on Öskjuhlíð hill, stating that it should be covered with mirrors, "So the Northern Lights can approach the feet of men— the roof should be decorated with crystal of every color and floodlights should be in the eaves to illuminate the whole area. It should answer to the light of day and the symbols of the night." The Pearl was built in 1991 to store 24,000 tons of the city's geothermally heated water, sitting atop six enormous cylindrical tanks. The structure is now home to a variety of exhibitions, ranging from a 100m-long manmade ice cave and a planetarium to immersive experiences that mimic the power of earthquakes and volcanic eruptions. The fourth floor is ringed by a viewing deck with fabulous views over the city and beyond; inside is a cafe whose main strength is ice cream. The top floor, which makes a complete circular revolution every 2 hours, has a restaurant; it's accessible only to diners.

Öskjuhlíð. www.perlan.is. ✆ **562-0200.** Admission 3,900kr adults; 1,950kr children 6–15; 7,800kr family. Observation deck only: 490kr (free ages 15 and under). Daily June–Aug 10am–11:30pm; Sept–May 10am–9pm. Cafe daily 10am–9pm. Restaurant daily 11:30am–9pm. Bus: 18.

Outskirts & Nearby
VIÐEY ISLAND ★

Viðey is hardly the most dramatically situated island off the Icelandic coast, but it provides a very nice afternoon escape from Reykjavík. The island has a surprisingly grand history, and is now a showcase for environmental art.

Viðey was inhabited as early as 900. From 1225 to 1539 it was the site of a prestigious Augustine monastery, which at one point owned 116 Reykjavík estates. In 1539, the Danish king appropriated the land in the name of the Protestant Reformation. Eleven years later, Iceland's last Catholic bishop, Jón Arason, took the island by force, but he was beheaded a few months later. At the beginning of the 20th century, the country's first harbor for oceangoing vessels was built on Viðey's eastern coast, but it was soon outmoded by Reykjavík's port. Viðey's population peaked in 1930 with 138 people, but by the 1950s the only inhabitants were birds enjoying the peace. In 1983 Viðey became city property.

Viðey has no cars and is only 1 square mile in area. It consists of **Heimæy (Home Island)** and **Vesturey (West Island),** linked by a narrow isthmus. You can bring a bike, but several free bikes are left out for any takers; some have baby seats and all have helmets. Visitors spend most of their time strolling along the easy trails. (Pick up the free trail map in the ferry ticket office.) Thirty bird species have been counted here. The most populous is the *eider,* the seafaring duck harvested on farms all over Iceland for its down feathers. Many birds nest in the grasses, so it's best to stick to the paths.

Visitors disembarking the **Viðeyjarferju ferry** (✆ 533-5055) won't miss **Viðey House (Viðeyjarstofa)** (✆ 533-5055; June–Aug daily 1–5pm), the country's first stone-and-cement structure, dating from 1755. It was originally home to Skúli Magnússon (1711–1794), who was appointed Royal Superinten-dent of Iceland by the Danish crown; it's now a cafe and event facility serving coffee and waffles in summer. Close by is **Viðeyjarkirkja,** the second-oldest church in Iceland, consecrated in 1774, with Skúli's tomb beneath the altar.

Vesturey's only manmade feature is Áfangar (Stages) ★, a vast yet under-stated work erected in 1990 by the American minimalist sculptor Richard Serra. Nine pairs of vertical basalt columns are spread across the land, their proportions determined by strict mathematical criteria. If you climb to the high point you can see all nine pairs, as well as a grand view of the surround-ing mountains. Viðey is also home to the **"Imagine Peace Tower,"** designed by Yoko Ono, featuring peace prayers in 24 languages, and—during late fall and on significant John Lennon dates—a shaft of light visible from the main-land, from one hour after sunset to midnight.

Elding (www.elding.is) operates a ferry (1,550kr adults; 1,000kr students; 900kr seniors; 775kr children 7–15 years old; free for children 6 and under) that departs throughout the day from Skarfabakki pier, Harpa, and Ægisgarður pier.

4

ELLIÐAÁR VALLEY

Árbær Open Air Museum (or Árbæjarsafn) ★ MUSEUM A 15-minute drive east of the city, this open-air folk museum is a re-created vil-lage with more than 20 traditional buildings surrounding a town square. Árbær, a division of the Reykjavík City Museum, was a working farm until 1948, and interior decorations are meant to represent a typical 1920s farm-house. (Look for a marvelous piece of homegrown artwork on the wall: a bird and bouquet constructed entirely from human hair.) Many of the buildings were slated for demolition in Reykjavík and around the country but found refuge here, such as an 1842 church transported from the north coast. From June to August, staff in period costume milk cows, weave wool, and cook chewy pancakes (*lummur*) on the farmhouse stove for visitors. What really makes a visit worthwhile is a guided tour (free with paid admission) of the original turf-roofed farmhouses, so time your visit accordingly. Without a guide you won't learn how to spin yarn, how meat was smoked (with sheep manure), and how everyone washed their hair (in urine). *Note:* Admission is included in the **Reykjavík City Card** (see p. 50).

Kistuhylur, in Artunsholt. http://borgarsogusafn.is. ✆ **411-6300.** Admission 1,650kr adults; 1,100kr students; free for seniors/children 16 and under. June–Aug daily 10am–5pm; 90-min. guided tours at 11am and 2pm; Sept–May daily only for guided tour at 1pm. Bus: 5 (to Strengur, a short walk from museum).

ORGANIZED TOURS

CityWalk ★ This upstart offers a daily 2-hour, tip-based **"Historical Walking Tour"** of Reykjavik each day. Operated by an amateur independent guide with a B.A. in history from the University of Iceland, the wheelchair-accessible route covers 2 kilometers in the oldest part of the city, mostly within the boundaries of Aðalstræti, Kirkjustræti, and Hafnarstræti streets. Tours depart from Austurvöllur square, usually between 10am and 3pm. The schedule is posted online 5 days in advance. Tours fill up, so making online reservations is essential. They also offer a **pub crawl** (2,500kr) and a **tour of Iceland's financial crisis** (3,500kr).

No phone. www.citywalk.is. Free, but tips expected.

Cooking Classes ★ **Salt Eldhús** (Icelandic for kitchen) teaches students how to cook local Icelandic ingredients like lamb and fish under the supervision of skilled instructors, including chefs from notable restaurants in the city. The "Cook and Dine" classes include instruction in a three-course meal, plus wine and a recipe folder. Limited class sizes ensure that each student gets attention.

Þórunnartún 2. www.salteldhus.is. ⓒ **551-0171.** 24,900kr adults; 12,500kr children 14 and under. Classes daily at 10am and 2pm.

Creative Iceland ★★ With a focus on highly interactive, personalized tours, small, independent agency Creative Iceland has brought an entirely new angle to Icelandic cultural experiences. It might be preparing a three-course meal in a cooking class, a graphic design course specializing in Icelandic letterpress, or a lecture on the "Elves and Hidden Peoples of Iceland." Prices range from about 2,900kr to 25,000kr per person, depending on the class.

Eiðistorg 13-15, Seltjarnarnes. www.creativeiceland.is. ⓒ **615-3500.**

Your Friend in Reykjavík ★ This family-run tour operator runs 2- to 3.5-hour walking tours around Reykjavík. The "Reykjavík Food Lovers" tour (14,900kr), weekends only, stops at five places to eat around the city, including a hot-dog stand and a market. Other tours include a Viking-centric tour and a beer tour that stops for samples of 10 Icelandic microbrews.

Tours start at Ingólfstorg Square. www.yourfriendinreykjavik.com. ⓒ **655-4040.**

Literary Walking Tours ★ On Thursdays at 3pm from June to August, the **City Library** sponsors free, little-known tours of Reykjavík, led by a literary critic or an actor. Tours, which last around 1½ hours, leave from the main branch and may include anything from the Settlement Museum (for a saga reading) to the cafe/nightclub **Kaffibarinn** (site of debauched scenes from the cult novel *Reykjavík 101*). Call ahead to make sure the time hasn't changed.

Tryggvagata 15. ⓒ **411-6100.**

Reykjavík Excursions ★ A 2½-hour **"Reykjavík Grand Excursion"** bus tour daily at 1pm lets you "do" the waterfront, Hallgrímskirkja, the Pearl, and the National Museum all before afternoon tea. The price is 5,499kr for adults, half-price for children 12 to 15, and free for children 11 and under, including museum admission and pickup/dropoff service. To go at your own pace, choose the **"Hop On–Hop Off"** tour, which runs 3 or 4 times a week (check website) June to August on open-topped double-deckers for 4,000kr adults, half-price for children 12 to 15, and free for children 11 and under. Departing from Harpa every 30 minutes, sights include Hallgrímskirkja, the Pearl, the National Museum, the old port, Kringlan Mall, and Laugardalur Park. The bus completes the loop once each hour, so you can stop wherever you like and catch another bus an hour or two later. Your ticket is valid for 24 hours from the first use, so you can continue hopping the next morning.

Harpa Concert Hall. www.re.is. ℰ **580-5400.**

OUTDOOR ACTIVITIES
Thermal Pools

The city operates seven **thermal pools** (www.spacity.is), all with changing rooms, lockers, showers, wading pools for small children, and "hot pots" (hot tubs), usually in a row with successively higher water temperatures. All but one have water slides and other delights for children. Entrance fees are typically 900kr for adults and 140kr for children ages 6 to 15, though you can get in free with the **Reykjavík City Card** (see p. 50). Swimsuit and towel rental are typically 500kr apiece.

Don't be dissuaded by poor weather. Icelanders still show up in the rain, and believe the combination of cold air and hot water is greatly beneficial to health. (They have very long life spans to show for it.) For a side of the city few tourists witness, show up at 7am, when Icelanders have a dip before work. For more on **pool etiquette,** see box p. 64.

REYKJAVÍK thermal POOL GUIDE

○ **Árbæjarlaug,** Fylkisvegur 9, Árbær, near Elliðaár River (ℰ **411-5200;** Mon–Thurs 6:30am–10pm; Fri 6:30am–8pm; Sat–Sun 9am–8pm all year round; bus: 19). This kiddie wonderland is full of water toys, but it has plenty for adults, too. A 15-minute bus ride from the city's heart, this pool is one of Reykjavík's less touristy. The city's largest public Jacuzzi is here, but you won't find anywhere to do laps.

○ **Laugardalslaug,** Sundlaugavegur 30, at the north end of Laugardalur Park (ℰ **411-5100;** Mon–Fri 6:30am–10pm; Sat–Sun 8am–10pm; bus: 14). In the eastern part of the city, this is the biggest and most populated pool, with several outdoor swimming areas, an Olympic-size indoor pool, a steam room reminiscent of a whale's belly, and a massage room.

○ **Sundhöllin,** Bergþórugata 16, at Bergþórugata, behind Hallgrímskirkja

(ℰ **411-5350;** Mon–Thurs 6:30am–10pm; Fri 6:30am–8pm; Sat 8am–4pm; Sun 10am–6pm; bus: 1, 6, or 13). A major renovation in 2017, adding an outdoor pool, a new reception area, and updated the locker facilities, turned this into one of the best pools in town. A line of hot pots outside offers views of the city. The historic pool building was designed by the architect of Hallgrímskirkja.

○ **Vesturbæjarlaug,** Hofsvallagata, at Melhagi (ℰ **411-5150;** Mon–Thurs 6:30am–10pm; Fri 6:30am–8pm; Sat–Sun 9am–8pm; bus: 11 or 15). This pool is a 15-minute walk from Tjörnin Pond, on the southwestern edge of the city, near the university and just a short distance from good shoreline strolling on Ægisiða. Nauthólsvík Beach is nearby, and you can pay extra to sit under sun lamps, a nice splurge on a gloomy day.

Spas

A few Reykjavík hotels offer fitness rooms, saunas, massages, and health and beauty treatments, but only at **Hilton Reykjavík Spa,** Suðurlandsbraut 2 (www. hiltonreykjavikspa.is; © **444-5090;** Mon–Fri 6am–8pm, Sat 6am–6pm, Sun 10am–4pm), do these combined services truly amount to "spa" status. NordicaSpa is especially adept at treatments featuring Iceland's natural resources, from geothermal mud massages to seaweed wraps. Non-guests of the hotel are welcome.

Laugar Spa ★   While it isn't going to knock the Blue Lagoon (p. 84) off its pedestal anytime soon, for many this mammoth complex that opened in 2004 is more than enough to fulfill their hot-water needs. Owners have spared no expense to wow patrons with the latest in super-deluxe spa and fitness technology. Features include indoor and outdoor pools, exhaustive beauty and massage treatments, and a health-food restaurant. The six saunas and steam rooms are set at different temperatures, and each has a thematic fragrance. Among the indoor and outdoor spa baths, choose freshwater or seawater. One pool is designed exclusively for foot soaking. To visit the "relaxation cave," which has a 20-foot-wide waterfall, you must have your retina scanned at reception; then at the cave entrance, your eye-print is acknowledged and the doors snap open. Children can be left in their own playrooms or watching movies while you attend to yourself.

Sundlaugavegur 30a, at the north end of Laugardalur park, next to Laugardalslaug pool. www.laugarspa.com. © **553-0000.** Admission 5,800kr. Gym and spa Mon–Fri 6am–11:30pm; Sat 8am–10pm; Sun 8am–8pm. Beauty salon Mon–Fri 9am–7pm; Sat 11am–6pm. Massage salon Mon–Fri 9am–9pm; Sat 11am–6pm. Bus: 14.

POOL etiquette

Icelanders are especially strict about pool rules, especially when they pertain to hygiene. (Remember that Icelandic pools are far less chlorinated than pools abroad, so the concern over spreading germs is not paranoia.) To avoid stern looks of disapproval—or even lectures by pool monitors—follow these simple procedures:

- Leave shoes and socks outside the locker room, unless a sign specifically authorizes you to take them in.
- Undress completely at your locker and then walk to the showers carrying your towel and swimsuit. Stash your towel by the showers.
- Shower first, and then put your suit on. Rarely will you find a shower curtain or stall to hide behind; if you feel shy, be assured that Icelanders are both respectful of privacy and very nonchalant about this everyday routine. (Also be prepared for voluntary nudity in steam rooms, which are sex-segregated.)

- When showering, use soap, which is usually provided. Most shower rooms post a notorious sign—often photographed by visitors—depicting a human body, with red blotches over the "trouble areas" requiring particular attention.
- Don't go down water slides headfirst.
- After your swim, shower again and dry off before entering the locker room. Dripping on the locker room floor is frowned upon.

Whale-Watching

Faxaflói Bay is a prime whale-watching area (though visitors headed to Húsavík on the north coast should probably wait and head out from there). The smaller and less dramatic minke whales are the most common sightings, but you stand a good chance of spying humpback whales, harbor porpoise, white-beaked dolphins, and orcas. From May to mid-August, whale tours also stop at **Lundey Island,** a puffin nesting site (see below). Trips last 2½ to 3 hours and leave from Ægisgarður, the easternmost pier of the old port.

All the tour companies are reputable, but a solid choice is **Elding** (www.elding.is; ✆ 555-3565), the largest operator, boasting a high whale-sighting success rate. If no whales are seen, you are given a complimentary ticket for another tour that's valid for 2 years. Tickets are 10,990kr adults, 5,495kr children ages 7 to 15, and free for children 6 and under. Boats depart June through August at 9am, 10am, 1pm, 2pm, and 5pm (also 10am and 2pm July through early Aug) and January through May and September at 9am and 1pm. The price includes warm overalls and raincoats, plus admission to the "Whale Exhibition" with a simple exhibition on marine life in Faxaflói. Most boats have a play area for kids. If you want to throw in some sea angling with your whale- and puffin-watching, **Special Tours** (www.specialtours.is; ✆ 560-8800) combines all three activities for 20,390kr, with departures May through September at 1pm and 2pm. They will even grill your catch for you as you sail back.

Puffin-Watching

West of Reykjavík, the small islands of **Lundey** and **Akurey** are home to some 50,000 puffins during breeding season. Many whale-watching tours include a puffin stop; but both **Elding** (www.elding.is; ✆ 555-3565) and **Special Tours** (www.specialtours.is; ✆ 560-8800) offer a shorter, less-costly tour for puffin fanatics (for more on puffins, see p. 213), and their boats are better designed for drawing close to the bird cliffs. Tours last 1 hour and leave from Ægisgarður pier at the old port. Tickets are 5,990kr for adults, 2,995kr for children 7 to 15. Boats sail May to mid-August, three times daily between 9am and 3pm.

Fishing

Not many world capitals have good salmon fishing within city limits. The season for Reykjavík's **Elliðaár River** extends from June 1 to August 31, and opens with the mayor throwing the first cast. Contact the **Angling Club of Reykjavík** (www.svfr.is; ✆ 568-6050) for information on permits and procedures. Also ask about trout and Arctic char fishing in nearby lakes. For tackle and equipment, try **Veiðihornið,** Síðumúli 8 (✆ 568-8410).

For **sea fishing, Elding** (www.elding.is; ✆ 555-3565) has a 3-hour sea-angling tour for 14,900kr from May to September, leaving daily at 9am and 1:30pm, with grills on board.

Other Outdoor Activities

Many local farms offer 2- to 4-hour **horseback-riding tours,** which may include lunch and hotel pickup. Several excellent companies near Reykjavík are **Laxnes Horse Farm** in Mosfellsdalur (www.laxnes.is; ℂ **566-6197**), **Eldhestar** in Hveragerði (www.eldhestar.is; ℂ **480-4800**), and Íshestar in Hafnarfjörður (www.ishestar.is; ℂ **555-7000**).

Reykjavík has a handful of **golf courses**. The **Reykjavík Golf Club** (www. grgolf.is; ℂ **585-0200**) runs two 18-hole courses: the oceanside **Korpúlfsstaðir** to the northeast (Thorsvegur, via Korpúlfsstaðir; bus: 24) and the difficult **Grafarholt,** Iceland's premier championship course, to the east (Grafarholtsvegur, off Route 1; bus: 15 or 18). Both are about a 15-minute drive from the city center and stay open during summer evenings. Course fees are 10,300kr, club rental is 5,700kr, cart rental is 6,900kr, and trolley rental is 1,400kr. About 20 minutes from the center is **Oddur Golf Club** (www.oddur.is; ℂ **565-9092**) in Urridavatnsdalir, which opened in 1997 and is widely considered one of the country's best courses. Surrounded by lava, it's a frequent host of international tournaments. Course fees are 11,500kr, club rental is 6,000kr, cart rental is 6,500kr, and trolley rental is 500kr. Closer to the center, in Seltjarnarnes, west of Reykjavík, is the casual 9-hole **Golfklúbbur Ness,** at the end of Suðurströnd (http://nkgolf.is; ℂ **561-1930**), with good ocean views (bus: 11).

Spectator Sports

The unique Icelandic form of wrestling known as *glíma* dates back to the Viking era. The main season for competitions is from September to April. For more information, contact the **Icelandic Glíma Association** (ℂ **514-4064**). Also keep an eye out for historical reenactments at museums or special events like the **Viking Festival** in Hafnarfjörður (p. 29).

Icelanders are fanatical about the unusual and exciting sport of **handball,** once described as "water polo without the water." Iceland finished fourth in the 1992 Barcelona Olympics, and eighth in the 2007 World Cup, but their moment of glory was at the 2008 Beijing Olympics when they won silver—the smallest nation ever to win an Olympic silver medal in a team sport. The height of the season is September until April. For more information, contact the **Icelandic Handball Federation** (www.hsi.is; ℂ **514-4200**).

The Icelandic national **soccer** team was ranked 37th in the world in 1994, and fell to as low as 117th position in 2007, before climbing up to 22nd position in 2018 while making quite a bit of noise in the World Cup and the UEFA Euro 2016. If you'd like to attend a game, you can check out a match at **Laugardalsvöllur Stadium,** Laugardalur Park (ℂ **510-2900**).

WHERE TO STAY

With once-empty buildings being transformed into new boutique hotels and seemingly every older Reykjavík hotel constantly in a state of renovation or expansion, not to mention entire apartment blocks being rented out on **Airbnb,** Reykjavík's entire accommodation landscape has raised its game considerably in the last few years. The downside is that nightly rates have been on the rise, but the upside is that you can expect high standards, as well as big discounts in the off-season. High season is longer in Reykjavík than in the rest of Iceland, so you are likely to encounter peak prices and limited availability in May, June, and September as well as during the country's peak months of July and August.

Places are generally classed as either a hotel or a "guesthouse," which is an Icelandic rendition of the B&B. Because offerings are similar at both, price and location are more likely to influence your choice. Be aware that many tour packages automatically place unsuspecting visitors outside the heart of the city. Conversely, light sleepers in downtown hotels may wonder why they paid more for the privilege of being in the middle of the late-night revelry.

Central Reykjavík
VERY EXPENSIVE

101 Hotel ★★★ Iceland's (and possibly Europe's) most exemplary example of a design hotel, the 101, named after the neighborhood's postal code, attracts Reykjavík's most fashionable crowd. Despite the stark exterior, everything from the fireplace and zebra-striped chairs in the lounge to the extensive collection of contemporary art from Icelandic artists is touched by cool. Someone who works nearby once told me that they go there whenever they have a break from work, just because it's so chic and neat the way they stack their art books. The rooms are sleek with glossy black and white surfaces, though far from over the top. Most suites and doubles add balconies, some with views of both the harbor and old town. Standard double and double balcony rooms have walk-in showers only; all others have walk-in showers and bathtub. The long, narrow restaurant and bar, **Kitchen & Wine,** sits beneath a glass ceiling and stay open relatively late.

Hverfisgata 10. www.101hotel.is. ⓒ **580-0101.** 38 units. 39,015kr–56,015kr double; 67,915kr and up for junior suite. Limited street parking. **Amenities:** Restaurant; bar; small exercise room; small spa with steam room; room service; free Wi-Fi.

Hótel Borg ★★ Classy and elegant, the iconic Borg was Iceland's first luxury hotel when it opened in 1930. The work of architect Guðjón Samúelsson, who also designed the even more iconic Hallgrímskirkja church, the hotel's castlelike features and prominent location overlooking Austurvöllur Square make it one of the city's most recognizable landmarks. Major renovations in 2007 swapped out the dated interiors for a chic Art Deco look with modern Scandinavian amenities like Bang & Olufsen flatscreens, plus period black and white bathrooms equipped with Philippe Stark fittings and heated marble floors. The two-level Tower Suite, with 360-degree views of the city center, might just be the most luxurious room in the city and often hosts visiting celebrities. Sadly, they also swapped out their New Nordic restaurant for a branch of **Jamie's Italian.**

Pósthússtræti 11, on Austurvöllur Sq. www.keahotels.is. ⓒ **551-1440.** 99 units. May–Sept and Dec 28–Jan 2 52,000kr double, 83,000kr suites. Rates 25% lower Oct 1–Dec 27 and Jan 3–Apr 30 except suites. Children 11 and under stay free in parent's room. Limited street parking. **Amenities:** Restaurant; bar; concierge; spa; free Wi-Fi.

Reykjavík Hotels & Restaurants

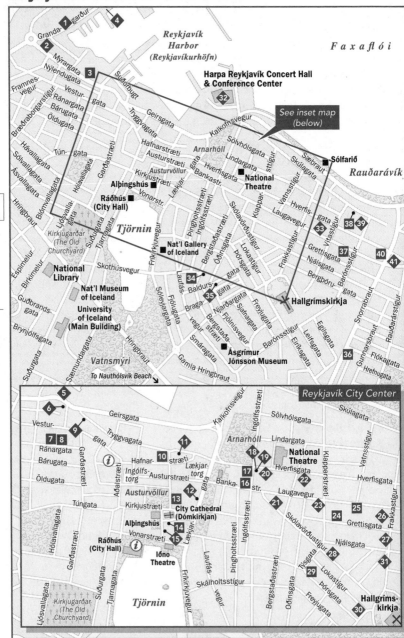

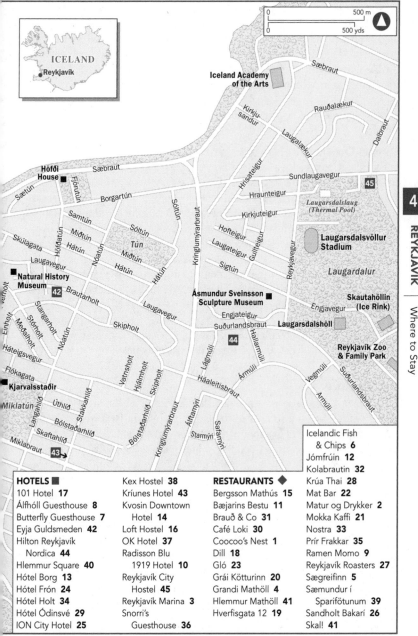

HOTELS ■
101 Hotel **17**
Álfhóll Guesthouse **8**
Butterfly Guesthouse **7**
Eyja Guldsmeden **42**
Hilton Reykjavík
  Nordica **44**
Hlemmur Square **40**
Hótel Borg **13**
Hótel Frón **24**
Hótel Holt **34**
Hótel Óðinsvé **29**
ION City Hotel **25**

Kex Hostel **38**
Kríunes Hotel **43**
Kvosin Downtown
  Hotel **14**
Loft Hostel **16**
OK Hotel **37**
Radisson Blu
  1919 Hotel **10**
Reykjavík City
  Hostel **45**
Reykjavík Marina **3**
Snorri's
  Guesthouse **36**

RESTAURANTS ◆
Bergsson Mathús **15**
Bæjarins Bestu **11**
Brauð & Co **31**
Café Loki **30**
Coocoo's Nest **1**
Dill **18**
Gló **23**
Grái Kötturinn **20**
Grandi Mathöll **4**
Hlemmur Mathöll **41**
Hverfisgata 12 **19**

Icelandic Fish
  & Chips **6**
Jómfrúin **12**
Kolabrautin **32**
Krúa Thai **28**
Mat Bar **22**
Matur og Drykker **2**
Mokka Kaffi **21**
Nostra **33**
Þrír Frakkar **35**
Ramen Momo **9**
Reykjavík Roasters **27**
Sægreifinn **5**
Sæmundur í
  Sparifötunum **39**
Sandholt Bakarí **26**
Skal! **41**

ION City Hotel ★★   After its luxe Golden Circle hotel was splashed on the pages of every travel magazine in the world, intimate Icelandic hotel brand ION set its sights on the capital, opening this modern design hotel in 2018. Using gray, white, and black tones throughout, the interiors mimic the Icelandic landscape. The standard rooms are smallish, yet designed well enough that every inch is utilized, while suites add extra amenities like balconies and even private saunas. The hotel's chic restaurant and bar, **Súmac ★**, fuses Icelandic ingredients with Mediterranean and Middle Eastern spices.

Laugavegur 28. http://ioncity.ioniceland.is. ✆ **578-3730.** 18 units. 36,720kr double; 52,445kr junior suite; 68,515kr suite. Rates include a complimentary mini-bar. **Amenities:** Restaurant; bar; grocer; laundry service; balconies (in some); free Wi-Fi.

Kvosin Downtown Hotel ★★★   Situated in one of the most attractive areas of downtown, between the lake and the square, this apartment-style hotel has a lot going for it. Designer Einar Geir Ingvarsson restored this landmark 1900 brick apartment building, formerly home to the city's Public Reading Society, with all sorts of cool Scandinavian accents like designer lamps and armchairs and various 20th-century modernist furnishings. Each oversized unit has a unique layout and set of amenities, ranging from terrace access to sofabeds to dining areas. Downstairs are an artisanal grocer and a hip bar with a long list of gin and tonics; plus, instead of a ho-hum on-site breakfast, guests are given a voucher for one at the excellent **Bergsson Mathús** (p. 77) next door.

Kirkjutorg 4. www.kvosinhotel.com. ✆ **571-4460.** 24 units. June–Aug and Dec 28–Jan 2 42,000kr junior suite; 149,000kr suite. rates include breakfast. Rates 40% lower Oct–Apr, except Dec 28–Jan 2. Limited street parking. **Amenities:** Bar; grocer; laundry service; balconies (in some); free Wi-Fi.

EXPENSIVE

Hlemmur Square ★★   This modish hotel/hostel amalgam from hotelier Klaus Ortlieb—who also created the Gotham Hotel in New York City and Claridge's in London—is proof of how diverse Reykjavík's hotel scene has become. Inside the five-story building, which dates to the 1930s, you'll find a mix of design elements, such as a lobby modeled after the colorful streetscapes of Reykjavík to contemporary rooms, most with balconies and spacious sitting areas, filled with colorful accents, neutral furnishings, and a minibar stocked with local products. The third and fourth floors are reserved for the hostel, where 4- to 14-bed dorms have large lockers under the bed, plus two guest kitchens and an extra lounge. Hostel-goers also have access to all hotel facilities. Plenty is happening downstairs too, such as a craft beer and cocktail bar, live music in the lobby, and a playroom for kids.

Laugavegur 105. www.hlemmursquare.com. ✆ **415-1600.** 18 units and 180 hostel beds. June–Aug and Dec 28–Jan 2 28,000kr—35,000kr double; 5,700kr–8100kr dorm bed. Rates 15% lower Feb–Mar and Sept–Oct; 25% lower Nov–Jan, except Dec 28–Jan 2. Limited street parking. **Amenities:** Bar; concierge; currency exchange; 2 guest kitchens; laundry service; room service; free Wi-Fi.

Hótel Holt ★   Home to Iceland's largest privately owned art collection, this tried-and-true classic is set on a quiet residential street just a 5-minute walk from downtown. Original owner Þorvaldur Guðmundsson, who passed away in 1998, was a great admirer of Icelandic art, and the work of some of the country's best-known artists, including Jóhannes S. Kjarval, adorn the rooms, lounges, library, and a ground-floor restaurant. Aside from the artwork, the rooms are rather classic, with leather chairs and dark wood furnishings. Some have access to a small balcony.

Bergstaðastræti 37. www.holt.is. ✆ **552-5700.** 41 units. June–Aug 39,436kr double; 46,552kr and up junior suite and suite. Rates 11%–12% lower Sept–May. Free parking. **Amenities:** Restaurant; bar; concierge; small health club/massage room; free access to nearby fitness studio; room service; free Wi-Fi.

Hótel Óðinsvé ★★   Set in an early-19th-century building on a quiet residential street and one block from the center's main commercial district, the Óðinsvé is a straightforward, sensible option. The rooms vary considerably in size and shape, with some of the singles being downright claustrophobic. However, most rooms get plenty of light and all feature a clean, minimalist design with light wood floors and Danish bedding. Standard rooms share a common balcony and patio, while the deluxe rooms and suites on the third and fourth floors have private balconies with fine views of Hallgrímskirkja and Mount Esja. Breakfast is served in the hotel's restaurant, **Snaps,** a modern Scandinavian bistro that's a popular go-to spot for neighborhood locals (main courses 2,390kr–4,990kr).

Óðinstorg Sq. (at the intersection of Þórsgata and Týsgi). www.hotelodinsve.is. ✆ **511-6200.** 50 units. May–Aug 32,596kr double; 45,996kr junior suite. Rates around 15% lower Sept; 30% lower Oct–Apr. Rates include buffet breakfast. Children 11 and under stay free in parent's room. Limited street parking. **Amenities:** Restaurant; concierge; car rental service; free Wi-Fi.

Radisson Blu 1919 Hotel ★★   The high-molded ceilings and grand marble central staircase of the posh, historic 1919 building (originally the headquarters of Eimskip, Iceland's first major shipping line) still remain in this slick downtown hotel. A favorite among business travelers, the hotel adds to its historic base with a modern Scandinavian design that eschews refinement in the avant-garde art installations that grace its lobby, the glitzy **1919 Restaurant** (main courses 3,500kr–4,500kr), and a lounge filled with cube stools covered in cowhide and floor-to-ceiling windows. The minimalist rooms are more subdued but are big and airy, with hardwood floors and dark fabrics. The upper-floor suites add even more space, plus skylights and private Jacuzzis in some.

Pósthússtræti 2. www.radissonblu.com/1919hotel-reykjavik. ✆ **599-1000;** 1800/333-3333 from U.S.; 800/3333-3333 from U.K. 88 units. June–Aug and Dec 28–Jan 2 34,4990kr double; 78,900kr and up for suite. Rates 20% lower Feb–Mar and Sept–Oct; 30% lower Nov–Jan, except Dec 28–Jan 2. Limited street parking. **Amenities:** Restaurant; bar and lounge; small exercise room; concierge; express laundry service; room service; free Wi-Fi.

4

REYKJAVÍK | Where to Stay

Reykjavík Marina ★   In the up-and-coming fishpacking district along the waterfront, this former paint factory is one of the Reykjavík's most all-around fun hotels. The colorful room decor is a nod to the area's nautical past, with things like fish hook hangers and rope knot wallpaper, merged with quirky modern design elements, like polished concrete walls and reclaimed wood tables. This place is amenity-rich too, with one of the city's premier cocktail spots (**Slippbarinn ★★**), a laidback bistro, a cinema showing Icelandic movies with English subtitles, and a fitness room with a small climbing wall.

Myrargata 2. www.icelandairhotels.com. ✆ **415-1600.** 108 units. 37,400kr double; 68,850kr and up for suite. Rates 40% lower Oct–Apr, except Dec 28–Jan 2. Rates include breakfast. Limited street parking. **Amenities:** Restaurant; bar; cinema; gym; free Wi-Fi.

MODERATE

Butterfly Guesthouse ★   Most visitors to Reykjavík have probably noticed Butterfly's green house with a massive butterfly on it without realizing what's inside. Though rather simply furnished, small, and lacking private bathrooms (in most), the pastel painted rooms are well kept and probably one of the best value stays in town. The two sky-lighted apartments, available for a minimum of 2 nights, each add a kitchen and balcony, as well as private bathrooms. Breakfast is self-serve from basics stocked in the pantry.

Ránargata 8a. www.butterfly.is. ✆ **894-1864.** 8 units, 4 without bathroom. Apts. have TV and kitchen. Late May through early Sept 22,500kr double without bathroom; 25,000kr double w/bathroom; 30,000kr apt. Limited street parking. **Amenities:** Car rental; shared kitchen; free Wi-Fi.

Eyja Guldsmeden ★   From the Danish-born eco-conscious hotel chain Guldsmeden, this stylish boutique hotel in a former office building has rooms adorned with Balinese-style furniture, four-poster beds, and the occasional sheepskin or cowhide. The only downside? It's on the farther reaches of Reykjavík's primary hotel scene, which means that prices are considerably lower than they would be a few blocks away. A second, more central property, the 52-room **Von Guldsmeden,** will open on Laugavegur sometime in 2019.

Brautarholt 10. www.guldsmedenhotels.com/eyja. ✆ **519-7300.** 65 units. 29,900kr double. Rates 25% lower Oct–Mar. **Amenities:** Restaurant; bar; gym; free Wi-Fi.

Hótel Frón ★   This four-floor hotel set within three adjoining buildings sits right in the middle of Reykjavík's primary shopping and nightlife zone. Parquet flooring and flatscreen TVs are about the only luxuries you will find here, aside from the street-facing rooms with balconies that look right over Laugavegur, one of the best people-watching seats in town. The hotel has 20 studio apartments with kitchenettes for only a slight rate increase over a double. The hotel gets extra props for getting early-morning arrivals into their rooms when possible at no extra cost.

Laugavegur 22a. www.hotelfron.is. ✆ **511-4666.** 96 units. May–Sept 24,000kr double; 25,500kr studio apt; 28,800kr apt. Rates around 30% lower Mar–Apr and Oct, and 40% lower Nov–Feb. Rates include breakfast. Free parking. **Amenities:** Restaurant; bar; kitchenettes (in apts. only); free Wi-Fi.

Kex Hostel ★★ Whoever said you need a lot of cash to stay at a hipster hotel? Even more than a place to sleep, Kex, set inside an old biscuit factory near the waterfront just a 10-minute walk southeast of the center, has become something of a scene with its lively gastropub **Sæmundur í Sparifötunum** (see below), heated outdoor patio, and vintage barber chair (where a third-generation barber actually gives cuts on Thurs nights). Decorated mostly with found and salvaged objects, the sparse, clean accommodations with polished concrete floors are divided between private rooms, some with an ocean view and private bathrooms, and 4- to 16-bed dorms, both coed and female only, with electrical outlets and lockers for each guest.

Skúlagata 28l. www.kexhostel.is. ⓒ **561-6060.** 43 units. June–Sept 27,700kr double without bathroom; 41,100kr double w/bathroom; 5,300kr and up dorms. Prices are 20%–25% lower outside of summer. **Amenities:** Restaurant; bike rental; book exchange; guest kitchens; gym; laundromat; lockers; luggage storage; tour desk; free Wi-Fi.

OK Hotel ★★ The reception at the OK Hotel, right in the middle of Laugavegur core shopping zone, is inside the restaurant below. The staff here will hand you your keys and an information packet, but other than that you are pretty much on your own. The two- to six-person studios are decorated in funky, mismatched vintage furniture and street art made from recycled materials, and are equipped with kitchenettes, iPod docks, and flatscreen TVs. Some rooms have balconies.

Laugavegur 74. www.ok.hotelreykjavik.net. ⓒ **578-9850.** 15 units. June–Aug and Dec 28–Jan 2 30,720kr double. Rates 30% lower Oct–Mar. **Amenities:** Restaurant; bar; luggage storage; free Wi-Fi.

INEXPENSIVE

Álfhóll Guesthouse ★ Centrally located on a quiet residential street downtown toward the old port, this summer-only 1928 guesthouse offers a variety of tasteful rooms that won't break the bank. All feature antique furnishings and each layout is unique, with some having more light than others. The three studio apartments on the top-level sleep up to four, and come with sloped ceilings and kitchenettes.

Ránargata 8. www.islandia.is/alf. ⓒ **898-1838.** 13 units. May 15–Sept 16,550kr double without bathroom; 29,000kr studio apt for 2–4 persons. Rates include breakfast (summer only). No credit cards. **Amenities:** Free Wi-Fi.

Loft Hostel ★ This lively, HI-affiliated hostel with a clean, minimalist vibe has become something of a hub of backpacker activity in Reykjavík. Most come for the four-, six-, and eight-bed dorm rooms, all of which come with en-suite bathrooms and lockers and include linens (but no towels), but the Loft also has a few (somewhat overpriced) private rooms. Extras include a bar with frequent live music, a lounge filled with vintage and recycled furnishings, and a large terrace with views over the downtown streets.

Bankastræti 7. www.lofthostel.is. ⓒ **553-8140.** 19 units. 6,465kr dorms; 23,000kr double. Rates up to 30% lower Oct–Apr. Free parking. **Amenities:** Cafe; bar; guest kitchen; book exchange; luggage storage; tour desk; free Wi-Fi.

Snorri's Guesthouse ★   On a busy avenue, though not far from the BSÍ bus terminal, Gistiheimili Snorra is a more than reasonable option for those willing to spend a little extra time walking from downtown and back. The room classes offer a range of amenities—from basic rooms without bathrooms or TVs to ensuite doubles and family rooms with TVs, DVD players, sofas, and refrigerators. The friendly staff is helpful in giving recommendations and helping with travel arrangements.

Snorrabraut 61. www.guesthousereykjavik.com. ⓒ **552-0598.** 23 units. May–Sept 20,900kr double without bathroom; 28,200kr double w/bathroom; 33,200kr family room w/bathroom. Rates 22%–27% lower Oct–Apr. Rates include breakfast buffet (except for sleeping-bag guests). Free parking. **Amenities:** Car rental; Flybus (ask driver for Flóki Inn across the street); tour desk; free Wi-Fi.

Outside the City's Heart

Perhaps you think of hostels as the exclusive domain of scruffy young backpackers, but Iceland's hotel prices have driven you to despair. While places like Loft Hostel and Kex have taken some of the crowd, **Reykjavík City Hostel** ★, Sundlaugavegur 34 (www.hostel.is; ⓒ **553-8110;** fax 588-9201; 40 units without bathroom; May–Sept 18,000kr double; 5,810kr dorm with linens; discounts Oct–Apr), is still a good option for the budget-minded. You don't need a membership card (though members get discounts). You'll see plenty of families and seniors and people from all walks of life. The hostel actually has more amenities than most hotels: guest kitchens, sauna, free parking, cafe/bar, game room, playground, free Wi-Fi, and laundry rooms, plus fun events like film showings and pub crawls. Many tour operators offer their lowest prices through the helpful front desk. Admittedly, the ambience is sterile and the location is not central, but Flybus and airport connections are easy, and you're right next door to the **Laugardalslaug pool** (p. 63). Book way in advance, particularly for doubles; summer rooms sell out as early as January.

EXPENSIVE

Hilton Reykjavík Nordica ★   When it opened in 1965 on a busy road east of downtown, this sleek hotel, with its chrome-glass and natural-wood interiors, was like nothing Iceland had ever seen. In 2007, it became a part of the Hilton chain and underwent a major renovation, putting it back in the spotlight. While other smaller hotels in the center are far more interesting and luxurious, this hotel's ability to maintain its high standards ensures that it remains in the conversation. The chic rooms are decked out with timber-beamed ceilings, Venetian fabrics, and marble bathrooms. Business and executive rooms are located on the eighth and ninth floors and include free access to the exceptional **Hilton Reykjavik Spa** (p. 64), as well as the **panorama lounge. Vox,** one of the city's first New Nordic restaurants, is not as groundbreaking as it once was, but it's still a convenient amenity on this side of town.

Suðurlandsbraut 2. www.hiltonreykjavik.com. ⓒ **444-5000.** 251 units. June–Oct 38,200kr double; 50,200kr and up executive; 74,500kr suite. Rates 25%–40% lower off-season. Free valet/self-parking. **Amenities:** Restaurant; bar; spa; room service; shuttle bus to city center; free Wi-Fi.

MODERATE

Kríunes Hotel ★★   It's hard to believe that this ranch-style hotel sitting pretty on the banks of a small peninsula overlooking Lake Ellidavat is just a 15-minute drive from the city center (and a shuttle is available to move you back and forth). The property has gone through several renovations and name changes since it opened in 1998, leading to a mish-mash of styles, though it's still family-run and as quaint as ever. The parquet-floored rooms follow a classic theme, with some adding hot tubs or fireplaces. The front desk can hook you up with canoes, kayaks, and foot-pedal boats for a fee; horse rentals and fishing excursions can also be arranged. The property is also a good place to see the Northern Lights.

Við Vatnsenda. www.kriunes.is. ✆ **567-2245.** 14 units. Early May–late Sept 26,999kr double; 49,999kr suite year-round. Rates include breakfast. Free parking. **Amenities:** Restaurant; hot tub; sauna; tour desk; free Wi-Fi.

WHERE TO EAT

Over the past 3 decades, Reykjavík has transformed from a culinary wasteland into a culinary destination. In years past, dining options were limited to greasy-spoon diners and overpriced tourist restaurants, as well as a few local standbys lost in the crowd. Now the dining scene has become downright dynamic. There are New Nordic bistros, cult coffee roasters, street food vendors, artisanal pizza shops, and hipster gastropubs with a dozen local craft beers on tap. Chefs are looking backward into the country's Viking past to rescue centuries-old food traditions and bring them into modern times. With relatively few venerated food traditions to uphold, innovative young chefs have been free to create Icelandic food in their own image, drawing inspiration wherever they find it. The quality and diversity of ingredients is astounding for such a remote outpost of the world, and little by little, one kitchen at a time, the rest of Iceland is catching on.

A few years ago, restaurant prices in Reykjavík seemed outlandish. Now, largely thanks to an exchange rate that helps tourists from just about anywhere, high-quality food is more affordable. Ingredients and staff are still so costly that all meals have a high base cost, but you're still getting good value at the margin: spend 5,000kr per person and you'll likely have a good meal; spend 8,000kr and you'll likely have a fantastic one. For the best balance, we recommend visiting the grocery store (and the hot-dog stand) a few times, filling up on your hotel's breakfast buffet, and then splurging on a few top-quality meals to remember.

While street food is limited to summer in Reykjavík (and generally mediocre), two food halls have opened in in town. The old Hlemmur bus station has been transformed into **Hlemmur Mathöll** (www.hlemmurmatholl.is), Laugavegur 107, a lively food court with a branch of the bakery Brauð & co, a small-plates restaurant and bar called **Skal!** (see p. 79), a coffee bar, a *banh mi* sandwich shop, and several other concepts. In the fishpacking district fronting the old harbor, **Grandi Mathöll** (http://grandimatholl.is/), Grandagarður 16, is set in a refurbished fish factory, offering up a similar array of concepts.

Expensive

Dill ★★★ NEW ICELANDIC   When Gunnar Karl Gíslason opened Dill in 2008 in the Nordic House, Iceland was on the verge of collapse. Even after all of his investors dropped out, local producers believed in him enough that they were willing to front him food and supplies. It's a good thing, too. No chef in Iceland has had more of a profound impact on the country's culinary evolution, reviving lost traditions and helping develop names for artisanal producers. In 2014, Gíslason, who now cooks in New York, moved the restaurant downtown into a restored old house that was more aligned with his original vision for the restaurant, and it quickly earned a Michelin star, the very first in the country. The tasting menus change often, sometimes daily, based on which ingredients are fresh and in season. The mostly natural wine pairing is far and above anything else in town. Despite being one of the top restaurants in all of Scandinavia, prices are still quite accessible.

Hverfisgata 12. www.dillrestaurant.is. ⓒ **552-1522.** Reservations recommended. 3-course menu 7,900kr; 5-course menu 9,900kr; 7-course menu 11,900kr. Wed–Sat 6pm–midnight.

Kolabrautin ★ INTERNATIONAL   Amid the glass panels on the fourth floor of Harpa, underneath a modernist reflective ceiling with a one-of-a-kind view of the old harbor and downtown, this sleek restaurant brings in an elite crowd of both glamorous locals and passing visitors. The menus fuses mostly Icelandic ingredients into eclectic, modern plates like lobster ravioli or duck breast with miso and spring-onion-filled potatoes. There's a wood-fired oven on-site to roast meats and sourdough pizzas, plus set concert menus where you can opt to have dessert after the show.

Austurbakki 2. www.kolabrautin.is. ⓒ **519-9700.** Reservations recommended. Main courses 3,400kr–5,700kr; 4-course menu 10,100kr. Daily 4–11pm.

Matur og Drykkur ★ ICELANDIC   Its name translating to "food and drink," this laid-back restaurant in an old salt fish factory beside the Saga Museum serves Icelandic specialties like cod liver with rowan berries, Arctic char with smoked buttermilk and beer mustard, and warm rye bread soup with ice cream. It's said that the chef's grandmother cried after sampling his halibut soup, a recipe that brought back memories from her childhood.

Grandagarður 2. www.maturogdrykkur.is. ⓒ **571-8877.** Reservations recommended. Main courses 3,590kr–4,990kr; 8-course tasting menu 10,990kr. Mon–Sat 11:30am–3pm; Mon–Sun 6–11pm.

Hverfisgata 12 ★★★ PIZZA   This quirky second-level space, sandwiched between fine-dining space Dill and the Mikkeller & Friends bar, has been a welcome addition to the city's dining scene. The space is a curio cabinet of weird flea-market finds, with a lively cocktail bar and several intimate dining spaces. In addition to the standard wood-fired pizzas, several more unusual ones pair things such as potatoes and sea truffles or skyr and various types of cheese. The appetizers—like spicy French fries and beef tongue with apple purée—are worth their weight in gold.

Hverfisgata 12. www.hverfisgata12.is. © **437-0203.** 2,450kr–3,450kr pizzas. Mon–Fri 5–11pm; Sat–Sun 11:30am–11pm.

Nostra ★★ NEW NORDIC   Two young chefs with experience in top restaurants in Iceland, Europe, and New York are helping reinvigorate Reykjavík's fine-dining scene in this modern space with a color-changing glass wall and open kitchen. Driven by the seasons, the adventurous menus consists of four-, six-, and eight-course tastings, including vegetarian, vegan, and pescatarian options. They don't shy away from unfamiliar ingredients, such as dried and shaved goat heart or blue mussels, but the technique is really the star here, from cooking carrots for 12 hours to freezing strawberry sabayonne with liquid nitrogen. The restaurant's attached bar, **Artson ★★**, stays open late and has some of the city's best cocktails.

Laugavegur 59. www.nostrarestaurant.is. © **519-3535.** 4-course tasting menu 8,900kr. Tues–Sat 5:30–9:30pm.

Mat Bar ★★ GASTROPUB   This corner pub with black-and-white-tile floors and a marble bar sided by leather stools seems to be every local's favorite eatery. Mat Bar has one of Reykjavík's most creative menus, serving dishes like rabbit-filled dumplings and reindeer steak with an arctic berry glaze—but it's all tied closely to the seasons, so nothing stays on the menu too long. Plates are small, so order two to three per person.

Hverfisgata 26. www.matbar.is. © **788-3900.** Main courses 1,500kr–4,700kr. Tues–Sun 5pm–midnight.

Þrír Frakkar ★★ ICELANDIC   The kind of dishes that Icelandic mothers and grandmothers make in their own kitchens, this is classic, home-style food, made with love and a rarity in the capital's restaurants. With nautically themed interiors and a residential location, this old-school spot is as tried and true as they come. The hashed fish with traditional Icelandic brown bread is a must, as are the cod cheeks when available. It's a good, less gimmicky place to try Iceland's more unusual delicacies—like *hákarl* (aka fermented shark) or cured fin whale—than the city's more touristy restaurants.

Baldursgata 14, at Nönnugata. www.3frakkar.is. © **552-3939.** Reservations recommended. Main courses 4,590kr–6,250kr. Mon–Fri 11:30am–2:30pm and 6–10pm; Sat–Sun 6–11pm.

Moderate

Bergsson Mathús ★★ INTERNATIONAL   This simple, soulful, farm-to-table eatery is Reykjavík's best breakfast spot. Whether you're looking for something light, say, a green juice or chia porridge, or something heavier, like bacon, eggs, and potatoes, this bright, cheery spot has you covered. In between meals, many stop in for coffee and cake. The lesser-known dinner service is also quite reliable, offering up a chalkboard menu of casual dishes like pan-fried ling and spinach lasagna. A second location has been added in the fishpacking district at Grandagarður 16.

Templarasund 3. www.bergsson.is. ✆ **571-1822.** Main courses 990kr–2,390kr. Mon–Fri 7am–7pm; Sat–Sun 7am–5pm.

Coocoo's Nest ★ INTERNATIONAL   This laid-back hipster deli with reclaimed wood-panel walls helped breath some life into the blossoming old harbor area when it opened in the summer of 2013. The emphasis is on fresh and healthy, with eclectic, always-changing menu items like creamy cauliflower soup or lamb sandwiches with salsa verde. There are special menus on some nights, such as taco Tuesdays or sourdough pizzas on Wednesdays and Thursdays. Get to their weekend brunches early, because seats fill up fast.

Grandagarður 23. www.coocoosnest.is. ✆ **552-5454.** Main courses 1,590kr–3,990kr. Tues–Sat 11am–10pm; Sun 11am–4pm.

Gló ★ VEGETARIAN   In a country where vegetables have traditionally been hard to come by, the success of a chain of vegetarian restaurants is a sign of how things are changing. Gló, with four locations around town, is the lifeblood of the Icelandic vegetarian and health-conscious eater. The sleek downtown location serves various raw and vegetable- or grain-based plates cafeteria style, offering a roster of dishes that changes daily.

Laugavegur 20b. www.glo.is. ✆ **553-1111.** Main courses 1,490kr–3,190kr. Daily 11am–9pm.

Icelandic Fish & Chips ★ FISH   Much of England's national snack uses fish from Icelandic waters, so it's no surprise that Iceland can make decent fish and chips too. At this organic bistro near the waterfront, the fish changes every day. There's usually some combination of cod, haddock, wolffish, red fish, blue ling, plaice, and pollock, and you can opt to have it battered and fried or made with some other preparation. For the chips, order a cup of the "skyronnes," the *skyr*-based house sauce with flavors like coriander-lime or ginger-wasabi.

Tryggvagata 11. www.fishandchips.is. ✆ **511-1118.** Main courses 1,390kr–5,290kr. Daily 11:30am–9pm; Sat noon–9pm.

Jómfrúin ★ DANISH   Although there is little trace left of Iceland's time as part of Denmark, some things are worth keeping around. The *smørrebrød,* an open-faced sandwich, is the cornerstone of pre-Noma Danish culinary culture. It's so big in Copenhagen that the city even has a *smørrebrød* school, and in 1995, Jómfrúin's head chef was the first male student ever to graduate. Most *smørrebrød* features a dense rye-bread base layered with different toppings like smoked salmon, pâté, bacon, fried onions, or herbs. There are dozens of varieties, but for an Icelandic twist try the *hangikjöt,* topped with smoked lamb, green peas, asparagus, and egg quarters.

Lækjargata 4. www.jomfruin.is. ✆ **551-0100.** Sandwiches 2,150kr–3,600kr. Daily 11am–10pm.

Sæmundur í Sparifötunum ★★ GASTROPUB   Inside the converted biscuit factory that also houses the Kex Hostel, this gastropub looks straight out of Williamsburg, Brooklyn, with its tattooed and bearded bartenders, extensive craft beer list (they also brew their own), and mismatched furniture. The menu is priced for the hostel crowd, though it's still one of the best and most reliable options in town. Courses range from elevated bar snacks like baked goat cheese to larger meals like pumpkin curry and fried chicken with fermented hot sauce. Live jazz is offered on occasion.

Skúlagata 28l. www.kexhostel.is/saemundur. ☏ **561-6060.** Main courses 1,900kr–2,790kr. Daily noon–11pm.

Skal! ★★★ NEW NORDIC   Chef Gísli Matthías Auðunsson has made a name for himself with Slippurinn in the Westman Islands, where he forages for native seaweeds and wild herbs while experimenting with traditional techniques like drying, salting, pickling, fermenting, and smoking. In 2017, he opened this bustling restaurant inside a food hall in the old Hlemmur bus station (see p. 75). Counter seating wraps around the open kitchen, where chefs prepare dishes ranging from small plates like Icelandic scallop ceviche to hot dogs to braised lamb ribs—and prices are some of the most accessible in town. The drink program here is superb, with an expertly crafted natural wine list and several herb-infused cocktails.

Laugavegur 107. www.skalrvk.com. ☏ **775-2299.** Main courses 1,000kr–2,500kr. Daily noon–11pm.

Inexpensive

Bæjarins Bestu ★★★ HOT DOGS   Everyone from Bill Clinton to Charlie Sheen has stopped by this famous hot-dog shack facing a parking lot that has operated continuously in the same location since 1937. Britain's *Guardian* newspaper even voted it the "Best Hot Dog Stand in Europe." The secret to the thin, long *pylsur* that just sticks out of the edges of the bun is anyone's guess. Some credit the rémoulade sauce, while others say there's some unknown cooking fluid. Order it *"eina með öllu,"* with all the fixings. Aside from one outdoor picnic table, there really isn't any seating. Most clientele simply take their dog standing up.

Tryggvagata 101, corner of Pósthússtræti. No phone. Hot dogs 500kr. Sun–Thurs 10am–1am; Fri–Sat 10am–4:30am.

Hot Dog Utopia

Icelanders are well aware that their *pylsur* (hot dogs) are among the best on the planet, and they consume them in enormous quantities—usually *ein með öllu,* or "one with everything." This expression is so ingrained in the national psyche that Akureyri began calling its Bank Holiday Weekend celebrations (p. 29) "Ein með öllu" a few years ago. A familiar and welcoming sight inside every filling station is the undulating metal rack that holds your hot dog as you dispense mayo, ketchup, and a tangy rémoulade (with finely chopped pickle) from enormous squeeze tubes. Toppings also include raw and crispy onions. The key ingredient, however, is the hot dog itself: The addition of lamb to the usual pork and beef mellows and deepens the taste experience. That's probably all you want to know about how they're made.

Krúa Thai ★ THAI This no-frills dive run by a Thai family has been a favorite for generations of students and backpackers. The menu is made up of nearly 50 standard Thai dishes that aren't toned down for non-Thai guests unless you specifically request it. The *tom yam,* chicken or seafood stew, is particularly soul-pleasing on cold winter days. Krúa Thai's three-course weekday lunch special is quite possibly the best-value dining option in town.

Skólavörðustígur 21. ℗ **555-2525.** Main courses 1,950kr–2,820kr. Daily 11:30am–9:30pm.

Ramen Momo ★ ASIAN All Asian cuisines seem to collide at Ramen Momo, which opened on the waterfront in 2014. It serves up steamed-bun sandwiches, *momo* dumplings, ramen, and sweets like black sesame pudding to just a few seats. Despite the exotic menu, most of the ingredients are sourced locally; they even make their own organic noodles in house. Available to go or for delivery as well.

Tryggvagata 16. https://ramenmomo.is. ℗ **571-0646.** Main courses 950kr–1,890kr. Mon–Sat 11:30am–9pm; Sun 5–9pm.

Sægreifinn ★★ SEAFOOD Despite the passing of its founding fisherman, who had become something of an Icelandic icon, the ramshackle "Sea Baron" carries on. Order at the counter and take your number to the long, communal wooden tables with stools made from fish containers. Most visitors come for the *humarsupa* (lobster soup), which will cure your ills on a wet, windy day. It's a touch sweet and creamy, with hints of celery, red pepper, tomato, cinnamon, clove, and coriander—plus a decent chunk or two of Icelandic lobster. Seasonal fish and shellfish, as well as whale, are also offered in kebab form.

Geirsgata 8 between Ægisgata and Tryggvagata. www.saegreifinn.is. ℗ **553-1500.** Main courses 1,600kr–2,600kr. Summer (usually May 15–Sept 15) daily 11:30am–11pm; off-season daily 11:30am–10pm.

Cafes

Various explanations are given for why Iceland runs on coffee: the former prohibition of beer, the high cost of alcohol, the long and dark winters, all the sudden downpours of rain, the need to digest heavy diets. Whatever the cause, Icelandic coffee is fine and strong, and coffeehouse culture thrives in Reykjavík, where international chains have yet to gain a foothold. Cafes are a great place to meet locals, second only to the pools. Magazines are usually lying around, refills are often free, and you can linger for hours without being glared at. Many cafes serve food by day and function as bars and clubs at night, closing at 1am or later on weekends. The number of cafes opening before 11am is steadily increasing, to cater to an emerging breakfast trend.

Brauð & Co ★★★ Just down the street from Hallgrimskirkja, this artisan bakery inside the graffiti-covered storefront became an instant classic when it opened in 2016. Their additive-free sourdough and pastries are something you will crave long after you leave Iceland, but don't miss their *snúður* (cinnamon buns), made with local, high-fat butter and often flavored with seasonal ingredients like blueberry or almonds. Expect a line out the door in the mornings, though additional locations, including at the Hlemmur food hall, have helped disperse the wait.

Frakkastígur 16. www.braudogco.is. ⓒ **456-7777.** Baked goods from 450kr. Mon–Fri 6am–6pm; Sat–Sun 6am–5pm.

Café Loki ★   Just beside Hallgrímskirkja church, Loki is a good cafe and restaurant for any time of the day for something uniquely Icelandic. For breakfast, try pancakes or rye bread with egg and herring. For lunch, there's meat soup, or for dinner, smoked lamb face. Of course, *kleina* (fried pastry) and coffee are served all day long.

Lokastígur 28. www.loki.is. ⓒ **466-2828.** Main courses from 2,400kr–3,300kr. Mon–Sat 9am–9pm; Sun 11am–9pm.

Grái Kötturinn ★   "The Grey Cat" is a favorite breakfast haunt for locals. The book-lined basement space with just a handful of tables is a favorite of the bohemian, intellectual set. Pancakes, bacon and eggs, and other American breakfast basics make up the menu. It's one of the few places that opens early, so many come here straight from the airport while awaiting check-in at their hotel.

Hverfisgata 16a. ⓒ **551-1544.** Main courses 850kr–1,850kr. Mon–Fri 7:30am–3pm (only sandwiches are available from 2–3pm); Sat–Sun 8am–3pm.

Mokka Kaffi ★   One of the oldest cafes in a town of old cafes, Mokka has been around since 1958. It's totally unpretentious and always a bit cramped and crowded, but it's full of local color. The coffee is decent, though you can find better, but when paired with their famous waffles with jam and whipped cream it becomes a mind-blowing cultural experience like none other.

Skólavörðustígur 3a. www.mokka.is. ⓒ **552-1174.** Sandwiches and waffles around 8500kr. Daily 9am–6:30pm.

Reykjavík Roasters ★★★   Originally called Kaffismiðja Íslands when it opened in 2008, Reykjavík Roasters quickly became a cult favorite after a rebranding effort in 2013 brought on by new partners. Now it's widely considered to be the finest roaster in Iceland and the center of coffee geekery in the capital. While two additional locations have now opened, the original, with its vinyl collection and creaky wood floors, not to mention the smell of roasting coffee beans, will always be a favorite.

Kárastígur 1. www.reykjavikroasters.is. ⓒ **517-5535.** Coffees from 850kr. Mon–Fri 8am–5:30pm; Sat–Sun 8am–5pm.

Sandholt Bakarí ★★   Family-run for more than a century, this artisanal bakery has managed to maintain a high quality despite its long-time popularity. Now headed by Ásgeir Sandholt, a former Nordic Champion of Cake Decorating and a national chocolate master, Sandholt is better than it has ever been, with new breads using local grains, cakes, pastries, and cookies being developed all the time. A great space in the back has a few tables for coffee, soups, sandwiches, or just indulging your sweet tooth.

Laugavegur 36. www.sandholt.is. ⓒ **551-3524.** Sandwiches around 1,350kr; pastries or cake 750kr–1,100kr. Daily 7am–6:30pm.

SHOPPING

Reykjavík is not the shopping mecca that Paris or London is, but a new wave of boldly conceptual store owners is gaining almost as much attention as the restaurateurs. Most shops are concentrated on **Laugavegur** and **Skólavörðustígur**—with some of the best discoveries in the network of streets in between. The two streets that extend the bottom of Laugavegur—**Austurstræti** and **Bankastræti**—are also good shopping areas.

Reykjavík is a smart place to buy supplies before hitting the rest of the country, where goods are even more expensive. General shopping hours are 9am to 6pm weekdays, and 10am to 4pm Saturdays. Almost everything is closed Sunday except for a few shops, particularly those selling knitted things and puffin snow globes. *Note:* Store listings below do not indicate opening hours unless they deviate from the norm.

Arts, Crafts & Photography

Fótógrafí ★   This one-room gallery focuses on the work of dozens of contemporary Icelandic photographers, such as photojournalists and landscape specialists. On sale are fine-art prints, posters, photo books, and old cameras. Skólavörðustígur 22. www.fotografi.is. © **821-5600.**

Kaolin ★   This ceramics gallery and shop features the work of several important Icelandic ceramicists, who take turns working the counter. It's named after a type of white clay that is used in the sculptures, tableware, and other items for sale. Skólavörðustígur 5. www.kaolinkeramikgalleri.com. © **555-2060.**

Kirsuberjatréð ★   Inside a historic 1888 building, this art and design collective, translated to "Cherry Tree," is run by 12 female Icelandic artists. Their

---

Save up to 15% with a VAT Refund

Iceland Refund (© **564-6400**) reimburses you the **Value-Added Tax** you pay (about 11%–24% of purchase price) under the following four conditions: 1) purchases must be taken out of the country; 2) each sales receipt must total at least 6,000kr—for less expensive items you can consolidate purchases at a single store; 3) purchases must be from an accredited store; and 4) you must leave the country within 3 months of purchase. When you make a purchase, request a **Tax Free form,** which must be signed by the salesperson. Your refund can be claimed from the following places: **Keflavík Airport,** at the Landsbanki Íslands Bank in the Leifur Eiriksson Terminal; the **Seyðisfjörður ferry** to Europe, onboard prior to departure; and **Reykjavík's Tourist Information Office** (p. 50). If the total value of your *refund* is less than 5,000kr (that is, if your total purchases amount to about 33,000kr or less), you can receive the refund directly in cash or have it credited to your credit card at the airport or the ferry; at the Tourist Information Office, you can only have it applied to your credit card. If the refund is more than 5,000kr, your only option is to have the refund applied to your credit card no matter where you claim it—and all goods (except wool goods) need to be shown at customs before check-in for your departing flight.

backgrounds are rather diverse (fashion designers, ceramicists, jewelry designers, a saddlesmith), resulting in an array of edgy ideas, from fish-skin wallets to colorful onesies for babies. Vesturgata 4. www.kirs.is. ✆ **562-8990.**

Books & Music

English-language books are not hard to come by, as many Icelanders prefer them to translated editions. (See p. 19 in chapter 2 for book recommendations.)

12 Tónar ★ With its own homegrown label and a second store at Harpa, 12 Tónar is one of the most important names in Icelandic music. Since 1998 they have produced dozens of albums from a variety of musical genres, and many others are offered for sale. It's a chilled-out spot where you can hang out on the couch and listen to a CD. Live performances are usually held every other Friday in the garden. Skólavörðustígur 15. www.12tonar.is. ✆ **511-5656.**

Eymundsson ★ Iceland's largest and oldest bookstore chain, founded in 1872, has branches all over the country, though this oversized location downtown is likely the first a foreign tourist will come in contact with. It has a considerable amount of English-language books and magazines, including Icelandic literature that has been translated into English. Austurstræti 18. www.eymundsson.is. ✆ **540-2130.**

Fornbókabúðin ★ This fantastically cluttered antiquarian bookseller, founded in 1964, was American chess champion Bobby Fischer's favorite bookstore when he lived in the city. He allegedly spent hours in the back reading and even had his mail delivered here. Among the English-language titles are old copies of the Icelandic sagas. Pay particular attention to the Norse mythology section in which some books are written in Old Norse. Klapparstígur 25–27 (at Hverfisgata). www.bokin.is. ✆ **552-1710.**

Lucky Records ★ What began in 2005 as a stall in the Kolaportið flea market has ballooned into one of the largest vinyl and CD shops in Iceland. The more than 40,000 items in the sprawling store near the old Hlemmur bus station cover a wide variety of genres, including jazz, soul, funk, and afrobeat, as well as rock, pop, and an impressive selection of Icelandic artists. Rauðarárstígur 10. www.luckyrecords.is. ✆ **551-1195.**

Sangitamiya—The Nectar Music ★ This pro-peace music store sells musical instruments from around the world, as well as instruments made locally. There is also literature about the place these instruments hold in the cultures they hail from. Most of the staff is musically trained, and one of them can usually give you a primer on how to play whatever exotic instrument you find. Keep an eye out for the traditional Icelandic *Langspil*—a simple but lovely stringed instrument. Grettisgata 7. www.sangitamiya.is. ✆ **551-8080.**

Clothing

Aftur ★ Founded in 1999, Aftur is best known for recycled clothes. No, not secondhand clothes. Recycled. Basically, they buy old clothes for the fabrics and cut them into small pieces and put them back together again to make high-fashion items. Several other funky brands are sold here as well. Laugavegur 39. www.aftur.is. © **775-1000.**

Geysir ★ Like an Icelandic hipster paradise, Geysir is one of Iceland's trendiest stores. Think of it as an Icelandic J. Crew, but with a bit more edge. Wool is a major element here, and the beautiful wool sweaters, blankets, and scarves are a huge step up in quality from the tourist shops, though they're pricey. Skólavörðustíg 16. www.geysir.is. © **519-6000.**

STEiNUNN ★ The studio of haute fashion label Steinunn, from designer Steinunn Sigurðardóttir, is on the second floor of a warehouse in the western piers. Taking inspiration from Iceland's wilderness (think endless twilights, cloud vaults, and sub-Arctic flora), she goes for pure, unmixed soft materials like silk and lambswool. The cuts are minimalist yet very feminine and textural with ruffles, bunches, and unexpected uses of fur or tulle. Grandagarði 17. www.steinunn.com. © **588-6649.**

Concept Stores

Blue Lagoon ★★ Yes, that Blue Lagoon, but don't expect a Hard Rock Café gift shop. Believe it or not, the skincare products produced in a lab beside the lagoon are world-class, not to mention expensive. Pick up scrubs, masks, and lotions made designed from the silica, algae, and minerals that are produced naturally at the facility (and the reason everyone started going here in the first place). Laugavegur 15. www.bluelagoon.com. © **420-8849.**

Iglo + Indi ★ This vibrant children's store, which also has a location in the Kringlan shopping mall, is inspired by a magical world that the owner noticed her daughter created in her drawings, "where rabbits and lions walk 'foot in paw' and where the real and the imaginary are equally tangible." The collections span sizes from newborns to 12 years of age and include clever details like prints, bows, ruffles, or elbow patches that make every piece unique. Skólavörðustíg 4a. www.igloindi.com. © **571-9006.**

Tulipop ★ Cuddly, gothic, colorful, inspired by nature…these are just some of the terms that describe this playful design shop geared to both kids and adults. They have their own fanciful line of stationery, plates, cutlery, and key chains. Many of the designs feature characters they have dreamed up, such as the gemstone-loving Mr. Tree or the mushroom boy bubble. Skólavörðustígur 43. www.tulipop.com. © **519-6999.**

Jewelry

Jewelry is relatively less expensive in Iceland, especially gold and silver. You'll find countless items inspired by the country's natural features and pagan history, often made from lava stones and native minerals. Most makers eagerly make up what you want, a good way to bring home a little piece of Iceland (especially since it's illegal to collect minerals yourself). For classic designs, try the well-stocked **Gull & Silfur,** Laugavegur 52 (© **552-0620**).

Aurum ★ Award-winning designer Guðbjörg Kristín Ingvarsdótir is the face of this chic, independent jewelry shop. Inspiration for her designs is taken largely from Icelandic nature, such as earrings that resemble the feathers of a raven or necklaces adorned with silver wildflowers. Bankastræti 4. www.aurum.is. ✆ **551-2770.**

Hringa ★ This quirky, independent jewelry shop launched in 2008 and releases several new lines each year, inspired by nature or urban trends. All materials used are recycled. Laugavegur 33. www.hringa.com. ✆ **551-1610.**

Markets & Malls

Kolaportið ★ While most of the items in this sprawling flea market, which harkens back to a different time in the country when it was far less prominent, are just utter crap, there is something still charming and authentic about it. Stalls are crammed with books, antiques, crafts, and clothes, with hardly any tourist schlock, though you'll have to hunt for treasures. The back corner is probably the most interesting section, where a small market and food court sells smoked salmon and birch cheese as well as more unusual delicacies like fulmar eggs, horse sausage, and fermented shark. Tryggvagata 19. www.kolaportid.is. ✆ **562-5030.** Sat–Sun 11am–5pm. Bus 1, 3, 4, 5, 6, 11, 12, or 13.

Kringlan ★ Within a 10-minute drive for 80% of the capital area's residents, this 80-store mall is understandably a big part of the social fabric here. It is so popular that the word "Kringlan" is now synonymous with "mall" in Icelandic. Most stores are European chain fashion and housewares shops, but it has some nice quirky places, too, plus a liquor store, food court, cinema, and grocery store. The restaurants and cinema stay open after hours. Parents will appreciate **Adventureland** (✆ **517-9025;** maximum 2 hr. for 1,600kr; Mon–Wed 3–6:30pm; Thurs, Fri 2–5pm; Sat 11am–6pm; Sun 1–5pm), a play area where you can leave your 3- to 9-year-olds while you shop. Kringlan has a free shuttle bus that departs from the Tourist Information Centre (Aðalstræti 2) and Harpa every hour (Mon–Sat 10am–5pm; Sun 1–4pm). Kringlan 4-12. www.kringlan.is. ✆ **517-9000.** Mon–Wed 10am–6:30pm; Thurs 10am–9pm; Fri 10am–7pm; Sat 10am–6pm; Sun 1–5pm. Bus 1, 3, 4, or 6.

Smáralind ★ More modern than Kringlan, Smáralind is the largest mall in Iceland, with more than 100 stores on three floors. The stores are mostly major chains, and the restaurants and cinema stay open after hours. Hagasmári 1, 201 Kópavogur. www.smaralind.is. ✆ **528-8000.** Mon–Wed and Fri 11am–7pm; Thurs 11am–9pm; Sat 11am–6pm; Sun 1–6pm. Bus 2.

Outdoor Gear

Cintamani at Laugavegur 11 (www.cintamani.is; ✆ **517-8088**), the upstart competitor of fashionable 66° North (see below), has slightly lower prices, more camping gear (tents, boots, maps, and so on), and a travel agency for adventure tours. Útilíf (www.utilif.is) is the best place for technical outdoor equipment, especially for camping, climbing, cycling, and fishing—or if you just forgot your swimsuit. Útilíf is found in both major shopping malls: Kringlan (© **545-1580**) and Smáralind (© **545-1550**).

66° North ★ What began by serving fishermen in the Westfjords village of Suðureyri, where the right clothing was a matter of life and death, has blossomed into a major international outwear brand. Pricey, but a great place to pick up waterproofs, fleeces, and ski gear for all ages. Aside from two downtown stores (the other is at Laugavegur 17-19), it has locations in both the Kringlan and Smáralind malls (see above). Bankastræti 5. www.66north.com. © **535-6680.**

Wool Garments

Over centuries of harsh weather, Icelandic sheep evolved a dual-layered wool: Inner fibers are soft and insulating; the outer ones water- and dirt-repellent. These qualities create knitwear that is surprisingly light, resilient, and wearable in all kinds of weather. Sweaters in traditional Icelandic patterns are well-known, and you'll also find wonderful hats, mittens, socks, and blankets. Don't wait until your return to Keflavík Airport to buy your sweaters; the selection isn't nearly what it used to be.

A miniature branch of the discount outlet in suburban Mosfellsbær (see p. 94), **Álafoss,** Laugavegur 1 (www.alafoss.is; © **562-6303**), offers marginal savings over its competitors, and has a decent selection of traditional wool sweaters and handicrafts.

Farmers & Friends ★★ Clothing line **Farmer's Market** has a flagship store in the harbor area, as well as a store downtown at Laugavegur 37. The brand is worth seeking out for its sexier, lighter, less bulky take on traditional Icelandic sweater patterns. The sweaters are made from Icelandic wool, but don't wear one into the Handknitting Association store (see below)—they're manufactured abroad. They're also available at the Keflavík airport, the Blue Lagoon (p. 84), and Geysir (p. 84). Hólmaslod 2. Skólavörðustígur 19. www.farmers market.is. © **552-1960.**

Handknitting Association of Iceland (Handprjónasamband Íslands) ★ Owned, run, and supplied by a cooperative of several hundred Icelandic women hand-knitters that was founded in 1977, this sizable store is stocked to the gills with traditional Icelandic sweaters, scarves, and hats. Less-expensive machine-knitted items are also available. Skólavörðustígur 19. www. handknit.is. © **552-1890.**

REYKJAVÍK NIGHTLIFE

Reykjavík rocks like a city 10 times its size, with more than 50 bars and clubs in the throbbing heart of the city. Thankfully there's much more to Reykjavík's famous nightlife than bar-hopping, and any evening in the city is full of cultural activity. For a current schedule of events, see "Visitor Information," at the beginning of this chapter.

Bars & Nightclubs

Until 1989, beer with an alcohol content above 2.2% was illegal, and other forms of booze were tightly restricted. Alcohol consumption in Iceland is actually lower than in most European countries, but when Icelanders do drink, they tend to make up for lost time. Late Friday or Saturday night, you'll occasionally witness dancing on every available surface, public urination, the occasional brawl, sexual goings-on, and so on. At least the 2007 smoking ban has made the air more hospitable.

The legal drinking age is 20, but it's not heavily policed. Some bars and clubs have a 22-and-over policy. Drinking on the street is prohibited, but the law isn't enforced. Reykjavík is a safe place, but as always, women should beware of accepting drinks that may have been tampered with. Many foreigners, usually men, come in search of reputedly loose Icelandic women and are disappointed.

Fashion in the club scene is surprisingly dressy for laid-back Iceland, though admittedly you don't see many Icelanders shopping downtown in their sweatpants during the day either. A certain divide has opened up between spiffier clubs and hangouts with too many hipsters, rockers, and bohemians for any sort of dress code.

On weekends, not much gets started before midnight, and clubs stay open as late as 6am. Weeknights, when bars are required to close at 1am, are far more relaxed. On Thursday nights, DJs and live music often take it up a notch. Most of the clubs are cafes by day and serve food until 10pm. Bars or clubs only have cover charges when there's live music.

Many locals save money by drinking at home and then heading out around 1am, when the boisterous lines start forming. At the end of the evening, many partiers wind down in Austurvöllur Square, near the biggest late-night taxi stand at Tjörnin Pond.

Hürra ★   With a huge dance floor, some of Iceland's best DJs, and a regular lineup of live music, this raucous hipster bar is one of the more popular options in the city center to get your groove on. The music can change considerably from night to night, ranging from jazz concerts to electronic sets. Tryggvagata 22. www.hurra.is. No phone.

JOINING THE party

o **Pub Crawl**   Nightlife comes in a package tour, starting on select nights at 10pm at a location passed along via Facebook or e-mail by **City Walk** (www.citywalk.is/pubcrawl). For 2,500kr, a team of guides will lead the group to several bars, where there will be drink specials. Around 40 others are along for the ride, Icelanders and tourists alike.

o **Beer Tasting**   The craft-beer scene in Reykjavík has exploded in the last few years and the city now has a dozen good bars with a selection of Icelandic microbrews. **Your Friend in Reykjavík** (www.yourfriendinreykjavik.com) offers 2.5-hour tours with tastes of 10 different Icelandic beers (9,990kr per person).

Dillon ★ When Dillon first opened in 1999 it was more of an English-style pub aimed at the student crowd. Now it has grown up a bit, calling itself a whiskey bar. There's occasionally live music, while on Saturdays the DJ is none other than white-haired local fave Andrea Jóns, the so-called "grandmother of Icelandic rock." Laugavegur 30. www.dillon.is. ✆ **511-2400.**

Kaffibarinn ★★★ A bit of celebrity cachet here—Björk stops in, scenes from the cult film *101 Reykjavík* were shot here, and Britpop entrepreneur Damon Albarn owned a share—but celebrity cachet doesn't go far in Reykjavík. Pretty much everyone just ends up at this bohemian spot by the end of the night. When the bars and clubs close, it always seems to be the last spot filled with people. DJs spin Wednesday to Saturday, but you can converse upstairs on weekends. Bergstaðstræti 1. www.kaffibarinn.is. ✆ **551-1588.**

Microbar ★ Located in the center of Reykjavík's nightlife row, this is a prime spot for sampling Icelandic craft beers, including the bar's own homebrews. Usually the crowd is quite laid-back, just a handful of local and foreign beer enthusiasts chatting over pints. Vesturgata 2. ✆ **847-9084.**

Mikkeller & Friends Reykjavik ★★★ This local branch of cult Danish gypsy brewer Mikkeller, which opened in 2015, is the most serious destination for beer geekery in the history of Iceland. Two floors above **Dill** ★★★, the city's top restaurant (p. 76), this intimate space has a list of taps pouring highbrow ales that are sometimes made in such small batches that they might be gone the next night. Hverfisgata 12. www.mikkeller.dk. ✆ **437-0203.**

Skúli Craft Bar ★ This laid-back pub (named after Reykjavík founder Skúli Magnússon, whose statue is just outside the bar) has perhaps the most diverse beer selection in Reykjavík. It's not limited to only Icelandic beers, though they do make an appearance, but serves top brews from around Scandinavia, such as Denmark's Evil Twin or To Øl. Aðalstræti 9. ✆ **519-6455.**

Slippbarinn ★★ Despite its seemingly innocent location inside the Hotel Marina, this is the city's premier cocktail joint. The mixologists here have created concoctions far more advanced than anything you will find elsewhere in town. Think barrel-aged cocktails, like chervil negronis and corpse revivers, or multi-person punch bowls. On Wednesday nights, local musicians perform. Mýragata 2. www.slippbarinn.is. ✆ **560-8080.**

Gay & Lesbian Nightlife

The perception among Reykjavík's gays and lesbians is that the city's wild nightlife doesn't extend as much to them. The population is just too small to support a major "scene." On the upside, gay and lesbian visitors feel personally welcomed, not lost in the crowd. Reykjavík is also more integrated than you might expect; there's no gay area, and only one bar has an officially gay identity. **Kiki Queer Bar** (www.kiki.is), Laugavegur 22, welcomes visitors into a small space (if you manage to get yourself through the blindingly pink doorway) that can quickly turn into a flaming dance floor on weekends. Upstairs is a quieter room with tables and an outside smoking area.

For more info and activities, the website **www.gayice.is** posts a schedule of events. The **Reykjavík Gay Pride Festival** (www.hinsegindagar.is/en) usually takes place in the first week of August.

Live Music

Since the late 1980s, especially since Björk's solo career took off, Iceland has enjoyed an outsized reputation as an incubator of alternative popular music. The **Iceland Airwaves** festival (p. 30) attracts more visitors to Iceland than any other single event. Good music can be heard virtually every night, often in galleries, stores, and other unpredictable venues, so check listings in the free circular the *Reykjavík Grapevine* (www.grapevine.is). Reykjavík's two alternative music store/labels, **12 Tónar** and **Lucky Records** (p. 83), are also prime places to tap into local happenings.

Why Iceland? Many look no further than Iceland's strong singing traditions. Others point to Reykjavík's ideal size: big enough to constitute a "scene," yet small enough that—with no real record industry or celebrity culture—the scene stays down to earth. Everyone is influenced by everyone else, styles easily cross-fertilize, and no one raises an eyebrow at the most outlandishly clashing double bills. Every record is reviewed in the press, though ironically many bands have risen only after gaining foreign attention.

The alternative scene roughly divides into three camps: hard rock, indie rock, and electronica. But don't mistake the hippest, edgiest alternative bands like Sigur Rós, Of Monsters and Men, and Gus Gus for the entire popular music scene. Iceland's version of *American Idol, Idol Stjörnuleit* (Idol Starsearch), was watched by half the country and was as unabashedly "pop" as its American forebear.

Check local listings for shows. Aside from Húrra (see p. 87), the arena-size **Laugardalshöll,** Engjavegi 8 (www.laugardalsholl.is; ✆ 553-8990), on a soccer ground in Laugardalur Park, hosts the biggest international acts.

Performing Arts: Music & Dance
CLASSICAL MUSIC

Although overshadowed by Reykjavík's popular music scene, classical music thrives here and even has its own celebrities: Vladimir Ashkenazy has been an Icelandic citizen since 1972, and best-selling operatic tenor Garðar Thór Cortes is regularly voted sexiest man in Iceland. As with popular music, concerts have unpredictable schedules and play in unpredictable venues, so check daily listings. A highly recommended experience is to see an organ recital or choral music in **Hallgrímskirkja ★** (p. 57) or the more intimate **Fríkirkjan (Free Church),** Laufásvegur 13 (www.frikirkjan.is; ✆ 552-7270), on the east side of Tjörnin Pond.

In July and August the **Sigurjón Ólafsson Museum ★** (p. 59) moves aside the sculptures in its main hall for a discriminating series of classical and jazz concerts Tuesday evenings at 8:30pm. Each concert is 1 hour with no interval. **Salurinn,** Hamraborg 6 (www.salurinn.is; ✆ 570-0400), is a state-of-the-art classical venue in the nearby suburb of Kópavogur. The hall is made from Icelandic materials (driftwood, spruce, crushed stone) and has fabulous acoustics.

The **Icelandic Symphony Orchestra** (www.sinfonia.is; ℂ **545-2500**), founded in 1950, is quite accomplished despite its short history. Sixty performances run each season from September to June. The most regular performance time is Thursday at 7:30pm. Since 2011, they have made **Harpa ★★★**, the flashy performance complex by the old harbor (see p. 54), their home.

The Icelandic Opera, Ingólfsstræti 101, between Laugavegur and Hverfisgata (www.opera.is; ℂ **511-4200**), was founded in 1978 and stages international and Icelandic operas. It also has a home at **Harpa.** Unfortunately for summer tourists, the northernmost opera house in the world only opens its doors in the spring and fall.

DANCE & THEATER

Most drama in Iceland is in Icelandic, but occasionally shows are put on with a tourist audience in mind, and these performances often provide a great (and amusing) insight into Icelandic culture. Ask at the Tourist Information Office and check listings in the *Reykjavík Grapevine.*

The **Icelandic Dance Company** (www.id.is; ℂ **568-8000**) focuses exclusively on contemporary dance and performs at the City Theatre, Listabraut 3. The **Reykjavík Dance Festival** (www.reykjavikdancefestival.com) includes choreographers from around the world and runs for 4 days in late August/early September.

Cinema

Most cinemas in Iceland are largely restricted to showing American blockbusters. Movies are subtitled, except for some children's films, which are dubbed. **Bíó Paradís** (www.bioparadis.is; ℂ **412-7711**), Hverfisgötu 54, is Reykjavík's first arthouse cinema, with four screens. It shows mostly European, Icelandic, and U.S. independent films, and occasionally Icelandic documentaries, shorts, and retrospectives of classic films. It opens at 5pm and tickets are generally 1,600kr. The daily newspaper *Morgunblaðið* has film listings in English, or go to www.kvikmyndir.is and click the "Bíó" tab. As for cinema etiquette, Icelanders are strangely averse to watching film credits; most rise from their seats even before credits start to roll and ushers become impatient with any lingerers.

Volcano House   The Volcano House cinema presents two unique documentaries covering two of the most powerful eruptions of Iceland over the last 40 years: the 1973 eruption on the Westman Islands and the 2010 eruption of Eyjafjallajökull in South Iceland. Each show (two films) is about 53 minutes and starts with a short personal introduction on volcano activity in Iceland. There is a short introduction on Icelandic geology before the show. Patrons are welcome to explore an on-site geological exhibition, where they can handle various samples of pumice, ash, and lava from Icelandic volcanoes. Tryggvagata 11. www.volcanohouse.is. ℂ **555-1900.** Tickets available at box office 30 min. before showtime. 1,990kr adults; 1,700kr students/seniors; 1,000kr children ages 12–16. In English, showtimes are every hour on the hour from 10am–9pm.

Reykjavík Nightlife

REYKJAVÍK

NEAR REYKJAVÍK

Visitors using Reykjavík as a home base will find an incredible wealth of scenery and activities within easy reach. Typical highlights of Icelandic nature and culture are only a day trip, or even a half-day trip, away. If you have limited time, or are taking advantage of Icelandair's free stopover on flights between North America and Europe, this southwest chunk of Iceland will provide you with a wealth of waterfalls, geysers, lava fields, and museums to see and plenty of activities to do.

Good bus tours are available, but we recommend renting a car—even just for a day—because many sights are otherwise inaccessible. Keep in mind that parts of West and South Iceland (chapters 6 and 8) are also only an hour or two away, in case you'd like to add a glacier or volcanic eruption site to your itinerary.

5

HAFNARFJÖRÐUR

10km (6 miles) S of Reykjavík.

From the main road, it's easy not to notice Hafnarfjörður, even though it's Iceland's third-largest town (pop. 26,000) and second-busiest port. Once you've reached the waterfront, however, the city's distinct identity becomes clear. Its port has been trading continuously since the 14th century, and by the early 15th century it had become a major trading hub, first with the British and then the Germans, before the Danish king imposed a trade monopoly in 1602. This history, combined with the shape of the port and its effect on centuries of town planning, gives Hafnarfjörður more the ambience of a Northern European seaside town than Reykjavík. Also unlike Reykjavík, the town is carved out of the surrounding lava field. If you're visiting in June and want kitsch overload, come to Hafnarfjörður for the **Viking Festival** (p. 29).

Essentials

GETTING THERE   The drive from Reykjavík is only 15 minutes; take Route 40 south to the Hafnarfjörður turnoff. Bus 1 runs every 30 minutes (more regularly Sept–May) from Hlemmur and Lækjartorg bus stations in Reykjavík to Hafnarfjörður's shopping area, near the tourist information office (and a 10-min. walk from

Reykjanes Peninsula

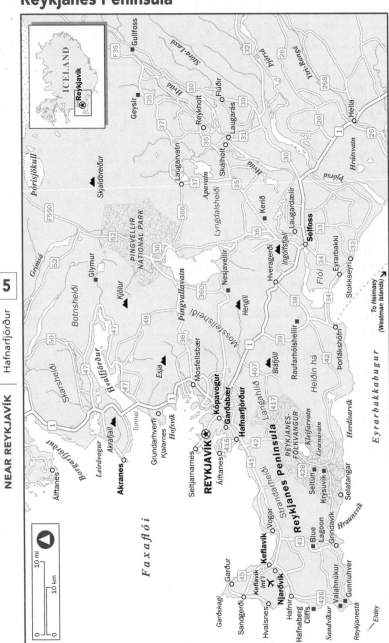

NOTES ON ENTERING THE countryside

You don't need to venture far from Reykjavík to feel as though you're in the countryside, or perhaps on another planet. Mossy lava fields abound, cliff tops swarm with thousands of squawking birds, and thin ribbons of waterfall are haphazardly strewn about mountainsides. But if you're leaving downtown Reykjavík for the first time since you arrived in Iceland, the dramatic landscape is an invigorating shock to the system. The land feels strangely unformed, caught in geological transition. Without trees or thick vegetation obscuring the view, the ever-distant horizon seems impossibly close, and the tops of mountains impossibly high. Iceland's original settlers found no natives to subdue, and never had to group their homes on hilltops in defensive clusters. Farmsteads, evenly spread throughout the land, have been the basis of Icelandic society until relatively recent history. Every farm has a name—often the same name it had 1,000 years ago—and its own road sign. The name is usually derived from its surrounding geography.

the Viking Village). The trip takes about 25 minutes. The **Flybus airport shuttle** (www.re.is; © **580-5400**) connecting Reykjavík and Keflavík also stops in Hafnarfjörður. For a taxi, call **AðalStöðin** (© **420-1212**).

VISITOR INFORMATION   The **tourist office,** Strandgata 6, inside the Town Hall (www.visithafnarfjordur.is; © **585-5780**), is open Monday to Thursday 8am to 5pm and Friday 9am to 5pm; from June to August it's also open weekends from 10am to 3pm.

Exploring Hafnarfjörður

Hidden Worlds ★   This 1½- to 2-hour walking tour takes you past all of the hiding places of Hafnarfjörður's "hidden people" (see p. 250), particularly elves. Guides stop at places like Hellisgerdi Park and the base of the cliff, Hamarinn, where it is said that the Royal Family of the Hidden Folk lives. Along the way, guides retell stories about magical hidden worlds and the town's harmonious development with the Hidden Folk, who occasionally appear.

Strandgata 6. www.alfar.is. © **694-2785.** Tickets 4,500kr including a "Hidden Worlds" map. Tues and Fri 2:30pm.

Where to Stay & Dine

Fjörukráin Viking Village Hotel ★   While the cheesed-out barbarity of the restaurant next door (see below) might scare some modern folks away from staying on-site, let it be known that this hotel is actually rather straightforward. The downstairs area is home to a cavernous bar, and rooms are relatively pleasant, with clunky wood tables, coffeemaking facilities, and LCD TVs. Some bathrooms even have jetted tubs, and there's a small hot pot in the back garden. Farther into the countryside, about 15 minutes away, is a second property, the **Hlið Fishermen's Village,** which has eight cottage-style rooms, overlooks the ocean, and has some turf roof buildings, as well as another restaurant (cottages from 42,000kr).

Strandgata 55. www.fjorukrain.is. ✆ **565-1213.** 42 units. Apr–Sept 25,200kr double. Rates around 30% lower Oct–Mar. Rates include breakfast. **Amenities:** Hot tub; sauna; free Wi-Fi.

Viking Restaurant ★ CONTINENTAL   Sure, this kitschy Viking-themed restaurant inside the Fjörukráin Viking Village hotel complex (see above) goes way overboard with its dragon heads carved on the roof, the Viking actor employees who kidnap visitors from arriving tour buses, and tapestries and runic symbols everywhere. But for children, or just those with a quirky sense of humor, it can be a fun place. The 350-seat Viking Restaurant is based on a Norwegian church, and dinner is the primary attraction, when actors in Viking and Valkyrie costumes sing, dance, and tell stories. There might be combat demonstrations or a presentation of "honorary Viking" certificates. Kidnappings direct from the tour bus are done on request. The "Viking Dinner" includes everything from the old days: fish soup, dried haddock, lamb shank, and *skyr* for dessert. There will even be a cube of putrefied sharkmeat with a tiny Icelandic flag in it and Brennivín, aka "Black Death," served in traditional lamb horns.

Strandgata 55 (at Viking Village). www.fjorukrain.is. ✆ **565-1213.** Reservations recommended. Main courses 2,700kr–6,500kr; Viking menu 9,560kr including drinks. Dinner daily 6–10pm; bar open late Fri–Sat.

Von Mathus & Bar ★ ICELANDIC   If the Viking Village fails to pique your interest, Hafnarfjörður has some good alternatives, like this homey neighborhood bistro. Focusing on seasonal Icelandic cuisine, the menu ranges from light starters like ceviche and mussels to heavier dishes such as lamb neck and tri-tip. Drinks include original cocktails, local craft beers on tap, and a well-rounded wine list.

Strandgata 75. http://vonmathus.is. ✆ **583-6000.** Main courses 2,900kr–4,900kr; Viking menu 9,560kr including drinks. Tues–Thur 11:30am–3pm and 5:30–9pm, Fri–Sat 11:30am–3pm and 5:30–10pm; bar open late Fri–Sat.

MOSFELLSBÆR

15km (9¼ miles) NE of Reykjavík.

This town hasn't been swallowed up by the overflowing city, but its day may soon come. The outskirts of Mosfellsbær yield to beautiful pastureland, where you'll find the town's main attraction: the former home of Halldór Laxness (p. 24), Iceland's greatest modern writer.

The **tourist office** (www.mos.is; ✆ 525-6700) is at the library in the Kjarni shopping mall (Þverholt 2).

Halldór Laxness Museum (Gljúfrasteinn) ★ MUSEUM   Halldór Laxness, who won the 1955 Nobel Prize for Literature, spent more than half of a century in this mid-20th-century country home, called Gljúfrasteinn. It became a museum in 2004, and much of the house has been left unchanged: the original furniture, the well-polished 1968 Jaguar in the driveway, and artwork by close friends Jóhannes Kjarval, Svavar Guðnason, and Nina Tryggvadóttir. Guests enter in the reception building for a multimedia presentation dedicated to Laxness's life and work, then spend the next 25 minutes with an audio tour that includes interview clips with Halldór and his wife, voiced over in English. Halldór was a fine pianist, and concerts are still held on his grand piano every Sunday at 4pm from June through August; tickets are only 1,500kr.

It's not easy to reach Gljúfrasteinn without a car. From central Mosfellsbær, hire a taxi to take you to near the museum. If you combine the museum visit with horseback riding at **Laxnes Farm** (see below), you may be able to strike a deal, because they offer hotel pickup (for not much more than bus fare) anyway.

Mosfellsbær 270. www.gljufrasteinn.is. ✆ **586-8066.** Admission 900kr adults; free for children 17 and under. June–Aug daily 9am–5pm; Sept–May Tues–Sun 10am–4pm. Closed weekends Nov–March. From Reykjavík by car, take Rte. 1 through Mosfellsbær, then turn right on Rte. 36; the museum is a few km ahead.

HORSEBACK RIDING Across the road from the Laxness Museum (above)—but no longer connected with Halldór Laxness's family—is **Laxnes Horse Farm** (www.laxnes.is; ✆ **566-6179**). A visit to the farm is recommended for those who would like a short horseback ride near the premises or a longer tour of the area. The cost is 11,900kr for a 2-hour ride, leaving daily 10am and 2pm (hotel pickup at 9am or 1pm usually available); it's generally not for children 5 and under.

SHOPPING Prices on the large selection of wool clothing and handicrafts at Álafoss **Factory Outlet,** Álafossvegur 23 (www.alafoss.is; ✆ **566-6303**), are 15% to 20% below Reykjavík levels. Coming by bus (bus 15 from Hlemmur, then 27 or 57) involves a 400m (¼ mile) walk from the nearest stop. By car, follow Route 1 north through three traffic circles in Mosfellsbær, then turn right off the fourth traffic circle onto Álafossvegur. The store is 320m (1,050 ft.) ahead on the left. Hours are Monday through Friday 9am to 6pm and Saturday 9am to 4pm. Other stores in this hub include **Knives of Distinction,** Álafossvegur 29 (www.knifemaker.is; ✆ **566-7408**), where you can watch Páll Kristjánsson at work carving knife handles and other trinkets from whale teeth and reindeer antlers.

ESJA, HVALFJÖRÐUR & AKRANES

Esja is 22km (14 miles) N of Reykjavík; Hvalfjörður is 25km (16 miles) N of Reykjavík; Akranes is 48km (30 miles) N of Reykjavík.

This coastal area north of Reykjavík is often bypassed by visitors, but the scenery is up to Iceland's high standards, particularly Iceland's tallest waterfall, **Glymur.**

Essentials

GETTING THERE Route 1 leads north from Reykjavík, passing Esja before reaching the tunnel across Hvalfjörður to Akranes. For Akranes, turn left after the tunnel on Route 51, then left again on Route 509. Nine buses make the trip from Reykjavík to Akranes on weekdays (six on weekends); the route—bus

15 from BSÍ station, connecting with bus 57 in Mosfellsbær—goes right past the Esja trailhead (tell the driver if that's your destination) but bypasses the coastline of Hvalfjörður by taking the tunnel.

VISITOR INFORMATION   Questions about Esja should be directed to the **tourist information office** in Reykjavík (p. 44). Hvalfjörður is in Akranes township. The **Borgarnes Tourist Information Office** (www.west.is; ✆ 437-2214) is also helpful for this area.

Exploring the Area

Climbing **Esja** ★ all the way to the top is formidable but rewarding, and the mountain's main trails are well-marked and negotiable. Many opt to linger on the gentle slopes at Esja's base, especially those with children. Several routes lead up Esja, which is more of a volcanic range than a single peak. The recommended and most popular trail starts at a parking area along Route 1. (Heading north from Reykjavík, it's at the base of the mountain; look for the sign "GÖNGULEIÐIR Á ESJU" just after a driveway marked "MÓGILSÁ.") From there it's a 780m (2,559-ft.), 4km (2½-mile) ascent to the marvelous Þverfellshorn lookout. Allow at least 5 hours for the return trip. The tallest peak (914m/2,999 ft.) is 3km (2 miles), but only tempts very devoted hikers. The excellent Myndkort "photomap," compiled from aerial satellite photographs, details all of Esja's trail routes.

North of Esja, drivers on Route 1 pass through a very deep, 6km (3¾-mile) **tunnel beneath Hvalfjörður,** completed in 1998. (*Beware:* It's a speed trap.) The tunnel shortened the drive by 47km (29 miles), but the old route around the fjord is a scenic drive and the only way to reach Glymur.

Hvalfjörður means "whale fjord," and, if you keep your eyes fastened on it, you might see why. At 30km (19 miles) it's the longest fjord in southwest Iceland, and was an important naval base for the Allies in World War II.

Glymur ★★ is the tallest waterfall in Iceland (200m/656 ft.), and what it lacks in raw power it makes up for in lithe beauty. Getting there is half the fun, with great views out to the fjord and surrounding countryside, and into a dramatic gorge filled with nesting birds in late spring and early summer. When the flow is substantial, Glymur is as breathtaking as **Gullfoss** ★★★ (p. 108) but with 99% fewer tourists, thanks to its inaccessibility to cars. Glymur is also relatively unknown because the path is somewhat dangerous: The trail requires real caution, good balance, and agility. Also, the waterfall is less spectacular when the flow tapers off; ask around at local hotels and information offices to get an educated guess based on rain and meltoff.

To reach the trail to Glymur, turn off the main road at the head of Hvalfjörður. The parking area is a few minutes ahead. From the parking lot, a fenced-off dirt road bears toward the right, but the trail bears slightly left, marked with yellow-painted stones. In 2 to 3 minutes the trail divides, again without posted signs, though both routes are still marked with yellow rocks. The trail bearing left takes you up the west side of the gorge. This trail is shorter and easier, but you don't get a good view of the waterfall. The right-hand path takes you across the river and up the east side of the gorge and is fully worth the extra effort. It reaches the river in 20 minutes or so; you have to wind through a cavity in the cliff to reach the shore, and then cross the river on a round wooden beam, while holding on to a steel suspension cable. Allow 2½ hours round-trip for the hike up the east side of the river.

Continuing west on Route 47 along the north shore of Hvalfjörður, you'll soon pass a deserted **whaling station.** At the tip of the peninsula is **Akranes,** a fishing and cement-factory town of around 66,000. The first settlers, who came as early as 880, are believed to have been Irish hermits. Akranes commemorates its founding with the **Irish Days festival** on the second weekend in July; events include a sandcastle competition, beach barbecue, and a contest to see who has the reddest hair. Just east of town is **Akrafjall,** the town's twin-peaked patron mountain. At 555m (1,804 ft.), Akrafjall's southern peak **Háihnúkur ★** is a less exhausting climb than Esja. A well-marked trail to the top runs along the edge of a cliff full of great black-backed gulls and other birds. The parking area is along Route 51, at the Akranes hot water utility.

Akranes Folk Museum ★ MUSEUM This small-town **Folk Museum** opened in 1959 on the ancient manor of Garðar, which had a church and parsonage that dates to the early days of Christianity in Iceland. Among the exhibits on display is a rowing boat with full rigging from 1874, and a selection of other items connected to seafaring and fishing. The exhibition **Iceland's Sport Museum** is more interesting, with artifacts like the bike hand-twisted by Jón Páll Sigmarsson, Iceland's four-time winner of the "World's Strongest Man" competition. Another section is a forge, sometimes in operation for guests, where blacksmiths hone their skills. The forge is sometimes in operation for guests. Several old fishing vessels lie outside on the lawn. Guided tours of the museum are offered on weekdays at 2pm.

Garðar. www.museum.is. ⓒ **431-1150.** Admission 500kr adults; 300kr seniors; children 15 and under free. June–Aug daily 10am–5pm; Sept–May daily 1–5pm. Entering Akranes on Rte. 509, turn left at first traffic circle onto Esjubraut; at next roundabout turn left onto Garðagrund; then take second left on Safnasvæði, and the museum is ahead on the left.

Where to Stay

Hotel Glymur ★★ This rural coastal fjord is an idyllic alternative to Reykjavík for those who prefer to commune with nature a bit, maybe even see the Northern Lights, on a first or last night in Iceland. This is no country-bumpkin lodge, however. It's actually quite stylish; all rooms have two floors and Italian leather furniture, along with views to the fjord. Spacious villas that sleep four to six people were added in 2010.

Rte. 47. www.hotelglymur.is. ⓒ **430-3100.** 22 units, 6 villas. May–Sept from 22,600kr double; 51,000kr villa. Rates around 15% lower Oct–Apr. 8,600kr for an extra bed. Rates include breakfast. Package offers available online. From the northern junction of Rte. 1 and Rte. 47 (the junction north of the tunnel), take Rte. 47 east for 12km (7½ miles). **Amenities:** Restaurant, bar; outdoor hot tub; free Wi-Fi.

Where to Eat

For an excellent "country chic" dinner in Hvalfjörður, make a reservation at **Hotel Glymur** (above). The menu includes the catch of the day, trout, lamb, chicken, and a vegetarian dish, for a set rate of 7,900kr. From noon to five it's a less expensive cafe, serving fish soup, fresh salad, and hot waffles.

In **Akranes,** the **Galito Restaurant,** Stillholt 16–18 (www.galito.is; ✆ **430-6767;** main courses 3,590kr–5,700kr; Sun–Thurs 11am–9pm, Fri–Sat 11am–10pm), has an untypical small-town menu with hot smoked minke whale, grilled horse tenderloin, and blackened cod, alongside standard burgers, sushi, and pizzas. The local bakery, **Brauða-og Kökugerðin,** Suðurgata 50a (✆ **431-1644**), makes sandwiches and serves coffee.

REYKJANES PENINSULA

47km (29 miles) NE of Reykjavík.

From Keflavík airport, this southwestern extremity of Iceland appears to be a bleak and uniform expanse of lava rock. In reality, Reykjanes is a wondrous and geologically varied landscape, which is why much of it has been declared a **UNESCO Global Geopark** (www.reykjanesgeopark.is). The north coast is indeed flat and contains most of the peninsula's population. The western, southern, and interior regions, on the other hand, have striking volcanic ranges, geothermal hotspots, and sea cliffs full of nesting birds. Some parts are so remote that only a few local farmers in search of stray sheep have ever set foot in them. A trail system is well developed, but hiking routes are often unmarked, and it can be difficult to find drinking water.

Essentials

GETTING AROUND   Reykjanes is really best accessed by car or tour. Regular bus routes do extend to Garður and Sandgerði in the northeast and Grindavík on the south coast, but stops aren't spaced with tourists in mind. **Strætó** (www.straeto.is; ✆ **540-2700**) connects Garður, Sandgerði, Grindavík, and Vogar to Keflavík and Reykjavík several times a day. **Reykjavík Excursions** (www.re.is; ✆ **580-5400**) connects Reykjavík and Grindavík several times a day depending on the season, stopping at the Blue Lagoon.

TOURS   Extreme Iceland (www.extremeiceland.is; ✆ **588-1300**) has a half-day Reykjanes Geopark, Lava Caves & Volcanoes tour for 17,200kr and a bus tour around the coast, with optional dropoff at the Blue Lagoon or airport. **Reykjavík Excursions** (www.re.is; ✆ **580-5400**) sets up tours to the Reykjanes UNESCO Geopark, ATV tours, and packages to the Blue Lagoon with transportation.

VISITOR INFORMATION   The **Reykjanes tourist office,** Krossmói 4, Reykjanesbær (www.visitreykjanes.is; ✆ **421-3520;** Mon–Fri 9am–5pm, Sat 10am–2pm), and Grindavík's **Saltfish Museum** (p. 100) are the best bets.

The Icelandic Touring Association's *Reykjanes Myndkort* ("picture map"), assembled from aerial satellite photographs, is an essential resource for identifying walking and hiking routes.

Exploring Reykjanes

The sights listed below follow a counterclockwise loop around the peninsula, but you can also follow the route in reverse.

GARÐUR & GARÐSKAGI

Garður, 15 minutes' drive northwest from Keflavík, is the northernmost town on the peninsula. Its main tourist draw is **Garðskagi,** a rocky point with two lighthouses and a quirky folk museum. To reach Garðskagi, drive through Garður and follow the coast toward the lighthouse in the distance. (As you leave town, consider stopping at Útskálakirkja, the lovely church visible from the road on your right.) The larger lighthouse, **Garðskagaviti,** is the tallest in Iceland; the outmoded 1897 lighthouse still stands close by. Built in 1944, Garðskagaviti was a gift from American servicemen grateful for being rescued from a sinking U.S. Coast Guard vessel. Visitors can climb to the 360-degree lookout platform at the top. (If it's locked, ask for a key in the museum.) The last stretch of the climb involves steep, narrow steps and a trap door. Garðskagi offers a broad, flat ocean vista, bird sightings, and lots of wind.

Most visitors to the lighthouse stop in at the **Garður Peninsula Historical Museum** (𝄐 422-7220; free admission; Apr–Oct daily 1–5pm), a folk and maritime museum with more than 60 midcentury boat engines, all in working condition.

SANDGERÐI

Sandgerði is a busy fishing village 5km (3 miles) south of Garður on Route 45.

Sudurnes Science and Learning Center ★ MUSEUM   This natural history museum is attached to a research center, operated in conjunction with the University of Iceland, that works closely with the aquaculture community for the prevention and cure of diseases in the wild. The museum side has lots of strange specimens that tend to delight young kids—things like barnacles, shark eggs, and the only stuffed walrus in Iceland. There are even a few live creatures to touch. Children can also go to the beach, gather seawater and bugs, and examine them under microscopes. The center is on the north end of town, in a cluster that includes two art galleries, a pizzeria, and a seafood restaurant.

Garðvegur 1, off Rte. 45, Sandgerði. www.thekkingarsetur.is. 𝄐 **423-7551.** Admission 1,000kr adults; 600kr children ages 6–12; free for ages 5 and under. May–July Mon–Fri 10am–4pm; Sat–Sun 1–5pm. Closed in winter.

THE WESTERN COAST

Two kilometers (1¼ miles) south of Hvalsneskirkja is a junction. The road bearing right dead ends at a bright yellow lighthouse. The road bearing left continues along the coast until it joins Route 44 near the sleepy town of Hafnir. Proceeding south along Route 425, the landscape is suddenly dominated by harsh black lava with little vegetation. This was one of three areas in Iceland used by the Apollo flight crew to practice moonwalking. About 5km (3 miles) south of Hafnir is a parking area on the right, with a small sign indicating the trailhead for the Hafnaberg Cliffs, a nesting site for guillemots, kittiwakes, fulmars, and razorbills. The 1½-hour round-trip hike is recommended for birders, but you'll find more visually dramatic seacliffs at Reykjanes, below. If you do walk to Hafnaberg, keep an eye out for whales.

Another 2km (1¼ miles) farther south is a turnoff for the **Bridge Between Two Continents,** a 15m (49-ft.) footbridge spanning a rift in the rock that is part of the jagged division between the North American and Eurasian tectonic plates. There are similar rifts all over the Reykjanes Peninsula without gimmicky bridges built across them.

REYKJANES

"Reykjanes" means "Smoky Point." The name originally referred only to this southwest corner of the peninsula, with its steamy geothermal hotspots. The highlight is **Valahnúkur ★★,** a magical stretch of coastline where you can clamber up grassy banks and peer over the indented cliffsides at crashing waves, while thousands of birds bob around in the wind currents. To get to Valahnúkur, turn right off Route 425 just before the power plant, and make your way past the lighthouse on the unsurfaced roads. The area can be fully explored in an hour or so. Be very careful at the cliff edges: Winds can be extremely gusty, and some grass-tufted patches of earth may not support your weight. The striking, near-cylindrical island **Eldey,** a bird preserve 15km (9¼ miles) offshore, is part of the same volcanic rift line that formed Valahnúkur.

You can return to Route 425 by a different dirt road, which runs south of the power plant and its runoff lake. Once you've passed the lighthouse, just head for the steam rising from a small hill. This is **Gunnuhver,** a typical geothermal field swathed with mineral shades and thick, eggy smells. Gunnuhver is named for Gunna, a woman who, according to legend, was accused of murder and thrown into the boiling hot spring. *Warning:* Tread carefully and stick to the trails—one false step could melt the rubber right off your soles.

GRINDAVÍK

The 17km (11-mile) stretch on Route 425 east from Reykjanes is practically deserted, so it's arresting to suddenly encounter **Grindavík**'s clustered mass of prefab houses and difficult-to-navigate port. With its technologically advanced fish-processing plant, the town gives off an industrious and forward-looking air. Reykjanes has little arable land, so local economies are especially dependent on fishing. A helpful **information desk** is inside the Saltfish Museum (see below).

Arctic Horses, Hestabrekka 2, Grindavík (www.arctichorses.is; ✆ **696-1919**), leads 90-minute rides around the scenic peninsula southeast of Grindavík (8,800kr per person).

The Icelandic Saltfish Museum (Saltfisksetur Íslands) ★ MUSEUM *Saltfiskur,* or dried and salted fish, was once Iceland's most valuable export. Grindavík, in particular, has long been among the most prolific centers of salted cod production. Great care was taken to re-create the history of dried salted cod processing through a model fishing village from the 1930s, the heyday of the salt cod industry.

Hafnargata 12a (between Ránargata and Mánagata). ✆ **420-1190.** Admission 1,000kr adults; 800kr children ages 8–16. Daily 11am–6pm.

SELATANGAR

Route 427 proceeds east from Grindavík to Krýsuvík, fairly close to the south coast. The route can be a bit rough, which has discouraged tourism to this wonderfully remote eastern region of Reykjanes Peninsula.

Twelve kilometers (7 miles) east of Grindavík, a small brown sign on the right points to **Selatangar ★**, a fishing settlement abandoned since 1880. The gravel road proceeds 1.7km (1 mile) to a parking area near the shore. From there it's a 10-minute walk east, mostly on black sand, to an assortment of crude stone foundations for huts and storehouses. The setting is stark and a little spooky. (Residents claimed they were chased out by a ghost named "Tumi.")

ROUTE 428

Returning to Route 427 and continuing east, the junction with Route 428 is 3km (2 miles) ahead. **Route 428 ★★**, a spectacularly scenic drive across an interior highland plateau, can be tackled in a conventional car in summer, but only by proceeding slowly and carefully. You'll need at least an hour to get to the Route 42 junction north of Kleifarvatn Lake. Along the way are several opportunities for short hikes to viewpoints on the ridges east of the road.

KRÝSUVÍK

If instead of turning on to Route 428, you continue straight on Route 427, you'll reach **Krýsuvík Church (Krýsuvíkurkirkja)** in 9km (5½ miles). This tiny, brown 1857 wood church once served the surrounding farm, which is now abandoned. The church is always open, even in the off-season. The altarpiece, mounted in summer only, is an abstract work in broad swaths of primary colors by **Sveinn Björnsson** (1925–1997), a sailor inspired by Picasso, primitivism, and the local scenery.

Just east of the church, Route 427 ends at Route 42. Turning right leads to a beautiful drive to Þorlákshöfn and Hveragerði. Turning left takes you north toward Reykjavík through the Reykjanesfólkvangur wilderness reserve.

REYKJANESFÓLKVANGUR

Only 40km (25 miles) from Reykjavík, **Reykjanesfólkvangur ★** was designated a nature reserve in 1975 to protect the region's lava formations around ridge volcanoes. Heading north from Krýsuvík on Route 42, the first notable landmark is **Grænavatn,** an oddly tinted green lake inside an explosion crater. A parking area is on the right, and it's worth a quick look. Another kilometer (¾ mile) north is the **Seltún geothermic field ★**. A short loop trail proceeds through the chemical smells and bubbling mud cauldrons.

Slightly farther north is **Kleifarvatn ★**, a large, deep, and starkly beautiful lake with black sand beaches. Intake and outflow of water is very limited, and in 2000, water levels dropped considerably after earthquakes opened fissures on the lake bottom. The scenery is well enjoyed from the spit of **Lambatangi,** a short walk from the road on the southern end of the lake. Watch out for Kleifarvatn's worm-like resident aquatic monster, said to be as large as a whale.

Where to Eat

Garðurs's folk museum has a **restaurant,** and Sandgerði has two **restaurants.** In Grindavík, **Salthúsið,** Stamphólsvegur 2 (www.salthusid.is; ✆ **426-9700;** Tues–Fri 5–9pm, Sat–Sun 3–9pm; main courses 3,700kr–5,100kr), special-izes in cod, especially salted, but it also serves other fish and lamb dishes with touches of international flavors in a log cabin setting.

THE BLUE LAGOON (BLÁA LÓNIÐ)

50km (31 miles) SW of Reykjavík.

The **Blue Lagoon ★★★** (www.bluelagoon.com; ✆ **420-8800;** Jan–May 24 8am–10pm; May 25–June 28 7am–11pm; June 29–Aug 19 7am–midnight; Aug 20–Nov 30 8am–10pm; Dec 1–Dec 31 8am–9pm) is the most popular tourist attraction in Iceland, with nearly 1 million visitors each year—more than double Iceland's entire population. The surreal image of bathers in milky blue water, faces smeared with white mud, amid an expanse of black lava, may be the most common photographic emblem of an Iceland visit.

WHAT IS THE BLUE LAGOON?   Well, not the age-old hot pool you might imagine. It's actually the by-product of the geothermal power plant, when deep boreholes were drilled to extract blazing-hot, mineral-rich water under pressure from thousands of feet underground. This water produces electricity by driving steam turbines. The runoff water, still very hot, is too salty to provide central heating for homes, so it was piped into the lagoon, which was dug out of the lava field. The water gets its pearly, bluish hue from the combination of algae, silica, and other minerals. (In high summer, when the algae is in full bloom, the water is more green than blue.) The fuss all started when an Icelander suffering from psoriasis popped in for a swim. He noticed an immediate improvement in his skin condition, and the rest is a textbook marketing success story. (The "Blue Lagoon" was named not long after the 1980 Brooke Shields movie.) A bank of lava was added a few years ago to shelter swimmers from the wind and to block views of the power plant.

The spa has drilled its own water boreholes to regulate the temperature and balance the mineral and salt content. The salinity matches ocean water and reduces the eggy smell normally associated with geothermal water. Other spas have mimicked the Blue Lagoon's success, but none can quite duplicate its water formula. Studies have apparently confirmed the water's effectiveness for pso-riasis, and the public health system even covers some visits here. Claims made for curing arthritis, baldness, negative karma, and the like are less reliable. In reality, the two most common ailments treated here are jetlag and hangovers.

Getting There

BY CAR   The Blue Lagoon is less than an hour from Reykjavík and just 15 minutes from Keflavík International Airport. From Route 41, which connects

Reykjavík and Keflavík, turn south on Route 43. After about 8km (5 miles), turn right on Route 426 and follow the signs.

BY BUS   A **public bus** goes to the Blue Lagoon from the BSÍ terminal (p. 46) in Reykjavík, but **bus tours** (see below) include the entrance fee and work out to almost the same price, plus they'll pick you up at your hotel.

TOURS   Tours usually don't include a guide and are really just shepherding. Transportation to and from the lagoon, from your hotel in Reykjavík or Keflavík, is hourly and can be made directly while booking for an extra $47. Other agencies, such as **Reykjavík Excursions** (www.re.is; ✆ **580-5400**), offer similar packages.

The Lagoon Experience

No orientation lecture here—basically, you arrive at the time you selected during purchase online and you're just handed a locker key and sent off to shower and jump in a hot lake. (Make sure to remove rings, bracelets, and such; the water damages precious metals, especially silver.) White silica mud, which conditions and exfoliates the skin, is scraped from the bottom and scooped out of buckets for guests to smear all over themselves at the Mask Bar. The water is around 100°F (36°–39°C), but the temperature can change abruptly as you move around. Watch out for the rectangular wood structures, where hot water is introduced. One billows steam just for effect.

Minerals in the lagoon water will temporarily coarsen and harden your hair. Conditioner—provided free in the showers—should be left in while you soak, and long hair should be tied up.

It's a very mixed scene: Icelanders are interspersed among visitors—some of whom aren't sure they want to share a bath with so many strangers. (Be reassured: The water is completely replaced by natural flow every 40 hours.)

Any time of year is great for a visit. Winter nights may be best of all, because you can watch the Northern Lights in complete comfort with icicles in your hair.

Basic admission ($85 adults; children 13 and under free) includes entrance to the lagoon, sauna rooms, a silica mud mask, a towel, and a drink of your choice. If you are willing to visit at odd hours in the early morning or at night, discounts are available. The Premium package ($110) includes the use of a robe, slippers, dinner reservations, and an extra mask in the lagoon; even more exclusive are the 4-hour spa experience packages at the **Retreat ★★★** ($601 at peak times; see below), which includes access to a spa circuit, steam cave, relaxation rooms, and a quieter, closed-off section of the lagoon, as well as skincare amenities and access to the main lagoon.

Once you've had an **in-water massage,** you might never go back to on-land ones. You lie floating on your back with a blanket over you, while the masseuse's hands slide between your back and the floating mat. A 30-minute massage ($86) is ideal. Call or check the website for a full menu of fabulous **spa treatments.** Book well in advance.

Where to Stay & Dine

It used to be that the only place to stay near the Blue Lagoon was a small collection of rooms called "The Clinic"; otherwise you would need to try the nearby **Northern Light Inn** (below) and several places in Grindavík (6km/3¾ miles away) or Keflavík (20km/12 miles away; p. 105). However, there are now two stunning hotels right on the Blue Lagoon property, not to mention several great dining options (two push-your-tray **cafeterias,** the casual **Lava Restaurant,** and the New Nordic fine-dining **Moss Restaurant**).

The Retreat ★★★   Redefining the Blue Lagoon experience, the Retreat is like another, more exclusive world within Iceland's biggest attraction. Hidden by high walls of lava, this luxurious, futuristic-looking compound is almost eerily quiet, lacking the crowds of the main lagoon, despite being connected to it. The stark, contemporary rooms, featuring floor-to-ceiling windows and a furnished terrace, are mini-spas in themselves, with rain showers and stand-alone bathtubs that look out over fields of lava. While this property isn't cheap, it does come with a considerable amount of extras like the complimentary minibar, some Blue Lagoon skincare amenities, daily yoga sessions, guided group hikes to Thorbjörn mountain, and access to the Retreat spa and a more exclusive lagoon. The property has two restaurants, a casual cafe and the fine-dining **Moss,** one of the best in Iceland.

Norðurljósavegur 9, 240 Grindavik. www.bluelagoon.com. ℂ **420-8800.** 62 units. 180,000kr double. Rates include breakfast. **Amenities:** 2 restaurants; bar; fitness center; free Wi-Fi.

Silica ★★   Originally known as the Clinic, when it was intended primarily for psoriasis patients, the Silica has expanded into a full-blown hotel. While many still come for health reasons and a team of doctors and specialists are on-site, the average tourists will appreciate the white exterior walls clashing with the black lava fields and blue lagoon waters. The Zen rooms feature wood floors and minimalist decor, as well as a small veranda. Guests have access to the hotel's 900m (3,000-ft.) private section of the lagoon and a small complex of pools, as well as access to the main lagoon, a short walk or ride away.

Norðurljósavegur 9, 240 Grindavik. www.bluelagoon.com. ℂ **420-8800.** 35 units. 67,000kr double. Rates include breakfast. **Amenities:** Cafe; hot tubs; indoor/outdoor pools; free Wi-Fi.

Geo Hotel ★   This modern hotel opened in the summer of 2015, right in the middle of the quiet fishing village of Grindavík, a short drive from the Blue Lagoon. The rooms feature a minimalist Scandinavian design that is far from typical in Reykjanes, plus there's a large terrace with hot tubs. The property makes considerable effort to get guests arriving on red-eye flights from North America into rooms on arrival.

Víkurbraut 58, 240 Grindavik. www.geohotel.is. ℂ **321-4000.** 36 units. June–Aug 34,946kr double. Rates around 25% lower off-season. Rates include breakfast. **Amenities:** Restaurant; bar; hot tubs; free Wi-Fi.

Moss Restaurant ★★★ ICELANDIC   Inside the Retreat at the Blue Lagoon, no expense has been spared to make this one of Iceland's top restaurants. The team of chefs, trained in Michelin-star restaurants, works out of an

The Blue Lagoon (Bláa Lónið) | NEAR REYKJAVÍK

open kitchen on the building's top floor, where bilevel dining areas look out over the lagoon. The five- and seven-course tasting menus source the best ingredients from around Iceland and change daily based on what's fresh. Expect courses like smoked arctic char tartar and beets topped with bleu cheese snow. Don't miss the wine cellar, an elevator ride below the restaurant, carved out of the lava rock.

Norðurljósavegur 9, 240 Grindavik. www.bluelagoon.com. © **420-8700.** 7-course tasting menu 15,900kr; drink pairing 12,500kr. Daily 6:30–9:30pm. Reservations required.

Guesthouse Borg ★ The cheapest option near the Blue Lagoon, this basic guesthouse with smallish single and double rooms is a reasonable option for those on a budget. Most guests here spend all their time at the Lagoon anyway, so the no-frills, family-run facilities don't seem to bother many.

Borgarhraun 2 (by Víkarbraut). www.guesthouseborg.com. © **895-8686.** 7 units w/ shared bathroom. May 15–Sept 15 14,400kr double. Rates around 25% lower off season. Rates include breakfast. **Amenities:** Guest kitchen; lounge area; free Wi-Fi.

Northern Light Inn ★ With more hotels now in the area, the Northern Light Inn doesn't have the lure it once did. Still, this little hotel in the middle of a vast lava field is a great place to stay. The rooms are large and have character (like flowered wallpaper), and common areas are intriguing, with a fireplace lounge and a cognac honesty bar. It's loaded with extras too: free breakfast buffet, free airport and Blue Lagoon transfers, and a viewing balcony for the Northern Lights. **Max's restaurant** (main courses 3,200kr–6,500kr), open daily from 7am to 9pm, tries hard to please, with smoked salmon from Ólafsfjörður and a Sunday roast.

Rte. 426, just east of Blue Lagoon. www.nli.is. © **426-8650.** 20 units. June–Aug 33,600kr double. Rates around 15% lower May and Sept, 30% lower Oct–Apr. Rates include breakfast. **Amenities:** Restaurant; free airport & Blue Lagoon transfers; free Wi-Fi.

KEFLAVÍK

47km (29 miles) SW of Reykjavík.

For many visitors, one look down from their descending plane on to Keflavík's sprawling Lego housing is all they need to know. But **Keflavík** ★ is an underrated town, and you could do much worse than spend your first or last night here. It's also a good base for all of Reykjanes Peninsula. On the first Saturday in September, the sea cliffs are dramatically lit up for the "Night of Lights," with live music, family entertainment, and a fireworks show. Keflavík maintains a strong fishing economy and has merged with Njarðvík to the east to form a single municipal entity called Reykjanesbær. The joint population is more than 15,000—by far the largest settlement on the peninsula.

Essentials

GETTING THERE Route 41 connects Reykjavík to Keflavík. **Strætó** (www. straeto.is; © **540-2700**) links Reykjavík and Keflavík with five to seven scheduled buses each weekday and three on weekends (1,840kr; ages 4–11 half-price). The bus leaves from BSÍ terminal in Reykjavík, stopping at Kringlan Mall, and makes several stops in Keflavík.

VISITOR INFORMATION   The Reykjanes Peninsula **tourist office** is at Krossmói 4, Reykjanesbær (www.visitreykjanes.is; ℭ **421-3520;** Mon–Fri 9am–5pm, Sat 10am–2pm).

Exploring Keflavík

If it's your last day in Iceland and you'd like one more stroll to commune with the ocean, proceed north from the Duus Hús on the well-worn **path along the cliff top.** On a clear day you can see Reykjavík or even Snæfellsnes Peninsula 100km (62 miles) away.

Duus Hús ★ MUSEUM   Set in a sprawling red warehouse near the harbor, this well-run and surprisingly diverse art museum and cultural exhibition is one of the more interesting free attractions in all of Iceland. The highlight is the collection of nearly 100 models of Icelandic fishing vessels, out of the several hundred that were built by local skipper Grímur Karlsson since his 1984 retirement. They range in size from 6m to 1.5m (2–5 ft.) and are meticulously detailed. There are also original pieces from Iceland's best-known painter, Jóhannes Kjarval, on the side wall.

Duusgata 2–10. ℭ **421-3796.** Free admission. Weekdays 11am–5pm; weekends 1–5pm.

Icelandic Museum of Rock 'n' Roll ★★ MUSEUM   When the now-closed American naval base was built during WWII in Keflavík, it brought not only personnel and equipment but a radio signal, which in turn brought rock 'n' roll. In the decades that followed, Keflavík became the epicenter of Iceland's rock scene, and dozens of the country's most important musicians have hailed from the small town. This museum, which opened in 2014, explores not only the history of these artists but the entirety of the Icelandic rock scene though exhibits and memorabilia, visited with the aid of an iPad loaded with music videos and audio tracks. The exhibits are highly interactive and include sound booths, mixing tables, and electric guitars that visitors can test out.

Hjallavegur 2. www.rokksafn.is. ℭ **420-1030.** Admission 2,000kr adults; 1,500kr seniors; free for children 16 and under. Daily 11am–6pm.

Where to Stay

EXPENSIVE

Hótel Keflavík ★   This always-reliable hotel, which has been Keflavik's leading accommodation since it opened in 1986, keeps getting better. In 2015 the property got a considerable facelift, particularly at the penthouse level, where the flashy five-star suites are as luxurious as any in Reykjavík. There they installed an insane amount of LED lighting and Scandinavian designer furnishings. The rest of the rooms are elegantly decorated too, infusing contemporary artwork with pseudo-Victorian wallpaper, red carpeting, and top-of-the-line electronics, including ensuite iPads; most have ocean views.

There's also a gym with free spinning classes, a sauna, and a solarium. Across the street a less expensive **guesthouse** has six rooms and access to all hotel facilities. Included in rates is a one-way taxi from the airport.

Vatnsnesvegur 12–14. www.kef.is. ✆ **420-7000.** Hotel: 70 units. 17,800kr double; 27,800kr junior suite. Guesthouse: 6 units. 33,600kr double. Rates include breakfast. **Amenities:** Restaurants; bar; free airport transfer; health club; room service; sauna; solarium; free Wi-Fi in public areas.

Park Inn by Radisson ★   This hotel has been managed by several hotel chains over the years, though the service and quality have remained relatively consistent. The rooms are smart and efficient, plus, there are all sorts of extras, like their OM Center, a spa and wellness center with yoga, pilates, and meditation sessions, as well as massages and a salon. There are also 8am check-ins for early flights, an art gallery, and a map to hiking trails.

Hafnargata 57. www.parkinn.com/airport-hotel-keflavik. ✆ **421-5222.** 81 units. 28,200kr double. Rates around 25% lower Apr–May and mid-Sept to Oct, and around 40% lower Nov–Mar. Rates include breakfast. **Amenities:** Restaurant; bar; spa; free airport transfer; free Wi-Fi.

MODERATE

Hótel Keilir ★   Right in the middle of downtown Keflavík, this uncomplicated Scandinavian minimalist hotel is walking distance to countless shops and restaurants. The rooms, half of which overlook Faxaflói Bay from cement balconies, are clean and sterile, with just some nature-photo pillowcases and artwork on the walls to liven them up.

Hafnargata 37. www.hotelkeilir.is. ✆ **420-9800.** 40 units. May 15–Sept 15. 32,200kr double. Rates around 40% lower Sept 16–May 14. Rates include breakfast. **Amenities:** Bar; free Wi-Fi.

INEXPENSIVE

B&B Guesthouse, Hringbraut 92 (www.bbguesthouse.is; ✆ **421-8989**), a short walk from Keflavík's main drag, has 10 comfortable and clean (if not cheery) doubles with shared bathroom for 13,600kr including breakfast. Amenities include a guest kitchen and free airport transfer.

Where to Eat/Nightlife

Keflavík's best down-to-earth local bar, **Paddy's Irish Pub,** Hafnargata 38 (✆ **421-8900;** Sun–Thurs 5pm–1am; Fri–Sat 5pm–5am), has live music Friday and Saturday with no cover—and, of course, Guinness by the pint.

Kaffi Duus ★ CAFE/SEAFOOD   On the north end of town near the harbor, this nautical-themed spot with outdoor seating is laid-back by day but comes alive at night. The menu is home to both standard international fare, like fish and chips or pasta, and more exotic plates like almond-and-Parmesan-crusted cod or chicken tikka.

Duusgata 10. www.duus.is. ✆ **421-7080.** Reservations required for dinner. Main courses 2,850kr–7,500kr. Daily 10am–10pm; bar open late Fri–Sat.

GOLDEN CIRCLE: ÞINGVELLIR, GEYSIR & GULLFOSS

Þingvellir is 49km (30 miles) NE of Reykjavík; Geysir is 118km (73 miles) NE of Reykjavík; Gullfoss is 125km (78 miles) NE of Reykjavík.

Each Golden Circle tour has its minor variations, but all include three major sights: **Þingvellir** ★★, meaning "Parliament Fields," where the Icelandic parliament first convened in 930; **Geysir** ★, a geothermal hotspot from which the English word geyser is derived; and **Gullfoss** ★★★, a majestic waterfall, whose name means "golden falls." The "Golden Circle" route as a whole isn't notably golden or circular, but "Mossy Green Triangle" is a less marketable title for the most popular day tour in Iceland. Nearby sights are often incorporated into the route, particularly the **Nesjavellir power plant, Kerið crater,** and **Skálholt,** once the most dominant settlement in south Iceland.

Essentials

GETTING THERE   Bus tours are popular and convenient, especially in less than perfect weather or for when you're in the mood to sit back and relax, keeping your eyes wandering across the landscape while a local provides insights about the geography and history of the area. Even so, many visitors prefer the flexibility of a rental car. This allows time for a hike into the valley at Þingvellir, and you might fit in **Hveragerði** (p. 117) or the **Þjórsárdalur valley** (p. 232). The roads are open all year but can be very slippery and dangerous in winter. *Note:* If you plan on taking the interior **Kjölur Route** (p. 302) to Akureyri, you can see Geysir and Gullfoss then.

By car, Þingvellir is less than an hour from Reykjavík; take Route 1 north of Mosfellsbær, then turn right on Route 36. From Þingvellir, continue east on Route 36, turn left on Route 365, and turn left again on Route 37 in Laugarvatn; when Route 37 ends, turn left on Route 35. From there it's a short way to Geysir, and another 10 minutes to Gullfoss.

Bus tours leave from Reykjavík's BSÍ terminal, and prices include free hotel pickup and dropoff. Standard tours generally last 8 hours and leave at 7am or 9am. **Reykjavík Excursions** (www.re.is; ✆ 580-5400) charges 6,399kr for the standard "Gullfoss Geysir Direct" tour, which includes Gullfoss, Geysir, and Thingvellir National Park and lasts 5½ hours. It runs both during the day and as an evening tour. Children ages 12 to 15 get 50% off; ages 11 and under ride free. The Golden Circle tour from **Grayline Iceland** (www.grayline.is; ✆ 540-1313) costs 7,500kr and lasts 8 hours, while **Iceland Total** (www.icelandtotal.is; ✆ 585-4300) has a Golden Circle tour focusing exclusively on the big three destinations for 6,000kr. If you want to make a bigger day of it, there are also combination tours, taking in a museum or a glacier; ask tour operators for details.

VISITOR INFORMATION   Þingvellir has two **tourist offices** (www.thingvellir.is). Approaching from Reykjavík, the first you come to is the **interpretive center,** at the top of the Almannagjá fault; the turnoff from Route 36 is marked "FRÆÐSLUMIÐSTÖÐ" (June–Aug daily 9am–7pm; Apr–May and Sept–Oct daily 9am–5pm; Nov–Mar Sat–Sun 9am–5pm). Fun and informative video displays explain the area's natural and cultural history, and books and maps are for sale. Along Route 36 is the **information office** (© **482-2660;** May–Sept daily 8:30am–8pm; cafe open Apr and Oct 8:30am–8pm and Nov–Mar Sat–Sun 9am–5pm) with a bookshop.

The modern **Geysir Center** (www.geysircenter.com; © **480-6800;** June–Aug daily 9am–10pm, May and Sept daily 9am–8pm, Oct and Apr daily 10am–4pm), across the street from the geothermal area, has an information desk, restaurant, cafe, and extensive souvenir shop.

The unstaffed **Gullfoss visitor center** (Mon–Fri 9am–6pm; Sat–Sun 9–7pm) is right next to a **cafe and gift shop** (© **486-6500;** Oct–Apr daily 8am–6pm; May–Sept 8am to as late as 10pm), where questions can be directed.

Þingvellir ★★

Þingvellir—a rift valley bounded by cliffs to the east and west, about 6km (3¾ miles) apart—is the symbolic heart of the Icelandic nation, though it's hardly clear why at first glance. Without obvious historical markers, such as significant ruins, knowing a little of the area's history beforehand makes a visit more interesting, and for the ultimate level of appreciation, reading an Icelandic saga or two will enable you to experience Þingvellir in the company of its many legendary ghosts.

The first Icelandic parliament (or *Alþing*) convened here in 930, where it remained off and on through 1798. (The Alþing, now in Reykjavík, is widely considered the oldest continuously operating parliamentary institution in the world; it was disbanded for many years by Iceland's colonial rulers, so the Isle of Man has its own claim to this streak.) To Icelanders, Þingvellir is not only where their political independence originated, but also where their oral and literary traditions were passed on, and where their very sense of peoplehood formed. In the 19th and early-20th centuries, Þingvellir became a potent symbol and meeting place for the growing nationalist movement for independence from Denmark. In 1930, marking the millennium of the first Alþing, Þingvellir became Iceland's first national park. When Iceland gained formal independence in 1944, 20,000 people—one-sixth of the population—gathered at Þingvellir. The proclamation of independence was read in the pouring rain, followed by 2 minutes of silence and the peal of church bells. In 2004, Þingvellir became a UNESCO World Heritage site. It's still used for national commemorations.

Þingvallavatn, the largest natural lake in Iceland, forms Þingvellir's southern boundary; 90% of its water comes from underground springs and fissures. Þingvellir sits directly on the continental rift: Land west of the **Almannagjá (Everyman's Gorge)** is moving west, and land east of the **Hrafnagjá (Raven Gorge)** is moving east. The entire plain is riven with small crevices from all this geological stretching.

Þingvellir National Park

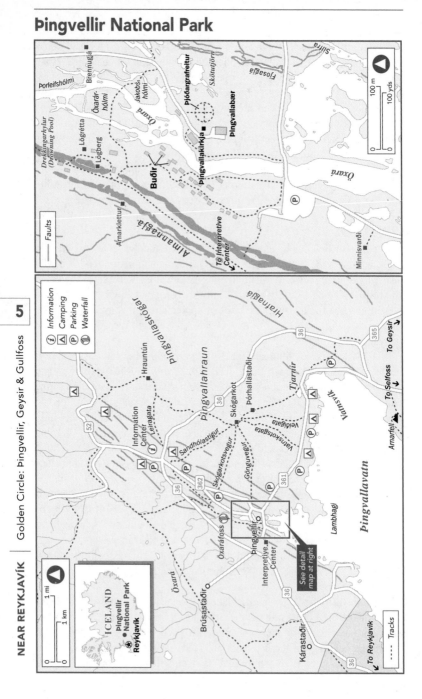

EXPLORING ÞINGVELLIR

Þingvellir is no Versailles; the only visible remnants of the old parliamentary gatherings are hardly more than lumps in the ground. All the main historical sites are clustered in the southwest corner of the park, and the vast majority of visitors never venture farther. This area was a good assembly site because the cliffs served as a natural amphitheater, the river provided fish and drinking water, and the plains held plenty of room for encampments. The rest of the park is undeveloped except for walking trails.

The parking areas closest to the sights are at the interpretive center and down in the valley off Route 362, about 150m (492 ft.) from the church. From the former there's a nice view of the latter, and a broad, well-tended path leads a short distance down through the **Almannagjá (Everyman's Fault)** to the designated **Lögberg (Law Rock),** marked by a flagpole. (No one knows for certain where the original rock was.) The **Lögsögumaður (Law Speaker),** the only salaried official at the Alþing, recited the laws from this podium by memory. Facing toward the south and the river, you can see bulges of earth and stone, the remains of temporary encampments called **búðir (booths).** The fault of **Flosagjá** forms the eastern border of the assembly. Northeast of the Law Rock, across the river, are the **Neðrivellir (Low Fields),** thought to be the meeting place for the **Lögretta (Law Council).**

The Öxará **(Axe River)**—so named, according to Icelandic folk legend, because this is where the axe that killed Jóra the troll washed up, an event predicted by the Norwegian king who had told Icelanders to set up their parliament wherever the axe was found—was probably diverted from its original course to provide drinking water for the assembly. North along the river is the **Drekkingarhylur (Drowning Pool),** where at least 18 women convicted of incest, infanticide, witchcraft, or adultery were tied in sacks and held under water. An informational panel marks the supposed spot. In the Christian millennial celebrations of 2000, a wreath was placed here in atonement for the executions. A short walk farther north is a pretty waterfall, Öxaráfoss.

Across the river is the simple and charming **Þingvellir Church (Þingvallakirkja)** (Jun–Aug 9am–7pm), which seats about 35. The first church at the site was built around 1016, with a bell and timbers sent by King Olaf of Norway. The current church was consecrated in 1859 and restored in 1970 to something close to its original condition, with the notable exception of the new copper roof.

Next to the church is the unremarkable farmhouse **Þingvallabær,** a summer residence for the Prime Minister—no security fence necessary. It was built in 1930 to commemorate the millennium of the first Alþing, and is not open to the public. Behind the church is **Þjóðargrafreitur,** a raised circular **graveyard.** Burial at this spot has been bestowed on only two men, Jónas Hallgrímsson (1807–1845) and Einar Benediktsson (1864–1940), both poets and key figures in Iceland's nationalist revival.

By the nearest parking area is a bridge overlooking the **Peningagjá (Money Fault).** Inside the fault is a clear, glistening pool that makes every child dream of diving down to collect all the coins.

WHY DOES ÞINGVELLIR church HAVE TWO ALTARPIECES?

Inside the church are two altarpieces. One depicts the Last Supper, and was painted on driftwood by local farmer and artisan Ófeigur Jónsson in 1834. The other, *Christ Healing the Blind Man*, from 1896, is by Danish painter Niels Anker Lund (1840–1922). Ófeigur's painting was the original altarpiece, but it was deemed too primitive and amateurish by church authorities and replaced by Lund's painting at great expense. Ófeigur's painting was bought for a pittance by a Victorian heiress named Mary Disney Leith (1840–1926). Leith, who had a lifelong fascination with Iceland, journeyed there 18 times, wrote travel memoirs, and translated some sagas. The piece ended up in the collection of St. Peter's Church, Shorwell, on the Isle of Wight, near Leith's estate. When Þingvellir church was renovated in 1970, Magnus Magnusson—the prolific author, saga translator, and longtime "Quizmaster" on BBC1's *Mastermind*—tracked it down with the help of Mrs. Leith's granddaughter. The congregation in Shorwell Church returned it in exchange for a replica made at Iceland's National Museum.

OUTDOOR ACTIVITIES

HIKING   Simplistic trail maps are available for about 500kr from the visitor offices, but trails are well marked, and you can probably just remember or jot down your route from signboards. More serious maps, including one called "The Golden Circle" (1,950kr), which covers this whole region, are available at bookstores and information offices.

Apart from the historical sites, and the north–south trails connecting the sites to the information office, all trails extend east into the **Þingvallahraun** lava field. All of the lava flowed about 9,000 years ago from **Skjaldbreiður (Shield Volcano),** a perfectly rounded, squat cone visible to the north. Named for its shape, Skjaldbreiður then lent its name (in translation) to all other shield volcanoes, just as Geysir lent its name to all geysers.

Virtually all the trails leaving from the western edge of the park converge halfway across the valley at the ruins of **Skógarkot,** a sheep farm abandoned since the 1930s. Each trail takes about 30 to 40 minutes. Farther east lies **Þórhallastaðir,** another farm ruin, but Skógarkot is more picturesque and enough to satisfy most day walkers. It's also an ideal picnic spot, with a great view over the lake to Hengill (p. 118) and the Nesjavellir geothermal power plant (below).

A **recommended loop itinerary** starts and ends at the information office. If you have 3 hours, head south along the fault to the historical sites, then take the trail east from the church to Skógarkot, cutting directly back to the office. With only 2 hours to spare, park near the historical sites and squeeze in a hike to Skógarkot and back. If you have just 1 hour, stick to the historical sites and venture north along the fault. You can time your trip to take advantage of the **free 1-hour guided tours** of the historical sites, leaving from Þingvellir Church (Þingvallakirkja) at 10am and 3pm weekdays June through August. Serious hikers follow a trail all the way to the eastern edge of the rift—near to where Route 36 climbs the eastern rift wall at Hrafnagjá—but it's too long for a return trip in 1 day, so you'd want to arrange a ride one-way.

Forty percent of all Icelandic flora can be found in Þingvellir, but nothing is taller than a dwarf birch. It's especially pretty late in the year. As you walk through the valley, be careful not to step into the many fissures along the trail, and keep a close eye on children.

SCUBA DIVING **Diving** in Þingvallavatn has taken off recently. Dives focus on dramatic fissures on the lake bottom, up to 40m (131 ft.) below the surface. Þingvallavatn is not recommended for beginners, however, given the cold temperatures and currents inside the fissures. **Silfra** is the most renowned of these otherworldly ravines in Þingvallavatn. Dives or snorkel tours can be arranged through **Dive Silfra** (www.divesilfra.is; ✆ **562-7000**), which also creates packages with day tours of the Golden Circle.

South of Þingvellir

Near the southwest shore of lake Þingvallavatn are the **Nesjavellir power plant** and the **Hengill hiking area** (p. 118), which is also accessible from Hveragerði to the south. The brochure "Hiking Trails in the Hengill Area" can be found at Nesjavellir and book stores.

Nesjavellir Geothermal Power Plant ★ Iceland's renewable energy sources, hydropower and geothermal power, are the envy of fossil-fuel-guzzling nations around the world. Nesjavellir, which produces the capital area's hot water and electricity from geothermal hot springs, is the country's second-largest plant. It was built in 1987 and attracts 20,000 visitors a year. Exhibits are informative, and the glassed-in observation platform affords a good view of the plant's gleaming pipery. **Reykjavík Excursions** (www.re.is; ✆ **580-5400**) and **Grayline Iceland** (www.grayline.is; ✆ **540-1313**) often include Nesjavellir in daylong bus tours combined with Þingvellir (above).

Off Rte. 360, around 12km (7½ miles) south of the Rte. 36/Rte. 360 junction. www.or.is. ✆ **480-2408.** Free admission. June–Aug Mon–Sat 9am–5pm, Sun 1–6pm; Sept–May no regular hours; call to inquire about group tours.

Geysir ★

The word "geyser" derives from this fascinating geothermal area full of hot springs, steaming creeks, mud marbled in mineral shades, turquoise pools encrusted with silica, and one reliable geyser. Geysir (*gay*-seerr), discovered and named in 1294, refers to both this general area and a specific geyser, which once spouted as high as 80m (262 ft.), but is now just a calm, steamy vent with occasional hisses and gurgles. Rocks and soap were often dumped into Geysir to make it erupt on demand, only accelerating its demise. Recent research has shown that if the water level were lowered 2m (6½ ft.), Geysir would again erupt every 30 to 60 minutes to a height of 8 to 10m (26–33 ft.). Thankfully **Strokkur (The Churn),** another geyser next to *the* Geysir, spouts reliably every 5 minutes or so. Each spout varies in size, so wait to see at least two or three.

The geyser mechanism is not completely understood, but scientists agree that the eruptions are basically caused by a pressure buildup formed when hot water and gas are trapped beneath a cooler layer of water. Strokkur's eruptions can reach as high as 35m (115 ft.). (Americans can be seen affecting nonchalance, because Old Faithful reaches 25–55m/82–180 ft., and Steamboat reaches 90–120m/295–394 ft.) The spouting water is steaming hot—around 257°F (125°C)—so be careful not to stand downwind.

Gullfoss ★★★

Along the Hvitá river, just 7km (4 miles) from Geysir, Gullfoss is Iceland's most iconic and visited waterfall, as elegant as it is massive. The waterfall is a 10-minute walk from the parking area, and you'll hear it well before you see it. Two smaller falls at the top lead to an L-shaped curtain cascade dropping another 21m (69 ft.) into a 2.5km-long (1½-mile) gorge. The two paths, one above and one below, give you plenty of different angles for viewing. Bring your raincoat for the lower one, as the spray can be heavy at times. When it's sunny, you can always expect a rainbow; in winter the falls are filigreed in beautiful ice formations. Near the falls is a **monument to Sigríður Tómasdóttir,** who probably saved Gullfoss from being submerged by a hydroelectric dam in the 1920s. The daughter of the farmer who owned the property, Sigríður threatened to throw herself over the falls if the project went through. The courts ruled against her, but the hydroelectric company gave in to public pressure and the contract simply expired in 1928. The **visitor center** (Mon–Fri 9am–6pm; Sat–Sun 9am–7pm) is right next to a **cafe and gift shop** (Oct–Apr daily 8am–6pm; May–Sept 8am to as late as 10pm).

Near the Golden Circle

The sights below are listed in the order you would encounter them in a return trip from Gullfoss to Reykjavík. **Kerið Crater** and **Skálholt** are included in some Golden Circle tours. With your own car, you might also consider a side trip to the **Þjórsárdalur Valley** (p. 232) or **Hveragerði** (p. 117).

SKÁLHOLT

Skálholt, about 40km (25 miles) from the town of Selfoss, is off Route 31, a short detour south from Route 35, which connects Gullfoss and Selfoss. Though few visible remnants exist today, Skálholt was once the most wealthy, populated, and influential settlement in Iceland. In 1056 it became the seat of Iceland's first Catholic bishop. A church built at Skálholt in the mid-12th century from two shiploads of Norwegian timber was the largest wooden structure in medieval Scandinavia (and twice the length of the current church). The clerical class got rich from land tenants, but was also an important force in bringing education for all: Laypersons of both sexes were enrolled, and classes were conducted in Icelandic as well as Latin. By the early 13th century, Skálholt was Iceland's largest settlement, with 200 people; just before the Reformation, it owned 10% of all land holdings in the country.

In 1550, Jón Arason, Iceland's last Catholic bishop—in fact, the last Catholic bishop of any Nordic country—was beheaded here along with his sons, after leading a rebellion against the Danish king's order to Lutheranize the country. They were buried without coffins at the back of the church, and by the following year, the monarchy had appropriated all church lands. Eighty meters (262 ft.) from the current church lies a crude relief on two slabs of stone, **a monument to Jón Arason.**

The current **neo-Romanesque church** was inaugurated in 1956. The altarpiece, by Icelandic artist Nína Tryggvadóttir (1913–1968), is an enormous mosaic of Christ with arms outstretched. The pulpit, which long predates the church, has a panel featuring the old Icelandic coat of arms: a filet of cod.

As you enter the church, a door to your left leads to a **museum** (✆ 486-8872; admission 1,000kr, free for children 11 and under; mid-May to Aug daily 9am–8pm; Sept to mid-May, ask for key from the office building during working hours) in an underground passage that once connected the medieval church with its school buildings. Skálholt's history is well annotated here, but the centerpieces are the bishops' tombstones and the sarcophagus of Bishop Páll Jónsson (1196–1211), carved from a solid block of sandstone.

Since 1975, the free **Skálholt Summer Concerts festival** ★ (www.sumartonleikar.is; ✆ 486-8824) features both contemporary and early Icelandic music (mostly baroque) with period instruments in 40 or so different concerts in the church. The festival, founded by harpsichordist Helga Ingólfsdóttir, begins the last week of June or first week of July and continues for 6 weeks. Concerts are usually Thursday at 8pm, Saturday at 3 and 5pm, and Sunday at 3pm. The Sunday 5pm performance is part of a church service.

KERIÐ CRATER

Passersby on Route 35 (15km/9¼ miles northeast of Selfoss) should hop out to see this small but shapely scoria crater, formed 6,500 years ago by a collapsing magma chamber at the end of a volcanic eruption. **Kerið** is 55m (180 ft.) deep, including the stagnant water at the bottom, and the sides are nicely streaked in red, black, and ochre. Björk once did a concert from a raft in the middle, but the acoustics weren't ideal. A path runs around the rim; take care and watch your footing.

Outdoor Activities

RIVER RAFTING The **Hvitá** is Iceland's most popular river for whitewater rafting, with fabulous scenery and easy to medium-difficulty rapids that don't require previous experience. Every afternoon from May through September, the recommended tour operator **Arctic Adventures** (Laugavegur 11; www.adventures.is; ✆ 562-7000) sets out from its Drumbóbase camp, signposted from Route 35 about a 10-minute drive south of Geysir. The 3-hour tour—with breaks for cocoa and cliff jumping—is 13,990kr per person, or 18,990kr with pickup/dropoff in Reykjavík (minimum age 12).

Where to Stay Along the Golden Circle

ÞINGVELLIR & NEARBY

ION Luxury Adventure Hotel ★★★   Jutting out on stilts from the base of Mount Hengill is this Brutalist glass, steel, and concrete luxury hotel. Opened in 2013, it is by far the top accommodation in the Golden Circle, if not all of central

Iceland. With its polished concrete, stacks of art books, and wool throws, it's Nordic chic in the wilderness. The property has won awards for its eco-friendly practices like water-saving showers and furniture constructed of driftwood. The rooms are not particularly interesting, and the water has that sulphur smell (the Nesjavellir Geothermal Power plant is nearby), but the common areas are quite refined. The hotel has a pricey New Nordic restaurant, **Silfra** (see below), and a glass bar with floor-to-ceiling windows protruding from the end of the building, where you can watch the Northern Lights. Outdoors, beneath the bar, is an oversized hot tub.

Nesjavellir vid Thingvallavatn. www.ioniceland.is. © **482-3415.** 46 units. June–Aug from 45,000kr double. Winter rates 10% less. **Amenities:** Restaurant; bar; hot tub; spa; tour desk; free Wi-Fi.

GEYSIR

Hótel Geysir ★   Directly across the street from the geothermal field, this midsize hotel is adjacent to all the action of the tourist center and the tour bus after tour bus stopping there. At press time, it was in the midst of a major renovation that will transform the hotel from 24 to 77 rooms and renovate the spa and restaurant. It is expected to reopen sometime in 2019.

At the Geysir Center. www.geysircenter.is. © **480-6800.** 77 units. Call for rates. **Amenities:** Restaurant; horse rental; spa; tour desk; free Wi-Fi.

GULLFOSS

Hótel Gullfoss ★   The only hotel within walking distance from the waterfall and just a short drive from Geysir, Hotel Gullfoss, beside the Hvita River, is a step up from most of the guesthouses in the area. The rooms are quite bland, though a **full-service restaurant** and outdoor hot tub make up for it. At the northeast corner of the Golden Circle, the hotel is also a convenient point for travelers driving over or back over the mountains from Kjölur.

On Brattholt farm, Rte. 35 btwn. Geysir and Gullfoss. www.hotelgullfoss.is. © **486-8979.** 16 units. Mid-Jun–Aug 31 28,800kr double. Rates around 25% lower Sept–mid-June. Rates include breakfast buffet. **Amenities:** Restaurant; bar; outdoor hot tub; free Wi-Fi.

FLÚÐIR

Icelandair Hótel Flúðir ★   With a central garden filled with hot tubs, this hotel is located in a pretty rural town known for its dairy farms and mushroom greenhouses. It definitely has that Icelandair chain feel, where it looks a little bit modern but also a little pre-fab. The village geothermal pool and fitness hall are close by, and the **restaurant** (decorated with original artwork from Tolli, one of Iceland's most famous painters) is very good and sources only locally grown vegetables and locally raised beef (main courses 3,000kr–6,500kr).

Vesterbrún 1, just off Rte. 30. www.icelandairhotels.is. © **444-4000.** 32 units. June–Aug from 18,000kr double. Special offers available online. Breakfast available (1,900kr). **Amenities:** Restaurant; bar; free Wi-Fi.

Where to Eat

Lindin ★ ICELANDIC   Halfway between Þingvellir and Gullfoss in a tiny valley resort town popular with Reykjavíkians, Lindin is one of the more interesting restaurants on the Golden Circle drive and relatively unknown by tourists. Much of the menu, created by a chef trained at the prestigious Culinary Institute of America in New York, is based on seasonal wild game, such as goose or guillemot. There's even a reindeer burger with basil-horseradish sauce.

Lindarbraut 2, 1 block from Rte. 37, Laugarvatn. www.laugarvatn.is. © **486-1262.** Reservations recommended. Main courses 3,600kr–5,850kr. May–Aug daily noon–10pm.

Silfra Restaurant & Bar ★★ NEW NORDIC   Named after the famed rift in Lake Þingvellir, this contemporary Scandinavian restaurant in the chic ION Luxury Adventure Hotel, with its tall windows looking out onto a lava field, could compete with many of Reykjavík's best fine-dining restaurants. Dinner showcases the restaurant's more adventurous side, with plates like lumpfish roe and sunchokes, beef cheeks, and a roasted saddle of lamb meant for sharing. The lunch menu is more casual, with a larger selection of sandwiches and straightforward fish and beef dishes. The wine and beer list is extensive.

Nesjavellir vid Thingvallavatn; www.ioniceland.is. © **482-3415.** Reservations recommended. Main courses 3,500kr–6,900kr. Daily noon–10pm.

HVERAGERÐI, SELFOSS & NEARBY

Hveragerði is 45km (28 miles) SE of Reykjavík; Selfoss is 57km (35 miles) SE of Reykjavík.

Unless you're planning a hiking expedition into Hengill, this region is usually more of an operational base or stopover. Nonetheless, don't pass through on the Ring Road without considering a hike into the geothermally active valley **Reykjadalur,** an exploration of the cave **Raufarhólshellir,** or a gluttonous lobster dinner at **Fjöruborðið** in Stokkseyri (all below).

Essentials

GETTING THERE   Hveragerði and Selfoss are both along Route 1. Frequent buses run daily from BSÍ terminal in Reykjavík to both towns, which are routine stops in many southern itineraries. A ticket to Selfoss is around 1,840kr, and from there buses run to and from Eyrarbakki and Stokkseyri.

VISITOR INFORMATION   The **regional tourist office** (www.south.is; © **483-4601;** Mon–Fri 9am–5pm, Sat 10am–2pm) for all of south Iceland is in Hveragerði, at Sunnumörk 2–4.

Exploring the Area
HVERAGERÐI

Hveragerði is at the southern end of an active geothermal region that extends north through Hengill to Lake Þingvallavatn. (One Hveragerði family recently discovered that a hot spring had erupted into their living room.) Since the 1920s, the town has harnessed this energy to grow fruits and vegetables in **geothermal greenhouses.**

The horse farm **Eldhestar** (www.eldhestar.is; © **480-4800**) on Route 1, about 2km (1¼ miles) east of Hveragerði, is highly recommended for short local rides or longer trips on horseback into the Hengill hiking area.

A DAY hike IN HENGILL

A hike to **Reykjadalur** ★★, or "Smoky Valley," is a great way to experience the Hengill area's best scenery—capped off with a swim in a natural hot spring—in as little as 2½ hours. It can be as gentle a hike as you choose.

From Hveragerði, head north on the main street, Breiðamörk, ascending to a level expanse surrounded by mountains. At a division in the road, bear left onto the gravel road marked "Reykjadalur." The road ends at a parking area at the base of the mountains, next to the Varmá River. Across the bridge is a signboard with a trail map of the area. The trail you're looking for is called Rjúpnabrekkur (Ptarmigan Slopes). It proceeds directly from the signboard and is marked with stakes painted like matchsticks.

After an initial ascent, a lesser descent leads into the Reykjadalur valley. The trail then crosses the stream and passes several gurgling mud pools. In just over an hour, you'll reach the head of the valley, with Ölkelduhnúkur mountain straight ahead of you. A hot, steaming stream leads uphill to the left (west) along the Klambragil Valley. A cold stream leads uphill to the right (east), where a camping hut is visible. Where the waters merge is the place to swim. If it's too hot, head back downstream to find a suitable temperature. Don't forget your bathing suit.

An enjoyable hour-long trail circumnavigates Ölkelduhnúkur. Several trails branch off from this loop trail, but if you stick with the inside route, you'll end up back at the swimming spot. The circuit is spoiled a bit by power lines but has several more geothermal hotspots. Ambitious hikers could continue all the way to Þingvallavatn in a day (after arranging transport on both ends).

NLFÍ Rehabilitation and Health Clinic ★ More medically inclined than most spas in Iceland, this well-regarded clinic has developed innovative treatments for arthritis and other medical conditions using natural materials. While rehabilitation treatments require a 3-week commitment, the clinic offers a range of general spa treatments, such as deep-heat mud baths, massages, and acupuncture. Additionally, an on-site geothermal pool facility (Mon–Fri 4–8:30pm, Sat–Sun 7:30am–4pm; 1,800kr adults, 900kr seniors/children 13 and under) has indoor and outdoor pools, hot tubs, and saunas. Frænmörk 10. www.heilsustofnun.is. ☏ **483-0300.**

HENGILL HIKING AREA ★★

Hengill is not Iceland's most dramatic or well-known hiking and camping region, but the mountain's august slopes and steaming geothermal valleys have a quiet authority and devoted following. The most common access points are Hveragerði to the south and Nesjavellir (p. 113) at lake Þingvallavatn to the north. Hengill itself is an 803m (2,634-ft.) active volcano, though its last eruption was about 2,000 years ago. Trail information is well mapped at all access points, and trails are clearly marked in varied colors.

RAUFARHÓLSHELLIR ★★

Of all the lava tube caves in Iceland, this one perhaps best combines accessibility and mystique. Raufarhólshellir is essentially an empty riverbed of lava, formed about 3,700 years ago. At 1,350m (4,429 ft.), it's Iceland's second-longest cave, with over 1km (⅔ mile) of complete blackness. The cave ceiling reaches as high as 10m (33 ft.) and averages 12m (39 ft.) in thickness. The ground is strewn with boulders and ice, making some passages difficult to traverse. The most spectacular lava contortions are at the very end, but fascinating ice formations can be seen throughout the route year-round. Entering the cave should not be attempted without a strong flashlight, warm clothing, and good shoes. A helmet and knee pads would be ideal. Exploring the full length of the cave should take around 2 hours. The unmarked parking area is just off Route 39, about 2km (1¼ mile) west of the Route 39/Route 38 intersection, between Hveragerði and Þorlákshöfn.

SELFOSS

With over 6,000 residents, Selfoss is an important trade hub and the largest town in south Iceland. Selfoss sprang into existence in 1891, when a bridge was built over the river Öfulsá, replacing ferry transport across the river to the south. The town itself doesn't really compel a visitor's attention, but the tourist office (p. 50) provides information and maps for all surrounding towns as well, and the **geothermal pool** (𝒸 **480-1960;** year-round weekdays 7:45am–9:15pm, weekends 10am–8pm; admission 650kr) makes a relaxing stop. Just east of town on an old dairy farm in Flóahreppur, you'll find **Olvisholt Brewery** ★ (www.olvisholt.is; 𝒸 **767-5000**), one of Iceland's first craft breweries. The tap room is open Monday to Friday noon to 3:30pm, while tours (3,000kr) are offered at 11am and 2pm and include an overview of the brewing process and a tasting of several beers.

EYRARBAKKI

From Selfoss, the coastal towns of Eyrarbakki and Stokkseyri can be reached in about 10 minutes by car. The route proceeds across the Flói marshland, an important breeding ground for birds. Both towns were once prominent fishing and trading centers, but neither had a natural port, so they were eclipsed by the bridge at Selfoss and a new harbor at Þorlákshöfn to the west. Eyrarbakki was once the largest community in southwestern Iceland and has an unusual concentration of turn-of-the-20th-century houses.

Kayakaferðir Stokkseyri, Heiðarbrún 24 (www.kajak.is; 𝒸 **896-5716;** closed Nov–Mar), runs 1- to 2-hour kayak tours (from 4,950kr) in nearby coastal lagoons and marshland canals full of birdlife.

Museums of Eyrarbakki ★ MUSEUM   Built around 1765 by Danish merchants who ordered it from a Scandinavian catalog, the House (**Húsið**) is the anchor of this complex of buildings on the western edge of town dedicated to documenting and preserving local history. For almost 2 centuries the house was the entry point for art and European culture in Iceland. Inside the restored wooden structure, the period-themed rooms have hit-or-miss artifacts—spoons carved from whale teeth, an old loom, and products from a defunct drugstore. The small **Egg House** in back has a nice collection of bird eggs and taxidermy. The **Maritime Museum,** included in the admission price, is 100m

(328 ft.) away across a field; look for the flagpole. Items on display include leather seaman outfits softened with fish oil, shark hooks and porpoise harpoons, and a 1915 fishing boat for 16 sailors.

Eyrargata. www.husid.com. ✆ **483-1504.** Admission 1,000kr adults; 850kr seniors 67+; free for children 11 and under. May 15–Sept 15 daily 11am–6pm; other times by arrangement.

Where to Stay
HVERAGERÐI
Frost and Fire ★ This pleasant guesthouse is situated on a bend in the warm-enough-to-bathe-in Varmá River, and the colorful rooms, hot tubs, and dining room all take advantage of the view. Each of the light-filled rooms has a private entrance and artwork from Icelandic artists. In the summer another six rooms in a country house called **Axelshús** are opened up to guests. It's set on a hill with views of the river, valleys, and town. A spa area includes an outdoor pool, steam room, and Kneipp baths.

Hverhamar (just off Breiðamörk, at the northern end of town). www.frostandfire.is. ✆ **483-4959.** 22 units. June–Aug 39,500kr double. Rates around 10% lower May and Sept; around 30% lower at other times. Rates include breakfast. **Amenities:** Restaurant; outdoor pool and hot tubs; sauna; free Wi-Fi.

Hótel Eldhestar ★ A smart country hotel primarily utilized by equestrians who have come to take advantage of one of Iceland's best horse farms, Eldhestar was the first lodging in Iceland to receive the Nordic eco-label, the Nordic Swan. The Icelandic horse inspires much of the decor on the property; walls are lined with old photos and notes describing the animal's importance through the ages. The rooms have a country feel to them too, with wool comforters and beds from Hästens in Sweden.

On Rte. 1, about 2km (1¼ miles) east of Hveragerði. www.hoteleldhestar.is. ✆ **480-4800.** 26 units. June–Aug 29,450kr double. Rates around 30% lower Apr–May and Sept–Oct, and 45% lower Nov–Mar. Rates include breakfast. **Amenities:** Restaurant; bar; hot tub; free Wi-Fi.

SELFOSS
Hotel Selfoss ★ This hulking, corporate-feeling property on the riverfront is one of the least atmospheric places to stay in Selfoss, but it still gets plenty of attention. It is one of the most complete hotels in the area, with lots of extras such as the **Riverside Spa,** with its thermal pool and sauna; an upmarket restaurant with floor-to-ceiling windows; a bar with a fireplace; a cinema; and extensive conference facilities.

Eyrarvegur 2. www.hotelselfoss.is. ✆ **480-2500.** 99 units. 29,450kr double. Rates around 25% lower Jan–Apr, 23% lower Oct–Dec. Rates include breakfast. **Amenities:** Restaurant; spa; free Wi-Fi.

Where to Eat
Fjöruborðið ★★ SEAFOOD Many Reykjavíkians trek all the way to this famed lobster house just for dinner at one of the most legendary restaurants in

the south of Iceland. The Icelandic langoustine, not actually a lobster, is the star of the menu here, appearing in a creamy soup or sautéed in garlic and butter. Fish, beef, lamb, and vegetarian dishes are also offered, but none but the langoustine warrants the special trip.

Eyrarbraut 3a, Stokkseyri. www.fjorubordid.is. © **483-1550.** Reservations recommended. Main courses 3,500kr–7,900kr. June–Sept Mon–Thurs, Sun noon–9pm, Fri–Sat noon–10pm; Oct–May not open for lunch on weekdays.

Friðheimar ★★ INTERNATIONAL Set within a sprawling geothermal-powered greenhouse complex, this one-of-a kind restaurant has a menu built around tomatoes, including the beer and coffee drinks. At tables surrounded by tomato plants, you can indulge in tomato soup, mussels or pasta served with tomato-based sauces, and tomato and apple pie. A small gift shop offers items produced at the greenhouse and local area. Tours of the greenhouses are available with advance notice, while horse shows take place outside during the summer months.

Bláskógabyggð, Selfoss; www.fridheimar.is. © **486-8894.** Reservations recommended. Main courses 1,900kr–2,600kr. Daily noon–4pm.

Rauða Húsið ★ CONTINENTAL An Eyrarbakki institution, the "Red House" is set in a 1919 building that has been lovingly restored without losing its sense of history. The menu is quite varied, with a cream of langoustine soup as the house special, plus sous-vide-cooked beef and a nut-and-seed loaf for vegetarians. But there are also plenty of classics, including pastas and grilled fish. The cellar pub, decorated with wooden casks, is a fine place for a nightcap.

Búðarstíg 4 (coastal Rd., at Bakarísstígur), Eyrarbakki. www.raudahusid.is. © **483-3330.** Main courses 2,850kr–8,250kr. Sun–Thurs 11:30am–9pm; Fri–Sat 11:30am–10pm.

WEST ICELAND

A breathtaking combination of rugged peaks, ambling waterfalls, and the Snæfellsjökull glacier growing in magnificence as it ducks in and out of sight along the coast-hugging road, the Snæfellsnes Peninsula feels worlds apart from Reykjavík despite being a short drive away. Just across the bay, the Westfjords are a place where stony mountains and narrow inlets hide isolated farms and fishing villages that have changed little in decades. Thanks to improved roads and tunnels, this still-undiscovered natural wonder is opening up more and more to the rest of the country. The area comprises a tenth of Iceland's landmass and a third of its coastline, and round every bend is some new variation on how mountains can tumble to the sea. Fjord after fjord provides a calming contrast, stretching out to the distant Atlantic horizon.

On a clear day, the glacier-topped Snæfellsjökull stratovolcano, the same one that contained a passage into the planet's core in Jules Verne's *Journey to the Center of the Earth,* is visible from Reykjavík. Visitors arriving at Keflavík airport should scan the northern horizon as they head toward Reykjavík, because for most this is the closest they will come to witnessing Iceland's beautiful western corner.

It's easy to imagine that a region such as this created the cliché "rugged beauty." Yet, while many places such as the Snæfellsnes Peninsula make a worthwhile day trip from Reykjavík, they tend to suffer the fate of being all too often glimpsed en route rather than considered destinations in themselves. The Westfjords are even more neglected, despite boasting some of Iceland's grandest bird cliffs, loveliest sand beaches, and loneliest upland moors. Winters are relatively long and harsh, and the population is around 7,400—less than one inhabitant per square kilometer, compared with the national average of three.

The image of the Westfjords as inaccessible, however, is exaggerated. The main road to Ísafjörður is now paved all the way to the Ring Road and even boasts its own Ring Road, sometimes dubbed the Ring Road 2 or the Green Circle. Plus, daily flights to Ísafjörður take just 40 minutes from Reykjavík. The next morning you could be boarding a boat for Hornstrandir Nature Reserve, one of Iceland's most ruggedly beautiful and pristine hiking areas. By afternoon you might be staring down at an Arctic fox, or peering over a dizzying bird cliff at the crashing surf, with the world left completely behind.

West Iceland has other oft-neglected gems, some sitting right on the Ring Road. Snæfellsnes, a 70km-long (43 mile) finger of land pointing westward, is closely identified with the Snæfellsjökull glacier near its tip, but the peninsula has plenty more to offer and can easily sustain 2 or 3 days of exploring. Circling it is one of Iceland's most enjoyable road trips, especially if outdoor activities are tacked on. Possibilities include some splendid coastal walks; whale-watching from Ólafsvík; horseback riding along beaches on the south coast; snowmobile trips to the glacier; and kayak or boat tours among the low-lying islands of Breiðafjörður, a thriving habitat for birds and seals.

BORGARNES, REYKHOLT & FARTHER INLAND

Overland routes from Reykjavík to all points in west Iceland pass through this region, which draws many history-minded visitors. Borgarnes has an engaging museum on the twin themes of the first settlers in Iceland and *Egil's Saga,* a classic of medieval European literature. Saga enthusiasts also make pilgrimages to **Reykholt,** once the residence of Snorri Sturluson, the most prominent historical figure of Iceland's saga-writing age. Farther inland are two of Iceland's most extensive lava caves: **Surtshellir** and **Víðgelmir.** From here, an alternate route south to Þingvellir passes between glacier-capped mountains for a taste of Iceland's starkly beautiful interior.

Essentials

GETTING THERE   Borgarnes is on the Ring Road, 74km (46 miles) north of Reykjavík. Reykholt is on Route 518, 39km (24 miles) inland from Borgarnes.

Straeto buses (www.straeto.is; © 540-2700) connect Reykjavík and **Borgarnes** up to five times daily during the summer, though less during the rest of the year. The trip costs around 1,850kr one-way and is 55 minutes, or 75 minutes with a stop at Akranes. From mid-May to mid-September, buses from Reykjavík to **Reykholt** leave daily at 8:30am, returning at 7pm or 7:45pm, with a one-way fare of 2,350kr. The bus stops at Borgarnes and makes several local stops between Borgarnes and Reykholt. See also "Bus Tours," p. 130.

VISITOR INFORMATION   Regional **tourist information** for West Iceland is in Borgarnes at the **Hyrnutorg shopping center,** Borgarbraut 58-60 (www.westiceland.is; © 437-2214; June–Aug Mon–Fri 9am–5pm, Sat–Sun 10am–6pm; Sept–May Mon–Fri 9am–5pm). The reception office at **Snorrastofa** (www.snorrastofa.is; © 433-8008; May–Sept daily 10am–5pm) provides information on Reykholt and nearby areas.

Exploring the Area
BORGARNES

Visitors tracing the footsteps of Egil Skallagrímsson, the warrior-poet hero of *Egil's Saga,* should pick up the free "Saga Trails of Iceland" brochure at the Settlement Center museum. The museum leads guided tours for groups by arrangement, and individuals can sometimes sign on by calling ahead.

The focal point of **Skallagrímsgarður Park,** a public garden on Skalla-grímsgata downtown, is a burial mound thought to contain the remains of Egil's father and son. Facing the mound is a relief sculpture of Egil on horse-back, his face twisted with grief as he carries his dead 17-year-old son.

The Settlement Center ★★ MUSEUM Founded in 2006, the Settle-ment Center's two exhibitions tell the story of the first 60 years of Icelandic settlement (around 870–930) and *Egil's Saga,* from Iceland´s most famous Viking and first poet Egill Skallagrimsson. Visitors strap on headphones for two 30-minute audio exhibits, available in 14 languages. The settlement exhibit is a basic primer and may feel a bit remedial to those well-versed in the subject, though for most first-time visitors to Iceland it serves as a great introduction. The successes of its interactive and multimedia features, such as a video of a re-created Viking ship, are perhaps a tribute to the background of the founders, an actor/playwright and a television reporter.

Egil's Saga is among the six most celebrated literary achievements of medi-eval Iceland. Egil is a volatile and ambiguous character, capable of masterful poetry and merciless barbarity. While *Njál's Saga* has more passages illustra-tive of everyday life in 10th-century Iceland, *Egil's Saga* has every dramatic hallmark, from pagan sorcery to bitter love triangles to gory battle scenes featuring outlaws and berserkers. The exhibit ably conveys the strangeness and horror of the story. Be warned, however, that the installations—like a life-size witch queen of Norway, rocking and grumbling over a fire, with a decom-posed beast's head impaled on a pole—may frighten young children.

Brákarbraut 13–15. www.landnam.is. ✆ **437-1600.** Admission 2,500kr; adults; 1900kr seniors/children 6–14; free for children 5 and under, but the *Egil's Saga* exhibition is not suitable for young children. Year-round daily 10am–9pm.

REYKHOLT

The historic settlement of Reykholt, less than an hour inland from Borgarnes, sits within the fertile, well-forested, and geothermally active Reykholtsdalur Valley. As the former home of chieftain, politician, scholar, and author Snorri Sturluson (1178–1241), Reykholt holds deep cultural resonance for Iceland-ers. Today the settlement is a cluster of buildings anchored by **Snorrastofa,** a research institute and museum dealing in medieval Iceland and Sturluson's literary works. An 1887 church is charmingly restored, though a 1996 church has taken over its functions, including the **Reykholt Music Festival** (mainly classical) held around the last weekend of July (www.reykholtshatid.is).

During the 1986 Reagan–Gorbachev summit in Reykjavík, a step toward ending the Cold War, Icelandic Prime Minister Steingrímur Hermannsson spoke to international reporters while relaxing in a hot tub at his local pool. In the early 13th century, Sturluson apparently held political powwows at Reyk-holt in an outdoor bath with crude taps for regulating hot and cold water flow. The exact site of the original **Snorralaug (Snorri's Pool)** is unknown, but in 1959 the National Museum settled on the current spot and built a reconstruc-tion, 4m (13 ft.) in diameter, with hewn blocks of silica stone and stone piping found during excavations. Next to the pool is an underground passageway, perhaps leading to the basement where Sturluson was murdered.

Snorrastofa ★ EXHIBIT   Partially curated by the National Museum of Iceland, this research institute and tourist reception center is home to the permanent exhibit "Snorri Sturluson and His Time." The exhibit explores Sturluson's life and oeuvres while examining specific facets of 13th-century Icelandic society, from education, language, religion, and music to the use of geothermal heat. Snorri was the likely author of *Egil's Saga,* and his own life story, packed with political intrigue and concluding in murder, is of saga-esque proportions. Snorri's other works include the *Prose Edda,* also known as *Snorri's Edda* or *Snorra Edda,* a kind of handbook for poets writing in the traditional skaldic style inherited from Iceland's pre-Christian past. This book provided a systematic account of Norse mythology, much of which might otherwise have been lost to history. The oldest calfskin copies of Snorri's works are held at the Culture House in Reykjavík (p. 52).

Rte. 518, 5km (3 miles) from the junction with Rte. 50. www.snorrastofa.is. Ⓒ **433-8000.** Admission 1200kr; free for children. May–Sept daily 10am–6pm; Oct–Apr Mon–Fri 10am–5pm.

INLAND

Hraunfossar (Lava Falls) is a kilometer-long succession of small waterfalls that drape over the lava rock on the north bank of the Hvitá River. The falls originate from cold springs and gush out from beneath trees, creating the impression of a giant water sculpture. From Hraunfossar, a short path leads upstream to **Barnafoss (Children's Falls),** a raging ravine renamed (from Bjarnafoss, or Bjarni's Foss) by the mother of two children who went missing and were presumed to have drowned there. Hraunfossar is marked from the southern branch of Route 518, about 18km (11 miles) east of Reykholt.

Plunging into the monstrous **Surtshellir** ★ lava tube cave is an exhilarating adventure but should not be attempted without good shoes, warm clothes, and a strong flashlight; helmet and gloves are also recommended. Proceed with extreme caution: The cave floor can be slippery or strewn with loose boulders, and the complete darkness can be disorienting. The main tube extends nearly 2km (1 mile), but narrow side passageways are the most fun to explore. To reach Surtshellir, take Route F578 for about 8km (5 miles) from the eastern-most point of Route 518. Regular cars should have no trouble reaching the marked parking area, which is a 5-minute walk from the cave entrance.

Víðgelmir ★ is 148,000 cubic meters (5,226,571 cubic ft.), making it the biggest lava cave in Iceland and one of the biggest in the world. Among its dramatic rock, ice, and mineral formations, smoothed, icy stalagmites create the impression of a Moomintroll-populated underground. Viking-era artifacts found inside Víðgelmir in 1993, including a fireplace and animal bones, are now on display at the National Museum in Reykjavík (see p. 56). The cave is close to Surtshellir but can only be accessed on guided tours led by **Fljóts-tunga Farm** (www.thecave.is; Ⓒ **435-1198**). Tours leave from May until September (10am, noon, 3pm, and 5pm) and by request during the off-season.

The basic 1½-hour tour is 6,500kr per person, with a minimum of two people, though a more intense tour lasts 3 to 4 hours and costs 39,000kr per person. *Note:* These tours are not suitable for young children.

From Route 518, east of Reykholt and close to Surtshellir and Víðgelmir, Route 550 cuts southwest through **Kaldidalur valley,** passing between the volcano Ok—formerly called the Okjökull glacier until it shrunk to the point that it could no longer sink and move under its own weight and lost its glacier status—and the Þórisjökull and Langjökull glaciers before joining Route 52, which continues south to Þingvellir. Regular cars proceeding slowly and carefully usually will not encounter problems between mid-June and mid-September. (The road is sometimes mistakenly identified as mountain road "F550," and "F" usually signifies "4WD only.") However, all drivers should beware of sandstorms in high winds. Kaldidalur is recommended to those who will not otherwise experience Iceland's gritty and desolate interior highlands. The road's highest point, at 727m (2,385 ft.) above sea level, is marked by a huge cairn and has a marvelous view of a rhyolite peak to the east.

Tours & Activities

CAVING See "Surtshellir" and "Víðgelmir," above.

GLACIER TOURS The region's much-hyped attraction, **Into the Glacier** ★★ (www.intotheglacier.is; ✆ 578-2550), offers three daily trips into a manmade ice cave with LED light walls, tunnels, a chapel, and interior chambers on the Langjökull glacier. Multiple daily tours leave from Husafell or Reykjavík and run in the summer, costing 19,500kr for a 3- to 4-hour excursion. Children 12 to 15 years old receive a 50% discount, while children 11 and under are free. Heli-tours, snowmobile tours, and Super Jeep tours on the glacier are also offered. Add-ons include other attractions, like stops at Hraunfossar and Þingvellir, carbon credits, or helicopter transportation from Reykjavík.

From May to August, **Mountaineers of Iceland** (www.mountaineers.is; ✆ 580-9900) offers a "Hot Spring and Cool Glacier" Super Jeep tour, including transport from Reykjavík, that stops at the Geysir hot spring, Langjökull, and a secret lagoon near Flúðir. It costs 39,900kr, plus add-ons for snowmobile rides on Iceland's second-largest glacier or excursions through ice tunnels.

GOLF Borgarnes has an excellent 18-hole course, **Hamarsvöllur,** run by Golfklúbbur Borgarness (www.gbgolf.is; ✆ 437-1663). The course fee, 9,975kr, includes clubhouse access. Midnight golf is available upon request.

JEEP TOURS Mountain Taxi (www.mountaintaxi.is; ✆ 544-5252) has a year-round "Iceland in a Nutshell" tour from 49,500kr, which includes Þingvellir, Kaldidalur, Langjökull Glacier, Surtshellir, Hraunfossar, and Reykholt and many optional activities such as riding snowmobiles.

Where to Stay

Located between Borgarnes and Reykholt, a guesthouse alternative to the pricier hotels is **Brennistaðir,** Rte. 515, 15km/9⅓ miles from Reykholt (www.brennistadir.is; ✆ 435-1193; 12,400kr double). Of the many farmsteads in the region that have been converted into guesthouses, we also recommend **Húsafell,** Rte. 518, 66km/41 miles from Borgarnes (sveitasetrid@simnet.is; ☎ **895-1342;** 14,000kr double),

EXPENSIVE

Hotel Húsafell★★   The jumping-off point for trips to the the Langjökull glacier, this chic hotel hidden within the brush, close to walking trails and fishing spots, is becoming base camp for West Iceland adventures. The minimalist rooms are quite straightforward, aside from paintings from Húsafell artist Páll Gudmundsson, with superior deluxe and suites adding a furnished patio. The main dining room is stunning, with good food to boot; but prices are astronomical, and when the nearby cafe closes there's little other option for dinner. Rates include access to a geothermal pool complex a short walk away. The hotel can also set up stays at two standalone cottages, a cabin, and a villa in close proximity.

Rte. 518, Stórarjóður. www.hotelhusafell.com. ☎ **435-1551.** 48 units. June–Aug 32,600kr double; 46,000kr deluxe; 66,800kr suite. Rates around 30% lower Oct–Dec, and around 40% lower Jan–Apr. Rates include breakfast. **Amenities:** 2 restaurants (with 4 dining halls); bar; pools; hot tubs; golf course; tour desk; free Wi-Fi.

Fosshotel Reykholt ★   Adjacent to the Snorrastofa research institute and a 45-minute drive from the Langjökull ice caves, this rather plain-looking yet reliable hotel makes a good base for exploring the area's attractions. Decor is somewhat outdated throughout and far from inspiring, though the rooms are spacious and the staff helpful. Plenty of extras are in place, though, like Northern Lights wakeup calls, outdoor hot tubs, and massage facilities.

Rte. 518, Reykholt. www.fosshotel.is. ☎ **435-1260.** 53 units. June–Aug 24,400kr double. Rates around 30% lower Oct–Dec, and around 40% lower Jan–Apr. Rates include breakfast. **Amenities:** Restaurant; bar; spa; hot tubs; bike rental; free Wi-Fi.

Hótel Hamar ★   Part of the Icelandair chain, this surprisingly modern single-story country hotel, beside the eighth-hole green of the Hamarsvöllur golf course, sits just outside of Borgarnes, making it an ideal stopover for those driving along the Ring Road. The rooms, decorated in neutral tones and a minimalist Scandinavian style, all feature under-floor heating and decks with outdoor seating; some add glacier views. Golf packages are available. The inhouse **restaurant** (main courses 2,400–6,300kr; daily 11:30am–9:30pm; reservations recommended in summer) has a menu heavy on fish, lamb, and local produce. Cod—served with cauliflower pureé, pak choi, miso, and sesame—is a nice break from typical preparations.

Rte. 1, 3km (2 miles) north of Borgarnes. www.icelandairhotels.is. ☎ **433-6600.** 44 units. June–Aug 21,060kr double; 31,000kr suite. Rates 25% lower May and Sept; around 35% lower Oct–Apr. Rates include breakfast. **Amenities:** Restaurant; bar; golf course; hot tubs; free Wi-Fi.

MODERATE

Ensku Húsin ★   In a secluded spot near the Langá River, 6km (3¾ miles) from Borgarnes, this is one of Iceland's oldest fishing lodges. Though it has passed through the hands of several families since it was built in 1884 by an

Icelandic cabinetmaker, much of the historic charm remains, and current owners have paid considerable attention to making it as true to the original as possible despite a 2007 renovation. The smallish rooms feature wood-paneled walls and ceilings and are decorated with antique furnishings. Its restaurant uses recipes that have been passed down in the house for generations.

Rte. 533 (just off Rte. 54, 6km/3¾ miles from Rte. 1), Borgarnes. http://enskuhusin.is. ✆ **437-1826.** 19 units, 11 w/bathroom. May 15–Sept 15 23,000kr double; 19,000kr double without bathroom. Rates around 10% lower Sept 16–May 14. Rates include breakfast. Closed Christmas–March 1. **Amenities:** Restaurant; free Wi-Fi.

INEXPENSIVE

Bjarg ★ This old farmhouse turned guesthouse on the outskirts of town makes up for its rustic vibe with astonishing views of the fjord. The rooms, with their wood-paneled everything and arched ceilings, are not half-bad considering that this is where the sheep and horses used to spend their nights.

Off Rte. 1, about 1km (⅔ mile) northeast of Borgarnes. bjarg@simnet.is. ✆ **437-1925.** 3 units (none w/bathroom), 1 apt. Mid-May to mid-Sept 17,300kr double. Rates around 25% lower w/sleeping bag. Rates around 25%–40% lower mid-Sept–mid-May. Rates include breakfast. **Amenities:** Guest kitchen; free Wi-Fi.

Where to Eat

Aside from the hotel restaurants listed above, there's also **Ljómalind market** (Sólbakka 2; www.ljomalind.is; ✆ **437-1400**), near the N1 station, which sells farm products from a women's cooperative. It's a good place to load up on smoked meats and *skyr* desserts as well as local handicrafts.

Mika ★ ICELANDIC Filling the void in Reykholt's once limited dining scene, this stylish eatery and chocolate shop saves you from having to eat at a sterile hotel restaurant. Owners pride themselves on using local ingredients and making everything from scratch, though the menu trends to the familiar: langoustines, pastas, and pizzas baked in a wood-burning oven.

Skolabraut 4, Reykholt. www.mika.is. ✆ **486-1110.** Main courses 3,990kr–6,990kr. June–Aug daily 11:30am–9pm; Sept–May daily 11:30am–6pm.

Settlement Center Restaurant ★ ICELANDIC Even if you are just passing through Borgarnes and not planning on visiting the museum, this upbeat cafe and restaurant is a worthwhile stop. Food borders on the traditional, from fish soup to mussels, though a few pasta dishes and salads add some diversity. The lunch buffet offers breads, soups, and salads for 2,400kr.

Brákarbraut 13, Borgarnes. www.landnam.is/eng/restaurant. ✆ **437-1600.** Reservations recommended for dinner in summer. Main courses 2,800kr–5,300kr. Daily 10am–9pm.

SNÆFELLSNES

The jagged outline of the peaks of **Snæfellsnes** ★★★, seen from Reykjavík on a clear day, leads one's gaze westward along the horizon to the glistening white cone of Snæfellsjökull glacier, the peninsula's star attraction. With its mountainous and glacier-carved spine, black and golden sand beaches, and

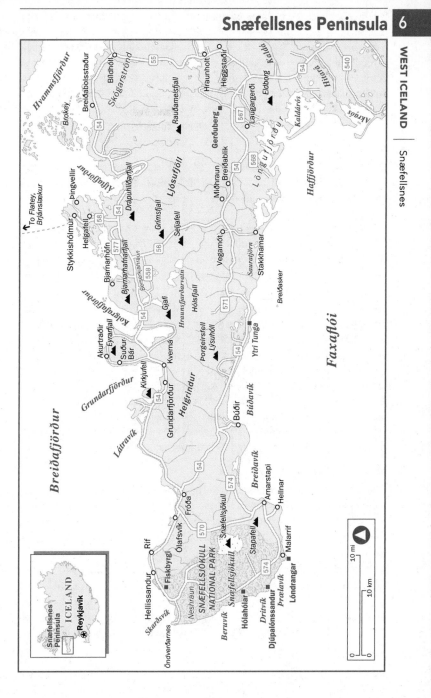

lava fields blanketed in luminescent moss, Snæfellsnes is almost an Iceland unto itself. Many come for a day, looping around the peninsula and heading back to the capital, though there is more than enough to do here to spend several. An activity tour is an ideal complement to a Snæfellsnes road trip, so before setting out, consider signing up for horseback riding or an expedition on the glacier. Another possibility is a boat tour of Breiðafjörður, leaving from Stykkishólmur, the largest town on Snæfellsnes. (Stykkishólmur and Breiðafjörður are covered later this chapter; see p. 139.)

Essentials

GETTING THERE & AROUND Snæfellsnes can be done on a long day trip from Reykjavík, but staying 2 days or longer is preferable. The peninsula has relatively good roads, and—with so many widely dispersed attractions—coming **by car** really pays off.

The **bus service** is somewhat limited. **Straeto** (www.straeto.is; ℐ **540-2700**) has a daily route from mid-June until August between Reykjavík and Stykkishólmur, where transfers to Hellissandur can be found, plus almost daily routes during the off-season (3–3¼ hr.; 3,750kr one-way), stopping at Akranes and Borgarnes.

VISITOR INFORMATION On the north coast, local information offices are in Ólafsvík, at Pakkhúsið, Route 574 (ℐ **433-9930;** May–Sept daily 11am–5pm), and **Stykkisholmur,** at the Sports Center, Borgarbraut 4 (ℐ **433-8120;** daily 10am–6pm). For **Snæfellsjökull National Park,** which includes the entire western tip of the peninsula, the Snæfellsjökull National Park Visitor Center in **Hellnar** (ℐ **436-6888;** mid-May–mid-Sept daily 10am–6pm) is on the main road through the village. A good resource outside Snæfellsnes is in **Borgarnes,** Brúartorg 1 (www.west.is; ℐ **437-2214;** June–Aug Mon–Fri 9am–6pm, Sat–Sun 10am–3pm; Sept–May Mon–Fri 9am–4pm).

A detailed map, *Snæfellsnes,* published by Mal og Menning, is available at bookstores, service stations, and tourist information offices.

Exploring the Area

The peninsula's southern coast has the most level land between mountains and sea, the best beaches for horseback riding and seal-spotting, and the most rain. The western tip is dominated by Snæfellsjökull and the lava that spouted from the volcano beneath it. The indented northern coastline has the best ports, and thus the vast majority of the population.

BUS TOURS **Reykjavík Excursions** (www.re.is; ℐ **580-5400**) offers a guided 10-hour "Wonders of Snæfellsnes" tour. Stops include Arnarstapi, Djúpalónssandur, and Ólafsvík. The tour costs 16,999kr, not including lunch, and leaves Reykjavík daily from June to August. **Grayline** (www.grayline.is; ℐ **540-1313**) has a similar tour for 19,900kr, departing daily June through August.

Tours & Activities

WHALE-WATCHING Whale-watching tours depart from Ólafsvík, with **Laki Tours** (www.lakitours.com; ℐ **546-6808**), at 9,900kr, from April to October. The most common sightings here are minke whales, which are 7m to

8m (23–26 ft.) long and only flash their backs for a few quick breaths. Dolphins turn up on two out of three occasions and put on a better show. Lucky passengers see orcas (aka killer whales), sperm whales, or blue whales.

SOUTHERN SNÆFELLSNES

Eldborg, a 200m-long (656 ft.) crater at the southeast base of the peninsula, has an elegantly symmetrical, oblong shape rising from the lava field it spawned some 5,000 to 8,000 years ago. More dramatic scoria craters are found elsewhere in Iceland—Hverfell at Lake Mývatn, for example—but for visitors sticking close to Reykjavík, Eldborg is a fairly interesting 2-hour round-trip hike. The best approach is from Snorrastaðir Farm (see box below); the turnoff from Route 54 is 35km (22 miles) from Borgarnes.

Gerðuberg, an escarpment of hexagonal basalt columns, is strikingly broad and rectilinear. Gerðuberg is a 1km (⅔ mile) detour from Route 54; the turnoff is about 46km (29 miles) from Borgarnes, on a dirt road almost directly opposite Route 567 to Hótel Eldborg.

Proceeding west, Route 54 passes Route 571 78km (48½ miles) from Borgarnes, and then moves close to the shoreline. Six-and-a-half kilometers (4 miles) after the Route 571 junction is a turnoff for **Ytri-Tunga Farm** on the left, and past the farmhouse is a beach with a seal colony, at least in June and July. The farm is private property, so be respectful of any signs, and do not disturb or try to feed the seals.

Icelanders love converting hot springs to swimming pools, however unlikely the location. The **Lýsuhóll geothermal pool** (✆ **433-9917;** mid-June–Aug 11am–6:30pm; admission 350kr) is so natural that you may find clumps of algae bobbing on the surface. The turnoff is on the north side of Route 54, 8.5km (5¼ miles) west of Ytri-Tunga.

HORSEBACK riding ON SNÆFELLSNES

The south coast of Snæfellsnes, with its sand beaches, lava fields, and sightings of birds and seals, is a wonderful setting for riders of all levels.

Snorrastaðir Farm (www.snorrastadir.is; ✆ **435-6628**), at the base of the peninsula, leads rides on the picturesque sands of Löngufjörur at an hourly rate of around 5,000kr. Accommodation, if needed, is in functional up-to-six-person private cabins (set at a weekly rate of 24,400kr per night). The turnoff from Route 54 is 35km (22 miles) from Borgarnes, and the farm is 2km (1¼ miles) farther ahead.

Hótel Eldborg (www.hoteleldborg.is; ✆ **435-6602**) has a 32,000kr package that includes a 4-hour ride on Löngufjörur,

a night's lodging (before or after the ride), three-course dinner, and breakfast. The hotel is in a school building and operates only from June 5 to August 20; the 16 rooms are simple, with shared facilities. To get there, exit Route 54 on to Route 567, about 46km (29 miles) from Borgarnes, and proceed 4km (2½ miles).

Lýsuhóll Farm (www.lysuholl.is; ✆ **435-6716**), the leading horse tour operator on the south coast, is based farther west, about 9km (5½ miles) east of the southern junction of Route 54 and Route 574 (next to the Lýsuhóll geothermal swimming pool). Tours range from 60-minute rides (6,000kr) or 8-day explorations of Snæfellsnes (23,000kr with full room and board).

Just west of Lýsuhóll, Route 54 passes **Búðavík,** a bay with lovely, broad sandbanks and the glacier as a backdrop. After Búðavík, Route 54 cuts overland to the north coast, while Route 574 continues along the south coast. Off Route 574, less than a kilometer from the Route 54 junction, a turnoff leads to Búðir, once a thriving fishing village and now just an 1848 church and an exclusive country hotel (see **Hótel Búðir,** p. 132). West of Búðir along the coast is the **Búðahraun lava field,** a protected nature reserve. Route 574 passes north of Búðahraun to **Breiðavík,** another idyllic bay for strolling beachcombers. The free brochure "Snæfellsnes: Magical Iceland" lays out walking routes in these areas.

For centuries **Búðir** was the most active trading hub on the south coast of Snæfellsnes. A hundred people lived here in 1703, the year Iceland's first census was taken. The **church** is restored and worth a look; ask for the key at the hotel. Búðir is the best starting point for walks across Búðahraun. A 2km (1¼-mile) trail heads southwest along the coast to **Frambúðir,** an anchorage dating to the Settlement Age. Ruins of fishermen's huts, fish-drying sheds, and trading booths are still visible, and whales are often spotted offshore. From Frambúðir, a trail cuts inland across the lava field to **Búðaklettur,** a volcanic crater 88 meters (289 ft.) deep. The surrounding lava flowed from here 5,000 to 8,000 years ago, and has since revegetated with mosses, wildflowers, heather, birch, and 11 varieties of fern. Unusual shade variations are found in the rock. To reach Búðaklettur from the hotel, allow 3 hours round-trip.

Arnarstapi, a growing cluster of cabins and restaurants on the western end of Breiðavík, is near a small, rocky cove. The village's coastline is popular with birdwatchers, though they could face attacks by Arctic terns, especially during the nesting season (May–June). The clunky **stone sculpture** set back from the sea cliffs represents Bárður Snæfellsás, a half-human, half-giant saga hero and local guardian spirit. Just outside Arnarstapi, Route 574 skirts the base of **Stapafell,** a mountain long thought to be an elf domicile, hence the doorways painted on the rocks.

The 2.5km (1½-mile) **Arnarstapi–Hellnar trail** ★★ between Arnarstapi and Hellnar, the next village to the west, lies within a protected nature reserve and is understandably the most popular seaside hiking route on Snæfellsnes. Of all the unusual forms of lava erosion seen from the cliff-top trail, the most striking is **Gatklettur,** a natural arch extending into the sea.

Situated on a blissful stretch of rocky coast, the fishing village of **Hellnar** (year-round population: 9) is a perfect rest stop, even for those not hiking the Arnarstapi–Hellnar trail. The Fjöruhúsið Café (see "Where to Eat," p. 132) has an outdoor deck overlooking some amazing layered lava rock formations and the **Baðstofa (Bathhouse),** a sea cave resounding with bird cacophony.

SNÆFELLSJÖKULL NATIONAL PARK (ÞJÓÐGARÐURINN SNÆFELLSJÖKULL)

Snæfellsjökull glacier lies atop a 1,446m-high (4,744-ft.) volcano that last erupted around the year 250. The national park, inaugurated in 2001, extends down from the glacier and volcano to the entire western tip of Snæfellsnes.

The **Snæfellsjökull National Park Visitor Center** (www.ust.is; ℂ **436-6860**; May 20–Sept 10 daily 10am–6pm) is in Hellnar, on the main road leading into the village. Park information is also found in Ólafsvík, at the **Pakkhúsið** on Route 574 (ℂ **433-6930;** May–Sept daily 11am–4pm). All these offices carry good topographical hiking maps of the park.

When seen from Reykjavík, 115km (71½ miles) away, **Snæfellsjökull** is a prominent knoll on the northern horizon, glittering by day and glowing red at dusk. With its near-symmetrical white cone and iconic stature, Snæfellsjökull could be compared to another dormant volcano: Japan's Mount Fuji. Both mountains have exerted an unusual grip on artists, writers, and spiritualists. Jules Verne, in his 1864 sci-fi novel *Journey to the Center of the Earth,* made Snæfellsjökull the entry portal for a scientific expedition to the Earth's core. In the Halldór Laxness novel *Under the Glacier,* Snæfellsjökull inspires an almost-hallucinatory religious transformation in a small Snæfellsnes community. New Agers make pilgrimages to the glacier, believing it to be one of the Earth's primary "energy points." Snæfellsjökull was exceptional even to the Vikings, who thought trolls lived inside it. But Snæfellsjökull—already one of Iceland's smallest glaciers—is shrinking rapidly. Since 1996, the icecap has dwindled from 14 sq. km to 11 sq. km (5¼ sq. miles–4¼ sq. miles).

ACTIVITIES ON THE GLACIER Because glacier conditions vary, you should consult the visitor center before you do any **climbing.** Generally, the best access is from Route 570, which skirts the eastern side of the glacier and connects with Route 574 on the south and north coasts, near Arnarstapi and Ólafsvík. Route 570 is an F road, so you will need a 4×4 to traverse it. Continuing 1.3km (0.8 mile) north on Route 570, you will come to a parking area near the **Sönghellir** "singing cave." About 100m (330 ft.) along the walking path is the tiny cave, and if you have a flashlight, peek inside at the graffiti dating back centuries. The cave's famous echoing potential is best exploited when you stand outside the entrance and sing.

Hiking routes from Route 570 to the summit are inconsistent from year to year. The usual advice is to walk on tracks formed by snowmobiles and snow tractors, lessening the chances of falling into a hidden crevasse. *Warning:* Conditions are worsening as the glacier melts, and as a rule no one should climb Snæfellsjökull on foot before mid-February or after late July. The best time for an ascent is from March to May. Always be prepared for a sudden onslaught of rough weather. No technical equipment is necessary, except at the spire of rock at the final summit, which is sometimes coated in ice, necessitating an ice axe and crampons. The crater, about 1km (⅔ mile) in diameter, is filled in with ice, and two lesser summits are along the ring. **Go West** (www.gowest.is; ℂ **695-9995**) offers technical hikes with gear on the glacier from July to September; it's 22,000kr from Arnarstapi, or 35,000kr from Reykjavik.

Snowmobile and "snow cat" tours up Snæfellsjökull are arranged by **The Glacier** (www.theglacier.is; ℂ **663-3371**), based in Arnarstapi. Scheduled trips run throughout the day from mid-February to mid-August, with

NORTHERN LIGHTS: aurora borealis

A brightly hued fog creeps across the night sky, shape-shifts into a solid green and red swirl stretching out from horizon to horizon, then suddenly breaks into dozens of daggers of light, piercing downward until they seem within reach. This is just one example of the *aurora borealis*, or Northern Lights (*norðurljós*), that I witnessed in Snæfellsnes; it is nature at its most magical. If you haven't seen this phenomenon before, Iceland is a great place to do so because the small population and big distances between towns make it easy to escape light pollution, even close to Reykjavík. If you need a lift to a more likely Northern Lights sighting than your hotel in the middle of town, the closest tourist information office will be able to provide details of tours. Northern Lights tours operate from mid-March to mid-April when they are best seen, but there are usually a few sightings up to early May, and occasionally even as early as late August; just keep an eye out. *Aurora borealis* occurs when Earth's magnetic field is intercepted by energy particles from the sun, which ionize atoms in the upper atmosphere. This is why solar activity is a good predictor of the intensity and duration of these auroral displays. Check out the updated aurora forecasts from the **Icelandic Met Office website** (https://en.vedur.is/weather/forecasts/aurora) for an idea about what times you might be able to see the activity each night.

If you want to capture the northern lights by photograph, bring a tripod if you have an SLR camera (or at least one that lets you leave the shutter open for 30 seconds or more).

additional 9pm and 11pm departures in summer to enjoy the midnight sun. Snow cats are tractor-like behemoths with bench space for up to 20 passengers. A snowmobile tour is 12,000kr per person (six-person minimum), and snow cat tours are 27,500kr. Prices include snowsuit, gloves, and helmet.

THE WESTERN COAST

The park map, available at all nearby tourist information offices, details many excellent alternatives to ascending Snæfellsjökull. The wild-looking peaks northwest of the glacier are particularly intriguing, with almost no tourist traffic.

At the peninsula's southwest end, **Malarrif ★** (Pebble Reef) is the starting point for a rewarding 40-minute round-trip walk east along the shore to Lóndrangar, a pair of beautiful sea pillars from a long-extinct volcano. The turnoff from Route 574 is 8km (5 miles) west of Arnarstapi, and the parking area is next to a lighthouse that looks like a rocket.

About 4km (2½ miles) northwest from Malarrif, Route 572 branches off from Route 574 and leads 2km (1¼ miles) to **Djúpalónssandur ★**, a black sand beach set amid strangely eroded clumps of lava. The partial remains of a British fishing trawler shipwrecked in 1948 lie scattered on the beach, with an information sign. The wreckage looks simply like litter, but may resonate as a symbol of Iceland's historic struggles with the British over territorial fishing waters. From Djúpalónssandur, a 15-minute trail leads to **Dritvík ★**, an equally scenic cove to the north. Remarkably, from the mid-16th to the mid-19th centuries Dritvík was the largest seasonal fishing station in all of Iceland, with as many as 600 men camped out here in spring and summer. Some remains of stone walls can still be seen.

Hólahólar, a crater cluster that is clearly visible from Route 574, can be reached by a marked turnoff 3km (2 miles) north of the Route 572 junction. The road proceeds right into the largest crater, Berudalur, which forms a natural amphitheater. A wonderful, easy seaside trail proceeds from Hólahólar 4km (2½ miles) north to Beruvík.

The northwest corner of Snæfellsnes is accessed via Route 579, a bumpy road extending 7km (4¼ miles) from Route 574. Within 2km (1¼ miles) the road passes Skarðsvík, an alluring golden-sand beach with a sign marking the Viking gravesite discovered here. Öndverðarnes is the small peninsula at the very northwest tip, a scene of multiple shipwrecks and bleak cliffs known as **Svörtuloft** (the "Black Skies"). The lighthouse here is disappointingly stubby, and the sad ruins of a well lie 200m (656 ft.) away.

At **Fiskbyrgi,** the ruins of centuries-old fish-drying sheds, simple structures of lava rock up to 600 years old, have taken on an eerie stateliness over the years. The 5-minute trail to the site starts at a parking area on the south side of Route 574, about 1km (⅔ mile) east of the Route 579 junction and just west of a 420m-high (1,378 ft.) radio transmitter once used by the U.S. Navy.

THE NORTH COAST

One of Iceland's oldest fishing villages, **Hellissandur,** is home to **Sjómannagarður** (© 481-3295; admission by donation; June–Aug Tues–Sun 10am–5pm), a humble maritime museum with a re-creation of a typical, turf-roofed fisherman's hut from the early 1900s. Sjómannagarður is on Route 574, across the road from and just west of the N1 filling station.

Ólafsvík is one of Iceland's oldest trade hubs, and today nets the most fish of any village in Snæfellsnes. The **Snæfellsbær Regional Museum (Byggðasafn Snæfellsbæjar,** the upper floor at Pakkhúsið), Route 574 at the corner with Kirkjtún 2 (© 433-6930; admission 500kr adults, free for seniors and children 11 and under; May–Sept 9am–7pm), is inside an 1841 trade post that also houses the tourist information office on the ground floor. The exhibits are mostly just antiquated household items and farm implements.

Grundarfjörður is the most picturesque town on the north coast. **Kirkjufell ★★**, its spectacular, oblong signature mountain, is dramatically located near a picturesque waterfall, making it the ultimate Instagram shot. It pokes up from a promontory west of town, while good trails lead south from town into the peninsula's mountainous spine. The **Eyrbyggja Heritage Center,** Route 54 at Hrannarstígur (© 438-1881; free admission; June–Aug daily 9am–5pm), which doubles as the tourist information office, has exhibits on the history of fishing and rural life on the peninsula and nonstop screenings of Icelandic documentaries and feature films.

The gloriously weird **Berserkjahraun ★** lies halfway between Grundarfjörður and Stykkishólmur. The lava flowed some 3,000 to 4,000 years ago and is young enough to retain all kinds of convoluted shapes, with fascinating hues and textural contrasts in the rock and thick mosses.

A SHORT HISTORY OF GOING berserk IN ICELAND

The term "gone berserk" originates from the **berserkers,** a faction of Norse mercenaries known for their savage battle frenzy. In Old Icelandic, *berserkr* meant "bear-shirted," so they may have worn bear pelts; but *berr* also meant "bare," so the name may have only signified fighting without armor. Berserkers disappeared by the 1100s, leaving a wake of mystery for future scholars. Some maintain they were merely symbolic archetypes to be invoked in wartime and as literary figures in the sagas.

The **Berserkjahraun** was named after a famous incident in the *Eyrbyggja Saga.* In the late 10th century, Vermundur the Slender of Bjarnarhöfn—a farm located just beyond the northwest boundary of the lava field—returned from Norway with two berserkers. They were difficult to handle, so Vermundur gave them to his brother Víga-Styrr (Killer-Styrr) at Hraun, now Hraunháls farm, at the northeast end of the lava field. One of the berserkers fell in love with Víga-Styrr's daughter Ásdís and demanded her hand. Víga-Styrr agreed, on the condition that the suitor clear a path through the lava field from Hraun to Bjarnarhöfn. The berserkers quickly finished this Herculean task, but Víga-Styrr reneged on the deal and killed them instead (by locking them inside a scalding hot sauna and spearing them as they tried to escape). In the saga, the berserkers are laid to rest in a hollow along the path.

The story could indeed have some basis in truth. A path through the lava field can still be found, and in a late-19th-century excavation alongside it, researchers uncovered the skeletons of two men—both of average height but powerfully built. To reach this path, exit Route 54 at its western junction with Route 577, marked "Bjarnarhöfn." After about 2km (1¼ miles), the road to Bjarnarhöfn branches off to the left. Stay on Route 577, and a sign for the "BERSERKJARGATA" trail is shortly ahead. The trail extends about 1km (⅔ mile) through the lava field, and halfway along is the hollow, now marked only by a stone cairn and a blank, weather-beaten sign. The best Berserkjahraun scenery, however, is south of Route 54, where the lava looks like a stormy sea frozen in time. Three access points lead from Route 54; the westernmost and easternmost are marked as Route 558, and the one in the middle is unmarked.

The same farm that figures in the *Eyrbyggja Saga* (above), **Bjarnarhöfn,** off Route 577, near the western junction of Route 577 and Route 54 (www.bjarnarhofn.is; ☏ **438-1581**), now produces Iceland's most indelicate delicacy: cured and putrefied Greenland shark, or *hákarl* (p. 26). Visitors can see a shark exhibit, tour the facilities, and sample the goods if they dare. **Hákarlasafn** has been featured on several TV cooking shows. Admission is 1000kr adults, free for children 13 and under (June to mid-Sept daily 9am–6pm or call ahead).

Where to Stay

The listings below—all excellent bases for exploring the entire peninsula—follow a clockwise pattern around the periphery. Places to stay in Stykkishólmur, the largest town on Snæfellsnes, are listed on p. 142.

SOUTH COAST
Arnarstapi Center ★ This cluster of stylish wooden buildings anchored by a busy restaurant have turned once sleepy Arnarstapi into a hub of activity

on the south coast of the Snæfellsnes peninsula. Rooms in both the hotel and the cottages feature wooden floors and large windows facing the sea. The standalone cottages are removed somewhat from the other buildings and are entered through a small patio.

Arnarstapi. ℗ **435-6783.** 36 units plus 10 cottages. May–Sept 28,200kr double; cottages from 36,800k. Rates about 25% lower Oct–Apr. Rates include breakfast. **Amenities:** Restaurant; free Wi-Fi.

Fosshotel Hellnar ★   Opened in 1998, with new wings added in 2004 and 2011, the Fosshotel Hellnar, near the Snæfellsjökull visitor center, is one of the more reliable hotels on the Snæfellsnes peninsula. The rooms vary in size and shape, though all feature shiny wood floors and modern bathrooms. The best rooms have views of Faxaflói Bay, while superior rooms are considerably larger and add a sitting area.

Hellnar, off Rte. 574. www.hellnar.is. ℗ **435-6820.** 39 units. June–Aug 31,440kr double; 56,647kr superior. Rates around 10% lower May and Sept. Rates include breakfast except for cottages. **Amenities:** Restaurant; bar; library; terrace; free Wi-Fi.

Guesthouse Hof ★   A few hundred meters from the beach, this simple wooden guesthouse on an old farmstead, with views of Snæfellsjökull glacier 30km (19 miles) away, is a good option for self-catering travelers. The plain original five flats are in the log cabin main building, along with some communal space. In 2012, nine standalone cottages were added, which are a variety of sizes, sleeping anywhere from 2 to 12 people.

Off Rte. 54, east of Búðavík Bay and just west of Ytri-Tunga Farm about 80km (49 miles) from Borgarnes. www.gistihof.is. ℗ **846-3897.** 6 units plus 9 cottages. May–Sept 16,400kr double; cottages from 25,000kr. Rates about 25% lower Oct–Apr. **Amenities:** Shared kitchen, hot tub; kitchenette (cottages); free Wi-Fi in public areas.

Guesthouse Langaholt ★   Open since 1978, this family-run guesthouse is one of the original lodging options on the Snæfellsnes Peninsula. Regular renovations and lots of love have kept it around. The basic yet cheerful rooms look toward the beach or mountains, while the little inhouse **restaurant** specializes in the local catch of the day, whether it's cod or monkfish.

Rte. 54, at Garðar Farm, east of Búðavík Bay about 89km (55 miles) from Borgarnes. www.langaholt.is. ℗ **435-6789.** 21 units, 12 with private shower. 28,800kr double. Rates include breakfast. **Amenities:** Restaurant; golf course; free Wi-Fi.

Hótel Búðir ★★★   Seemingly all alone on the south coast, aside from a historic church and the seals that swim by directly in front of the hotel, this is a special place. The atmosphere here is what many other hotels have tried to re-create with little success. It's partially because of the spectacular views, especially when the days are clear, when an entire spine of snow-capped mountains and windswept beaches—not to mention the glacier and a waterfall—come into view. The hotel maintains a country elegance, neatly decorating the walls with clusters of picture frames and taxidermied animals from the surrounding area without seeming tacky. Rooms are individually outfitted with their own collection of quirky knickknacks and artwork. Then there is the locavore **dining room,** the beautiful **lounge** with a golden telescope to admire the birdlife that dots the beaches nearby, and a **bar** stocked to the nines with single malt scotches and Icelandic craft beers.

At Búðir, off Rte. 574, near the southern junction of Rte. 574 and Rte. 54. www.budir.is. ⓒ **435-6700.** 28 units. May–Sept 34,900kr–52,900kr double; 68,500kr suite. Rates around 30% lower Oct–Apr. Rates include breakfast. **Amenities:** Restaurant; bar; free Wi-Fi.

NORTH COAST

Hótel Framnes ★   This former fishermen's hostel in Grundarfjörður is one of the area's most reliable options. Opt for the east-facing rooms with views of the fjord, where you may even spot a whale if you look hard enough on the right day. Extras include a full 60-seat **restaurant** with Icelandic specialties, as well as a mechanical massage chair, sauna, and hot tub with ocean views.

Nesvegur 8, Grundarfjörður. www.hotelframnes.is. ⓒ **438-6893.** 37 units. June–Aug 15,000kr double; 21,000kr triple. Rates around 10% lower May and Sept; around 30% lower Oct–Apr. Rates include breakfast. **Amenities:** Restaurant; free Wi-Fi.

Hótel Hellissandur ★   An unassuming crash pad on the main road, the Hellissandur is more than efficient. The views alternate between mountain and glacier views, though all have the same outdated furniture and surprisingly roomy, tile-floor bathrooms. Additionally, it has little extras like the complimentary use of fishing poles and hiking maps, plus they rent bicycles.

Klettsbúð 9, Hellissandur. ⓒ **430-8600.** 20 units. June–Aug 22,000kr double. Rates around 30% lower Sept–Dec and May; 40% lower Jan–Apr. Rates include breakfast. **Amenities:** Restaurant; bar; free Wi-Fi.

Vogur Country Lodge ★   Overlooking Snæfellsnes Glacier and Breidafjördur Bay, this converted farmhouse is several dozen kilometers down a gravel road. If isolation is what you are after without sacrificing comfort, this is a plus. The bright yet simple rooms were renovated in 2014. Salmon, lamb, and other regional specialties are served in the **restaurant,** though guests may grill their own dishes in the BBQ hut with meat bought on-site.

Fellsströnd, Búðardalur. www.vogur.org. ⓒ **894-4396.** 24 units. June–Sept 15 26,950kr double. Rates around 10% lower May and Sept; around 30% lower Oct–Apr. Rates include breakfast. **Amenities:** Restaurant; BBQ hut; sauna; hot tub; TV lounge; kitchen; free Wi-Fi.

Where to Eat

SOUTH COAST

Choices were once limited in this sparsely populated region, and many visitors used to stock up on groceries in Borgarnes, but options have grown wildly in recent years.

Between Vegamót and Búðir, the best dinner option is the buffet at **Guesthouse Langaholt,** Route 54, at Garðar Farm, east of Búðavík Bay (ⓒ **435-6789;** 4,200–7,900kr; May–Sept 7–9pm), with a large selection of dishes made with fish fresh-caught from local fishermen; be sure to call ahead, especially in May or September.

The most gourmet option by far is **Hótel Búðir ★★**, off Route 574, near the southern junction of Route 574 and Route 54 (© **435-6700;** reservations recommended; main courses 4,500kr–5,950kr; Mar–Oct daily 6–10pm, Nov–Feb Fri–Sun 6–10pm), with a pared-down, seasonal menu strong on fresh, local ingredients, such as lamb with celery root or honey-glazed carp and fried langoustine. On the main road into Arnarstapi, **Arnarbær** (© **435-6783;** main courses 1,800kr–3,800kr; daily 10am–10pm) is a reliable and unpretentious choice, with lamb and seafood specials as well as the usual burgers, though you'll find better fish and chips at **Mönsvagninn ★**, aka the Munch Wagon, a seasonal food truck parked right outside (daily noon–8pm Apr–Sept). In Hellnar, **Fosshotel Hellnar ★** (© **435-6820;** reservations recommended; main courses 2,900kr–5,500kr; Sept–May daily 7–9pm) serves intercontinental dishes (and you can sometimes see orcas right from your table), while **Fjöruhúsið ★** (© **435-6844;** light fare 1,000kr–3,300kr; May 15–Sept 15 daily 10am–10pm) is a tiny seaside cafe with limited seating, a sublime atmosphere, and a famed fish soup.

NORTH COAST

The north coast has a greater array of dining options than the south, but nothing worth planning your trip around—an array of hotel restaurants serving simple, good-quality dishes, the village restaurant-bar, and fast food at the filling station. In most cases you are better off stopping off in Stykkishólmur.

In Hellissandur, the **Hótel Hellissandur,** Klettsbúð 7 (© **430-8600;** reservations recommended; main courses 3,700kr–5,500kr; mid-May to mid-Sept daily 7:30am–9pm), serves the best of the Icelandic mainstays, such as fresh fish or lamb soup and a vegetarian option, at reasonable prices.

In a black building on the outskirts of Heilisandur, **Viðvík ★★** (© **430-1026;** reservations recommended; main courses 3,700kr–5,500kr; Thurs–Sun 6–10pm) opened in 2017 and has drawn much praise for its Icelandic gastro-pub fare sourced from local producers, plus craft beers and good cocktails. In Grundarfjörður, **Bjargarsteinn ★**, Sólvellir 15 (bjargarsteinn.is; © **436-6770;** main courses 3,500kr–6,600kr; daily 5–10pm), is the most elegant choice, set in a 1908 house that was actually transported from Akranes; call in advance, especially in May or September. **Café Emil**, Grundargata 35 (© **897-0124;** main courses 1,250kr–3,100kr; daily 9am–6pm), is also a good option, with homemade soups and cakes.

STYKKISHÓLMUR & BREIÐAFJÖRÐUR

As the largest town on Snæfellsnes Peninsula—and with a ferry link to the Westfjords—Stykkishólmur is often the presumed base or transit hub for any trip in west Iceland. Actually, any place on Snæfellsnes is a good base if you have a car, and most visitors headed to the Westfjords drive or fly, bypassing Stykkishólmur altogether. Yet Stykkishólmur is an attractive place in its own right, at the tip of a peninsula amid Breiðafjörður's scattering of mirage-like islands, an area rich in wildlife. Despite its name, Breiðafjörður is more bay than fjord, and its extensive shallows, mudflats, and rocky coastlines sustain one of the most flourishing and diverse ecosystems in Iceland, making it the primary source of those delicious blue mussels you see everywhere. Breiðafjörður has around 2,500 islands, but its pronounced tidal fluctuations make the final tally unknown. Most of Breiðafjörður falls within a strictly regulated nature reserve, and tours from Stykkishólmur provide opportunities for kayaking, fishing, birding, seal-spotting, and shellfish-slurping. The car ferry *Baldur* links Stykkishólmur to the south coast of the Westfjords, docking along the way at Flatey Island, a historic settlement and the only populated island in Breiðafjörður.

Essentials

GETTING THERE & AROUND Stykkishólmur is 172km (107 miles) from Reykjavík, with good roads the entire way. **Straeto buses** (www.straeto. is; ✆ **540-2700**) connect Reykjavík and Stykkishólmur (2½ hours; 4,7140kr one-way), with one or two departures almost daily (not always on Wed) in each direction year-round. Another route—also with one or two departures daily—covers the north coast of Snæfellsnes from Stykkishólmur to Hellissandur (65 min.; 1,700kr one-way), with stops at Grundarfjörður, Ólafsvík, and Arnarstapi.

The car ferry ***Baldur*** (www.seatours.is/ferrybaldur; ✆ **433-2254**) makes a scenic crossing of Breiðafjörður, linking Stykkishólmur to Brjánslækur in the Westfjords, with a stop at Flatey Island. For detailed information, see p. 141.

VISITOR INFORMATION Stykkishólmur's **travel information center,** Borgarbraut 4 (www.stykkisholmur.is; ✆ **438-1750;** June–Aug Mon–Fri 9am–10pm, Sat–Sun 10am–7pm), marked from the main road into town, is in the sports/swimming hall.

Exploring the Area
STYKKISHÓLMUR

The **downtown waterfront** is worth a stroll, because Stykkishólmur has admirably preserved and maintained its older buildings. To continue the walk, head past the ferry landing along a narrow causeway to **Súgandisey Island,** which protects the port and has wonderful views of Stykkishólmur's brightly painted buildings and the islands of Breiðafjörður.

Four kilometers (2½ miles) due south of Stykkishólmur is **Helgafell,** a conspicuous, knobby hill of columnar basalt, 73m (240 ft.) high. Helgafell was held so sacred by early pre-Christian settlers—who believed they would enter it upon death—that a decree forbade anyone to gaze upon it unwashed. Meaning "Holy Mountain," Helgafell figures prominently in two of Iceland's best-known sagas, *Eyrbyggja Saga* and *Laxdæla Saga*. A steep, 10-minute trail leads to the top, which affords great views of Breiðafjörður and surrounding mountains. At the summit are the remains of a small stone structure that may have been a chapel. The 1903 church near Helgafell's base is also worth a peek. The turnoff to Helgafell is marked from Route 58.

Eldfjallasafn Volcano Museum ★ MUSEUM   This small museum contains volcano-themed artwork, objects, artifacts, and lava rocks from the collection of volcanologist Haraldur Sigurdsson, who has carried out research on the world's volcanoes worldwide for more than 40 years. Sigurdsson, or his assistant, is usually on hand to guide you through the exhibit.

Aðalgata 6. www.eldfjallasafn.is. ⓒ **433-8154.** Admission 1,000kr. May 1–Sept 30 daily 10am–5pm; Oct 1–April 30 Mon–Fri 9am–4pm and Sat 1–4pm (other times open by request).

Library of Water (Vatnasafn) ★ MUSEUM   With Iceland's glaciers rapidly shrinking, this installation may yet become an important environmental archive. The heart of the collection, a permanent architectural installation inside a former library on a hill overlooking Breiðafjörður, are the 24 floor-to-ceiling transparent columns created by New York–based artist Roni Horn, who has toured widely in Iceland for more than 30 years. Each of the columns is filled with water from one of Iceland's primary glaciers. English and Icelandic adjectives associated with weather are inscribed on the rubber floor.

Bókhlöðustígur 17. www.libraryofwater.is. E-mail: vatnasatn@gmail.com. Free admission. June 1–Sept 1 daily 1–6pm; May & Sept weekends 1–6pm; Oct–April Sat 2–6pm.

Norwegian House (Norska Húsið) ★ MUSEUM   The town's folk museum is set in an 1832 building built with timber from Norway by a wealthy trader and ship owner. The exhibits—collections of everything from saddles to sewing machines from the original owner—retell the history of Stykkishólmur, whose natural harbor made it a critical trade link between Iceland and mainland Europe. An excellent gift shop is on the ground floor.

Hafnargata 5. ⓒ **433-8114.** Admission 1,250kr adults; 1,000kr seniors. June–Aug daily noon–5pm or by arrangement.

FLATEY ISLAND

For most of Icelandic history, Flatey—measuring a mere 1×2 kilometers— was the commercial hub of Breiðafjörður, peaking in the mid-19th century. Today the island has around 25 gaily painted homes, but only five year-round residents, who like to feel time has passed them by (though it's nice to have modern, satellite-fuelled phone coverage, too). Visitors simply take in views of Snæfellsnes and the Westfjords, stroll along the low bird cliffs, and keep the world at a manageable distance. The 1926 church is adorned with frescoes painted in the 1960s by Kristjana and Baltasar Samper; the side walls depict scenes from island life, complete with ducks and puffins, while the altarpiece portrays Jesus in a white Icelandic sweater standing over two sheep farmers. The yellow building behind the church, from 1864, is Iceland's oldest, smallest, and cutest library. Visitors in early summer should remain on the lookout for divebomb attacks by Arctic terns defending their nesting grounds.

The ferry ***Baldur*** (www.seatours.is/ferrybaldur; ⓒ **433-2254**), which connects Stykkishólmur to Brjánslækur on the southern coast of the Westfjords, docks at Flatey four times a day (twice in each direction) from around June 10 to August 22. A visitor could, for instance, board the 9am ferry from

Stykkishólmur, arrive at Flatey at 10:30am, and head back to Stykkishólmur at 1:15pm or 8pm. Departures continue year-round but are more limited outside of summer. The one-way fare to Flatey is 3,920kr. Passengers taking the full route between Stykkishólmur and Brjánslækur (5,760kr) may disembark at Flatey and re-embark later that day—or the next day. The ferry has an acceptable restaurant.

Flatey's one place to stay is **Hótel Flatey** (www.hotelflatey.is; ✆ **555-7780;** June–Aug 28,500kr double including breakfast; closed Sept–May), with snug, old-fashioned, en suite rooms inside converted warehouses that flank the market square. It contains the only **restaurant** on the island (June–Aug Sun–Thurs 8:30am–10pm; Fri–Sat 8:30am–midnight), which serves up blue mussels harvested in the bay, lamb, and light fare.

Tours & Activities

The dominant tour operator in Stykkishólmur is **Seatours,** Smiðjustígur 3 (www.seatours.is; ✆ **433-2254**), whose most popular offering is a 2-hour cruise called the **Viking Sushi Adventure** (departures daily May 15–Sept 15; 7,700kr adults, free for children 14 and under). Breiðafjörður's endless islands, abundant birds and seals, and unusually strong tides are encountered aboard a 120-passenger catamaran with a restaurant. Nets are dropped overboard so that passengers can slurp the celebrated local sea urchins and scallops straight from the shell. **Kontiki,** Austurgötu 2 (www.alternativeiceland.com; ✆ **691-5663**), offers 2- to 3-hour sea-kayaking trips around the bay, leaving multiple times per day during the summer months, starting at 9,900kr. For visitors based in Reykjavík, **Reykjavík Excursions** (www.re.is; ✆ **580-5400**) and **Grayline Iceland** (www.grayline.is; ✆ **540-1313**) incorporate the cruises into bus tours of Snæfellsnes.

BIRD-WATCHING Breiðafjörður has 65% of Iceland's rocky shores and 40% of its mudflats, attracting a rich concentration of seabirds, waders, geese, and—the most coveted sighting of all—white-tailed eagles. Flatey Island and Seatours' "Viking Sushi Adventures" (see above), are sure to please bird lovers. Seatours also schedules 3-day nature cruises of Breiðafjörður, departing from Reykjavík, with 2 nights on Flatey.

Where to Stay

Fosshotel Stykkishólmur ★ The hulking, chainlike structure that is the Fosshotel Stykkishólmur feels somewhat out of place in the uber-authentic village that is Stykkishólmur, yet it's still the most reliable hotel in town, particularly outside of high season. The contemporary style in the lobby fizzles out into a watered-down, characterless vibe as you move into the spacious guest rooms.

Borgarbraut 8. www.hotelstykkisholmur.is. ✆ **430-2100.** 79 units. Mid-June to Aug 28,500kr double; 34,000kr triple; 58,100kr suite. Rates 15%–40% lower Sept to mid-June. **Amenities:** Restaurant; bar; room service; laundry; free Wi-Fi.

Harbour Hostel Guesthouse ★   This popular hostel, artfully decorated with vintage furniture, is located beside the harbor in the historic Sjávarborg house, built in 1914 as an ice storage facility. It has 4-, 8-, and 12-bed dorms, plus a few private rooms. All rooms share bathrooms and come with linens.

Hafnargötu 4. www.harbourhostel.is. © **517-5353.** 6 units, none w/bathroom. 18,000kr double; 4,990kr dorm. Breakfast available for 1,490kr. **Amenities:** Guest kitchen; laundry; self-service bar; free Wi-Fi.

Höfðagata Guesthouse ★★   The oldest B&B in town, the quaint, centrally located Höfðagata is all-around pleasant with its garden and veranda looking out toward the bay. The cheery attic rooms and reclaimed wood furniture make it seem straight out of a Pottery Barn catalog.

Höfðagata 11. www.hofdagata.is. © **694-6569.** 6 units, 2 w/bathroom. 25,500kr double w/private bathroom; 16,500kr–21,500kr double w/shared bathroom. Rates include breakfast. **Amenities:** Guest kitchen; hot tub; free Wi-Fi.

Hótel Breiðafjörður ★   Part hostel (set in an 1897 schoolhouse with a communal kitchen, dining area, and balcony) and part hotel (in a no-frills house with a balcony), this centrally located, family-run property has been serving visitors to Stykkishólmur in some form for 3 decades. The rooms are quite basic no matter where your bed is, though they get plenty of light.

Aðalgata 8. www.hotelbreidafjordur.is. © **433-2200.** 11 units. June–Aug 28,200kr double; 11,800kr hostel double w/shared bathroom; 4,500kr dorm bed. Rates 20%–25% lower Sept–May. Rates include breakfast. **Amenities:** Cafe; free Wi-Fi.

Hótel Egilsen ★★   Contemporary design meets Icelandic history in this beautifully restored red house that dates to 1867 on Stykkish's main drag. Small and intimate, it's the most charming building in one of Iceland's most charming harbors. You can mingle with guests with a glass of wine and a cookie in the lounge or retreat to the smallish but tidy rooms with coconut fiber mat beds, goose-down duvets, and iPads.

Adalgata 2. www.egilsen.is. © **554-7700.** 10 units, none w/bathroom. 31,700kr–39,500kr double. Rates include breakfast. **Amenities:** Bar; lounge; free Wi-Fi.

Where to Eat

Narfeyrarstofa ★★★ ICELANDIC   Don't let the cutesy house with its lace curtains and antique wood furnishings fool you; this is not your typical village eatery. Seafood is the specialty here, all of it coming from the boats docked a few minutes away in the harbor. Try the blue mussels, the smoked salmon, or Breiðafjörður's famous scallops with Icelandic barley. All of it will knock your wool socks off. The wine list is small but superb, as is the selection of craft beer, including one brewed with a hint of smoked whale testicle. In between services, coffee and homemade cakes are usually available.

Aðalgata 3. www.narfeyrarstofa.is. © **438-1119.** Reservations recommended. Main courses 2,200kr–4,950kr. Daily 11:30am–9pm.

Sjávarpakkhúsið ★ ICELANDIC   In an old bait and fishing-gear warehouse on the waterfront, Sjávarpakkhúsið has a more straightforward menu than Narfeyrarstofa, though the seafood is just as fresh. Try the cod cheeks in beef broth followed by a rhubarb brûlée.

Hafnargata 2. www.sjavarpakkhusid.is. ⓒ **438-1800.** Main courses 2,690kr–3,650kr. May 15–Sept 15 daily 5–10pm.

WESTFJORDS: THE SOUTHWEST COAST

The Westfjords region feels almost like an island—which would be the case, if not for a 7km (4¼-mile) bridge of land at its base. The Ring Road bypasses the area altogether, though Westfjorders like to say they have a ring road of their own (comprised of Routes 60 and 61). To other Icelanders, the Westfjords conjure historic images of fugitives, shipwrecks, and remote villages hemmed in by pack ice through long winters. Westfjorders are sometimes stereotyped as resilient, hard-nosed survivors; as eccentrics; and—having contributed a disproportionate share of Iceland's prominent statesmen—as natural-born leaders.

Látrabjarg proper, at the southwestern tip of Látrabjarg Peninsula, is Iceland's largest sea cliff, stretching 14km (8¾ miles) and peaking at a height of 441m (1,447 ft.). Many visitors walk along the rim for an hour or two and zoom off again, but the entire peninsula, with its wonderful beaches and trails, handsomely rewards those who linger. May is optimal for birdwatchers because access to Látrabjarg is unrestricted during nesting season and few other tourists are around. Most birds are gone by September, but after that visitors can bask in the solitude and ponder the *aurora borealis.*

For drivers continuing northeast from Látrabjarg Peninsula, this section also covers the next three coastal villages—Patreksfjörður, Tálknafjörður, and Bíldudalur—and their enviable surroundings.

Essentials

GETTING THERE & AROUND

Many visitors tour the Westfjords by flying to Ísafjörður and renting a car.

BY CAR The condition of the main road to Ísafjörður has improved substantially in the past few years and is now paved all the way to the Ring Road, but the terrifyingly steep and unfenced drops remain, and the secondary roads remain quite rough. With forbearance and caution, however, drivers in regular cars can get around as much as elsewhere. Drivers coming from north Iceland have a choice of shortcuts from the Ring Road over to Route 60, which follows the south coast of the Westfjords before looping back around. Currently the best all-year link is Route 59, but the summer road Route 605 (via Route 61) is better when weather permits.

BY FERRY The car ferry *Baldur* (www.seatours.is; ⓒ 433-2254) links Stykkishólmur (on Snæfellsnes Peninsula) to Brjánslækur (on the south coast of the Westfjords) in a 2½-hour trip with a stop at Flatey island (p. 141); a restaurant is on board. Drivers headed from Reykjavík straight to the Westfjords do not

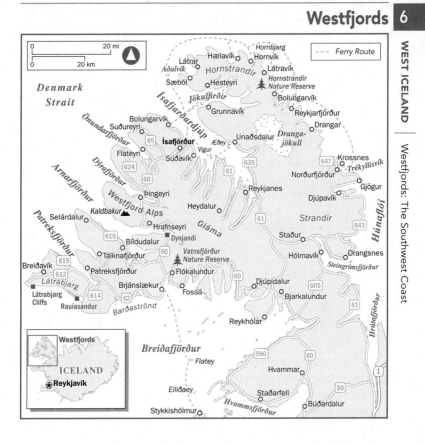

save time by taking the ferry, but can enjoy the Breiðafjörður views and bypass some bumpy roads. Drivers coming from Snæfellsnes may save a short amount of time. From around June 10 to August 22, the ferry departs Stykkishólmur daily at 9am and 3:45pm, returning from Brjánslækur at 12:15pm and 7pm. For the rest of the year, the ferry departs Stykkishólmur at 3pm Sunday to Friday and 11am some Saturdays, returning from Brjánslækur 3 hours later. One-way tickets are 5,760kr adults, 4,610kr seniors, 2,880kr children ages 12 to 15, and free for children 11 and under, plus 5,760kr per car. Passengers with cars are advised to book in advance. Winter prices are about 20% less.

BY BUS   Straeto (www.straeto.is; ⓒ **540-2700**) connects Reykjavík and Króksfjarðarnes (3½ hr.; 5,980kr) or Hólmavík (3¾ hr.; 6,900kr), at the eastern base of the Westfjords, 3 or 4 days per week, extending another 50 minutes to Reykhólar on Sundays. This route is a dead-end in terms of public transport, however.

Daily from June through August, **Westfjords Adventure** (www.westfjords adventures.com; © **456-5006**) runs a bus from Ísafjörður to the **Látrabjarg cliffs** and back (20,900kr), with stops at Brjánslækur, Patreksfjörður, and Örlygshöfn (Látrabjarg Peninsula). The bus continues to Látrabjarg if passengers book in advance; otherwise, it turns back at Patreksfjörður. The full route, which is 4½ to 5 hours each way, can be taken as a round-trip day tour from Ísafjörður (35,700kr), with 90 minutes to walk along the cliff top. The bus stops at Brjánslækur at 12:15pm (on the way to Látrabjarg) and 6:45pm (on the way back) for ferry connections. Hótel Breiðavík (p. 149) can supply van transport around Látrabjarg Peninsula for guests.

BY PLANE **Eagle Air** (www.eagleair.is; © **562-2640**) flies between Reykjavík and Bíldudalur (a village on the southwest coast of the Westfjords) every day but Saturday. Flights take 40 minutes, and one-way fares start at 24,700kr. Although flights to Ísafjörður are generally cheaper, Bíldudalur is closer to Látrabjarg, so if planned carefully, flying to Bíldudalur in conjunction with the Westfjords Adventures buses (above) could allow for a visit to Látrabjarg en route to Ísafjörður without as much back-tracking.

VISITOR INFORMATION
The tourist information office in Ísafjörður (p. 155) can provide help for any destination in the Westfjords. On **Látrabjarg Peninsula,** information is provided at the **Egill Ólafsson Folk Museum** (© **456-1511;** June–Sept 10 daily 10am–6pm).

Exploring the Area
LÁTRABJARG PENINSULA

Entering the peninsula along Route 612, the landscape's allure is soon apparent. Three kilometers (2 miles) from the Route 62 junction is a picnic table, where the fjord view opens up, extending past a stranded ship, a lovely waterfall, and a mountain alley to the ocean.

From Route 612, Route 614 works its way south over the spine of the peninsula to **Rauðisandur ★**, a spellbindingly beautiful settlement, named for its broad, red-tinted sandbanks sheltering a large lagoon. Once Route 614 winds down from the mountains, a road branches to the right and leads west along the coast for a few kilometers. At the end, past Saurbær church, is **Kaffihús Rauðasandi,** Iceland's most absurdly remote cafe, serving coffee, cake, and waffles (late June/early July–Aug 10 daily 1–6pm). Rauðisandur is situated just beyond the eastern boundary of the Látrabjarg cliffs, and makes a great starting point for a coastal hike; see "Hiking Routes," below.

Local history is admirably and painstakingly preserved at Egill Ólafsson Folk Museum, Route 612, at Hnjótur Farm, by the waterfront at Örlygshöfn on the north coast (www.hnjotur.is; © **456-1511;** admission 1000kr adults, 700kr seniors, free for children 15 and under; May 9–Aug 31 daily 10am–6pm). However, old saw blades, drill bits, and other trifles overwhelm the more deserving artifacts. The most unusual holding is a Russian plane that was stranded in Iceland in 1993.

CLIFF-SCALING ICELANDERS TO THE rescue

As you gaze over Látrabjarg, think of December 12, 1947, when the British fishing trawler *Dhoon* ran aground 500m (1,640 ft.) from the base of the cliff, prompting the most famous and dramatic rescue of shipwrecked sailors in Iceland's history. No roads reached Látrabjarg in 1947, and it took the first rescuers several hours to walk to the cliff's edge in the dark with one pack horse. (In December, the Westfjords region has only 4 hours of daylight.) When the sky lightened on the following day, 12 men descended the 120m (394 ft.) cliff by rope, while three remained on top to hold the rope fast. A rescue line was fired over to the boat, and all 12 British sailors were brought to land suspended on a flotation buoy. When darkness and the tide set in, only seven sailors and one rescuer had been hoisted up the cliff. The rest spent the night huddled together on a small outcrop. It took all of the next day, in heavy winds and rain, to hoist up the remaining men, who then had to spend the night in tents near the cliff top. The next morning, they turned down the horses that were brought over to transport them—after the 75-hour ordeal, they were too cold not to walk.

Each summer, **Látrabjarg ★★**, the largest if not the tallest sea cliff in Iceland, hosts about four nesting birds for every living Icelander. Every major Icelandic cliff-nesting species is found here. Puffins, sure to be the avian stars of your photos, start arriving at the end of April and disappear en masse in mid-August. Látrabjarg is the world's largest nesting area for razor-billed auks, identified by their black head and back, white breast, raven-like beak, and long tail. In May and June, locals rappel down the cliff sides to collect eggs, a skill that came in handy for the *Dhoon* rescue of 1947 (see the "Cliff-Scaling Icelanders to the Rescue" box, above).

The usual way to see Látrabjarg is to park at the end of Route 612, by the lighthouse, and walk east on the well-established trail along the cliff top. The highest point of the cliffs is reached in about an hour. To hike the full length of Látrabjarg, see "Hiking Routes," below.

HIKING ROUTES The south coast of the peninsula from Látrabjarg cliffs to Rauðisandur makes for a memorable **one-way hike** over 1 or 2 days. The shorter route starts along the un-numbered road to Keflavík, a small bay at the eastern edge of the cliffs, and leads 10km (6 miles) west to the lighthouse at the end of Route 612. The road to Keflavík branches off from Route 612 a short way south of Breiðavík, and should be negotiable in a regular car up to the trailhead. The equally enticing **2-day route** begins in Rauðisandur, with an overnight in the Keflavík mountain hut, which sleeps nine on a first-come, first-served basis; there is no way to reserve.

Hótel Breiðavík (p. 149), with advance notice, can arrange transportation at one or both ends of the journey, and can also drop off or pick up supplies at Keflavík. The cost is usually around 10,000kr per trip, regardless of the number of passengers. The hut almost never fills up, but having Hótel Breiðavík deliver supplies could be a good insurance measure. The hut has no formal price, only instructions on how to make a voluntary contribution later. For other worthwhile hiking routes on the peninsula, consult Hótel Breiðavík and the *Vestfirðir & Dalir* hiking map of Látrabjarg. The map is widely available on the peninsula, and can be ordered in advance from www.galdrasyning.is.

PATREKSFJÖRÐÐUR TO BÍLDUDALUR

The coastal route north from Látrabjarg Peninsula soon passes through or near the villages of Patreksfjörður, Tálknafjörður, and Bíldudalur. All three are stunningly situated and have restaurants, places to stay, and other basic services (including free Wi-Fi within village limits). Patreksfjörður is the third-largest village in the Westfjords, with about 700 residents.

Tálknafjörður has a standard geothermal village pool, 25m (82 ft.) long, with hot tubs, but **Pollurinn**—a little spring-fed beauty overlooking the fjord—is outside of town, completely unmarked, unadvertised, and disguised from the road. To get there, take Route 617 northwest from the village for 2 or 3km (1–2 miles); a driveway on the right leads to the pool, just uphill round the bend. The tiny facilities include showers, changing rooms, a shallow tub shaped like a recliner, and a deeper tub, often too hot for all but the most intrepid soakers. Admission is free all year-round.

The Sea Monster Museum, Strangata 7, Bíldudalur (www.skrimsli.is; ✆ **456-6666;** admission 1,250kr; May 15–Sept 6 daily 10am–6pm) is the primary reason to visit this cute village on the shores of Arnarfjörður. The museum entertains visitors with the history of sea monster sightings in Icelandic history, folk culture, and literature. A disproportionate number of such sightings have occurred in and around Arnarfjörður.

From Bíldudalur, Route 619 extends 25km (16 miles) northwest along a wondrous stretch of coast to Selárdalur, a remote settlement with one remaining farm, a church, and **Listasafn Samúels** (www.facebook.com/Listasafn-Samúels-323068613584/), a museum devoted to the painter, sculptor, and former resident Samúel Jónsson (1884–1969). Since the church didn't need a new altarpiece, Samúel built his own makeshift church to display his work. Outside are several crude concrete sculptures, including a statue of Leifur Eiriksson and a replica of the Alhambra Palace in Granada, Spain. Although his works could be dismissed as amateurish, his life sets a compelling example of how to reconcile artistic pursuits with poverty and seclusion. Samúel's church is left open from mid-June to August, with a box requesting donations.

Where to Stay

The tourist office in Ísafjörður (p. 155) can help locate hotels and provides comprehensive listings on its website.

THE SOUTH COAST OF THE WESTFJORDS

The few hotels scattered along this barely populated stretch of coast sometimes come in handy for those en route to Látrabjarg.

The family-run **Hótel Bjarkalundur,** Route 60, about 100km/62 miles from Route 1 (www.hotelbjarkalundur.is; ✆ **434-7762;** 28,900kr double, including breakfast; 26,500kr cottages; closed Oct–Apr), in operation since

1947, is the oldest summer hotel in Iceland, and has 16 presentable, well-priced rooms with sinks, plus six wood cottages that were added in 2014. It's an all-around pit-stop with a **restaurant,** bar, fuel, and small store.

Proceeding west, the next option is **Djúpidalur,** Route 60, about 122km (76 miles) from Route 1 (☎ **434-7853;** 10,800kr double without bathroom; no credit cards), a sheep farm in a geothermal valley popular among trout and salmon fishermen. Lodgings are straightforward, with a guest kitchen and indoor geothermal swimming pool.

The next place on Route 60—located 100km (62 miles) west of Djúpidalur, near the Route 62 junction, and 6km (4 miles) from the Brjánslækur ferry terminal—is **Hótel Flókalundur** (www.flokalundur.is; ☎ **456-2011;** 17,500kr double, including breakfast; closed mid-Sept to mid-May), with 15 small en suite rooms and a serviceable **restaurant.** A 5-minute walk from the hotel is a fabulous outdoor geothermal pool, lined with natural stones and overlooking the fjord.

LÁTRABJARG PENINSULA

Fosshotel Westfjords ★ National chain Fosshotel must have had a hunch that Westfjords tourism would be growing incrementally when they decided to open this hotel on a remote fjord. Although the setting isn't nearly as enchanting as that of the Breiðavík (see below), the rooms are more comfy and modern, with shiny wood floors, flatscreen TVs, and working Wi-Fi.

Aðalstræti 100, Patreksfjörður. www.fosshotel.is. ☎ **456-2004.** 40 units. May–Sept 25,800kr double. Closed Oct–Apr. **Amenities:** Restaurant; bar; conference room; free Wi-Fi.

Hótel Breiðavík ★★ Only 12km (9 miles) from the Látrabjarg cliffs, the westernmost point in Iceland, Breiðavík's natural surroundings are about as good as it gets in a country where spectacular vistas are not hard to come by. For making it this far out (and very few do), the reward is a pristine, barely touched bay, with a 5km-long (3-mile) golden beach backed by towering mountains. The property itself is quite basic, with size-challenged rooms and picture frames that don't seem to go with anything. The owners can set up excursions to the bird cliffs or transportation to and from the property.

Rte. 612. www.breidavik.is. ☎ **456-1575.** 30 units, 14 w/bathroom. May 15–Sept 15 33,000kr double; 22,600kr double without bathroom; 16,500kr sleeping-bag accommodation. Rates include breakfast (except sleeping-bag accommodation). Closed Sept 16–May 14. **Amenities:** Restaurant; bar; laundry; kitchen; free Wi-Fi.

Hótel Látrabjarg ★ Beside the largest bird cliffs in Europe, this former schoolhouse turned basic guesthouse is frequented by hardcore birders—few others make it out this far west. The rooms all have en-suite facilities now, with some adding ocean or mountain views. Horses and fishing trips can be arranged at the front desk.

Rte. 615, 3km (2 miles) from the Rte. 612 intersection. www.latrabjarg.com. ☎ **825-0025.** 10 units. May–Sept 41,400kr double. Rates include breakfast. Closed Oct–Apr. **Amenities:** Free Wi-Fi.

PATREKSFJÖRÐUR & TÁLKNAFJÖRÐUR

Patreksfjörður boasts a boutique hotel: **Ráðagerði,** Aðalstræti 31 (www. radagerdi.net; © **456-1560;** 30,900kr double), which opened in summer 2010. The hotel, renovated over 3 years by a designer-architect duo, boasts a beautiful interior and equally stunning views across the fjord. **Patreksfjörður** also has several inexpensive choices, all with guest kitchens.

Where to Eat

LÁTRABJARG PENINSULA

The restaurant at **Hotel Breiðavík** is open daily in summer, with soup and bread starting at noon; cakes and waffles at teatime; and, from 7 to 9pm, a wholesome set dinner menu for 4,800kr. **Hótel Látrabjarg** also serves dinner by advance request. **Egill Ólafsson Folk Museum** (p. 146) has a cafe. See also **Kaffihús Rauðasandi** in Rauðisandur (p. 146).

PATREKSFJÖRÐUR TO BÍLDUDALUR

In Patreksfjörður, **Eyrar,** Aðalstræti 8 (© **456-4565;** Mon–Fri 9am–6pm), is the resident cafe and bakery. Patreksfjörður and Tálknafjörður each have a restaurant on the standard small-town Icelandic model, serving local fresh fish, plenty of lamb, plus pasta burgers, pizzas, and sandwiches. The nod goes to the well-priced **Þorpið,** Aðalstræti 73, Patreksfjörður (© **456-1295;** main courses 1,400kr–2,800kr; June–Sept 15 Mon–Fri 11am–9pm, Sat–Sun 12:30–9pm; Sept 16–May 31 daily 11am–2pm and 6–9pm).

CENTRAL WESTFJORDS

The Westfjords are Iceland's oldest landmass, with no active volcanoes for the last 10 million years. Glaciation created more than half of Iceland's fjords but little lowland suitable for agriculture. The central coastal region of the Westfjords—with Arnarfjörður to the south and Ísafjarðardjúp to the north—is particularly mountainous, and in winter, roads to nearby towns can be cut off for days at a time. Highlights of this area include Dynjandi, the largest and most resplendent waterfall in the Westfjords; the "Westfjords Alps," a prime hiking area; and the village of Suðureyri, where locals invite visitors to experience the fishing life.

Essentials

GETTING THERE & AROUND   Route 60 is the main artery of the central Westfjords. The distance from Bíldudalur to Ísafjörður, the Westfjords capital, is 145km (90 miles), and the road is now paved all the way. Thanks to a long, three-pronged tunnel built in 1996, Ísafjörður is only 25 minutes from Suðureyri, 20 minutes from Flateyri, and 45 minutes from Þingeyri.

Two **airports** with scheduled flights from Reykjavík are just outside the central Westfjords; to the south is Bíldudalur (p. 148), and to the north is Ísafjörður (p. 153).

From June until August, **Westfjords Adventure** (www.westfjordsadventures. com; © **456-5006**) runs a **bus** from Patreksfjörður to Látrabjarg peninsula and back (20,900kr round-trip), with **ferry connections** to Snæfellsnes Peninsula at Brjánslækur; in addition to scheduled stops along the way, a pickup or dropoff along Route 60 can usually be arranged informally.

F&S Hópferðabílar (𝒞 893-1058) operates the municipal buses that connect Ísafjörður to **Suðureyri, Flateyri,** and **Þingeyri** on weekdays year-round. The schedule is posted at www.westfjords.is, but you shouldn't have trouble figuring it out. One-way fares are 320kr, and buses leave Ísafjörður from the N1 gas station on Pollgata, behind Hótel Ísafjörður.

VISITOR INFORMATION   The **tourist information office** in Ísafjörður (p. 155) covers the entire Westfjords, though most towns have an ad hoc information kiosk, such as at service stations, museums, or guesthouses.

Exploring the Central Westfjords

Dynjandi ★, meaning "booming" or "resounding," comprises six waterfalls. The tallest is Fjallfoss, an astonishing 100m (328-ft.) waterfall that drapes its way down ever-broadening cascades in the shape of a tiered wedding cake. The five smaller falls beneath—Hundafoss, Strokkur, Göngumannafoss, Hrísvaðsfoss, and Sjóarfoss—add to the charm of the area, an ideal picnic stop. Dynjandi is clearly marked from Route 60, near the head of Dynjandisvogur, an inlet of Arnarfjörður. Heading south on a clear day you will see it from the road before the turnoff.

A settlement on the north shore of Arnarfjörður, **Hrafnseyri** was the childhood home of nationalist hero Jón Sigurðsson (1811–1879). **Byggðasafnið Hrafnseyri** (www.hrafnseyri.is; 𝒞 **456-8260** or 845-5518; admission 900kr; June–Sept daily 11am–6pm) focuses on Jón, but it is also an excellent museum, giving visitors a sense of 19th-century Icelandic life. It has a pleasant cafe if you need a rest stop. Phone to arrange visits outside opening hours/dates.

In aerial photos, the Westfjords region is often identified by successions of table-topped mountains, formed by eruptions beneath the crushing weight of thick icecaps. The **Westfjords Alps ★★**, on the peninsula between Arnarfjörður and Dýrafjörður, were so named by breaking this pattern: Not only are these "Alps" particularly tall—Kaldbakur, at 998m (3,274 ft.), is the highest peak in the Westfjords—but they're topped with razorback ridges that delight photographers and entice every hiker's inner tightrope walker.

The *Vestfirðir & Dalir* series provides the best map of **hiking routes.** Given the vertiginous ridges, loose scree, and exposure to the weather, it's a good idea to register your route with the tourist office in

> ### Iceland's Only Castles
>
> All are welcome to participate in an annual **sandcastle competition** held the first Saturday of August at a beach on Önundarfjörður (from Route 60, head just over a kilometer northwest on Route 625).

Ísafjörður before heading out. **Kaldbakur** is the most challenging and rewarding climb, with stunning panoramic views extending to Snæfellsnes Peninsula. Trails approach the peak from both the north and south. At the summit is a 2m (6½ ft.) cairn—with a guestbook inside—artificially raising Kaldbakur's height to four digits.

In 1995, an avalanche crashed into the small fishing village of **Flateyri** on Önundarfjörður, killing 20 people and damaging or destroying 30 homes. As a result, the slope behind Flateyri now has a colossal, A-shaped barricade—1.5km long, 15 to 20m high, and 45 to 60m thick (1 mile × 49–66 ft. × 148–197 ft.)—designed to deflect tumbling boulders and snow into the fjord.

From 1889 to 1901, Flateyri was the largest whaling station in the North Atlantic, with most trade controlled by Norwegians. The old Flateyri bookstore, **Gamla Bókabúðin,** Hafnarstræti 3–5 (daily 1–5pm), has a small exhibit on village history.

When the fishermen of **Suðureyri ★** began taking steps to ensure an environmentally sustainable future, they were hardly scheming to lure tourists. Later came the knowledge that tourism revenue, together with carrying the banner of environmental responsibility, could form a virtuous circle. The fishermen make short, fuel-efficient trips in fiberglass boats. All fish are caught by hook and bait, a method far less harmful to marine ecosystems than the practice of dragging weighted nets across the ocean floor. No fish parts are wasted; bones are powdered for animal food, and heads are dried and shipped to Nigeria. All Suðureyri homes are heated by underground hot springs piped through radiators, and all power comes from a hydroelectric facility.

An aptly named tour operator called **Fisherman** (Skipagata 3, Suðureyri; www.fisherman.is; ✆ **450-9000**) arranges popular a **Seafood Trail ★** tour (1½ hours; 5,000kr) that takes in a fish processing plant and a local food trail to sample regional delicacies. Tours are offered daily from May to October.

Where to Stay

The welcoming and idyllic **Korpudalur Kirkjuból Hostel** (www.korpudalur. is; ✆ **456-7808** or 893-2030; 6 units, none w/bathroom; June–Aug 14,800kr double; 5,800kr per person w/sleeping-bag; breakfast available for 2,200kr; closed Sept–May) is a 1912 farmhouse at the head of Önundarfjörður (on Route 627, 5km/3 miles southeast of Route 60). Ísafjörður is only 17km (11 miles) away, and airport or bus pickup can be arranged. The hostel is also an excellent resource for arranging kayaking, sailing, and sea-angling trips.

Fisherman Hotel ★★   Friendly owner Elias has carved out his own tourist hangout in the middle of town, taking over several typical houses, which he has turned into accommodations, a cooking school, tour operator, a cafe, and the excellent **Fisherman Kitchen** (see "Where to Eat," below). His efforts have helped give visitors a window into the life of Suðureyri's fishing livelihood (see **Seafood Trail ★,** above). For this reason, many opt to stay here rather than in Ísafjörður, which is just a short drive away. The simple yet clean and cheerful self-catering hotel rooms (named after local fish) beside the restaurant are some of the best in the region, with modern bathrooms with tile floors plus the amenities of much pricier hotels. The rooms in the guesthouse are just as nice, only a little smaller and with shared bathrooms.

Aðalgata 14, Suðureyri. www.fisherman.is. © **450-9000.** 5 units in the hotel plus 13 w/ shared bathroom in the guesthouse. 26,500kr double; 17,700kr double without bathroom. Rates include breakfast. **Amenities:** Restaurant; tour operator; guest kitchen; free Wi-Fi.

Where to Eat

Dining options between Þingeyri and Bíldudalur (in the southwest Westfjords) or Flókalundur (on the south coast) are rather limited to the **Byggðasafnið Hrafnseyri cafe** and Þingeyri's **Simbahöllin Café** (www.simbahollin.is; © **899-6659;** Fjarðargata 5), a homey coffeehouse set in a 1915 grocery store with goodies like waffles with rhubarb jam and cream. Þingeyri is just 45 minutes from Ísafjörður, so many drivers headed north aim to reach the Westfjords capital by dinnertime.

Café Kaupfélag ★ CAFE   Opposite Fisherman Kitchen in an old storehouse and part of the Fisherman complex, this charming cafe (opened in 2015) is an inviting place for a coffee or light meal, or even a draft beer or two after a day at sea. Food options are limited, though fish soup is always available.

Aðalgata 11, Suðureyri. © **450-9000.** Drinks and snacks 500kr–1,400kr. Daily 6–10pm.

Fisherman Kitchen ★★ ICELANDIC   Newly remodeled, this Suðureyri restaurant, just 25 minutes from Ísafjörður, is all about the fish. Even the menus are wrapped in cured fish skins. Most of the ingredients are foraged for or grown right in the fjord, including rhubarb in a dessert that is "stolen" from a neighbor's garden. Starters include cured salmon and haddock with mustard seeds and dill, while main courses include pan-fried Atlantic wolffish in a cream and cognac sauce. Non-fish options are also available.

Aðalgata 14, Suðureyri. © **450-9000.** Main courses 3,490kr–5,200kr. Daily 8am–10pm. Closed Oct 2–April 30.

ÍSAFJÖRÐUR & ÍSAFJARÐARDJÚP

Icelandic towns present a compelling contrast of isolation and worldliness, with no better example than **Ísafjörður** ★, the likeable and sophisticated hub of the Westfjords. Even in such a remote and unlikely setting, you'll find nice restaurants, trendy shops, and cafes full of laptop users. Built on a gravel spit in a fjord within a fjord, Ísafjörður possesses an ideal natural port and has been one of Iceland's busiest trading hubs since the late 18th century. In the late 19th century, it was the same oasis it is today, with two hotels, several gaming clubs, and a drama club. The current population is under 3,000, more than half the Westfjords total. Its steep, mountainous backdrop and conscientiously preserved architecture encourage relaxing strolls around town.

Boats leaving Ísafjörður soon enter Ísafjarðardjúp (p. 159), the enormous fjord that nearly cleaves the Westfjords in half; the lovely, winding drive east along its southern shore is also the fastest route to Reykjavík.

Essentials

GETTING THERE & AROUND

BY PLANE **Air Iceland** (www.airicelandconnect.is; ✆ **570-3030**) connects Reykjavík and Ísafjörður two or three times daily year-round. The flight is 40 minutes, and ticket prices are from around 11,500kr (check website for specials—sometimes considerably less). Sitting on the left side of the plane grants views of Snæfellsjökull and the most picturesque Westfjords coastline. All flights from Akureyri to Ísafjörður connect through Reykjavík.

An **airport shuttle** operated by **Sophus Magnússon** (✆ **893-8355**; 750kr) starts from Bolungarvík and stops at Hótel Ísafjörður approximately 45 minutes before flight departure times. The shuttle also picks up arriving passengers and stops at the hotel on the way back to Bolungarvík. The driver will stop at other hotels in Ísafjörður on request. Call ahead for reservations or ask at your hotel reception.

BY CAR Drivers heading from Reykjavík to Ísafjörður have three main options. The fastest route (441km/273 miles; 6½ hr.) follows this road sequence: Ring Road (Route 1)—Route 60—Route 608—Route 61. The entire route is paved, and has been further streamlined by a bridge over Mjóifjörður. Another route (455km/283 miles; 7½ hr.) follows Route 60 from the Ring Road all the way to Ísafjörður. This route is more scenic and provides access to the southwest and central Westfjords. About a third of the route is unpaved, however. The third option is to take the *Baldur* **car ferry** (p. 151) from Stykkishólmur (on Snæfellsnes Peninsula) to Brjánslaekur (in the Westfjords), and then continue to Ísafjörður on Route 62 and Route 60. The total travel time is around 8 hours, but the driving distance is cut to 294km (183 miles). Drivers headed to Ísafjörður from north Iceland should simply take Route 61 from the Ring Road.

Ísafjörður has several **rental** agencies, including **Europcar/Bílaleiga Akureyrar** (www.holdur.is; ✆ **461-6000**) and **Budget** (www.budget.is; ✆ **562-6060**). Both are airport-based, but also deliver cars anywhere in town.

BY BUS Bus travel is usually not a convenient or cost-efficient means of getting to Ísafjörður from outside the Westfjords, but if you're coming from Reykjavík or Snæfellsnes, combining the bus with the car ferry has some sightseeing advantages.

Three connecting buses lead from Reykjavík or Akureyri to Ísafjörður. The first leg, with **Straeto** (www.straeto.is; ✆ **540-2700**) leads to Brú, on the Ring Road. Morning buses approach Brú both from the south, starting in Reykjavík, and from the north, starting in Akureyri. The next leg, also with Sterna, goes from Brú to Hólmavík. The final leg from Hólmavík to Ísafjörður runs only June to August on Tuesday, Friday, and Sunday and is serviced by **Westfjords Adventure** (www.westfjordsadventures.com; ✆ **456-5006**).

For the bus–ferry route from Reykjavík, the first leg is the morning **Straeto** bus from Reykjavík to Stykkishólmur, arriving around 11am from June 1 to 15, or 10:35am mid-June through August. The ferry then goes from Stykkishólmur to Brjánslækur in the Westfjords. The ferry does not leave Stykkishólmur until 3:45pm, so you'll have some time to kill there; from mid-June until August you might throw in the 11am **"Unique Adventure Tour"** offered by **Seatours** (Smidiustigur 3, Stykkisholmer; ww.saeferdir.is; ✆ 433-2254). The connecting bus from Brjánslækur to Ísafjörður—with service only from June to August on Monday, Wednesday, and Saturday—is handled by **Westfjords Adventure** (9,600kr; see p. 146 for other connections to the southwest Westfjords). The total travel time is 12 hours from Reykjavík to Ísafjörður, or 7¾ hours on the way back (except the first half of June, when visitors need to overnight in Stykkishólmur).

For buses connecting Ísafjörður to the southwest Westfjords, see p. 146. For municipal buses connecting Ísafjörður to Suðureyri, Flateyri, and Þingeyri, see p. 151.

The main bus stop in Ísafjörður is the N1 service station on Pollgata.

BY TAXI   Leigubílar Ísafirði (✆ 456-3518) is on call 24/7.

BY BIKE   West Tours, Aðalstræti 7 (www.westtours.is; ✆ 456-5111) rents good mountain bikes for 6,000kr per day.

VISITOR INFORMATION

Ísafjörður's **tourist office,** Aðalstræti 9 (www.westfjords.is and www.isafjordur.is; ✆ **450-8060;** June–Aug Mon–Fri 8:15am–6pm, Sat–Sun 11am–2pm; Sept–June Mon–Fri 11am–4pm), is very efficient and provides information and hotel assistance for the Westfjords.

Exploring Ísafjörður

Ísafjörður is laid out on a coastal spit shaped like the number "7" in a small fjord called Skutulsfjörður. The northernmost part of town—from the mainland to the elbow of the "7"—is known as *Hæstikaupstaður,* which loosely translates to "Uptown." Hæstikaupstaður has most of Ísafjörður's historic homes, built by fish merchants in the 19th and early 20th centuries. Before walking around town, pick up the "Ísafjörður History" **map** at the tourist office, or visit the Heritage Museum (below), which has an accessible exhibit on town history. **West Tours** (below) offers a 2- to 3-hour town walking tour on request (around 9,900kr per person, including admission to Heritage Museum; minimum two people), which smartly combines historical sites with introductions to local characters—including an accordion-playing barber.

Miðkaupstaður (Midtown), bounded by Silfurgata to the north and Mjósund to the south, is Ísafjörður's commercial hub. The main drags are Hafnarstræti and Aðalstræti, which converge at Silfurtorg, the town square. The information office is on Aðalstræti, at Miðkaupstaður's south end. The Heritage Museum, the waterfront, and most of the warehouses and industrial buildings are in *Neðstikaupstaður* (downtown), the southernmost section of Ísafjörður.

WHAT TO SEE & DO

While **Iceland Airwaves** (p. 30) in Reykjavík each October is the country's reigning alternative/indie music festival, Ísafjörður's **Aldrei fór ég suður** ★ (www.aldrei.is) is a more intimate (though very well-attended) festival held on the Friday and Saturday before Easter. Its name means "I never went south," an expression used by locals who have resisted the waves of migration to the city. Like Airwaves, international acts are included; but, unlike Airwaves, every performance is free. Flight and accommodation packages are sold by **West Tours** (below).

Other events during Easter Week include art exhibitions and **Ski Week (Skíðavikan),** featuring trail competitions, snowboard jumps, and a family day. Check with the Ísafjörður tourist office for details.

If you have an hour to kill, the quirky **Hversdagssafn: Museum of Everyday Life** ★ (© 694-4266; June–Sept Mon–Fri 10am–5pm, Sat 11am–2pm), Hafnarstraeti 5, gives insight into the daily life of people from around the region.

The Westfjords Maritime and Heritage Museum (Byggðasafn Vestfjarða) ★ MUSEUM

Set in one of four side-by-side pre-1800s buildings, this fish and fishing-industry-centric museum near Ísafjörður's southern tip is one of the town's most visited attractions. There's an informative primer on Westfjords regional history with scannable displays, plus an engaging documentary on open rowboat fishing that is screened continuously, with English subtitles. Film screenings and other events are held from mid-June to mid-August on Monday and Thursday evenings; call or check with tourist information for schedules.

Suðurgata, near southern tip of Ísafjörður (look for flagpoles). © **456-3291.** Admission 1,200kr adults; 950kr seniors; free for children ages 15 and under. June Mon–Fri 10am–5pm, Sat–Sun 1–5pm; July Mon–Fri 10am–6pm, Sat–Sun 10am–5pm; Aug daily 10am–5pm.

TOURS & ACTIVITIES

West Tours, Aðalstræti 7 (www.westtours.is; © **456-5111**), the dominant tour operator in the Westfjords, is highly recommended and has an imaginative range of offerings, from birding and sea kayaking to fox-spotting and berry picking. A particularly exciting **day tour** is the 12-hour boat and hiking excursion to Hornvík in Hornstrandir Nature Reserve. (For tours to **Hornstrandir** ★★★, see p. 166.) West Tours rents **mountain bikes** and can suggest fantastic routes, such as the coastal road around the peninsula between Arnarfjörður and Dýrafjörður.

In winter, options are abundant, particularly for cross-country or backcountry skiers.

HIKING The "Ísafjörður-Dýrafjörður" trail map (part of the *Vestfirðir & Dalir* map series), on sale for 1,400kr at bookstores and the tourist office, thoroughly outlines local trails. A pleasant, short hike (about an hour round-trip) starts from Route 61, directly across the fjord from the southern tip of Ísafjörður and ascends 220m (722 ft.) along a creek to **Naustahvilft,** a bowl-like indentation in the mountainside (Icelanders call such formations "troll seats"). A recommended **all-day hike** (20km/12 miles; 8 hr.) starts from Ísafjörður's northern suburb Hnífsdalur, ascending Hnífsdalur Valley before descending through Seljalandsdalur Valley and back into town. A municipal bus goes to Hnífsdalur roughly once an hour on weekdays (7:15am–6:45pm; schedule at www.isafjordur.is). An equally recommended and somewhat less exhausting hike (16km/10 miles; 6½ hr.) starts by a bridge at the base of Skutulsfjörður and ascends through **Engidalur Valley** along the Langá River past a hydroelectric power station, with a detour to Fossavatn lake.

Where to Stay in Ísafjörður

For places to stay in Suðureyri and Önundarfjörður (within a 25-min. drive of Ísafjörður), see p. 152.

EXPENSIVE

Hótel Ísafjörður ★★   Right on Silfurtorg Square in the center of town, this comfortable, modern hotel is one of the few reliable accommodations options in the Westfjords. There are pleasant water views from most of the rooms, which are decorated in a very light Scandinavian style, while staff is extremely friendly. The restaurant, **Við Pollinn ★** (see p. 158), is one of the best in town and is open all year.

Silfurtorg 2. www.hotelisafjordur.is. © **456-4111.** 36 units. June–Aug 23,000kr double. Rates 30%–40% lower Sept–May. Rates include breakfast. Internet specials available. **Amenities:** Restaurant; bar; free Wi-Fi.

MODERATE/INEXPENSIVE

Gamla Guesthouse ★   Operated by Hótel Ísafjörður, this 1896 ex-nursing home on a historic residential block has nine decent-size, simple, and serene rooms. Corridors are lined with old photos, and the breakfast room is bright and inviting. Additional rooms are rented in a separate house, 100m (328 ft.) down the street, with a TV lounge and large guest kitchen.

Mánagata 5. www.gistihus.is. © **456-4146** or 897-4146. 14 rooms, none w/bathroom. May–Sept 13,600kr double. Rates around 20% lower Oct–Apr. Rates include breakfast. **Amenities:** Guest kitchen; Internet terminal; free in-room Wi-Fi.

Hótel Edda Ísafjörður ★   Set near the entrance to town, this uninspiring chain hotel feels a little bit like a college dorm. Actually, it is one during the school year. Rooms are basic and bare, with just a bed and a desk.

Off Skutulsfjarðarbraut (Rte. 61). www.hoteledda.is. © **444-4960.** 33 units. Double from 23,5000kr. Breakfast available (2,450kr). Closed Sept–May. **Amenities:** Kitchenettes; free Wi-Fi.

Hótel Horn ★   The sister hotel to Hótel Ísafjörður down the street, the Horn opened in 2014. It has a fresh, new, almost modern feeling that you don't often find in the Westfjords, with glossy wood floors, black and white photography, and flatscreen TVs. The top-floor rooms have higher ceilings and an almost industrial feel.

Austurvegur 2. www.hotelhorn.is. ☏ **456-4611.** Double from 29,600kr, including breakfast. **Amenities:** Free Wi-Fi.

Where to Eat in Ísafjörður

EXPENSIVE

Við Pollinn ★ ICELANDIC   Despite its chic interior—a four-tiered wooden ceiling, panoramic windows facing the harbor, and light wood floors—the Hotel Ísafjörður's menu is quite ho-hum. It has a couple of high points, like spiced cod with mashed potatoes or the (hard to fail in Ísafjörður) fish of the day, but the rest of the menu is comprised of things like a chicken burger and steak sandwich. Keep your expectations low, and you might enjoy it.

In Hótel Ísafjörður, Silfurtorg 2. http://isafjordurhotels.is/torg. ☏ **456-3360.** Main courses 2,500kr–4,200kr. Sun–Thurs 7:30am–3pm and 6pm–10pm; Fri–Sat 7:30am–3pm and 6pm–10:30pm.

MODERATE

Edinborg ★ ICELANDIC   In the barnlike building that also houses the tourist information center, this stylish pub and restaurant staring at the waterfront is one of the more reliable lunch or dinner options in town. It's a local hotspot mainly; most tourists head either to Tjöruhúsið or Hotel Ísafjörður. The menu is casual, just a few grilled fish dishes, steaks, and burgers.

Adalstraeti 7. www.edinborgbistro.is. ☏ **456-4400.** Main courses 2,490kr–4,490kr. Daily 11:30am–10pm.

Tjöruhúsið ★★★ SEAFOOD   Few seafood lovers have ever walked out of here disappointed. One of Iceland's classic regional restaurants, Tjöruhúsið sits in a 1781 fish warehouse beside the Heritage Museum. With bench seating and long wooden tables, it's got an atmosphere that never goes out of style. The lunch menu is simple: Waiter points to the fish on a chart to let you know what is fresh, and you pick the preparation. Your lunch is then served still sizzling in the pan alongside potatoes, tomatoes, lettuce, grapes, and lemon slices. Portions are big enough for two. For dinner, the meal is served buffet style, with everyone seated at the same time.

Suðurgata. ☏ **456-4419.** Reservations recommended. Main courses 3,200kr–6,500kr. June to mid-Sept daily noon–2:30pm and 6–10pm.

INEXPENSIVE

Thai Koon ★ THAI   This no-frills Thai canteen in an unassuming strip mall is probably the only place you'll find something spicy in the entire Westfjords. The combo plates are served cafeteria style and taste better than you might expect from the food-court-like surroundings.

Neisti Shopping Center, Hafnarstraeti 9–11. ☏ **456-0123.** Main courses 1,290kr–2,500kr. Mon–Sat 11:30am–9pm; Sun 5–9pm.

CAFES & BAKERIES

Gamla Bakaríð ★ The embossed tin ceilings and everything-locally-produced feel to this elegant patisserie give it a character lacking in most other places in town. It's mostly grab and go, but there's a small seating area where you can sip an herbal tea and enjoy a *kleinur* (cruller-like pastry).

Aðalstræti 24. ℭ **456-3226.** Pastries 150kr–1,050kr. Daily 7am–6pm.

Shopping/Nightlife

Ísafjörður's boutique stores and souvenir shops are all arrayed along Aðalstræti and Hafnarstræti. For **outdoor gear,** head downtown to **Hafnarbúðin,** Suðurgata (ℭ **456-3245;** Mon–Fri 9am–6pm, Sat 10am–2pm), near the Heritage Museum.

The only dance club in town is **Krúsin** (no phone; Fri–Sat nights only), but **Edinborg** (see above) is also good for a drink on the weekends.

Ísafjarðardjúp
BOLUNGARVÍK

Fourteen kilometers (9 miles) northwest of Ísafjörður, Bolungarvík—the second-largest town in the Westfjords—braves exposure to raw weather conditions to lie close to fertile fishing grounds. Bolungarvík's **tourist office,** Vitastígur 1 (www.bolungarvik.is; ℭ **450-7010;** June–Aug Mon–Fri 9am–4:30pm; Sat 2–5pm) is next to a crafts shop and the Natural History Museum.

For dining, there's **Kjallarinn Krá,** Hafnargata 41 (ℭ **456-7901;** main courses 2,400kr–4,200kr; June–Aug daily 11am–11pm, Sept–May Fri–Sat 6–11pm), where the menu focuses on fresh catch from the waterfront.

Natural History Museum (Náttúrugripasafn Bolungarvíkur) ★ MUSEUM This museum was created primarily to house a polar bear, shot 64km (40 miles) offshore after drifting from Greenland on pack ice, that was part of a strange legal battle among the gunmen and the authorities. Most of the display cases feature stuffed animals and bird eggs, seemingly one of every species ever found in Iceland, including one lost Chilean flamingo that followed some swans, as well as the rock collection of Steinn Emilsson, a geologist who was also the local elementary school principal.

Vitastígur 3. www.nave.is. ℭ **456-7005.** Admission 1,000kr adults; free for children 15 and under. Mon–Fri 9am–5pm; June 15–Aug 15 also Sat–Sun 10am–5pm.

Ósvör Museum ★ MUSEUM This maritime museum is far less museum than a restored, seasonal fishing station. The encampment is home to several buildings, including a turf-insulated stone hut and a salting shed. A restored rowboat helps to gives a good idea of the kind of ships that were used for fishing during that time. The best part, however, is the curator, who wears a sheepskin suit similar to the ones Icelandic sailors wore back in the day and doesn't break character.

Rte. 61, 1km (⅔ mile) east of Bolungarvík. www.osvor.is. ℭ **892-1616.** Admission 1,000kr adults; free for children 15 and under. Early June to mid-Aug daily 10am–5pm.

SÚÐAVÍK

Around 20km (12½ miles) southeast of Ísafjörður, the main attraction of Súðavík is its **Arctic Fox Centre** (www.arcticfoxcentre.com; ✆ 862-8219; June–Aug 9am–6pm, May and Sept 10am–6pm, Oct–April Mon–Fri 10am–2pm; 1,200kr admission). This nonprofit opened in 2010 and holds exhibitions, screens films, and doubles as a research station focusing on Iceland's only native land mammal, the Arctic fox, best seen in the nearby **Hornstrandir Nature Reserve** (the center staff can set up tours into the reserve). An on-site cafe re-creates the diet of the Arctic fox for human consumption.

VIGUR ISLAND

Owned and occupied by the same family for four generations, Vigur is not the most scenically compelling island in Iceland, but most visitors are pleased enough gazing at the local birds—especially puffins—and vicariously experiencing the solitary island life (which in this case, we notice, has satellite TV). The family has 25 sheep and also earns money from puffin hunting and harvesting down feathers from eider-duck nests.

Every afternoon from mid-June through late August, **West Tours** (p. 166) offers a 3-hour tour of Vigur for 11,500kr, starting with a 35-minute boat ride from Ísafjörður. The walking is very leisurely, as photographers loiter to inch their way closer to puffins on the low cliff ledges. (Be aware that puffins fly south en masse in mid-Aug, and on sunny days they often go off fishing for sand eels.) Other notable sights include seals and an **1830 windmill,** the only one left standing in Iceland. Tours end with coffee and cake at the farmhouse.

HEYDALUR ★

This picturesque valley near the head of Mjóifjörður, about 135km (84 miles) southeast of Ísafjörður, provides a wonderful interlude in any journey along the Ísafjarðardjúp coast on Route 61. Tours organized by the **Heydalur Country Hotel** (www.heydalur.is; ✆ 456-4824) include horseback riding (60 min.; 8,000kr); sea kayaking, usually accompanied by curious seals (2 hr.; 7,000kr); and an hour's hike up the valley to a trout fishing lake (4,500kr rod rental). All activities wind down with a soak in a fabulous outdoor geothermal pool.

The hotel has nine simple, pleasant en suite **guest rooms** (18,500kr double) and an atmospheric **restaurant** (main courses 1,800kr–4,500kr; June–Aug daily 11am–10pm) inside a restored barn.

THE STRANDIR COAST

Flanking Húnaflói bay, at the northeast edge of the Westfjords, the Strandir coast has a mysterious allure that's difficult to account for. In many ways, the region accentuates what is already exceptional about the Westfjords. Winters are unusually harsh, and pack ice often remains into late spring. Lowland is scarce, and inhabitants are especially dependent on the sea; even the sheep have been known to taste like seaweed, their backup diet. Strandir's topography is more varied than most of the Westfjords, and the abundance of driftwood lends an enchanting and melancholic cast to the shoreline. Historically,

Strandir's villages have been among the most isolated in the country; outlaws have sought refuge on its austerely beautiful upland moors. Whatever the cause, visitors often describe the Strandir coast in quasi-mystical terms.

Those not keen on roughing it in Hornstrandir—or without the time to spare—can still reach the astonishing sea cliffs at **Hornbjarg ★★★** on day tours from Norðurfjörður twice a week in summer (see p. 166).

Essentials

GETTING THERE No public buses venture up the Strandir coast past Hólmavík and Drangsnes, so a rental car is indispensable. Car rental is not available in Hólmavík or Gjögur, Strandir's only airport, so drivers usually arrive from Reykjavík, Ísafjörður, or Akureyri. Hólmavík, a village at the base of Strandir, is along Route 61, 224km (139 miles) from Ísafjörður and 274km (170 miles) from Reykjavík. A few kilometers north of Hólmavík, Route 643 branches off from Route 61 and heads up the coast, ending 96km (60 miles) later at Norðurfjörður.

Eagle Air (www.eagleair.is; ✆ **562-2640**) flies two to three times a week from Reykjavík to Gjögur (from 28,000kr one-way; 40 min.), 16km (10 miles) southeast of Norðurfjörður.

Straeto buses (www.straeto.is; ✆ **540-2700**) connecting Ísafjörður to towns outside the Westfjords stop at Hólmavík; see below.

VISITOR INFORMATION The tourist office for all of Strandir is in **Hólmavík,** Norðurtún 1 (✆ **451-3111;** June 10–Aug daily 9am–5pm), at the community center.

Exploring the Strandir Coast

The coastal route from Hólmavík to Norðurfjörður on Route 643 is among the most scenic, rugged, and hypnotic drives in all of Iceland. Norðurfjörður has a general store with basic groceries, fuel (operable 24 hr. by credit card), and a bank (open weekdays 1–4pm). Also make sure to pick up a **hiking map** at the Hólmavík tourist office (above).

HÓLMAVÍK

Museum of Icelandic Sorcery and Witchcraft (Galdrasýning á Ströndum) ★ MUSEUM Unlike the rest of Europe, mass hysteria regarding witches and sorcerers never really took hold in Iceland. The Strandir Coast, however, was a relative hotspot of sorcery. From 1625 to 1685, around 120 alleged sorcerers were tried across the country, with 25 burned at the stake (23 of them men), plus many others accused, tried, or flogged. Admission into the two-level exhibit includes a 30-minute audio tour that explains each of the display cases, which contain creepy items, mostly re-created accessories like the "necropants," which are made of human skin and allegedly used by Icelandic sorcerers. The only real artifact here is an ancient "blood stone" used for animal sacrifices. Most appreciate the attached **restaurant** more than the museum.

Höfðagata 8–10. www.galdrasyning.is. (Sorcerer's Cottage ✆ **451-3525.**) Admission 950kr adults; free for children 11 and under. June–Sept 15 daily 11am–6pm; rest of year by request.

DJÚPAVÍK ★★★

The little village of Djúpavík lies on the stunningly beautiful inlet of Reykjarfjörður fjord. The soulful **Hótel Djúpavík** is the ideal base for exploring Strandir. Activities arranged by the hotel (see "Where to Stay," p. 163) include sea fishing and sea kayaking—no experience necessary—and touring the ruins of a herring factory next door, where art exhibitions are frequently held.

Djúpavík's first houses went up in 1917, soon after herring were discovered in Reykjarfjörður. The factory, finished in 1935, was an engineering marvel and the largest concrete structure in Europe. The herring trade was so lucrative that the factory paid for itself in a single 5-month season. During peak summers, 200 workers—mostly teenage girls—worked the machinery round the clock. In the early 1950s, the herring simply failed to show up, and in 1971 Reykjarfjörður was completely abandoned. Today the only winter residents are the members of a growing family who have run the hotel since 1985.

Guided 45-minute tours of the factory ruins start at 2pm daily from mid-June through August; the 1,000kr cost includes an informative photo-and-text exhibit in an anteroom. The factory is certainly atmospheric, but interest will vary; for some it's just crumbling concrete and rusting metal, while for others it's equal to the Roman Coliseum. Exploring on your own is prohibited for safety reasons.

For further information on Djúpavík, and an extensive online photo gallery of the Strandir coast, visit the hotel website, **www.djupavik.com**.

GJÖGUR, TRÉKYLLISVÍK & NORÐURFJÖRÐUR

Gjögur, near the tip of the peninsula north of Reykjarfjörður, has a cluster of summer homes. A crude road winds past Gjögur's minuscule airport to **Gjögurstrond ★**, an evocative stretch of beach and rocky coastline, with steam drifting from underground hot springs.

The next bay to the north is **Trékyllisvík,** and on its south shore is the 19th-century church at Árnes. In February 1991, during a severe windstorm, the church was lifted off its foundation and deposited a few feet over, but nothing inside was damaged. Next to the church is the small museum **Minja-og Handverkshúsið Kört** (kort@trekyllisvik.is; ✆ **451-4025;** admission 500kr; June–Aug daily 10am–6pm), with a haphazard, regional collection of textiles, dolls, and various fishing and farming artifacts.

Norðurfjörður, a tiny village at the north end of Trékyllisvík, has the only market and fuel beyond Hólmavík. From late June to mid-August, a boat departs from here three times a week for Hornstrandir Nature Reserve (p. 164). Route 643 ends at Norðurfjörður, but a coastal road continues another 4km (2½ miles) to Krossnes farm. Shortly after passing the farm, a driveway on the right leads downhill to **Krossneslaug ★★**, or Krossnes, about 90 minutes beyond Djúpavík and one of Iceland's most sublime geothermal pools. A gorgeous stone beach is just a few feet away, and some intrepid souls brave the freezing ocean water before scrambling back to the heated pool. (Do not attempt this without shoes for traversing the rocks.) The pool is large enough to swim laps, and the temperature is perfect. The pool is open any time, but twilight is especially idyllic. The changing facilities were renovated in 2015.

OUTDOOR ACTIVITIES

HIKING The *Vestfirðir and Dalir* ("Westfjords and Valleys") hiking map series, available at the Hólmavík tourist office (and sold online at www.strandir.is/hikingmaps), includes several maps covering the Strandir area and details the most worthwhile hikes, with thorough directions, distances, and difficulty ratings. The hikes recommended below are of moderate difficulty.

A 5km (3-mile) **loop hike** from Hótel Djúpavík heads up a steep cleft behind the hotel, then east along a plateau with fabulous fjord views before descending to meet Route 643; allow 3 hours to stop and smell the mosses.

Starting from Naustvík on the north shore of Reykjarfjörður, an ancient footpath heads through a scenic mountain pass to Árnes on Trékyllisvík Bay; the route is 3.5km (2 miles) and about 90 minutes each way.

Just north of Gjögur is **Reykjaneshyrna,** a small mountain and sea cliff rising conspicuously between the road and the ocean. You can either approach from the Gjögur airfield, or park much closer—at a blue sign for Reykjaneshyrna along Route 643—to make the 90-minute round-trip climb. The top has great views in all directions.

Another excellent hike is a 4- to 5-hour clockwise loop starting from **Krossneslaug.** Walk back to Norðurfjörður, then turn right on Route 647, which heads overland to Munaðarnes Farm, on the coast of Ingólfsfjörður. Then continue around the peninsular coastline—first on an unmarked trail, then along a road—back to Krossnes for a triumphal dip in the pool.

Where to Stay

Djúpavík and Norðurfjörður, on the northern stretch of the Strandir coast, are the most memorable places to stay. If you need lodging anywhere in Strandir's southern portion, contact the **Hólmavík information center** (p. 161) or visit **www.westfjords.is**.

Hótel Djúpavík ★★ Dating to 1938, when Djúpavík was a major name in the herring trade, this former boardinghouse for female workers is one of the most atmospheric on the Strandir coast, if not all of Iceland. Although it's not luxurious—rooms lack bathrooms, beds are small, and everything is faded—there's just something about this place that is hard not to fall in love with. Rooms get booked up months in advance for the summer season, and owners open up extra spaces at the less-expensive Lækjarkot and Álfasteinn Cottages, though turning up without a reservation is not recommended. Árneshreppur, 522. www.djupavik.com. ✆ **451-4037.** 8 double rooms, none with bathroom. 22,600kr double. Breakfast available (1,800kr). **Amenities:** Restaurant; tours; free Wi-Fi in common areas.

NORÐURFJÖRÐUR

Gistiheimilið Bergistanga (www.bergistangi.is; ✆ **451-4003;** 6,500kr sleeping-bag accommodation; no credit cards) has serviceable rooms with sleeping-bag accommodations (made-up beds on request). It serves breakfast, but only on request (1,800kr). A 10-minute walk from the general store is **Valgeirsstaðir mountain hut (Gistiskáli Ferðafélag Íslands)** (© **451-4017;** 3,200kr per person sleeping-bag accommodation; closed Sept–June), with a well-equipped kitchen, a hot shower, and eight rooms, each accommodating up to six people in sleeping bags. Booking must be done online through the hiking group **Ferðafélag Íslands** (www.fi.is; © **568-2533**). If you show up and space is available, you won't be turned away.

Where to Eat

Hólmavík has a large **supermarket** for stocking up on supplies; Norðurfjörður has a far more rudimentary one. No restaurants are north of Hótel Djúpavík.

Cafe Riis ★ ICELANDIC   The driftwood floorboards and carved magic symbols on the bar inside Hólmavík's oldest building give Cafe Riis a very localized feel. The food is mostly above-average pub grub like pizza and burgers, with a few local dishes thrown in.

Hafnarbraut 39, Hólmavík. © **451-3567.** Main courses 2,090kr–4,290kr. Sun–Fri 11:30am–11:30pm; Sat 11:30am–3am; kitchen closes daily 10pm.

Galdur ★★ ICELANDIC   Although a sorcery museum is probably not the first place you think of for a nice meal, this made-to-order restaurant has some of the best dishes in the Westfjords. The menu is classic, centering on regional specialties like steamed blue mussels or leg of lamb, as well as veggie burgers.

Höfðagata 8–10, Hólmavík. www.galdrasyning.is. © **451-3525.** Main courses 1,800kr–4,900kr. Daily 11am–6pm in summer.

Hótel Djúpavík ★ ICELANDIC   The only reason you'll ever dine here is if you are staying at the hotel or passing through on your way to or from the pool at Krossneslaug, but it's still one of the better dining options in the region during the summer. Some of the recipes have been passed down through the house or are just all-around home-cooked classics, like the fish soup. Other dishes have touches of Asia or the Mediterranean. Toward the end of summer, ask for the *skyr* with freshly picked berries. If you are just stopping by, call ahead and let them know.

Rte. 643, Djúpavík. http://djupavik.is. © **451-4037.** Main courses 2,650kr–4,990kr. Mid-June to Aug daily 8am–9:30pm, with dinner starting at 6pm; other times of year call ahead.

HORNSTRANDIR NATURE RESERVE

Among Iceland's coastal areas, **Hornstrandir ★★★**—the spiky peninsula at the northern tip of the Westfjords—is the truest wilderness. Because of its harsh climate, few Icelanders ever settled here, and the last full-time residents left in 1952. It has no roads, no airstrips, no powerful rivers for hydroelectricity, and just one hot spring for geothermal heat. Hornstrandir was designated a nature reserve in 1975; since grazing by horses and sheep is forbidden, the vegetation—from mossy tundra to meadows full of wildflowers—now resembles that from when the Vikings first arrived. Arctic foxes, seen scurrying by day and heard cackling at night, are also protected. The coast is lined with idyllic sandy bays, spooky abandoned homes, and rugged sea cliffs teeming with birdlife. Other visitors are few and far between.

Visiting Hornstrandir can require careful planning, but the logistics are not as difficult as they're often made out to be. The best time to come is from late June to mid-August; to cut weather risks, most visitors arrive the second half of July or the first week of August.

Essentials

VISITOR INFORMATION   The best source is the tourist office in Ísafjörður (p. 155). The Environment Agency website **www.ust.is** (click "Protected Areas," then "Tourist Information") has very useful general information.

GETTING THERE & AROUND   For those not taking a tour, the general procedure is to sketch out an itinerary in sync with ferry schedules. Most visitors take **ferries** to Hornstrandir from Ísafjörður or Bolungarvík, the village 14km (9 miles) northwest of Ísafjörður. The other option is ending up in Norðurfjörður on the Strandir coast, though it is a 16km (10-mile) **walk** between Norðurfjörður and the tiny Gjögur airport (p. 161), which has one weekly **flight** to and from Reykjavík. Hardcore hikers sometimes walk into Hornstrandir over several days, starting from Unaðsdalur, at the end of Route 635 on the north shore of Ísafjarðardjúp.

Contrary to what many have heard, **camping** is not necessary in Hornstrandir (see "Where to Stay," p. 167). If you like to camp but don't enjoy lugging your tent and gear around in a heavy backpack, the ferry system allows you to set up base camps from which to explore. **West Tours** (below) acts as an agent for all ferries below and can even arrange for packages to be sent in.

> ## Don't Stand Up the Ferry Man
>
> If you're touring independently in the Nature Reserve, your ferry operator will ask when and where you expect to be picked up. If your plans change, relay a message to the boat operator through a guesthouse or another visitor. Otherwise, an expensive search-and-rescue mission will probably be launched.

Sjóferðir (www.sjoferdir.is; © **456-3879**), based in Ísafjörður, has a weekly ferry service to Grunnavík, Hesteyri, Aðalvík, Veiðileysufjörður, Hrafnfjörður, and Hornvík from late June to late August. The schedule at the website is misleading, because many listed departures are only for arranged tours with West Tours (below).

The ferry run by **Borea Adventures** (www.boreaadventures.com; © **456-3322**) leaves from Bolungarvík and has irregular service (phone to check or book) to Grunnavík, Hesteyri, and Aðalvík from mid-June through August (all prices one-way).

Tours

If you'd like a private guide instead of a group tour, contact the Ísafjörður tourist office, which keeps a list of licensed guides.

West Tours, Aðalstræti 7, Ísafjörður (www.westtours.is; ✆ **456-5111**), the most reputable tour operator, offers scheduled day tours to Hesteyri (9 hr.; 18,900kr) and Hornvík (12 hr.; 32,900kr), guided day hikes from Sæból (in Aðalvík) to Hesteyri (12 hr.; 25,850kr), and spectacular 4-day, 3-night camping expeditions to Hornvík (82,000kr).

Iceland's premier hiking group, **Ferðafélag Íslands,** Mörkin 6, Reykjavík (www.fi.is; ✆ **568-2533**), leads a variety of Hornstrandir trips into October.

Borea Adventures, Hlíðarvegur 38, Ísafjörður (www.boreaadventures. com; ✆ **899-3817**), offers marvelous 6-day Hornstrandir trips (252,000kr, including food and equipment) aboard its 18m (60-ft.) racing yacht. Participants alight from the yacht for kayaking, observing wildlife, or, in winter, backcountry skiing.

Hiking Hornstrandir

The *Vestfirðir & Dalir* series (p. 151) includes the best Hornstrandir map. The maps indicate which trails are passable only at low tide, and the Ísafjörður information office can supply tide tables. Also make sure to bring a compass, shoes for fording streams, and plenty of warm clothing. Most clear running water is safe to drink, unless it passed through bird nesting areas. Hiking alone is not a good idea.

When sketching out an itinerary, always allow extra time to get from one place to another. Harsh weather or thick fog could roll in, and even the few marked trails can be difficult to follow. (It never gets completely dark, so you can always take your time.) Trails at higher altitudes may have deep snow even in July. Take note of nearby emergency huts, which have radios, heaters, and food. Check weather reports and review the challenges of your route with the Ísafjörður tourist office.

No one itinerary stands out in Hornstrandir, but one sight is decidedly worth putting at the top of your list. **Hornbjarg ★★★,** a sea cliff on Hornstrandir's north coast, just east of Hornvík bay, is the most spectacular landmark on Iceland's coastline. From its narrow summit, the inland slope descends in a surreal parabolic curve. Gazing down at the birds and surf from the 534m (1,752-ft.) ledge—which is also the highest point on Hornstrandir—is exhilarating and unforgettable. Campers stationed in **Hornvík ★★,** the bay just west of Hornbjarg, should venture to the sea cliff **Hælavíkurbjarg ★★,** the canyon river **Gljúfurá ★,** and **Hornbjargsviti ★,** the lighthouse at Látravík. The guesthouse connected to the lighthouse is almost as convenient a base as Hornvík.

On the south side of Hornstrandir, which is more accessible from Ísafjörður, the ghost town of **Hesteyri ★** is another excellent base camp for hikes. Hesteyri's population peaked at 80 in the 1930s, when the herring trade was in full swing, and a forlorn, long-abandoned whaling station lies close by.

Hornstrandir's other main settlement was at **Aðalvík** ★★, a 6-hour hike overland from Hesteyri. Some hikers continue from Aðalvík to Straumnes lighthouse, the Rekavíkurvatn lagoon, Fljótsvatn lake, and back to Hesteyri in a memorable, 3-day clockwise loop. The hike between Hesteyri and Hornvík is somewhat demanding and takes 2 days, with an overnight in Hælavík.

This brief overview hardly exhausts the endless hiking and camping possibilities in Hornstrandir, not to mention the equally pristine wilderness south of the nature reserve, including Snæfjallaströnd peninsula and the uplands surrounding Drangajökull, the biggest glacier in the northern half of Iceland.

Campers are trusted to respect the land and pick up after themselves. The truly responsible don't even leave a trace of toilet paper. Fires are prohibited. Make sure to keep food inside your tent at night so as not to attract foxes.

Where to Stay

All guesthouses in Hornstrandir require that you bring your own sleeping bag. All have guest kitchens and are open from around mid-June to mid-August. If any guesthouse proves difficult to reach, **West Tours** (p. 156) can act as a booking agent. *Note:* No Hornstrandir guesthouses accept credit cards.

Within the nature reserve, the best place to stay is **Kvíar Lodge,** a restored farmhouse run by **Borea Adventures** (www.boreaadventures.com; ✆ **456-3322**), with 15 beds, a wood-burning sauna, kayaks, and Zodiacs. Guests usually book accommodation as part of a tour package. The most accessible guesthouse from Ísafjörður is **Læknishúsið** (www.hesteyri.net; ✆ **456-1123;** 16,000kr per person); this former doctor's house is in Hesteyri, an abandoned village on Hornstrandir's south coast. On the north coast, a few kilometers east of Hornvík, a building adjoined to the **Hornbjargsviti Lighthouse** sleeps 40 in seven separate rooms (www.fi.is; ✆ **566-6752;** 8,500kr per person).

Grunnavík, at the tip of the Snæfjallaströnd Peninsula south of Hornstrandir, is included in some ferry routes and has the guesthouse **Ferðaþjónustan Grunnavík** (grunnavik@grunnavik.is; ✆ **862-8411;** 6,500kr per person).

Wild camping in the nature reserve is free. All the above have tent sites for around 3,000kr per person, including use of facilities.

NORTH ICELAND

The north of Iceland is tucked just beneath the Arctic Circle and Greenland Sea, but the weather is relatively hospitable and the land forgiving. Northerners gloat about their climate, which is sunnier and drier than the southwest in summer. The multiform northern coast bears little resemblance to the south coast, which is dominated by glaciers and worked over by the flow of glacial sediments. The north has the highest population of any region outside the southwest corner; even cod and puffins are migrating to the north coast as the oceans warm.

Most visitors cluster in the near northeast region comprising **Akureyri,** Iceland's thriving northern capital; **Mývatn,** a wonderland of lava forms, multi-hued geothermal fields, and birdlife; **Húsavík,** Iceland's whale-watching mecca; and **Jökulsárgljúfur,** an extensive canyon full of magisterial rock formations and waterfalls.

Touring within this so-called "Diamond Circle"—a bit of marketing one-upmanship based on the popular "Golden Circle" in the southwest—you may keep seeing the same tourists, who can access all these sights by day from the same accommodation. Venture west of Akureyri or east of Jökulsárgljúfur and the tourist sightings quickly diminish. Visitors zoom past Húnaflói on the Ring Road, but would not regret an excursion to a seal colony on its Vatnsnes peninsula, or the stone church at Þingeyrar.

The Skagafjörður region offers **Glaumbær,** Iceland's best museum of preserved 19th-century farm buildings; **Hólar,** seat of Iceland's northern bishopric in the Catholic era; and **Siglufjörður,** a fjord town as scenically situated as any in the country. The Arctic Circle cuts right through the tiny island of **Grímsey,** which exerts a mystical pull on those visitors who can't resist remote islands. The northeast corner of Iceland, with its driftwood beaches, sea cliffs, lonely moors, and misty lakes and lagoons, is a wonderful place to forget about hectic, goal-oriented travel.

HÚNAFLÓI

Húnaflói (Bear Cub Bay) lies between the Westfjords and Skagi Peninsula, and its environs are among the least tourist-trodden in the country. Drivers heading from Reykjavík to Akureyri on the Ring Road mostly see undulating agricultural land, but few dramatic landmarks to beckon them off course. Anyone passing

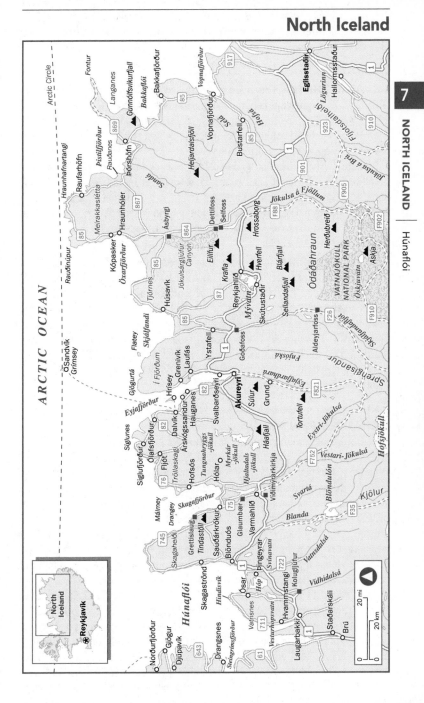

through, however, should consider a daytime or overnight detour, particularly for **seal-watching** on Vatnsnes peninsula or visiting the **19th-century stone church** at Þingeyrar.

Essentials

GETTING THERE   The main hubs in Húnaflói are Hvammstangi and Blönduós. Hvammstangi is 6km (3¾ miles) north of the Ring Road on Route 72, 197km (122 miles) north of Reykjavík, and 203km (126 miles) west of Akureyri. Blönduós is along the Ring Road, 243km (151 miles) from Reykjavík and 145km (90 miles) from Akureyri.

Straeto (www.straeto.is; ✆ **540-2700**) runs at least one **bus** daily year-round between Reykjavík and Akureyri, stopping at Hvammstangi and Blönduós. Reykjavík to Hvammstangi is 3 hours and 20 minutes; a ticket costs 5,980kr; Akureyri to Hvammstangi is 3 hours and costs 4,600kr; Reykjavík to Blönduós is 4 hours for 7,360kr; Akureyri to Blönduós is 2 hours and 10 minutes and costs 3,220kr.

VISITOR INFORMATION   The best tourist info for Húnaflói is in **Blönduós** (www.northwest.is; ✆ **452-4520;** June 1–Aug 23 daily 8am–8pm), just off the Ring Road on Brautarhvammur; look for the international flagpoles. In **Hvammstangi,** tourist info is at the **Icelandic Seal Center (Selasetur Íslands),** Brekkugata 2 (www.selasetur.is; ✆ **451-2345;** June–Aug daily 9am–6pm, Sept 1–15 Mon–Fri 10am–4pm). In the off-season, rely on the regional tourist office at **Varmahlíð** (www.visitskagafjordur.is; ✆ **455-6161;** June 1–14 and Sept daily 9am–5pm, June 15–Aug daily 9am–7pm, Oct–May daily 10am–3pm) in nearby Skagafjörður.

Exploring Húnaflói

VATNSNES PENINSULA

Húnaflói is home to the majority of **Icelandic harbor seals** (plus a few gray seals), and the best place to spot them is on this nubby peninsula west of Blönduós. The peninsula's only town, **Hvammstangi,** is at its southwestern base. Vatnsnes has a mountainous interior, but its shores blend wild coastline with fertile grazing land for horses and sheep. Seals can be viewed any time of year. Centuries of hunting have not made the seals any less curious about humans, and they like to shadow your movements from a distance. The seal population is just a third of what it was in 1980, but not because of the viral disease that has affected seal populations in Europe. It is extremely important not to disturb or try to feed them.

The "World of the Sea People" exhibit at Hvammstangi's **Icelandic Seal Center (Selasetur Íslands),** at Brekkugata 2 (www.selasetur.is; ✆ **451-2345;** June–Aug daily 9am–5pm, Sept 1–30 Mon–Fri 10am–2pm) is a good primer on seal biology, seal/human relations, and seal-related folklore, and the staff are very helpful and give updates on current seal-viewing locations. Admission is 1,100kr adults and 750kr for children ages 12 to 16.

From Hvammstangi, Route 711 follows the periphery of Vatnsnes. On clear days, the west side of the peninsula has **great views** of the Strandir coast.

Signs are sometimes posted at turnoffs for viewing platforms to spot seal colonies. A particularly accessible **seal colony** is on the peninsula's western shore, about 15km (9 miles) north of Hvammstangi and just north of the Hamarsrétt sheep round-up pen, which is marked from the road.

About 26km (16 miles) farther along the western coastal road of the Vatnsnes peninsula on Route 711 from Hvammstangir is **Illugastaður,** currently the best place to view the seal colonies. From the main parking lot, a trail leads about 900m (3,000 ft.) to a viewing platform with superb views of Strandir. Illugastaðir also has a coffee shop (② **451-2664;** June 20–Aug 20 daily 2pm–6pm) with camping (1,200kr adults, free for children 15 and under) and bathroom facilities. The area is closed between April 20 and June 20 because of eider-duck nesting.

Ósar ★ is the most idyllic spot on Vatnsnes for an overnight stay and another great place to watch seals (see Ósar Youth Hostel, p. 173). **Hvítserkur ★**, just off the shoreline near Ósar, is a bizarre, M-shaped, 15m-high (49-ft.) basalt crag with its own bird population. To reach this must-do photo stop, turn off Route 711 a short distance north of Ósar and proceed to the parking area. Scramble down to the black sand beach and, if the tide is low, walk into Hvítserkur's arches. Head south along the beach for 20 minutes, past the resident ducks and harbor seals that are likely lounging on the sands across the channel (one or two seals will probably swim over to investigate). From this part of the beach, it's a 10-minute walk uphill to Ósar.

ÞINGEYRAR

The distinctive stone **Þingeyrar Church ★** (② **452-4473;** free admission; June–Aug daily 10am–5pm) lies on pastureland east of Vatnsnes peninsula. It was built between 1864 and 1877, and financed entirely by Ásgeir Einarsson, a local farmer and member of parliament. While most Icelandic churches from this time are sided with sheets of corrugated iron made to resemble painted wood, Þingeyrar was constructed at great expense from hewn basalt and limestone. The interior layout varies from the ultra-rectangular Icelandic norm. The apse—the semicircular projection on the eastern end of the church that normally holds just the altar—is deepened and broadened to encircle everything in front of the pews ("apsidal choir" is the technical term). Many Icelandic church ceilings have a few hundred gold stars mounted on square panels; Þingeyrar church has about a thousand gold stars on a smooth, dark-blue ceiling, which is half-domed over the apsidal choir.

The altarpiece, made in Nottingham, England, in the 15th century, illustrates biblical scenes with appealingly crude alabaster figures in relief. (A similar altarpiece at Hólar is more compelling; see p. 177.) It once had wing panels, lost during a failed attempt to sell the altarpiece abroad. The baroque-style canopied pulpit and matching baptismal font were made in the Netherlands in the late 17th century. The church's best-known feature is the "Apostles Collection": small, painted oak-wood figurines, placed between the railings of the gallery. The originals were made in Germany in the late 16th century, sold from Þingeyrar in the early 20th century, and then donated to the National Museum. What you see here are expert 1983 replicas.

To reach Þingeyrar Church, exit on to Route 721 from the Ring Road, 20km (12 miles) west of Blönduós, and proceed 7km (4¼ miles) to the end.

BLÖNDUÓS

This coastal town and agricultural trading hub is the largest settlement in Húnaflói, with nearly 1,000 residents.

Textile Museum (Heimilisiðnaðarsafnið) ★ MUSEUM   Founded by the Women's Union in East Húnavatnssýsla, this museum has been open since 1976, though it was relocated to a new, modern building in 2003. Not everyone will be captivated by century-old crocheted nightgowns and exquisitely embroidered undergarments, but it's hard not to be impressed by the dedication put into this nationwide textile collection. An important piece of the museum is dedicated to Halldóra Bjarnadóttir, a magazine publisher and founder of a wool and textile college in Svalbarði. She collected varieties of weaving and knit patterns, plus objects related to wool and textile processing, and all were donated to the museum. One room is full of mannequins sporting the national costume in several late-19th-century variations—the best such display in Iceland. Another section hosts temporary exhibits of Icelandic textile artists. Make sure to see the portrait made from lint.

Árbraut 29. www.textile.is. © **452-4067.** Admission 1,200kr adults; 1,000kr seniors; free for ages 16 and under. June–Aug daily 10am–5pm. From the Ring Road, turn on to Húnabraut, then bear left on Árbraut, following the northeast side of the river Blanda.

Outdoor Activities

HORSEBACK RIDING   **Gauksmýri** (www.gauksmyri.is; © **451-2927**), about 50km (31 miles) west of Blönduós, is a reputable horse farm that offers short tours of the Húnaflói area. Rides start at 8,000kr for 1 hour and can include introductory lessons. Guided stable visits are also available for 800kr. In addition, Gauksmýri is an eco-minded **lodge and restaurant;** see "Where to Stay," below.

Arinbjörn Jóhannsson at **Brekkulækur Farm** (www.abbi-island.is; © **451-2938**) has been putting together epic 3- to 15-day riding adventures for 3 decades. Tour itineraries, outlined on the website, usually include highlands, coastal regions, and some mingling with locals.

Where to Stay

VATNSNES PENINSULA & NEARBY

Gauksmýri ★   Opened in 2006, this laid-back rural lodge on a farmstead in the isolated Línakradalur valley, exactly halfway between Reykjavík and Akureyri, is aimed at horseback riders, though it's a perfectly fine place for non-riders too. The country-chic rooms come equipped with horse-themed blankets and photos. Buffet-style meals are served for lunch and dinner in the 70-person **dining room,** with floor-to-ceiling windows overlooking the farm.

Birdwatchers will appreciate the proximity to Lake Gauksmýrartjörn, home to 35 different species.

Rte. 1, about 50km (31 miles) west of Blönduós and 4km (2½ miles) east of the Rte. 1/ Rte. 72 junction. www.gauksmyri.is. ✆ **451-2927.** 27 units, 18 w/bathroom. June–Sept 25,000kr per person in a double or single room. Rates around 15% lower Oct–May. Rates include breakfast. **Amenities:** Restaurant; bar; Internet terminal; free Wi-Fi.

Ósar Youth Hostel ★   Near the large seal colony at Hvítserkur (p. 171), 25km (16 miles) north of the Ring Road, this isolated HI-affiliated hostel is situated on a working dairy farm. The rambling farmhouse, with dramatic views of the mountains and beach, has a variety of basic rooms available, from private doubles to dorm beds, plus a few standalone cabins. Breakfast is available, but bring your own food for lunch or dinner; the nearest market and restaurant is in Hvammstangi, 25 minutes away. Book well in advance for summer.

Rte. 711. Coming from the west, turn left from the Ring Road onto Rte. 711 and proceed about 30km (19 miles). Coming from the east, turn right from the Ring Road onto Rte. 716, then turn right again on Rte. 711 and proceed about 19km (12 miles). www. hihostels.com/hostels/osar. ✆ **862-2778.** 10 units without bathroom. 13,200kr double; 20,900kr triple; 5,500kr sleeping-bag accommodation in dorm bed; 1,500kr sheet rental for entire stay. Breakfast available (1,800kr). Closed Nov–Apr. **Amenities:** Guest kitchen; bar; free Wi-Fi.

BLÖNDUÓS

Glaðheimar Cottages ★   This rustic cottage facility is right off the Ring Road overlooking the Blanda River. Cottages vary from 15 to 58 sq. m (49–190 sq. ft.), come with private terraces, and sleep two to eight people. Some units have their own geothermal hot tub and BBQ facilities, and a couple have a sauna.

Blöndubyggð 10. www.gladheimar.is. ✆ **820-1300.** 20 units, 1 w/bathroom. May–Sept 14,700kr without bathroom; 27,200kr with 2-bedrooms, bathroom, and hot tub. Rates around 25% lower Oct–Apr. **Amenities:** Guest kitchen; Wi-Fi (reception only).

Where to Eat

See also **Gauksmýri** in "Where to Stay," above.

HVAMMSTANGI

Sjávarborg ★ ICELANDIC   This minimalist dining room overlooking the water is surprisingly sophisticated for little Hvammstangi. Design elements like exposed ceiling beams, mussel floats made into light fixtures, and reclaimed wooden tables have turned this old slaughterhouse into one of the most unique eateries in the north. The dishes are more creative than you might expect in this part of Iceland, ranging from lobster Alfredo to lamb ragú, and use the highest-quality ingredients. For a dessert to write home about, try the ice cream made with Rauður Ópal Icelandic schnapps.

Hafnarbraut 4. www.sjavarborg-restaurant.is. ✆ **451-3131.** Main courses 2,350kr–4,550kr. Sun–Thurs 11am–10pm; Fri–Sat 11am–1am.

SKAGAFJÖRÐUR

About 4,000 people live along this broad fjord or in the fertile valley at its head: Sauðarkrókur, 25km (16 miles) north of the Ring Road, is a likable coastal town with over half of the region's population. Near Sauðarkrókur, Glaumbær Folk Museum is the most engaging of Iceland's many 19th-century turf-roofed farmsteads. Inside the fjord are the strangely shaped islands of Drangey and Málmey. Hólar, home to Iceland's northern bishop from 1106 to 1798, retains some vestiges of its former glory. Hofsós, halfway up Skagafjörður's eastern shore, was a launch point for Icelandic emigrants to North America, and many of their descendants return there to visit the Emigration Museum and genealogical center. Siglufjörður, the most beautifully situated town in north Iceland, is 55km (35 miles) northeast of Hofsós: The main draws here are the **Herring Era museum** and the surrounding mountains. Skagafjörður is famous across Iceland for its horse breeding and horsemanship, and for adrenaline-seekers, the Eystri-Jökulsá is one of Iceland's fiercest rivers for whitewater rafting.

Essentials

GETTING THERE

BY CAR   The Ring Road passes to the south of Skagafjörður's major sights. Route 75 meets the Ring Road at Varmahlíð—294km (183 miles) from Reykjavík and 94km (58 miles) from Akureyri—and proceeds north to the Glaumbær Folk Museum, Sauðarkrókur, and western Skagafjörður. From the Ring Road 5km (3 miles) east of Varmahlíð, Route 76 leads 97km (60 miles) to Siglufjörður, along the east side of Skagafjörður, past the roads to Hólar and Hofsós. The only **car rental agency** in Sauðárkrókur is **Europcar/Bílaleiga Akureyrar** (www.holdur.is; ℂ **461-6000**).

BY BUS   Straeto (www.straeto.is; ℂ **540-2700**) runs at least one bus daily year-round between Reykjavík and Akureyri, stopping at Varmahlíð (twice daily during the summer). Reykjavík to Varmahlíð takes 5 hours and costs 7,820kr; Akureyri to Varmahlíð takes 85 minutes and costs 2,760kr. A bus between Varmahlíð and Sauðárkrókur runs at least twice daily, May to September, and is timed to connect with the Reykjavík–Akureyri bus. Another bus running between Sauðárkrókur and Siglufjörður stops at Hólar and Hofsós and Fjlót. Departures are every day but Saturday, June until September, and are timed to connect with flights from Reykjavík. Always check the website before leaving.

VISITOR INFORMATION

Skagafjörður's tourist information office is in **Varmahlíð** (www.visitskagafjordur. is; ℂ **455-6161**; June 1–15 daily 9am–5pm, June 16–Aug 15 daily 9am–7pm, Sept 1–May 31 daily 10am–3pm), in a turf-roofed building beside the gas station. The website **www.northwest.is** has good listings of local services.

Exploring Skagafjörður

NEAR VARMAHLÍDÐ

Glaumbær (Skagafjörður Folk Museum) ★★ MUSEUM   Although it's not the only museum inside preserved 19th-century turf buildings,

WHY BUILD A house WITH TURF?

By the mid-12th century, Iceland's climate had cooled considerably, and most of the country had been deforested. Turf housing became the norm and remained so even into the 20th century. Wood was scarce and expensive, and Icelanders roamed the coasts monogramming driftwood to claim it. Roof sod was supported by grids of flat stones and wood rafters. Icelandic grass (which is very thick, with enduring roots) held the turf together. A turf house could last as long as 100 years in areas with moderate rainfall. The roof slope was critical: too flat and it would leak, too steep and the grass would dry out. Glass was costly, too, so windows were often stretched animal skins or abdominal membranes. Turf construction lent itself to small rooms, maze-like interiors, and easy lateral expansion, but it required constant repair. Even the best turf house was leaky, damp, dark, cold, and unventilated, with lingering smoke from the burning of peat and dried manure. Sleeping quarters were often directly over the stables, to take advantage of the animals' body heat.

Glaumbær, which was inhabited until 1947, is one of the best. While the farm is believed to have been worked since the Age of the Settlements (A.D. 900), the current buildings date to the mid-18th century. With connecting corridors between them and their central kitchens, Glaumbær is a reminder of how Icelanders were once homebound in residences such as this through long, dark winters as recently as a single generation ago.

Aside from the usual fishskin shoes and animal bone toys, Glaumbær's more unique holdings include driftwood desks, primitive brain teasers, and a snuff box made of a whale tooth. For Icelanders, the most treasured piece is a basket allegedly made by Fjalla-Eyvindur, the beloved 18th-century outlaw. The near-waterproof basket, expertly woven from willow roots, is inside an unmarked glass case at the back of room #5. The church next door is worth a quick look to see the six disassembled panels from a 1685 Danish pulpit.

Áskaffi, in an adjoining 1886 clapboard house, serves hot drinks, cakes, sandwiches, old-fashioned pancakes, fresh *skyr*, and cake.

Rte. 75, between Varmahlíð and Sauðárkrókur. www.glaumbaer.is. © **453-6173.** Admission 2,000kr adults; 1,000kr students; free for children 15 and under. June–Sept 10 daily 9am–6pm, other times by appointment.

Víðimýrarkirkja ★ CHURCH This 1834 turf-roofed church, built by parliamentarian Jón Samsonarson from Keldudalu, is a masterpiece of Icelandic architecture. The timber frame interior, all original, is rather simple and elemental, though it contains several important artifacts. The 1616 altar painting, probably Danish, is a Last Supper exhibiting the characteristic exaggeration of folk art: Judas holds a moneybag. The pulpit dates to the 17th century, but the paint has mostly worn off. The two bells were cast in 1630.

Off Rte. 1, 5km (3 miles) west of Varmahlíð. © **453-5095.** Admission 1,000kr adults; free for children 15 and under. Daily 9am–6pm.

SAUÐARKRÓKUR ★

This colorful town of 2,550 inhabitants is a convenient regional base with a main street filled with lively shops, restaurants, and small hotels. Consider unwinding at the **town pool,** which has two large whirlpools (ask to have the bubbles turned on).

Gestastofa Sútarans ★ TANNERY   The only tannery in Europe that makes fish leather, Gestastofa Sútarans is where fish skin is processed to make high-quality leather. Guided tours of the tannery, at 10am and 2pm or by arrangement, show how the material is processed before it's ready to be shipped off to international fashion houses like Prada and Dior. The shop allows visitors to purchase leather and hides directly from Atlantic Leather and Loðskinn, the two companies that operate the tannery.

Borgarmýri 5. ⓒ **512-8025.** Admission 500kr. June–Sept 15 Mon–Fri 11am–5pm, Sat 11am–3pm.

DRANGEY ★ & MÁLMEY ★

These two uninhabited, bird-rich islands—whose fantastical shapes look like artists' creations—make for an ideal joint tour. Drangey is surrounded by vertical cliffs reaching 180m (591 ft.). From a distance it appears cylindrical, but a closer look reveals strange contortions and indentations in the rock face. It's the ultimate fortress, and in *The Saga of Grettir the Strong* (aka *Grettis Saga*), one of Iceland's best-known legends, the outlaw Grettir spends the last 3 years of his life here. Sheep once grazed on Drangey's smooth top and had to be hoisted up and down with ropes. From the single landing spot, a steep path ascends to the top with ladders and cable handrails. Málmey is larger, with an elegant S-shaped contour, and reaches 156m (512 ft.) high. A family farm prospered here before burning down in 1950. **Drangey Tours** (www.drangey. net; ⓒ **821-0090**) leads tours of both islands on request, leaving from Reykir on Skagafjörður's west coast daily at 11am and lasting 4 hours. The price is 13,500kr per person. If you'd like to include fishing, Drangey Tours have guided trips for 25,000kr per hour for rental of the entire boat. Similarly, **Haf og Land** (sailinginskagafjordur.is; ⓒ **861-9803**), based in Hofsós, runs sailing trips to either island, leaving at 9:30am throughout the summer for 9,000kr per person, with a minimum of four people.

GRETTISLAUG ★

In *Grettis Saga,* Grettir swims from Drangey to the western shore of Skagafjörður, where he bathes in a geothermal spring and then fetches some glowing embers to bring back to the island. In 1992, 962 years later, Jón Eiríksson, "the Earl of Drangey," built **Grettislaug,** a pool in open surroundings at Grettir's legendary bathing spot. An adjacent pool was added in 2006. Both are constructed with natural stones and remain at bathwater temperature. For a memorable swim at Grettislaug, drive north from Sauðárkrókur on Route 748 to the end of the road. Facilities are basic and bathers are asked to contribute 1,000kr into a metal box.

HÓLAR ★

Hólar (© **455-6333;** free admission; all sites open daily 9am–6pm unless otherwise specified), also known as Hólar Í Hjaltadalur, was the northern seat of power in Iceland's Catholic era. Today's visitors see little direct connection to its bygone prestige, but the present cathedral, **Hóladómkirkja,** displays perhaps the best artifacts of any church in Iceland.

In 1056, Iceland's first Catholic bishop was installed at Skálholt in the southwest. Northern Icelanders complained that he was too far away, and 50 years later a second diocese was added at Hólar. Just before the Reformation, the Hólar bishopric owned a 70-ton ship, invaluable manuscripts, stockpiles of gold and silver, and large holdings of land and livestock—all ripe for confiscation by the Danish king, who, like other European monarchs of the time, understood that Protestantism would ease his financial problems. Hólar's last Catholic bishop, Jón Arason (1484–1550), was beheaded at Skálholt, after leading a rebellion against the king. Lutheran bishops remained at Hólar until 1798, when the two bishoprics were consolidated and relocated to Reykjavík. Hólar is now home to about 110 people and **Hólaskóli,** a small university with courses in equine sciences, rural tourism, and aquaculture.

Hólaskóli's main building holds a restaurant, pool, and guesthouse. In the lobby you'll find the free brochure "Hólar History Trail," which lays out the nearby sights in walking-tour format. **Nýibær** is a preserved 19th-century turf farmhouse, but it's empty and hardly worth visiting with **Glaumbær ★★** (p. 168) so close by. **Auðun's House (Auðunarstofa)** is a reconstruction of a bishop's residence from the early 14th century, built in 2002 with only 14th-century building methods. A 13th-century chalice, vestments, and medieval manuscripts are stored in the basement.

Built in 1763, the current cathedral, though large by Icelandic standards, is the smallest ever built at Hólar. It's also Iceland's oldest stone church, built with local red sandstone and basalt. The detached bell tower was consecrated in 1950; just inside the entrance is a 1957 mosaic of Jón Arason by the well-known contemporary artist Erró, then barely out of art school.

Inside the cathedral, a glass case holds a 1584 Bible, the first printed in Icelandic. A painting of a Hólar bishop, from 1620, is the oldest known portrait of any Icelander. On the side wall is a crucifix from the early 16th century. Its large size is uncharacteristic of Lutheran churches, and it's surprising to learn that it was imported in the mid-17th century after the Reformation, probably from southern Europe. The 1674 baptismal font is made of soapstone, which—according to popular lore—drifted to Iceland on an ice floe from Greenland. More likely, it was imported from Norway.

The **altarpiece ★★**, made around 1500, is an impressive, painted wooden sculpture depicting the Crucifixion story with apostles and saints on the wings. Jón Arason bought the piece in Holland, though it's thought to be German. Both side panels swivel inward, revealing paintings on their back sides; on the right side, St. Sebastian spurts blood from several arrow wounds, while St. Lucy is indifferent to a sword through her neck. Make sure to ask the attendant to draw out these back panels for you. An even older English altarpiece, from Nottingham, made of alabaster and also in sculpted storybook form, hangs over the side entrance. An attendant is always on hand for questions, but tours (650kr) are only given for groups, so call ahead.

HOFSÓS & NEARBY

Hofsós, a trading post dating back to the 16th century, has maintained its throwback feel by preserving some of its 18th-century buildings and replicating others. Built in 2010, the **swimming pool** in Hofsós (✆ **455-6070;** admission 1,000kr adults, 500kr children ages 7–18; open Mon–Fri 7am–1pm and 5:15–8:15pm, Sat–Sun 11am–3pm) sits on the cliff tops, with superb views of the fjord and Mount Tindastóll. While swimming, you feel like you could swim directly to the islands in the fjord.

Icelandic Emigration Center (Vesturfarasetrið) ★ MUSEUM

Founded in 1996, this center traces the Icelandic emigration of the late-19th and early-20th centuries. Four exhibits in three buildings explore the new lives that Icelanders created in the New World in settlements from Utah to Brazil. (In "New Iceland," a settlement founded in 1875 on Lake Winnipeg, Manitoba, many older people still speak Icelandic as a first language.) A gallery with more than 400 photographs of these emigrants is displayed, as is a specific story of an Icelandic settlement in North Dakota. Visitors researching their family roots should contact the museum in advance; general inquiries are free, and more intensive archival research can be hired at an hourly rate.

Suðurbraut 8. www.hofsos.is. ✆ **453-7935.** Admission 1,500kr adults for all three exhibits, or 700kr for individual; 1,200kr seniors; free for children 11 and under; free admission for genealogy room. June–Aug daily 11am–6pm; other times by arrangement.

FLJÓT ★★

Just 30 km (19 miles) northeast of Hofsós on the coast road to Siglufjörður (Route 76) is one of Iceland's best-kept secrets. Sparsely populated Fljót is the northernmost settlement in Skagafjörður and certainly stunning across all seasons. In the summer, the wild Icelandic flowers still reign and green pastures contrast perfectly with the snow-capped, convoluted mountains of Tröllaskagi. The valley is divided by one of Iceland's best fishing rivers, Fljótaá, where the salmon are so superior the rights to fish in it were snapped up quickly by a fishing club in Siglufjörður. The abundant snowfall in the winter transforms the area into a wonderland of snow illuminated with hues of purple, pink, and gold by the winter sun. The stars and Northern Lights are much clearer in this area because of its northerly location.

There's a filling station and small grocery store, **Ketilás** (✆ **467-1000**), at the junction of Route 76/82.

Tucked away inland in the Fljót Valley is the ultra-luxury resort, **Deplar Farm ★★★** (www.elevenexperience.com; ✆ **970-349-7761**), which is open year-round and offers experiences like heli-skiing, fly-fishing, and whale-watching. The property includes a farm-to-table restaurant, a geothermal indoor/outdoor pool, Isopod flotation tanks, and an outdoor Viking sauna, among other perks.

SIGLUFJÖRÐUR ★★

Lovingly dubbed "Sigló" by the locals, the impossibly picturesque town of Siglufjörður is inside a short, steep-sided fjord less than 40km (25 miles) from the Arctic Circle. With a steady population of 1,200, it was for many years only accessible by a single road that winds along a pretty stretch of remote coastline. In December 2010, a tunnel east to Ólafsfjörður increased access to Siglufjörður, also cutting 2 hours off the road trip to Akureyri, and some major developments have since followed.

Siglufjörður, which still runs on fish, was a herring boomtown in the early and mid-20th century. During the herring heyday, hundreds of ships were docked here, and hordes of girls came for the summer to gut, salt, and pack the fish in barrels for export. Overfishing aided by sonar equipment caused herring populations to plummet after World War II, and, in 1969, the herring failed to show up entirely.

The town has preserved its older buildings well, though a cluster of new buildings, including a hotel, marina, and restaurants, have helped revive the once-sleepy waterfront. Besides strolling around town, say, or shooting a round of golf on the **nine-hole course,** the main activities for visitors are the **Herring Era Museum** and the fine hiking nearby. From July to the first week in August, time your visit for a Saturday, when **herring-salting demonstrations** are presented at 3pm, complete with costumes, song, dance, and accordions. Tickets are 1,400kr and include museum admission. On the first weekend of August, a celebratory holiday across the country, Siglufjörður draws hundreds of visitors for its nostalgic **Herring Adventure Festival,** with musical performances, family entertainment, and yet more fish preparation demos. In early July, a 5-day **folk music festival** (www.folkmusik.is) includes workshops as well as concerts day and night by Icelandic and international artists.

The Siglufjörður area offers several first-rate **hiking routes.** Avid hikers can sustain themselves with two full-day trips, one to the west of the fjord and one to the east. The excellent and widely available trail map "Gönguleiðir á Tröllaskaga II: Fljót, Siglufjörður, Ólafsfjörður, Svarfaðardalur" has no descriptions in English, but you can still deduce estimated walking times and altitudes. A short hike on the fjord's eastern shore leads to the Evanger herring factory, destroyed by an avalanche in 1919. Two routes head east overland to Héðinsfjörður, a wild and beautiful fjord abandoned in 1951; the shorter route is at least 4 hours one-way. A popular hike follows the old road leading west through the 630m (2,067 ft.) Siglufjörðarskarð Pass; this road is usually free of snowdrifts and passable in 4WD vehicles from early July to late August. Instead of taking the full 15km (9-mile) route one-way, and having to arrange transportation back, you could cut north along the ridge and then descend into town in a strenuous but very rewarding 6- to 7-hour loop.

Folk Musik Center (Þjóðlagasetur) ★ MUSEUM The center is located in the house where the Rev. Bjarni Thorsteinsson, a collector who spent a quarter of a century researching his opus, *Icelandic Folk Songs,* lived from 1888 to 1898. Aside from his collections of unique Icelandic instruments, the museum features videos of traditional music, from *rímur* chanting to nursery rhymes. Concerts are held Saturday evenings in July and August.

Norðurgata 1. www.folkmusik.is. ⓒ **467-2300.** Admission 1,000kr adults; free for children 15 and under. June 1–Aug 31 daily noon–6pm, by appointment the rest of the year.

Herring Era Museum (Síldarminjasafnið) ★★ MUSEUM   The herring trade was for Icelanders what the California Gold Rush was for Americans, and at some point in the country's history, it accounted for a quarter of Iceland's export income. Siglufjörður was the epicenter of this trade, earning it the nickname "Herring Capital of the World," until the 1969 collapse. This award-winning, ambitious museum is spread across three buildings; one replicates an entire 1950s quayside, complete with nine herring vessels of various sizes, and another reconstructs a processing factory for herring meal and oil. Most affecting are the old living quarters for the herring girls, with tiny beds that each slept two. Information posted in English increases every year, and the staff is very helpful and informative. The admission fee here includes access to the **Folk Musik Center** (see above) and the **Ura Museum** (a watch and silversmith workshop). Salting performances are held on the deck of Róaldsbrakki each Saturday in July, with local "herring girls" filling barrels and demonstrating old salting practices, with traditional song and dance.

Snorragata 15. www.sild.is. ⓒ **467-1604.** Admission 1,800kr adults; 1,000kr seniors and ages 16–20; free for children 15 and under. June 1–Aug 31 daily 10am–6pm; May 15–June 15 and Aug 21–Sept 15 daily 1–5pm.

Dalvík

This fishing town of just under 2,000 people, on the western shore of Eyjafjörður 44km (27 miles) north of Akureyri, may provide a diversion worth adding to a ferry trip to Hrísey or Grímsey. Little-known among tourists, **"The Great Fish Day" (Fiskidagurinn)** is a huge outdoor festival that takes place on the first or second weekend of August. Everything is free: food, soft drinks, live music, folk dancing in traditional costume, short films, and, of course, exhibitions of fish in tubs full of ice. The local fish factory is the main sponsor, and all workers are volunteers. On Saturday from 11am to 5pm, the largest grill in Iceland cooks up cod, haddock, salmon, and about 12,000 fish burgers. The night before, around 70 Dalvík families place two torches outside their doors, a signal that anyone is welcome to stop in for fish soup.

GETTING THERE
BY CAR   Take Route 82 from the Ring Road 10km (6¼ miles) north of Akureyri. **Straeto** (www.straeto.is; ⓒ **540-2700**) runs three **buses** between Akureyri and Dalvík on weekdays year-round; the ride is 45 minutes and costs 1,840kr.

Dalvík's **tourist office,** Svarfaðarbraut (www.dalvik.is; ⓒ **466-3233;** June–Aug Mon–Fri 6:15am–8pm, Sat–Sun 10am–9pm; Sept–May Mon–Fri 6:15am–8pm, Sat–Sun 10am–4:30pm), is at the local swimming pool, and the website has information in English.

Hvoll Folk Museum (Byggðasafnið Hvoll) ★ MUSEUM   Many of the thousands of artifacts in this cultural museum were donated by local residents. A central focus is on Svarfaðardalur natives who became nationally famous, such as Jóhann Pétursson (1913–1984), who during his lifetime was the world's second-tallest person. Standing at 2.3m (7 ft., 8 in.) in U.S. size 24 (62 European) boots, he appeared in Viking costume as "Jóhann the Giant" in U.S. and European circuses and made several Hollywood cameos. He was understandably ambivalent about his work and stage name, and returned to Dalvík in his final years.

Karlsrauðatorg. www.dalvik.is/byggdasafn. ⓒ **460-4928.** Admission 650kr adults; 500kr seniors; 150kr children ages 6–16. June–Aug daily 11am–6pm; Sept–May Sat 2–5pm.

Outdoor Activities

HIKING   Bergmenn Mountain Guides (www.bergmenn.com; ⓒ **698-9870**) are the best agents in the area for **hiking tours** and **ski mountaineering** on the beautiful Tröllaskagi Peninsula (including the fabulous 2- to 3-day route from Dalvík west to Hólar).

HORSEBACK RIDING   The farms below offer lessons and short rides as well as multi-day adventures for all ability levels.

Flugumýri (ⓒ **895-8814**), on Route 76, 3km (2 miles) off the Ring Road, presents exhibitions for groups, showing off the talents of the Icelandic horse; call ahead, and, if an exhibition is scheduled, you can sign up for 4,000kr, including coffee and cake. **Hestasport** (www.riding.is; ⓒ **453-8383**), a respected outfit just outside Varmahlíð, has several good route options for summer including the Hofsós and Hólar area, the Kjölur Route (p. 186) through the interior to Gullfoss and Geysir, and local sheep round-ups. This company also offers winter tours with snowmobiling and skiing options. **Lýtingsstaðir** (www.lythorse.com; ⓒ **453-8064**), on Route 752, 20km (12 miles) south of Varmahlíð, has a good range of highland tours, including horse and sheep round-ups. The tours vary in length and theme depending on the time of year; the longer tours include full board and accommodation.

RIVER RAFTING   The rivers feeding Skagafjörður provide the best river rafting in North Iceland. The Eystri-Jökulsá has difficult class III and IV+ rapids, while the Vestari-Jökulsá has easier class II rapids, as well as a cliff-jumping ledge and a hot spring (where rafters gather to make cocoa). Several operators, including **Bakkaflöt** (www.bakkaflot.com; ⓒ **453-8245**) and **Viking Rafting** (www.vikingrafting.is; ⓒ **823-8300**), run trips to rivers around the region, ranging from super-tame trips on the Blanda River (ages 6 and up) to an exciting 3-day adventure down the Eystri-Jökulsá, starting deep within the desert interior. The Eystri-Jökulsá trip lasts 6 to 7 hours and costs around 25,000kr all-inclusive, with a minimum age of 18. The Vestari-Jökulsá trip lasts 4 to 5 hours and costs about 16,000kr, minimum age 12. Trips run from May to early October.

WHALE-WATCHING   Most visitors to north Iceland save their **whale-watching** for Húsavík, which has better infrastructure—more scheduled departures, waterfront coffeehouses, the whale museum—but only a marginal advantage in whale sightings. **Arctic Sea Tours** (www.arcticseatours.is; ✆ **771-7600**), based in Dalvík, leads 3-hour whale-watching tours (9,900kr adults, 5,000kr children ages 7–16; June 1–30 daily 9am, 7pm; July–Aug 26 9am, 7pm, 11pm), and sea-angling trips by arrangement. **Whale-Watching Hauganes** (www.whales.is; ✆ **867-0000**), based 30km (19 miles) north of Akureyri and 14km (8¾ miles) south of Dalvík, has comparable services.

Where to Stay

VARMAHLÍÐ ★

Hótel Varmahlíð ★   A good stopping point for Ring Road drivers, or those beginning or ending the drive over the Kjölur pass, this unassuming hotel serves its purpose. The rooms are big but lack character. The on-site **restaurant** (see "Where to Eat," p. 184) is one of the few that opens daily in the area.

Rte. 1. www.hotelvarmahlid.is. ✆ **453-8170.** 19 units. May–Sept 32,000kr double. Rates around 30% lower May–June 14 and Sept; around 45% lower Oct–Apr. Rates include breakfast. **Amenities:** Restaurant; free Wi-Fi in public areas.

SAUDÐÁRKRÓKUR

Guesthouse Mikligarður ★   This completely remodeled 1931 house, overlooking Sauðárkrókur´s beautiful 20th-century church, is more reliable than the other budget options in town. Since coming under the management of Arctic Hotels in 2007, it has been well-maintained.

Kirkjutorg 3. www.arctichotels.is. ✆ **453-6880.** 14 units, 2 w/bathroom. May 1–Sept 30 20,900kr double w/bathroom; 12,550kr double without bathroom. Rates 5%–20% lower Sept 16–May 14. Rates include breakfast (May 15–Sept 15 only). **Amenities:** Guest kitchen; TV lounge; free Wi-Fi.

Hótel Mikligarður ★   This hulking orange building is a school dormitory outside of the summer months, but it really doesn't have an institutional feel. Rooms are cheerful and all have private facilities, plus there's a TV lounge on each floor and a wine bar on the ground floor. It's a 1km (⅔ mile) walk from the center of town.

Skagfirdingabraut (by Sæmundarhlíð). www.arctichotels.is. ✆ **453-6880.** 65 units. June–Aug 23,650kr double. Rates include breakfast. Closed Sept–May. **Amenities:** Restaurant; bar; free Wi-Fi in reception.

Hótel Tindastóll ★★   Allegedly the oldest hotel in all of Iceland and one of the 20 oldest wooden houses, Tindastóll was shipped in pieces from Norway and assembled in Hofsós between 1820 and 1829, before being moved to Grafarós for a few decades. It was moved to its current location in 1884 to be used as a hotel to help fill the demand for the growing number of emigrants departing for North America. Management has done a great job of retaining the original feel of the structure, with wood floors, handcrafted furnishings and beamed ceilings (not to mention the sea-stone walls lining the downstairs breakfast nook/lounge). There's a natural-stone hot pool in back, plus bathrobes in every room to get you there. A more contemporary annex with nine rooms was added next door in 2012.

Lindargata 3. www.hoteltindastoll.com. © **453-5002.** 19 units. June–Aug 30,760kr double. Rates 10%–30% lower May and Sept; 20%–40% lower Oct–Apr. Rates include breakfast. **Amenities:** Bar; hot tub; free Wi-Fi.

HOFSÓS

If researching your family tree keeps you in Hofsós overnight, the **Icelandic Emigration Center** (p. 178) can find you accommodation. **Gistiheimilið Sunnuberg,** Suðurbraut 8 (© **453-7310;** June–Aug 15,600kr double; Sept–May 10,350kr double), has five acceptable rooms with private bathrooms.

Lónkot ★ This country resort is situated on a beautiful, remote stretch of Lónkot oceanfront north of Hofsós. The rooms vary in shape and size, though all feature vintage '70s furniture. The hotel doubles as an artists' retreat: The lounge exhibits the works of a particular artist each summer, while the garden is home to a collection of sculptures from top Icelandic sculptors. The slow-food-inspired **restaurant** makes use of local flowers, herbs, and berries.

Lónkot, 13km (8 miles) north of Hofsós. www.lonkot.is. © **453-7432.** 5 units, 3 w/ bathroom. June–Aug 36,000kr double; 25,900kr double w/shared bathroom; 59,100kr family suite. Rates 10%–20% lower Sept–May. Rates include breakfast. **Amenities:** Restaurant, lounge; hot tub, free Wi-Fi in public areas.

SIGLUFJÖRÐUR

The Herring House ★ This four-bedroom guesthouse is perched on a hillside overlooking the center of town, a short walk from most of the restaurants and facilities on the harbor. The quaint, cozy rooms lack private bathrooms, but make up for it with quirky charm. Additionally, it has a small cottage (2-night min.) with a kitchenette and private toilet, though note that the shower is shared and outside.

Hlíðarvegur 1. www.theherringhouse.com. © **868-4200.** 5 units. 16,500kr–21,650kr double without bathroom; 28,350kr cottage. **Amenities:** Free Wi-Fi.

Siglo Hótel ★★★ Part of a larger development, a marina village that includes various shops and restaurants, the Siglo, which opened in 2015, has helped completely transform this once-faded waterfront. The colorful new buildings have brought new life and a surge of tourists to the sleepy town. Siglo's modern Scandinavian rooms are far more sophisticated than anything this remote village has ever seen, with HDTVs and high-thread-count sheets. The suites are considerably larger and add terraces. Around sunset, most guests congregate in the large hot pots overlooking the water. The hotel has one fine-dining restaurant, **Sunna,** inside the main building, and several others on the other side of the marina.

Snorragata 3. www.siglohotel.is. © **461-7730.** 6 units, none w/bathroom. June–Aug 43,300kr double; 77,000kr suite. Rates include breakfast. **Amenities:** Restaurant; cafe, bar; hot tub, sauna, tour desk; free Wi-Fi.

Where to Eat

VARMAHLÍÐ

Hótel Varmahlíð ★ ICELANDIC It's part of the Skagafjörður "Food Chest" program, in which restaurants use ingredients that have been produced or processed in the Skagafjörður region. The soulful, homestyle dishes, such as lightly salted cod heads and rhubarb cobbler, are above and beyond what you might expect from a straightforward Ring Road pitstop. In the winter the restaurant opens for groups only with advance notice.

Rte. 1. ⓒ **453-8170.** Main courses 2,650kr–5,700kr. June–Aug daily 6–9:30pm; May and Sept daily 7–9pm; Oct–Apr by request in advance.

SAUÐÁRKRÓKUR

The bakery **Sauðárkróksbakari,** Aðalgata 5 (ⓒ **455-5000;** June–Aug 7am–6pm, Sept–May 8am–4pm), one of Iceland's oldest bakeries, is perfect for breakfast, a soup and sandwich lunch, or a pastry. Try the chocolate cake with coconut sprinkles. Also, don't miss the craft-beer bar, **Grand-Inn,** Aðalgata 19 (ⓒ **844-5616**), which has a wide selection of Icelandic, Scandinavian, and Belgian beers.

Kaffi Krókur ★ ICELANDIC This bistro and coffeehouse is set in an 1887 house originally built for the town sheriff. It was badly damaged in a fire in 2008, but reopened a year later better than ever. The interior is pub-like, with booth seating and lots of woodwork. The menu is far superior to the more humdrum spots down the street, with pan-fried lamb, fish, and lobster/shrimp sandwiches.

Aðalgata 16b. www.kaffikrokur.is. ⓒ **453-6299.** Main courses 1,000kr–8,490kr. June–Aug daily 11:30am–11pm.

HOFSÓS & NEARBY

Within the village, your only choice is **Solvík** (ⓒ 453-7930; June 1–Aug 31 daily 11am–9pm), a pleasant, summer-only restaurant/cafe next to the Emigration Center (p. 178).

Lónkot Rural Resort ★ ICELANDIC On the fjord north of Hofsós, this slow-food-inflected restaurant in the Lónkot resort pays close attention to seasonal changes in flowers and herbs, which it incorporates into its menu. Expect dishes like Arctic char tartare, puffin with blueberries, or violet ice cream. Call in advance to let them know you're coming.

Rte. 76, 11km (7 miles) north of Hofsós. www.lonkot.is. ⓒ **453-7432.** Reservations recommended for dinner. Main courses 3,700kr–5,900kr. June–Sept 15 8am–midnight; kitchen closes at 10pm.

SIGLUFJÖRÐUR

With the growing crop of restaurants opening in and around the marina village, Siglufjörður's dining options have improved dramatically in recent years. The bakery **Aðalbakari,** Aðalgata 36 (ⓒ **467-1720;** daily 7am–5pm), serves breakfast and lunch, with sandwiches, pastries, and cakes. For craft beer in one of the world's northernmost breweries, visit the tasting room at **Segull 67** (www.segull67.is; ⓒ **863-2120**), at Vetrarbraut 8-10, inside an old fish factory that's a short walk from the harbor.

Hannes Boy Café ★ CONTINENTAL   Inspired by Siglufjörður's herring-centric past, this rustic-chic eatery is named after an old sailor who used to hang out on the docks. The menu is quite eclectic, offering burgers, seafood pasta, and *smælki,* deep-fried potatoes served with shrimp, chicken, or smoked salmon. The clunky wooden tables, beamed ceiling, and old herring-barrel furniture complete the atmosphere.

Gránugata 23. www.hannesboy.is. ✆ **461-7730.** Reservations recommended for dinner. Main courses 2,350kr–3,890kr. June–Aug Sun–Thurs 11:30am–10pm, Fri–Sat 11:30am–11pm.

Harbor House Café ★ SEAFOOD   Set inside a wooden fishermen's shack beside the harbor, this quaint eatery gets lost behind the fishing boats and more modern hotel and restaurant complex that is quickly surrounding it. The small, nautically inspired dining room holds just a handful of tables and serves up a short menu of Icelandic classics like smoked herring, seafood soup, and pan-fried arctic char.

Gránugata 5b. ✆ **659-4809.** Main courses 2,500kr–3,990kr. May–Sept Wed–Thurs 6–11:30pm, Fri 6pm–1:30am, Sat noon–1am, Sun 9am–9pm.

AKUREYRI

Nestled at the head of Eyjafjörður, Iceland's longest fjord, **Akureyri** ★ is north Iceland's largest fishing port, as well as its cultural, industrial, and trade hub. It's often called Iceland's "second city," but residents don't seem to take this the wrong way. Akureyri has only around 19,000 people, so just reaching the status of "city" is an unrivaled achievement outside the Reykjavík metropolitan area. (Technically, Akureyri is Iceland's fourth-largest city, after the Reykjavík suburbs of Kópavogur and Hafnarfjörður.) Akureyri is a sophisticated and thriving place, and Akureyrians boast of their superior weather, warmer and drier than drizzly Reykjavík in summer, with more frost and snow in the winter.

Akureyri's first known settler was Helgi the Lean, who arrived around 890. By 1602 it was an active trading post, and by 1900 it had 1,370 residents. The trade cooperative KEA, formed in 1886, still owns large shares of several Eyjafjörður businesses, and in 1915 Akureyri had the country's first social-democratic government. The University of Akureyri, established in 1987, is the only state-run university outside of Reykjavík.

Akureyri sees about 200,000 visitors a year, and has no shortage of restaurants and museums. The annual Summer Arts Festival, which includes concerts, exhibitions, dance, and plays, lasts from mid-June to late August.

Essentials
GETTING THERE & AROUND
Akureyri is on Route 1 (the Ring Road), 388km (241 miles) from Reykjavík and 265km (165 miles) from Egilsstaðir. The downtown, clustered around Hafnarstræti, with Ráðhústorg Square at its northern end, is easily navigable **on foot.** Much of Akureyri is spread along a steep incline, so a car is helpful.

BSO taxi (☏ 461-1010) is on call 24 hours and operates a **taxi stand** on Strandgata at Hofsbót, with at least one wheelchair-accessible car.

BY PLANE **Air Iceland** (www.airicelandconnect.com; ☏ 460-7000) has eight 45-minute flights daily between Reykjavík and Akureyri. One-way tickets average 11,100kr but go as high as 20,000kr and as low as 9,000kr with early booking online. From Akureyri, direct flights go to Vopnafjörður and Grímsey Island; all other destinations are routed through Reykjavík. **Akureyri Airport (AEY)** is on the Ring Road, 3km (2 miles) south of town.

BY CAR Rental agencies at the airport are **Avis** (www.avis.is; ☏ 824-4010), **Hertz** (www.hertz.is; ☏ 522-4440), and **Bílaleiga Akureyrar** (www.holdur. is; ☏ 461-6000), which has another office at Tryggvabraut 12. All agencies should offer to pick you up anywhere in town. If you rent in Akureyri and leave the car in Reykjavík, the dropoff fee will likely be 10,000kr to 12,000kr.

Parking—clustered along Skipagata, one block east of the pedestrian-only stretch of Hafnarstræti—is free, but during working hours you need to dash into a store or bank and ask for a "parking disc," a windshield sticker with attached clock hands. Signs indicate how long the parking spot is good for, from 15 minutes to 2 hours. Set the clock hands ahead to the time the spot expires.

BY BUS **Straeto** (www.straeto.is; ☏ 540-2700) connects Reykjavík and Akureyri twice daily in summer via the Ring Road (6 hr.; 10,120kr) and also has daily summer connections between Akureyri and Dalvík (45 min.; 1,840kr), and Egilsstaðir (4 hr.; 8,280kr).

SBA-Norðurleid (www.sba.is; ☏ 550-0700) includes sightseeing stops in its routes, often with guides. One bus connects Reykjavík and Akureyri daily in summer through the Kjölur route (9 hr.; 18,500kr), with brief stops at Geysir, Gullfoss, and Hveravellir. Other daily summer routes connect Akureyri to Mývatn, Húsavík, and Jökulsárgljúfur Park in various combinations. The winter tour to Mývatn is 19,500kr, where the snow and frost transforms the lake into a scene from a fairy tale.

Buses within Akureyri are free—yes, *free*—with four routes (numbered 1, 2, 3, 4) that run hourly on weekdays from 6am to as late as 10:30pm. No buses run on weekends or holidays. All routes leave from Ráðhústorg Square, by the shop named *Nætursalan*. No routes go to the airport. For schedule and route information, pick up a brochure at the tourist information office, call ☏ 462-4929, or visit www.akureyri.is/ferdamenn/samgongur/straetisvagnar.

VISITOR INFORMATION

The very competent **tourist information office** (www.visitakureyri.is or www.nordurland.is; ☏ 553-5999; June 15–Sept 6 Mon–Fri 7:30am–7pm) is in the hulking modernist **Hof Cultural Center** (p. 188) at Strandgata 12, a 5-minute walk east from Ráðhústorg Square. The office is useful for all of north Iceland, and the staff can help with accommodations.

Anyone planning a hiking adventure in north Iceland or the interior can buy maps and get free advice from the local hiking club, **Ferðafélag Akureyrar,**

Akureyri

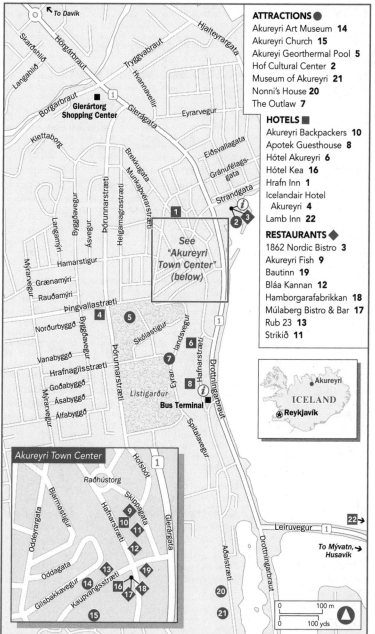

ATTRACTIONS ●
Akureyri Art Museum **14**
Akureyri Church **15**
Akureyi Georthermal Pool **5**
Hof Cultural Center **2**
Museum of Akureyri **21**
Nonni's House **20**
The Outlaw **7**

HOTELS ■
Akureyri Backpackers **10**
Apotek Guesthouse **8**
Hótel Akureyri **6**
Hótel Kea **16**
Hrafn Inn **1**
Icelandair Hotel
Akureyri **4**
Lamb Inn **22**

RESTAURANTS ◆
1862 Nordic Bistro **3**
Akureyri Fish **9**
Bautinn **19**
Bláa Kannan **12**
Hamborgarafabrikkan **18**
Múlaberg Bistro & Bar **17**
Rub 23 **13**
Strikið **11**

Strandgata 23 (www.ffa.is; ✆ 462-2720; June–Aug Mon–Thurs 3–7pm, Fri 4–7pm; Feb–May Fri 4–7pm). This is also where you register your itinerary, so in the event that you don't return, they'll know where to come looking for you.

[FastFACTS] AKUREYRI

Banks/Currency Exchange Banks are generally open weekdays 9am to 4pm and have commission-free currency exchange and 24-hour ATMs. The main bank is **Landsbanki** (✆ 460-4000) at Strandgata 1, open weekdays from 9am to 4pm.

Cellphones For thorough information, see p. 334. Phones and calling plans are available at **Síminn** (✆ 800-7000), **Nova** (✆ 519-1000), or **Vodafone** (✆ 599-9000), all located in the Glerátorg Mall, open Mon–Fri 10am–6:30pm, Sat 10am–5pm, and Sun 1–5pm.

Drugstores Apótekar-inn (✆ 460-3456; Mon–Fri 9am–5:30pm) is downtown at Hafnarstræti 95. Drugstores with extended hours are **Apótekið,** Furuvellir 17, Hagkaup Market (✆ 461-3920; Mon–Fri 10am–7pm, Sat 10am–4pm, Sun noon–4pm), and **Lyf & heilsa,** Glerátorg Mall (✆ 461-5800; Mon–Fri 10am–6:30pm, Sat 10am–5pm, Sun 1–5pm).

Emergencies Dial ✆ 112 for ambulance, fire, or police. See also "Medical Help," below.

Internet Access Wi-Fi hot spots are found all over town, including nearly all hotels and most restaurants and cafes.

Laundry Þvottahúsið Höfði, Hafnarstræti 34 (✆ 462-2580; Mon–Fri 8am–6pm), a full-service laundry, 3,000kr for up to 5kg/11 lb. Hostel **Akureyri Backpackers,** Hafnarstræti 98 (✆ 571-9050), has similar rates.

Libraries Akureyri Library, Brekkugata 17 (✆ 460-1250; June–Sept Mon–Fri 10am–7pm; Sept–May Mon–Fri 10am–7pm, Sat noon–5pm), has cheap Internet access and a decent collection of English-language books and magazines; tourists can borrow books for free.

Luggage Storage The **tourist information office** (see "Visitor Information," p. 186) can hold bags for up to 1 night, but does not have a secure room.

Medical Help For an ambulance, call ✆ 112. **Akureyri Hospital** (Spítala-vegur, by Eyrarlandsvegur; main number ✆ 463-0100, emergency room ✆ 463-0800, 24-hr. telephone service, consultation

✆ 848-2600; Mon–Fri 5am–9pm, Sat–Sun 7am–noon and 2–4pm) is just south of the botanical garden. **Heilsug-æslustöðin Clinic,** Hafnarstræti 99 (✆ 460-4600; daily 8am–4pm), is downtown.

Police For emergencies, dial ✆ 112. The police station (✆ 464-7700) is at Þórunnarstræti 138.

Post Office/Mail The **post office** (✆ 580-1000; Mon–Fri 9am–6pm) is at Standgata 3, in the middle of the city.

Supermarkets Supermarkets include **Bónus** (Langhólt 1), **Haugkaup** (Furuvellir, near Hjalteyrar-gata), and **Nettó** (Glerátorg Mall). Supermarkets open late include **10-11** (Þingval-lastræti at Mýrarvegur; 24 hr.) and **Samkaup Strax** (Borgar-braut at Hlíðarbraut; 24 hr.).

Taxis See "Getting There & Around," p. 185.

Telephones Public phones are available at the **tourist information office** (see "Visitor Information," above), **Akureyri Hospital** (see "Medical Help," above), **Spítalavegur** (by Eyrarlandsvegur), and the **city pool** (p. 195).

Exploring Akureyri
HEART OF THE CITY

The latest attraction in Akureyri is the **Hof Cultural Center** (**Menningar-húsið Hof**) on Strangata 12 (www.menningarhus.is; ✆ 450-1000), which opened officially in August 2010. As with many Icelandic buildings, the beauty is on the inside, where the modern, acoustically designed hall hosts concerts, conferences, and performances.

Akureyri Art Museum (Listasafníð á Akureyri) ★ MUSEUM   This umbrella venue, converted from several disused industrial buildings, includes three exhibition venues and fronts gallery street Kaupvangsstræti, just uphill from Akureyri Church. Founded in 1993, the well-designed museum has no permanent collection and is devoted mostly to contemporary Icelandic art, with international shows on occasion. The oldest art museum outside of the capital region, it has helped launch the careers of several important figures, such as Icelandic artists Erró and Kjarval, as well as the American photographer Spencer Tunick and French photographer Henri Cartier-Bresson.

Kaupvangsstræti 12. www.listak.is. © **461-2610.** 1,500kr admission. May–Sept 10am–5pm; Oct–April noon–5pm.

Akureyri Church ★ MUSEUM   The symbol of Akureyri, this bravura concrete church's twin Art Deco spires have drawn mixed critical responses but rarely fail to make an impression. The hilltop location, face-forward design, and beckoning, outstretched spires lend the frontal exterior an animal vitality. The church was consecrated in 1940 and designed by Guðjón Samúelsson, the state architect responsible for the even larger Hallgrímskirkja in Reykjavík. However distinctive his bold geometric outlines, Guðjón's signature is just as evident in the fine details, such as the basalt-inspired hexagonal columns above the doorway and the obsessive tiering in the ceiling, archways, and surrounding lawn. Be sure to inspect the lovely tilework in Iceland spar—a native crystal used to make light prisms—on the pulpit and the illuminated cross hanging from the ceiling. The midsection of the stained-glass window directly behind the altar comes from the original Coventry cathedral, one of England's great casualties in World War II. Take note of the unusually large 3,200-pipe organ.

Off Eyrarlandsvegur. www.akureyrarkirkja.is. © **462-7700.** Mon–Fri 8:30am–10pm; until 8:30pm Wed. June–Sept Sun service 11am; Oct–May Sun service 11pm. Prayers Thurs noon.

SOUTH OF THE CITY CENTER

The riveting 1901 sculpture **The Outlaw (Útlaginn) ★**—easy to miss amid the greenery in the traffic island formed by Eyrarlandsvegur and Hrafnagilsstræti—established the reputation of Iceland's best-known sculptor, Einar Jónsson. A wild-looking outlaw dressed in skins carries his dead wife over his back, a spade in one hand and his little boy asleep on his other arm. He wants to bury her in consecrated ground, but would be put to death if captured, so he comes secretly at night. This cast-metal version conveys tension and detail lacking in the plaster model at the **Einar Jónsson Museum ★★** in Reykjavík (p. 57).

Museum of Akureyri (Minjasafn Á Akureyri) ★ MUSEUM   This museum is in the oldest section of town, a 15-minute walk south of the modern part, and holds a permanent exhibit on the cultural history of life in

Akureyri from the 19th century to present day. It also has temporary exhibits on a sub-theme, such as collections of maps of Iceland that date back to the 16th century or a rundown of the 82 different Yule lads, the Icelandic version of Santa Claus.

Aðalstræti 58. www.minjasafnid.is. ℂ **462-4162.** Admission 1,500kr adults; 750kr seniors; free for children ages 15 and under. June 1–Oct 1 daily 10am–5pm; Oct 2–May 31 daily 1–4pm.

Nonni's House (Nonnahús) ★ MUSEUM   This museum is squeezed inside the tiny childhood home of Jón Sveinsson (1857–1944), author of a semi-autobiographical children's book series famous throughout Iceland and Germany. ("Nonni" applies to Jón *and* his fictional boy-hero.) Sveinsson left for France at age 12 to become a Jesuit priest and missionary and never returned, but his boyhood adventures continued to inspire him long after he left. The fictional Nonni, along with his younger brother Manni, live on an isolated north Iceland farm and run into all kinds of family drama and adventure, including a brush with polar bears. The books were written in German, but English translations are sold at reception. The museum, founded in 1957, is full of manuscripts and personal items. Nonnahús and the Museum of Akureyri offer discounted joint admission.

Aðalstræti 54. www.nonni.is. ℂ **462-3555.** Admission 2,000kr adults; free for children 15 and under. June–Aug daily 10am–5pm; Sept Thurs–Sun 10am–5pm.

Where to Stay
EXPENSIVE

Hótel Akureyri ★★   Though it's just a few blocks' walk from the center of town, Hótel Akureyri—in a quaint four-story building (*note:* no elevator) just off the waterfront on a small incline backed by birch trees—feels removed from what little hustle and bustle Akureyri has. The rooms, most of which face the fjord (book well in advance for these during the summer), are more functional than luxurious, but are well-kept and come with cozy duvets. An inviting **lounge** with a full bar is on the ground floor, while the breakfast buffet (1,990kr) is one of the best around, with homemade breads, little jars of *skyr* with preserves and granola, and pastries. The staff is all-around helpful.

Hafnarstræti 67. www.hotelakureyri.is. ℂ **462-5600.** 19 units, 6 apts. May–Sept 20,370kr–25,950kr double; rates higher with ocean view. Rates around 25%–50% lower Oct–Apr. **Amenities:** Lounge; free Wi-Fi.

Hótel Kea ★★   At the base of the long stairway to Akureyri Church, this centrally located, modern Scandinavian property is the city's most luxurious. Though it was built in 1944, it underwent extensive renovations in 2011, when it swallowed up the neighboring hotel and added several dozen more rooms. The stately rooms feature handsome dark-wood furnishings and plush beds, plus smallish bathrooms covered in white tiles. Deluxe rooms add an extra sitting area and nicer artwork, while the suite adds a balcony overlooking Eyjafjörður fjord. The **Múlaberg Bistro & Bar** ★ (see p. 192) is one of the better dining options in Akureyri. Kea Hotels also has a second property a few blocks away, **Hotel Nordurland,** that's considerably less expensive.

Hafnarstræti 87–89. www.keahotels.is. © **460-2000.** 104 units. June–Aug 40,550kr double; 90,800kr suite. Rates around 20% lower May and Sept, 30% lower Oct–Apr. Rates include breakfast. **Amenities:** Restaurant; bar; room service; free Wi-Fi.

MODERATE

Icelandair Hótel Akureyri ★   Open since 2011, this chic hotel from the Icelandair chain is set in a renovated historical building that formerly housed the University of Akureyri. Standard classic rooms are rather cozy, with the toilet and shower rooms literally right behind where the bed pillows sit, though all other rooms are more spacious, with room for a couch. Big windows allow for lots of light and views of the Akureyri pool and the fjord. Family rooms add an extra set of bunk beds for kids. Breakfast is available for 2,280kr. Skiers will appreciate the heated storage room with secure lockers for equipment.

Reception and apts at Geislagata 10. www.icelandairhotels.is. © **444-4000.** 3 units, 6 apts. May–Sept 30,000kr double; 35,000kr family room; 40,000kr suite. Rates 10%–15% lower Oct–Apr. **Amenities:** Restaurant; bar; patio; ski storage room; free Wi-Fi.

Lamb Inn ★   Set on a sheep farm 10km (6¼ miles) south of Akureyri, this 1830s farmhouse is a pleasant alternative to the city hotels for those with their own transportation. It's an excellent base camp for Northern Lights watching. The bright, simple rooms have wood floors and views of the surrounding countryside, though many have shared bathrooms. A popular **restaurant,** lamb-centric of course, is set in a converted barn with original timber.

Rte. 829, 10km (6¼ miles) south of Akureyri. www.lambinn.is. © **463-1500.** 17 units. June–Aug 25,700kr double; 31,300kr triple. Rates around 10% lower Oct–Apr. Rates include breakfast. **Amenities:** Restaurant; bar; hot tub; free Wi-Fi.

INEXPENSIVE

Akureyri Backpackers ★   Smack in the middle of Akureyri's main shopping street, this lively three-floor hostel has captured the attention of the young, backpacking crowd. The old building has 16 four- to eight-person dorms with bunk beds and seven plain and simple private rooms. The hostel's popular **bar** and **restaurant,** open until 1am on the weekends, is a good place to catch up on travel tales. It has a free tour-booking service.

Hafnarstræti 98. www.akureyribackpackers.com. © **571-9050.** 23 units. 20,000kr double; 5,600kr dorm bed. **Amenities:** Restaurant; bar; tour desk; guest kitchen; sauna; laundry; free Wi-Fi.

Apotek Guesthouse ★   Opened in 2015 in a restored building near the waterfront, this small, central guesthouse is bright and clean, with a fresh, minimalist decor. The rooms are spacious and have either shared or private bathrooms. A penthouse apartment adds a full kitchen, living area, and three bedrooms.

Hafnarstræti 104. © **469-4104.** 44 units, 8 w/bathroom. May–Sept 17,800kr double; 15,530kr double without bathroom; 39,100kr penthouse. Rates around 15% lower Oct–Apr. **Amenities:** Shared kitchen; balcony; TV lounge; free Wi-Fi.

Hrafn Inn ★ This laidback guesthouse is close to the bus terminal, though still walking distance to the center. Rooms are smallish but come with wood floors, flatscreen TVs, and private facilities. Common room is lacking, aside from a cramped sitting area with Victorian furnishings and a shared kitchen facility where you can make your own breakfast.

Brekkugata 4. www.hrafninn.is. ✆ **462-2300.** 40 units, 1 w/bathroom. May 15–Sept 24,000kr double. Rates around 20% lower Sept–May. Rates do not include breakfast. **Amenities:** Guest kitchen; free Wi-Fi.

Where to Eat

Reykjavík's restaurants are hard to match, but Akureyri puts on a respectable showing and makes the most of local strengths. The Eyjafjörður Valley is a big beef- and dairy-producing region, and *skyr*—Iceland's famous whipped whey concoction—was invented here. Delicious blue mussels are cultivated in Eyjafjörður. Perhaps we shouldn't tell you that Eyjafjörður's excellent smoked lamb is smoked "the traditional way"—with dried manure. Iceland's first and only microbrewery, *Kaldi,* is in the tiny village of Árskógssandur, although the beer is made with grain imported from the Czech Republic.

EXPENSIVE

Múlaberg Bistro & Bar ★ INTERNATIONAL   On the ground floor and the patio of the Hotel Kea, this sleek hotel restaurant is proof of Akureyri's evolving tastebuds. The eclectic kitchen dishes out everything from finger foods and *moules frites* to ceviches using local seafood and smoked duck breast. A daily happy hour runs from 4 to 6pm.

Hafnarstraeti 87-89. ✆ **460-2020.** Main courses 2,290kr–6,290kr. Sun–Thurs 11:30am–11pm; Fri–Sat 11:30am–1am.

Rub 23 ★ INTERNATIONAL   Spice rubs like Indian or Caribbean Creole, which customers can pick and add to their choice of fish or meat, are the backbone of this concept restaurant. Sure, it's a little gimmicky, and with ingredients this fresh, especially the fish, the rubs and sauces are better left off, but few chefs in the north really know how to work the products quite like they do. Each main course also comes with a tray of house-made sauces, like mango chile or roasted garlic and coriander, plus some roasted potatoes and sweet potato puree. There's also a lengthy sushi menu, which ultimately might be the better option. With a vaulted ceiling and contemporary art, the modern space is one of the more attractive establishments in town.

Kaupvangsstræti 6. www.rub23.is. ✆ **462-2223.** Main courses 4,990kr–6,490kr. Daily 5:30–10pm.

Strikið ★ ICELANDIC   The view from its fourth-floor porch—whether from the interior dining room with its tall windows or the ample terrace—gives Strikið a vantage point to take in the sea, mountains, and Akureyri town center. If the fun ended there, most guests would still probably leave satisfied. Yet the eclectic menu doesn't disappoint, giving Asian touches to Icelandic products without seeming gimmicky, such as the shellfish soup with lemongrass and ginger or the langoustine tempura.

Skipagata 14. ✆ **462-7100.** Reservations recommended. Main courses 2,800kr–6,200kr. Mon–Thurs 11:30am–10pm; Fri–Sat 11:30am–11pm; Sun 5–10pm.

MODERATE

1862 Nordic Bistro ★ SCANDINAVIAN   Named after the year Akureyri was founded by Danish King Frederik VII, this modern Scandinavian bistro inside the Hof cultural center lacks soul, but with high-quality ingredients and a great space, you probably won't care. The menu includes Danish open-faced sandwiches, traditional lamb soup, and even a vegan nut steak. A Sunday brunch buffet from 11am to 2pm is 3,250kr.

Strandgötu 12, inside the Hof Cultural and Conference Center. www.1862.is. ✆ **466-1862.** Main courses 2,500kr–4,400kr. Mon–Sat 11:30am–8pm; Sun 11am–6pm.

Bautinn ★ ICELANDIC   This stalwart, family-friendly eatery on Akureyri's busiest corner serves a large, all-around menu with something for everyone. Foodies will appreciate the sprinkling of local dishes, like hashed fish or guillemot with lingonberry sauce, while less adventurous diners have pastas, sandwiches, and pizzas to choose from. All main courses, which come with fried vegetables and potatoes, also include the soup and salad bar.

Hafnarstræti 92. www.bautinn.is. ✆ **462-1818.** Main courses 1,890kr–4,290kr. Daily 9am–11pm.

Hamborgarafabrikkan ★ BURGERS   Also known as the Hamburger Factory, this quirky gourmet burger chain launched in Reykjavik in 2010. This branch beneath Hotel Kea is their first outside of the capital. A multicolored cow just inside the door and Christmas lights on the ceiling liven up the semi-industrial space. If you are tired of mediocre burgers at hotel restaurants around the Ring Road, these meaty, square burgers make for a nice change from pan-fried Arctic char. There are dozens of variations, including an Icelandic lamb burger, as well as chicken wings and salads, *skyr* cake for dessert, and even oversized fishbowl cocktails.

Hafnarstræti 87–89. www.fabrikkan.is. ✆ **575-7575.** Main courses 2,295kr–2,995kr. Daily 11:30am–11pm.

INEXPENSIVE

Akureyri Fish ★ INTERNATIONAL   This divey, one-room seafood spot near the waterfront is the simplest option for indulging in Akureyi's extra-special fresh fish access. Battered and fried fish and chips, served with homemade sauces like lemon pepper dill or béarnaise, are the specialty. Traditional Icelandic *plokkari*, or grilled chicken, is discounted during lunch.

Skipagata 12. ✆ **414-6050.** Main courses 1,390kr–2,390kr. Daily 11:30am–10pm.

Bláa Kannan ★ CAFE   Spilling onto Akureyri's main pedestrian street, this lively cafe is perhaps Akureyri's best people-watching spot. When the weather is nice, there is no better place to sit outside checking your e-mails with a coffee in hand. If you need a light snack, it offers sandwiches and various baked goods, like cakes and quiche.

Hafnarstræti 96. ✆ **461-4600.** Main courses 1,250kr–1,650kr. Mon–Sat 9am–11pm; Sun 10am–11pm.

Outdoor Activities

Akureyri's best travel agency for booking tours is **Nonni Travel,** Brekkugata 5 (www.nonnitravel.is; ✆ **461-1841;** Mon–Fri 9am–5pm). The **tourist information office** (p. 186) can also book many tours.

AERIAL TOURS   Seeing Iceland from an airplane may seem decadent or extravagant, but few regret this memorable and exhilarating experience. **Mýflug Air** (www.myflug.is; ✆ **464-4400**) offers sightseeing trips from 20 minutes up to 2 hours; prices range from 19,000kr to 57,000kr. Logical destinations include Mývatn, Jökulsárgljúfur, Herðubreið, Askja, and Kverkfjöll; for all these places, however, it's cheaper to take off from Mývatn. Eagle Air and Mýflug flights can be booked through the tourist office.

DIVING   Since 2010, **Strytan Dive Center** (www.strytan.is; ✆ **862-2949**) has been operating diving trips for 437,000kr for single guided dives, to geothermal chimneys, Ásbyrgi canyon, and Grímsey Island, as well as PADI certification and multi-day tours.

GOLF   **Golfklúbbur Akureyrar** (www.gagolf.is; ✆ **462-2974**) runs the world-class course **Jaðarsvöllur** (course fee 8,500kr; club rental 5,500kr; cart rental 5,700kr; June–Aug 8am–10pm), which hosts the 36-hole **Arctic Open** (www.arcticopen.is; entry fee 42,400kr) in late June; contestants tee off into the morning hours under the midnight sun. The course is up the hill southwest of the city, off Eikarlundur.

HIKING   The best local hiking is southwest of Akureyri in and around Glerárdalur Valley, which is surrounded by small glaciers and some of north Iceland's tallest mountains. Most routes are strenuous, and hikers should be aware that harsh weather, even snowstorms, could set in without warning. The best place to start is **Ferðafélag Akureyrar,** Strandgata 23, Akureyri (www.ffa.is; ✆ **462-2720**), which maintains the **Lambi mountain hut** in Glerárdalur, and publishes the *Glerárdalur* hiking map (800kr).

HORSEBACK RIDING   **Pólar Hestar** (www.polarhestar.is; ✆ **463-3179**), one of Iceland's most well-established horse tour companies, is recommended for everything from 1-hour rides (6,000kr) to multi-day pack trips through the interior. Pickup from Akureyri can be arranged.

FISHING   **Iceland Fishing Guide** (www.icelandfishingguide.com; ✆ **660-1642;** 40,000kr per person; two-person min.) offers 6-hour fishing tours to lakes and rivers around northern Iceland, including lunch and equipment.

SKIING   **Hlíðarfjall** (www.hlidarfjall.is; ✆ **462-2280**) is Iceland's premier ski area, sitting on the banks of the fjord with lovely watery views. Best conditions are usually in February and March, and the slopes are floodlit during the darkest winter days. The longest run is 2.5km (1½ miles) with a 500m (1,640 ft.) vertical drop, and the area is served by six lifts including four-man chairs. Hlíðarfjall also offers cross-country trails, a snowboarding course, a ski school, equipment rental, and a restaurant. Hlíðarfjall is 7km (4¼ miles) west of town; take Hlíðarbraut or Þingvallastræti to Hlíðarfjallsvegur. A taxi costs about 4,000kr each way.

SWIMMING   The **Akureyri Geothermal Pool ★**, Þingvallastræti 21 (**⌀461-4455;** admission 950kr adults; free for children 4 and under; June–Aug Mon–Fri 6:45am–10pm, Sat–Sun 8am–7:30pm; Sept–May Mon–Fri 6:45am–9pm, Sat–Sun 10am–4:30pm), is a water wonderland, with indoor and outdoor pools, a children's pool, two waterslides, hot tubs, massaging water jets, a steam bath, fitness equipment, an ice cream stand, and, for an extra charge, a sauna. Bring a towel to avoid the 800kr rental fee.

WHALE-WATCHING   Whale-watching in Eyjafjörður is traditionally based at Hauganes and Dalvík, north of Akureyri (p. 198), though **Ambassador** (www.ambassador.is; ⌀ **462-6800**) also offers two or three daily 3-hour departures direct from Torfunefsbryggja harbor in downtown Akureyri (10,990kr adults; 4,445kr children 7–15).

Shopping

Most Akureyri shopping can be quickly scanned by perusing Hafnarstræti (especially the northern, pedestrian-only stretch), Skipagata, and Ráðhústorg Square, where the two streets meet. Along Glerárgata, just north of the Glerá River, is **Glerártorg Mall** (⌀ **461-5770;** Mon–Fri 10am–6:30pm; Sat 10am–5pm; Sun 1–5pm), two restaurants, a drugstore, a supermarket, and 37 stores, including the trendy Icelandic outerwear company 66° North.

Flóra ★   This concept store and workshop utilizes recycled, handcrafted, and handmade items from local designers. You'll find everything from gourmet goods like honey and Icelandic herbs to cutesy candles and hand-knitted woolen accessories. Hafnarstræti 90. www.floraflora.is. ⌀ **661-0168.** Mon–Fri 10am–6pm; Sat 10am–4pm.

Kista ★   This contemporary design store in the Hof sells various Icelandic-made products, from a shaggy foot stool to wool items to candles. Strandgötu 12, inside the Hof Cultural and Conference Center. www.kista.is. ⌀ **897-0555.** Mon–Fri 10am–6pm; Sat–Sun 11am–4pm.

Penninn Eymundsson ★   An inviting bookstore on Akureyri's busiest corner, this shop has a variety of English-language books, plus maps, souvenirs, Wi-Fi, and a cafe. Hafnarstræti 91–93. www.eymundsson.is. ⌀ **540-2180.** Mon–Fri 9am–10pm; Sat–Sun 10am–10pm.

Akureyri Nightlife

Most nights in summer, activities are not limited to loud bars and clubs; the *Listasumar* brochure delineates everything from Thursday-night jazz sets to choral concerts and evening "history sailing" in the fjord. Akureyri's bars and nightclubs are within a 10-minute walk of each other, so roam (as Icelanders do) until you find a scene to your liking. Only live music commands a cover charge, and you'll never be pressured to buy drinks. On Friday and Saturday nights, teenagers drive around town at a crawl, dressed as if they're cruising Miami Beach in a '50s convertible, honking and gabbing out the car windows.

The main nightspots are **Café Amour,** Ráðhústorg 9 (© **461-3030**), which has a wine bar downstairs and small DJ room upstairs with holographic bordello wallpaper; and **Græni Hatturinn,** Hafnarstræti 96 (© **461-4646**), a dedicated music venue inside one of Akureyri's oldest houses. **Akureyri Backpackers ★** (see p. 191) has a lively cafe that turns more publike as the night wears on, serving a few basic cocktails and Icelandic craft beers.

NEAR AKUREYRI

Akureyri is a great base for excursions fanning out in several directions. **Eyjafjörður,** with its broad, smoothly sloping bowl shape and rich farmland, seems to welcome human habitation more than other Icelandic fjords. **Safnasafnið** and **Smámunasafn** are two of Iceland's most offbeat and inspiring museums. The inhabited islands of **Hrísey** and **Grímsey,** both full of birdlife, are fascinating worlds unto themselves. Farther afield, **Goðafoss** and **Aldeyjarfoss** are among Iceland's most exquisite waterfalls. Some sights, notably **Safnasafnið** and **Goðafoss,** are on the Ring Road and can fit into trips to Mývatn, Húsavík, and Jökulsárgljúfur.

Hrísey Island ★

Heimaey (Home Island) in the Westman Islands is Iceland's largest and most populated offshore island; Hrísey is second on both counts, with about 180 residents. With its paved roads, well-tended homes, and geothermal swimming pool, the village does not feel particularly marginal. Hrísey has been inhabited since the 10th century but sprouted rapidly in the 19th century as a base for processing and exporting herring. The herring vanished at the end of the 1960s, and in 1999 the fish-freezing plant closed, forcing many residents to leave.

Hrísey has a clear view to the northern horizon, and is perfect for witnessing the scooping midnight sun in early summer. Fjord views on the island are heart-stirring if not heart-stopping. In mid-July, Hrísey plays at being a sovereign nation during its Independence Day **Family Festival:** Guests pass through customs, get their Hrísey passport stamped, then enjoy tractor and fishing trips, dancing, and a children's singing competition.

ESSENTIALS

The main **ferry** to Hrísey, **Sævar** (www.hrisey.is; © **695-5544;** round-trip ticket 1,500kr adults, 750kr children 12–15, free for children 11 and under;

departures every 2 hr. daily 9:30am–11pm) leaves from Árskógssandur, a small village on the western shore of Eyjafjörður, 35km (22 miles) north of Akureyri. The ride lasts 15 minutes.

Hrísey's **information office** is inside a shark museum called **"The House of Shark Jörundur,"** the oldest house on the island, on Norðuvegur 5 (www.hrisey.is; © **695-0077;** mid-June to mid-Aug daily 10am–4pm). A crafts store, **Pearl Gallery,** is located by the ferry landing.

EXPLORING HRÍSEY ISLAND

In summer, as you disembark the ferry, you'll likely see **Tractor Trips** in action (© **695-0077**) where tourists take 2-hour **birdwatching tours** in a tractor-pulled hay cart, which has seats and a loudspeaker so the driver can commentate. Call in advance to make reservations.

Free **trail maps** are available on the ferry. The main trail ascends to Hrísey's highest point in a 2.3-km (1.4-mile) loop, but the longer trails are best for bird sightings. The far northern section of Hrísey, **Ystabæjarland,** is a private nature reserve accessible only with the owner's permission; consult the information office if you hope to hike all the way there. Permission is usually not granted until mid-July, to protect birds during nesting season.

Hrísey's **bird populations** chose their residence well. Hunting is prohibited, and no foxes or mink have made it out to the island. Hrísey is a quarantine station for imported pigs and cattle, so Icelandic horses and sheep—which never interbreed with foreigners, at least not in Iceland—are kept off the island to keep them safe from species-hopping diseases. This leaves more vegetation for ground-nesting bird species.

WHERE TO STAY & DINE

The only accommodations are at **Brekka** (www.brekkahrisey.is; © **466-1751;** Jun–Aug daily 11:30am–9pm, Sept–May Fri–Sat dinner only), a yellow building visible from the water's edge. The restaurant is far better than you might anticipate, with first-rate fish and lamb dishes (2,790kr–6,700kr). Four basic doubles with shared bathroom and ocean views go for 11,000kr.

bombs AWAY!

Arctic terns, which harass and sometimes attack anything that comes near their eggs, are a serious menace and can turn a Hrísey walk into a Hitchcockian nightmare. Terns are very agile and the attack comes in a quick swoop, with furious flapping and hideous shrieks. (The Icelandic word for tern, *kría*, comes from the shrieking sound.) The worst time is June, when walkers should carry some sort of stick or umbrella over their heads for protection.

Ptarmigans, on the other hand, haven't the slightest fear of people, and in early September waddle right into village streets and yards seeking protection from falcons. The spindly-legged and needle-billed godwits, around from mid-May to mid-August, are another endearing sight.

Grímsey Island ★

Many visitors studying a map of Iceland notice an obscure speck, 41km (25 miles) north of the mainland and bisected by the Arctic Circle, and feel strangely compelled to go there. Grímsey is indeed a worthwhile and exotic destination (more for the Arctic location than any exceptional topography) with 85 hardy inhabitants, basalt cliffs reaching 105m (344 ft.), and abundant birdlife. Many visitors come in late June to see the midnight sun "bounce" off the horizon, but this involves a tradeoff. June and early July is also when Arctic terns most aggressively defend their nests, sometimes drawing blood from the scalps of unwitting tourists (see "Bombs Away!" box, above).

ESSENTIALS

GETTING THERE   Until 1931, the only way to get to Grímsey was on a mail boat that came twice a year. Today, **Air Iceland** (www.airiceland.is; ✆ 570-3030) flies from Akureyri daily at 8:30 to 9:30am (1pm Saturdays) and returns to Akureyri at 11am. The flight is 25 minutes and costs around 9,950kr one-way; or from Reykjavík with a stop is around 19,800kr one-way. **Mýflug Air** (www.myflug.is; ✆ 464-4400) has a 2-hour tour for 48,000kr, leaving from Mývatn in a plane that does aerial sightseeing along the way.

From May 15 until the end of August, the *Sæfari* **ferry** (www.samskip.is; ✆ 853-2211; round-trip from Dalvík 1,500kr adults, 750kr seniors and children ages 12–15, free for children 11 and under) sails from Dalvík to Grímsey on Mondays, Wednesdays, and Fridays. A bus leaves Akureyri at 7:50am and connects with the ferry, which leaves at 9am and arrives at noon. The return trip is at 4pm, reaching Dalvík at 7pm, where another bus bound for Akureyri waits. From September until mid-May, the ferry departs for Grímsey at the same times, but heads right back to Dalvík after unloading.

One-way tickets for Air Iceland flights and the ferry are half-price, so it makes sense to mix and match. Taking the ferry there and the flight back, for instance, gives you more than 8 hours on Grímsey.

VISITOR INFORMATION   Consult **Akureyri's tourist information office** (p. 186), or visit www.grimsey.is.

EXPLORING GRÍMSEY ISLAND

Grímsey is flat-topped and only 5.3sq. km (3⅓ sq. miles), with the highest cliffs on the east side, and walks are a straightforward matter. The island is home to more than 60 **bird species.** The most popular are puffins, which can be observed from May to mid-August.

For the right price, someone is always willing to take you **sea fishing, bird hunting,** or, in May or June, **egg-collecting;** contact either guesthouse listed below.

Gallery Sól, Sólberg (✆ 467-3190), a gallery, souvenir shop, and cafe, opens up to greet arriving and departing visitors from the ferry or plane. The **community hall** has a library endowed by David William Fiske (1831–1904), a wealthy American who never set foot in Grímsey but was touched by how much the locals were dedicated to chess.

WHERE TO STAY & DINE

Most of Grímsey's houses are in the village of Sandvík, which has a small **market**.

Guesthouse Básar ★ Just a few steps from the Arctic Circle, this no-frills, family-run guesthouse has simple rooms, plus a shared kitchen and living area. Some rooms accommodate up to three or four. Dinners and sea-angling tours can be arranged by advance request.

Básar. www.gistiheimilidbasar.is. ✆ **467-3103.** 8 units, none w/bathroom. 16,000kr double; 6,000kr per person sleeping-bag accommodation. Breakfast available (1,500kr). **Amenities:** Guest kitchen; free Wi-Fi in public areas.

Guesthouse Gullsól ★ Above Gallery Sól, the island's de facto welcome center, this simple property features a shared TV lounge and guest kitchen. It's one of the liveliest places on the island, though that's not saying much on Grímsey. The friendly owners can help set up birdwatching or fishing trips around the island.

Sólberg. www.gullsol.is. ✆ **467-3190.** 6 units, none w/bathroom. 13,000kr double. **Amenities:** Guest kitchen; no Wi-Fi.

Restaurant Kría ★ Basically the only real restaurant on the island, Kría serves up local specialties such as fish, lamb, and puffin, as well as the standard burgers and sandwiches. It has a nice view of the harbor, and they also rent bicycles (1,500kr for 3 hr.).

Nýja-sjáland. ✆ **467-3112.** Main courses 1,900kr–4,600kr. May–early Sept daily noon–9pm; bar open late Fri–Sat. Early Sept–Apr usually closed, but call ahead.

Upper Eyjafjördður

Icelanders tolerate and even nurture their single-minded eccentrics, as evidenced by the three sights below. All are on Route 821, which heads directly south from Akureyri.

Christmas House (Jólagarðurinn) ★ SHOP The fireplace is always lit and hung with stockings at this year-round, fire-engine-red Christmas dreamhouse topped with giant candy canes. All things Christmassy are on sale inside, while outside you'll find an enormous advent calendar inside a faux medieval turret and perhaps the most festive restroom in the world. Beware Grýla the troll, who lives downstairs.

Rte. 821, 11km (7 miles) south of Akureyri. ✆ **463-1433.** Free admission. June–Aug daily 10am–10pm; Sept–Dec daily 2–10pm; Jan–May daily 2–6pm.

Grundarkirkja Church ★ CHURCH A church has existed at Grund in some form since medieval times. This curious 1905 incarnation, atypically aligned north to south, has several Romanesque spires, an onion dome, and a balconied interior reminiscent of an opera house. It's the largest Icelandic church financed by an individual, farmer Magnús Sigurðsson, and is atypical of most Icelandic churches of the late-19th and early-20th centuries, which tend to be simple structures with square belfries, sometimes elongated, and topped by a kind of narrow-brimmed hat. A chalice from the 15th century and a church chair from the times of Þórunn, the daughter of bishop Jón Árnason, found at the church are now at the National Museum of Iceland (see p. 56).

Rte. 821, 18km (11 miles) south of Akureyri.

Sverrir Hermannsson's Sundry Collection ★ MUSEUM   This oddball museum is essentially a junk collection meticulously sorted and arranged by master carpenter Sverrir Hermannsson (1928–2008), whose reconstruction work can still be seen on many of the most famous buildings in the region. Exhibits include mounted arrays of nails, cocktail napkins, perfume bottles, fake teeth, hair elastics, waffle irons, and unbroken spirals of pencil shavings. You'll have to decide for yourself whether the patterns and repetitions are artistic or simply obsessive. Sverrir marked most items with the initials of the original owner, and many bear the word *gámur,* meaning they were rescued after being thrown out. A cafe is on-hand, and up the hill is **Saurbær Church,** a typical turf church from 1858.

Rte. 821, 27km (16¾ miles) south of Akureyri. www.smamunasafnid.is. ✆ **463-1261.** Admission 1,000kr adults; 500kr seniors; free for children 15 and under. May 15–Sept 15 daily 11am–5pm.

Northeast of Akureyri

Laufás ★ FARM MUSEUM   Of the many 19th-century turf-covered farms that are now museums, Laufás—a parsonage built in the 1860s, in a meadow overlooking Eyjafjörður—was the most prosperous. The old rectory is considered to be the prototype of Icelandic architecture, though it is much larger than other examples. Twenty to thirty people lived in the labyrinthine interior at a time, with rooms designated for weaving, cleaning birds, and dressing brides. The damp and claustrophobic rooms have only thin shafts of light from high windows, but contemporaries would have envied the wood floors and crafting of the walls, with their alternating layers of stone and tweed-patterned sod. There are no guided tours, and little information is in English.

Laufás earned money harvesting eider down, which explains a gable carving of a woman's head crowned by a duck. The 1865 church is well restored and typical of its time; the most endearing feature is the **1698 pulpit,** with unschooled but talented carvings of five saints grinning like dolls. An old-fashioned **cafe** serves flatbread with smoked trout, rhubarb pie, and bread with mountain moss baked inside (originally eaten to keep Icelanders from dying of scurvy). On a Sunday in mid-July, Laufás hosts a historical event with staff in period costume carving wood, cooking pancakes, and mowing with scythes.

Rte. 83 (about 10km/6¼ miles from Rte. 1 and 30km/19 miles from Akureyri). www. akmus.is. ✆ **463-3196.** Admission 1,500kr adults; 750kr for children 16 and under. May 15–Sept 15 daily 10am–6pm.

Safnasafnið ★★ MUSEUM   The admirable concept behind this enjoyable and penetrating museum is to erase boundaries between folk art, "outsider" art, and contemporary art—and the results here are highly successful.

The 5,000-plus pieces extend far beyond paintings and sculptures to include dolls, toys, embroidery, tools, and anywhere that creative expression can be found. Established artists are included, but curators also scour the country in search of compelling work by anyone, including those with no formal training. Safnasafnið expanded in 2007 and puts on 12 to 15 exhibitions a year, in any conceivable artistic genre. The two constants are a rotating exhibit from the Icelandic Doll Museum, and a hands-on toy exhibit inspired by optical illusions. Wondering about that blue-and-yellow cube on the wall? Stare at it for a minute, then focus on the white wall and its inverse image appears.

Rte. 1, 11km (7 miles) northeast of Akureyri. www.safnasafnid.is. ✆ **461-4066.** Admission 1,200kr adults; free for children 13 and under. Early May to mid-Aug daily 10am–5pm; Apr–Oct by appointment.

Between Akureyri & Mývatn
GOÐAFOSS ★

Located right off the Ring Road, about 50km (31 miles) east of Akureyri and 53km (33 miles) west of Reykjahlíð, Goðafoss (Waterfall of the Gods) is not very tall or powerful, but admirers point to the separate cascades forming an elegant semicircular arc, the swirling patterns in the blue-green (or sometimes brown) water, and the strange bubbliness of the surrounding lava. According to legend, Goðafoss was named in the year 1000 when the Law Speaker of the Icelandic parliament, after proclaiming Iceland a Christian country, tossed his pagan statuettes into the falls.

Just downstream is the restaurant and guesthouse **Fosshóll** (www.godafoss. is; ✆ **464-3108;** 25,935kr double; May 15–Sept daily 6–10pm; closed Oct–May 14), which serves local trout on top of the usual road-stop fare. You can park right by the falls, but walking upstream from Fosshóll is a more satisfying approach.

ALDEYJARFOSS ★★

This stunning waterfall is worth the substantial detour from the Ring Road. The falls have a powerful churning force, and the freakish basalt formations are enough to make spectators wonder what planet they've been transported to. To reach Aldeyjarfoss, turn south on Route 842 from the Ring Road, just west of Goðafoss, and proceed 41km (25 miles) to the marked turnoff. Buses on the Sprengisandur route from Mývatn to Landmannalaugar all make a sightseeing stop here.

MÝVATN & KRAFLA

Iceland's president Ólafur Ragnar Grímsson wrote: "The Old Testament teaches us that God created the world in 6 days and then rested. This is not altogether true. Iceland was forgotten when He went to rest." The **Mývatn–Krafla region** ★★★—a volcanic smorgasbord of surreal lava fields, boiling and burping mud pools, sulfurous steam vents, explosion craters, and pseudocraters—is Iceland's most varied place to see the earth in mid-formation. Lake Mývatn is also a unique ecosystem and the largest migratory bird

Lake Mývatn

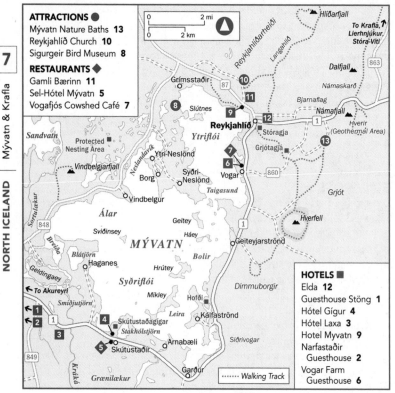

ATTRACTIONS ●
Mývatn Nature Baths **13**
Reykjahlíð Church **10**
Sigurgeir Bird Museum **8**

RESTAURANTS ◆
Gamli Bærinn **11**
Sel-Hótel Mývatn **5**
Vogafjós Cowshed Café **7**

HOTELS ■
Elda **12**
Guesthouse Stöng **1**
Hótel Gígur **4**
Hótel Laxa **3**
Hotel Myvatn **9**
Narfastaðir
  Guesthouse **2**
Vogar Farm
  Guesthouse **6**

sanctuary in Europe, with thousands of waterfowl feeding on bugs and algae in the warm, shallow waters.

Mývatn is part of the greater Krafla volcanic system, a swath of faults and fissures 4 to 10km (2½–6 miles) wide and 80km (50 miles) north to south, with Krafla caldera at its center. Krafla's last two eruption periods were 1724–1729 and 1975–1984. Both times, multiple fissures shifted and dilated, with sporadic eruptions and lava fountains, but much of the magma never surfaced, petering out laterally underground. Today, the most active geothermal areas are Krafla and Bjarnarflag, each with a geothermal power plant. The Krafla region is ideal for plants harnessing geothermal energy, because eruptions are infrequent and foreshadowed by a year of tectonic grumbling.

Mývatn–Krafla is well-touristed, and places to stay fill up quickly in summer, so the May or September shoulder season is advantageous. In high season, it may be a good idea to visit here early in your itinerary, before you've been spoiled by solitude elsewhere. On June weekends, there may be choral concerts in the church or at Dimmuborgir. Mývatn–Krafla is also a compelling winter destination. Despite the multitude of sights, 2 days here is sufficient.

Essentials

GETTING THERE & AROUND

The only village in the area is **Reykjahlíð,** on the northeast shore of Mývatn. **Skútustaðir,** on the south side of the lake, has a small cluster of tourist services.

BY CAR   Reykjahlíð, along Route 87 just off the Ring Road, is 103km (64 miles) east of Akureyri and 166km (103 miles) west of Egilsstaðir. The nearest place to arrange **car rental** is in Akureyri.

BY BUS   The **Strætó bus** (www.straeto.is; ✆ **540-2700**) connecting Akureyri and Egilsstaðir stops at Skútustaðir and Reykjahlíð. It runs daily from June until August. The cost is 2,760kr from Akureyri or 5,980kr from Egilsstaðir. **SBA Norðurleið** (www.sba.is; ✆ **550-0700**) has Mývatn–Krafla **sightseeing day tours** departing from Akureyri and Mývatn. The tour from Akureyri (17,100kr) hits Goðafoss (p. 201), Stóra-Víti, Hverir, Grjótagjá, and Dimmuborgir. From Reykjahlíð, the main daily tour (8,000kr; 3¼ hr.) hits Dimmuborgir, Grjótagjá, Stóra-Víti, Hverir, and the Mývatn Nature Baths. Unforgivably, neither tour goes to **Leirhnjúkur ★★★** (p. 206). All Sterna and SBA buses leaving Reykjahlíð board at the tourist information office (below) next to the N1 filling station.

BY BIKE   Bike **rental** is available from **Hike & Bike** (www.hikeandbike.is; ✆ **899-4845**) for 5,000kr a day, while **Ferðaþjónustan Bjarg** (ferdabjarg@ simnet.is; ✆ **464-3800**) rents out bikes for 4,500kr a day, but like cows and horses they must be returned to the shed every evening by 9pm.

ON FOOT   Touring the sights by foot is possible, but most visitors find bus tours, car rental, or bike rental more practical. All hotels, restaurants, and services in Reykjahlíð are within walking distance of one another.

VISITOR INFORMATION

Mývatn's **tourist information office** is at Hraunvegur 8 (www.visitmyvatn.is; ✆ **464-4390;** June–Aug daily 9am–6pm; call for off-season opening hours).

Exploring the Area

AROUND MÝVATN

The following sights form a clockwise route around the lake, starting in Reykjahlíð. The distance around the lake is 36km (22 miles) by car.

In 1729, at the height of the Krafla eruption, a lava stream gobbled up two farmhouses and was headed straight for **Reykjahlíð Church.** At the last moment, the stream split and flowed into the lake. The church site is slightly elevated, but prayer was credited for averting disaster. The current church dates from 1962, and the vivid pulpit carving depicts the old church with the eruption in the background and "27 AUGUST, 1729" written in psychedelic font. All that remains of the old church is a foundation wall in the graveyard, and menacing heaves of lava are still clearly visible just beyond the graveyard wall.

The road to the church (and campsite and airfield) leads uphill from Hótel Reynihlíð. Near the end of the road, a pleasant trail leads west over the

Eldhraun lava field, before crossing Route 87 and heading back to town along the north shore of the lake; allow 2½ to 3 hours round-trip.

Stóragjá, Grjótagjá, Hverfell, and **Dimmuborgir** (below) are connected by a recommended and well-marked trail, 7km (4.3 miles) or 2½ to 3 hours in each direction. The **trail** begins from the Ring Road near Reykjahlíð, a few meters east of the Route 87 junction. Between Grjótagjá and Hverfell, the trail has two marked junctures—one coinciding with the Hverfell parking area—where you can detour to **Mývatn Nature Baths ★★★** (p. 206).

The steamy **Grjótagjá fissure ★** is set amid a geothermal valley of red and black gravel. Grjótagjá is 2km (1¼ miles) from the Stóragjá–Dimmuborgir trailhead, and also reachable by car on Route 860, which connects with the Ring Road at two points. (Approaching from the west requires opening a sheep gate.) Near the parking area, two portals in the heaving lava lead to an enticing hot spring and pool. You can climb down and sit by the water, but it's too hot for swimming and fogs up camera lenses.

Hverfell ★★—the striated black mound shaped like a dog bowl—is unmistakable. The name "Hverfell" is a controversial subject; for the past 150 years it's been Hverfjall (*fjall* meaning "mountain"). However, a local man took the matter to court and won his case to have it returned to its original Hverfell (*fell* meaning "small hill"). Hence signs that say Hverfell (Hverfjall). Either way, it was formed between 2,500 and 2,900 years ago, when rising magma met with groundwater, forcing a massive explosion of steam, ash, and rock. The rim is 1km (⅔ mile) in diameter, and the crater is 140m (459 ft.) deep, with a round nub in the middle. Hverfell's solemn, elemental grandeur cannot be fully appreciated without walking up to the crater rim. It's a 3km (1.9-mile) walk south from Grjótagjá, but you can also drive from the Ring Road to a parking area on Hverfell's north side. From there it's a 25-minute ascent. The trail loops completely around the rim, and the descent of the southern slope toward Dimmuborgir is steep and more challenging.

Meaning "Dark Castles," **Dimmuborgir** is a surreal lava field 1km (⅔ mile) in diameter. Its most distinctive features are the contorted crags and pillars reaching 20m (66 ft.) in height; nothing quite like them exists elsewhere, except on the ocean floor. Dimmuborgir was created around 2,200 years ago, when molten lava formed a lava lake on the site. Eventually the lava found an outlet and drained into Mývatn, but hardened pillars had formed around steam vents and were left behind. The surface of the lava lake had half-congealed, and left all kinds of crusty "watermarks" on its way out. The best time of year to visit is at the end of summer when the fiery hues of the birch contrast spectacularly with the black lava formations; plus the air is free of midges.

Dimmuborgir is a 2km (1-mile) walk from the southern face of Hverfell, and can also be reached by car off the Ring Road. Plan on walking for an hour or two among the well-marked loop trails. The recommended **Kirkjuvegur trail** leads to **Kirkjan (Church),** a lava chute forming an archway. The more hazardous **Krókastígur trail** cuts through the middle of the site, past some of the most bizarre formations.

Höfði, a lakeside park on a small promontory, makes for a nice hour-long stroll along peaceful forested pathways. The fragrant spruce and other trees were planted by Höfði's former owner. After entering the park, the trail branching off to the right leads to another juncture where you can detour uphill to a fantastic viewpoint. If you bear left after the park entrance and circle the promontory clockwise, you'll pass a clearing overlooking Kálfarströnd.

The name **Kálfarströnd** ★ refers to a farm on a grassy peninsula extending into Mývatn, and also to a series of lava columns *(klasar)* rising like strange mushrooms in a cove between the peninsula and Höfði Park. The turnoff from the Ring Road is 1km (⅔ mile) south of Höfði. After parking, pass through the farm gate, and the 30-minute, staked loop trail past the klasar is shortly ahead on the right. Kálfarströnd is sublime on a calm, soft-lit evening, with the klasar looming, the sky reflected in the aquamarine shallows, Höfði's evergreens in the background, and Mývatn's trim green islands etched in the distance. Bring your head net.

If Mývatn had a visual trademark, it would be **Skútustaðagígar,** the cluster of pseudocraters surrounding Stakhólstjörn pond, at the southwest shore of the lake. Pseudocraters, found primarily in Iceland (and on Mars), are so named because they were never conduits for emerging lava. They're formed when lava flowing above ground heats sub-surface water, causing explosions from steam and gas buildup. The Skútustaðagígar pseudocraters, each around 20m (66 ft.) deep, are quite striking from the road (or from Vindbelgjarfjall, below); but when viewed from the rims, they're simply grassy bowls. The walk around Stakhólstjörn takes an hour; or a 30-minute circuit begins opposite the Skútustaðir gas station or from Hótel Gígur (p. 208).

The best all-around vista of Mývatn is from the top of **Vindbelgjarfjall mountain** ★, near the northwest shore. The 2-hour round-trip hike to the summit leaves from Vagnbrekka farm, off Route 848, 4km (2½ miles) from the junction with the Ring Road. From the farm to the base of the mountain, the trail traverses a protected nesting area for waterfowl. The protected area is off-limits from May 15 to July 20, but does not extend to the trail. The ascent is all scree and a bit slippery, but manageable.

THE KRAFLA GEOTHERMAL AREA

The Krafla central volcano crater is difficult to see from the ground because its shape is broken and irregular, yet its overall diameter is as large as that of Mývatn. Krafla is the name of a small mountain in the area, just east of the Víti crater but not to be confused with the Krafla central volcano. The Krafla Geothermal Area is within the Krafla central volcano and includes the areas Leirhnjúkur and Stóra-Víti, while Mývatn Nature Baths, Hverir, Námafjall Ridge and Bjarnarflag are south of the Krafla Geothermal Area.

Hverir ★, a large geothermal field, full of bubbling mud cauldrons and hissing steam vents, is 7km (4¼ miles) east of Reykjahlíð and easy to spot from the Ring Road. Walking through Hverir feels unreal, as minerals and chemicals in the earth form an exotic spectrum unlike anything normally associated with nature. Some patches of ground are hot enough to cause severe burns, so stick to the paths. From Hverir, an hour-long trail ascends Námafjall, cuts north to a parking area off the Ring Road at Námaskarð Pass, and then loops back to Hverir. Views are fabulous, but, again, be cautious, stay on the trail, and look out for scalding-hot patches of pale earth. The crust might look solid and not particularly hot on the surface, but underneath may lie a pocket of boiling mud. The walk can be seriously gloppy after rain.

Just east of Hverir, Route 863 branches off the Ring Road and leads north into the Krafla caldera. Gritty as burnt toast, the **Leirhnjúkur lava field ★★★** is the best place to witness remnants of the 1975 to 1984 eruptions—and may be the most surreal landscape you will ever see. The parking area is clearly marked from Route 863, and from there it's a 15-minute walk to a geothermal field at the edge. Some visitors make the drastic mistake of looking at the boiling gray mud pots and color-streaked earth, and then heading back to their cars. Allow at least another hour for circling the trails and peering at the subtle range of color, texture, and moss inside each steamy rift. A good way to start is by proceeding from the geothermal field toward a bowl-shaped pseudocrater visible to the north. A recommended trail known as the **Krafla Route** leads straight from here to Reykjahlíð and takes 3 to 4 hours one-way.

Route 863 dead-ends at a parking area by the rim of **Stóra-Víti,** a steep-sided explosion crater, formed in 1724, with a blue-green lake at the bottom when not covered in snow. A trail circles the rim and descends on the far side to an interesting hot spring area. The route, which is worthwhile but not essential, takes about an hour round-trip and is not advised during muddy conditions.

Mývatn Nature Baths (Jarðböðin Við Mývatn) ★★★ GEO-THERMAL POOL   Hidden amid the lava fields and hillsides is this popular geothermal pool facility. Like the Blue Lagoon, the water is said to contain a unique solution of minerals, silicates, and microorganisms that equal countless benefits for the skin and bones. Although the facilities are not nearly as impressive as the Blue Lagoon, improvements in recent years have added a gift shop and restaurant. Though it may seem like a lot of money for a swim, it's the best way to unwind after a strenuous day of touristing, and saunas are included in the admission price. The water remains at a comfortable bath temperature, between 36°C and 39°C (96.8°F–102.2°F). Remove any copper or silver you might be wearing; it will be damaged by sulfur in the water. Bring your own towel and swimsuit—rental for each is 700kr.

Rte. 1, 3km (2 miles) east of Reykjahlíð; turn right at blue sign for "JARÐBÖÐIN VIÐ MÝVATN." www.myvatnnaturebaths.is. ✆ **464-4411.** Admission 5,000kr adults; 3,300kr seniors/ students; 2,200kr children ages 12–15; free for children 11 and under. June–Aug daily 9am–midnight, no entry after 11:30pm; Sept–May daily noon–10pm, no entry after 9:30pm.

Sigurgeir Bird Museum ★ MUSEUM   Just north of Reykjahlíð, on the Ytri-Neslönd farm beside the lake, this museum builds on the work of Sigurgeir Stefansson, who collected birds while living at the farm. The interactive display contains a specimen of nearly all of the Icelandic breeding birds; it also holds a logbook of recent sightings, telescopes set up to watch the birds on the lake, and a remote camera on one of the lake's islands.

Rte. 1, 5km (3 miles) north of Reykjahlíð; turn right at blue sign for "JARÐBÖÐIN VIÐ MÝVATN." www.fuglasafn.is. ℂ **464-4477.** Admission 1,500kr adults; 800kr seniors and children ages 7–14; free for children 6 and under. June–Aug daily 9am–6pm; Sept–May daily noon–4pm.

Outdoor Activities

Mývatn is a common launch point for tours of the interior, especially to Askja Caldera and Kverkfjöll. The bus that takes the Sprengisandur route across the interior highlands to Landmannalaugar also leaves from Mývatn. Askja, Kverkfjöll, and Sprengisandur are covered in chapter 12.

AERIAL TOURS **Mýflug Air** (www.myflug.is; ℂ **464-4400**), based at the small airfield just outside Reykjahlíð, runs sightseeing tours of Mývatn–Krafla, Jökulsárgljúfur, Askja, Kverkfjöll, Vatnajökull, Grímsey, and other natural spectacles with a fleet of two six-seaters and a ten-seater. Tours range from 20 minutes (19,000kr) to 2 hours (57,000kr) with a minimum of two passengers, or three for Grímsey. Flights are weather-dependent.

CAVING **Saga Travel** (www.sagatravel.is; ℂ **659-8888**) arranges 5-hour guided tours of **Lofthellir,** a lava cave alive with lustrous and ghostly ice formations. The cost is 19,900kr adults and 9,950kr children ages 6 to 12, with a two-person minimum. Gloves, helmets, flashlights, and studded boots are provided. Tours run June until September. Dress warmly.

DOG SLEDDING From October to May, **Inspiration Iceland** (www.inspiration-iceland.com; ℂ **865-9426**) has day or Northern Lights husky tours, for 3 hours from 27,500kr. Longer excursions combined with Super Jeep rides visit top Mývatn attractions like Goðafoss and the Mývatn Nature Baths, at 153,000kr for a party of two.

HORSEBACK RIDING **Safari Hestar** (www.safarihestar.is; ℂ **464-4203**) has 1-hour tours with a choice of destinations for 7,000kr per person; a 2-hour excursion is 11,000kr. **Saltvík** (www.saltvik.is; ℂ **847-9515**), based 5km (3 miles) outside Húsavík, leads unforgettable multi-day tours in Saltvík and the Mývatn–Krafla area.

SUPER JEEP **Sagatravel** (www.sagatravel.is; ℂ **659-8888**) offers a 6- to 7-hour excursion covering Krafla and Leirhnjúkur (34,900kr adults; 17,450kr children ages 6–12). The tour includes stops at Herðubreiðalindir Oasis, Drekagil Gully, Víti explosion crater, and Askja Caldera. Departures, by reservation only, are June to October at 8am, with a four-person minimum. Trips to Dettifoss and Jökulsárgljúfur run year-round. From September to May, **Sel-Hótel Mývatn** (www.myvatn.is; ℂ **464-4164**) runs Super Jeep and snowmobile tours of Mývatn, as well as other off-road tours; call in advance for bookings and prices.

Where to Stay

All options below are around Mývatn, mostly in Reykjahlíð, the village on the northeast corner of the lake, and Skútustaðir, a small settlement on the south side. On short notice, the information office can tell you which have vacancies, but in July and early August, every single room could well be occupied. Two guesthouses west of Mývatn are good, relatively inexpensive backups: **Guesthouse Stöng** (www.stong.is; © **464-4252**) and **Narfastaðir Guesthouse** (www.farmhotel.is; © **464-3300**).

EXPENSIVE

Hótel Gígur ★ This quiet, south-shore, summer-only hotel on the lakefront has one of the most idyllic locations in Mývatn. Despite the cramped rooms, renovations have hooked them up with modern amenities and simple Scandinavian decor. The stylish **restaurant** overlooks the Skútustaðagígar pseudocraters, which makes it worth a stop even if you're not staying here. Rooms with lake views are booked well in advance.

Rte. 1 at Skútustaðir. www.keahotels.is. © **464-4455.** 37 units. May 15–Aug 32,900kr double. Rates include breakfast. Closed Sept–May 14. **Amenities:** Restaurant; bar; Internet terminal; free Wi-Fi.

Hótel Laxa ★★ Posh Laxa opened in 2014 in the quiet southwest corner of the lake, perched on a small ridge with endless views of the landscape. It is the area's largest hotel and the only property to give design any consideration, from the turf-roofed buildings stacked like shoeboxes to the wood facade. The slick common areas feature clean, straight lines and place large windows at every angle to take advantage of the view.

Rte. 848, 8km (5 miles) west of Skutustadhir. www.hotellaxa.is. © **464-1900.** 80 units. June–Aug 26,250kr double. Rates around 30%–50% lower Sept–May. Rates include breakfast. **Amenities:** Restaurant; bar; lounge; room service; free Wi-Fi.

Hótel Myvatn ★ This classic lake hotel was long the region's only upscale property, until Laxa came along in 2014. It's still better than most, though calling it luxurious would be a stretch. A 2018 renovation by Icelandair Hotels added rooms and modernized the decor and amenities. Many rooms have lake views, though all vary considerably in size and shape.

Rte. 87, Reykjahlíð, on lake side of road. www.icelandairhotels.com. © **464-4142.** 59 units. July–Aug 20 37,400kr double. Rates around 20%–35% lower Sept–May. Rates include breakfast. **Amenities:** Restaurant; free Wi-Fi.

MODERATE

Eldá ★ This stalwart operation is set in three different Reykjahlíð houses in a small residential complex. Each of the houses is rather basic and functional. The check-in is at Helluhraun 15. The breakfast buffet is surprisingly good, with fresh-baked bread and smoked salmon.

Helluhraun 15, Reykjahlíð. www.elda.is. © **464-4220.** 27 units, none w/bathroom. June 21–Aug 31 24,700kr double; 30,000kr triple. Rates 10%–20% lower off-season. Rates include breakfast in summer. Just north of the N1 filling station, turn on Hlíðarvegur, then make first right on Helluhraun. At the T junction, turn right; Eldá is shortly ahead on the left. **Amenities:** Guest kitchen; free Wi-Fi.

Vogar Farm Guesthouse ★ Taste fresh milk from the cows during their 7:30am feeding on your way to breakfast while staying at this working dairy farm (see **Vogafjós Cowshed Café** ★★, below). The guesthouse consists of two loghouses with 10 rooms each, plus a loghouse with additional rooms. All come with private bathrooms, high ceilings, and wood-lined walls. The property sits 3km (2 miles) south of Reykjahlíð, far from any bus stop. Check-in is at the cafe. Book well in advance for the summer.

Rte. 1, 3km (2 miles) south of Reykjahlíð. www.vogafjos.is. ✆ **464-4303.** 26 units. June–Aug 27,100kr double. Rates up to 50% lower Sept–May. Rates include breakfast. **Amenities:** Cafe; free Wi-Fi.

Where to Eat
EXPENSIVE
Sel-Hótel Mývatn ★ ICELANDIC This average hotel restaurant with nice views of the lake is best known for its **lunch buffet,** which is a favorite stop for passing tour groups before or after visiting the Skútustaðagígar pseudocraters nearby. You might find Icelandic "specials" like putrefied shark or sheep-head jelly in the buffet, though the a la carte menu—with dishes like smoked lamb with blueberry cream and pan-fried trout with prawns and almonds—is more reliable.

Rte. 1, Skútustaðir. www.myvatn.is. ✆ **464-4164.** Reservations recommended. Main courses 1,450kr–3,490kr; lunch buffet 3,900kr. June–Aug daily noon–2pm and 6–8:30pm; Sept–May 7–9pm.

MODERATE
Gamli Bærinn ★ ICELANDIC The chalkboard menu of seasonal dishes based on what's fresh is a good sign at this bustling tavern, though most of the dishes are quite simple. The kitchen serves a traditional Icelandic lamb soup and sources its beef from a local farmer who raises Galloways, which is about as good as it gets in Iceland. The menu also includes goulash and smoked Arctic char served on geysir-baked rye bread. The tavern hosts live acoustic music some nights.

Rte. 87, near Hótel Myvatn. ✆ **464-4270.** Reservations recommended. Main courses 950kr–3,200kr. Daily 10am–11pm.

Vogafjós Cowshed Café ★★ CAFE Sharing a barnlike structure with a milking shed, with windows giving you a peek at the cows inside from the gift shop, this farmhouse restaurant is the region's most authentic. The Mývatn area has a plethora of traditional products, such as smoked trout and lamb or geysir-baked rye bread, and this restaurant is a fine place to try them all. Milking times are 7:30am and 5:30 or 6pm; otherwise the cows are usually outside the shed.

Rte. 1, 3km (2 miles) south of Reykjahlíð; look for cow-shaped sign. ✆ **464-4303.** Reservations required for dinner. Main courses 3,250kr–5,400kr. May 15–Sept daily 11am–10pm; other times call ahead.

HÚSAVÍK & NEARBY

Húsavík, once a busy whale-hunting port, is now Exhibit A in making the case that whale-watching tours are a better source of income. Packaging itself as the "European Capital of Whale-Watching," this pretty fishing town of 2,300 complements the tours with pleasant waterfront eateries and a compelling whale museum. A visit to Húsavík is usually just a 1-day wonder in travel itineraries that dwell longer in Akureyri, Mývatn, and Jökulsárgljúfur.

Essentials

GETTING THERE   Húsavík is on Route 85, 92km (57 miles) from Akureyri, 54km (34 miles) from Mývatn, and 65km (40 miles) from Ásbyrgi in Jökulsárgljúfur. The only **car rental agency** in town is **Húsavik Car Rental,** Garðarsbraut 66 (www.bilaleigahusavikur.is; ✆ **464-1888**).

Strætó bus (www.straeto.is; ✆ **540-2700**) has a daily direct bus from Akureyri to Húsavík and Húsavík to Akureyri from mid-June through August; the cost is 2,760kr one-way.

VISITOR INFORMATION   Húsavík's **tourist office,** Garðarsbraut 5 (www. nordausturland.is; ✆ **464-4300;** June–Sept Mon–Sat 9am–7pm, Sun 10am–6pm), is on the main street in the middle of town.

HÚSAVÍK

Most tourist activity—including whale-watching ticket booths, four eateries, a bookstore, a market, a handknit woolens store, and the Whale Museum—are clustered on two parallel streets: Hafnarstétt, which runs right along the waterfront, and Garðarsbraut, just uphill.

WAS ICELAND'S first SETTLER NOT A VIKING?

Húsavík's beginnings pose a vital challenge to the way Icelandic history is told. In the 860s, a few years before the Norse settlement of Reykjavík, a Swede named Garðar Svavarsson spent a winter at Húsavík. According to later accounts, one of Garðar's men, Nattfari, escaped with two slaves—a man and a woman—and stayed behind, settling across the bay and then farther inland. Nattfari's identity, motives, and ultimate fate remain a mystery. He may have been a slave himself. His name isn't Norse, and probably means "Night Traveler," but his origins are unknown. Still, Nattfari may well have been Iceland's first permanent settler—not Ingólfur Arnarson, who is traditionally assigned this role.

Why was Nattfari left out of the picture? The introduction to the *Book of Settlements*, a key Icelandic text from the 13th century, suggests a motive: "… we think we can better meet the criticism of foreigners when they accuse us of being descended from slaves or scoundrels if we know for certain the truth about our ancestors." Ingólfur was Norse, with superior class status, and his emigration to Iceland seemed more deliberate and heroic. In 1974, Iceland held its official 1,100-year celebration of Icelandic settlement. Four years before, the people of Húsavík held their own ceremony for Nattfari and his two companions.

THE saga OF ICELANDIC WHALING

Icelanders can be touchy about whaling. Mere mention of the subject could provoke an impassioned speech about how Iceland is unjustly judged by a sanctimonious and hypocritical outside world.

In 1986, the International Whaling Commission (IWC)—formed in 1946 to promote cooperation among whaling nations—placed a moratorium on commercial whaling. The moratorium had no legal authority, but Iceland withdrew its IWC membership in protest. Iceland rejoined in 2002, but 2 years later resumed whaling under the pretense of scientific research. This meant that studies were conducted on the whales' stomach contents—and on the resulting implications for fish stocks—before the meat was sold off. In 2006, Iceland dispensed with the scientific cover and set a commercial whaling quota in open defiance of the moratorium.

Whaling supporters point out that minke whales, which comprise the vast majority of victims, have a worldwide population of 900,000 and are not an endangered species. Evidence does suggest that minke whales reduce fish stocks, particularly cod, which alone account for as much as 20% of Iceland's export income.

Icelanders have hunted whales for more than 300 years and consider it part of their cultural heritage. From the time of settlement, beached whales were such a precious resource that the Icelandic word for beached whale, *hvalreki*, also means "windfall" or "godsend." Icelanders also feel they have fought too long and hard for control of their territorial waters to let foreigners once again meddle.

Opponents highlight the gruesome details of whale hunting; from the first harpoon strike, these noble and intelligent creatures can take a full hour to die. Whales may compete with fishermen for cod, but whaling provides only a few seasonal jobs, and demand for whale meat is low. Tourists have shown some interest, but few Icelanders eat whale. Whale meat costs less than chicken in Icelandic supermarkets, and often ends up as animal food. The main foreign buyer, Japan, is increasingly wary of toxins found in the meat of North Atlantic whales.

Since Iceland resumed whaling, Greenpeace has led a tourist boycott. Within Iceland, however, most antiwhaling activists would prefer tourists come and spend money on whalewatching tours. Decades ago, tourist buses took a 1-hour trip from Reykjavík to Hvalfjörður to watch whales being sliced up and processed. Now nearly 100,000 tourists a year watch Icelandic whales that are very much alive.

In August 2007, Iceland's fisheries minister announced a halt to commercial whaling. In 2008, the ministry issued a new quota of 40 minke whales. Despite opposition from Icelanders and diplomatic pressure from at least 26 countries, in 2009 commercial whaling was allowed to continue with an extended quota of 150 fin whales and 100 minke; however, a rare hybrid blue and fin whale was slaughtered in 2018, much to the outrage of the rest of the world.

The German- and Swiss-inspired design of **Húsavík Church (Húsavíkurkirkja)**—located along Garðarsbraut—stands out in Iceland, as do the 1907 church's cruciform shape and absence of a pulpit. The lovely patterns painted on the interior walls are from 1924 and feature the Lutheran symbol of a cross within a heart. The 1931 altarpiece depicts Jesus raising Lazarus from the dead, as an onlooker faints.

Húsavík Museum (Safnahúsið) ★ MUSEUM Icelandic museums based on regional histories are often too esoteric, but Safnahúsið has an unusually broad range of interesting artifacts within its two permanent exhibitions. On the first floor, the maritime exhibit screens old-time fishing documentaries, and just outside is an authentically stinky baiting-shack and the skull and chinbone of a blue whale. The second-floor exhibit, "Man vs Nature: 100 Years in Þingeyjarsýslum," explores the region's natural history, from a stuffed polar bear shot at Grímsey Island in 1969 to a rare albino eider duckling, which are normally stomped to death by their mothers to protect siblings from predators. Among the folk arts, don't miss the whalebone carvings or the display case marked "Hárfínt Handbragð," full of necklaces and collars made from ladies' hair. The third floor is dedicated to art and photo exhibitions.

Stórigarður 17. www.husmus.is. ✆ **464-1860.** Admission 1,000kr adults; 700kr seniors; free for children 15 and under. June–Aug daily 10am–6pm; Sept–May Mon–Fri 10am–4pm.

Húsavík Whale Museum (Hvalasafnið á Húsavík) ★ MUSEUM This engaging and informative museum inside a former slaughterhouse examines all things whale: whale biology, whale sociology, whale hunting, whale-watching. A more authentic scene than Reykjavík's more kid-oriented whale museum can be found here, where full skeletons of 10 species hang from the ceiling. Screens show gripping footage of whales underwater, whales being hunted and processed, and Icelanders gathering to push stranded whales back into the ocean. The museum is sponsored by environmental groups, but wisely avoids any preachiness, letting the facts on whaling speak for themselves. A new wing built to house a 25m (82-ft.) **blue whale skeleton** found in 2010 in Skagi, in the northwest, opened in 2016.

Garðarsbraut. www.hvalasafn.is. ✆ **464-2520.** Admission 1,990kr adults; 1,500kr seniors/students; 500kr children ages 10–18. June–Aug daily 8:30am–6:30pm; May and Sept 9am–5pm; Oct 10am–4pm.

TJÖRNES

Northeast from Húsavík, Route 85 follows the periphery of this stubby peninsula. Fossil devotees should stop for a look at the **Ytritunga Fossils:** millions of sea shells—deposited when sea levels and water temperatures were far higher—in steep banks where the Hallbjarnarstaðaá stream meets the ocean. The turnoff from Route 85 is about 12km (7½ miles) northeast of Húsavík, just past Ytritunga Farm, and marked by a sign with "FOSSILS" in small lettering. Be careful on the road's final descent to the ocean; if it's washed out, you may never get back up.

OUTDOOR ACTIVITIES

SWIMMING The Geosea Geothermal Sea Baths (www.geosea.is; ✆ **464-1200**), located on a grassy hill that's a 20-minute walk from the center, is the latest major spa facility to open in Iceland and the most modern in the north. Using a natural mixture of sea and geothermal water that was oddly being used for cheese-making until the spa moved in, the facility was designed by the same architects of the Blue Lagoon and features a series of stunning infinity pools overlooking the ocean. It's open May to September 9am to midnight; October to April noon to 10pm. Prices are 4,300kr adults, 2,700 seniors, and 1,800kr children 16 and under. Towel rental is 800kr.

HORSEBACK RIDING   **Saltvík** (www.saltvik.is; *℘* **847-9515**), 5km (3 miles) outside Húsavík, offers a popular 2-hour strut along the seashore for 9,900kr per person.

SAILING/BIRDWATCHING   **North Sailing** (www.northsailing.is; *℘* **464-2350**) offers a memorable 3½-hour "Húsavík Original Whale Watching and Sails" tour on a two-masted schooner, combining whale-watching with a visit to **Lundey,** an island bristling with puffins. Passengers can help set sails or even take the helm. Tickets are 12,500kr for adults, half-price for children 14 and under, with one or two departures daily from early May to late August. (After Aug 15, you're unlikely to see puffins.)

SEA FISHING   Húsavík's whale-watching companies, such as **Gentle Giants,** offers fishing trips in pursuit of cod and haddock. Expect to pay around 16,900kr for a 2- to 3-hour tour, with all equipment and arrangements made for grilling the catch. Gentle Giants schedules regular departures at 4pm in summer, but requires a four-person minimum.

WHALE-WATCHING   Húsavík lies close to whale migratory lanes, and whale-watching prospects are somewhat better than elsewhere in Iceland; but visitors should keep expectations in check. Tour companies boast a 98% success rate, but "success" could be a fleeting glimpse of a minke whale, which is relatively small and doesn't put on much of a show. The most acrobatic performer is the humpback whale, whose feeding technique involves blowing a vertical spiral of bubbles—halting the fish within—and then launching itself open-mouthed up through the spiral and into the air. Humpbacks appear two times out of three. Odds of seeing a white-beaked dolphin are one in three; a harbor porpoise, one in five. The very lucky see the world's largest creature, the blue whale, whose heart is the size of a VW beetle. These leviathans have only been appearing in Skjálfandi bay for the past decade.

Húsavík has two rival whale-watching tour operators, **Gentle Giants** (www.gentlegiants.is; *℘* **464-1500**) and **North Sailing** (www.northsailing.is; *℘* **464-2350**). While your chances of seeing whales are good with either, North Sailing went carbon neutral in 2015 and tends to be less aggressive with its boats crowding around whales (which they don't like). Gentle Giants charges 10,400kr, 4,400kr for children 7 to 15, and free for children 6 and under. North Sailing costs 10,500kr, 3,500kr for children 7 to 15, and free for children 6 and under. Those who have difficulty making decisions might consider that Gentle Giants has snazzier jumpsuits and gives away twisted donuts called *kleina,* while North Sailing hands out cinnamon rolls and also runs 8-day trips to Greenland. Each has a ticket kiosk on the main road.

The season runs from late April until October, when whales start returning south to breed. From June to August, as many as six tours with either company may depart daily from 8:45am to 8pm. In late April, May, and September, three tours depart daily, the latest at 1:30pm. In October, Gentle Giants has morning tours on Saturday and Sunday only. The standard tour lasts 3 hours.

> ### Whale-Watching Tip
>
> Take the insulated jumpsuits that are supplied to all passengers.

Tours are sometimes canceled in rough weather, so anyone coming from out of town should call ahead. Seasickness pills are a good idea (ginger also works well), even if conditions seem calm.

Where to Stay

For those who don't like switching beds every night, Húsavik can be a base for exploring Jökulsárgljúfur and the Mývatn area. The Aðaldalur Valley between Akureyri, Húsavík, and Mývatn is often overlooked, but also makes for a good operational headquarters. **Icelandic Farm Holidays** (www.farm holidays.is; ✆ **570-2700**) lists several places in and around Aðaldalur. The nicest hotel in Aðaldalur is **Hótel Rauðaskriða** (Rte. 85, about 18km/11 miles from Rte. 1; www.hotelraudaskrida.is; ✆ **464-3504**; 37,000kr double including breakfast), with a restaurant, bar, and hot tubs.

EXPENSIVE

Fosshotel Húsavík ★ Walking distance from the harbor, this whale-themed hotel, the only fully functional property in town, underwent a major renovation in 2016 that added an extra 41 rooms and sleek conference facilities. Rooms are more functional than chic and range in size from shoebox in the singles to surprisingly spacious in the deluxe. The decent on-site **restaurant/ bar** is whale-themed, of course.

Ketilsbraut 22. www.fosshotel.is. ✆ **464-1220.** 110 units. June–Aug 33,900kr double; 38,600kr deluxe. Rates around 30% lower Sept–May. Rates include breakfast. **Amenities:** Restaurant; bar; conference rooms; tour desk; free Wi-Fi.

MODERATE

Kaldbaks-Kot ★ These self-catering, timber log cabins are situated on the waterfront, just before the entrance to town. Each is equipped with a double bed, bathroom, living room with pullout sofa, kitchenette, and a terrace with outstanding views across the bay. Ask about discounts for stays of 3 nights or more.

Rte. 85 just south of Húsavík. www.cottages.is. ✆ **464-1504.** 17 units. July to mid-Aug 24,800kr double cabin; 28,800kr cabin w/sleeping loft. Rates 10% lower June and late Aug; 20% lower Sept and May. **Amenities:** Free Wi-Fi.

INEXPENSIVE

Árból Guesthouse ★ Set in a 1903 house, the former residence of the district governor, Árból Guesthouse is situated beside a pleasant stream and park. It's the best guesthouse in town, with lots of original character like antique furnishings and attic rooms with ocean views and pinewood floors and walls.

Ásgarðsvegur 2. www.arbol.is. ✆ **464-2220.** 10 units, none w/bathroom. 21,100kr double. Rates include breakfast. Rates 20% lower Oct–Apr. **Amenities:** Free Wi-Fi.

Where to Eat

If other places are full, **Fosshotel Húsavík** (above) has a standard-issue restaurant called **Moby Dick,** with an above-average reindeer burger. The **Bákari** (Garðarsbraut, off Mararbraut; ✆ **464-2901;** Mon–Fri 8am–6pm, Sat 10am–2pm, Sun 8am–6pm), indeed a bakery, has sandwiches as well as baked goods and could pass for lunch.

Gamli Baukur ★ SEAFOOD   This snug wooden building with a nautical theme serves a variety of standard seafood plates. I recommend sticking to the simpler options, like fish and chips and seafood soup; otherwise you might be disappointed. The terrace has some of the best views of the whale-watching boats returning from sea.

Hafnarstétt 9. www.gamlibaukur.is. ✆ **464-2442.** Snacks 1,850kr–4,250kr. April 15-Oct 15 daily 8am–9pm.

Naustið ★ SEAFOOD   Choose between the spacious patio or the pleasant interior with reclaimed-wood walls and tin-can lanterns at this family-run spot on the harbor. It's known for having some of the freshest seafood in town; the fish can literally be tossed from the fishing boats since they dock so close. There's an excellent seafood soup and grilled fish of every sort. The sushi you can probably skip.

Naustagardi 2. ✆ **464-1520.** Main courses 1,950kr–4,000kr. March–Oct daily noon–10pm.

Salka ★ ICELANDIC   Salka, set in a heritage home with a large terrace beside the Whale Museum, has the most interesting menu in town. It is the only restaurant here to really focus on local dishes and ingredients like puffin, salted cod, and langoustines, though they have standard international plates too. It also has an extensive pizza list and will even deliver it to your hotel.

Garðarsbraut 6. www.salkarestaurant.is. ✆ **464-2551.** Main courses 2,050kr–4,750kr. Daily 11:30am–9pm.

VATNAJÖKULL NATIONAL PARK

Jökulsárgljúfur ★★★ is now part of Vatnajökull National Park (Europe's largest national park), which has extended to encompass the entirety of the Vatnajökull Glacier. **Jökulsárgljúfur Canyon** is Iceland's most celebrated canyon, which channels Iceland's second-longest river, the Jökulsá á Fjöllum. The river's opaque, gray water carries sediments from Iceland's largest glacier, Vatnajökull. A comparison to America's Grand Canyon and the Colorado River is tempting, but Jökulsárgljúfur does not register on such an instantly overwhelming scale. Rather, its treasures—including an extraordinary range of basalt formations, waterfalls, and plant life—unfold at each turn.

The ideal way to experience Jökulsárgljúfur is by taking a 2-day hike from bottom to top, but day hikes suffice for most. The busiest season is mid-June to mid-August, so if you crave solitude—and wish to avoid rowdy visitors at campsites—aim for late May to early June or late August and September.

Essentials

GETTING THERE & AROUND

BY CAR Jökulsárgljúfur—a mouthful that simply means "Glacial River Canyon"—is aligned north to south. Roads run along the east and west sides, connecting Route 85 in the north to the Ring Road in the south. In general, regular cars have more access to park sites from the north. On the west side of the canyon, you can navigate Route 862 from Route 85 as far south as the Vesturdalur campsite, near Hljóðaklettar—though potholes can be treacherous, especially in late summer. You might even get as far as the Hólmatungur parking area, but check with your car-rental company, as this could void your insurance. On the east side of the canyon, regular cars can take Route 864 between Route 85 and Dettifoss—and usually all the way to the Ring Road, depending on conditions. Those with 4WD vehicles can probably get from the Ring Road to Route 85 on either side of the canyon, but Route 864 on the east side is far easier.

BY BUS For the time being, no public transport connects Ásbyrgi with either Húsavík/Akureyri or Dettifoss/Mývatn. From mid-June into August, **SBA Norðurleið** (www.sba.is; ✆ **550-0700**) has a marathon 13-hour bus tour from Myvatn to Akureyri (on the west side of the canyon), stopping at Krafla, Dettifoss, Ásbyrgi, and Húsavík. A one-way trip is 15,300kr, half-price for children.

ON FOOT Park trails are well-marked and well-tended, with maps posted at trailheads, but it's still a good idea to secure maps and trail brochures at the information office before setting out. Visitors are asked not to venture off the trails, as sub-Arctic vegetation is fragile and slow to recover from trampling.

Hiking the full length of the park over 2 days can proceed in either direction, but almost everyone heads downstream, from south to north, starting at the parking area for Dettifoss (on the west side of the river) and ending at Ásbyrgi. The only legal campsite along the 34km (21-mile) route is at Vesturdalur. The warden at Vesturdalur is happy to store bags during the day, so clever planning can lighten your load. Visitors with cars could drop supplies at Vesturdalur, then park back at Ásbyrgi and take the daily SBA bus (which starts in Akureyri) from Ásbyrgi to Dettifoss, arriving around 1:20pm. (Make sure you can reach Vesturdalur before dark.) Those without cars can still jump off the bus at Vesturdalur and leave things with the warden before continuing on to Dettifoss. The hike has challenging segments and route variations, so make sure to review your plans with the park visitor information office (see below).

VISITOR INFORMATION

Tourist information can be found at the **visitor office** in Ásbyrgi (www.vjp. is; ☏ **470-7100;** May 1–May 31 and Sept 1–Sept 30 10am–4pm; June 1–June 20 and Aug 16–Aug 31 9am–7pm; June 21–Aug 15 9am–9pm), which is on Route 861; exit Route 85 at the filling station, and it's shortly ahead on the left.

Exploring Jökulsárgljúfur

Our top three walking areas are: Ásbyrgi, the wooded horseshoe canyon at the park's northern end; **Hljóðaklettar** and **Rauðhólar,** in the middle of the park; and on the south end of the park, a triumvirate of waterfalls: **Hafragilsfoss, Dettifoss,** and **Selfoss.** All three areas could be crammed into 1 day, but 2 days or even 3 are preferable. Another prime walking area is **Hólmatungur ★★**, with its luxuriant cascades and vegetation, but access is more limited (see "Getting There & Around," above).

ÁSBYRGI ★

This broad canyon, near Route 85 and west of the Jökulsá á Fjöllum River, forms a "U" shape about 3.5km (2 miles) north-to-south and 1km (⅔ mile) across, with a forested plain on the bottom and a rock "island" called Eyjan in the middle. Geologists believe Ásbyrgi was gouged out by catastrophic flooding from Vatnajökull somewhere between 8,000 and 10,000 years ago, and again around 3,000 years ago. Apparently these flood bursts had 2,000 times the force of the Jökulsá á Fjöllum today. The river then shifted east to its current location, leaving Ásbyrgi dry. The Vikings had their own explanation for Ásbyrgi: Clearly the god Óðinn's horse, Sleipnir, had left an enormous hoofprint with one of his eight legs.

Walks in Ásbyrgi can start from the information office or from a parking area at the southern end of the "U," near the base of the cliffs. Route 861, which splits off from Route 85 at the N1 filling station, passes the information office and ends at the parking area. No one path asserts itself among the walking routes, so if you have a car, it makes sense to drive to the parking area and scan the many options from there. Beautiful ferns and orange lichen inhabit the cliff walls, along with 1,200 pairs of nesting fulmars. If you decide to see Ásbyrgi from the rim above, backtrack to the information office and find the trail leading to Tófugjá, where you can ascend the rim with the aid of ropes.

HLJÓÐÐAKLETTAR & RAUÐÐHÓLAR

Hljóðaklettar (Echo Rocks) ★★ and **Rauðhólar (Red Hills) ★★** form an ideal 2-hour loop hike, starting from a parking area shortly past the Vesturdalur campsite on the west side of the canyon. The trail has tricky footing in spots, but is not otherwise difficult. The area is covered in the national park map *Jökulsárgljúfur,* available at the visitor office (300kr). The trail weaves through some of Iceland's most intriguing basalt configurations, often eroded from below to form honeycomb patterns. The human-sized trees along the trail feel oddly companionable, and the woolly willow is easily noted by its light-green, fuzzy leaves. Hljóðaklettar earned its name from certain locations where the sound of the river echoes and seems to come from the wrong direction. The best spot to witness this phenomenon is right by the marked turnoff for Kirkjan (Church), a fabulous cave once sought out by sheep during storms. Rauðhólar, a crater row tinted with red gravel, marks the northern end of the loop and has great panoramic views. Some trekkers take the bus to Vesturdalur and continue all the way to Ásbyrgi.

HAFRAGILSFOSS, DETTIFOSS & SELFOSS

Moving progressively upstream along the Jökulsá á Fjöllum River, the magnificent waterfalls **Hafragilsfoss, Dettifoss** ★★, and **Selfoss** ★ are a kind of three-course meal. Hafragilsfoss, at 27m (89 ft.) high and 91m (299 ft.) across, is captivating and monstrously powerful. The best view is from the Sjónnípa lookout point, a 1km (⅔-mile) hike north from the parking area. Hafragilsfoss is overshadowed, however, by Dettifoss, Europe's mightiest waterfall. On average, the milky-gray glacial water cascades over the 44m (144-ft.) drop at a rate of 200 cubic meters (656 sq. ft.) per second. Selfoss is only 11m (36 ft.) high, but its unusual breadth and parabolic shape are well worth seeking out as a pleasing finale.

Most visitors see the waterfalls from the east side of the river, because the parking areas on the west side are not accessible to regular cars. Those in 4WD vehicles often approach Dettifoss from the west side, where the view is somewhat better. The SBA buses (p. 216) also stop on the west side. On the east side, however, views of Selfoss are slightly improved and Hafragilsfoss is much more accessible. The drive to the waterfalls from Ásbyrgi—on Route 864, down the eastern side of the canyon—takes about 40 minutes. Selfoss is reached by walking 1.5km (1 mile) south from the Dettifoss parking areas on either side of the river.

Where to Stay

PARK CAMPGROUNDS   Camping within the park is restricted to three campgrounds on the west side of the river: Ásbyrgi, on the park's north end; **Vesturdalur,** in the middle; and **Dettifoss,** on the south end. Ásbyrgi and Vesturdalur are supervised from June through September 15 and accessible to regular cars. Ásbyrgi has showers, a shop and snack bar, laundry machines, and facilities for trailers and camper vans. Vesturdalur is for tents only and has no showers, so the party crowd gravitates to Ásbyrgi. Ásbyrgi can be a zoo late at night, especially on summer weekends, despite the quiet policy after 11pm. The Dettifoss campground has minimal facilities—just outhouses and a water tap—and is only meant for hikers who traverse the park north to south and then continue toward Mývatn. The campsites rarely if ever run out of tent space, but it's still a good idea to call in advance to see if the site is crowded through the information office (above).

Camping is 1,900kr per person per night, 800 for children ages 13–16, and free for children 12 and under. Showers at Ásbyrgi are 500kr.

OUTSIDE THE PARK   The option below is on Route 85, near Ásbyrgi.

Hótel Skúlagarður ★   Set in a former boarding school and community hall that was built in 1953, this relatively plain property, split between two buildings, is the area's best hotel option, if that tells you anything about your options. Its high point is that it puts you in close proximity to Ásbyrgi for a morning jaunt.

Rte. 85, 14km (9 miles) west of Ásbyrgi. www.skulagardur.com. (𝄐 **465-2280.** 47 units, none w/bathroom. May 15–Aug 25,200kr double; 8,500kr per person sleeping-bag accommodation. Rates around 30% lower Sept–May 14. Breakfast available (1,800kr). **Amenities:** Restaurant; bar; guest kitchen; free Wi-Fi.

Where to Eat

The only dining option near Ásbyrgi is the **shop/snackbar** (𝄐 **465-2260**) next to the **filling station** on Route 85, and in high season the few tables are often full. Some kind of fish plate is added to the usual burger and sandwich offerings. Hours are 9am to 10pm from mid-June through August, with earlier closing times in the off-season.

THE NORTHEAST CORNER

"Land of Fire and Ice," the number-one cliché of Iceland's travel industry, has little bearing on Iceland's peaceful and remote northeast corner, which has no fearsome volcanoes, no mighty glaciers, no one-of-a-kind geological marvels. You'll see no romantic villages nestled in majestic fjords. Not a single restaurant, hotel, museum, church, or saga site exerts any significant pull. Yet visitors come here time and again, just to gaze at birds on misty moors and walk to lonely lighthouses. It may have no star attractions, but the northeast corner is an ideal meeting of pristine beauty and blessed solitude.

Essentials

GETTING THERE & AROUND

BY PLANE   **Air Iceland** (www.airiceland.is; (𝄐 **570-3030** or 473-1121) connects Akureyri to Vopnafjörður about four times a week. There are also flights from Reykjavík to Þórshöfn Monday to Friday. Typical airfares to Þórshöfn from Reykjavík are between 16,500kr to 32,000kr, while Akureyri to Vopnafjörður start at 6,080kr each way. Book online for a cheaper bonus fare.

BY CAR   In September 2010, a new road cutting across Hólaheiði and Hófaskarð at the base of the peninsula was laid, shortening the 300km (186-mile) distance from Húsavík to Vopnafjöður by 53km (27 miles). The new road takes the number of the old coastal road (Route 85), and the old coastal road around Melrakkaslétta has a new number (Route 870). At the same time, another new road was laid to Rauðarhöfn (Route 874), branching off the new Route 85 across Hólaheiði at Ormarsá. This road has shortened the distance to Raufahöfn by 21km (11 miles).

In Vopnafjörður and Þórshöfn, the only car-rental agency is **National/ Bílaleiga Akureyrar** (www.holdur.is; ✆ **461-6000**).

BY BUS   At present, there is no public transport to or from Þórshöfn, though in the past **SBA Norðurleið** (www.sba.is; ✆ **550-0700**) offered a bus on weekdays throughout the year from Akureyri.

VISITOR INFORMATION

The **tourist information office** in Akureyri (p. 186) can offer general help. In **Þórshöfn,** tourist information is at the local swimming pool, Langanesvegur (www.langanesbyggd.is; ✆ **468-1515;** mid-June to Aug Mon–Fri 8am–8pm, Sat–Sun 11am–5pm; Sept to mid-June Mon–Thurs 4–8pm, Fri 3–7pm, Sat 11am–2pm). In **Vopnafjörður,** tourist information is next to the fish factory at Hafnarbyggð 4 (✆ **473-1331;** June 20–Aug 20 10am–6pm).

Exploring the Northeast

For outdoor activities in this region, arrangements can be made informally. Someone is always willing to take you hiking, birdwatching, fishing, canoeing, or horseback riding, but no specific tours are advertised.

The following sites form a clockwise route around the northeast corner.

MELRAKKASLÉTTA

Melrakkaslétta, which means "Arctic Fox Plains," is the only general name for the broad peninsula extending to the northernmost point of the Icelandic mainland. Shingle beaches full of driftwood and wading birds are seen along the mostly low-lying coastline, while small lakes, moors, boggy tundra, and eroded hills form the interior. Most farms on the peninsula have been abandoned.

An excellent new **hiking map** for Melrakkaslétta, the fifth in the Útivist & Afþreying series, is widely available in the region.

Rauðinúpur ★, the headland at the northwest tip of the peninsula, has a lighthouse, sea stacks, bird cliffs tinted with red slag, and that end-of-the-Earth allure. The turnoff from Route 85 is roughly 22km (14 miles) north of the village of Kópasker (and 3.5km/2 miles *after* a turnoff that heads along the coast to Grjótnes). In 8km (5 miles) the road ends at Núpskatla crater, and Rauðinúpur is visible to the left. Walk along the rocky shore, which can be slow going, then past the lighthouse to the sea cliffs. Allow 2 hours for the round-trip.

ATTACK OF THE terns

Beware of attacks by Arctic terns, especially in early summer, and have a stick handy to raise over your head in defense. Puffins are seen in large numbers, and one of the sea stacks hosts a gannet colony.

Hraunhafnartangi is a promontory at the peninsula's northeast corner, less than 3km (2 miles) from the Arctic Circle. (Hraunhafnartangi was once thought to be the northernmost point of the mainland, but Rifstangi, a few kilometers to the west, wins that title by a hair.) The solitary lighthouse is visible from the road, and a 1.7km (1-mile) 4WD track leads directly there along the shore (going toward the lighthouse, the ocean will be on your left). The dock by the lighthouse was active in the saga age, and a large cairn marks the gravesite of hero Þorgeir Havarsson. Be on the lookout for attacks from nesting birds.

The eastern region of Melrakkaslétta is dotted with endless **lakes** and ponds, treasured by a small coterie of fishermen and birdwatchers. A lovely, peaceful trail leads 5km (3 miles) from the village of Raufarhöfn to Ólafsvatn Lake; from Hotel Norðurljós, walk up to the power line and follow the staked route.

RAUFARHÖFN

Raufarhöfn, the **northernmost village on the Icelandic mainland,** was a major processing hub for herring into the 1960s but now numbers less than 250 inhabitants. Erlingur at Hotel Norðurljós is Raufarhöfn's one-man **tourist bureau** and the best resource for any outdoor activities in Melrakkaslétta. He's also behind a scheme called **Arctic Henge** (www.arctichenge.com), a Stonehenge-inspired sundial structure, 54m (177 ft.) in diameter with 72 stones, on a hill just north of town.

If you're staying in Raufarhöfn, consider a walk along the Raufarhafnar-höfði headland, a pleasing locale for observing birds on sea cliffs and watching boats come in and out of the harbor. A 2km (1.2-mile) loop trail starts from the church.

RAUÐANES

The 7km (4-mile) circuit of this small cape halfway between Raufarhöfn and Þórshöfn is one of the best walks in the northeast corner. The route follows the bluffs, with views of sea pillars and archways, and one opportunity to clamber down to a beach. The turnoff from Route 85 is about 35km (22 miles) south of Raufarhöfn, and leads to a farm called Vellir. The trailhead is about 2km (1.2 miles) from the turnoff, on the right side of the road. After circling the periphery of Rauðanes counter-clockwise, the trail ends up farther down the road.

ÞÓRSHÖFN & LANGANES

Anyone with a taste for truly out-of-the-way places should look into **Langanes ★**, a 45km-long (28-mile) peninsula shaped like a duck's head. Much of the landscape is moorland full of lakes and ponds, with a few mountains reaching 719m (2,359 ft.) on the east side, some bird cliffs, and a good range of vegetation and wildflowers. The near-total solitude, abandoned farms, driftwood beaches, persistently foggy climate, and remote lighthouse at the narrow tip of the peninsula all give Langanes its own forlorn enchantment.

The village of **Þórshöfn** is the launch point for excursions into Langanes. A regular car can proceed about 33km (20½ miles) beyond Þórshöfn on Route 869, and a 4WD road extends 12km (7 ½ miles) along the northwest coast of the peninsula all the way to the lighthouse at Fontur, with side routes branching off to the southeast. Worthwhile destinations include the ruins of Skálar, a village abandoned since 1954; the bird cliffs of Skálabjarg, just southwest of Skálar; the staked trail at Hrollaugsstaðir, where Hrollaugsstaðafjall mountain meets the sea; and the Fontur lighthouse, which has a guestbook to sign. All the hiking and 4WD routes are detailed in English on an essential hiking map, the eighth in the Útivist & Afþreying series.

To plan a trip to Langanes, start with tourist information at Þórshöfn (p. 220). The **Sauðaneshúsið museum** (© 468-1430; June 10–Aug 31 daily 11am–5pm), 6km (3¾ miles) north of Þórshöfn on Route 869, is devoted to relics of Langanes, and the caretaker is very knowledgeable about the region. The farm hostel **Ytra-Lón** (www.ytra-aland.is; © 468-1242) is located even farther into Langanes. From May 15 to June 10, the **egg-collecting club of Þórshöfn** leads expeditions into Langanes where visitors can rappel down cliffsides snatching bird eggs. The friendly staff at the **Ytra-Áland farm accommodation** (www.ytra-aland.is; © 468-1290) can arrange trips, and can also set up 4WD expeditions to Langanes or take you on day tours.

VOPNAFJÖRÐÐUR & BUSTARFELL

Vopnafjörður is the largest town in the region, with around 680 people, an airport, and one police officer. Drivers continuing south along the coast on Route 917 toward Egilsstaðir are treated to incredible views as they pass through **Hellisheiði,** Iceland's highest coastal mountain pass (656m/2,152 ft.), on the steep descent into Fljótsdalshérað Valley. Anyone headed west from Vopnafjörður to Mývatn should be sure to fill up the gas tank. The two sights listed below are some distance outside of town.

Bustarfell Museum ★ MUSEUM   This well-preserved 18th-century turf farmhouse has the unusual characteristic of having remained in the same family for 400 years, though it is now in the care of the Icelandic National Museum. Bustarfell's more unique holdings include hand-carved chess pieces, snuff boxes made from animal bones, a driftwood shoulder harness with sheephorn hooks, granddad's winning dark-green bridegroom suit, and a pair of baby booties knitted from human hair. English signage is limited, and it's difficult to get the full import of the exhibit without asking staff. (Many visitors, for instance, see the short beds and assume Icelanders have become much taller—when in fact they slept partially upright to aid digestion of their low-fiber diets.) The museum's **Croft Cafe** serves old-fashioned cakes and cookies.

Rte. 85, about 20km (12 miles) southwest of Vopnafjörður. www.bustarfell.is. © **471-2211.** Admission 1,100kr adults; 300kr children ages 9–13; free for children 8 and under. June 10–Sept 10 daily 10am–5pm.

Vopnafjörður Pool ★ SWIMMING POOL   Vopnafjörður is the rare Icelandic settlement without a geothermally heated pool inside the village proper. Many residents, however, feel privileged to have this idyllic alternative next to the Selá, an elite salmon-fishing river once used by George H. W.

Bush. The simple 12m (40-ft.) pool was built in 1949, and at 32 to 33 degrees Celsius (90°F–91.5°F), it's warmer than most Icelandic pools. It has two hot tubs, a wading pool for children, and changing rooms. The turnoff from Route 85, about 9km (5½ miles) north of Vopnafjörður, is marked by the usual swimming pool icon. The pool is 3km (2 miles) from the turnoff.

ⓒ **473-1499.** Admission 400kr adults; 200kr children. Mon–Fri 10am–10pm; Sat–Sun noon–10pm.

Where to Stay
RAUFARHÖFN
Hótel Norðurljós ★   Originally a boardinghouse for up to 200 "herring girls" who worked at a nearby fish processing plant, this boxy structure was converted into a hotel more than 40 years ago. Rooms are more functional than pretty; all are en suite. The hotel has a large **restaurant,** a **lounge** with books on Iceland, and a pleasant terrace overlooking the waterfront.

Aðalbraut 2. www.hotelnordurljos.is. ⓒ **465-1233.** 15 units. 25,100kr double. **Amenities:** Restaurant; bar; lounge; free Wi-Fi.

ÞÓRSHÖFN & NEARBY
Guesthouse Lyngholt ★   This 1958 home has been continually restored since the current owners purchased it in 1999. The rooms are tight and simple but well-kept, and they get lots of light. The guesthouse has an additional six rooms above the police station.

Langanesvegur 12. www.lyngholt.is. ⓒ **897-5064.** 7 units, none w/bathroom. June 1–Aug 31 15,500kr double. Rates 10% lower Sept–May. **Amenities:** Guest kitchen; free Wi-Fi.

Ytra-Áland ★   Just west of Þórshöfn, this remote, oceanfront farmstead is one of the few authentic places to rest your head in the northeast. Instead of the cookie-cutter accommodations you often find elsewhere, this family-run guesthouse has a parlor with lace curtains and Victorian chairs. A few hiking trails lead right from the property, and the owners can arrange 4WD excursions. **Dinner** is served on request for 2,900kr to 4,500kr.

Off Rte. 85, 18km (11 miles) west of Þórshöfn. www.ytra-aland.is. ⓒ **468-1290.** 6 units, 2 w/bathroom. 17,000kr double; 14,000kr double without bathroom; 4,500kr sleeping-bag accommodation per person; 15,000kr cottage for 3–8 people. Rates include breakfast, except for cottage. **Amenities:** Guest kitchen; free Wi-Fi.

VOPNAFJÖRÐÐUR
Hótel Tangi ★   In the northeast wilds you might be surprised to find a room with flatscreen TVs and working Wi-Fi, even if the hotel it's in is quite standard. Splurge for the rooms with the private bathrooms; the others are considerably smaller.

Hafnarbyggð 17. www.hoteltangi.com. ⓒ **473-1203.** 17 units, 4 w/bathroom. 24,200kr double; 13,800kr double without bathroom. Rates include breakfast. **Amenities:** Restaurant; bar; free Wi-Fi.

Where to Eat

The villages of Raufarhöfn, Þórshöfn, and Vopnafjörður each have one restaurant, usually in a hotel, and an **N1 filling station** grill.

Barán Bar and Restaurant ★ ICELANDIC   The local hangout is this restaurant and bar near the dock. The TV is always blaring, and late nights see a rather hard-drinking crowd, but you will find sustenance in the clam chowder, burgers, and pizza.

Eyrarvegur 3, Þórshöfn. www.baranrestaurant.is. © **468-1250.** Main courses 2,000kr–4,300kr. Mon–Thurs 11am–10pm; Fri–Sat 11am–3am; Sun noon–10pm.

SOUTH ICELAND

A masterpiece of nature and home to some of Iceland's most celebrated wonders, the south provides a dynamic feast for the visitor's senses. Presiding majestically over the region is Europe's greatest glacier, Vatnajökull, a multi-tongued monster stretching east and thrusting its force down upon 8% of the country. The frozen white mass—crowned by Iceland's highest peak, Hvannadalshnúker, which surfaces just above the sub-glacial tongue, Öræfajökull—creates a well-focused distinction against the black deserts to the south.

The area is also the location of Eyjafjallajökull (that's *Ay*-yah-*fyatl*-ah-yer-kutl), the unpronounceable volcano, which in April 2010 brought European air traffic to a standstill.

The Ring Road (Route 1) threads 374km (235 miles) across this diverse landscape from Þjórsárdalur to Höfn, stitching together a progression of magnificent sights, each with its own collection of folk tales and legends.

In *Njáls Saga* country around Hella and Hvolsvöllur, every rock, knoll, and crag seems to have a story. The 4-day trek connecting Landmannalaugar and Þórsmörk—each an unbeatable hiking area in its own right—is the most celebrated trail in Iceland. Active tour opportunities abound, from horseback riding to dogsledding. On the enchanting Westman Islands, you can explore dramatic bird cliffs by boat, or by sidling close to puffins on the ledges.

The south was the last stretch of coastline to be fully claimed by settlers. Most early Norse arrivals took stock of the sand deserts, glaciers, and heavy surf, then moved on to better ports and more forgiving habitats. Even today, the largest town in southern Iceland is Heimaey (Home Island), on the Westman Islands, with a population of 4,500; no town on the mainland tops 1,000.

Most of the south is well served by buses in summer, and the Ring Road bus extends at least to Höfn year-round. But if you're connecting a lot of dots, a rental car is the ideal transport.

Destinations such as Gullfoss, Geysir, and Kerið, though geographically located in the south, are covered in the "Near Reykjavík" chapter because so many people visit as part of the Golden Circle day trip (p. 108).

For the best visitor information online, consult **www.south.is**.

WESTMAN ISLANDS (VESTMANNAEYJAR)

In traditional annals, Norse settler Hjörleifur Hródmarsson was killed on Iceland's south coast around the year 870 by his Irish slaves. The slaves fled to the islands offshore, but were later hunted down and killed by Ingólfur Arnarson, Reykjavík's first settler and Hjörleifur's brother-in-law. The Norse referred to Irishmen as "west men," and the islands have since been known as the **Westman Islands (Vestmannaeyjar)** ★★★. Herjólfur Bárðarson was thought to be the first Norse inhabitant of the Westmans around 900, but archaeological evidence points to a Norse settlement as early as the 7th century.

The Westmans became world famous in 1963, when a new island, **Surtsey,** was created by a series of volcanic eruptions 120m (394 ft.) beneath the ocean surface. As the magma fought its way out of the sea, huge clouds of steam and ash sailed into the stratosphere. New land was being cooked up right on television. Surtsey was 1.7 sq. km (1 sq. mile) when the eruptions subsided, but has since eroded to half that area. It's now a nature reserve accessible only to scientists, who are studying how life takes root on barren foundations. (See "Tours & Activities," p. 230, for trips that circumnavigate Surtsey.)

Of the 15 Westman Islands, only the largest, **Heimaey (Home Island),** is inhabited. Westman Islanders have a strong local identity; a common joke refers to the mainland as "the sixteenth island." A few even dreamed of independence from Iceland, especially because the Westmans are relatively wealthy and contribute more in taxes than they receive in services. But their dependence on the Icelandic state became all too clear when, on January 23, 1973, a volcano right next to Heimaey town erupted after 5,000 years of dormancy. When the molten rock finally stopped flowing on July 3, 30% of the town was buried in lava and ash, and 400 buildings were destroyed. Heimaey had also grown by 2.5 sq. km (1 sq. mile).

The first weekend of August is a huge party in Heimaey, as Islanders join thousands of visitors at the campgrounds for live music, fireworks, and bonfires through the night.

Essentials

GETTING THERE

BY AIR Flying to Heimaey is an exciting and sometimes terrifying experience, because planes are often buffeted in the wind. Flights are regularly cancelled because of weather conditions. The airline listed below offers day packages, which might include a bus tour of Heimaey or a round of golf. A taxi ride into town costs around 1,400kr, or you could walk there in about 20 minutes. Taxis often wait for flights, but if not, call **Eyjataxi** (© **698-2038**).

Eagle Air (www.eagleair.is; © **562-4200**) makes 20-minute flights once or twice daily to and from the Westman Islands. From June until August, the price is from 16,900kr.

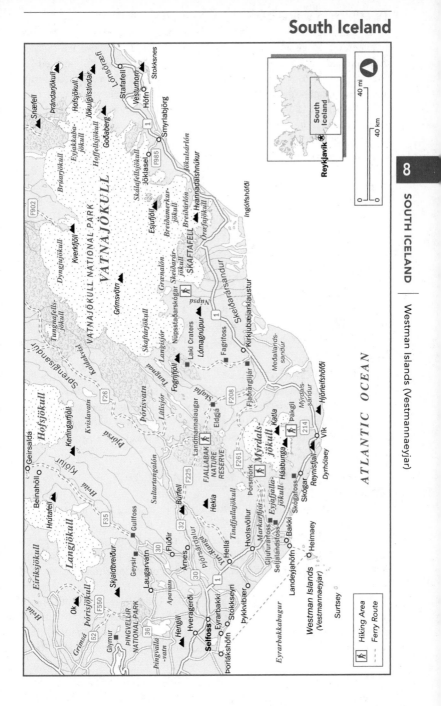

BY FERRY   **Landeyjahöfn** (www.herjolfur.is; ℂ **481-2800**) is a port on the tip of Iceland's south coast, which is a model of environmentally friendly architecture and engineering. Since it opened, it has shortened the journey from the mainland to **Heimaey** from 3 hours to 30 minutes and doubled the number of daily trips. The ferry *Herjólfur* now makes 32 weekly round-trips in summer (June–Aug) between Landeyjahöfn and Heimaey; five daily trips from Thursday to Sunday; and four trips a day from Monday to Wednesday. One-way tickets are 1,380kr adults, 680kr seniors and children ages 12 to 15, and free for children 11 and under. Transporting cars starts at 2,200kr and goes up depending on the size. For all schedules, call ahead or check the website. The ferry sometimes sells out for cars, but rarely for passengers, except possibly the first weekend of August. **Straeto buses** (www.straeto.is; ℂ **553-3737**) from Reykjavík to Landeyjahöfn are aligned with the ferry schedule and depart from the **BSÍ bus terminal** at Vatnsmýrarvegur 10. One-way bus fare from Reykjavík is 4,600kr.

It may seem indulgent to take a car, but it's not a bad idea, because Heimaey has a good road system and attractions are quite spread out. If you do bring a car, make sure to reserve in advance. Even if car reservations are full, you have a decent chance of getting in on standby; register your name at the ticket office, which opens an hour before departure. *Note:* The ferry is sometimes cancelled due to bad weather, or the return can change within a few hours' notice to the port at Eyrarbakki, near Selfoss, a 2-hour drive from Landeyjahöfn.

VISITOR INFORMATION

The **tourist information office** (www.vestmannaeyjar.is; ℂ **481-3555**) is located in City Hall *(Ráðhús)*. **Visit Westman Islands** (www.visitwestman islands.com) is also useful. Make sure to pick up the free **walking map** from the tourist office (open May 15–Sept 15 Mon–Fri 10am–6pm, Sat–Sun 11am–5pm; Sept 16–May 14 call ahead).

Exploring the Westman Islands
HEIMAEY TOWN

Heimaey is the most profitable fishing port in Iceland, bringing in 12% to 13% of the country's annual catch, or about 200,000 tons of fish. During the 1973 eruption, lava threatened to cut off the port entirely, so Iceland's geologists proposed a novel and successful strategy: pumping seawater onto the molten rock to create a hard outer layer and retard the flow. Ironically, the port ended up more sheltered than before.

Facing the innermost waterfront is a rope hanging from a cliff. This is where local children are trained in **spranga,** the "national sport" of the Westmans. The sport originated with egg collecting and involves all sorts of daredevil cliff-scaling. Egg-collecting season is in May and June, and it's fun to watch.

Eldheimar ★★ MUSEUM   The 1973 Heimaey eruption buried roughly 400 houses beneath volcanic rock, and archeologists are still uncovering what remains of some of the buildings, giving the island the nickname "Pompeii of the North." This museum has been built around the remains of one of the homes. Audio guides describe the history and events that transpired before, during, and after the eruption.

Gerðisbraut 10. www.eldheimar.is. ⓒ **488-2700.** Admission 2,300kr adults; 1,200kr children 10–18; free for children 9 and under. Daily 11am–6pm.

Sæheimar Aquarium ★ AQUARIUM   The bulk of this small aquarium are 12 fish tanks donated by local fishermen and filled with unusual sea creatures. The highlight, though, are the live puffins, which visitors are allowed to hold—they are completely tame. A separate touching tank allows children to play with crabs, starfish, and sea urchins.

Heiðarvegur 12. www.saeheimar.is. ⓒ **481-1997.** Admission 1,200kr adults; children 10–17 500kr; free for children 9 and under. May 1–Sept 30 daily 10am–5pm; Nov 1–April 30 Sat 1–4pm.

SKANSINN
Skansinn is on the east side of town, where the lava meets the port. A partially crushed water tank at the lava's edge is a vivid illustration of the volcano's destructive power. The English built a fortification here in the 15th century, when they were Iceland's biggest trading partners. This was of little use in 1627, when Algerian pirates landed on Heimaey's southeast coast. Of the island's 500 inhabitants, about half were taken to Algiers and sold into slavery. Many others were herded into a storehouse and burned alive. The few remaining islanders survived by hiding in caves or rappelling down cliffs. Only 39 of the captives were eventually ransomed and returned to Copenhagen.

The Stave Church (Stafkirkjan) ★ CHURCH   The Norwegian government presented this building to Heimaey in 2000, on land formed during the 1973 eruption, to commemorate the millennium anniversary of Iceland's official adoption of Christianity. In the year 999 or 1000, the king of Norway sent emissaries to the annual Icelandic assembly *(Alþing)* to lobby against paganism. According to saga accounts, their instructions were to build a church wherever they first set foot on land. The location of the original site is under dispute, and the new church is based on the medieval Norwegian Haltdalen Stave Church. In keeping with the saga, the church was built in 2 days.

Skansinn. Free admission. May 15–Sept 15 daily 11am–5pm.

AROUND THE ISLAND
Eldfell & the "New Lava"   Locals refer to the red volcanic cone created in 1973 as **Eldfell** (Fire Mountain), and the surrounding lava as **"the new lava,"** or *nýjahraun,* to distinguish it from the "old lava" *(eldhraun)* around Helgafell on the south side of town. Take a rambling drive or walk through the new lava to witness how islanders are improvising on and shaping their new landscape. Some have built lava gardens, or sculptures, or memorials for homes that are buried directly underneath. The 5m (16 ft.) wooden cross at the base of Eldfell is a good starting point for an ascent. The cone is still steaming slightly, and the ground is still warm if you scratch beneath the surface. Just

THE GREAT puffling RESCUE

With their orange beaks and feet, tuxe-doed 18cm-tall (7-in.) bodies, and sad clown eyes, puffins are by common consent among the world's cutest creatures. Their air speed can reach 80kmph (50mph), yet they flap awkwardly and frantically, like cartoon animals who suspend themselves momentarily before crashing to earth. For centuries, Icelanders have hunted puffins by waving a kind of giant butterfly net over cliff ledges to catch them in mid-air. Most puffins breed in Iceland, and the Westman Islands boast Iceland's largest puffin colony. In 2007, however, puffin numbers declined alarmingly; speculation is that warmer ocean waters have pushed their main food source, sand eels, farther north.

Puffins are usually monogamous for life, and—unless they end up on a dinner plate—have an average lifespan of 25 years. They usually return to the same breeding area, if not the same cliff-top nesting burrow, and the females lay two eggs per year, but only one at a time. The pufflings hatch in around 42 days, and both parents gather fish for them. In mid-August the parents abandon the nest, and the pufflings are left to fend for themselves.

In late August, hundreds of hungry pufflings are attracted and disoriented by Heimaey's lights and end up crashing into yards and streets. Locals lock their cats inside, but let children stay up late to gather the pufflings in boxes lined with soft fabric. The pufflings stay in the families' homes overnight. The next morning, the children return the pufflings to the sea.

southeast of the cone is **Páskahellir,** a lava tube that should not be entered without a strong flashlight; the easiest trail access is near the airport.

Other Walks   A trip to the Westmans is not complete without a good walk. A thrilling, vertiginous, and somewhat dangerous **hiking trail** starts on a 4WD road behind the N1 service station by the port; continuing along Heimaey's northeastern cliffs, eventually connecting with equally harrowing trails that ascend from Herjólfsdalur, near the golf course. Ropes and chains guide you up and down the steep sections. A gentler trail along **Ofanleit-ishamar** on the west coast is great for puffin close-ups. The lighthouse at **Stófjörði,** on the southern tip of the island, is officially the windiest spot in Iceland. In the southeast, the sea cliffs of **Litlihöfði** are another picturesque spot for puffins.

Tours & Activities

Boat tours ★★ led by avian experts offer an entirely different viewpoint on coastal caves and bird cliffs around Heimaey. You might also see seals, dolphins, or even orcas, which populate the sea around the Westmans.

Viking Tours (www.vikingtours.is; ✆ **488-4884**), headquartered at Tangagötu 7, near the ferry landing, offers a 90-minute circle tour of the island; the captain will likely enter a sea cave and demonstrate the acoustics by playing saxophone for an audience of thousands of nonplussed birds. Tickets are 8,200kr for adults, 7,200kr for children ages 9 to 14, and free for children 8 and under. Other options include bus tours (with plenty of walking), whale-watching, and dinner sailings. Viking also offers a tour of Surtsey, though the boat is not permitted to land. **Eyja Tours** (https://eyjatours.com; 🕐 **852-6939**), also located near the ferry, offers a similar range of tours.

You can rent bikes or electronic trike bikes from **Booking Westman Islands** (https://bookingwestmanislands.is; 🕐 **626-3340**), while **Ribsafari** (www.ribsafari.is; 🕐 **661-1810**) offers tours on inflatable boats that explore caves and puffin nesting sites and look for orcas. **Vestmannaeyjavöllur** (www.gvgolf.is; 🕐 **481-2363**) is the only Icelandic golf course situated inside a volcano crater and is considered one of the top courses in Europe. It may also be Iceland's most scenic course, though you never know where the wind will take the ball. Course fees are 7,500kr, with inexpensive club rental, and tournaments take place most weekends in summer.

Where to Stay

Additional options are available at **www.vestmannaeyjar.is.**

EXPENSIVE

Hótel Vestmannaeyjar ★★ Since adding a new wing in 2014 that nearly doubled the number of rooms, not to mention a name change, this hotel in the center of town really stands out from the pack. The rooms are snazzy, with flatscreen TVs, wood floors, and contemporary Scandinavian furniture. There are plenty of extras too, like an excellent **restaurant,** hot tubs, a sauna, and billiards.

Vestmannabraut 28. www.hotelvestmannaeyjar.is. 🕐 **481-2900.** 43 units. May–Sept 26,775kr double; 33,915kr suites. Rates around 10% lower Oct–Apr. Rates include breakfast. **Amenities:** Restaurant; hot tubs; sauna; free Wi-Fi.

MODERATE

Hótel Eyjar ★ Although the Eyjar lacks the extra amenities of Hótel Vestmannaeyjar, the nicely renovated rooms are at least comparable. The doubles are well-maintained, albeit small, while the apartments add kitchenettes, plus a fold-out sofa in the larger ones. On the ground floor is an Eymundsson bookstore, tourist information center, and a **coffee shop.**

Bárustígur 2 (at Strandvegur). www.hoteleyjar.is. 🕐 **481-3636.** 11 units. June–Aug 35,100kr double; 45,640kr suite for 2–3 people. Rates around 10% lower Sept–May (except suites). Rates include breakfast during the summer, otherwise available for 2,500kr. **Amenities:** Free Wi-Fi.

INEXPENSIVE

Lava Guesthouse ★ The clean, minimalist rooms at this pleasant property in a 1911 house in the center of town came on the market in 2018. Rooms are a bit cramped and the slanted ceilings in some don't help; however, extras like a shared terrace and kitchen help make up for it. The guesthouse also rents out a sleek three-bedroom apartment with a full kitchen nearby.

Bárustígur 13. Lavaguesthouse.com. 🕐 **659-5400.** 6 units. May–Aug 13,800kr double w/shared bathroom; 31,400kr family room; 47,400kr apartment. Rates around 20%–30% lower Sept–Apr. **Amenities:** Guest kitchen; free Wi-Fi.

Where to Eat

In addition to the places mentioned below, you can grab a drink at the tasting room and bar of Ölstofa The Brothers Brewery (http://tbb.is), at Vesturvegur 5, in the center of town; it's open Thursday to Saturday.

Einsi Kaldi ★ ICELANDIC   Named after a well-known sailor from Vestmannaeyjar, this stylish restaurant inside the Hótel Vestmannaeyjar is headed by a chef who worked in top Reykjavík kitchens before returning to his hometown. The menu is seafood-heavy, with scallops, blue mussels, langoustines, and wolffish prepared in various ways.

At Hótel Vestmannaeyjar, Vestmannabraut 28. www.einsikaldi.is. ✆ **481-1415.** Reservations recommended. Main courses 2,890kr–6,890kr. Daily 11:30am–9pm.

Gott ★ ICELANDIC   Sometimes simple food can be the best. Fresh-baked bread in the morning. Organic coffee. Fish right from the boat. Chef Siggi Gislason, a former member of the Icelandic culinary team, has written several bestselling cookbooks with his wife, so despite the homey, straightforward-sounding dishes, a lot of love goes into them. The colorful bistro, with tables crafted from old doors, also has sidewalk seating. A second location is in Reykjavík.

Bárustígur 11. https://gott.is. ✆ **481-3060.** Main courses 2,190kr–2,690kr. Daily 11am–9pm.

Slippurinn ★★★ ICELANDIC   Some restaurants in Iceland do a better job of capturing a sense of place than others. Then some do a spectacular job. The kitchen team at Slippurinn forages for wild herbs, which are used in cocktails and to infuse oils. Traditional cooking techniques are emphasized in innovative ways throughout the menu, such as in the arctic thyme-cured halibut or the whole glazed cod heads that get finished tableside with a torch. Three- and five-course tasting menus are on offer, though Slippurinn is still very much a spot for locals as much as tourists, so it has something for everyone, including a daily pan-fried-fish option. The Slippurinn is family-run: The chef's sister redesigned the old machine workshop, while his mother occasionally waits tables. On weekends, the bar stays open until midnight.

Strandvegur 76. www.slippurinn.com. ✆ **481-1515.** Main courses 3,400kr–4,900kr. Daily 11:30am–3pm and 5–10pm. Closed Oct–Apr.

Stofan Bakhús ★ BAKERY/CAFE   This always-busy bakery and cafe is your best option for something quick and easy. It sells typical Scandinavian-style pastries and cakes, plus sandwiches and soups.

Bárustígur 7. ✆ **481-2664.** Small dishes 850kr–2,500kr. Mon–Fri 7:30am–5:30pm; Sat 7:30am–4pm; Sun 10am–4pm.

ÞJÓRSÁRDALUR & HEKLA

Dominated by Iceland's legendary Mount Hekla, Þjórsá is Iceland's longest and mightiest river, and its valley—Þjórsárdalur—holds what is believed to be the world's most voluminous lava flow since the end of the last Ice Age. The flow is about 8,000 years old and covers around 805 sq. km (499 sq. miles). In the river's lower reaches, the lava has yielded to fertile grazing land. The upper reaches near Hekla remain bleak, thanks to ash fallout from Hekla's periodic eruptions. The valley may be considered by some to be off the beaten track, but it attracts many Icelandic campers during the summer.

Essentials

GETTING THERE   Fifteen kilometers (9 miles) east of Selfoss, Route 30 branches off from Route 1 and follows the northwest side of the Þjórsá. At Árnes (your last chance for a hot dog), turn on to Route 32 to continue along the river. Eventually Route 32 bridges the Þjórsá and dead-ends at Route 26. To the left are Hrauneyjar (p. 307) and the Sprengisandur route to the north (p. 306). A right turn leads back to Route 1 on the opposite side of the river, passing near the base of Hekla.

VISITOR INFORMATION   The best resource is the regional tourist office at **Hveragerði** (Sunnumörk 2–4; www.south.is; ✆ **483-4601**). Þjórsárdalur's website is **www.sveitir.is**.

Exploring the Area

This region makes for an ideal day trip from Reykjavík or anywhere within reach. The highlights listed below follow a circular route up the northwest side of the Þjórsá on Route 32, and back down the southeast side on Route 26. No bus tours cover the area, so you'll need a car. Come prepared for a long stretch without food or facilities. If you're planning a hike in the Stöng/Gjáin/Háifoss area, bring a map.

ALONG ROUTE 32

Returning to Route 32 and continuing east for approximately 2km (1¼ miles), you'll see a turnoff for **Hjálparfoss,** a picturesque waterfall that breaks through the breadth of lava rock. It's certainly worth the 1km (⅔-mile) detour. Clamber up to the vantage point above the cascade.

Return to Route 32 from Hjálparfoss, turn right, and immediately cross a bridge. Within another 1km (⅔ mile) you'll come to a gravel road (Route 327) on the left. It's marked with a small sign for the ancient site of Stöng, which is 7km (4⅓ miles) down the gravel road. The road is very rough, but usually passable—if only just—in a conventional car. From the parking area, look for the red-roofed building that houses the ruins. All that remains of **Stöng** are the simple stone foundations of a 12th-century Viking longhouse, but it's probably the most intact Saga Age building yet excavated. The ruins were preserved by ash from the first recorded Mt. Hekla eruption in 1104. As many as 20 farms once occupied this area, which is hard to believe from the bleak vistas you see today. Informative panels map the layout of the women's quarters, central fireplace, barn, smithy, and reconstructed driftwood church.

The lush, peaceful gorge of **Gjáin ★★**, in the Rauðá (Red River), full of wildflowers and curious rock formations, is only a 10-minute walk from Stöng; the well-worn trail leaves right from the ruins. Gjáin (pronounced

Gyow-in) is so lovely that several people are said to have had their ashes spread there.

A very short distance past the turnoff to Stöng and reached by a marked right turn off Route 32, **Þjóðveldisbærinn** (www.thjodveldisbaer.is; ✆ **488-7713;** admission 750kr adults, free for seniors and children 12 and under; June to early Sept 10am–5pm) is an ambitious reconstruction of a Viking-era homestead—the only such project in Iceland. The longhall design is mostly based on the excavated ruins at Stöng, but is meant to represent all similar settlements from the 11th and 12th centuries. (Consider visiting Þjóðveldisbærinn before Stöng, to better understand what Stöng once looked like.) It's striking to compare the Vikings' commodious interiors to the damp, claustrophobic living quarters in 19th-century turf farmhouses preserved all over Iceland. Viking settlers had more access to wood for construction and were not as concerned with insulation—Iceland was warmer before the mid-12th century. The builders of Þjóðveldisbærinn restricted themselves to the same technology available to the Vikings 900 years ago. The exhibit also explains Viking home economics, such as how many kilometers a woman had to walk in circles to spin a length of cloth.

Háifoss ★, a beautiful waterfall, the third tallest in Iceland at 122 meters (400 ft.), is reached by a rough gravel road. The turnoff, marked "Háifoss" and "Hólaskógur," is on the left side of Route 32, roughly 10km (6 miles) past the turnoff for Þjóðveldisbærinn. (Soon after exiting for Háifoss, another road branches off to the left toward Gjáin and Stöng, which should not be attempted without 4WD.) Hólaskógur is a mountain hut 2km (1¼ miles) from Route 32, and Háifoss is roughly 6km (3¾ miles) farther.

HEKLA & ENVIRONS

Shortly after the turnoff for Háifoss, Route 32 crosses the Þjórsá and dead-ends at Route 26. A right turn leads you back to the Ring Road, passing close to the base of **Hekla,** Iceland's most notorious volcano. After a few kilometers (about 2 miles), you'll pass the 4WD road F225 to Landmannalaugar on the left. About 4km (5 miles) later, look out to the right until you see **Tröll-konuhlaup,** a short but broad and commanding waterfall with an island in the middle; the turnoff is unmarked, but you can easily find your way to the step-ladder that climbs over the fence.

At this point you're as close as the road will come to **Hekla,** the majestic, oblong, snow-crested peak rising from the plains. Hekla is the second most active volcano in Iceland, and its white collar masks its molten heart: *Hekla* means "hood," a name derived from the clouds that usually obscure the peak.

For most nationalities, natural disasters are just periodic intervals in their collective memory. In Iceland's national story, Hekla and its ilk are vital players. A 1585 map of Iceland pictures Hekla in mid-eruption, with the caption: "Hekla, cursed with eternal fires and snow, vomits rocks with a hideous sound." Hekla's first recorded eruption in 1104 blanketed every farm and village within a 50km (31-mile) radius. Since then it's erupted more than 100 times and about once a decade since the 1970s, with the last occurrence in

ASCENDING hekla

Hekla remained unclimbed until 1750—perhaps because in popular mythology, it was the gateway to hell. (The rumblings heard for months after each eruption were said to be tormented souls.) Climbing Hekla is no piece of cake: A round-trip hike to the 1,491m (4,892 ft.) summit takes at least 7 hours (4 hr. up, 3 hr. down). A trail on the north side is well-marked, but don't attempt it without a good map and expert advice on current conditions. One good source is the **Hekla Center** (© 487-8700) at Leirubakki Farm on Route 26, near the mountain (see below).

Mountain Taxi (www.arcticsafari.is; © **544-5252**), based in Reykjavík, leads a 10- to 12-hour circuit of Hekla in Super Jeeps, with a stop for a dip in the Landmannalaugar hot spring, for 39,500kr.

2000. An enormous **reforestation project** (the largest attempt at reforestation anywhere in Europe), covering 1% of Iceland's entire land surface, is projected to surround Hekla with trees.

Hekla Center (Heklusetur) ★ EXHIBIT   This small but well-designed multimedia exhibition, open since 2007, explores the history of Mount Hekla and its influence on human life in Iceland from the time of settlement. Video screens display eruption footage, a seismometer keeps track of current grumblings, and screen-saver-like software artistically renders the seismometer. At the end, Hekla itself is framed on the wall—through a window. To reach the exhibit, continue southwest on Route 26; it's at the Leirubakki Farm.

www.leirubakki.is. © **487-8700.** Admission 1,000kr, adults; 500kr children ages 6–11; children 5 and under free. Daily 10am–10pm.

Where to Stay & Dine

For other options in the vicinity, see "Hella, Hvolsvöllur, & Markarfljót Valley," later in this chapter. **Rjúpnavellir** (www.rjupnavellir.is; © **892-0409**) is ideally located for access to Landmannalaugar, Veiðivötn (p. 307), and Fjallabaksleið. It offers basic bungalows with kitchens for 19,600kr. The resort, near the base of Hekla, comprises two cottages, providing room for a total of 48 people.

Fosshotel Hekla ★   Not nearly as close as Leirubakki is to Hekla, this functional inn (from a chain known for providing little more) is a good default option on the return from the highlands. Its wood-floor rooms lack authenticity, but a **restaurant** with locally sourced ingredients and a hot tub save the day.

Brjánsstaðir. www.fosshotel.is. © **486-5540.** 46 units. May–Sept 14 30,000kr double. Rates around 25% lower Sept 15–Apr. Rates include breakfast. **Amenities:** Restaurant; hot tub; sauna; free Wi-Fi.

Leirubakki ★   This pleasant country hotel sits under the shadow of the Hekla volcano and has long served as its unofficial visitor center. The farmstead has a surprisingly sophisticated multimedia exhibition (above) and a **restaurant** with well-executed local dishes and a fantastic view of Hekla (main courses 2,500kr–7,200kr; reservations recommended), as well as a hot tub, sauna, and heated outdoor pool that's carved out of stone and lava walls, known as the "Viking Pool." Horse rental is available.

Rte. 26. www.leirubakki.is. © **487-8700.** 14 units. May–Sept 14 31,000kr double w/ bathroom. Family rooms available for 4 and 6 people. Rates around 35% lower Sept 15–Apr. Rates include breakfast (except for sleeping-bag accommodation). **Amenities:** Restaurant; heated outdoor pool; hot tub; sauna; free Wi-Fi in public areas.

LANDMANNALAUGAR, FJALLABAK & SURROUNDINGS

Naming Iceland's best hiking area is a pointless exercise, but if the proverbial gun were put to our heads, **Landmannalaugar** ★★★ would edge out the competition. In photographs, this area is usually represented in two ways: by the rhyolite mountains, with their astonishing mineral spectra, and by deeply contented bathers in the natural hot spring by the main camp. But Landmannalaugar is a much wider world unto itself—with glacial valleys, marshes, canyons, moss-covered lava fields, tephra desert, and plentiful geothermal hotspots—and can sustain several days of exploring. The ideal follow-up is the **Laugavegurinn** (p. 237), the world-famous 4-day trek to Þórsmörk.

Landmannalaugar proper is a flat, gravelly area 600m (1,969 ft.) above sea level, set between a glacial river and a lava flow dating from the 15th century. But the name Landmannalaugar is commonly applied to its surrounding area as well, all part of the **Fjallabak Nature Reserve.** Landmannalaugar is reached from the west by two mountain roads: F225 from Hekla, and F208 from the Hrauneyjar area. F208 continues east (on what is known as "the Fjallabak Route") past the volcanic rift Eldgjá and eventually joins the Ring Road west of Kirkjubæjarklaustur.

Essentials

GETTING THERE From June 15 to September 13, daily buses from **Reykjavík Excursions** (www.re.is; © **580-5400**) connect Reykjavík and Skaftafell in both directions via Landmannalaugar and the Fjallabak route. The bus from Reykjavík leaves at 7:15am and from Skaftafell at 3pm. The bus from Reykjavík ends at Landmannalaugar and returns to Reykjavík the same day. Buses from Reykjavík—with stops at Hveragerði, Selfoss, Hella, and Leirubakki—arrive at Landmannalaugar at 7pm, and leave at 12:30pm. A one-way ticket between Reykjavík and Landmannalaugar is 9,500kr for adults and 4,750kr for children 11 and under.

From July 27 to August 24, another Reykjavík Excursions bus connects Landmannalaugar to Mývatn in the north, via the **Sprengisandur Route** through the interior (p. 306). The bus departs at 9:30am three times a week in each direction, and takes 10 hours, with some sightseeing stops, for 17,500kr.

It's possible to reach Landmannalaugar by **driving** a conventional car, but only from Hrauneyjar via Route F208, which opens up around the end of June. Insurance for rental cars is usually voided on "F" roads, however, so it's probably not worth the risk. The bus to Landmannalaugar uses Route F225 for scenic reasons, but even drivers with 4WD vehicles should check with the Landmannalaugar hut about road conditions before attempting this route; a particularly hazardous ford is close to Landmannalaugar. Coming from the east, a car could take Route 208/F208 from the Ring Road as far as Eldgjá, but the same insurance problem applies. *Note:* Fuel stops are nonexistent between Hrauneyjar and Kirkjubæjarklaustur.

Where to Stay & Dine

Landmannalaugar has just one place to stay, a two-story mountain hut open mid-June to early October and run by **Ferðafélag Íslands** (www.fi.is; © **568-2533**). The hut is perhaps the most overburdened in Iceland; reservations should be made at least 6 months in advance if possible, especially for July and August. Reservations must be made online, with advance payment. Vouchers are sent to you by mail and must be shown to the wardens. If you show up without a reservation and they have room, you can pay with cash, MasterCard, or Visa.

The basic wooden structure has 78 sardine-style beds in four bedrooms, with kitchen, toilets, and showers, which cost 500kr. Beds are 9,000kr for adults, 4,500kr for ages 7 to 18, and free for ages 6 and under, but you must bring your

THE laugavegurinn

This 55km (34-mile) route between Landmannalaugar and Þórsmörk is Iceland's best-known trek, and for good reason. The scenery is breathtaking, endlessly varied—from ice caves and geothermal fields to glacial valleys and woodlands—and perfectly choreographed through each leg of the journey. Sleeping-bag huts with kitchens, toilets, and (usually) showers are spaced at roughly 14km (9 mile) intervals. Some energetic hikers sprint the entire route in 2 days, but 4 or even 5 days are ideal for fully digesting your surroundings. The trail opens up anytime from late June to mid-July and remains passable until some point in September. The season could be extended a little on either end by bringing an ice axe and crampons for steep, icy sections.

Either bring a tent or book somewhere to stay well in advance. **Ferðafélag Íslands** (www.fi.is; © **568-2533**) runs the hut at Landmannalaugar, all three huts along the route, and one of the three huts at Þórsmörk (p. 246). The

costs and payment procedures are the same as for the Landmannalaugar hut. It's a great luxury to have your bags carried from hut to hut by 4WD; see "Tours and Activities," p. 238. You must pack in all of your own food, unless provisions are part of your arranged tour.

You'll also want good hiking shoes, a full weatherproof outfit, extra footwear for fording rivers (supportive rubber sandals are best), and a map and compass, even though the trail is heavily used and well-marked. The Landmannalaugar hut sells a standard hiking map of the route, as well as a small book, *The Laugavegurinn Hiking Trail*, by Leifur Þorsteinsson, with good detail on sights along the trail as well as potential side trips.

The route can be hiked in either direction, but most trekkers head from Landmannalaugar to Þórsmörk. This route evens out the strenuousness of each day, and has a slight net loss of altitude. Many hikers continue from Þórsmörk on the 2-day trek to Skógar (p. 247).

own sleeping bag. Camping costs 2,000kr per person, and gives you access to the toilets and showers but not the kitchen. Some visitors assume they'd prefer sleeping indoors, but the hut can get hot, and noisy, so bring earplugs.

Exploring the Area

Landmannalaugar can be enjoyed in day tours, afternoon visits, and 2-hour bus layovers, but 2 to 4 nights is ideal. Arriving by bus one afternoon and leaving the next doesn't allow time for hikes that take the better part of a day. **Fjallabak** is often drizzly, so it's smart to include an extra day in your itinerary for insurance.

Available at the hut for 1,800kr, **maps** of the Landmannalaugar area lay out the trails in detail. Wardens and fellow hikers are happy to detail routes of any length or difficulty. Recommended destinations include **Brandsgil Canyon, Frostastaðavatn Lake,** the summits of **Bláhnúkur** and **Brennisteinsalda,** and the unjustly named **Ljótipollur (Ugly Puddle),** a red crater with a lake full of brown trout. Almost all visitors complete the day with a dip in the famous **hot spring** near the hut.

East of Landmannalaugar, the roughest stretch of Route F208 leads to **Eldgjá ★,** or the "Fire Canyon." This 30km-long (19-mile) volcanic fissure reaches a depth of 270m (886 ft.) and width of 600m (1,969 ft.), revealing reddish rockslides and a pretty waterfall named Ófærufoss. The buses heading both east and west stop at Eldgjá for around 45 to 60 minutes.

Tours & Activities

Many tour companies in Reykjavík offer day trips to Landmannalaugar by 4WD, combined with some sightseeing around Þjórsárdalur and Mt. Hekla, but you'll probably feel cheated by having so little time. Also, 4WDs are prohibited from venturing off-road, so they do not offer the freedom of access you might anticipate.

Enlisting in a **Laugavegurinn hiking tour** has several advantages. All tours include transportation to and from Reykjavík, huts with showers, a guide, and plenty of companionship, usually including Icelanders. Best of all, your bags are delivered from hut to hut.

From July into early September, **Trex** (www.trex.is; ✆ **587-6000**) leads a few Laugavegurinn tours. The cost is 169,900kr per person.

Útivist (www.utivist.is; ✆ **562-1000**), equally recommended, has even more Laugavegurinn departures for a slightly higher fee: 72,000kr per person (half-price for children 6–16). As with Ferðafélag Íslands, a meal at Þórsmörk is included. Útivist also offers a choice between more strenuous 4-day trips and less strenuous 5-day trips. Cross-country-skiing trips to Landmannalaugar leave in spring, and a 4WD tour of the Fjallabak reserve leaves in late August. Útivist also leads a few 4-day trips to **Sveinstindur–Skælingar ★★★** in July and August for 64,000kr (half-price for children 6–16). This remote and otherworldly landscape northeast of Eldgjá is far less known than Landmannalaugar and Þórsmörk. The medium-difficulty trip features a mountain climb and long traverse of a lovely, river-braided glacial valley. Bags are transported by 4WD.

Icelandic Mountain Guides (www.mountainguide.is; ☏ **587-9999**) hosts several Laugavegurinn tours for groups of 6 to 14 from 139,900kr per person, depending on amenities. All meals are included and prepared for you.

HORSEBACK RIDING

Riding in this area is spectacular, but may not be suitable for beginners. **Eld Hestar** (www.eldhestar.is; ☏ **480-4800**) offers 7-day horseback riding tours to and around Landmannalaugar. *Note:* The service is available only on select summer dates. **Hekluhestar** (www.hekluhestar.is; ☏ **487-6598**) arranges 5-, 6-, and 8-day riding trips around Hekla, Landmannalaugar, and the Fjallabak reserve. The 6-day Hekla–Landmannalaugar pack trip, including horses, equipment, guide, and full board, costs 319,000kr per person.

HELLA, HVOLSVÖLLUR & MARKARFLJÓT VALLEY

Proceeding east from Reykjavík along the southern coast, this area represents the last broad expanse of agricultural land before mountains and glaciers press more tightly to the coast. The villages of Hella and Hvolsvöllur are right along the Ring Road; east of Hvolsvöllur, the broad Markarfljót river valley leads inland toward Þórsmörk. (For the lower route through the Markarfljót valley to Þórsmörk, see p. 246.)

Prior to the volcanic eruptions in spring 2010, this area was more famous for raising horses and as the home country of *Njáls Saga,* perhaps the most famous of Icelandic tales. Since the eruptions, the area has seen a huge increase in volcano tourism, with off-the-beaten-track areas such as Fljótshlíð suddenly being invaded with an army of traffic. A number of quality tour operators in the area lead various tours to the volcano site (p. 240).

Eyjafjallajökull might not be Iceland's biggest and best volcano, but it's certainly the one everyone wants to see. If you watched open-mouthed as the amazing images of Eyjafjallajökull erupting filled your TV screen for days, if not weeks, now's your chance to see the celebrity in person. To get a close look at the now resting beast, the best place to view it is from Fljótshlíð, about 25km (13 ½ miles) east of Hvolsvöllur and a 130km (70-mile) drive from Reykjavík. To get there by car, take the Ring Road (Route 1) to Hvolsvöllur and then turn left on to Route 261 and drive all the way to the end of the road; the last 7km (4 miles) of the road is unpaved. In good weather the volcano is clearly visible, with the white surface of the glacier emerging slowly from underneath a thick blanket of black ash. Every now and then the restless sleeper vents a plume of steam. To get even closer you need to take a tour (see below).

Essentials

GETTING THERE   All buses headed from Reykjavík to Þórsmörk, Vík, and Höfn stop at Hella and Hvolsvöllur en route, with plenty of daily options; contact **Sterna** (www.sterna.is; ☏ **553-3737**) or **Reykjavík Excursions** (www. re.is; ☏ **562-1011**), and check bus schedules for the South.

THE ring OF FIRE

On March 20, 2010, a new star of Icelandic tourism was born on the volcanic stage. The show started with the opening of a vent fissure in **Fimmvörðuháls**. The tourist companies in Iceland were quick to arrange an army of tourist pursuits, including helicopter trips and 4WD tours to the volcano site. One of the more extravagant excursions, offered by **Hótel Holt ★** (p. 71), shuttled people by helicopter to the site and prepared for them a red-carpet champagne dinner cooked on the newly laid lava field! After 3 weeks of activity the show ended, only to be upstaged by an even bigger and more dangerous eruption beneath the glacier **Eyjafjallajökull** directly to the west of the first. After a protracted second act, the world was waiting for sleeping sister **Katla** to awake and perform the grand finale.

Since the eruptions took place, the area has now been dubbed the "Ring of Fire." If you are lucky enough to be visiting Iceland during one of these spectacular performances of nature, the following tour operators are likely to host special volcano tours: **Glacier Guides** (www.glacierguides.is; ✆ **571-2100**), a popular tour company with Super Jeep rides to the best possible view at a safe distance; **Extreme Iceland** (www.extremeiceland.is; ✆ **565-9320**) is a similar company with Super Jeep rides to the volcanic areas; for an entirely different perspective, **Norðurflug** (www.nordurflug.is; ✆ **562-2500**) operates unforgettable helicopter tours of active volcanoes. Tours are, of course, always changing depending on the level of volcanic activity.

VISITOR INFORMATION In **Hvolsvöllur,** tourist information (www.hvolsvollur.is; ✆ **487-8043**) is located in the community hall **Hvoll (Félagsheimilið Hvoll)** on Austurvegi, just off the Ring Road.

Exploring the Area
HELLA

If you want to try out the manageable and good-tempered Icelandic horse in Iceland's premier horse-farming area, consider combining a ride with a **farm stay.** Some offer packages for anything from overnights to weeklong trips.

Hekluhestar, on Austvaðsholt Farm, Route 272, 9km (5½ miles) northeast of Hella (www.hekluhestar.is; ✆ **487-6598**), is mentioned above for its 6- and 8-day trips around Mt. Hekla and the Fjallabak reserve. Like many of the horse farms, it will negotiate just about any trip in the vicinity. Hekluhestar welcomes you to take part in farm life, which can be especially delightful during lambing season in late April/early May, foaling season in late May, and the sheep roundup in September.

Hestheimar, on Route 281, just off Route 26, 7km (4⅓ miles) northwest of Hella (https://hestheimar.is; ✆ **487-6666**), is an appealing guesthouse that offers horseback riding and renowned home cooking. In addition to six cottages, the guesthouse has four rooms, two with private bathroom, and a barn loft with sleeping-bag accommodation for up to 18; amenities include a guest kitchen and hot tub.

HVOLSVÖLLUR

LAVA Center ★★ MUSEUM   Opened in 2017, this interactive museum explores Iceland's volcanic systems and seismic activity through some impressive displays like an earthquake simulator, a walk through an ash-like cloud, and HD films of actual eruptions. A 360-degree viewing platform offers looks at three different volcanoes. It also has a large **restaurant** and souvenir shop.

Austurvegur 14. www.lavacentre.is. ✆ **415-5200.** Admission 2,400kr; 3,200kr with cinema. Daily 9am–7pm.

The Saga Center ★ MUSEUM   This educational exhibit avoids the gimmicky costumes and displays that other saga-related museums tend to rely on. The central theme is *Njál's Saga* (see box, *"Njál's Saga* & Its Sites," p. 242), the story of a bloody 50-year feud, and the walk-through exhibits are quite word-heavy, with extensive information panels, illustrations, and props explaining the historical context and literary significance of the sagas.

Rte. 261 (just off Rte. 1). www.njala.is. ✆ **487-8781.** Admission 900kr adults; free for ages 16 and under. Audio tour included w/admission price. May 15–Sept 15 daily 9am–6pm; off-season, call in advance.

MARKARFLJÓT VALLEY

Before the Markarfljót river was diked and bridged in the 1930s, it would swell with meltoff from Mýrdalsjökull and Eyjafjallajökull and change course, creating havoc downstream for farmers and tourists. From Hvolsvöllur, Route 261 proceeds east along the northern side of the Markarfljót valley for 27km (17 miles) to the Fljótsdalur Youth Hostel (see "Where to Stay," p. 243), where it turns into mountain road F261. The valley becomes progressively narrower, and Þórsmörk seems very close by, but the river is uncrossable.

If you can't get to Þórsmörk, a day hike up **Þórólfsfell** ★★ is a very worthy substitute. The 3-hour round-trip walk from the Fljótsdalur hostel isn't too strenuous, and wandering around the flat-topped peak yields fabulous views. With no single route or marked trail up Þórólfsfell, the best approach is from its northwest side, not from F261 to the south, which is much steeper. In good weather, your destination is clearly visible, but if fog rolls in, it's best to have a map and compass. From the top, you could descend the east side of the mountain and walk back to the hostel along F261.

The most ambitious hikers tackle the 9-hour round-trip from Fljótsdalur to the **Tindfjallajökull icecap** ★★; ask at the youth hostel about trail conditions.

THE NJÁL'S SAGA TRAIL

The sites below follow a roughly clockwise pattern.

Þingskálar   In Njál's time, this was the annual spring assembly site for the Rangá river district, and the scarce remains of 37 temporary encampments have been found. Several scenes are set here, including one in which Ámundi the Blind regains his eyesight just long enough to kill Lýtingur á Sámsstöðum. East

njál's saga & ITS SITES

Of Iceland's medieval sagas, *Njál's Saga* is by critical consensus the most lasting literary achievement, and the only one set in south Iceland. It is a heroic tale of love, feuds, sword-wielding, and bloody murder; Conan the Barbarian, eat your heart out. It has also been an invaluable historical resource, providing, for example, the most thorough account of Iceland's conversion to Christianity in the year 1000. The book was written around 1280 by an anonymous author, and purports to recount events almost 300 years earlier. The well-crafted story revolves around Njáll Þorgeirsson and his friend Gunnar Hámundarson, both actual historic figures.

Sites associated with *Njál's Saga* are heavily featured in tourist literature and roadside information panels: Just look for the "s" icon. The history recounted in *Njál's Saga* has left almost no human trace on the landscape, but the vividly described natural settings are much the same as they were in Njál's time (p. 241). Farmers often recount saga events that took place on their property as if they happened yesterday.

For a **horseback-riding tour** of the *Njál's Saga* sites, try **Njála Tours** (www.njala.is; ☏ **487-8781**), which operates out of Miðhús farm on Route 262, 2km (1¼ miles) north of Hvolsvöllur.

of the ruins stands a large boulder named the **Sacrifice Stone (Blótsteinn);** according to folklore, the stone was used to slaughter sentenced criminals.

From the Ring Road, 2km (1¼ miles) east of Hella, exit on to Rte. 264 heading north. In about 7km (4⅓ miles), turn left on Rte. 268 and proceed another 8km (5 miles); Þingskálar is on the left.

Bergþórshvoll Once Njál's home, Bergþórshvoll is now just a low hill amid marshy land 3km (2 miles) from the ocean. In the saga account, Njál's family is burned alive inside the house in the year 1011. Excavations from 1927–28 and 1951–52 proved that there was indeed a fire around this time.

Exit the Ring Road onto Rte. 255, 4km (2½ miles) south of Hvolsvöllur. When 255 ends, turn left on Rte. 252. Bergþórshvoll is 5km (3 miles) ahead on the left.

Gunnarssteinn In a savage battle scene, Gunnar Hámundarson and his allies are ambushed at this rock, which can be reached on foot from Keldur. Excavations turned up a skeleton and a bracelet engraved with two hearts. This bracelet might have come from Gunnar's brother Hjört (Heart), who in the saga was slain at Gunnarssteinn.

At Keldur, ask to be directed to the Gunnarssteinn trail, which leads 3km (2 miles) to the Rangá river, crosses a bridge, and follows the river south for 1km (⅔ mile).

Hlíðarendi Once Gunnar's home, this pretty spot overlooking the Markarfljót valley now holds a few farm buildings and a nicely restored country church. After Gunnar was killed here, he turned over in his grave and spoke cheerfully to his sons in verse. Ruins only amount to simple mounds in the earth. Bergþórshvoll (above) is barely discernible in the distance.

A sign for Hlíðarendi is marked on the left side of Rte. 261, about 17km (11 miles) from Hvolsvöllur.

Keldur   This ancient farm just northeast of Hvolsvöllur is said to be the location of the oldest buildings in Iceland. According to *Njál's Saga,* it was the home of Ingjald Höskuldsson, the uncle of Njál's love child, around the year 1000. It is now a modern dairy farm with more than 20 preserved buildings from the 19th century. The most notable survival is a 15th-century hall with stave construction and a 12th-century hidden underground passageway. This kind of tunnel (Jarðhús) is mentioned in the sagas and was probably used as an escape route when the farm was under attack.

At the easternmost point of Rte. 264, about 20km (12 miles) east of Hella. ℂ **487-8452.**

Where to Stay

On Route 261, 27km (17 miles) east of Hvolsvöllur in Markarfljót valley, the remote **Fljótsdalur Youth Hostel ★** (www.hostel.is; ℂ **487-8498;** 2 units without bathroom; Apr 1–Oct 31 4,500kr bunk; 900kr sheet rental; closed Nov 1–March 31) is practically a mountain hut. Yet, with its turf roof, beautifully tended garden, library full of yellowing travelogues, and incredible views toward Eyjafjallajökull, it could hardly offer more ramshackle appeal. Book well in advance, and remember that all food must be brought in.

Hellishólar ★   This rural farmstead has an accommodation for every type of traveler. There's the oversized log-cabin-like hotel, called Eyjafjallajökull, with a terrace and its own bar. The latest addition to the compound, it has the newest, most modern rooms, though they are still relatively basic. The unpretentious guesthouse has basic rooms with shared baths, while the cottages come in different sizes, but all have kitchenettes. There's even camping and space for RVs. Horseback riding can be arranged with a nearby farm, and an 18-hole golf course is on the property. The loud, boisterous **restaurant** has views of the surrounding farmland and can seat up to 180 people. All of the dishes are served on tableware that is handmade on the premises and painted with volcanic glazes; it can be purchased at the restaurant.

Rt. 261, 11km (7 miles) east of Hvolsvöllur, in Markarfljót Valley. www.hellisholar.is. ℂ **487-8360.** 40 units. 30,200kr hotel double; 11,400kr guesthouse double; 24,500kr cottage for 3–5 people. Rates around 30% lower off-season. **Amenities:** Restaurant; bar; hot tubs; golf course; free Wi-Fi.

Hótel Rangá ★★   Hótel Rangá is what hotels would look like if the elves had won the war. A giant stuffed polar bear greets you in the lobby, before you move down long, wood-lined corridors with checkered orange-and-white tile floors. Whimsical day beds are woven from thin tree branches, while quirky theme suites are decorated after different continents. Despite the high prices, it's hard not to like. It sits beside one of Iceland's choicest salmon fishing rivers, the Rangá, and hot tubs strategically placed outside every few patios allow you to really soak in the view. Opt for the river-facing suites rather than those that face Mt. Hekla and the parking lot. The **restaurant**'s long menu has a stellar reputation. With its isolated location and easy access from Reykjavík,

Rangá is an excellent destination to watch the Northern Lights, and you can even opt for a wakeup call if there's activity.

Off Rte. 1, 7km (4⅓ miles) east of Hella. www.hotelranga.is. ✆ **487-5700.** 52 units. June–Aug 80,000kr double; 110,500kr suite. Rates around 25% lower Apr–May and Sept–Oct; 33–40% lower Jan 5–Feb and Nov–Dec 23. Rates include breakfast. Closed Dec 24–25 and Dec 31–Jan 1. **Amenities:** Restaurant; 2 conference rooms; lounge; bar; hot tubs; in-room massage; tour desk; room service; free Wi-Fi.

Where to Eat

Árhús ★ ICELANDIC   Overlooking the Rangá River near town, a convenient Ring Road lunch stop, this kitschy, barn-like eatery sits across the street from the cottage hotel of the same name. Although the service is painstakingly slow, what comes out of the kitchen is usually worth the wait, such as the tender horse tenderloin with béarnaise sauce and an enormous plate of fish and chips that's enough for two to share.

Rte. 1, in the center of Hella. arhus.is. ✆ **487-5577.** Main courses 1,850kr–4,900kr. Daily 11:30am–9pm.

Eldstó Art Café & Bistro ★ CAFE   Local staples, like pan-fried Arctic char and *Kjötsupie* (lamb soup) with homemade bread, are offered up at this popular road stop.

Rte. 1, across from the N1 service station, Hvolsvöllur. www.eldsto.is. ✆ **482-1011.** Main courses 2,090kr–4,590kr. Daily noon–9:30pm.

Hótel Rangá ★★ SCANDINAVIAN/MEDITERRANEAN   This farm-to-table hotel restaurant, with tall windows on three sides to take in the excellent view of the highlands, is the most gourmet option in the Hella area. Dishes are highly seasonal, so you might find more local game like guillemot or reindeer at some times than others. The four-course gourmet menu, which changes every few months, is the most common dinner option, and it's only slightly more than a main course and appetizer or dessert. The dining room tends to get crowded in the evenings.

Off Rte. 1, 7km (3⅓ miles) east of Hella. www.hotelranga.is. ✆ **487-5700.** Reservations required. Main courses 4,400kr–10,500kr; 4-course chef's menu 11,900kr per person. Daily 6:30–10pm; closed Dec 24–25 and Dec 31–Jan 1.

Kaffi Langbrók ★ CAFE   This itsy-bitsy wooden cabin turned cafe is full of only-in-Iceland quirks, like the 200-year-old whale vertebra on the wall and the saga-inspired escape hatch. Homemade waffles with cream are the specialty. Get them with a side of free Wi-Fi. Other light meals and snacks include soup, sandwiches, and cakes. If you are lucky, you will walk in on musical group Hjónabandið singing at the restaurant, as they often do.

Rt. 261 (about 12km/7½ miles from Rte. 1), in the Markarfljót Valley. ✆ **863-4662.** Mon–Fri noon–11:30pm; Sat–Sun 11:30am–1am.

ÞÓRSMÖRK

Thór, the hammer-wielding Norse god of farmers and seafarers and pioneers, has always been especially revered by Icelanders, who see in him a personification of the persevering Icelandic character. **Þórsmörk ★★★** (Thór's Wood) has an aura of enchantment in the minds of Icelanders, as its name suggests. Surrounded by broad, silt-covered river valleys and three towering glaciers, Þórsmörk is a kind of alpine oasis; ask any sheep who has sought shelter there. Scenic surprises lie around every corner, from waterfalls, twisted gorges, and dripping, moss-covered caves to wildflowers, mountain grasses, and birch trees.

Come prepared: Only basic food supplies are available, and temperatures are colder than in coastal regions. Þórsmörk can be visited on day tours, but staying 1 to 3 nights is recommended.

Essentials

GETTING THERE Þórsmörk is accessed via Route 249/F249, which proceeds 30km (19 miles) east from the Ring Road along the southern edge of the Markarfljót Valley. Only 4WD vehicles with good clearance can reach one of Þórsmörk's three places to stay (Básar), and possibly another (Skagfjörðsskáli), though it's often safer to park and walk the final kilometer by crossing a pedestrian footbridge a short way downstream. Even 4WD vehicles should not drive directly to the third option, Húsadalur; drive to Skagfjörðsskáli (or the pedestrian bridge) and walk the 30 to 45 minutes to Húsadalur from there.

From June 15 until September 12, **Reykjavík Excursions** (www.re.is; ✆ **580-5400**) has a daily bus that leaves Reykjavík for Húsadalur, with stops in Hveragerði, Selfoss, Hella, and Hvolsvöllur. (The bus is cancelled only two or three times a year after surges of glacial meltwater.) It leaves at different times throughout the year, so check RE's website for updated information. From June 15 until August, a second daily bus is added. A one-way adult ticket from Reykjavík to Þórsmörk is 7,850kr.

VISITOR INFORMATION For general information, contact people where you'll be staying (see "Where to Stay," below). An excellent **hiking map,** "Þórsmörk og Goðaland," is for sale at all the huts (1,500kr).

Where to Stay

All three places here have tent sites, guest kitchens, and showers. Húsidalur has options of made-up beds, sleeping-bag accommodation, or sheet rental. To beat the summer rush, be sure to book at least a few weeks in advance.

Básar (✆ **893-2910**), run by and booked through Útivist (www.utivist.is; ✆ **562-1000**), comprises a small hut (sleeps 23) and a large hut (sleeps 60). Both are open May until October, and a warden is on hand. From November until April the smaller hut remains open, but you need to get a key in advance. Básar is notorious for late-night partying on summer weekends because it's the most easily accessible to 4WD vehicles. Sleeping-bag accommodation is 7,000kr per night.

Volcano Huts (www.volcanohuts.com; ✆ **552-8300**) is open from May 1 to October 31. It has the best facilities in the area, with an extensive compound of mountain huts, cabins, glamping tents, a cafe lounge, and a geothermal pool and sauna. The cafe, open until 9:30pm, sells drinks, *skyr,* soup, buffet meals, and basic sandwich supplies. Unlike the other two options, some sleeping quarters have private doubles and made-up beds. Sleeping-bag accommodation in a mountain hut is 8,400kr per person per night, doubles are 26,000kr, and cottages sleeping 1 to 2 people are 28,000kr. Sheets and towels are available for rent. The LavaSPA, with a pool and sauna, are included, but yoga classes and massages are extra. Of the three huts, Volcano has the least picturesque location, but the best hiking areas are within easy reach. Volcano is also the most peaceful after hours, since quiet time is more strictly enforced.

Skagfjörðsskáli (✆ **893-1191**), also known as "Langidalur" or simply "Þórsmörk Hut," is run by and booked through **Ferðafélag Íslands** (www. fi.is; ✆ **568-2533**). The hut, open from mid-May until the end of September, sleeps 75 people in three well-packed rooms. Sleeping-bag accommodation, at 8,000kr, is more expensive than that of the competition. A tiny store sells chocolate, soap, and a few other necessities. Vehicles must cross the Krossá River (just by the hut), which can sometimes get quite deep; ask at the hut to view the photo album, which contains an interesting history of vehicles getting stuck.

Exploring Þórsmörk

For 37,500kr per person you can sign up for a Super Jeep tour with **Mountain Taxi** (www.mountaintaxi.is; ✆ **544-5252**), which includes a short hike.

See p. 238 for arranged tours of the Laugavegurinn trail between Þórsmörk and Landmannalaugar.

THE ROUTE TO ÞÓRSMÖRK Route 249/F249 to Þórsmörk from the Ring Road is fabulously scenic, with the Markarfljót Valley on one side, and waterfalls and glacial tongues on the other.

Seljalandsfoss waterfall, just a short distance up Route 249, is easily spotted from the Ring Road, and is accessible to regular cars. Buses to Þórsmörk often stop for a few minutes so passengers can walk behind the falls, where spray fills the air and the roaring sound is dramatically magnified. The waterfall is brilliantly illuminated and especially enchanting in the evenings.

A short distance along Route 249, **Gljúfurárfoss** ★ is lesser-known but more mysterious and alluring, as the water falls into an enclosed cavern. Park at the farm with the neat lawn and the turf-roofed houses. From there, it's a precarious 3-minute clamber, aided by a chain and ladder, to a good viewpoint. *Warning:* Once you've climbed the final stretch of rock, it can be very difficult to get back down. A safer alternative is to wade up the stream into the cavern.

Close to Þórsmörk, the bus usually makes a photo stop at the small azure lake **Lónið,** with floating icebergs calved from the glacial tongue **Gígjökull.**

HIKING The hiking map *Þórsmörk og Goðaland,* available at the huts, sorts out the dense tangle of trails and is essential for exploring the area. The

THE FIMMVÖRÐUHÁLS trek

How many treks are there where you can actually walk on a steaming lava field and peer into crevices still glowing with brimstone? This spectacular 20km (12-mile) hike connecting Þórsmörk and Skógar, which traverses the 1,093m (3,586-ft.) Fimmvörðuháls Pass between Eyjafjallajökull and Mýrdalsjökull, now has a new dimension, compliments of Mother Nature. The trek was closed for a few months in 2010 after the vent fissure eruption spewed lava over a vast area, consuming at least 200m (656 ft.) of the famous trekking path. The path reopened later in the summer of 2010 with a new path marked out around the lava, and trekkers can now get close up and even walk on and explore the newly laid lava field. A few sections are steep and vertiginous, but no special equipment is usually required between early July and early September. The entire route could be done in 1 exhausting day, but most trekkers spend the night in the **Fimmvörðuskáli hut,** a short detour west of the trail near the top of the pass and about 3km (1 mile) from the lava field. The hut sleeps 20 in snug double-bed sleeping-bag bunks, and must be reserved in advance through Útivist (www.utivist.is; ✆ **562-1000**), at a cost of 7,000kr per person. Facilities include a kitchen but no showers (or water supply of any sort). No camping is allowed outside the hut or anywhere along the trail. Always check weather forecasts before setting out.

The trek can be done in either direction. Hikers going north to south (Þórsmörk to Skógar) have often started on the Laugavegurinn (p. 237), forming a continuous 6-day journey from Landmannalaugar to Skógar. The north-to-south route has the advantage of a net loss of altitude, but the south-to-north route affords a dramatic descent into Þórsmörk.

Arranged tours all go from south to north, to give visitors the option of spending another 1 to 3 nights at the huts in Þórsmörk. The best tour leader is Útivist (www.utivist.is; ✆ **562-1000**), which offers Fimmvörðuháls treks every few days in summer. The very reasonable 30,000kr cost includes transportation from Reykjavík to Skógar and Þórsmörk to Reykjavík, a group guide, and accommodation at the Fimmvörðuskáli hut, but no food.

map is less helpful for calculating the length of your hike, so get an estimate from the wardens.

Technically, only the area north of the Krossá River is Þórsmörk. The area south of the Krossá is called Goðaland (Land of the Gods), and the hiking there is generally harder and steeper. Þórsmörk and Goðaland are connected by a pedestrian bridge near the base of Valahnúkur, a short distance west of the Skagfjörðsskáli hut in Langidalur Valley. Climbing Valahnúkur is a good introduction to the area: Reaching the summit takes less than an hour from Húsadalur or Langidalur. Most hikers stay north of the Krossá and fashion a loop trail to the east, starting and ending at Langidalur. A 6-hour loop will take you as far east as Búðarhamar and around the peak Tindfjöll. An ambitious and rewarding 8-hour round-trip hike leads through Goðaland to the Tungnakvíslarjökull glacial tongue.

Iceland's most famous trail, the Laugavegurinn, connects Þórsmörk and Landmannalaugar in a 4-day hike (see box, p. 237).

SKÓGAR, VÍK & MÝRDALSJÖKULL

Here marks the opening stretch of the southern coast's most dramatic scenery. Tall mountains press against the Ring Road, and a long succession of waterfalls originates from the glaciers looming above. This region also boasts Iceland's best folk museum at Skógar, south Iceland's best coastal walks at Vík, and some lesser-known inland detours toward Mýrdalsjökull Glacier. If you are passing this way, add at least 2 nights to your itinerary to take in Vík's environs, including the Þakgil camp.

Essentials

GETTING THERE   All sights in this section are arrayed on or near Route 1 and can be reached by regular car. Skógar is 155km (96 miles) from Reykjavík, and Vík is 31km (19 miles) farther. In summer, two daily buses connect Reykjavík and Skógar (3,850kr) and two daily buses connect Reykjavík and Vík (4,600kr). Service continues through the winter, with departures at least three times per week. For tickets, contact **Straeto** (www.straeto.is; © **540-2700**).

VISITOR INFORMATION   The regional tourist office at **Hveragerði** (Sunnumörk 2–4; www.south.is; © **483-4601**) covers this area; the local office in Hvolsvöllur (p. 240) also services the area but is only open during the summer. In **Skógar,** limited tourist information can be found at the **folk museum** (p. 249), and at the **Fossbúð market** en route to Skógafoss. In **Vík,** the information desk is in the **Brydebúð Museum,** Víkurbraut 28 (www.visitvik.is; © **487-1395**), open June 15 to September 15 Monday to Friday from 10am to 8pm, Saturday to Sunday 1 to 8pm.

Exploring the Area

WEST OF SKÓGAR

Seljavallalaug ★ GEOTHERMAL POOL   In this "only in Iceland" geothermal swimming pool in a narrow valley beneath infamous Eyjafjallajökull, one wall is actually a mountainside from which the natural hot water trickles in. The 25m (80-ft.) pool is semi-abandoned and therefore free of charge. The pool is not monitored, but it is cleaned at regular intervals. Built in 1923, it is the oldest still-standing pool in Iceland.

May–Sept. From the western junction of Rte. 1 and Rte. 242, take Rte. 242 for 1km (⅔ mile), and then continue straight as Rte. 242 curves off to the right. Seljavellir is about 2km (1¼ miles) ahead. From the parking area walk 15 min. to Seljavallalaug.

SKÓGAR

Skógar feels more like an outpost than a village, but it's been continuously settled since the 12th century. It is best known for its waterfall and folk museum and as a launching point for the 2-day Fimmvörðuháls trek to Þórsmörk (p. 247).

For a wonderful day hike—especially if you like continuous and varied waterfalls—walk north from Skógafoss waterfall along the **Fimmvörðuháls trail** ★★ for about 2 hours, then head back along the same route.

Clearly visible from the Ring Road, the powerful, 62m (203-ft.) **Skógafoss** ★ waterfall looks ordinary from a distance but rewards closer inspection. Walk as close as you can on the gravel riverbed to be enveloped in the sound and spray and refracted light. A metal staircase leads to the top, where you can look down at nesting fulmars.

The prolific and affecting **Skógar Folk Museum (Skógasafn)** ★★★ (www.skogasafn.is; ✆ **487-8845**) is all the work of Þórður Tómasson, who has been gathering artifacts from local farms for almost 70 years. Since Þórður started the museum in 1949, countless imitations have sprung up all over Iceland, but none match the inspiration of the original. A pair of ice skates with blades made from old cow bones. A cask made from a hollowed-out whale vertebra, another used as a kitchen stool. A barometer made from a cow's bladder, which shrivels at the approach of bad weather. Most displays are annotated in English, but guided tours are free with admission for groups. Þórður officially retired from the museum in 2013 at age 93.

Admission to Skógasafn is 2,000kr adults, 1,500kr seniors and students, 1,000kr children 12 to 17, and free for children 11 and under (June–Aug daily 9am–6pm; May and Sept daily 10am–5pm; Oct–Apr 11am–4pm). From Route 1, on the eastern side of Skógar, follow signs for "Byggðasafnið í Skógum."

MÝRDALSJÖKULL

A short distance east of Skógar, Routes 221 and 222 provide the easiest Ring Road access to **Mýrdalsjökull,** the country's fourth-largest glacier. **Sólheimajökull,** a projectile of Mýrdalsjökull, just 5km (3 miles) from the Ring Road via Route 221, is a worthwhile diversion if you are not bound for greater glories east at Skaftafell and Jökulsárlón. Sólheimajökull is retreating up to 100m (328 ft.) every year, a vivid demonstration of the effects of global warming. Some visitors walk atop the glacier, but taking a tour is much safer. Watch out for quicksand at the glacier's edge.

Icelandic Mountain Guides, Vagnhöfði 7, 110 Reykjavík (www.mountain guides.is; ✆ **587-9999**), leads daily glacier walks of Sólheimajökull in summer, with explorations of crevasses and an introduction to basic climbing techniques. A 3-hour tour is 14,900kr (9,900kr for children), not including transportation from Reykjavík or elsewhere, while a 3- to 4-hour climbing tour is 19,900kr. The minimum age for the short tour is 10, the climbing tour, 14.

Arcanum Adventure Tours (www.arcanum.is; ✆ **487-1500**) is based at the Sólheimaskáli hut, 10km (6 miles) from the Ring Road on Route 222, and offers snowmobile, ice-climbing, and Super Jeep tours of Mýrdalsjökull. A snowmobile costs around 26,990kr per person for an hour. Road conditions on Route 222 vary, so ask if you'll need a ride from the Ytri-Sólheimar lodge at the base of the road.

DYRHÓLAEY ★★

This coastal bird sanctuary gets its name (meaning "doorway hill island") from a massive sea archway that photographers—and daredevil pilots—find irresistible. Dyrhólaey is not an island but a promontory, with a shallow inland lagoon full of wading birds, clifftops rife with puffins, and grassy slopes full of ground-nesting avian species. It's ideal walking territory, with some eye-catching sea stacks offshore. Dyrhólaey is closed during nesting season, from May 1 to June 25, though you can still take a guided tour with Dyrhólaeyjarferðir.

Route 218 leads to Dyrhólaey from the Ring Road, crossing a narrow isthmus and rounding the sanctuary. Consider parking at the far end of the isthmus and walking clockwise around the perimeter to the lighthouse, then cutting through the middle back to the shallows. This circuit takes about 3 hours and has fabulous views in all directions. Those who want to cut to the chase can proceed directly to the famous doorway arch on the south side of the sanctuary.

Exploring Vík & Environs ★★

Almost at the southern tip of the mainland, the town of Vík (also known as Vík í Mýrdal) is quaintly poised between mountains, sea cliffs, and a long, beautiful black sand beach. Vík's visual trademark is **Reynisdrangar,** a row of spiky basalt sea stacks that looks like a submerged stegosaurus and has long served as a navigational point for sailors. Lore has it that Reynisdrangar was formed when two trolls were unable to land their three-masted ship before dawn and turned to stone—as happens when trolls are caught in sunlight. The pillars reach up to 66m (217 ft.) in height and have their own bird populations. In good weather, the coastal walk along the Reynisfjall cliffs west of the town is spectacular.

Brydebúð ★ MUSEUM   The tourist information desk, Halldórskaffi, and a local museum are concentrated in this 1831 timber house, which was actually transported to Vík from the Westman Islands in 1895 by ship. The museum has an art gallery and exhibitions on town history, shipwrecks, and the Katla volcano.

Víkurbraut 28. http://brydebud.vik.is. ✆ **487-1395.** Museum admission 500kr adults; free for children 15 and under. June 15–Sept 15 Mon–Fri 11am–8pm, Sat–Sun 1–8pm.

REYNISFJALL

On a clear day or summer evening, the cliffs along **Reynisfjall mountain ★★** west of Vík make for the most beautiful walk on Iceland's southern coastline.

TROLL tales

Trolls arrived in Iceland as stowaways on Viking ships and took to the local landscape, making their homes in caves and cliffs. Their boats are made of stone, and they can fish without line or bait. Most trolls never appear in sunlight, lest they turn into stone themselves.

To Icelanders, trolls are tough, menacing, ugly, and often lonesome—anything but *cute*. It's best not to cross them, though they'll keep their word if you reach an agreement. Trolls who live in bird cliffs are often a great danger to egg-collectors. In an emergency, Christianity can help drive trolls off.

Trolls have not survived in the modern age nearly as well as elves. In fact, many people believe them to be extinct. Electricity hasn't been good for hidden people: Electric light makes the outer dark darker, diminishing the half-dark in which hidden people take form.

ACTIVE volcanoes

The south of Iceland has the highest concentration of known sub-glacial volcanoes in the world. These spectacular forces of nature are a magnet for geo-tourists, but also produce a variety of potentially lethal hazards, such as risk of lightning, tephra fallout (ash), and *Jöklahlaups:* sudden flood bursts of melted glacial ice mixed with ash, mud, huge chunks of ice, and toxic chemicals.

Since the eruption of Eyjafjallajökull in April 2010, all eyes have been focused on one of her angry sisters: **Katla**—a nearby sub-glacial volcano under the Mýrdalsjökull cap, directly north of Vík. This volcano has a history of erupting almost in unison with other local volcanoes and is long overdue. Since 1721, it has erupted five times at 34- to 78-year intervals, but there hasn't been an eruption since 1918.

Anyone visiting this area should be aware of the hazard areas and the evacuation procedures, especially in Vík, clearly set out in the widely available brochure "Eruption Emergency Guidelines."

The most common approach is from Vík, where the ascent must be made inland along the 4WD road that winds its way up. If you have a 4WD vehicle and want to drive up, the road meets the Ring Road at the village's western border. In a regular car, you can shorten the trip a bit by driving to a parking area at the base of the ascent; turn off the Ring Road right next to the "Velkomin Til Vikur" sign. Allow 3 hours total so you can round the cliffs far enough to take in the views north toward the mountains and glaciers and west toward Reynisfjara Beach, Dyrhólaey, and the Westman Islands. The vibrant bird life includes puffins. Reynisfjall can also be climbed from its western side, by driving south on Route 215 and following the trail that leads up from the Reyniskirkja church, near the power lines. You could also use this route to *descend* from Reynisfjall and extend your walk from Vík all the way to Reynisfjara.

REYNISFJARA

The black-pebble beach of **Reynisfjara ★★** at the southern end of Route 215 forms a 2.5km (1½-mile) spit, extending from Reynisfjall almost to Dyrhólaey (p. 249), that divides the ocean from Dyrhólaós Lagoon. Reynisfjara is even more beautifully situated than the beach at Vík, but it's less frequented. On the eastern edge of the Reynisfjara, at the base of Reynisfjall, is the phenomenal basalt sea cave **Hálsanefshellir ★★**. It's inaccessible at high tide, so time your visit accordingly. For tidal schedules, ask around, call the **Icelandic Coast Guard** (© **545-2000**), or use the "Marine Reports" link at www.myforecast.com.

ÞAKGIL & MÆLIFELL

Four kilometers (2½ miles) east of Vík, Route 214 extends 15km (9⅓ miles) north from the Ring Road to the Þakgil campground, situated in a sheltered enclave amid dramatic mountain scenery near Mýrdalsjökull Glacier. Route 214 itself is a fantastic drive, rough but passable in a regular car. At a high point halfway to Þakgil, the road passes some primitive wood shelters built for the movie set of *Beowulf and Grendel* (critics loved the scenery). A crude but serviceable **hiking map** is available at the campground or online at www.thakgil.is. One great hike follows a rough 4WD track, built for rounding up sheep, to the base of Mýrdalsjökull in a 4-hour round-trip. Another 4-hour loop includes the viewpoint at **Mælifell.** Two long but rewarding trails—about 7 hours apiece—lead to Þakgil all the way from Vík; the one farther east, through Fagridalur and Bárðarfell, is slightly more picturesque.

Where to Stay

The stretch of coast from Markarfljót to Vík is teeming with idyllic farms to stay at, so **Icelandic Farm Holidays** (www.farmholidays.is; ✆ **570-2700**) is a good backup resource to our recommendations below.

WEST OF SKÓGAR

Country Hótel Anna ★★★   Named after the Icelandic travel writer Sigríður Anna Jónsdóttir, whose first book was entitled *A Dairy Maid Travels the World,* this absolutely charming country hotel is full of life and personal character. The uniquely decorated rooms feature antique furnishings and elegant striped wallpaper. For more space, opt for the two high-ceilinged rooms on the top floor. A small exhibition space upstairs has photos and artifacts from the life of the hotel's namesake.

Moldnúpur (easternmost farm on Rte. 246). www.hotelanna.is. ✆ **487-8950.** 7 units. June–Sept 15 28,300kr double. Rates around 38% lower Sept 16–May. Rates include breakfast. **Amenities:** Restaurant; hot tub; sauna; free Wi-Fi.

Guesthouse Edinborg ★   With Eyjafjallajökull within view and the Seljavallalaug thermal swimming pool just up the road, few settings are as enchanting as this one. This old Norwegian wooden house has been completely renovated, and owners have done well in making the best of its small size. The two cottages have kitchenettes and sleep up to six.

Lambafell farm (on Rte. 242, close to western junction of Rte. 242 and Rte. 1). www.greatsouth.is. ✆ **846-1384.** 6 double units w/bathroom. May–Sept 19,300kr double. Rates include breakfast. **Amenities**: Internet terminal; billiards; free Wi-Fi.

Skálakot Manor Hotel ★★   On a seventh-generation family horse farm, this stylish manor house has quickly become one of South Iceland's most sought-after hotels. The Art Deco–inspired interiors have decadent accents like wingback armchairs and rich colors; some add fireplaces or standing baths. The **restaurant** focuses on local and seasonal ingredients, while horseback-riding tours, their specialty, and fishing trips in the Írá river can be arranged.

Öldubakki 5, Hvolsvöllur. skalakot.is. ✆ **487-8953.** 14 units. June–Aug 42,200kr double. Rates around 20% lower in the winter. Rates include breakfast. **Amenities:** Restaurant; bar; hot tub; room service; tour desk; free Wi-Fi.

SKÓGAR

Hotel Skógafoss ★   The basic rooms at this average hotel are smallish, and the more expensive waterfall views can be obscured by trees or other buildings. The better-than-average **restaurant,** with floor-to-ceiling windows and great views of most of the waterfall, serves a hearty and varied menu.

Close to Skógafoss waterfall. www.hotelskogafoss.is. ✆ **487-8780.** 20 units without bathroom. June–Aug 21,100kr double. Rates include breakfast. **Amenities:** Restaurant; bar; free Wi-Fi.

Hotel Skógar ★   It's one of the farthest properties on the block from the falls, though from the garden you can catch a glimpse of them, as well as the Eyjafjöll glacier. Rooms are plain yet tasteful, with wood floors and a balcony in the deluxe room. A four-bedroom farmhouse comes with a full kitchen and sleeps up to eight.

Close to Skógafoss waterfall. www.hotelskogar.is. ✆ **487-4880.** 12 units, including farmhouse. June–Sept 32,000kr double; 80,000kr farmhouse. Rates include breakfast. Closed Oct–Apr. **Amenities:** Restaurant; hot tub; Internet terminal; sauna; free Wi-Fi.

BETWEEN SKÓGAR & VÍK

Hótel Dyrhólaey ★   When it opened as a simple farm guesthouse in 1993, it only had six rooms. Given the popularity of the location, on the bay near Dyrhólaey and Reynisfjara, it has not been able to keep up with summer demand. Now it has 88 basic rooms in a series of interconnected, barn-like buildings. The front desk can arrange snowmobile tours and hiking trips on the glaciers, as well as puffin-spotting trips.

Brekkur farm (Off Rte. 1, 2.5km/1½ miles east of the Rte. 1/Rte. 218 junction). www.dyrholaey.is. ✆ **487-1333.** 88 units. June–Sept 15 19,300kr double. Rates around 40% lower Sept 16–May. Rates include breakfast. **Amenities:** Restaurant; free Wi-Fi.

VÍK & ENVIRONS

On a slope with great views overlooking the town, the **Vík Youth Hostel,** Suðurvíkurvegur (www.hostel.is; ✆ **487-1106;** 10 units, 36 beds, none w/ bathroom; open year-round 6,500kr per bed per night; breakfast available for 1,500kr; closed Nov 16–Mar 14), is a low-budget option that has more in common with a guesthouse.

Icelandair Hótel Vík ★★   Despite the corporate connections, this glass and concrete structure does a fine job of blending in with the cliffs and black-sand beaches that surround it without feeling forced. Should we admit how much we like the wood floors, stone walls, tree-trunk bedside tables, and earth-toned fabrics throughout the interiors? Swing by the bar for happy hour, and then stop by the **restaurant,** which is the most sophisticated in the area

Klettsvegi 1. www.icelandairhotels.is. ⓒ **487-1480.** 36 units. 79,350kr double. Rates include breakfast. **Amenities:** Restaurant, bar; free Wi-Fi.

Þakgil ★ Situated between Höfðabrekkuafrétti and Mýrdalssandur, this crowd-favorite campsite-and-cabin resort is 15km (9⅓ miles) from the Ring Road. The 10 cabins have kitchenettes, but little else. There are plans to generate hydroelectricity from the creek and tunnel into the mountain and furnish the rooms, but for now guests will have to be satisfied with the dining room in the naturally formed cave.

4km (2½ miles) east of Vík, take Rte. 214 from the Ring Road for 15km (9⅓ miles). www. thakgil.is. ⓒ **893-4889.** June–Sept 15 25,000kr cabin; 1,500kr camping. Closed Sept 16–May. No Wi-Fi.

Where to Eat

Several places listed above have good restaurants. **Country Hótel Anna,** west of Skógar, is open for dinner from mid-June until August, 7 to 8:30pm; two-course meals are 3,800kr to 4,900kr and include salmon, trout, and lamb. The kitchens of **Höfðabrekka** are also home to the famous Icelandic ghost Jóka. The restaurant at **Hótel Skógar** (p. 253) is the choicest option, with a small menu of fish and lamb courses averaging 4,500kr. It's open from noon to 3pm and 6 to 10pm; reservations are recommended for dinner.

Halldórskaffi ★ CAFE In a late-1800s house, this town hangout beside the museum and tourist office is known for its eclectic country-cafe menu. Comfort foods are the norm, with an extra-long menu that lists burgers, pizzas, and grilled fish or lamb dishes.

Víkurbraut 28, Vík. www.halldorskaffi.com. ⓒ **487-1202.** Reservations recommended for dinner. Main courses 1,890kr–4,890kr. June–Aug daily 11am–10pm.

Restaurant Berg ★ ICELANDIC This contemporary dining room inside the Icelandair Hótel Vík (p. 253) has dramatic views of the Reynisdrangar Pillars. The menu emphasizes local products, even going as far to name the farmers and fishermen who provided many of them. Among the many highlights are scallops with tapioca and lemon oil or the Icelandic lamb filet that's grilled on a stone from the black beach.

Klettsvegi 1. www.icelandairhotels.is. ⓒ **487-1480.** Reservations recommended. Main courses 2,990kr–6,290kr. Daily 11am–4pm and 6–9pm.

KIRKJUBÆJARKLAUSTUR & LAKI CRATERS

The 272km (169 miles) between Vík and Höfn—the most austerely beautiful stretch of the Ring Road—contain just one small village, Kirkjubæjarklaustur. (You can just call it "Klaustur," as locals do.) Klaustur means "cloister" and refers to a Benedictine convent located here from 1186 until the Reformation.

Today the village is not much more than a few houses and a pit stop, but it also serves as a crossroads for the interior route to Landmannalaugar and the Fjallabak reserve (p. 239). Another road leads to the Laki Craters, one of Iceland's most awe-inspiring volcanic formations.

Essentials

GETTING THERE   Kirkjubæjarklaustur lies along Route 1, 73km (45 miles) northeast of Vík and 259km (161 miles) from Reykjavík. This route with sightseeing stops is handled by **Reykjavík Excursions** (www.re.is; ✆ **580-5400**). In summer, one **bus** per day connects Reykjavík and Höfn via the Ring Road, stopping at Kirkjubæjarklaustur. Another **bus,** from Vík to Höfn, runs daily. During the winter, services are reduced to three times a week. From mid-June to early September, Reykjavík Excursions also connects Reykjavík to Kirkjubæjarklaustur and Skaftafell daily through the interior Landmannalaugar/Fjallabak route.

VISITOR INFORMATION   Kirkjubæjarklaustur's **tourist information office** (✆ **487-4620**) is on Klaustuvegur 10 opposite the chapel. Opening times are June to August Monday to Friday from 9am to 1pm and 3pm to 9pm, Saturday and Sunday 10am to 8pm.

Exploring the Area

A single road leads through town. It turns to gravel at **Systrafoss,** a pretty waterfall. At the top of Systrafoss is **Systravatn,** a pleasant lake surrounded by pasture. If you don't have a car to reach Fjaðrárgljúfur and just need a satisfying walk, a path ascends to Systravatn from the far side of the falls. Alternatively, the road continues past Systrafoss and soon ends at a parking area, where a path continues along the Skaftá River. Within a 15-minute walk is the **Systrastapa,** a freestanding crag that looks like a giant molar. According to local folklore, two nuns were buried on top of Systrastapa after being burned at the stake—thus the name, which means "Sisters' Crag." A steel cable and chain descend from opposite sides of the crag, but footing is dangerous.

Kirkjugólf (Church Floor), a designated national monument near Route 203 north of the central roundabout, is a kind of natural stone terrace formed by a cross-section of hexagonal basalt columns.

FJAÐRÁRGLJÚFUR

For a short hike or picnic spot along this stretch of the Ring Road, look no further than **Fjaðrárgljúfur ★★**, a 100m-deep (328-ft.) gorge formed during the Ice Age 2 million years ago. Its proportions aren't mind-boggling, but it wins high aesthetic marks for its indented cliffsides full of spikes, arches, and scary ledges. The walk along the eastern ledge is not challenging, and the most compelling views can be seen in a 1-hour round-trip.

To reach Fjaðrárgljúfur, turn on to Route 206 from the Ring Road, 6km (3¾ miles) west of Kirkjubæjarklaustur. In 2km (1¼ miles) or so, Route F206 branches off to the right; continue straight and the parking area is shortly ahead.

LAKI CRATERS (LAKAGÍGAR)

Those with an eye for beauty within bleakness should particularly admire the **Laki crater row ★★★**, formed during the largest lava eruption ever witnessed. Starting in 1783 and continuing for 8 months, an estimated 14.7 cubic km (3½ cubic miles) of lava emerged from over 100 craters along a 25km-long (16-mile) fissure, flowing as far as 60km (37 miles). The eruption could be seen all over Iceland and was followed by several earthquakes. The sun-obscuring haze lowered temperatures for the entire Northern Hemisphere by about 3°F (1°C–2°C) and reached as far as Asia and North Africa. Within 3 years, 70% of Iceland's livestock had died, mostly from fluorine poisoning. Most water and food was not contaminated, but cold weather and famine, combined with an outbreak of smallpox, killed 22% of the population. Today, Lakagígar's splattered, scabby landscape has a forlorn grandeur, and the volcanic craters are carpeted in gray mosses that turn bright green after a rainfall.

The crater row could be explored for days, but all visitors should at least climb Mt. Laki, the tallest of the craters, for astounding 360-degree views of the boundless lava flows and distant glaciers. The climb is not difficult, and takes about 45 minutes one-way from the parking area.

Reykjavík Excursions (www.re.is; © **580-5400**) has one daily bus in July and August from Skaftafell to the Laki Craters and back, with a stop at Kirkjubæjarklaustur and 3½ hours to explore the crater row on foot. From Kirkjubæjarklaustur the price is 16,900kr.

The Laki Craters are reached via Route 206/F206, which joins the Ring Road 6km (3¾ miles) west of Kirkjubæjarklaustur. This route has difficult river crossings, and should only be attempted in 4WD vehicles with high clearance; always check road conditions in advance.

Where to Stay & Dine

Hörgsland ★   This sprawling camping site, guesthouse, and cottage collection was launched in 2003, 8km (4.5 miles) northeast of Klaustur. It's sort of like a mini village. During the summer months, there will be people hanging out in the outdoor hot pots, families dining in the cafe, and backpackers setting up tents. Each of the cottages has terraces with BBQs, a kitchen, two bedrooms, and a sleeping loft, while guesthouse rooms are more basic. A three-course dinner is offered for 5,500kr with advanced notice.

Rte. 1, 7km (4⅓ miles) east of Kirkjubæjarklaustur. www.horgsland.is. © **487-6655.** 21 units, 18 with bathroom. 23,100kr guesthouse double; 27,700kr cottage. Rates include breakfast. **Amenities:** Cafe; hot tubs; free Wi-Fi.

Hótel Klaustur ★   Clean, efficient, and modern: That's the Icelandair hotel way. Aside from the geothermal pool, this rather uninteresting hotel supplies everything you need for a comfortable night, such as a good meal at the **restaurant,** a comfortable bed, and working Wi-Fi. Like most Icelandair hotel restaurants (main courses 2,650kr–4,590kr), this one is reliable and has high standards. The 150-seat dining room offers a little bit of everything, from special-occasion wild-game dinners to a locally sourced international menu, with grilled fish, pizza, and pan-fried Arctic char with Danish rye bread.

Klausturvegur 6. www.icelandairhotels.com. © **487-4900.** 57 units. June–Aug 36,100kr double. Rates about 18% lower Apr–May and Sept–Oct; about 33% lower Nov to mid-Dec and Feb. Breakfast available (1,500kr). Closed mid-Dec to Jan. **Amenities:** Restaurant; bar; terrace; free Wi-Fi.

Systrakaffi ★ ICELANDIC BISTRO   This pleasant bistro doesn't shy away from old-school Icelandic foods like rotten shark or *Plokkfiskur* (a traditional fish stew), though burgers and BBQ ribs also are served. The one-room cafe attracts locals as well as tourists.

Klausturvegur 13. www.systrakaffi.is. © **487-4848.** Main courses 1,950kr–4,700kr. Children's menu. Daily noon–9pm; closed Jan–Feb.

VATNAJÖKULL, SKEIÐARÁRSANDUR & SKAFTAFELL

East of Kirkjubæjarklaustur, the Ring Road enters a long, townless stretch in the shadow of **Vatnajökull,** the largest icecap between the Arctic and Antarctic circles. South of Vatnajökull is a stupendously bleak glacial floodplain called **Skeiðarársandur,** or just "The Sandur." The main regional attraction is **Skaftafell** ★★, a popular hiking area bordering Vatnajökull. Most of Skaftafell's day hikes are on scrubby grassland, amid a panorama of spiky mountains and glistening ice.

Essentials

GETTING THERE   Skaftafell is along the Ring Road, 327km (203 miles) east of Reykjavík. In summer, two buses a day connect Reykjavík and Skaftafell via the Ring Road. Reykjavík to Skaftafell takes 6 hours, and the route continues to Höfn. The route, with sightseeing stops, is handled by **Straeto** (www.straeto.is; © **540-2700**) and takes almost 6½ hours, ending at Skaftafell. From mid-June to early September, Sterna and Reykjavík Excursions also connect Reykjavík and Skaftafell daily through the interior Landmannalaugar/ Fjallabak route, which is more bumpy, expensive, scenic, and time-consuming. From mid-September until May, three weekly Þingvallaleið buses connect Reykjavík and Höfn, stopping at the Freysnes service station, 5km (3 miles) east of the park entrance.

VISITOR INFORMATION   The **Skaftafell tourist office** (www. vatnajokulsthjodgardur.is; © **478-1627**) is well marked from the Ring Road. Basic **trail maps** are available there for 400kr, and can also be printed from the website. The office is open daily from 9am to 7pm June 16 to August; daily from 9am to 6pm June 1 to 15 and September; and daily from 10am to 3pm October to April.

THE glacier MYSTIQUE

Those who have never seen a *jökull* (glacier) can find it hard to understand why these huge, dirty sheets of ice arouse so much interest. Part of the appeal is sheer magnitude, but the destructive power of glaciers also inspires respect. Only 10% of Iceland's land mass is covered by glaciers, but 60% of its volcanic eruptions occur beneath them, often causing catastrophic floods. In Icelandic folklore, someone crossing a glacier might plunge into a hidden crevasse, only to be heard singing hymns from the same spot for decades. But size and might are only part of the glacier mystique. Like an organism, its bodily matter replaces itself over time. Vatnajökull's oldest ice was formed around 1200, but rock, sediment, and human victims also churn through its messy digestive system. Stray airplane parts or ski poles from decades or centuries past often pop out from the glacier's edge. Glaciers also provide endless aesthetic variety. The same glacier can appear pink or white at a distance, brown- and black-streaked on nearer inspection, and a more translucent blue up close. Evidence suggests that glaciers aren't losing their hold on the Icelandic imagination: More than 150 living Icelandic men are named Jökull.

Exploring the Area

Halfway between Kirkjubæjarklaustur and Skaftafell, on the western edge of the Skeiðarársandur, **Núpsstaður**—a tiny, turf-roofed 17th-century chapel and collection of old farm buildings—is under the care of the National Museum. It was once home to the brave postmen and river guides who, until 1970, crossed the dangerous glaciers and rivers alone. Access is free at all hours, so consider a stop to contemplate this remote settlement between a waterfall, the table mountain Lómagnúpur, and the lifeless sands.

Núpsstaðarskógar ★★, near the western edge of Skeiðarárjökull along the Núpsá river, is a scrubland area rife with beautiful gorges, waterfalls, and glacier views; yet it remains one of Iceland's better-kept hiking secrets The only way to get there is by signing up for a tour with **Icelandic Mountain Guides** (www.mountainguide.is; ✆ **587-9999**). This recommended group leads 5-day hikes between Núpsstaðarskógar and the Laki Craters (p. 256), and a 4-day hike through Núpsstaðarskógar to Skaftafell, traversing the Skeiðarárjökull, for 149,000kr. Participants carry their own camping gear.

A sandur is not just any desert. *Sandur* is the Icelandic (as well as English) term for a floodplain full of sand and sediment deposited by sub-glacial volcanoes. **Skeiðarársandur,** formed by flood bursts from Vatnajökull, is the largest sandur in the world. This flat, interminable expanse, braided in meltwater streams and drained of life and color, was impassable until the Ring Road was completed in 1974.

In 1996, after a volcanic eruption at Grímsvötn, underneath Vatnajökull, a huge flood burst was anticipated for several days. Shortly after the film crews from the foreign media got bored of waiting and went home, a torrent of water and sediment rivaling the Amazon in size and force crashed down into the Skeiðarársandur, with house-sized icebergs bobbing along like corks. Once the sediment had settled, Iceland was 7 sq. km (2¾ sq. miles) larger. No one was killed or injured, and no communities were destroyed.

Approaching Skaftafell from the west, the Ring Road crosses three bridges. The first, Núpsvötn, was undamaged by the 1996 flood burst, even though water cascaded right over the roadway. The second bridge, Gígjukvísi, was pounded by icebergs and completely washed away. The third and longest bridge, Skeiðará, was partially demolished. A temporary road was ready in 3 weeks, and replacement bridges were completed in 9 months. A **monument** to the 1996 eruption, constructed from twisted hunks of the demolished bridges, lies between the new bridges and the Skaftafell park entrance.

SKAFTAFELL NATIONAL PARK ★★

Skaftafell is located in the southern territory of Vatnajökull National Park. The area has been conserved since 1967, and the variety of vegetation, wildflowers, and butterflies shows what can happen when grazing sheep are kept out for 40 years. The park's hiking trails for this area are mostly on the **Skaftafellsheiðl** (Skaftafell heath), a scrubby green oasis wedged between Iceland's largest glacier and its floodplains. The glacier next door makes the weather milder and more hospitable to plant life. Most visitors, however, are not leafing through their field guides but gazing at the astonishing vistas, some of Iceland's most imposing and picturesque mountainscapes, as well as the glacier and the vast black desert to the south.

GETTING THERE   Visitors should park next to the tourist office. The walk from the official parking area leads you past three nice waterfalls (Þjófafoss, Hundafoss, and Magnúsarfoss). The office is essential if you don't have a trail map. It also has an exhibit on local flora and fauna, and continuous screenings of thrilling footage from the 1996 Grímsvötn eruption.

HIKING   Skaftafell is most rewarding for those who penetrate farthest into the park. The easiest trail leads from the office to the glacial tongue **Skaftafellsjökull,** and takes about 30 minutes each way. This walk is perfectly nice but rather misses the point of the park, because you can drive right up to several equally interesting glacial tongues east of here. **Svinafellsjökull ★,** a stranger, spikier, less touristy version of Skaftafellsjökull, is reached by leaving the park and turning left on a signposted gravel road, just east of the entrance. You can park 300m (984 ft.) away and walk right up to it, though climbing on it is unsafe. (See also **Kvíárjökull ★,** p. 262.)

An ideal 2- to 3-hour hike takes in the magnificent Svartifoss waterfall, the Sjónarsker viewpoint, and the turf-roofed Sel farmhouse, built in 1912. **Svartifoss ★★** (Black Waterfall) is a wonder of natural architecture and was named for its striking formation of black basalt columns. Eroded from below, it forms an overhang resembling a pipe organ. These unique characteristics inspired many of the 20th-century buildings by Guðjón Samúelsson, including the Icelandic National Theater. The **Sjónarsker viewpoint** is about 20 minutes past Svartifoss. The farm site known as **Sel** (which simply means "Hut") was originally 100m (328 ft.) farther downhill, but was relocated in the mid-19th century to escape the encroaching sands.

Skaftafell's three premier hikes are much longer but worth the effort. One ascends through **Skaftafellsheiði** past Skerhóll and Nyrðrihnaukur and loops back along the eastern rim of Skaftafellsheiði, with incredible views throughout. An easier (if slightly less recommended) hike heads northwest, sloping down off the Skaftafellsheiði into **Morsárdalur** (the Morsá river valley). The trail then crosses a footbridge and leads to the Bæjarstaður, Iceland's tallest stand of birch trees. From there, continue southwest along the edge of Morsárdalur, past streams descending from the Réttargil and Vestragil gorges. On the far side of Vestragil, a trail leads uphill to a small, natural **geothermal pool** that's not shown on the park map. It's often perfect bathing temperature—and built for two. On the way back to the parking area, take the easier route through Morsárdalur without re-ascending Skaftafellsheiði.

TOURS   **Icelandic Mountain Guides** (www.mountainguide.is; ⓒ 587-9999) sets up a base camp at Skaftafell from March to October, and runs several recommended hiking and ice-climbing tours on Svinafellsjökull and Vatnajökull. Another trip connects Skaftafell and Núpsstaðarskógar (p. 258), while **Local Guide of Vatnajökull** (www.localguideofvatnajokull.com; ⓒ 478-1682) offers a range of adventurous glacier excursions on Svinafellsjökull and Vatnajökull, including hikes, ski mountaineering, and ice climbing.

Where to Stay

For information on the **Skaftafell park campground** (where you might be kept up late by partiers and visited by pesky ptarmigans), contact the tourist office (p. 257).

The large **Road 201 Guesthouse,** Skatárhreppur (www.road201.is; ⓒ 487-4785; 25 units without bathrooms; Mar–Oct 16,100kr double, 11,100kr–21,500kr sleeping-bag rooms for 3–5 people; closed Nov–Feb), has clean and functional rooms at a pretty riverside location 25km (16 miles) east of Kirkjubæjarklaustur and 45km (28 miles) west of Skaftafell, on Route 201, 2.5km (1½ miles) south of the Ring Road; look for the Hvoll sign. You can call them up off-season, and if you ask nicely they will accommodate you. If you're going by bus, you can arrange for the proprietors to pick you up at the junction and then ask the bus driver to drop you there.

Hótel Skaftafell ★   Some of the rooms at this ordinary hotel in an extraordinary location have a view to the Vatnajökull Glacier. The former Foss Hotel property is 5km (3 miles) east of the park entrance and the only thing closely resembling a fully functional hotel. The en suite guest rooms are basic and dated, though the staff is eager to help guests with plans. The **restaurant** is, well, there. All and all, it's as comfortable a base as you will find on the frontier.

Freysnes, on Rte. 1 opposite the Shell station. www.hotelskaftafell.is. ⓒ **478-1945.** 63 units. June–Aug 41,500kr double. Rates around 25% lower May and Sept; around 50% lower Oct–Apr. Rates include breakfast. **Amenities:** Restaurant; bar; free Wi-Fi.

Where to Eat

The Skaftafell park visitor office has a small selection of snacks. **Söluskálinn** (ⓒ **478-2242;** June–Aug daily 9am–10pm, Sept–May 1–6pm), at the Shell station 5km (3 miles) east of the park entrance, has a mini-mart, plus a grill and seating area.

Hótel Skaftafell ★   From the windows of this second-floor restaurant, you can just catch a glimpse of the Vatnajökull glacier. The 100-seat eatery is your only formal dining room in the vicinity of the park. The food includes your typical mix of Icelandic protein dishes or burgers and can be inconsistent.

Rte. 1, 5km (3 miles) east of the park entrance. www.hotelskaftafell.is. ✆ **478-1945.** Reservations recommended. Main courses 2,490kr–5,990kr. May–Sept noon–2pm and 6–9pm.

BETWEEN SKAFTAFELL & HÖFN

In the 136km (85-mile) stretch from Skaftafell to Höfn, **Vatnajökull** is among mountains, but the view is often blocked by clouds. Much of this area is considered part of the region known as Öræfi (Wasteland). This name was earned after a 1362 eruption under the Öræfajökull glacier, which explosively splattered ash, dust, and rock over a wide radius. The region's most famous attraction by far is **Jökulsárlón,** a fantastical lake full of icebergs calved from the glacier. **Ingólfshöfði,** a bird sanctuary on the cape, and glacier tours from Jöklasel earn some attention as well.

Essentials

GETTING THERE   During the rest of the year, three buses travel in each direction weekly. From mid-June until August, **Reykjavík Excursions** (www. re.is; ✆ **580-5400**) has departures twice daily from Skaftafell to Jökulsárlón and back, with 2 to 2½ hours at Jökulsárlón.

VISITOR INFORMATION   No tourist information offices serve the area between Skaftafell and Höfn.

Exploring the Area
INGÓLFSHÖFÐI ★

This flat-topped wedge of coastal land seems to hover above the shimmering flats as you drive east from Skaftafell. Around the year 870, Reykjavík's founder, Ingólfur Arnarson, probably spent his first Iceland winter here—thus the name, which means "Ingólfur's Cape." It then had a sheltered port and was surrounded by grasslands and scrub; now it's separated from the mainland by an expanse of black volcanic sand. Ingólfshöfði is a nature reserve protected from everyone except seven local families, who have been hunting and egg-collecting the land for centuries. The birds most common to the reserve are puffin and *skua,* a large ground-nesting species.

The most popular way to visit Ingólfshöfði is on the bird-watching tour led by **Extreme Iceland** (www.extremeiceland.is). Tours last 2½ hours and run from May 1 to August 31, departing at noon from the Ingólfshöfði parking lot about 22km (14 miles) east of Skaftafell Park along the Ring Road. The cost is 8,900kr, and reservations are accepted. Bring sunglasses to protect your eyes from sand in high winds, and pack a lunch.

This is no smooth bus tour—more of a 30-minute bumpy adventure in a tractor-drawn hay-cart. If the tide is right, you may see the sand flats covered with a thin layer of reflective water. The walking is leisurely on Ingólfshöfði, which peaks at 76m (249 ft.). The guide walks in front holding a walking pole aloft, in case of attack from a skua protecting its eggs. The tour group usually inspects a nest of these intimidating birds, while the mother squawks nearby.

INGÓLFSHÖFÐI TO JÖKULSÁRLÓN

The sites below are arranged geographically with turnoffs along the Ring Road.

Kvíárjökull ★ Thirty-nine kilometers (24 miles) east of Skaftafell, this glacial tongue and its scenic valley make for an easy, charmed hour-long hike. The turnoff from the Ring Road is marked "Kvíárjökulskambar," and a parking area is shortly ahead; Kvíárjökull is clearly visible in the distance.

Fjallsárlón ★ About 10km (6 miles) east is a marked turnoff for this lake—a kind of Jökulsárlón for loners. The waters are muddier and less sprinkled with icebergs, but the sight of Fjallsjökull calving into the lake is remarkable. The road to Fjallsárlón divides a few times, but all routes end up in the same place, within a 10-minute walk of the best glacier views.

Breiðárlón This lake is a similar variation on nearby Fjallsárlón and Jökulsárlón. The access road is well-tended but unmarked from the Ring Road, about 3km (1½ miles) northeast of the Fjallsárlón turnoff. The number of icebergs can vary greatly, but on a good day you'll be glad you came.

JÖKULSÁRLÓN ★★

Nothing quite prepares you for the carnivalesque spectacle of a lake full of icebergs broken off from a glacier. "Calf ice" from glaciers takes on crazier shapes than "pack ice" in the sea. Calf ice is also marbled with photogenic streaks of sediment. Jökulsárlón's clear water creates a magical play of light and tints the icebergs blue. Glacial ice takes a long time to melt, and the icebergs here can last up to 5 years. The creaking, groaning, and crashing sounds at the glacier's edge are otherworldly. About 60 seals have established a colony at Jökulsárlón; they can also be seen from the ocean side of the Ring Road.

Jökulsárlón did not exist 75 years ago, when Breiðamerkurjökull reached almost to the ocean. In the last few years, warming temperatures have accelerated the glacier's retreat and clogged the lake with growing numbers of smaller icebergs—an aesthetic demotion, unfortunately.

Glacier Lagoon Tours (www.jokulsarlon.is; ✆ **478-2222**), which run May 15 to 30 (daily 10am–5pm), June to August (daily 9am–7pm), and September 1 to 15 (daily 10am–5pm), set out in amphibious vehicles or Zodiacs and last 40 minutes. Tickets are 5,700kr for adults and 2,000kr for children ages 6 to 12 in the amphibious vehicles (free for children 5 and under); or 9,800kr for ages 13 and up and 5,000kr children ages 10 to 12 in the Zodiacs. Walking along the shore is almost as nice, but it's worth the money to float among the icebergs and view the glacier up close.

Vatnajökull Tours from Jöklasel ★

The vast **Vatnajökull glacier** covers about 8,000sq. km (3,089 sq. miles), with an average thickness of 400m (1,312 ft.) and a maximum thickness of 950m (3,117 ft.). Being atop Vatnajökull is truly transporting, and returning to sea level feels like re-entry from outer space. F985 dramatically ascends 16km (10 miles) to **Jöklasel** (𝒞 **478-1000**), a base camp at the edge of Vatnajökull, 840m (2,756 ft.) above sea level. Jöklasel is open from June 1 to September 10, 11:15am to 5pm, and the small cafe there serves a daily lunch buffet from 11:15am to 2pm. Jöklasel can be reached in a good 4WD vehicle, but the road is nerve-racking and often thick with fog.

Most visitors come to Jöklasel for the snowmobile and Super Jeep tours based there. (Some visitors take walks on the glacier from Jöklasel, but they're at risk of falling into a crack or getting lost if fog closes in.) Jöklasel's two tour operators are **Glacier Jeeps** (www.glacierjeeps.is; 𝒞 **478-1000**) and **Glacier Guides** (www.glacierguides.is; 𝒞 **571-2100**). The most popular tour is the 3-hour snowmobile package, which costs 24,000kr and includes pickup from the intersection of the Ring Road and Route F985 (about 35km/22 miles east of Jökulsárlón and 42km/26 miles west of Höfn) plus an hour on snowmobiles. **Glacier Jeeps** has scheduled departures at 9:30am and 2pm from late April to September 10 (reservations required). **Straeto** (www.straeto.is; 𝒞 **540-2700**) runs a daily scheduled bus from Höfn to Jöklasel to Jökulsárlón, Some tour operators combine round-trip transfers with snowmobiling and/or a boat trip at Jökulsárlón.

Snowmobile riders are outfitted with helmets, jumpsuits, rubber boots, and gloves. Make sure to bring sunglasses; tour operators don't supply goggles. Tours set out rain or shine and reach a height of 1,220m (4,003 ft.). Your views will depend entirely on the weather: You might see 100km (62 miles) in all directions, or just blankets of cloud. Normally you'll at least rise above the cloudline for clear views of the vicinity. Weather conditions are impossible to predict from sea level, so call ahead. Even snowmobile novices may find the riding too tame; everyone proceeds single file at the speed of the most cautious driver. Both tour companies also lead Super Jeep tours on Vatnajökull, from short joyrides to multi-day excursions.

Where to Stay & Dine

The recommended places below are listed in order of location, from west to east along the Ring Road.

The **cafe at Jökulsárlón** (𝒞 **478-2222;** June–Aug daily 9am–7pm; May 15–30 and Sept 1–15 daily 10am–5pm) has good seafood soup, plus sandwiches and waffles. Two of the places listed have good restaurants. **Hotel Smyrlabjörg's** enormous dinner buffet—with no less than nine fish dishes, plus lamb, pork, and beef—is open to non-guests from 6 to 8:30pm, June until mid-September; the cost is 6,500kr and no reservations are necessary. In the off-season, Smyrlabjörg serves set-dinner menus, but only with advance notice.

Hólmur ★   This comfy, unpretentious farmhouse with views of the Fláa-jökull glacier is one of the better-value places to bed down for the night. Overnight guests have access to a zoo filled with Icelandic farm animals and a surprisingly great restaurant and brewery, **Jón Ríki,** set in a converted cow house, serving traditional food based around seasonal ingredients. Reindeer tours are offered in winter, though they can be seen on the property year-round.

Rte. 1 (33km/21 miles) west of Höfn). www.holmurinn.is. ⓒ **478-2063.** 8 units without bathroom. June–Sept 15,600kr double; 6,500kr sleeping-bag accommodation. Rates around 30% lower Oct–May. Breakfast available. **Amenities:** Guest kitchen; free Wi-Fi.

Smyrlabjörg ★   This no-nonsense rural inn, set on a working farm only 2km (1¼ miles) off the road to Jöklasel, has clean, efficient rooms with en suite facilities. Some have views of the ocean, while others look toward the mountains. The massive dining hall is sometimes swarming with tour groups.

Rte. 1 (2km/1¼ miles west of Rte. 1/Rte. F985 junction). www.smyrlabjorg.is. ⓒ **478-1074.** 45 units. May 20–Sept 1 16,600kr double. Rates include breakfast. **Amenities:** Restaurant; bar; free Wi-Fi.

EAST ICELAND

The east has long been the domain of the dedicated explorer and a place for the tireless treasure hunter. Its remote location means that this quarter of Iceland is often left out of standard tourist itineraries, which concentrate mainly on the areas near Reykjavík, the south, the north, and the Snæfellsnes Peninsula. Ferries from Europe arrive in the east, at Seyðisfjörður, but through-routes from there bypass some of Iceland's most stunning coastal scenery.

Visitors to the Eastfjords can expect to encounter a contrast of extremes, where the valleys are lush and greener, the lakes and fjords deeper, and the mountain slopes steeper. The east is at the forefront of reforestation efforts, and Iceland's reindeer herds are concentrated in its highlands.

Not surprisingly, local economies are dominated by fishing. In the heyday of the herring, cod, and whaling industries, the east's rich fishing grounds attracted many Norwegian and French-speaking fishermen. Today most fjords have their own fish-processing plant, and other fjords lie abandoned or near-abandoned in all their pristine majesty.

Two of Iceland's best hiking districts are in the east: Lónsöræfi, a mountainous reserve near Vatnajökull, and Borgarfjörður Eystri, the northernmost region of the Eastfjords. Seyðisfjörður is the region's prettiest and most culturally thriving coastal town. Southwest of Egilsstaðir are some of Iceland's most ruggedly beautiful highlands. In summer, the east has the country's sunniest and warmest weather—though precipitation is actually higher, and winters are colder.

The main transit hubs for the east are Egilsstaðir and Höfn. During the summer, main bus services from Reykjavík reach the east through Akureyri and Höfn. During the winter, local companies continue to connect Höfn and Akureyri to Egilsstaðir and the Eastfjords.

The website **www.east.is** is an excellent resource for service listings, culture, and history.

HÖFN

Höfn (often used interchangeably with "Hornafjörður") simply means "dock." This busy fishing port lies on a narrow neck of land within shallow, protected waters. The town has only just over 2,000

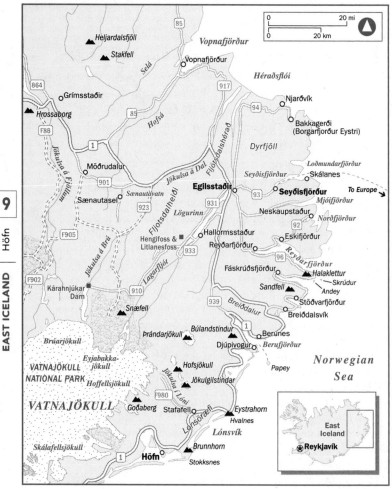

people, but that qualifies it for regional hub of the southeast. For tourists, Höfn is simply a stopover or a base for trips to Vatnajökull, Lónsöræfi, and elsewhere in the area. Höfn gets a major share of Iceland's lobster catch, and a **Lobster Festival** *(Humarhátíð)* is held here the first weekend in July, with all sorts of family entertainment.

Essentials

GETTING THERE & AROUND

BY PLANE   **Eagle Air** (www.eagleair.is; ⓒ **562-2640**) flies from Reykjavík to Hornafjörður (Höfn) twice daily on weekdays (once on Sat and Sun). The

Höfn

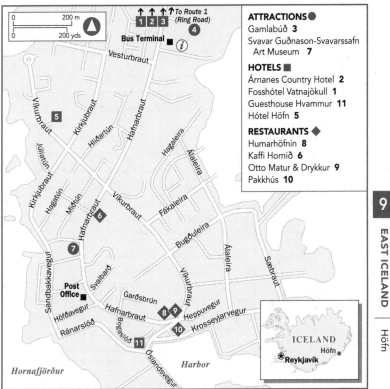

ATTRACTIONS ●
Gamlabúð **3**
Svavar Guðnason-Svavarssafn
  Art Museum **7**

HOTELS ■
Árnanes Country Hotel **2**
Fosshótel Vatnajökull **1**
Guesthouse Hvammur **11**
Hótel Höfn **5**

RESTAURANTS ◆
Humarhöfnin **8**
Kaffi Hornið **6**
Otto Matur & Drykkur **9**
Pakkhús **10**

trip lasts roughly an hour and costs around 25,400kr with discounts for children ages 2 to 11 (50%), as well as students and seniors (10%). **Hornafjörður Airport** (☏ **478-1250**) is a 10-minute drive northwest of town on Route 1, just off the Ring Road. Taxis do not wait at the airport, but you can call them at ☏ **865-4353.** The fare into town is around 4,000kr.

BY CAR Car rental agencies at the airport are **Eurpcar/Bílaleiga Akureyrar** (www.holdur.is; ☏ **461-6000**).

BY BUS The **Straetó** bus line (www.straeto.is; ☏ **540-2600**) connects Höfn to Reykjavík (8 hr.) and Egilsstaðir (3½ hr.). From May 15 until September 15, one bus travels daily between Reykjavík and Höfn in each direction, leaving from either city in the morning. For the rest of the year, the bus runs three times a week. From May until September 15, buses run between Höfn and Egilsstaðir, though service has been sporadic in recent years.

VISITOR INFORMATION

The **Höfn information office** is at the **Gamlabúð Visitor Centre** (www.vatnajokulsthjodgardur.is; ☏ **478-1833;** June–Aug daily 8am–8pm, May and

Sept daily 10am–6pm, Oct–Apr Mon–Fri 10am–noon and 4–6pm) at Heppuvegur 1.

Exploring the Area

For glacier tours on Vatnajökull, see **Vatnajökull Tours** from Jöklasel (chapter 8, p. 263).

Gamlabúð ★ MUSEUM   This 1864 warehouse, which is also home to the tourist information center and visitor center for the southern area of Vatnajökull National Park, has a small exhibition on the region's geology, glaciers, and culture. This is not Iceland's best folk museum, but it's free and represents what you'll find elsewhere: carved spoons, old medicine vials, the national costume, stuffed animals, and so on. Of particular interest, to some, are the ornamented bridles and saddles. Regular screenings of a 50-minute film from the 1960s are in Icelandic only, with demonstrations of traditional fishing and farming techniques.

Heppuvegur 1. ✆ **478-1833.** Free admission. June–Aug daily 8am–8pm; May and Sept daily 10am–6pm; Oct–Apr Mon–Fri 10am–noon and 4–6pm.

Svavar Guðnason-Svavarssafn Art Museum ★ GALLERY   This gallery is dedicated to the work of Svavar Gudnason, a native of Höfn who was one of Iceland's best-known contemporary painters. In his early work, the natural surroundings of the southeast inspired his landscape paintings, which propelled him to new heights internationally long after moving away. Seasonal exhibitions rotate the work of other regional artists.

Hafnarbraut 27. ✆ **470-8000.** Free admission. Mon–Fri 9:15am–noon and 12:45–3pm, Sat–Sun noon–5pm summer; Mon–Fri 9am–noon and 1–3pm winter.

EXPLORING HÖFN

For a view of Vatnajökull Glacier, take a short stroll along the water on the northwest side of town, behind Hótel Höfn (below). For an **easy 2-hour walk** ★, head to the Ring Road, drive 16km (10 miles) east, turn right shortly after exiting the tunnel, and proceed 2km (1¼ miles) beyond the farm buildings until the road ends. The walk south along the coast is uneventful for the first 30 minutes but eventually reaches a secluded and romantic expanse of sand, surf, and grassy tufts backed by steep mountains. Around the peak of Eystrahorn is another gorgeous beach.

Where to Stay

For farm accommodations between Höfn and Skaftafell Park, see p. 263.

EXPENSIVE

Fosshotel Vatnajökull ★   Located 10km (6 miles) north of town, near the airport, this run-of-the-mill chain property has nice views of the Vatnajökull glacier from some rooms. The rooms are clean and modern, though some are cramped. The windows are big, though, bathrooms are good, and a few rooms have balconies. A good restaurant on-site serves Hornafjarðar´s langoustine.

Route 1. www.fosshotel.is. ✆ **478-2555**. 66 units. June–Aug 33,900kr double. Rates around 20%–30% lower in winter. Rates include breakfast. **Amenities:** Restaurant; free Wi-Fi.

Hótel Höfn ★ Since it opened in 1965, this standby hotel has been regularly expanding and remodeling piece by piece. Standard rooms can be small, and upgrading to a superior only adds a small sitting area. And although superior rooms might not justify the high price—they're more functional than interesting—they have wood floors and large windows that take in views of town and glacier.

Víkurbraut 24. www.hotelhofn.is. ✆ **478-1240**. 68 units. May–Sept 40,700kr double; 48,500 superior. Rates around 30% lower Oct–Apr. Rates include breakfast. **Amenities:** Restaurant; free Wi-Fi.

MODERATE

Árnanes Country Hotel ★ This family-run lodge is just outside of Árnanes in Nesjahverfi, and 6km (3¾ miles) west of Höfn. The rural setting allows for sweeping views of the surrounding mountains, and several of the wood-trimmed rooms have small terraces to take advantage of them (plus blackout curtains for summer's eternal sunshine). Riding and glacier tours, plus a **restaurant** with Icelandic dishes and access to a 9-hole golf course, are offered.

Route 1. www.arnanes.is. ✆ **478-1550**. 22 units, 11 w/bathroom. June–Aug 32,900kr double w/bathroom; 26,900kr double without bathroom. Rates around 15% lower May and Sept; around 30% lower Oct–Apr. Rates include breakfast. **Amenities:** Restaurant; free Wi-Fi.

Milk Factory ★ This modern B&B on the north end of town is set inside, you guessed it, a former dairy factory. The minimalist rooms are spacious, with wood floors and tile bathrooms. Family rooms add a staircase that lead up to a small loft bed that's great for kids (though tight for two adults).

Dalbraught 2. www.milkfactory.is. ✆ **478-8900**. 17 units. 30,000kr double; 39,500 family rooms. Rates include breakfast. **Amenities:** Tour desk; free Wi-Fi.

INEXPENSIVE

Guesthouse Hvammur ★ While the multi-bedroom apartments in this small guesthouse by the harbor are rather stylish, with fine woodwork and Scandinavian designer furniture, the standard rooms are more basic. Each has a TV and washbasin, but some have tiny windows that let in only a minimal amount of light. If the rooms are full, the same owners have another property, a slightly more stylish roadhouse, on Route 1, **Höfn Inn.**

Ránarslóð 2. http://guesthouseinhofn.is. ✆ **478-1503**. 13 units, none w/bathroom. May–Sept 22,000kr–26,600kr double; 62,900kr 2-bed apt. Rates around 10% lower Oct–Apr. Breakfast available (1,500kr). **Amenities:** Guest kitchen; free Wi-Fi.

Where to Eat

Humarhöfnin ★★ SEAFOOD Translating to "lobster harbor," this is the best restaurant for langoustines in the best town for langoustines. The small, flavorful, lobster-like crustaceans are served in soup, on pizza, on a baguette, or grilled whole. It's set in a 1936 building, with checkered-tile floors and an Art Deco staircase, which once housed a farmer's co-op.

Hafnarbraut 4. www.humarhofnin.is. ⓒ **478-1200.** Main courses 2,900kr–8,600kr. May–Sept daily noon–10pm; April, Oct–Nov noon–9pm. Closed Dec–Jan.

Kaffi Hornið ★ CAFE While it's more casual than the competition, this log-cabin restaurant also attracts more locals, which has to mean something. Aside from the standard Icelandic and international fare, there are reindeer burgers, langoustine sandwiches, and pan-fried chickpea cutlets for vegetarians. Be sure to make reservations in summer.

Hafnarbraut 42. ⓒ **478-2600.** Main courses 2,700–5,800kr. May–Aug daily 10am–11:30pm; Sept–October 15 daily 10am–10pm; October 16–May Mon–Sat 10am–9pm.

Otto Matur & Drykkur ★★ ICELANDIC This atmospheric Nordic bistro is set on the harbor in the very first family house in Höfn, built by merchant Otto Tulinius in 1897. The owners have preserved the building's historic feel, with plank-wood floors, wall lanterns, and an old piano in one of the dining rooms. The menu is creative, with local ingredients (langoustine tails, loin of lamb, etc.) prepared unlike anywhere else in town. Here, for instance, langoustine soup is flavored with cognac and cream, while grilled chicken is spiced with anise.

Hafnarbraut 2. ⓒ **478-1818.** Reservations recommended. Main courses 3,200kr–5,900kr. April–Nov daily noon–10pm.

Pakkhús ★ ICELANDIC Set in a renovated two-level warehouse on the harbor with original product stamps on the walls, this lively eatery emphasizes ingredients from around the Vatnajökull region, including langoustines and wild game.

Krosseyjarvegi 3. www.pakkhus.is. ⓒ **478-2280.** Main courses 2,500–6,500kr. Daily noon–10pm.

LÓNSÖRÆFI

The next bay east of Höfn—Lónsvík, or "Lagoon Bay"—is dominated by a large lagoon (Lón), fed by the Jökulsá í Lóni (Glacial River of the Lagoon). The mountainous interior region that feeds the Lón is called **Lónsöræfi ★★★**, or "Lagoon Wilderness." This striking and varied landscape, now a 320sq.-km (124-sq.-mile) private nature reserve, is one of Iceland's best hiking territories.

The best parts of Lónsöræfi are undeveloped. Glacial streams wind down steep valleys of subtle mineral spectra; yellow rhyolite rocks gleam from streambeds; and reindeer herds can be seen grazing. Only one primitive road leads partly in, and accommodations are limited to basic mountain huts.

Essentials

GETTING THERE   Forty kilometers (25 miles) east of Höfn, the Ring Road crosses the main branch of the Jökulsá í Lóni River. Northeast of the river valley, just past the main bridge, a road branches off inland and leads a few kilometers into Lónsöræfi, past several summer houses. Some short hikes can kick off from here, but the best routes are accessed by mountain road F980, which meets the Ring Road on the southwest side of the river valley. Route F980 is 25km (16 miles) long and ends at Illikambur, a 1-hour hike from the Múlaskáli mountain hut. The route is technically passable in a 4WD vehicle with good clearance, but definitely not advised, because the river crossings are volatile and dangerous. From June through August, daily buses traveling between Höfn and Egilsstaðir stop on request at Stafafell. Check **www.publictransport.is** for updated times.

VISITOR INFORMATION   The best source of information and advice is the **Stafafell Guesthouse** (see below). Basic information can be found at **www.ust.is**; click "Protected Areas" and "Nature Reserves." From July 1 to August 15, a **warden** is stationed at Múlaskáli hut, where there is no phone reception, though it's possible to reserve lodging through the **FI office** (fi@fi.is; ✆ **568-2533**). The best **map** of Lónsöræfi is made by Mál og Menning.

Exploring the Area

HIKING   **Stafafell Travel Service** (www.stafafell.is; ✆ **478-1717**), based at the Stafafell Guesthouse (p. 272), is the best resource for planning your hiking trip. They can book the F980 bus, arrange transport from Höfn, reserve mountain huts, discuss your route and preparations, and sell you a map.

The Snæfell–Lónsöræfi Trek

One of Iceland's better-known treks goes from Lónsöræfi to Snæfell (p. 284), a 1,833m (6,014 ft.) peak northeast of Vatnajökull. The hike takes at least 4 days, and can be extended to 7 days if the start or endpoint is Stafafell. Mountain huts are spaced along the route at intervals of no greater than 17km (11 miles). The trek's northern half is very different from Lónsöræfi, because it traverses the glacier Eyjabakkajökull and a more desolate, less mountainous landscape. This trek is for experienced outdoorspeople:

Hikes are fairly strenuous, trails are often poorly marked, and you may need rope, crampons, and an ice axe. The trek can head in either direction, but going from Snæfell to Lónsöræfi gives you a net loss of altitude and saves the most interesting scenery for last. The **Stafafell Guesthouse** ★ (p. 272) is your best travel resource; make sure to review trail conditions beforehand. Snæfell is reached via Egilsstaðir by car, so be prepared for a long one-way trip to reconnect with your belongings.

Útivist (www.utivist.is; ✆ **562-1000**) doesn't run scheduled trips, but it's possible to book a group tour between May and September.

Several interesting **day hikes** are directly accessible from Stafafell, without taking the bus up Route F980. One particularly nice route leads through Seldalur to **Hvannagilshnúta,** a gorge surrounded by rockslides of brightly streaked rhyolite. However, the scenery in these lower reaches of Lónsöræfi pales in comparison to the interior regions.

Remember to bring extra shoes for stream crossings; the flow comes mostly from the glacier and is very unpredictable. Keep a map handy, because trails can be poorly marked. Also bear in mind that Lónsöræfi has one of the country's highest precipitation rates.

Where to Stay & Dine

The main accommodation for this area is the rather worn-down yet reliable **Stafafell Guesthouse ★** (www.stafafell.is; ✆ **478-1717;** 14 units, 1 w/bathroom; June–Sept 15 21,000kr double w/bathroom; 15,000kr double without bathroom; 5,000kr sleeping-bag accommodation; rates 33% lower Sept 16–May; no breakfast available but guest kitchen on premises). Guests can stay in two-bedroom cottages with kitchens, bathrooms, and living rooms, or in the owner's restored 19th-century farmhouse, which is humble and down-to-earth. Follow Route 1, 1km (⅔ mile) east of the main bridge over Jökulsá í Lóni.

All food must be brought into the area. The nearest **markets** are in Höfn and Djúpivogur. Most of the mountain huts have kitchens.

LOWER EASTFJORDS: DJÚPIVOGUR TO FÁSKRÚÐSFJÖRÐUR

Djúpivogur is at the tip of a peninsula 104km (65 miles) northeast of Höfn. Proceeding farther northeast, three more villages lie in this southern third of the Eastfjords, each with its own fjord or bay: Breiðdalsvík, Stöðvarfjörður, and Fáskrúðsfjörður. Tourism slackens off east of Höfn, and, after Djúpivogur, the coast is bypassed by the direct route to Egilsstaðir and the north.

Anyone passing this way, however, should not skip the Eastfjords entirely. On a road trip from the south, the scenery enters yet another glorious phase. The Eastfjords are steeper and less convoluted than the Westfjords, and each fjord has a kind of singular grandeur. Although activities are limited, you can spend a day or two hiking, horseback riding, or sea fishing, with perhaps a visit to Papey Island or Petra's mineral museum.

Essentials

GETTING AROUND Heading from Höfn toward Egilsstaðir, the Ring Road cuts inland at Breiðdalsvík, while the coastal Route 96 continues to Stöðvarfjörður and Fáskrúðsfjörður, then on through a 6km (3¾ mile) tunnel to Reyðarfjörður. But the most direct route between Höfn and Egilsstaðir uses the **Route 939 shortcut**. Route 939 is being incorporated into the Ring Road and connects with it at the head of Berufjörður, northwest of Djúpivogur, and reconnects with it 43km (27 miles) south of Egilsstaðir. Although it is a rough gravel road, Route 939 is manageable, and the alternative stretch of the Ring Road is not entirely paved either. The Route 939 shortcut bypasses everything in this section except for Djúpivogur, which is also the gateway to Papey Island. From Egilsstaðir, the fastest route to Fáskrúðsfjörður and Stöðvarfjörður is via routes 92 and 96, past Reyðarfjörður.

From June to August, **Straetó** (www.straeto.is; © **540-2600**) connects Höfn to Egilsstaðir (3½ hr.) via Djúpivogur, Berunes, and Breiðdalsvík. However, service has been diminishing to practically nonexistent in recent years.

VISITOR INFORMATION   The **Djúpivogur information office** (www. djupivogur.is; © **478-8288**; June–Aug daily 10am–6pm; weekends 10am–11:30am) is at the Langabúð museum by the port. **Breiðdalsvík's information office** (© **470-5560**; Mon–Fri 8am–noon and 1–4pm) is at Ásvegur 32; the **Hótel Bláfell**, Sólvellir 14 (www.blafell.is; © **475-6770**), is another good source. Tourist information for Stöðvarfjörður is handled at the regional information office in Egilstaður, Kaupvangur 10 (www.east.is; © **471-2320**). This office also covers the area farther north, including Eskifjörður, Reyðarfjörður, Neskaupstaðir, and Mjóifjorður.

Exploring the Area

HIKING   The trail map "Gönguleiðir á Suðurfjörðum Austfjarða," the fourth in the *Gönguleiðir á Austurlandi* series (500kr), covers the coastal region from Berufjörður to Fáskrúðsfjörður, though trail descriptions are in Icelandic only. Two mountain climbs, Sandfell and Halaklettur, are especially recommended for their breathtaking coastal scenery; don't leave the peaks before signing the guestbook.

Sandfell is a distinctive 743m (2,438 ft.) rhyolite mountain between Stöðvarfjörður and Fáskrúðsfjörður. The best approach is from the south side of Fáskrúðsfjörður. The trail leaves the coastal road between Víkurgerði and Vík farms and proceeds along the Víkurgerðisá River before cutting west. (On the map, the trail begins as #13 and becomes #14.) The scenery is excellent en route, with views of Fáskrúðsfjörður and Andey and Skrúður islands. Allow 5 hours for the round-trip.

The 573m (1,880 ft.) peak at the tip of the peninsula between Fáskrúðsfjörður and Reyðarfjörður is **Halaklettur.** Trail #7 starts at the north shore of Fáskrúðsfjörður, just east of the Kolfreyjustaður church. The ascent is less interesting than on Sandfell, but the superior view from the top takes in Fáskrúðsfjörður, Reyðarfjörður, the Vattarnestangi lighthouse, and Andey and Skrúður islands. Allow 4 hours for the round-trip. *Warning:* Don't go if you're afraid of heights.

DJÚPIVOGUR ★

This small, charming fishing village dates from 1589, when merchants from Hamburg were licensed by the Danish king to trade here. After the Danish trade monopoly was imposed in 1602, Djúpivogur became the only commercial port in southeast Iceland. Today, most visitors to Djúpivogur are primarily interested in tours to Papey Island.

Those who spend the night should know about the network of trails at the tip of the peninsula. It's a wonderfully peaceful area of shifting black sand dunes, active birdlife, and nice coastal views.

The long red building on the seafront, which dates back to 1790, houses a cafe and cultural center, **Langabúð Djúpavogi** (✆ **478-8220;** May 15–Oct 1 Sun–Thurs 10am–6pm, Fri–Sat 10am–11:30pm), with light meals, drinks, and occasional live entertainment. Outside, the sculpture known as "Eggin í Gleðivík" (Eggs in Happy Bay), by the celebrated artist Sigurður Guðmundsson, is a must-see in Djúpivogur. The 34 different stone eggs can be seen on the coast, approximately 1 km (⅔ mile) from the village.

PAPEY ★

Papey is not just another set of bird cliffs and a lighthouse; for centuries it was the only inhabited island off Iceland's east coast. Daily 4-hour tours with the **Gísli í Papey ferry** (https://djupivogur.is; ✆ **478-8119;** tickets 12,000kr adults, 6,000kr children ages 7–12, free for children 6 and under) leave Djúpivogur marina every day at 1pm from June until September 15 if weather permits.

Papey, a Celtic name, means "Friar's Island." Two 12th-century Icelandic sources affirm that Irish monks founded a hermitage here, perhaps after being chased off the mainland by the Norse; but excavations have not yet discovered evidence of habitation predating the 10th century. Papey was quite independent of the mainland because of dangerous tidal currents. Settlers lived a mostly self-sufficient life growing potatoes, tending sheep, and eating birds, bird eggs, fish, seals, and sharks. Later generations earned income by harvesting down feathers from eider-duck nests. Papey's population peaked in 1726, at 16. The last full-time resident was a man named Gisli, who bought the island in 1900, lived here 48 years, and lies buried here. The island still belongs to his family, and his granddaughter spends her summers here knitting and collecting eggs.

The best time to visit is June/July, when Papey is packed with guillemots, though puffins and other birds stay until mid-August. The seas are often choppy, so ask about conditions before your departure and have seasick pills at the ready. The 1-hour boat trip passes close to a rock shelf frequented by sunbathing or frolicking seals. Before docking at Papey, the boat enters a cove surrounded by low cliffs with chattering birds nesting on every ledge. The tour allows 2 hours for strolling around the island and visiting **Iceland's oldest wooden church,** which dates from 1807.

BREIÐDALSVÍK & BREIÐDALUR

Breiðdalsvík is a traditional coastal town of just over 200 people at the base of Breiðdalur (Broad Valley), a fertile enclave that attracts reindeer from the highlands in winter. The Ring Road cuts inland through Breiðdalur, and the surrounding mountains of sloping basalt strata are gorgeous at twilight. Breiðdalur is the longest and widest valley in the Eastfjords and surrounded by a spectacular view of towering mountains. It's popular for salmon fishing in Breiðdalsá, and its waterfalls attract ice climbers in winter. Breiðdalsvík hosts an annual strongman competition called **Austfjarðatröllið (Eastfjords Troll)** during the second week of August.

STÖÐVARFJÖRÐUR

This sleepy town 18km (11 miles) from Breiðdalsvík is best known for a great-grandmother's rock collection (see below). **Galleri Snæros,** Fjarðarbraut 42 (www.gallerisnaeros.is; ℂ **475-8931;** daily 11am–5pm June-Sept), is an arts and crafts gallery that exhibits and sells paintings, ceramics, and textiles by regional artists.

Steinasafn Petru ★ ROCK COLLECTION This collection of rocks and minerals is magnificent, but what brings in 20,000 visitors a year is its personal story. Everything was gathered by Petra Sveinsdóttir, who was so devoted to the stones that she once refused an invitation to a special dinner celebrating her work at the president's residence because she believed the stones should have received the recognition, not her. Sveinsdóttir passed away 2012 in her mid-80s, but kept working until her last years. The museum is in her former house and garden. A gift shop sells rocks with googly eyes stuck on.

Sunnuhulið. www.steinapetra.is. ℂ **475-8834.** Admission 1,500kr adults; free for children ages 14 and under. Daily 9am–6pm. Closed Oct 15–April 30.

FÁSKRÚÐSFJÖRÐUR

Formerly known as Búðir, Fáskrúðsfjörður was settled by French-speaking sailors (mostly Belgian and Breton) in the 1800s as a fishing base for half the year. In the cod boom of 1880 to 1914, about 5,000 French and Belgian fishermen came to east Iceland each season. Cod fishing was one of the world's most dangerous professions; over 4,000 French-speaking fishermen alone died in Icelandic waters between 1825 and 1940. In Fáskrúðsfjörður, they introduced locals to cognac and chocolate, stole eggs and sheep, and built a local chapel and hospital. Street signs are in Icelandic and French, and a cemetery east of town along the shore holds the graves of 49 French and Belgian sailors. For 4 days in late July, Fáskrúðsfjörður celebrates its French heritage with the *Franskir Dagar* **(French Days)** family festival.

In 2005, a 6km (3¾-mile) tunnel opened up between Fáskrúðsfjörður and Reyðarfjörður, shortening the route by 34km (21 miles). Fáskrúðsfjörður became close enough to Reyðarfjörður's new aluminum smelter to share in its economic resurgence.

Einar Jónsson, Iceland's leading sculptor, designed the **Memorial to the Shipwreck of Dr. Charcot,** an intriguing tribute to Arctic explorer Jean-Baptiste Charcot (1867–1936), shortly after Charcot's death in a shipwreck off the Icelandic coast. A guardian angel watches over a line of men, who ascend heavenward in a formation evoking a ship's prow. The sculpture is on Buðave, just east of the museum.

ANDEY & SKRÚÐUR ISLANDS

These two islands near Fáskrúðsfjörður beckon, yet are not covered by tours. Skrúður is especially intriguing, with a large puffin colony, 160m (525-ft.) cliffs, and an enormous cave. If weather permits, Skruður's owner occasionally offers a sightseeing tour by boat around the island; inquire at **Hótel Bjarg** (below).

Where to Stay

The friendly, well-managed **Berunes Youth Hostel** ★ (www.berunes.is; ✆ **869-7227;** 15 units, none w/bathroom; May–Sept 15,000kr double; 6,000kr sleeping-bag accommodations; breakfast available from 1,500kr; closed Nov–March), open since 1973, is along the Ring Road 25km (16 miles) south of Breiðdalsvík. It has comfortable rooms and great views of Berufjörður, as well as access to a guest kitchen and washer/dryer. Berunes itself is a very dignified-looking settlement: The house, farm buildings, church, and accommodations all blend harmoniously. The church is always open, and guests are welcome to play the organ.

Hótel Bjarg ★   Directly over a small stream, this inexpensive, straightforward hotel has a beautiful view of the fjord from its hillside perch. Rooms are small and the walls are thin; it's otherwise pleasant for the price. It also has a games room with table tennis, pool, foosball, and video games. The chatty, friendly owner used to live in the States.

Skólavegur 49, Fáskrúðsfjörður. www.hotelbjarg.com. ✆ **475-1466.** 8 units, 5 w/bathroom. 20,500kr double; 16,000kr double without bathroom. Rates around 20% lower in winter. Rates include breakfast. **Amenities:** Bar; hot tub; free Wi-Fi.

Hótel Bláfell ★   Family-run, this timber-lined hotel in the town center is like an oversized log cabin. The rooms are well-maintained and comfortable, and all have private bathrooms; some add a small balcony. In the evenings, wind down on the terrace or in front of an open fireplace in the lounge.

Sólvellir 14, Breiðdalsvík. www.blafell.is. ✆ **475-6770.** 34 units. June–Sept 15 26,500kr double. Rates 30% lower Sept 16–May. Rates include breakfast. **Amenities:** Restaurant; bar; sauna; library; Wi-Fi in lobby/lounge; free in-room Wi-Fi.

Hótel Framtíð ★★   Set in a 1909 house overlooking Djupivogur Harbor, this cozy hotel has lots of original details. Rooms are simple yet atmospheric, most lined with wood-plank walls. The cottages add a small terrace and cooking facilities, while the modern apartments have up to three bedrooms and balconies with stunning views.

Vogaland 4, Djúpivogur. www.hotelframtid.com. ✆ **478-8887.** 42 units. June–Aug 34,900kr double; 36,900kr cottage; 57,800kr apartment. Rates 25% lower Sept–May. Breakfast available for 2,500kr. **Amenities:** Restaurants; bar; sauna; laundry facilities; Wi-Fi in lobby.

Hótel Staðarborg ★   Converted from a former schoolhouse in 2000, this hotel still looks the part from the exterior. Inside, however, it's not nearly as institutional. The comfortable rooms are indeed basic, but livened up with contemporary artwork. The facilities are good too, from a lounge with billiards to a full-service **restaurant.**

Rte. 1, 7km (4⅓ miles) west of Breiðdalsvík. www.stadarborg.is. ✆ **475-6760.** 30 units. May–Sept 13,500kr double; 29,400kr family room; 6,500kr sleeping-bag accommodation. Rates 30% lower Jan–Apr. Rates include breakfast, except sleeping-bag accommodation. **Amenities:** Restaurant; bar; Jacuzzi; free Wi-Fi in some rooms.

Where to Eat

In Djúpivogur, the waterfront cafe at the **Langabúð** cultural building serves soup, sandwiches, and cake from 10am to 6pm daily.

Serving Breiðdalsvík, **Hótel Bláfell** and **Hótel Staðarborg,** listed above, both have decent restaurants. Bláfell's restaurant is a bit more traditional.

For a tipple, try **Beljandi Brugghus** (✆ **866-8330**), a craft brewery founded by two locals inside an old slaughterhouse in the center of Breiðdalsvík, open Friday and Saturday nights.

Café Sumarlína ★ ICELANDIC   There's usually a soccer game on and an older gentleman or two drinking pints of lager in the corner at this kitschy bistro down by the fjord. The pizzas stand out on this eclectic menu, though the egg and béarnaise-topped burger is tempting. During *Franskir Dagar* (French Days), there are usually live performances from passing musicians.

Búðavegur 59 (along Rte. 96, close to the dock), Fáskrúðsfjörður. www.sumarlina.is. ✆ **475-1575.** Main courses 1,500kr–5,000kr. Daily 11am–9pm.

Gestastofa ★ ICELANDIC   The family restaurant of the owners of the Berunes Youth Hostel is open for breakfast year-round. Ingredients from the Eastern Fjords are prized here and used in seasonal three-course dinners (4,500kr) on summer weekends. Make sure to call ahead.

Rte. 1, 25km (16 miles) south of Breiðdalsvík, in Berufjörður. ✆ **478-8988.** Apr to late Sept 8–10am and 6:30–10pm.

Havarí ★★ VEGETARIAN   Only a lonely country road between Breiðdalsvík and Djúpivogur, this cafe and music venue is owned by Icelandic rock star Svavar Pétur Eysteinsson of Prins Póló and his wife, Berglind. The menu is based on produce from their own organic farm, with eclectic items like grilled-cheese sandwiches, creamy squash soups, veggie sausages and burgers, as well as waffles and cakes. On summer weekends the the farm becomes east Iceland's biggest party destination, attracting major music acts from around Iceland. Check the website for events listings.

Karlstaddir Farm, 22km (14 miles) south of Breiðdalsvík. www.havari.is. ✆ **842-1808.** Main courses 3,500kr–5,250kr. June–Aug daily 8am–9pm; Sept–May daily 8am–4pm.

Hótel Framtíð ★ ICELANDIC   In the 1904 building that makes up the oldest part of this hotel compound, this charming restaurant is more refined than what you might expect in a backwater like Djúpivogur. Start with the goose-breast carpaccio and follow with roasted lamb in thyme sauce as you

Lower Eastfjords: Djúpivogur to Fáskrúðsfjörður

stare out over the harbor. You won't go wrong with the locally caught plaice, redfish, cod, or halibut.

Vogaland 4, on the harbor, Djúpivogur. www.hotelframtid.com. © **478-8887.** Reservations recommended. Main courses 3,860kr–6,400kr. June–Aug noon–2pm and 6–9pm; Sept–May noon–1:30pm and 6:30–8:30pm.

MIDDLE EASTFJORDS: REYÐARFJÖRÐUR, ESKIFJÖRÐUR & NESKAUPSTAÐUR

In Iceland, Reyðarfjörður is now inescapably associated with Alcoa, the world's largest aluminum company, which in 2005 built a 2km-long (1¼-mile) smelting plant on the outskirts of town. The smelter, powered by new hydroelectric dams in the country's interior, remains a very contentious subject (p. 287). However short-sighted this project may turn out to be, Reyðarfjörður and its satellite towns are bustling with energy after years of economic stagnation and population decline. A housing boom is rushing to meet the needs of hundreds of foreign workers, and locals no longer have to drive to Egilsstaðir to go to the movies or a shopping arcade. Resident opinion runs strongly in support of the smelter; alas, the needs of tourists—whose fjord views have been blighted by power lines, factory buildings, and ugly housing developments—were left out of the equation. The three towns are the largest in the Eastfjords, and each still has a range of attractions, dining, and places to stay; an abundance of information can be found at **www.east.is**.

Essentials

Route 92 connects Egilsstaðir to Reyðarfjörður, Eskifjörður, and Neskaupstaður, a distance of 71km (44 miles). By bus, **SVAust** (© **470-9000**) links all four towns (best to call and inquire; the schedule changes three to four times a year). **Regional tourist information** is in **Fáskrúðsfjörður's** City Hall *Ráðhús,* Hafnargata 2 (www.fjardabyggd.is; © **470-9000**).

Exploring the Area

Neskaupstaður, the easternmost town in Iceland, is more picturesque and remote than Reyðarfjörður and Eskifjörður, and its surrounding coastline is full of wonderful bird cliffs, sea caves, inlets, and pebble beaches. **Kayakklúbburinn Kaj** (www.123.is/kaj; © **863-9939**) leads kayak trips.

As with all the Eastfjords, peninsular hiking trails offer great coastal scenery. A good **hiking map** with trail descriptions in English is "Gönguleiðir á Fjarðaslóðum," number II in the *Gönguleiðir á Austurlandi* series.

If you have a strong flashlight and pass near Eskifjörður, consider poking around **Helgustaðanáma,** an abandoned spar quarry. **Iceland spar,** a type of calcite that can be cut along different planes to make light prisms, has been used in everything from microscopes to machines studying the emission of light from atoms. The shaft is 80m-long (62 ft.), and the calcites shimmer in the light. (Taking anything is illegal.) To get there from Eskifjörður, take the gravel road east of town along the coast. After 9km (5½ miles), there is a sign for Helgustaðir and a marked trailhead; park at the quarry information sign and walk 10 minutes uphill.

Icelandic Wartime Museum (Íslenska Stríðsárasafnið) ★ MUSEUM
Reyðarfjörður was a military base for British forces in World War II, and this museum is housed next to (and inside) some of the original barracks, the landing strip, and small gun shelters. The museum has plenty of artifacts, but the best way to bring the era alive is to reminisce with the old Icelanders who work there.

Spítalakampi, Reyðarfjörður. ✆ **470-9063.** Admission 850kr adults; free for children and seniors. June–Aug daily 1–5pm.

EGILSSTAÐIR

All roads in east Iceland fan out from Egilsstaðir, a hub for the eastern towns. The regional airport is here, and ferry passengers from Europe pass through after docking at Seyðisfjörður. The town has expanded slightly in the wake of the Kárahnjúkar hydroelectric project (p. 287). About 3,500 people live in greater Egilsstaðir, but most workers are here temporarily.

Egilsstaðir lies next to Lagarfljót (aka Lögurinn), Iceland's third-largest lake (53 sq. km/33 sq. miles). Most services—supermarket, service stations, bus depot, bank, camping, tourist info, shops—are clumped together off the Ring Road. The store for **outdoor equipment** is **Verslunin Skógar,** Dynskógar 4 (✆ **471-1230**), near Hótel Valaskjálf.

Essentials
GETTING THERE & AROUND
Egilsstaðir is on the Ring Road (Route 1), 186km (116 miles) northeast of Höfn and 265km (165 miles) southeast of Akureyri. The distance from Egilsstaðir to Reykjavík is 653km (406 miles) by the northern route, or 635km (395 miles) by the southern route—though with the Route 939 shortcut, the difference is negligible.

BY PLANE Flights from Reykjavík are generally cheaper than bus tickets, and in good weather you get an aerial tour of Vatnajökull. **Air Iceland** (www.airiceland.is; ✆ **570-3030**) flies from Reykjavík to Egilsstaðir six times daily in each direction. Typical airfare is 8,860kr to 16,200kr one-way. **Taxis** are at the airport. *Tip:* Book flights online for a cheaper ticket.

BY CAR Car rental agencies at the Egilsstaðir airport are **Europcar/Bílaleiga Akureyrar** (www.holdur.is; ✆ **461-6000**), **Avis** (www.avis.is; ✆ **660-0623**), and **Hertz** (www.hertz.is; ✆ **522-4450**).

BY BUS Travel between Reykjavík and Egilsstaðir requires an overnight in Akureyri or Höfn and costs more than flying unless you have a **bus passport**

Egilsstaðir

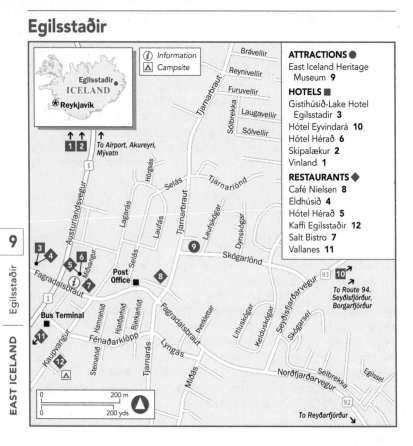

ATTRACTIONS ●
East Iceland Heritage
  Museum **9**

HOTELS ■
Gistihúsið-Lake Hotel
  Egilsstaðir **3**
Hótel Eyvindará **10**
Hótel Hérað **6**
Skipalækur **2**
Vinland **1**

RESTAURANTS ◆
Café Nielsen **8**
Eldhúsið **4**
Hótel Hérað **5**
Kaffi Egilsstaðir **12**
Salt Bistro **7**
Vallanes **11**

(p. 336). From June to September 15, **Straeto** (www.straeto.is; ℂ **587-6000**) runs sporadic buses between Akureyri and Egilsstaðir. From June until December, **SBA Norðurleið** (www.sba.is; ℂ **550-0700**) runs a service both ways connecting Egilsstaðir to Akureyri. The service runs daily until Sept 15, but is reduced in the winter. The winter service from January to May continues several times a week, but check with SBA for the right service provider.

SVAust (ℂ **470-9000**) connects Egilsstaðir to the surrounding towns of Breiðdalsvík, Stöðvarfjörður, Fáskrúðsfjörður, Reyðarfjörður, Eskifjörður, and Neskaupstaður (identified as "Norðfjörður") year-round Monday to Saturday. **Ferðaþjónusta Austurlands** (www.sfk.is; ℂ **472-1515**) connects Egilsstaðir to Seyðisfjörður in summer (p. 288). **Jakob og Margrét** (ℂ **472-9805** or 894-8305) takes passengers by van between Egilsstaðir and Borgarfjörður Eystri on weekdays (p. 293).

BY TAXI The two drivers to contact are Jón Björnsson (ℂ **898-2625**) and Jón Eiður (ℂ **892-9247**).

VISITOR INFORMATION

Egilsstaðir's excellent **tourist information office,** Miðvangur 1, (www.east. is; © **471-2320**) serves all of east Iceland, and also offers free Internet access.

Exploring the Area

For activities around Lake Lagarfljót (aka Lögurinn), see p. 285.

East Iceland Heritage Museum (Minjasafn Austurlands) ★

MUSEUM   This above-average folk museum holds a diverse collection of local artifacts, including a restored turf farmhouse and a few pre-Christian relics. Special attention is paid to reindeer and the dangers they face in the region, as well as some of the uses that result from hunting them. Information in English is limited, but the staff is usually eager to show visitors around. On summer weekends, the museum often holds spinning and weaving demos or offers horse-drawn carriage rides.

Laufskogar 1. www.minjasafn.is. © **471-1412.** Admission 1,000kr adults; free for children ages 17 and under; free admission Wed. June 1–Aug 31 daily 10am–6pm; Sept–May Tues–Fri 11am–4pm.

Where to Stay

The tourist office (above) has a full list of what is available, or check at **www.east.is.** There is also a good **campsite** (© **471-2320**) on Kaupvangur, opposite **Kaffi Egilsstaðir** ★ (p. 284); another campsite sits beside the restaurant.

EXPENSIVE

Gistihúsið–Lake Hotel Egilsstaðir ★★   The town of Egilsstaðir is named after this country estate, and not the other way around. The farm sat at what was one of the busiest crossroads in east Iceland, so guests naturally began turning up asking to sleep there. Eventually, around 1903, owner Eiríkur Halldórsson was forced to begin charging for accommodations. The oldest part of the house dates to 1903, with tasteful touches like antique furnishings and original woodwork, though a major expansion that added most of the rooms is less interesting. Each unit varies in size; those with views of Lake Lagarfljót are the first to go. The restaurant, **Eldhúsið,** prides itself on its local farm produce.

Rte. 932, approx. 0.5km (¼ mile) west of Rte. 1/Rte. 92 intersection. https://lakehotel.is. © **471-1114.** 50 units. June–Aug 42,700kr double. Rates around 30% lower Oct–Apr. Rates include breakfast. **Amenities:** Restaurant; bar; spa facilities (additional fee); free Wi-Fi.

Hótel Hérað ★   A clean, contemporary vibe runs throughout this reindeer-country chain hotel in the middle of town. It lacks views or any major defining characteristics, though the business-class amenities in the down-to-earth rooms are more than suitable for a short, comfortable stay. Interactive services, like daily high tea with hors d'oeuvres or a novelty-themed happy hour in the modern lounge with a fireplace, help bring life to the common areas.

Miðvangur 5–7. www.icehotels.is. ✆ **471-1500.** 60 units. June–Sept 15 28,400kr double. Rates around 25% lower Apr–May and Sept 16–Oct 31; around 40% lower Nov–Mar. Rates include breakfast. Closed Dec 23–Jan 3. **Amenities:** Restaurant, bar; room service; free Wi-Fi.

MODERATE

Hótel Eyvindará ★   With Egilsstaðir just off in the distance, 2km (1¼ miles) away, you are close enough to town to walk there, yet far enough away to still get a taste of the countryside. Woodlands surround this unassuming hotel, and rooms are spread out among a main building, an annex (where they add a terrace with a table and chairs), and freestanding cottages. Dinner is offered with advance notice during the summer.

Rte. 94, 1km (⅔ mile) north of the Rte. 94/Rte. 93 junction. www.eyvindara.is. ✆ **471-1200.** 16 units, 5 w/bathroom. 28,500kr double; 20,000kr double without bathroom; 32,000kr cottages for 2–4 people. Rates discounted off-season. Rates include full breakfast. **Amenities:** Restaurant; free Wi-Fi.

Skipalækur ★   One of Iceland's original farmstays, this sprawling rural compound is 3km (2 miles) northwest of Egilsstaðir in the village of Fellabær along the lake. Within 12 different houses are a range of doubles, with shared or private bathrooms, all varying in size, plus camping and lakeside cottages with kitchenettes and verandas. Horseback riding can be arranged, and fishing permits are also available.

Rte. 931, off the Ring Road, and across the bridge from Egilsstaðir. www.skipalaekur.is. ✆ **471-1324.** 20 units, 6 w/bathroom. 24,000kr double; 20,000kr double without bathroom; 25,500kr cottage for 2–4 people; 29,000kr cottage for 5–6 people; 4,500kr per person sleeping-bag accommodation. Rates around 10% lower off season. Rates include breakfast, except sleeping-bag accommodation. **Amenities:** Guest kitchen; free Wi-Fi in reception area.

Vinland Guesthouse ★   Across the bridge from Egilsstaðir in Fellabær, this welcoming metal-sided, prefab house is about as delightful as a metal-sided, prefab house can be. All of the rooms are identical, with private entrances and plain, cookie-cutter decorations, but include a few bonuses, like a minifridge and heated towel racks.

Signposted off Rte. 1 in Fellabær. www.vinlandhotel.is. ✆ **893-2989.** 6 units. 20,700kr double. Rates 29% lower Sept–May. **Amenities:** Free Wi-Fi.

Where to Eat

EXPENSIVE

Café Nielsen ★ ICELANDIC   Set inside a Danish-built home that dates to 1944, this intimate, family-operated restaurant with a shady terrace has an atmosphere that the hotel restaurants just cannot provide. Reindeer steaks with blueberry sauce are the specialty, though the menu extends to small plates like bacon-wrapped scallops and larger oven-baked or pan-fried local fish plates. At 1,850kr, the weekday lunch buffet is a fine deal.

Tjarnarbraut 1. www.cafenielsen.is. ✆ **471-2626.** Reservations recommended. Main courses 2,950kr–7,500kr. June–Aug Mon–Thurs 11:30am–11:30pm; Fri 11:30am–2am; Sat 1pm–2am; Sun 1–11:30pm.

Eldhúsið ★ ICELANDIC   This restaurant is set in the oldest part of Lake Hotel Egilsstaðir, which dates to 1904, with nice views of the lake. The intimate dining room has wood floors, white tablecloths, and crystal stemware. The kitchen favors beef and cheese produced right on the farm, along with organic produce and trout from the lake, though the menu is quite simple and straightforward. It is particularly busy on the days when the ferry gets in.

Rte. 932 approx. 0.5km (¼ mile) west of Rte. 1/Rte. 92 intersection. www.lakehotel.is. ✆ **471-1114.** Reservations recommended. Main courses 2,900kr–5,600kr. Daily noon–9:30pm.

Hótel Hérað ★ ICELANDIC   Completely renovated in 2013, this elegant, modern Icelandic restaurant sources almost everything it uses from local farmers, fishmongers, and hunters. The quality shows. A reindeer burger is grilled over a Spanish Motilfrit charcoal oven with barley bread from the local bakery and Icelandic Camembert that's really something special. Try the goose-leg confit with beets and feta to start. After dinner, retreat to the bar for a local craft beer or glass of wine.

Miðvangur 5–7. ✆ **471-1500.** Reservations recommended. Main courses 1,990kr–7,500kr. Daily 11:30am–2pm and 6–9pm.

MODERATE

Salt Bistro ★★ ICELANDIC   Simple comfort food with fresh ingredients made really well, that's the philosophy here. It's a local hangout, where Icelanders come to sip a beer in one of the booths and munch on homemade pizza. Salt Bistro has burgers made with local beef, grilled lamb from the region, and even a tandoor oven where they turn out a few Indian dishes. Look for nightly specials as well.

Midvangur 2. www.saltbistro.is. ✆ **471-1700.** Main courses 1,800kr–4,200kr. Mon–Sat 10am–10pm; Sun noon–10pm.

Vallanes ★★★ ICELANDIC   For breakfast only, this iconic organic farm, where the owners have planted an astounding 1 million birch trees and single-handedly revived Icelandic barley, offers a "from field to table" breakfast with advance reservations (minimum 4 people). It includes a tour of the farm along with a full breakfast based on wholesome, local, and organic ingredients set inside a beautiful greenhouse. The visit lasts approximately 1½ hours. You can also buy various products produced here from the on-site farm shop. The farm takes volunteers, though there's a 3-week minimum and reserved spots get filled up at the beginning of the year.

Vallanes (off Route 931, 2km/1.25 miles west of Route 1). www.vallanes.is. ✆ **471-1747.** 3,500kr per person. May–Sept Tues–Sat 8:30am–9am (cafe); June–Aug Mon–Fri 9am–6pm (shop).

Kaffi Egilsstaðir ★ CAFE   Opposite the campground, this casual cafe and restaurant occupies a renovated '50s house spruced up with red chairs and modern light fixtures. There's a daily lunch buffet and a list of international favorites like burgers and pizza. The bar stays open late on the weekends.

Kaupvangur 17 (across from the new campsite). ⓒ **470-0200.** Main courses 1,690kr–3,300kr. Sun–Thurs 10am–11.30pm; Fri–Sat 10am–10pm.

INLAND FROM EGILSSTAÐIR: LÖGURINN, SNÆFELL & KÁRAHNJÚKAR

Southwest of Egilsstaðir, the Lagarfljót River widens into a 38km (24-mile), narrow lake known as Lögurinn—or still Lagarfljót, as "fljót" implies a very wide river. A round-the-lake drive is a popular and agreeable day trip, though much of its appeal derives from forestation projects and social campground retreats, both primarily attracting Icelanders. Locals are fond of their changing foliage, but New Englanders might opt for the Eastfjords instead.

Roads from Lögurinn branch off into the interior highlands, where reindeer roam through ruggedly beautiful scenery. Serious hikers are lured by Snæfell, the tallest Icelandic mountain not underneath Vatnajökull. A paved road leads to Kárahnjúkar dam, part of a controversial hydroelectric project (p. 287).

Essentials

GETTING THERE   No scheduled buses head in this direction. Route 931—which meets the Ring Road both 10km (6 miles) south of Egilsstaðir and 3km (2 miles) north of Egilsstaðir—circumnavigates the lake, crossing a bridge near the southwest end. Route 933 branches off from Route 931 on both sides of that bridge, and forms its own loop via another bridge farther southwest. Route 910 branches off from Route 933 (on the lake's northwest side) toward Snæfell, Kárahnjúkar, and elsewhere in the interior. Those headed directly from Egilsstaðir to Route 910 should take the north side of the lake for slightly less distance, or the south side for better roads.

VISITOR INFORMATION   This entire area is covered by the **Egilsstaðir tourist information office** (p. 281). **Snæfellsstofa's** tourist office (www.vjp. is; ⓒ **470-0840;** May–Sept daily 9am–7pm) is in Skriðuklaustur off the main ring road on Route 933 *past* the Route 910 turnoff (about a 40-min. drive from Egilsstaðir). There's a souvenir shop and an innovative exhibition called Veraldarhjólið (the cycle of the world).

Kárahnjúkar, the **Végarður tourist office** (ⓒ **470-2570;** June–Aug 31 daily 1–5pm) is about 2km (1¼ miles) farther down the road. **Ferðafélag Fljótsdalshéraðs** (ferdafelag@egilsstadir.is; ⓒ **863-5813**), which runs the Snæfell mountain hut, is a great source of information for hiking the highlands.

Exploring the Area

The following destinations follow a circular path around Lögurinn.

Hallormsstaðaskógur, 24km (15 miles) from Egilsstaðir on Lagarfljót's southeastern shore, is Iceland's largest forest—a fact that never fails to amuse passing tourists. Iceland, which was substantially forested when settlers first arrived, currently leads the world in annual per capita planting of trees. Hallormsstaðaskógur has far more diversity than Iceland's original forests, with larch, red spruce, and other species added to native birch, rowan, and willow. A free **trail map** of Hallormsstaðaskógur is available at the Shell station along Route 931. A more formal **arboretum**—the best in Iceland, for what it's worth—is on the lake side of the road, marked "SKÓGRÆKT RÍKISINS/ TRJÁSAFN/ARBORETUM" on a brown wooden sign. A pleasant trail from the parking area leads to the lake.

Atlavík, a lakeshore campground, is the departure point for evening cruises on the *Lagarfljótsormurinn* (© **471-2900**). This 110-passenger ship, named for the Loch Ness–style sea monster supposedly dwelling in Lagarfljót, takes groups on lake cruises involving cookouts, fishing, and even live music (mid-June to Aug); call to see if an expedition is scheduled.

Gunnar Gunnarsson (1889–1975) didn't mean much in his native Iceland until late in his career, but from 1920 to 1946 he was Germany's second best-selling author, after Goethe. Gunnar was best known for historical fiction— notably *The Black Cliffs (Svartfugl),* based on a double murder case in the Westfjords along Route 933, 2km (1¼ miles) south of the Route 933/Route 910 junction. Gunnar's distinctive stone house, where he lived from 1935 to 1948, is now the **Gunnarstofnun Cultural Institute** (www.skriduklaustur.is; © **471-2990;** admission 1,000kr adults, 750kr students, 500kr seniors, free for children 16 and under; May 26–Aug 31 daily 10am–6pm; May 5–25 and Sept 1–16 daily noon–5pm), which includes a lovingly curated, permanent exhibit on the author (with some of his books for sale), temporary exhibits on local themes, an art gallery, and a first-rate cafe, **Klausturkaffi ★★**. Outside is an archaeological excavation of **Skriðuklaustur,** an Augustinian monastery founded in 1500 A.D. Findings are exhibited inside, where bored children can make use of the playroom full of toys and art materials.

Located 3km (2 miles) southwest of Skriðuklaustur, the **Végarður Visitor Center** has free exhibits on the Kárahnjúkar hydroelectric project; see below for details.

A 90-minute round-trip hike with nice views over the lake leads along the Hengifossá River uphill for 2.5km (1½ miles) to two photogenic waterfalls: **Hengifoss ★** and **Litlanesfoss ★**. The parking area is clearly marked from Route 933, between the junctions with Route 910 and 931. Hengifoss, at 118m (387 ft.), is Iceland's third-highest waterfall and has a distinctive pattern of red clay stripes wedged between thick layers of black basalt. Unless the flow is especially strong, you can climb up to a cave behind the falls.

Litlanesfoss, halfway along the trail, is no less beautiful, with fantastical formations of columnar basalt.

SNÆFELL, KÁRAHNJÚKAR & THE INTERIOR

From Lagarfljót, the newly paved Route 910 winds steeply up the hillside and finally levels off in **Fljótsdalsheiði ★**, a highland environment distinct from the lake below. Chances are good you'll see a reindeer herd in this austerely beautiful landscape, dominated by rocky tundra, lakes, clumpy moss, lichen, and scrub. Compared to interior deserts such as Sprengisandur, it's positively lush. Route 910 reaches **Kárahnjúkar dam** within an hour's drive, passing close to the northern slopes of the imposing 1,833m (6,013 ft.) peak **Snæfell.**

The controversial Kárahnjúkar project (p. 287) encompasses five dams, of which the Kárahnjúkar dam itself is the largest. Water is tunneled from the new reservoirs to a hydroelectric power station built into a mountainside substation on the northwest bank of the Jökulsá í Fljótsdal River, about 10km (6 miles) southwest of the Route 933/Route 910 junction.

The substation is open to visitors at certain hours through prebooking. For accessibility to this high-tech wonder, contact the **Végarður tourist office** (see p. 284), on Route 933, about 5km (3 miles) southwest of the Route 933/Route 910 junction. Végarður is run by the Icelandic power company Landsvirkjun (www.landsvirkjun.com), and the video presentation on Kárahnjúkar's engineering marvels is very effective PR.

The paved road ends at a viewpoint overlooking Hálslón Reservoir, which is as large as Lögurinn (Lagarfljót), covering 57 sq. km (22 sq. miles). The more interesting and revealing viewpoint would look downstream from the dam, where the once-raging Dimmugljúfur Gorge has been reduced to a trickle. There are no tours of this area, but **Tanni Travel** (www.tannitravel.is; ✆ **476-1399**), based in Eskifjörð, will take group bookings.

HIKING & CLIMBING The **"East Iceland Highlands" map,** produced by Iceland's national power company Landsvirkjun, details several rewarding hiking routes in the Snæfell–Kárahnjúkar area, with trail descriptions and difficulty ratings. (The map is not available online, but you can contact Végarður tourist office, above, and ask them to send you one.) Few trails are pegged, however, and some hikes require experience and advance planning.

Route 910 passes within 12km (7½ miles) of the **Snæfell mountain hut** (snaefellsstofa@vjp.is; ✆ **842-4367**). A 4WD track leads all the way there, though you may encounter difficult river crossings. The hut is on Snæfell's western side, about 800m (2,625 ft.) above sea level, and sleeps 45, with a kitchen, tent sites, and showers. **Ferðafélag Fljótsdalshéraðs** (www.fljotsdalsherad.is/ferdafelag; ferdafelag@egilsstadir.is; ✆ **863-5813**) operates the hut, leads occasional hiking tours, and is the best source for information on regional hiking. The website provides information on tour dates, destinations, and activities; the more ambitious hiker can pursue their "Pearls" scheme, which involves hiking to 9 of 18 locations of varying difficulty to be rewarded with a "Sprinter" certificate. **Snæfell** presides royally over its surroundings, and its

KÁRAHNJÚKAR: ICELAND'S lost WILDERNESS

Among Iceland's natural resources, renewable energy—generated from geothermal heat and flowing water—is second only to fish. Aluminum smelting, which requires abundant energy and ready access to ports, seems the perfect fit.

Enter Kárahnjúkar—a $3-billion hydroelectric network of dams, reservoirs, water tunnels, generators, and 52km (32 miles) of monstrous power lines in the eastern interior highlands—all built to power the aluminum plant at Reyðarfjörður in the Eastfjords. This mile-long behemoth is run by the American company Alcoa, the world's largest producer of aluminum products. Processed alumina powder is shipped in from as far away as Australia, and aluminum is produced in enormous vats cooked to 900°C (1,652°F).

Kárahnjúkar led to a worldwide protest campaign. In 2002, one in six Icelanders petitioned against the project, but the parliament approved it by a large majority. Many foreign activists staged protests near the construction sites, creating blockades or chaining themselves to the chassis of vehicles and obstructing workers.

Support for Kárahnjúkar still runs high in the east, where sagging local economies have already been boosted. Local fishermen were often idle after being outbid for fishing quotas. Iceland relies on dwindling fish stocks for most of its export income, and needs to diversify its economy. Kárahnjúkar's backers also stress that hydroelectric power is a "green" energy source: If aluminum plants were built elsewhere and powered by fossil fuels, they would produce 10 times the carbon emissions. Alcoa even has a relatively good environmental track record.

Kárahnjúkar's opponents, however, saw no reason to sacrifice Iceland's pristine wilderness just to feed the world's energy gluttony and lower the cost of beer cans. Kárahnjúkar has soaked up capital that could have been invested in more forward-looking sectors, such as scientific research institutions or software companies. Not to mention that the dams have drastically altered the most intact and extensive glacier-to-sea ecosystem in Iceland and flooded 57 sq. km (22 sq. miles) of Europe's largest unspoiled wilderness. The feeding grounds of reindeer and nesting grounds of pink-footed geese and other birds have already disappeared. Sand and clay have washed down from construction sites and devastated local fishing grounds. Soil erosion now sends storms of dust and sand on to farmland. The dams could also prove vulnerable to volcanoes and earthquakes. Vatnajökull glacier, the source of the dammed rivers, is melting rapidly and reservoirs could eventually dry up.

Support for Kárahnjúkar among Icelanders has slipped, and support for similar planned projects is waning. In April 2007, residents of Hafnarfjörður voted to reject a $1.2-billion smelter expansion by the Alcan corporation.

9

EAST ICELAND | Inland From Egilsstaðir: Lögurinn, Snæfell & Kárahnjúkar

spiky 1,833m (6,014 ft.) snow-capped peak tempts many climbers. A pegged trail leads up the western slope to the summit, but the climb requires some experience and equipment (crampons at the very least). Consult with the hut warden beforehand, and allow at least 7 to 9 hours round-trip. Hikes around the periphery of Snæfell are also recommended, and the full circuit is 29km (18 miles); check the "East Iceland Highlands" map for details.

For the glorious multi-day trek from **Snæfell to Lónsöræfi,** see p. 271.

Where to Eat

If driving around Lagarfljót, your best lunch option is the **cafe at Skriðuklaustur** ★★ (p. 285), which doesn't require museum admission. A fabulous, homemade, all-you-can-eat lunch buffet is served until 2pm, costing only 3,000kr for adults, 1,575kr for children 6 to 12. A cake buffet from 2pm to museum closing time costs 2,000kr adults, 1,000kr for children. In **Hallormsstaðaskógur,** the **Hotel Hallormsstaður** off Route 931 has a summer-only restaurant.

SEYÐISFJÖRÐUR

Icelandic villages nestled in fjords are likened to pearls in a shell, and none fit this description better than **Seyðisfjörður** ★★. The 17km (11-mile) fjord is lined with sheltering, snow-capped mountains and tumbling waterfalls. The dizzying descent into the fjord makes drivers feel like swooping gyrfalcons. The village, enlivened by Norwegian wood kit homes from the 19th and early-20th centuries, is a popular summer retreat for artists and musicians; the ferry from Europe arrives here weekly.

Seyðisfjörður is an ideal port, and it became a trading hub in the early 18th century. In the late 19th century, it became a boom town, thanks to the herring trade, largely controlled by Norwegian merchants. In 1906, Seyðisfjörður was chosen as the entry point for Iceland's first undersea telegraph link to the outside world. During World War II, Allied forces built a camp on the fjord, and a German air raid sank the *El Grillo* oil tanker, which still lies at the fjord bottom. Seyðisfjörður's economy remains reliant on fishing, and is prone to the same uncertainties faced by other Eastfjord villages.

Essentials

GETTING THERE

BY CAR Seyðisfjörður is at the end of Route 93, only 26km (16 miles) from Egilsstaðir. From the Ring Road, take Route 92 through central Egilsstaðir, then turn left on Route 93. Route 93 to Seyðisfjörður is often foggy, which could reduce your breathtakingly scenic drive to a blind, harrowing crawl.

About 7km (4⅓ miles) before reaching Seyðisfjörður, a gravel road branches off to the left. In 1885, Seyðisfjörður suffered the most deadly avalanche in Icelandic history. Twenty-four people were killed, many more were injured, and several houses were knocked right into the fjord. In 1996, another avalanche leveled a factory, but no one died. A **memorial sculpture** made from the factory's twisted girders stands in the town, at the intersection of Ránargata and Fjarðargata.

BY BUS From June through August, **Ferðaþjónusta Austurlands** (www. visitseydisfjordur.com/project/local-bus-schedule; ✆ **472-1515**) connects Seyðisfjörður and Egilsstaðir with two **buses** daily on weekdays, an extra bus on Thursdays, and one bus a day on weekends. Tickets are 1,250kr for adults, 950kr for seniors and teens (13–19 years), and 500kr for children (5–12 years).

VISITOR INFORMATION

The **tourist office** (www.visitseydisfjordur.com; ⓒ **472-1551;** May 1–Sept Mon–Fri 9am–noon and 1–5pm; Jan–Apr Tues–Wed 9am–noon and 1–5pm) is inside the ferry terminal building. It is closed from October to December but should be open on ferry arrival days. The staff sells bus passes and can help book places to stay.

Exploring the Area

Among Iceland's smaller towns, Seyðisfjörður has perhaps the best concentration of **historic buildings and homes.** Most compelling are the chalet-style houses, inspired by German and Swiss models, clustered along Bjólfsgata and Norðurgata streets. Well-off merchants imported these houses from Norway—assembly required—roughly between 1890 and 1910. The free brochure "Historic Seyðisfjörður," which can be found all over town, provides an in-depth history and walking tour of the architectural highlights.

Despite Seyðisfjörður's reputation as a magnet for Iceland's artsy community, the population is under 700, and visitors should not expect to find streets bustling with shops and galleries. Things do liven up the nights before and after the ferry arrival, however. It's also a good idea to check with the tourist office for **special events.** The various cultural festivities known as Á seyði are concentrated in early June but extend through July. The less-known **LungA festival** (www.lunga.is; ⓒ **861-5859**) takes place in mid-July and invites young people ages 16 to 25 to join workshops led by artists focusing on everything from visual art to circus performance to fashion design. Non-Icelanders are welcome, and the week culminates with live concerts by prominent Icelandic bands. Classical concerts are presented in **Bláa Kirkjan** (www.blaakirkjan.is; ⓒ **472-1775**), a blue-painted church in the middle of town, on six consecutive Wednesdays from July 7 to August 11 at 8:30pm. Tickets cost 2,800kr adults; 1,800kr senior and students; free for children 16 years and under; and go on sale half an hour before the performance.

The **Skaftfell Center for Visual Arts,** located above the Skaftfell bistro (listed below in "Where to Eat," p. 293) is the main hub for visual artists in the east of Iceland. The bistro is dedicated to young, experimental contemporary artists. The space was founded in the memory of the late artist Dieter Roth (known for his book creations and biodegradable works) and furnished in the spirit of his art; some of his book works are on display. In 2012, German artist Lukas Kühne installed a site-specific sound sculpture, *Tvisongur,* on a mountainside above town. The concrete structure consists of five interconnected domes, ranging in size between 2 and 4 meters, and covering an area of about 30 square meters. Each dome has its own resonance that corresponds to a tone in the Icelandic musical tradition of five-tone harmony, and works as a natural amplifier to that tone. To get there, walk down the gravel road that starts at the Brimberg Fish Factory for about 20 minutes, though it's best to ask at the tourist office for a map. From mid-May to mid-September, a **crafts market (handverkmarkaður)** is held on Austurvegur 23 from 1 to 5pm every day; call ✆ **866-7859** or contact the tourist office for an update. The tax-free shop **Þrýði,** Norðurgata 8 (✆ **472-1535;** Mon–Fri 3–6pm), sells souvenirs, woolens, and local handicrafts.

Technical Museum of East Iceland (Tækniminjasafn Austurlands) ★ MUSEUM   Seyðisfjörður was quite the cradle of modern technology in Iceland, with the first telegraph station (1906), the first machine shop to run on hydroelectricity (1907), and the first modern electric power station (1913). This museum encompasses the original telegraph station and the machine shop, which has original belt-driven metalworking machines, turbines, a foundry furnace, and a blacksmith's forge. Upstairs from the machine shop is an exhibit recounting Seyðisfjörður's technical triumphs and an old telephone switchboard to play with.

A DAY hike IN SEYÐISFJÖRÐUR

The 5- to 6-hour hiking route from **Stafdalur to Vestdalur** ★★ is a spectacular traverse through peaceful upland heath, past the mountain-sided lake Vestdalsvatn, and down into Seyðisfjörður along the cascading Vestdalsá River. Other than a steep downhill stretch at the end, the trail isn't overly strenuous. It's a one-way route, and you'll need to arrange transport at either end. Any clear day from late June to early September is suitable, though late June and early July have the best show of wildflowers. The trail is poorly staked, so bring a topographical map. Be sure to ask about snow conditions and bring sunglasses to protect your eyes from glare.

The trail begins from a ski lift along Route 93, about 8km (5 miles) outside of Seyðisfjörður. The turnoff is indicated by a large sign with the Shell Oil logo and the words "VELKOMIN Á SKÍÐASVÆÐIÐ Í STAFDAL." The trail is marked with yellow-tipped stakes and leads north, away from Route 93, with Stafdalsfell mountain

on the left and the boggy Stafdalsá River Valley on the right. In the pass between Stafdalsfell and Bjólfur peaks, the trail crosses the Stafdalsá. At this point, you are about halfway to Vestdalsvatn Lake. Make sure to round the lake clockwise; another yellow-staked trail takes the near side of the lake and will lead you astray. At the northeast corner of Vestdalsvatn, you can sign the guestbook in the Vatnsklettur shed. From there it's all downhill, due east, along the Vestdalur Valley, with waterfalls and fabulous fjord views the whole way. Upon reaching the Vestdalsá River, the trail divides and proceeds down both banks; the southern (right-hand) trail is a little easier. Both trails end up on the coastal road, 2km (1¼ miles) north of the village.

The reverse route uphill from Seyðisfjörður through Vestdalur to Vestdalsvatn, then back the same way, does not require one-way transport and is almost as rewarding. Allow 5 hours for the round-trip, or 6 if you start from the village.

The highlight is the telegraph station, located 100m (328 ft.) from the machine shop inside a blue-gray house, bought from a rich Norwegian merchant in 1905. That same year, a telegraph cable was laid under the ocean to the Faeroe Islands, and then on to Scotland and the rest of Europe. In the summer of 1906, a crew of over 300 Icelanders and Norwegians planted 14,000 telegraph poles in a 614km (382-mile) course from Seyðisfjörður to Reykjavík.

The devoted staff maintains the original telegraph equipment, which must be seen in action to be truly appreciated. Ask them to demonstrate the transmission of Morse code onto hole-punched rolls of paper, using a machine powered by a spring and hand crank. A specially adapted typewriter then converts the paper to words. The 3-day **Blacksmith Festival** takes place annually on the grounds in late July, with courses such as blacksmithing, knife-making, whittling, and metal casting as well as live music.

Hafnargata 44. www.tekmus.is. ☎ **472-1596.** Admission 1,000kr adults; 800kr seniors; free for children ages 18 and under. Free admission Fri. June–Sept 15 Mon–Fri 11am–5pm; Sept 16–May Mon–Fri 1–4pm.

Tours & Activities

Local sailor **Hlynur Oddsson** (hlynur@hotmail.de; ☎ **865-3741**) offers individually tailored **fishing, cycling, and kayaking** trips. Fishing trips generally pursue cod, haddock, and coalfish. Mountain-bike rental starts at 2,000kr for a half-day. Guided kayak tours range from 1 hour (4,000kr) to more advanced 10-hour excursions to Tröllanes and back (25,000kr).

For **bird-watching tours** of Skálanes, 19km (12 miles) from Seyðisfjörður, see below.

VENTURING FROM SEYÐISFJÖRÐUR

The lonely, pristine, and beautiful fjords north and south of Seyðisfjörður make for wonderful adventures off the beaten track. The best **topographical hiking map** of this entire region, including Borgarfjörður Eystri to the north, is titled "Víknaslóðir: Trails of the Deserted Inlets."

A road leads along the **north shore** of Seyðisfjörður, reaching halfway to the tip of the peninsula. At the end of the road, a 4WD track extends another 5.5km (3½ miles) to **Brimnes,** an abandoned farm with a lighthouse, and a good destination for a coastal walk. Campers should definitely consider the hike overland to **Loðmundarfjörður,** which once had several farms but was abandoned in 1973. Loðmundarfjörður is an 8-hour walk from the village, or 6 hours from farther up the coastal road. For more on Loðmundarfjörður and other deserted inlets to the north, see **Borgarfjörður Eystri ★★★** (p. 293). Another wonderful trek leads from the southern shore of Seyðisfjörður overland to **Mjóifjörður**—one more incredible find for connoisseurs of obscure fjords. Mjóifjörður is particularly long, steep, and narrow, with a beautiful series of waterfalls at its base, abundant crowberries in August, and about 35 inhabitants. A gravel road (Rte. 953) leads back to Egilsstaðir.

The isolated **Skálanes Nature and Heritage Center** ★ (www.skalanes. com; ✆ **690-6966** or 861-7008; May 15–Sept 15), 19km (12 miles) from the village on Seyðisfjörður's south shore, is a great day trip from Seyðisfjörður, especially for bird-watchers. Skálanes leads guided tours of the area that include high cliffs and a beach popular with seals. The lack of privacy is compensated for by uninterrupted views of the surrounding landscape and a dining room offering hearty meals—largely fish, lamb, reindeer, and eggs harvested by the staff. Meals are by reservation only, but traditional Icelandic soup is usually on hand for drop-ins. Cars can reach within 6km (3¾ miles) of Skálanes, and 4WD vehicles go all the way. Transportation can be arranged from as far as Seyðisfjörður; other options include biking or kayaking with the help of Hlynur Oddsson (see "Tours & Activities," above). **Hótel Aldan** ★★ (see "The Old Bank" below) also puts together a Skálanes package.

Where to Stay in & Around Seyðlsfjörður

The ferry from Europe arrives on Thursdays, so it's nearly impossible to find a room for Wednesday or Thursday nights in summer without booking far in advance. Early June is also difficult, because of the Á seyði festival. Many arriving passengers move on to Egilsstaðir, which has more choices and is only 26km (16 miles) away. Check with the tourist information office (p. 289), which can help book places to stay anywhere in the region.

The eco-friendly, offbeat **Hafalden Hostel,** Suðurgata 8 (www.hafaldan.is; ✆ **611-4410;** 7 units, none w/bathroom; 15,400kr double; 9,800kr sleeping-bag accommodation in four-person room; 600kr sheet rental; closed Oct 16– Apr 14), set in a hospital renovated in 2013, has straightforward bunk-bed rooms, free Wi-Fi, and access to a guest kitchen, Internet terminal, and washer. The common room, with large windows overlooking the fjord, is a perfect spot for writing postcards.

In Mjóifjörður, 30km (18 miles) away on the other side of the peninsula, **Sólbrekka** (www.mjoifjordur.weebly.com; ✆ **476-0007**) offers a few bedrooms with a guest kitchen, plus two cottages with small private kitchens (14,000kr double; 28,000kr cottage; 4,000kr sleeping-bag accommodation). A basic **cafe** (1–6pm daily July 1–Aug 15) serves sandwiches and cakes.

The Old Bank ★★ In a refurbished turn-of-the-20th-century building that once housed a bank and, before that, the nicest hotel in Iceland of the time, the Old Bank, aka Hótel Aldan, is east Iceland's most elegant hotel. The decor takes a nod from buildings past, outfitted with antique furnishings, embroidered rugs, and pinewood floors, with only modern bathrooms and flatscreen TVs bucking the trend. The layout is rather flexible, so most rooms can be combined to form suites or family rooms. Book well in advance for the summer, particularly around festival times.

Oddagata 6 (reception in Hótel Aldan restaurant, Norðurgata 2). www.hotelaldan.com. ✆ **472-1277.** 9 units. June–Aug 32,400kr double; 35,400kr triple/suite. Rates around 13% lower May and Sept; around 27% lower Oct–Apr. Rates include breakfast. **Amenities:** Laundry/dry-cleaning service for stays of 3 nights or more; free Wi-Fi.

Hótel Snæfell ★★ Part of the Hótel Aldan umbrella (above), Snæfell is set in a three-story wooden house that dates to 1908 and was used as a post office until 1943. It is situated by the mouth of the Fjardara River and has nice views of the bay. It's only a slightly simpler version of the Aldan.

Austurvegur 3 (reception in Hótel Aldan restaurant, Norðurgata 2). www.hotelaldan. com. ✆ **472-1277.** 9 units. June–Aug 26,200kr double; 32,000kr triple. Rates around 15% lower May–Sept; around 20% lower Oct and Apr. Rates include breakfast. Closed mid-Oct to Apr. **Amenities:** Free Wi-Fi.

Where to Eat in & Around Seyðlsfjörður

Hótel Aldan's Nordic Restaurant ★★ NORDIC Local, seasonal dishes are served at this stylish hotel restaurant with 1920s decor. Since opening in 2003, the small menus have become increasingly more sophisticated. The pan-seared Icelandic cod, always a safe bet, comes straight from the bay and is served with spiced cauliflower and hummus. On the meatier side, the rack of lamb has a nutty crust. Follow either with a hot rhubarb crumble or old-fashioned date cake. Tables in the smaller room have the best waterfront views.

Norðurgata 2. www.hotelaldan.com. ✆ **472-1277.** Reservations required. Main courses 3,100kr–4,600kr. May–Sept 15 daily 7:30–10am, 11:30am–2pm, and 6–10pm. Closed Sept 16–Apr.

Norð Austur ★★★ SUSHI Since 2015, one of the most exciting restaurant concepts in all of Iceland appears each summer in a sleek space above the Hótel Aldan's Nordic Restaurant. This annual pop-up pairs the seafood of the Eastern fjords with Japanese traditions, creating what many claim is Iceland's best sushi. Order a la carte or go for the eight-course omakase menu for original creations like deconstructed *fiskibollur* (fish balls) or cod ceviche.

Norðurgata 2. www.nordaustur.is. ✆ **787-4000.** Reservations required. Main courses 2,190kr–5,290kr; 8-course omakase 7,500kr. June-Aug Tue-Sun 5–10pm. Closed Sept–May.

Skaftfell ★ CAFE/BISTRO Come to this popular, art-themed bistro, housed in the Center for Visual Art, for the scene surrounding it more than the food. The vibrant setting features polished concrete floors and wood-panel walls lined with art, along with colorful red chairs and tables topped with the doodles of customers. The menu is less adventurous, featuring pizzas, a great veggie burger, lasagna, plus a range of cakes and coffees.

Austurvegur 42. www.skaftfell.is. ✆ **472-1633.** Reservations recommended Wed–Thurs in summer. Main courses 2,400kr–4,500kr; pizzas 1,500kr–2,300kr. May 1– Sept 30 Mon–Sun noon–9pm. Oct–April open weekends, or call ahead for group bookings.

BORGARFJÖRÐUR EYSTRI

Borgarfjörður Eystri ★★★ is one of Iceland's supreme hiking areas, but recognition has been slow in coming. Road access is bumpy and limited; some of the best trails are free of snow for only 3 months, from early June to early September; and the scenery lacks immediate, overwhelming visual impact. It's the second-biggest rhyolite area in Iceland, with mountainsides draped in silky swaths of minerals in bright shades, but it can't compete with Landmannalaugar. The fjords, inlets, and coastline are lovely but don't match the majestic grandeur of Seyðisfjörður or the staggering cliffs of Hornstrandir. The flowering plants may be the most beautiful and diverse in all of Iceland, yet the vegetation does not overtake the senses as it does in Þórsmörk. Put all of its assets together, however, and the comparisons fade away. Most hikers here are Icelanders, ahead of the tourist curve.

Borgarfjörður Eystri means "East Borgarfjörður," to distinguish it from Borgarfjörður in the west. The main village in the area, Bakkagerði, is in the fjord Borgarfjörður and sometimes refers to itself as Borgarfjörður. Borgarfjörður Eystri can refer to the village, the fjord, the village and the fjord, or the entire municipality, north to Njarðvík and south to Loðmundarfjörður.

Getting the best of Borgarfjörður Eystri requires venturing far from the village of Bakkagerði and ideally spending 2 or more nights by the abandoned inlets of Breiðavík, Húsavík, and Loðmundarfjörður, which have mountain huts with 4WD access. Trails are well-marked and signposted, and there are excellent arranged tours.

Essentials

GETTING THERE   Bakkagerði is 71km (44 miles) from Egilsstaðir. From the Ring Road, take Route 92 through Egilsstaðir, turn left on Route 93, and turn left again 1km (⅔ mile) later on Route 94, which goes all the way to Bakkagerði. Transportation between Egilsstaðir and Bakkagerði is available in the postal van with **Jakob Sigurðsson** (hlid@centrum.is; ℂ 472-9805 or 894-8305). Tickets are 2,500kr adults, 2,000kr seniors, and 1,500kr for children ages 12 and under. Departures are on summer weekdays only, leaving Bakkagerði at 8am and the Egilsstaðir tourist information office at noon.

VISITOR INFORMATION   Egilsstaðir's tourist information office (p. 281) covers this area and is a good place to buy a map. In Bakkagerði, limited tourist information is available at **Alfasteinn** and the **Fjarðarborg** tourist office (fjardarborg@simnet.is; ℂ 472-9920 or 848-5515; June–Aug daily noon–10pm), both of which should stock maps. The best website is **www.borgarfjordureystri.is**. The essential map **"Víknaslóðir: Trails of the Deserted Inlets,"** with trail descriptions in English, costs 1,050kr and is widely available in the summer.

Group & Self-Guided Tours

You can arrange camping or lodging at the three mountain huts independently, but guided tours have definite advantages. Tour companies have 4WD access all the way south to Loðmundarfjörður and can transport baggage and food. Guides are also well-versed in local history, geology, flora, and fauna, and can lead you to that unique milky waterfall, rare wildflower, or elf church off the main trail routes.

Ferðafélag Fljótsdalshéraðs (www.fljotsdalsherad.is/ferdafelag; ferdafelag@ egilsstadir.is; ℘ 863-5813) operates the mountain huts at Breiðavík, Húsavík, and Loðmundarfjörður and occasionally leads tours in the area.

Elftours (Ferðaþjónustan Álfheimar), Borgarfjörður Eystri (www. alfheimar.com; ℘ 471-2010), offers tours of Borgarfjörður Eystri under the heading "Myths and Magical Mountains." Costs start from 112,000kr for 3-day tours, including accommodations in double rooms, transportation from Egilsstaðir, a local guide, a day tour to Mývatn, and full board.

Hafþór Snjólfur Helgason (hshelgason@gmail.com; ℘ 472-9913), in Bakkagerði, leads trips and knows everything about the area. He can also put together **self-guided tours,** with food and supplies delivered to the huts. Four-wheel-drive delivery services are offered by Fjarðarborg and Guesthouse Borg; see p. 298. You can drive the routes yourself in a 4WD vehicle.

Exploring the Area

Route 94 traverses Fljótsdalshérað Valley before entering Borgarfjörður Eystri through a dramatic mountain pass. From Fljótsdalshérað, **Mt. Dyrfjöll**—distinctively notched, like the blunt end of a razorblade—is visible on the right. After the mountain pass, the road descends steeply into **Njarðvík,** a tiny settlement northwest of Bakkagerði. Near the bottom of the descent, on the right-hand side of the road, look for a sign for **Innra-Hvannagil ★**, a narrow rhyolite gorge. A 5-minute trail leads from the parking area into the gorge, which has banks of rock shards, a vertical surface of intricately patterned stone, and a stream running over slabs of gleaming yellow rhyolite. Walking farther into the gorge is impossible.

After Njarðvík, the road follows a sinuous, knuckle-whitening coastal route along the **Njarðvíkurskriður** (Njarðvík Screes), steep banks of loose rock at the base of the cliffs and mountains. On the ocean side is the **Naddakross,** a wooden cross with the Latin inscription *Effigem Christi qui transit pronus honora. Anno 1306* ("You who pass the sign of Christ, bow your head in reverence. Year 1306"). This marks the legendary spot where, in 1306, a farmer named Jón Árnason killed a half-human, cave-dwelling monster named Naddi by wrestling him into the ocean. Naddi had been gnawing loudly on rocks and striking terror into the hearts of anyone crossing the screes after nightfall. The present cross dates from the 1950s.

BAKKAGERÐI (BORGARFJÖRÐUR) ★

Njarðvík and Bakkagerði are the only inhabited parts of Borgarfjörður Eystri, with a total population of around 145. Borgarfjörður has a nice seaweedy **beach,** and seals often congregate on the eastern shores. A **submarine mine** from World War II is mounted along the main road. On the south side of the village, the Álfacafé store and cafe, Iðngarðar (℘ **472-9900;** May 20–Aug

In polls, only about 20% of Icelanders rule out the existence of elves. Construction projects can still be thwarted by fears of disturbing elf dwellings. In 1996, as ground was prepared for a graveyard in a Reykjavík suburb, two bulldozers leveling a suspected elf hill mysteriously broke down. Elf arbitrators were called in. "We're going to see whether we can't reach an understanding with the elves," the project supervisor told Iceland's daily newspaper, *Morgunblaðið*.

Many Icelanders are tired of being asked if they really believe in elves, because they can't give a simple yes or no answer. Saying "yes" would not mean they believe, in the most literal sense, that little people emerge from rocks every night and dance around. And saying "no" would not mean they dismiss related supernatural concepts and phenomena.

Icelanders by necessity have always been strongly attuned to their strange and harsh environment. Spend enough time outdoors in Iceland's long twilights—which play strange tricks on the eyes—and Icelanders' unwillingness to rule out hidden people starts to make intuitive sense.

daily 11am–8pm, Sept–May 11am–5pm), sells souvenirs made from rock, including candle holders, clocks, and, of course, trolls.

Borgarfjörður takes its name from Álfaborg, the rocky hill behind the village. Álfaborg is home to the elf queen herself—the name translates either to "elf rock" or "elf town." A stroll up the hill is a pleasant way to orient yourself to the valley. At the top is a view disc identifying the surrounding mountains.

Bakkagerðiskirkja ★ is a 1901 church, and aligned facing the fjord, rather than east–west, like every other Icelandic church of its day. According to local legend, the town planned to build the church on top of the Álfaborg, but an elf appeared to a town elder in a dream and requested the current site. Bakkagerðiskirkja hosts the town's most treasured possession: an **altarpiece painting** of Christ on the Mount by Jóhannes S. Kjarval. Christ stands on what looks like a miniature Álfaborg, with the unmistakable outline of Dyrfjöll in the background. The townspeople commissioned the painting in 1914, when Kjarval was 29 and studying in Copenhagen. Iceland's bishop hated the painting and refused to consecrate it.

On the main street is **Lindarbakki,** an oft-photographed, turf-roofed house with reindeer horns over the door. If you knock, the friendly summer resident will probably invite you in to sign the Gestabók. Note the now-framed rat skeleton she found in the wall.

Six kilometers (3¾ miles) northeast of the village, next to the fishing boat dock, **Hafnarhólmi** ★ has two excellent platforms for viewing puffins and cliff-nesting birds. The best time to visit is in the morning or late afternoon, when puffins are least likely to be off fishing. The platforms are closed in May for nesting season, and open from 11am to 7pm in June and July. In August, the platforms are open 24 hours, though the puffins disappear by mid-month. The fence atop the cliff is to prevent puffins from digging burrows in the territory of eider ducks, whose nest feathers are harvested once the nests have been abandoned. The lower platform is ideal for observing the kittiwakes.

HIKING ROUTES

As mentioned above, "Víknaslóðir: Trails of the Deserted Inlets" is essential for exploring the region. Trails are well-marked from the main road, and a map is posted at each trailhead. The best time for hiking is from early July to early September, though many routes are clear of snow by June. In late August you can eat your fill of *krækiber* (black crowberries)—keep an eye out for the rare albino variety. The weather is rainier in September.

The best trips in Borgarfjörður Eystri last 2 to 7 days, but if you have just 1 day (and no access to a 4WD vehicle), the two best **day hikes** are to Stórurð and Brúnavík. Both destinations take around 5 to 6 hours round-trip.

Stórurð ★★ is a mystical jumble of oddly-shaped boulders around a blue-green stream and pond with grassy banks. Don't come before early July, when the snow lifts. The best trail route (marked #9 on the "Víknaslóðir" map) starts at the 431m (1,414-ft.) Vatnskarð pass on Route 94, west of Njarðvík, and crosses the 634m (2,080-ft.) Geldingafjall peak, before descending into Stórurð. This trail has some ankle-twisting stretches of loose gravel and scree. Somewhat easier trails (#8 and #10) reach Stórurð from different parts of the road, but #9 has the best approach to Stórurð, as well as astounding views of Njarðvík, Fljótsdalshérað Valley, and even Snæfell and Vatnajökull.

Brúnavík ★★, the first cove east of Borgarfjörður, has a lovely beach of rhyolite sand and was inhabited by two families until 1944. Two trails lead to Brúnavík from the coastal road on Borgarfjörður's eastern side. For the dramatic descent into Brúnavík, the best circular route is clockwise, heading to Brúnavík through the 345m (1,132-ft.) Brúnavíkurskarð Pass (the trail marked #19 on the map) and returning through the 321m (1,053-ft.) Hofstrandarskarð Pass (trail #20).

The trails and 4WD tracks—and the best **multi-day trips**—extend all the way south to **Loðmundarfjörður,** or perhaps even to Seyðisfjörður. Loðmundarfjordur had 87 residents at the outset of the 20th century, but the last ones left in 1973 after failing to convince authorities to build a road around the coast from Seyðisfjörður. A partially restored 1891 church is still standing but stays locked up. (Húsavík also has a cute church near the ocean; it dates from the late 1930s and always remains open.)

The scenic highlights of Borgarfjörður Eystri are manifold, but **Hvítserkur** should be singled out, as many consider it the most strangely beautiful mountain in Iceland. The main bulk is pale-rose rhyolite, but glacial erosion has exposed dark basaltic ribbons that look like paint splattered by Jackson Pollock. Hvítserkur's best side faces south, and can be seen from Húsavik and the 4WD road leading there.

Where to Stay

The **mountain huts** at Breiðavík *(Breiðuvíkurskáli)* and Húsavík *(Húsavíkurskáli)* are operated by **Ferðafélag Fljótsdalshéraðs** (ferdafelag@egilsstadir. is; ☏ **863-5813**). The Breiðavík hut has a warden in the morning and evening. Both huts sleep 33 in bunks (5,500kr adults; 2,250kr children ages 7–12), and neither has reception for phones.

Camping is allowed at Bakkagerði (next to the Breiðavík), Húsavík, and Loðmundarfjörður mountain huts (2,000kr per night).

Álfheimar ★ This sustainable country hotel on a family farm is operated by a tour agency that offers various trips around Borgarfjörður Eystri. The rooms are divided among three buildings and are simple yet spacious. All come with private bathrooms and patios, with some adding sea views. The small **restaurant** uses fresh food from local fisherman and small-scale farmers.

Álfheimar, Borgarfjörður Eystri. www.alfheimar.com. ☏ **471-2010.** 32 units w/bathroom. 30,800kr double. Rates include breakfast. Closed Sept–May. **Amenities:** Restaurant; free Wi-Fi.

Blabjorg Guesthouse ★ Rooms in this bright, clean guesthouse, designed from a former fish factory, are equipped with underfloor heating, and most look over the water. A studio apartment has a separate living area and kitchen, making it perfect for a small family or two couples. The two- and three-bedroom apartments are also good for families or groups. The property has a small **wellness center** that includes a hot tub and infrared sauna, plus an outdoor wooden barrel sauna and wooden hot tub; guests get a discount.

Gamla Frystihusid, Borgarfjörður Eystri www.blabjorg.com. ☏ **861-1792.** 11 units w/ bathroom. 16,800kr double; from 35,000kr apartment. Closed Sept–May. **Amenities:** Spa; shared kitchen; free Wi-Fi in public areas.

Guesthouse Borg-Njardvík ★ Set in two separate houses, the basic rooms here come with access to shared bathrooms, a lounge, and a kitchen. There are on-site laundry facilities and breakfast, and a to-go lunch bag can also be arranged.

Bakkagerði, 720 Borgarfjörður Eystri (off Rte. 946). ☏ **472-9870.** 11 units, none w/ bathroom. 19,450kr double. Breakfast available (1,800kr). **Amenities:** Guest kitchen; free Wi-Fi.

Where to Eat

Consider stocking up at Egilsstaðir's **supermarkets** before heading to Borgarfjörður Eystri. Since Bakkagerði has few dining options, all places to stay have guest kitchens, and food must be brought in to mountain huts. From June to August, the community office **Fjarðarborg** (above) offers passable burgers, soup, sandwiches, vegetable pitas, lamb chops, and fried fish from 11:30am to 9pm daily. Main courses are 1,800kr to 3,800kr. Álfacafé (p. 295) has a limited cafe serving drinks, snack food, and 1,950kr servings of tasty fish soup with traditional Icelandic brown-rye flatbread.

FLJÓTSDALSHÉRAÐ VALLEY

Fljótsdalshérað is the broad, flat valley that extends from Egilsstaðir northeast to the ocean, providing an outlet for two major rivers, Jökulsá á Brú (aka Jökulsá á Dal) and Lagarfljót. The Jökulsá á Brú has been drastically affected by the Kárahnjúkar Dam (p. 286), far upstream. The diversion of water and blockage of sediments is disrupting the local ecosystem and could devastate the hundreds of seals that breed in the river delta. Nonetheless, the valley—walled in by mountains, with plenty of pretty farms and bird ponds—is a beautiful place to do some **horseback riding.**

Want to feel totally removed from the world in an adorable rustic farmhouse, cooking your own meals and riding horseback along peaceful ocean beaches, grasslands, and riverbanks in search of birds and seals? If so, **Húsey** ★ (www. husey.de; ✆ **471-3010** or 847-8229), a picturesque farm at the headwaters of the Jökulsá á Brú, is the place for you. Horse trips are tailored for both beginners and experts and range from 2-hour seal-watching jaunts to 2-day excursions to a historic farmstead. Non-riders may be perfectly content walking the trails. Breakfast is available for 2,000kr, but all other food must be brought in and can be prepared in the guest kitchen. For more places to stay, visit **www. fljotsdalsherad.is.**

The drive from Egilsstaðir to Húsey is about an hour. Take the Ring Road north for 26km (16 miles), then turn right on Route 925, just before the Jökulsá á Brú bridge (ignore the earlier junction with Rte. 925). At the farm Litlibakki, as Route 925 turns off to the right, go straight on Route 926 and continue to the end. If you need a ride, inquire at Húsey. For up to six people, the round-trip price is 19,200kr from Egilsstaðir, or you can get a lift to the main road for 11,200kr for bus connections to Akureyri, Egilsstaðir, and Höfn. A taxi will cost far more.

EGILSSTAÐIR TO MÝVATN

The lonely 167km (104 miles) stretch of the Ring Road between Egilsstaðir and Mývatn can be a blur of barren, gravelly plains—but it also affords beautiful vistas, especially on a clear day when Mt. Herðubreið is visible to the south. Make sure your gas tank is full before setting out.

Almost halfway from Egilsstaðir to Mývatn and 13km (8 miles) south of the Ring Road, **Sænautasel** ★ (✆ **892-8956**)—a reconstructed turf farm on a 60km-long (37-mile) heathland called Jökuldalsheiði—is a great detour to break up the trip. Sænautasel was abandoned in 1875 after the Askja eruption fouled the area with ash. In 1992, a descendant of Sænautasel's first settler reconstructed the original farm, which now welcomes visitors daily from June through August 31 (10am–10pm). To reach Sænautasel, exit the Ring Road at its western junction with Route 901, roughly 70km (43 miles) northwest of Egilsstaðir. A few kilometers later, turn left on Route 907 and continue for another 10 minutes. After desolate expanses of nothingness, the road arrives at a vision from another age: two turf-roofed houses next to a pleasant lake surrounded by vegetation. Pancakes and coffee are served inside the **Welcome building.** Admission to the farmhouse, close to the Welcome building, costs 850kr for adults, and is free for children 11 and under.

Buses connecting Egilsstaðir and Mývatn stop at **Möðrudalur,** an isolated sheep-farming settlement along Route 901, 8km (5 miles) south of Route 901's western junction with the Ring Road. Möðrudalur dates back to the Saga Age, and at 469m (1,539 ft.) above sea level, it is Iceland's highest working farm. **Fjallakaffi** (www.fjalladyrd.is; 𝄐 **471-1858** or 894-8181) offers pastries, lamb and vegetable soups, sandwiches, and hot dogs. The owners can also arrange 4WD trips to Vatnajökull, Askja, and Kverkfjöll.

THE INTERIOR

Almost a third of Iceland is covered by highland plateaus blanketed with volcanic gravel, and punctuated only by glacial rivers, scattered mountains and lakes, smatterings of vegetation, and perhaps a stray boulder. Amid this pristine desert wasteland, visitors often pose for pictures next to directional signs at road junctions. The signs seem to point nowhere, and, in the photo, the visitor invariably grins at the absurdity—and otherworldly beauty—of the scene. The Apollo astronauts ventured to Iceland's interior to train for moon walks, and until moon tourism is a reality, this place may be the closest substitute.

Known as the *hálendið*, or highlands in Icelandic, the interior is often described as Europe's last great untouched wilderness. This is somewhat misleading, as much of the land was vegetated before settlers and their voracious sheep first arrived.

Early settlers often traversed the interior for parliamentary meetings at Þingvellir, but many routes were closed when temperatures cooled in the 13th century and, with the advent of the ring road and interior flights centuries later, were never resurrected. In popular mythology, the interior became a refuge for outlaws and outcasts, much like the Wild West in the American imagination.

The two main south–north routes through the interior are Kjölur, in the western half of the country, and Sprengisandur, right in the middle. The Kjölur Route is relatively hospitable, and can be crossed easily in a 4WD vehicle. The Sprengisandur Route passes through Iceland's most fantastically bleak territory, with more hazardous road conditions. Farther east is the **Askja caldera,** a dramatic ring of mountains formed largely in the aftermath of a catastrophic 1875 eruption.

South of Askja is **Kverkfjöll,** where intense geothermal activity and the Vatnajökull glacier surreally converge. Some interior highland destinations find their place elsewhere in this book, notably **Landmannalaugar** and **Þórsmörk** in the south (chapter 8), **Snæfell** in the east (chapter 9), and the **Kaldidalur Route** in the west (chapter 6).

Travel season into the interior is generally restricted to midsummer, though a snowstorm is never out of the question. In July, the sparse plant life heroically blooms, but August is prettier, because more snow has lifted. Higher water levels can make river crossings more difficult in July, when it can also be buggier.

High winds and severe temperature fluctuations are endemic to the highlands. Volcanic sands are lightweight and swirl easily in the wind, so eye and face protection can be crucial. Driving in the interior presents serious challenges; see "Getting Around," in chapter 11 (p. 318), for details, and don't forget to check the website of the **Public Roads Administration** (www. vegagerdin.is) before setting off; it lists road closings and hazards in real time.

KJÖLUR ROUTE

Leaving aside the much shorter Kaldidalur Route in the west, Kjölur—which runs from Geysir and Gullfoss in the southwest to Húnaflói and Skagafjörður in the north—is the most accessible, most trafficked, and least barren route through Iceland's highland interior. The highest point of the road, 600m (1,968 ft.) above sea level, is in the valley between Langjökull and Hofsjökull, Iceland's second- and third-largest glaciers. Strictly speaking, Kjölur refers only to this valley, but the word commonly applies to the entire 165km (103 miles) course of mountain road F35. Kjölur is often called a "shortcut" to Akureyri, but this only makes sense if you're already near Geysir and Gullfoss—*and* you have a 4WD car.

Essentials

GETTING THERE The Kjölur Route opens in early- to mid-June, and can remain open even into October. If you're **driving,** note that the region has no gas stations, so be sure to fill your tank before setting out and bring gas cans for the rest of the way.

From mid-July through August, **SBA Norðurleið** (www.sba.is; ✆ **550-0700**) connects Reykjavík and Akureyri via Kjölur 4 days a week for most of the year (mid-June until early Sept), in both directions, leaving Reykjavík at 8am and Akureyri at 8:30am. The price is 17,900kr one-way and includes stops at Hveragerði, Selfoss, Geysir, Gullfoss, Hvítárnes, Kerlingarfjöll, Hveravellir, Svartábrú, and Varmahlíð, with short sightseeing breaks at Geysir, Gullfoss, and Hveravellir. The total trip takes 12 hours in either direction.

VISITOR INFORMATION The best information sources for Kjölur are the people or groups who run accommodations along the route. The hiking group **Ferðafélag** Íslands (www.fi.is; ✆ **568-2533**) operates several mountain huts around Kjölur and has the most regional expertise. The folks at **Ásgarður** (www.kerlingarfjoll.is; ✆ **894-2132**) know the Kerlingarfjöll area, while **Hveravallafélag** (www.hveravellir.is; ✆ **452-4200** or 894-1293) maintains Hveravellir, and has maps of all hiking routes from there.

Outdoor Activities

HIKING Ferðafélag Íslands (www.fi.is; ✆ **568-2533**), Iceland's premier hiking group, leads a few multi-day trips around Kjölur each year.

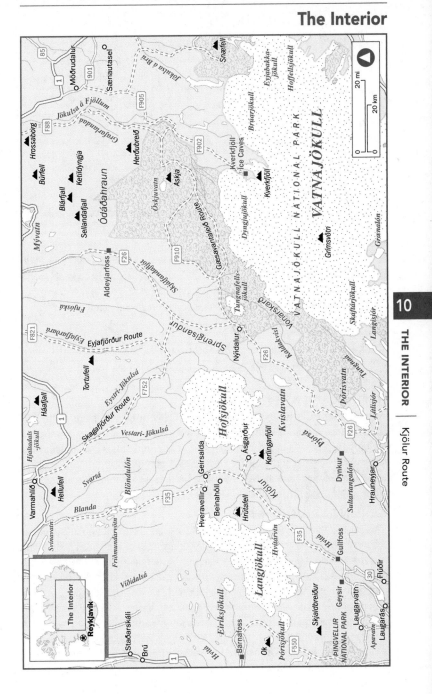

THE KJÖLURVEGUR trek

The **Kjölurvegur** ★★ (aka Kjalvegur) is a rewarding and very manageable 3-day hike along an old horse trail from Hvítárnes to Hveravellir, with mountain huts spaced at 4- to 6-hour (12–14km/7½–9-mile) intervals. The route skirts Langjökull, with interesting but optional detours from the Þjófadalir hut east through the Kjalhraun lava field or west toward Langjökull. Buses stop at both ends of the Kjölurvegur, though you'll have to walk the 6km (4 miles) from Route F35 to the Hvítárnes hut. (Reserving bus seats in advance is recommended.) Online, **www.fi.is** has a day-by-day breakdown of the route—under the heading "Hveravellir–Hvítárnes (the Old Kjalvegur Hiking Trail)"—but it takes you from north to south. Hiking south to north lets you end the trek with a valedictory dunk in Hveravellir's **geothermal pool.** To reserve space in the huts, see "Where to Stay," p. 305.

HORSEBACK RIDING Two of Iceland's most reputable stables run Kjölur tours on horseback. The Íshestar (www.ishestar.is; ✆ **555-7000;** 327,000kr per person) tour is 7 days, as is the one from **Eldhestar** (www.eldhestar.is; ✆ **480-4800;** 313,400kr per person); both give you 6 days in the saddle. Food, accommodation, and transportation are included.

Exploring the Area

The map "Kjölur: Arnarvatnsheiði–Kerlingarfjöll," available at tourist offices and online at **www.nordicstore.net,** has good detail on hiking and driving routes.

HVÍTÁRVATN & HVÍTARNES ★

Around 45km (28 miles) northeast of Gullfoss, a turnoff from Route F35 leads 6km (4 miles) to Hvítárnes, a well-vegetated, marshy plain overlooking Hvítárvatn, a broad aquamarine lake, its surface sometimes dotted with floating icebergs calved from Langjökull. The scenery is austere but captivating, and the Hvítárnes mountain hut, built in 1930, is a charming throwback, with white gables and turf-insulated side walls.

KERLINGARFJÖLL ★★

This vast volcanic system near the southwest corner of Hofsjökull is one of the most glorious and underappreciated hiking areas in Iceland. The highland scenery is astounding, with peaks ranging in height from 800m to 1,477m (2,625 ft.–4,846 ft.); rhyolite mountainsides in spectral shadings of red, yellow, and green; shimmering glaciers; chiseled ravines; and steaming geothermal hotspots, some with swimmable ponds and springs. If Landmannalaugar is not on your itinerary, Kerlingarfjöll is a very worthy alternative, with comfortable accommodations. Spending 2 or 3 nights here is an ideal way to break up the Kjölur Route. The website **www.kerlingarfjoll.is** has downloadable maps of all the hiking trails.

Kerlingarfjöll is reached via Route F347, which branches off from Route F35 about halfway between Hvítárnes and Hveravellir. The places to stay at Ásgarður (see below) are about 10km (6 miles) down the road. If you're coming by bus, note that the SBA bus can drop you at the crossroads, but only the Trex bus goes right to Ásgarður.

HVERAVELLIR ★

About 93km (58 miles) from Gullfoss, Route F735 detours 2km (1¼ miles) from Route F35 to reach Hveravellir (Hot Spring Plains), an intriguing geothermal hot spot and Kjölur's main summer service hub, with a restaurant, bar, small market, and sleeping-bag accommodation in mountain huts. There is no filling station here, but they have a supply of fuel for emergencies. Hveravellir's weather station is staffed year-round, providing one of Iceland's best jobs for loners. The geothermal field is worth a stop, especially to bathe in the waist-deep pool, or to see Öskurhólshver, a white-crusted conical fumarole hissing eggy steam. Stick to the boardwalks to protect both yourself and the land. Hveravellir is also a terminus for the Kjölurvegur trek; see box, p. 304.

Where to Stay & Eat

The only **restaurants** along the Kjölur Route are at Ásgarður (in Kerlingarfjöll) and Hveravellir, which also has a small **market.**

For mountain huts in **Hvítárnes** and along the **Kjölurvegur Route** (except for Hveravellir), sleeping-bag space must be reserved online and at least 1 month in advance through **Ferðafélag** Íslands (www.fi.is; ✆ **568-2533;** 6,000kr per person per night). All huts have kitchens but no utensils. None have showers, and only Hvítárnes has a warden. All food must be brought in, and all rubbish must be packed out.

At **Kerlingarfjöll,** from mid-June until the end of September, **Ásgarður** (www.kerlingarfjoll.is; ✆ **664-7878**) offers a wide range of lodging, from sleeping-bag accommodation in a bunk room for 28 people (5,800kr) to a hotel with 20 double rooms with private bathrooms (32,500kr) to chalets for up to six people (54,000kr). All rates include breakfast. Facilities include guest kitchens, a restaurant, and a bathhouse with showers and hot tubs. All cottages have heat and electricity, and the website outlines rooming options, with photos.

The mountain huts at **Hveravellir** are run by **Hveravallafélag** (www. hveravellir.is; ✆ **452-4200** or 894-1293; 7,500kr sleeping-bag accommodation) and are open between June and September (depending on weather conditions and road access). One hut has three bedrooms and sleeps 33, while the other sleeps 20 and is split into three rooms. Both have fully equipped kitchens and hot water. It's possible to book meals in advance; otherwise, soup and sandwiches are available. Private rooms sleep up to three (28,800kr; 1,500kr for linens or breakfast). Just off the Kjölur Route, 38 km (23.6 miles) north of Hveravellir, the Áfangi Mountain Hut sleeps 32 in eight rooms with bunk beds (7,500kr per person), plus adds a kitchen, dining area, and hot pot.

SPRENGISANDUR ROUTE

Sprengisandur, the desert expanse at Iceland's heart, is a true moonscape—so much so, in fact, that some conspiracy theorists believe this is where the U.S. government "faked" the moon landing. Such bleak, lifeless scenery is transporting and sublime to some, depressing and monotonous to others, but on a clear day, no one can fail to be impressed by the grand tableau of mountains and glaciers in all directions. If you've ever doubted that the world is round, come here and witness the sky arching overhead.

The Sprengisandur Route, the longest stretch between north and south, has no strict beginning or end, but loosely corresponds to Route F26, which spans 196km (122 miles) from the Hrauneyjar highland area to the Aldeyjarfoss waterfall. However desolate the route, opportunities for exploration abound.

Essentials

GETTING THERE

BY CAR With its rough surfaces and hazardous river fords, Route F26 is only for rugged 4WD vehicles with good clearance. The road's opening date varies, but usually falls at the end of June or early July. The **Public Roads Administration** (www.vegagerdin.is; ✆ **522-1000** or the inland service ✆ **1777**; weekdays May–Oct 8am–4pm, Nov–April 6:30–10pm) continually monitors road conditions; but for the latest on water levels or other dangers at river crossings, the warden at **Nýidalur** (✆ **854-1194**) is the better source. Traffic on the Sprengisandur Route has increased greatly, so in high season—as long as you stick to Route F26—driving in convoy is not a necessary precaution.

From the south, Route F26 is reached via Route 26 or Route 32; for sights en route, see "Þjórsárdalur & Hekla," p. 232.

Three significant interior routes branch off from Route F26. A few kilometers north of Nýidalur, Route F910 links Route F26 to Askja. This road—also known as the **Gæsavantaleið Route**—has incredible scenery but should only be attempted by experienced drivers in convoy; allow 9 hours from Nýidalur to Askja's Drekagil huts. Route F752, also known as the **Skagafjörður Route,** links Route F26 to the town of Varmahlíð and Skagafjörður. Routes F881 and F821, jointly known as the **Eyjafjörður Route,** link Route F26 to Akureyri. At its north end, Route F26 connects with Route 842, which leads 41km (25 miles) through the Bjarðardalur valley to the Ring Road near Goðafoss. The northern end of Route F26 is far more dependable than the Skagafjörður and Eyjafjörður routes, which are sometimes closed to traffic altogether.

BY BUS **Reykjavík Excursions** (www.re.is; ✆ **562-1011**) connects Landmannalaugar and Lake Mývatn via the Sprengisandur Route from July 3 to August 31. Departures from Mývatn (Reykjahlíð) are on Fridays at 8am, and

> ### Last Gas for 149 Miles!
>
> Fuel is not available on Route F26, and the service stations at Hrauneyjar and Goðafoss are 240km (149 miles) apart. (Unprepared drivers are often seen begging for fuel at Nýidalur.)

departures from Landmannalaugar are on Thursdays, also at 8:30am. The full one-way trip lasts 10 hours and costs 18,000kr, with stops at Hrauneyjar, Nýidalur, and Skútustaðir, plus sightseeing breaks at the Aldeyjarfoss and Goðafoss waterfalls. Passengers taking the bus from Mývatn to Landmannalaugar must wait until the following day for connections to Reykjavík and elsewhere. The duration of stops can differ, so be sure to keep informed of the time: You don't want to be left behind in no-man's land. The Sprengisandur Route is included in the **Iceland On Your Own** bus package deal (p. 324).

VISITOR INFORMATION

No specific tourist information office is assigned to the Sprengisandur Route, but regional offices in Hveragerði, Varmahlíð, Akureyri, and Mývatn can provide help. The **Hrauneyjar Highland Center** (www.hrauneyjar.is; ✆ **487-7782**) is a useful resource, and the warden at **Nýidalur** (✆ **860-3334**; July–Aug) is usually happy to answer questions.

Tours

HORSEBACK RIDING   Eldhestar (www.eldhestar.is; ✆ **480-4800**) offers an 8-day Sprengisandur traverse with 6 days spent on the saddle (382,400kr).

Exploring the Area

At the northern end of Route F26, make sure to stop at the enthralling waterfall **Aldeyjarfoss** (p. 201).

Hrauneyjar Highland Center, a year-round highland oasis at the southern terminus of the Sprengisandur Route, has a hotel and restaurant (see "Where to Stay & Eat," below), an information desk, and the last service station for the next 240km (149 miles). A trail map of the surrounding area is available at reception.

As a base, Hrauneyjar is best for those with their own 4WD transport. The Highland Center arranges tours only for groups, and the best local destinations—such as the **Veiðivötn lakes** (below), or the lovely **Dynkur** ★, a waterfall on the Þjórsá river—are inaccessible to regular cars. Hrauneyjar is especially handy for visitors who want to explore Landmannalaugar by day and then retire to a private room with a made-up bed. Landmannalaugar is an hour from Hrauneyjar via Route F208, which opens up in late June.

The Hrauneyjar area has some excellent fishing, and the Highland Center sells permits and rents rods. Prices are steep, however, with permits starting around 2,000kr per rod, per day in lakes.

VEIÐIVÖTN ★

Trout fishermen are particularly drawn to this idyllic and peaceful cluster of 50 volcanic crater lakes, located close to Landmannalaugar but accessed through Hrauneyjar on Route F228. Fishing permits (9,000kr per rod, per day) and sleeping-bag accommodation (10,500kr per person) in four bunk-style cottages are handled by the **Landmannahellir tourist service** (www.landmannahellir.is; ✆ **893-8407**). Make sure to book well in advance; accommodation and fishing permits are usually sold out by April.

NÝIDALUR ★

An overnight stay at this remote desert outpost, combined with a day hike east to **Vonarskarð Pass ★★**, makes for a memorable episode along the Sprengisandur Route. Nýidalur is right on Route F26, about 120km (74 miles) from Hrauneyjar and 20km (12 miles) from the northwest corner of Vatnajökull. Vonarskarð forms a dramatic saddle between Vatnajökull and the small glacier Tungnafellsjökull, and the hiking route skirts some restless geothermal fields. Sudden releases of glacial meltwater can make stream crossings difficult, so speak to the warden before setting out. Those just passing through Nýidalur can take the short easy hike east with panoramic views.

Where to Stay & Eat

No food is sold anywhere on the 240km (149-mile) stretch between Hrauneyjar and Goðafoss.

Hrauneyjar may be the last outpost at the desert frontier, but for those with 4WD vehicles, it's also a central base for exploring Þjórsárdalur, Hekla, Landmannalaugar, and Veiðivötn. Hrauneyjar's two hotels, run by the same management, are 1.4km (1 mile) apart, and each has a restaurant (see below).

The **Nýidalur mountain huts** (© 860-3334; 7,000kr sleeping-bag accommodation; July–Aug) sleep 79 people and are operated by **Ferðafélag Íslands** (www.fi.is; © 568-2533). Advance bookings can be made online, but walk-ins are usually accommodated. Showers cost an additional 400kr, and the kitchen has pans and utensils. Camping in the area costs 1,600kr per person. All food must be brought in. Come prepared to sleep in a packed room with 30 other visitors, or in tiny bunks for two.

The Highland Center ★ The only real high-end accommodation in the entire Icelandic highlands, as recently as 2005 this hotel was still a rustic farmstead. Although it won't win any design awards, the fact that the property has the array of amenities that it does—a hot tub, flatscreen TVs, a helipad, and Northern Lights wakeup calls—is quite a feat. Sleeping-bag rooms are more basic, but after any time in the desert, the hotel's hot water and electricity will feel like the Four Seasons. There's even a full-service **restaurant ★** (dinner only) on-site, open from 7 to 10pm with the standard mix of sandwiches or meat dishes (main courses 1,400kr–3,700kr).

Rte. 26, Hrauneyjar. www.thehighlandcenter.is. © **487-7750**. 91 units. June 15–Sept 27,000kr–35,000kr double; 14,600kr sleeping-bag accommodation. Rates include breakfast. **Amenities:** Restaurant; bar; hot tub; sauna; free Wi-Fi.

ASKJA, KVERKFJÖLL & EASTERN INTERIOR ROUTES

Among the scenic landmarks of Iceland's desert highlands, the vast stratovolcano **Askja ★★** is the most visited—and not just for its stark, elemental beauty and grandeur. If the weather cooperates, you can take a warm, unforgettable swim in a crater lake of milky-blue, sulfurous water. Trips to Askja often extend to **Kverkfjöll** ★★, a mountain spur protruding from the northern margin of Vatnajökull amid a bleak expanse of rugged hills and gritty lava. The Kverkfjöll region is suffused with geothermal activity, and hot springs sculpt elaborate ice caves as they emerge from the glacier's edge.

These areas can only be accessed in sturdy 4WD vehicles or on group tours. The only places to stay are mountain huts, and all food must be brought in. Clear skies can switch suddenly to rain, and snowstorms can arise even in midsummer. Askja can be reached on day tours from the Mývatn, but seeing Kverkfjöll requires at least 1 night away from Instagram. Two nights at Kverkfjöll should be the minimum, because the best hikes take a full day.

Essentials

GETTING THERE The 4WD roads to Askja and Kverkfjöll generally remain open from mid-June through mid-September or later. No mountain roads (designated by an "F" before the route number) in the region have fuel stops. Inexperienced drivers may have trouble negotiating rock shards, potholes, and fords over rivers.

The standard route to **Askja** is Route F88, which branches off from the Ring Road (Route 1) 32km (20 miles) east of Mývatn and stretches 95km (59 miles) to the Drekagil mountain hut at Askja's outskirts. From there, it's a bouncy 8km (5 miles) drive on Route F894 to the Vikraborgir parking area, a 2.5km (1½-mile) walk from Víti crater in central Askja.

Drivers headed from Askja to **Kverkfjöll** backtrack from Drekagil on Route F88 and then take Route F910 southeast to Route F902 (confusingly, another branch of Route F910 heads directly from Drekagil west to Nýidalur in Sprengisandur). Those headed straight from the Ring Road to Kverkfjöll usually start on Route F905 (by the Möðrudalur filling station/cafe, 65km/40 miles east of Mývatn) and then take Route F910 to Route F902. The distance from Möðrudalur to the Sigurðarskáli hut at Kverkfjöll is 108km (67 miles).

For **bus travel** to Askja and Kverkfjöll, see "Tours," below.

VISITOR INFORMATION Offices in Akureyri, Mývatn, and Egilsstaðir can all provide information on the Askja and Kverkfjöll region. For consultation on hikes in the Askja area, contact **Ferðafélag Akureyrar** (p. 313). This group runs the mountain huts at **Þorsteinsskáli,** Route F88, at Herðubreiðarlindir (© **822-5191**), and **Drekagil,** Route F88, at Drekagil (© **853-2541**), and the hut wardens have current information on road and weather conditions. For hikes in the Kverkfjöll area, the authority is **Ferðafélag Fljótsdalshéraðs** (p. 313), which runs the **Sigurðarskáli hut** (p. 313); again the wardens have the local lowdown. The huts are generally staffed from mid-June to August or mid-September; see "Where to Stay" below.

Tours

Most visitors to Askja and Kverkfjöll come on arranged tours, which makes sense, given the poor roads and other logistical hassles. However, except for the infrequent hiking trips led by Ferðafélag Akureyrar and Ferðafélag

Fljótsdalshéraðs, no tours allow extensive time for exploring. For Askja, Mývatn Tours is usually willing to leave you at the Drekagil hut and pick you up a day or two later. The SBA-Norðurleið tour allows 2 nights and a day at Kverkfjöll, but for more time, you'll need a 4WD vehicle.

Mývatn Tours (www.myvatntours.is; *©* **464-1920**) leads a classic 11- to 12-hour guided tour of Askja, starting from the Mývatn information kiosk, for 22,900kr adults. Departures are daily from July 1 to September 7. Bring lunch, warm clothes, strong shoes, and a bathing suit and towel. **Saga Travel** in Akureyri (www.sagatravel.is; *©* **659-8888**) offers roughly the same tour, but in Super Jeeps instead of a bus. The cost is 34,900kr for adults, half-price for children 12 and under, with a two-person minimum. Off-road driving is prohibited, however, so the much higher price is hard to justify. Departures are from June 15 until October 31 by advance request.

From early July 5 to August 15, **SBA-Norðurleið** (www.sba.is; *©* **550-0700**) offers a 3-day trip from Akureyri or Mývatn to Askja and Kverkfjöll, with 2 nights at Kverkfjöll's Sigurðarskáli hut. Departures are Mondays only, and the 58,500kr price (half-price for children ages 4–11) includes a guide but no food or accommodation. If you ask, they can at least reserve a bed for you at the hut.

Ferðafélag Fljótsdalshéraðs (www.fljotsdalsherad.is/ferdafelag; *©* **863-5813**; see p. 313) occasionally leads hiking trips in the Askja–Kverkfjöll region; tours can also be arranged with the staff.

For **aerial tours** of Askja and Kverkfjöll from Mývatn, see p. 207.

Exploring the Area
ROUTE F88 TO ASKJA

Starting from the Ring Road, the first 60km (37 miles) of Route F88 follow the western side of the Jökulsá á Fjöllum—the same river that forms the canyon in Jökulsárgljúfur farther downstream. Just south of the Ring Road and west of Route F88 is **Hrossaborg,** a 10,000-year-old crater formed when rising magma heated groundwater, prompting a massive explosion of steam and rock. Horses were once grazed well into the winter around the area; the horses would sometimes seek shelter in Hrossaborg during bad weather—hence the name, which means "Horse City." A small road leads from Route F88 right into Hrossaborg's natural amphitheater through a collapsed crater wall.

In roughly 40km (25 miles), Route F88 comes to its first major ford at the **Grafarlandaá river,** known for its pure-tasting water. Twenty kilometers (12 miles) farther south is **Herðubreiðarlindir,** a lovely highland oasis of moss, wildflowers, and springs gushing from beneath the lava rock to converge on the Lindaá River. **Herðubreið ★**, a majestic table mountain, looms 6km (3¾ miles) to the west. Herðubreiðarlindir has a mountain hut and summer warden, and is also the launch point for the Öskjuvegurinn ★, a memorable 5-day trek through some of Iceland's starkest wastelands. (Most of the route traverses the Ódáðahraun, which translates to "Lava Field of Evil Deeds.") The Öskjuvegurinn skirts Herðubreið, and reaches Askja's Drekagil hut on the

THE INTERIOR | Askja, Kverkfjöll & Eastern Interior Routes

second night. For further details on all the huts along the route, contact **Ferðafélag Akureyrar** (p. 313).

A 5-minute trail leads from Herðubreiðarlindir to the remains of a tiny underground shelter, where Fjalla-Eyvindur—Iceland's most legendary outlaw—reportedly survived the winter of 1774–75 on a diet of raw horsemeat and angelica roots. The original shelter collapsed and was renovated in 1922. A map available at the hut outlines other short, pleasant hikes in the Herðubreiðarlindir area.

In clear weather, the view of Herðubreið is awe-inspiring. Its name means "Broad Shoulders," and its flattened top is the result of eruptions beneath the crushing weight of a glacier. With its steep screes and vertical cliff faces, Herðubreið is a very challenging and somewhat dangerous climb. If you do make the attempt, consult the warden at Herðubreiðarlindir first, and allow 12 hours for the round-trip.

ASKJA ★★

In Iceland's recorded history, no cataclysm produced more ash than the 1875 volcanic eruption at Askja, which means "caldera" in Icelandic. The ash blanketed 10,000sq. km (3,861 sq. miles) of land, killing livestock and forcing hundreds of Icelandic farmers to emigrate to North America. Askja—designated a stratovolcano because of its layers of lava from periodic eruptions—erupted most recently in 1961, but the current topography took form in 1875. Increased seismic activity since 2010 has many speculating on the next eruption.

Askja is also Iceland's most dramatic illustration of a subsidence cauldron, formed when underground passageways of molten rock empty and collapse, leaving an enormous bowl in the middle of the volcanic edifice. Askja's collapsed heart, dominated by **Öskjuvatn Lake,** is 4.5km (3 miles) wide and still sinking. Öskjuvatn is Iceland's deepest lake, at 220m (722 ft.).

The mountain hut closest to Askja is at **Drekagil gorge,** 33km (21 miles) from Herðubreiðarlindir. From Drekagil, Route F894 extends 8km (5 miles) to **Vikraborgir,** a crater row formed during the 1961 eruption. Tour buses park at Vikraborgir for the easy 35-minute walk south to **Víti ★,** a lake-filled crater formed in 1875 and separated from Öskjuvatn by a narrow ridge. (*Víti*, by the way, means "Hell.") The Icelanders are usually the least hesitant to scoot down Víti's steep walls and plunge into the warm, opaque, eggy-smelling water, which reaches a depth of 60m (197 ft.). The water temperature ranges from 72°F to 86°F (22°C–30°C)—a bit tepid at times, but it's warmer if you swim out to the middle. You can also dig your toes into the hot mud on the lake floor. Trails proceeding from Víti around Öskjuvatn are difficult, dangerous, and often blocked by signs prohibiting access, so check with the warden at Drekagil before setting out.

A longer, more suspenseful approach to Víti starts at the Drekagil hut and proceeds through Dyngjufjöll, bypassing Vikraborgir. Consult the warden on the status of the trail, and allow 3 hours each way. A stroll up the Drekagil gorge is also worthwhile.

KVERKFJÖLL ★★

The Kverkfjöll volcanic system—which reaches 1,929m (6,329 ft.) in height and extends 10km (6 miles) on a south–north axis—is mostly buried beneath Vatnajökull, but its northern rim protrudes from the glacier's edge. With so much geothermal activity churning beneath Europe's largest mass of ice, Kverkfjöll is usually seen as a collision of natural extremes. Yet the most lasting impressions are of its austere and solemn beauty: the hypnotic pattern inside an ice cave, perhaps, or a view over reddish-black wastes with the barest etching of pale gray lichen.

> ### Hiking Tips
>
> The most common tourist mistake? Wearing sneakers, which shred on lava trails and soak through in snow or mud. Also remember to bring a water bottle, because it can be difficult to find drinking water free of silt.

HIKING ROUTES   The wardens at Sigurðarskáli, the only mountain hut in the Kverkfjöll vicinity, sell hiking maps and dispense excellent advice.

From Sigurðarskáli, a well-marked, manageable trail leads up **Virkisfell ★** for fabulous views; allow at least 90 minutes for the round-trip. From the mountain, the trail continues past several volcanic fissures to **Hveragil ★**, a river gorge and oasis of vegetation nurtured by hot springs, a wonderful natural bathing pool fed by a waterfall. Hveragil is 12km (7½ miles) from Sigurðarskáli, and the round-trip hike takes 7 hours. A rough 4WD track extends to Hveragil from Route F903, but talk to a warden before braving it.

A road extends 4km (2½ miles) from the hut to the edge of the Kverkjökull glacial tongue; a more direct walking trail is only 3km (2 miles). From the end of the road, it's a 10-minute walk west to where a river emerges from a spectacular **ice cave** (Íshellir) **★★** at the edge of the glacier. The play of light on the sculpted hollows and undulating walls is utterly entrancing. Eerie crashing sounds emanate from deep within the cave, and venturing inside is very dangerous. The escaping river is warmer in winter, when hot springs are less diluted by glacial meltoff.

Each day in summer, a Sigurðarskáli warden leads a **day hike ★★** onto Kverkjökull. The maximum group size is 20, and slots often fill up; call the hut and reserve in advance. The price is low—just 6,000kr to 13,000kr, depending how long the hike is—and includes crampons, walking poles, and safety harnesses. In good weather, the hike lasts 8 to 10 hours and extends past the Langafönn slope to **Hveratagl ★**, an expanse of steaming springs, bubbling mud cauldrons, and ice caves along the glacier's margin. The hike may continue farther to **Gengissig,** a pretty lagoon next to a small mountain hut. For independent hikers, it's possible to spend the night here and continue to **Skarphéðinstindur,** Kverkfjöll's highest mountain; from the peak, the trail loops more directly back to Sigurðarskáli by a different route. All unguided hikes on the glacier are discouraged, but if you do go, be sure to tell the wardens where you're headed and stick to established trails.

Where to Stay

Mountain huts in the Askja–Kverkfjöll region are generally open from mid-June to mid-September. Expect costs to be around 7,500kr per person per night, with an extra charge for showers (usually around 500kr). The Þorsteins-skáli, Drekagil, and Sigurðarskáli huts all have kitchens with cookware and utensils. No food is sold at the huts, and you must bring your own sleeping bag. As usual, guests are packed into large rooms with minimal privacy. If you bring a tent, expect to pay around 1,800kr per person for use of the facilities. In July and August, advance reservations are strongly advised.

All mountain huts in the Askja area, including **Þorsteinsskáli** and **Drekagil,** are owned and operated by **Ferðafélag Akureyrar,** Strandgata 23, Akureyri (www.ffa.is; ✆ **462-2720**). The wardens at Þorsteinsskáli (✆ **822-5191**) and Drekagil (✆ **822-5190**) can be reached directly, but reservations are made with Ferðafélag Akureyrar by e-mail (ffa@ffa.is).

The **Sigurðarskáli hut,** Route 902, at Kverkfjöll (✆ **863-9236**) sleeps up to 75 people and is booked through **Ferðafélag Fljótsdalshéraðs** (www.fljotsdalsherad.is/ferdafelag; ✆ **863-5813**). The remote hut at Gengissig—simply known as **Kverkfjöll hut**—has no electricity or running water and sleeps six (or 12, more intimately). For reservations, contact the **Icelandic Glaciological Society** (skalar@jorfi.is; ✆ **893-0742**).

10

PLANNING YOUR TRIP

This chapter is designed to help you with practical matters in planning your trip to Iceland: when to go, how to get there, how to get around, how to prepare. Advance planning is especially important in high season (mid-June to August), because tourism is booming and services have trouble meeting demand.

WHEN TO GO

Iceland has a concentrated tourist season, peaking from mid-June until the end of August. Many Icelanders think the summer tourists don't know what they're missing. Iceland offers plenty to do in the other seasons, even winter, when prices are dramatically lower for airfares, car rentals, and places to stay. Icelanders are avid Christmas celebrators, and the *aurora borealis* is remarkably vivid in winter. Most off-season visitors use Reykjavík as a home base, and combine city culture and nightlife with activities such as horseback riding, snowmobiling, and visiting spas.

High Season

On the other hand, high season is high season for good reason. Most tours and adventure trips to Iceland's most renowned natural attractions end after September. Roads in the hinterlands are generally closed from October to mid-May, and some don't open until early July. Precipitation increases in September, peaking from October to February, and frequent storms and driving rain are enough to dissuade many would-be winter adventurers.

The tourist **high season** corresponds with holiday time for Icelanders, but things don't shut down the way they do in, say, France. Icelanders work longer hours than most Europeans, and students fill seasonal service jobs. Some cultural institutions (theater, symphony, and opera) take the summer off, while most museums outside Reykjavík are open *only* in summer. Arts and cultural festivals are also clustered in summer, except in Reykjavík, where they gravitate to the "shoulder" seasons (April–May and Sept–Oct). In timing your visit, consider also that the number of daylight hours can have unanticipated physical and emotional effects. In early

The items below are hardly a complete packing list, just a few suggestions:

Bathing Suit   Yes, even in winter. Icelanders love their geothermal pools and hot tubs year-round, and so should you.

Binoculars   These aren't just for bird nerds; you'll be glad to have them when whales, seals, dolphins, and foxes appear in the distance.

Compass/GPS Locational Device   The latter is better, especially because compasses can be thrown off by Iceland's magnetic minerals.

Earplugs   Icelanders can get pretty noisy late Friday and Saturday nights.

First Aid Kit   It's easy to scrape yourself on Iceland's endless lava rocks, so at the very least bring bandages and antibacterial ointment.

Flashlight   There's a good chance you'll visit a cave; bring a strong one.

Hair Conditioner   The mineral content of Iceland's geothermal water can be pretty rough on hair.

Hiking Shoes   Even the most sedate tours often involve walking over rough terrain. Water-resistant shoes with ankle support are best.

Insect Repellent   You'll need this if you plan on visiting the interior or the Mývatn area, especially in spring or early summer. A **head net** is even better.

Motion Sickness Pills   Longer ferry rides, as well as whale-watching and sea-angling trips, traverse stretches of open sea. Iceland's winding, bumpy roads can also cause motion sickness.

Raingear   Icelanders prefer **raincoats** to umbrellas, since the wind blows rain (and umbrellas) in all directions. It's not *always* windy though, and if you visit any bird cliffs in nesting season an **umbrella** is ideal to protect against attacks by Arctic terns. Bring **rainpants** since Iceland is pretty darn rainy.

Sleeping Bag   This could save you lots of money; see "Sleeping-Bag Accommodation" in "Tips on Accommodations," p. 329.

Sleeping Mask   The midnight sun can make sleeping difficult.

Sunglasses   The Icelandic terrain can produce lots of glare, and with the sun so low on the horizon, sunglasses are essential for driving.

Sunscreen   The sub-Arctic sun can cause sunburn even when the weather's cool, and the landscape offers few places to hide.

Towel   Renting one every time you go to a geothermal pool adds up.

Tupperware   Visitors to remote parts of Iceland often have to carry food.

Windbreaker or Windproof Shell   Iceland is windy...penetratingly windy.

summer there is never complete darkness and the sun stays low on the horizon, creating an ongoing play of light and shadow. Spring and fall daylight hours are roughly the same as in North America or Europe. Days in midwinter have only 4 or 5 hours of sunlight. These fluctuations are even more extreme in the northern part of the country.

Average Monthly High/Low Temperatures

	JAN	FEB	MAR	APR	MAY	JUNE	JULY	AUG	SEPT	OCT	NOV	DEC
TEMP (°F)	28/36	27/36	28/36	32/45	37/48	43/52	46/55	45/55	41/54	34/46	30/39	27/36
TEMP (°C)	-2/2	-3/2	-2/2	0/7	3/9	6/11	8/13	7/13	5/12	1/8	-1/4	-3/2

Off-Season

Tourists arrive en masse in June and disappear just as abruptly in early September—so it's no wonder Icelanders compare them to flocks of migrating birds. More and more visitors are coming in the off-season, however, particularly for short vacations in Reykjavík. Nightlife and spas are major draws, and winter adventure travel—particularly backcountry skiing, glacier snowmobiling, and 4WD touring—is also catching on. With fewer tourists around, locals can be especially hospitable and welcoming. Prices are dramatically lower for airfares, hotels, and car rentals, but don't expect major price breaks from mid-December to mid-January.

Most museums and many restaurants outside Reykjavík shut down in the off-season, while some Reykjavík cultural institutions—notably the Icelandic Opera, headquartered at the world's northernmost opera house—are open *only* off-season. With fewer tours to choose from, visitors usually depend on rental cars to get around. Most major roads are plowed all year, including all of the Ring Road (Route 1). Winter driving conditions can be hazardous, however, and in the dead of winter some villages can be completely cut off for days at a time. Most mountain roads and interior routes are impassable in the off-season, except in specially adapted "Super Jeeps."

Icelandic winters are surprisingly moderate, but they have only 4 to 6 hours of daylight. Late winter has more sunlight than early winter, with a corresponding increase in arranged tours. From September until March the night is dark enough to see the *aurora borealis,* the startling electromagnetic phenomenon in which shafts and swirls of green (and sometimes orange or blue) light spread across the sky. Of course, depending on the weather, some off-season visitors may see only clouds.

The shoulder seasons—April to May and September to October—can be wonderful times to visit, though some destinations are inaccessible. A good general strategy is to shoot for the outlying weeks of the high season for each destination.

OUTDOOR ACTIVITIES

Many outdoor activities can be enjoyed in the off-season. Of particular interest are aerial tours, dog sledding, fishing, glacier tours, hiking, horseback riding, jeep tours, pools and spas, and skiing and ski touring. Icelanders even like to golf on snow-covered courses, using bright orange balls.

REYKJAVÍK & NEARBY

Reykjavík remains equally vibrant year-round—the weather has little bearing on its appeal. Cultural activities and nightlife show no signs of winter weariness, and Reykjavíkians still throng to their outdoor geothermal pools even if snow gathers in their hair. The capital is particularly lively and heartwarming during the Christmas season. Each weekend, starting in late November, the neighboring town of **Hafnarfjörður** hosts an elaborate **Christmas Village** with caroling choirs, trinket stalls, and costumed elves. On New Year's Eve,

If you've ever wanted to explore Green-land, your trip to Iceland could be an ideal opportunity. Iceland is Greenland's closest access point by plane, and you can even visit on a day tour. **Air Iceland** (www.airicelandconnect.com; ⓒ **570-3030**) flies year-round from Reykjavík to Greenland's east coast, and once or twice a week in summer to south or east Greenland.

many visitors shuttle to Reykjavík just to take part in the bacchanalian celebrations.

Day tours from the capital are less varied but hardly in short supply. The popular **Golden Circle** tour runs year-round, and two of its principal highlights—the **Strokkur geyser** and **Gullfoss waterfall**—are even more captivating in winter. Various companies also lead nightly **Northern Lights tours** in search of the *aurora borealis*. The **Blue Lagoon spa** in Reykjanes Peninsula is strange and magical in wintertime, with far fewer crowds.

OUTSIDE THE CAPITAL AREA

Compelling winter destinations outside Iceland's southwest corner are too numerous to list, but two regions deserve special mention: **West Iceland** and **Lake Mývatn–Krafla Caldera** in the north.

In the west, the wondrously varied scenery of **Snæfellsnes Peninsula** makes for a great road trip year-round, and **Hótel Búðir,** an idyllic getaway on the peninsula's south coast, is always open. **Ísafjörður,** the appealing **Westfjords** capital, is especially buzzing during its Easter Week music and ski festivals. Two marvelous country retreats in the Westfjords remain open all year: the **Heydalur Country Hotel,** along Ísafjarðardjúp Bay, and **Hótel Djúpavík,** on the entrancing **Strandir Coast.**

Akureyri, Iceland's northern capital, is alive and kicking in the off-season, with the country's best ski slope, **Hlíðarfjall,** close by. Many winter visitors fly to Akureyri, rent a car, and spend a couple of days surveying the myriad volcanic spectacles of **Mývatn** and **Krafla.** The geothermally heated lagoon of **Mývatn Nature Baths** remains open, and **Sel-Hótel Mývatn** arranges jeep and snowmobile excursions, horseback riding, and go-cart joyrides on the lake. The cross-country skiing is fabulous from February onward, and, in April and May, the lake twitches with bird-watchers ushering in the tourist season.

GETTING THERE

Virtually all international arrivals come through **Keflavík International Airport (KEF)** (www.isavia.is/en/keflavik-airport; ⓒ **425-6000**), about 50km (31 miles) southwest of Reykjavík. KEF is sometimes called "Leifur Eiríksson Air Terminal" or "Reykjavík Airport," even though Reykjavík has a small, domestic airport in the city proper, **Reykjavík City Airport**

Duty-Free Alcohol

Alcohol prices in the airport may seem high, but they're far lower than elsewhere in Iceland, so consider buying duty-free before you leave the airport. Icelandair prohibits alcohol from being transported in carry-on luggage, so if you're taking this airline and want to buy duty-free, wait until you arrive in Keflavík. Customs limits you to 1 liter of wine or 6 liters of beer, plus 1 liter of spirits. If you're not carrying spirits or beer, then you can bring in 2.5 liters (5⅓ pints) of wine.

(www.isavia.is/en/reykjavik-airport). Extensive renovations to Keflavík International were completed in 2007, and the airport sees nearly 9 million passengers each year. Arriving passengers must go through another **security check** before clearing Customs. The airport has a **tourist information** desk with brochures galore, but the staff cannot make hotel or tour reservations.

Until recently only Icelandair and WOW Air flew to Iceland, but many additional airlines have opened up routes. **Peak season** is June to August, plus the 2 weeks before Christmas and the 2 weeks after the New Year.

Icelandair (www.icelandair.com; ✆ **800/223-5500** U.S. and Canada) flies to Keflavík from 21 North American cities. Flights from North America are usually overnight, though from May to October daytime flights are available from New York and Boston a few times per week. Icelandair offers a good range of discount packages combining airfare, hotels, and sometimes tours. Midweek flights are often significantly cheaper. Fares between the U.S. and Europe can include a free stopover for up to 7 days in Iceland. All fares, except for some special offers, are discounted for children 11 and under.

With average prices that are considerably lower than Icelandair's, **Wow Air** (www.wowair.com; ✆ **1866/512-8364** in U.S. and Canada, 590-3000 in Iceland) is a growing force, flying out of nearly as many North American cities as Icelandair.

GETTING AROUND
By Car

Icelanders love their cars for good reason: Iceland has **no train transport,** and many of Iceland's most beautiful sights are far from populated areas. A private vehicle can be even more necessary during the "shoulder season" (Apr–May and Sept–Oct), when most buses and tours are not operating. Renting a car is costly when you take the price of gas into consideration, but it often stacks up well against air and bus travel, especially if you have three or four passengers. Reykjavík is easy to get around without a car, and parking there can be a nuisance, so many visitors only rent a car upon leaving the city.

Route 1, usually referred to as "The Ring Road," is 1,328km (825 miles) long and circles the entire island. Almost all of it is paved, and it's cleared all winter. Only about a third of Iceland's total road network is paved, however.

It's generally cheaper to rent a car before you arrive at the airport. If you rent in Reykjavík (as opposed to at the airport, which is over 48km/30 miles away), most agencies will deliver the car to your hotel (or deliver you to the car) and then pick up the car (or deliver you to your hotel) when you're done.

Most agencies offer a choice between limited and unlimited mileage plans. Expect to pay at least 5,000kr per day for a small car with unlimited mileage. For a 4WD vehicle, prices start around 18,000kr. If you pick up the vehicle in one location and drop it off in another, the drop-off fee is usually at least 6,000kr. Renting a car usually requires a credit card as a form of deposit.

The **major car-rental agencies** in **Reykjavík** include **Avis,** Reykjavík City Airport (www.avis.is; ✆ **591-4000**); **Holdur/Europcar,** Skeifan 9 and Reykjavík City Airport (www.holdur.is; ✆ **461-6000**); **Budget,** BSÍ bus terminal (✆ **562-6060**) and Reykjavík City Airport (www.budget.is; ✆ **551-7570**); and **Hertz,** Holtavegur 10 and Reykjavík City Airport (www.hertz.is; ✆ **562-6060**).

Although the majors will have more pickup and dropoff locations, and often better resources for dealing with breakdowns and mishaps, **local agencies** are generally reliable and slightly cheaper, and you're usually getting the same product. Consider taking the **Flybus airport shuttle** (www.re.is; ✆ **580-5400**) from the airport to Reykjavík, then renting from a local agency once you're ready to leave the city. Agencies in the Keflavík area can also meet you at the airport. Recommended local agencies that can meet you at Keflavík International Airport include **Geysir,** Blikavöllur 5 (www.geysir.is; ✆ **893-4455**); and **SS Car Rental,** Iðjustígur 1, Njarðvík (www.carrentalss.com; ✆ **421-2220**). Recommended local agencies that will deliver a car to your hotel in Reykjavík include ÁTAK Car Rental, Smiðjuvegur 1, Kópavogur (www.atak.is; ✆ **554-6040**), which carries automatics; **Sixt,** Keflavík (www.sixt.com; ✆ **540-2221**); and **SAD Cars** (www.sadcars.com; ✆ **577-6300**), which, believe it or not, gives new life to used cars (max 5 years old).

The travel agency **Touris** (Frostaskjól 105, Reykjavík; www.tour.is; ✆ **551-7196**) has good deals on packages combining 4WD rentals with lodging.

AGE LIMITS & LICENSES Generally you must be 21 to rent a regular car in Iceland and 23 to rent a 4WD vehicle, but company policies vary. No maximum age limit is in effect. All national drivers' licenses are recognized, so you do not need an international one.

INSURANCE Basic third-party liability insurance is included in car-rental rates. Cars usually come with a standard collision damage waiver but a high deductible; in other words, if you get into a scrape you are liable for, say, the first 195,500kr in damages, beyond which the insurance pays. For an extra cost—say, 2,500kr per day—you could bring the deductible down to 25,500kr on a standard car. This is often a good idea as cars face hazardous conditions.

Driving on **prohibited mountain roads** will void your insurance on regular cars. The letter "F" precedes the numbers of mountain roads on maps and road signs. Even with 4WD vehicles, insurance is often voided if you attempt to cross rivers. Standard insurance does not cover damage to the car from a collision with an animal, and you may have to compensate the animal's owner as well. Even for minor accidents, be sure to get a police report so your insurance will cover it. *Note:* Many agencies offer sand and ash insurance, which confuses nearly everyone. Freak sand storms with heavy winds, sometimes called ash storms, can blow dry earth onto vehicles and severely damage the paint job. They usually happen in the winter, occasionally in the spring or fall, and are limited primarily to the south of the country. If you're not going to the south, don't worry about it.

AUTOMATIC VS. MANUAL TRANSMISSION   Even the major Icelandic car-rental companies have very few cars with automatic transmissions. They must be reserved in advance, and usually cost about 10% more.

2WD VS. 4WD   Many of Iceland's most beautiful landscapes are accessible only to 4WD vehicles, so if you're in a regular car, be prepared for serious envy as you watch the 4WD vehicles turn off the Ring Road into the great unknown. All the major agencies rent 4WD vehicles and can provide you with ropes, shovels, fuel cans, and GPS navigational systems. On the other hand, the vast majority of roads are accessible to regular cars, and for the more difficult traverses, you can take buses or sign up for 4WD tours. This saves money on fuel, and the environment will thank you.

CAMPERS   Icelanders often travel in campers, and the concept of a "portable hotel" holds great appeal in a country with so much open space and so many accessible campgrounds. As hotel prices continue to rise, it is becoming an increasingly popular option for traveling around the country. Some recommended agencies, all of which have a wide range of vehicles, include **Happy Campers** (https://happycampers.is), **KúKú Campers** (www.kukucampers.is), and **Go Campers** (www.gocampers.is).

DRIVING LAWS   Icelanders drive on the right side of the road. Unless otherwise marked, speed limits are 30kmph (18 1/2 mph) in residential areas, 50kmph (31 mph) in towns, 80kmph (50 mph) on unpaved roads, and 90kmph (56 mph) on paved roads. No right turns are allowed at red lights. In rotaries (aka roundabouts), right of way goes to the driver in the inside lane. Headlights must always be on.

Seat belts are mandatory in both front and back seats, and children under 6 must be secured in a car seat designed for their size and weight; these are usually available for rent, but you may want to bring your own. No one less than 140cm (4ft. 7in.) tall, weighing less than 40kg (88lb.), or under the age of 12 is allowed to ride in a front seat equipped with an airbag. Talking on phones is prohibited unless you have a hands-free system. Many intersections in the capital have automatic cameras to catch traffic violators.

The blood alcohol limit is extremely strict at .05%, so getting behind the wheel after just one drink could make you guilty of a crime. Drivers stopped under suspicion for drunk driving are usually given a "balloon" or breathalyzer test, which cannot be refused.

To protect the fragile sub-Arctic vegetation, all off-road driving is strictly prohibited, except on some beaches.

DRIVING SAFETY Iceland is not for Sunday drivers. Weather conditions are erratic; roads are winding and narrow, with no guardrails and many blind spots; and most routes are unpaved. We cannot stress enough how important it is not to speed; the majority of fatal car accidents in Iceland involve travelers unfamiliar with the country's driving hazards.

Before you set out, ask your car rental agency about potentially difficult road and weather conditions, especially in the off-season. For road conditions, Icelanders rely heavily on information continually updated by the **Public Roads Administration** at ✆ **354-1777** (May–Oct 8am–4pm; Nov–Apr 8am–5pm) or www.vegag.is. For weather, contact the **Icelandic Meteorological Office** (www.vedur.is; ✆ **902-0600,** press "1" for English).

Most roads are steeply sided and do not have shoulders—two seconds of inattention and you could topple off the road into great danger. Many road signs indicate dangers ahead, but few specify how much to reduce your speed, so always be on the safe side. Slow down whenever pavement transitions to gravel; tourists often skid off **gravel roads,** unaware of how poor traction can be on loose dirt and stones. Flying stones launched by oncoming traffic are another hazard on gravel roads, often cracking car windows; slow down and move to the side, especially if a larger vehicle is approaching. For traction, it's often safer to slow down by lowering the gears rather than using the brakes.

Most **bridges** in Iceland are single lane—signposted *Einbreið brú*—and the first car to reach it has right of way.

Always bring sunglasses in the car with you. **Glare** is a common hazard, and the sub-Arctic sun is usually low on the horizon.

Be on the lookout for **sheep** on the road, particularly when a lamb is on one side and its mother is on the other.

MOUNTAIN ROADS & FORDING RIVERS Do *not* attempt highland interior routes in a 2WD car. Roads that require 4WD vehicles are indicated by the letter "ꜰ" on road signs and maps. The safest procedure on these roads is to travel with other cars. Always carry repair kits and emergency supplies, and on particularly remote routes, inform someone of your travel plans before setting out. If you don't have a GPS navigation system, at least bring a compass.

Unbridged river crossings for 4WD vehicles are marked on maps with the letter "v." Water flow at these crossings can change dramatically and unpredictably from hour to hour. A sudden increase in flow can be caused not only by rain, but also by the sun melting glacial ice. Water levels are usually lower earlier in the day. Several drivers have drowned in river crossings; always seek advice if you have any doubts. Many drivers wait and watch other vehicles cross before making their own attempt. Sometimes it's necessary to check the water depth by walking into the current; bring sturdy rubber sandals, a life jacket, and a lifeline for this purpose. Before crossing, make sure the 4WD is engaged. Drive in first gear and use "low" drive if you have it. It sometimes helps to cross diagonally in the direction of the current.

OFF-SEASON   In winter the weather is particularly volatile and daylight hours are limited. Most roads are open by April or May, but some interior routes are impassable as late as early July. Make sure your vehicle has snow tires or chains, and always pack blankets, food, and water in case you get stranded.

FILLING STATIONS   Iceland has many long gaps between fuel stops, so keep your vehicle filled and know how far you can go before you have to refill the tank. Many pumps are automated and remain open 24 hours. Machines for swiping your credit or debit card usually expect you to know the card's PIN. The machines also ask you to input the maximum amount you want to spend, but you are only charged for what is pumped. **N1** and **Olís,** the companies with the most stations in Iceland, both sell prepaid cards. Some small-town stations indicated on maps are tiny operations, so you may want to call ahead to make sure they're open.

ROAD MAPS   The **Iceland Road Atlas** (Stöng Publishers), updated every 2 years, is a phenomenal compendium of maps and information and a must-have for any serious road trip. It's nearly impossible to find online or abroad, but it is available at most Iceland car-rental agencies and many fuel stops and bookstores. Each map is focused narrowly on short stretches of individual roads, so you may prefer a simpler road atlas that gives you the big picture; these are easy to find.

CARPOOLING   **Samferða** (www.samferda.net) effectively connects people looking to carpool on specific routes at specific times. Anyone receiving a ride is expected to share costs of fuel or car rental. The bulletin board at **Reykjavík City Hostel** (p. 74) is also popular with those looking to split costs.

By Bus

Iceland's bus system is reliable and punctual. Public buses link all major towns, and even some barren interior routes are covered in summer. (Icelandic buses are impressive machines, chugging right across rocky terrain and raging rivers.) Buses are up to European standards of comfort.

Several bus companies operate in Iceland, but all scheduled routes are coordinated by Iceland's main bus company, **BSÍ** (www.bsi.is; ✆ **562-1011;** daily 4:30am–midnight). Bus schedules are available online or at bus stations and tourist information offices across the country. The website **www.nat.is** is also great for bus timetables and bookings; click "Travel Guide," then "Transportation," then "Bus Schedules and Rental." Most long-distance bus routes run only in summer.

Buses on the Ring Road do not require reservations, and you can pay on board with cash or credit card. In small towns the bus stop is usually the main filling station. Coverage of the Ring Road is complete from June through August, but from September through May it extends only from Reykjavík to Akureyri in the north and to Höfn in the southeast.

OUTDOOR safety

Icelanders visiting the U.S. are amused by all the warning signs and guardrails. If Iceland tried to match these precautions, it would quickly be bankrupted. Always use care in Iceland's untamed outdoors. Thoroughly research the potential hazards of any journey, and talk to someone with local knowledge before setting out. Bring a first-aid kit to any remote destination.

Be prepared for Iceland's notoriously abrupt shifts in weather. For forecasts, check with the **Icelandic Meteorological Office** (www.vedur.is; (𝄞) **522-6000** and 902-0600). Keep in mind that the temperature usually drops about 1° for every 100m (328 ft.) of elevation. Even near the coastline in summer, night temperatures can drop below freezing. Always carry warm and waterproof clothing and footwear, even in summer. Bring a map and compass for longer walks or, ideally, a GPS unit. A cellphone is also useful for emergencies, though coverage is unlikely in remote areas.

ROCKS & FOOTING Rocks and rock faces in Iceland are often loose and crumbly. Hiking shoes with good ankle support are advised. Be careful not to loosen rocks that could tumble onto someone below you, and be aware of potential rock falls or avalanches. Take special care to have solid footing on mountaintops and cliff tops, where winds are strongest.

GEOTHERMAL AREAS & VOLCANOES In geothermal hotspots, most tourists know better than to stick their fingers in boiling mud pots, but other dangers are not so obvious. Sometimes unwary visitors step right through a thin crust of earth into boiling mud below, getting their feet stuck—and badly burned—in the mud. Lighter soil is usually the most dangerous. The crust looks solid and is not particularly hot, but underneath there may be a pocket of mud boiling its way upward. Stick to paths and boardwalks when provided, and always seek advice before you approach active

volcanoes. If you're visiting an active volcanic area you should be aware of the hazards and the evacuation procedures, clearly set out in the widely available brochure "Eruption Emergency Guidelines."

GLACIERS Even road-trippers who seldom stray from their cars are likely to encounter a glacier. Do not set off on a glacier without some experience or advice from a local expert. Tours with professional guides are the safest route. Glaciers can collapse without warning, and even a smooth surface can disguise deadly crevasses. If you walk onto a glacier despite the danger, follow other footprints or snowmobile tracks. Generally, the best time for glacier traverses is from mid-February to mid-July, with optimal conditions between March and May. Never venture into ice caves; even experienced guides seldom lead groups there. And beware of quicksand that can form from meltoff at the glacier's edge.

EMERGENCY SHELTERS The **Icelandic Association for Search and Rescue** (www.icesar.com; (𝄞) **570-5900**) maintains several bright orange emergency shelters in remote interior and coastline locations, and along some roads, often in high mountain passes. The shelters are identified on most maps and are stocked with food, fuel, and blankets. These are to be used *in emergencies only.* If you are forced to use something, make sure to sign for it so it can be replaced.

SEARCH & RESCUE Locals constantly encourage visitors to inform someone before venturing into risky areas alone. For most trips you can simply leave your name and itinerary with a local tourist information office or park warden. For more risky ventures, you should register at the Reykjavík office of the **Icelandic Association for Search and Rescue,** Skógarhlíð 14, Reykjavík (www.icesar.com; (𝄞) **570-5900**); local and online registration is in the works.

more economical. An enjoyable way to see Iceland is on **Reykjavík Excursions** (www.re.is; ℂ **580-5400**) bus passes, available online or at the BSÍ terminal in Reykjavík. For example, the **Iceland On Your Own** bus pass includes coverage on all routes, including through the interior, for 30,200kr.

By Plane

Air travel in Iceland is common, easy, cost-efficient, and often necessary, especially in winter. Booking online and in advance is likely to save you money. Some routes are very frequent (like Reykjavík to Akureyri, 10 flights per day in summer) and some far less so (Reykjavík to Gjögur, once per week).

Air Iceland (www.airiceland.is; ℂ **570-3030**) handles most domestic air travel, serving seven destinations inside Iceland (Reykjavík, Akureyri, Egilsstaðir, Ísafjörður, Grímsey, Þórshöfn, and Vopnafjörður) as well as the Faroe Islands and Greenland. Children 11 and under get 50% off on Air Iceland.

Eagle Air (www.eagleair.is; ℂ **562-4200**) connects Reykjavík to Westman Islands, Sauðárkrókur, Hornafjörður (Höfn), Bíldudalur, and Gjögur, and also offers sightseeing tours.

One-way prices from Reykjavík began at 16,200kr to the Westman Islands (25 min.), 11,500kr to Akureyri (45 min.), and 16,600kr to Egilsstaðir (1 hr.).

Note: Because of Iceland's high winds and unpredictable weather, you should always be prepared for delays and cancellations, especially in winter.

By Boat

Iceland's **ferry system** is often used by tourists. The only ferries that take cars are the *Baldur,* which connects Stykkishólmur on the Snæfellsnes peninsula to Brjánslækur in the Westfjords, and the *Herjólfur,* which connects Landeyjahöfn to the Westman Islands.

RESPONSIBLE TOURISM

Each time you take a flight or drive a car, carbon dioxide is released into the atmosphere. You can help neutralize the damage by purchasing "carbon offsets," from organizations such as **Carbonfund.org** (www.carbonfund.org) in the U.S., Iceland has its own reputable **Iceland Carbon Fund** (Kolviður; www.kolvidur.is); the website helps you calculate your damages and choose a tree-planting project or other remedy. Once in Iceland you can base your activities on hiking, biking, horseback riding, or other activities that do not consume fossil fuels.

Several Icelandic companies have earned certification from **Blue Flag** (www.blueflag.global), a Danish association that certifies beaches, marinas, whale-watching tours, and other businesses for sustainable oceanside development. **Nordic Eco Label** (www.nordic-ecolabel.org; ℂ **08/5555-2400**) certifies places to stay for adhering to strict environmental practices.

EarthCheck (www.earthcheck.org) is another important eco-certification label (formerly known as Green Globe). Several Icelandic tourist businesses

In addition to the resources for Iceland listed above, the following websites provide valuable wide-ranging information on sustainable travel. For a list of even more sustainable resources, as well as tips and explanations on how to travel greener, visit www.frommers.com/planning.

- **Responsible Travel** (www.responsible travel.com) is a great source of sustainable travel ideas; the site is run by a spokesperson for ethical tourism in the travel industry. **Sustainable Travel International** (www. sustainabletravel.org) promotes ethical tourism practices, and manages an extensive directory of sustainable properties and tour operators around the world.
- In Canada, **www.greenlivingonline. com** offers extensive content on how to travel sustainably.
- **Carbonfund** (www.carbonfund.org) and **TerraPass** (www.terrapass.com)

provide info on "carbon offsetting," outlining ways to offset the greenhouse gas emitted during flights.

- **Greenhotels** (www.greenhotels.com) recommends green-rated member hotels around the world that fulfill the company's stringent environmental requirements. **Environmentally Friendly Hotels** (www.environmentally friendlyhotels.com) offers more green accommodation ratings.
- For information on animal-friendly issues throughout the world, visit **Tread Lightly** (www.treadlightly.org). For information about the ethics of swimming with dolphins, visit the **Whale and Dolphin Conservation Society** (www.wdcs.org).
- **Volunteer International** (www. volunteerinternational.org) has a list of questions to help you determine the intentions and the nature of a volunteer program.

have received the Green Globe—as has *every* community on the Snæfellsnes Peninsula (p. 128).

Environmental issues often come up in conversation with Icelanders, so you may want to read up on the hot topics. Iceland has resumed whaling, and the subject often provokes emotional responses (p. 211). For information about the ethics of whaling, visit the **Whale and Dolphin Conservation Society** (www.icewhale.is). The website **www.savingiceland.org** has a pronounced radical slant but contains links to informative articles on environmental issues facing Iceland.

SPECIAL INTEREST TRIPS & TOURS

Special Interest & Educational Tours

Smithsonian Journeys (www.smithsonianjourneys.com; ✆ **877/338-8687**), affiliated with the Smithsonian Institution, hosts several educational trips focusing on geology, hydropower, and Icelandic culture.

Discover the World (www.discover-the-world.co.uk; ✆ **01737-214-250**) lead educational trips to Iceland for schools, with four scheduled itineraries focusing on different topics, such as geography and biology. **Ísafold Travel**

(www.isafoldtravel.is; ⓒ **544-8866**) has educational tours in geology and energy technology.

Icelandic Ancestry

The Snorri Program (www.snorri.is; ⓒ **551-0165**) provides an opportunity for young North Americans of Icelandic descent to explore their heritage. The main 6-week program (mid-June through July) is for ages 18 to 28, but older visitors can join a modified 2-week program in late August.

Vegetarian Travel

Icelandic diets are meat-heavy, but fresh vegetables have become more widely available in recent years, partly because of local production in geothermally heated greenhouses. And, of course, there's plenty of fish. Pasta dishes are common on menus. The few vegetarian restaurants and health-food stores in the country are concentrated in Reykjavík and Akureyri. **Happy Cow's Vegetarian Guide** (www.happycow.net) is a good resource.

Volunteer & Working Trips

Seeds Iceland (www.seeds.is; ⓒ **845-6178**) sets up volunteer 2-week "work camps" for projects ranging from environmental cleanups and trail marking to preparation for local cultural festivals.

WWOOF (www.wwoofinternational.org) connects travelers who want to stay and work on organic farms, usually from a few weeks to a few months. In return, farms offer food and accommodation. Several important Icelandic farms are plugged into the network, including the enchanting **Móðir Jörð,** just south of Egilsstaðir.

Go Abroad (www.goabroad.com) maintains an excellent database of volunteer vacation opportunities, with several options in Iceland.

Women's Tours

Canyon Calling (www.canyoncalling.com; ⓒ **928/282-0916**), based in Sedona, Arizona, leads a cost-conscious 8-day multi-activity trip for women in early July. Activities include sightseeing, hiking, rafting, whale-watching, and horseback riding.

Escorted General-Interest Tours

Many visitors reflexively dismiss tours and packages, but Iceland is a good place for even the most independent-minded to reconsider. Many of the most fascinating parts of the country are difficult to access on your own, and tour companies can save you lots of time in research and planning. Icelanders themselves often sign up with the same tour companies used by tourists.

MAJOR ICELANDIC OPERATORS

o **Icelandair** (www.icelandair.com; ⓒ **570-3030**) has all kinds of tours and packages, and its domestic counterpart **Air Iceland** (www.airiceland.is; ⓒ **570-3030**) offers day tours to Lake Mývatn, the Westfjords, and other locations. Icelandair offers the usual air/hotel packages and a good selection of outdoor adventure tours and special-interest tours, including a "Game of Thrones Iceland Tour."

- **Reykjavík Excursions** (www.re.is; ✆ **580-5400**), Iceland's largest tour company, has an enormous selection of tours to choose from; most but not all rely primarily on bus travel.
- **Grayline** (www.grayline.is; ✆ **540-1313**), Iceland's second-largest tour company, is equally prolific and reputable.
- **Iceland Travel** (www.icelandtravel.is; ✆ **585-4300**), one of Iceland's biggest travel agencies, rounds out the big three.
- **Nordic Adventure Travel** (www.nat.is; ✆ **898-0355**) is an excellent resource for outdoor adventure tours, often with online booking discounts.
- **Guðmundur Jónasson Travel** (www.gjtravel.is; ✆ **511-1515**), a long-established company, has an interesting range of cross-country adventures, and is especially good for tours that involve light hiking.
- **Nonni Travel** (www.nonnitravel.is; ✆ **461-1841**) is the leading tour operator in Akureyri, Iceland's "second city." Offerings include rafting, whale-watching, and other adventures, as well as the usual bus tours.
- **West Tours** (www.westtours.is; ✆ **456-5111**), a recommended company with a creative range of tours, is the leading operator in the Westfjords.

NORTH AMERICAN OPERATORS

- **Adventures Abroad** (www.adventures-abroad.com; ✆ **800/227-8747**) has a well-designed 12-day cultural tour of Iceland in August.
- **Borton Overseas** (www.bortonoverseas.com; ✆ **800/843-0602**), a Minneapolis-based specialist in Scandinavia, has a good range of Iceland offerings.
- **Butterfield & Robinson** (www.butterfield.com; ✆ **866/551-9090**), a prestigious upscale company, has a very well-designed 5-day winter tour, and a trip for families with children 8 and up.
- **Continental Journeys** (www.continentaljourneys.com; ✆ **800/601-4343**) is a good clearinghouse for a wide variety of Iceland tours, both escorted and independent, summer and winter. The affiliated **Great Canadian Travel Company** in Winnipeg (✆ **800/661-3830;** www.greatcanadian travel.com) has a good range of tours, including cruises and a 10-day "Iceland on a Budget" self-drive tour starting at $1,300, not including airfare.
- **Mountain Travel Sobek** (www.mtsobek.com; ✆ **888/831-7526**) offers 10-day hiking excursions in the Eastern fjords.
- **Nordic Saga Tours** (www.nordicsaga.com; ✆ **800/848-6449**), based in Edmonds, WA, has a carefully selected list of Iceland tours.
- **Odysseys Unlimited** (www.odysseys-unlimited.com; ✆ **888/370-6765**), a well-regarded company based in Newton, Massachusetts, has an excellent 11-day escorted tour crisscrossing the country for $4,997 and up, including airfare.

- **Scanam World Tours** (www.scanamtours.com; ✆ **800/545-2204**) is a prominent Scandinavian specialist based in Cranbury, New Jersey, with a good range of Iceland options.
- **Scantours** (www.scantours.com; ✆ **800/223-7226**), based in Los Angeles, has an enormous range of Iceland tours impressively laid out by type and departure date. The site is especially useful for scoping out off-season trips, spa trips, and cruise options.

TIPS ON ACCOMMODATIONS

Options

HOTELS

The word "hotel" generally signifies the most luxurious choice in town, but not all hotels are superior to or more expensive than guesthouses (see below), and not all "hotel" rooms even have private bathrooms. Expect to pay at least 10,000kr for the most basic hotel double with a private bathroom, 8,000kr for one without a private bathroom, or 20,000kr for an average business-style room.

International chains have few footholds in Iceland. Icelandic chains are more common. **Icelandair Hotels** (www.icelandairhotels.com; ✆ **444-4000**) has nine three- and four-star hotels around the country. Its subsidiary **Edda Hotels** (www.hoteledda.is; ✆ **444-4000**) has eight summer-only hotels, mostly in student housing; **Hotels of Iceland** (www.hotelsoficeland.is; ✆ **514-8000**) has 17 hotels ranging from one to four stars; and **Kea Hotels** (www.keahotels.is; ✆ **460-2000**) has 11 two- to four-star hotels.

GUESTHOUSES

Gistiheimilið (guesthouses) are a time-honored Scandinavian institution closely related to the bed-and-breakfast. Rooms, usually in private houses, are most often cheaper than hotels and range in quality from the equivalent of a two-star hotel to a hostel. Private bathrooms are rare, but most guesthouses are likely to have cooking facilities, sleeping-bag accommodation (see below), or a family-size apartment fitting four to six people. Because Icelanders have a highly developed sense of personal privacy, the proprietors often live in a separate house. Standards of cleanliness are usually very high.

Prices vary; a double with a shared bathroom ranges from 6,000kr to 25,000kr. About half of Icelandic guesthouses include breakfast in the room price, and the rest usually offer breakfast for an extra 1,200kr to 1,800kr or so per person.

CABINS

Small timber cabins for visitors are sprouting up all over Iceland, often in rural areas and usually in conjunction with an existing hotel or guesthouse. Some visitors seek them out for their comparative privacy, quiet, and convenience. The cabins are often designed for family groups of around four, with

THE case FOR HOSTELS

Iceland's dozens of youth hostels are hardly the exclusive domain of young backpackers. All have good basic standards of service and cleanliness. Some are almost indistinguishable from guesthouses or farm stays. Some offer doubles, though most rooms sleep three to six; private bathrooms are rare. All hostels give you the option of sleeping-bag accommodation or sheet rental and have guest kitchens; some offer meals and self-service laundry. In some remote destinations, hostels may be your only option for lodging and dining, and an excellent source of tourist information.

All youth hostels in Iceland can be booked through one convenient **central office** (www.hostel.is; ✆ **575-6700**). The website includes good deals on adventure tours and a popular car-rental package with hostel vouchers. Hostels tend to fill up even faster than hotels and guesthouses in high season, so plan ahead. Many hostels close in winter. Children ages 5 to 12 usually stay for half-price.

A **Youth Hostelling International membership (www.hihostels.com)**, which gives you a 20% discount on rates, can be purchased before you leave home.

private bathrooms and cooking facilities. Prices are comparable to regular doubles.

FARM HOLIDAYS

Staying at farmhouses is the classic Icelandic way to travel. Every farm has its own road sign, and farm names are often unchanged from the Age of Settlement.

A farm stay is simply a guesthouse in farm surroundings; comforts are similar to those of a European bed-and-breakfast. **Hey Iceland** (www.hey iceland.is) lists more than 60 farm holidays.

SLEEPING-BAG ACCOMMODATION

For hardy visitors on a budget, the Icelandic custom of *svefnpoka gisting,* or "sleeping-bag accommodation," can feel like a gift from the travel gods. In many guesthouses, farm stays, and even some hotels—though not in Reykjavík—visitors with their own sleeping-bags can get around 35% to 50% off on room rates. For the most part, the beds, rooms, and amenities are the same, though you'll rarely find a private bath; you're simply sparing the management the trouble of washing sheets.

Camping

Iceland's heavy winds and rains present a serious challenge for campers, but Iceland's many campsites make the country far more accessible to visitors of limited means, provided they have the appropriate equipment. Camping typically costs only 800kr to 1,600kr per person per night, and a few municipal campsites are free. Icelandic campsites are safe, conveniently located, and plentiful: Virtually every village has one. Some have washing machines, electricity, hot showers, and kitchens; others have only a cold-water tap and toilets. Most campsites are only open June through mid-September.

MONEY-SAVING tips on accommodations

- **Book rooms with access to a kitchen.** Restaurants are particularly expensive in Iceland, and you can save money by cooking for yourself.

- **Ask about apartments and "family rooms" if you are in a group of three or more.** These types of rooms are very common in Iceland, but not always well advertised.

- **Act noncommittal.** Many Icelandic guesthouses quote different prices to different people. Always ask for a price before committing, even if the guesthouse has a published rate. They could quote something lower to snag your business.

- **Be wary of packages and group tour rates.** Icelandic guesthouses often quote a *higher* rate to a travel agent than to an individual calling directly, especially outside of Reykjavík.

- **Ask about special rates or other discounts.** You may qualify for corporate, student, military, senior, frequent flier, trade union, or other discounts. Children's discounts are very common in Iceland.

- **Book online.** Internet-only discounts are very common in Iceland; many places have a standard discount every time you book online. Some supply rooms to Priceline, Hotwire, or Expedia at rates lower than the ones you can get through the hotel itself.

- **Remember the law of supply and demand.** You can save big on hotel rooms by touring in Iceland's off-season or shoulder seasons, when rates typically drop, even at luxury properties.

The **Camping Card** (www.campingcard.is) grants you (plus spouse and up to four children under the age of 16) up to 28 nights in more than 40 campsites across the country for the entire summer for only 15,500kr. The website has a list and map of participating sites. The card can be purchased online or in Iceland at Olis stations and post offices. **Nordic Adventure Travel** (www.nat.is) also has a helpful map of the sites. The free **directory** *Tjaldsvæði Íslands* is available at tourist information centers.

Reykjavík Center (www.reykjavikcenter.is) takes it up a notch by indicating availability of rooms or sleeping spaces within a specified time frame. Despite its name, it covers the whole country.

Landing the Best Room

Visitors often assume they want a room with lots of natural light. In the non-stop daylight of Iceland's early summer, however, you might want to request a room with less sun exposure and/or good blackout curtains.

If you're a light sleeper, ask for a quieter room away from vending or ice machines, elevators, restaurants, bars, and nightclubs. Icelanders have a well-earned reputation for late-night partying on Friday and Saturday nights.

Note: Top sheets are generally not even an option in Iceland. Also, filter coffeemakers are rare: coffee/tea-making facilities usually consist of an electric hot water kettle, instant coffee, and teabags.

ATMs ATMs are the most practical and reliable way to get cash at fair exchange rates. Upon arrival at Keflavík International Airport, you'll easily find ATMs and the currency exchange desk, both run by **Landsbanki Íslands,** which has fair exchange rates. ATMs are found in most villages around Iceland, though not all are accessible 24 hours. Icelandic ATMs generally accept all major debit, credit, and cash-only cards. **Cirrus** (www.mastercard. com; ☏ **800/424-7787**) and **PLUS** (www.visa.com; ☏ **800/843-7587**) cards are almost universally accepted in Icelandic ATMs.

Traveler's checks are still widely accepted in Iceland.

Tip: Avoid exchanging money at hotels, which tend to have high transaction fees.

Credit Cards Credit cards are safe, convenient, and generally offer good exchange rates, though many banks assess a 1% to 3% "foreign transaction fee" on all charges you incur abroad. You'll need a PIN to withdraw cash advances on your credit card. You will *not* need a PIN for most credit card purchases, but occasions may arise (particularly at automated fuel pumps).

Icelanders love credit and debit cards, and will commonly whip one out just to buy an ice cream. Most shops and tourist establishments accept credit cards; you can even charge a taxi ride. Visa and Master-Card are the most widely accepted, while American Express and Diner's Club are not nearly as useful. Electron, Maestro, and EDC debit cards are sometimes accepted at retail stores.

Customs:

Arriving in Iceland *All riding and angling gear must be disinfected,* including gloves, boots, and waders. You'll need proof of disinfection from an authorized vet, or the gear will be disinfected upon arrival at your expense. For more information, contact the **Agricultural Authority** (☏ **530-4800**).

Visitors at least 20 years of age may bring 1 liter (33.8 oz.) of wine or 6 liters (6 ½ qt.) of beer, plus 1 liter of spirits (33.8 oz.). If you're not carrying spirits or beer, you can bring in 2.5 liters (2½ qt.) of wine.

There are no limits on foreign currency.

You may bring up to 3kg of food into Iceland, but no raw eggs, raw meat, or milk.

All animals require a permit from the Agricultural Authority (above). Permits are hard to get, and the animal must undergo 4 weeks of quarantine, so traveling with pets is usually not an option.

Visitors 18 or older may bring up to 200 cigarettes or 250g (½ lb.) of tobacco, but no "moist snuff."

For complete listings of permitted items, visit the **Directorate of Customs** website (www.tollur.is).

Leaving Iceland Icelandic law forbids the export of birds, bird eggs, bird nests, eggshells, many rare minerals, all stalactites and stalagmites in caves, and 31 protected plant species. Objects of historical or archaeological interest may not be taken out of the country without special permission. **U.S. Citizens:** For specifics on what you can bring back, download *Know Before You Go* online at **www.cbp.gov** or contact the **U.S. Customs & Border Protection** (general inquiries: ☏ **1-877/CBP-5511**; from outside the U.S.: 703/526-4200). **Canadian Citizens:** For a clear summary of Canadian rules, pick up the booklet *I Declare,* issued by the **Canada Border Services Agency** (www. cbsa-asfc.gc.ca; ☏ **800/461-9999** in Canada, or 204/983-3500).

Disabled Travelers Iceland has more options and resources for visitors with disabilities than ever before, but you must call well in advance to secure your plans. Reykjavík and Akureyri are fairly accommodating, and new public buildings have to meet a strict code for wheelchair access. Accessible facilities are few and far between in the countryside, however, and tours often involve traversing long distances over rough ground or unpaved paths. (Iceland's top tourist attraction, the **Blue Lagoon** [p. 102], has good wheelchair access.)

Always make specific inquiries at hotels before booking. The website **www. whenwetravel.com** lists wheelchair-accessible hotels around the world; although listings for Iceland are not great at present, the situation will hopefully improve in the future.

Most museums and other tourist attractions offer reduced admission prices for travelers with disabilities.

All **airlines** flying to and from Iceland can accommodate visitors with disabilities, and Air Iceland, the main domestic airline, generally has no trouble with wheelchairs. **Buses** in Reykjavík are all wheelchair-accessible, and the largest tour operators each have a few wheelchair-accessible buses. Most **car ferries** are wheelchair-accessible.

Tour operator **Nordic Visitor** (Laugavegur 26, Reykjavík; www.iceland visitor.com; ✆ **511-2442**) has experience in putting together tours for visitors with disabilities.

Sjálfsbjörg, Hátun 12, Reykjavík (www.sjalfsbjorg.is; ✆ **550-0300;** Mon–Fri 8am–4pm), Iceland's association for people with disabilities, can answer questions or offer advice on your itinerary.

Doctors & Hospitals
Iceland has very high-quality medical care and more doctors per capita than any

other country on earth. Virtually all doctors speak English reasonably well. Reykjavík and larger towns have hospitals. Most smaller towns have at least one doctor and one pharmacy (apótek); if you need a doctor, ask at any local pharmacy or business. Most pharmacies are open 9am to 6pm, and over-the-counter medicines are accessible, if expensive. Iceland's barren interior is another story entirely, however: You could be hours from even the most rudimentary form of care.

Electricity   Icelandic electricity runs at 220 volts, 50 Hz AC, and electric sockets have two round plugs; you may need an "international" power adapter that regulates the current to prevent damage, particularly if you are bringing your laptop. Icelandic phone jacks are the same as in North America.

Emergencies   For emergencies in Iceland, dial ✆ **112.** If you get sick, you can usually just call or show up at the nearest hospital or health center.

Family Travel   Iceland is a wondrous and magical place no child will ever forget. Most tour companies welcome children (with the exception of the most rigorous trips) and charge 50% less for children 11 and under. Discounts are usually available for transportation and tourist attractions, and sometimes for places to stay as well. **Air Iceland,** the main domestic airline,

offers 50% off for children ages 2 to 11 when tickets are booked over the phone; even greater discounts may be available online.

Many hotels, guesthouses, and farms offer **"family rooms"** sleeping three to five people, sometimes with cooking facilities. Even youth hostels commonly have family rooms. Often a place has only one or two such rooms; the only way to be sure is to ask. The **Icelandic Farm Holidays** network of farm accommodations (www.farmholidays. is; ✆ **570-2700**) is usually cheaper than hotels and offers children a glimpse of Icelandic country life.

Iceland is a safe and personal enough country that parents may feel comfortable leaving their children with local babysitters. You can always ask the staff at your accommodation to recommend someone. The comprehensive **My Family Travels** (www. myfamilytravels.com) offers trip planning and has plentiful information on Iceland.

Remember: Iceland cannot possibly install guard ropes and warning signs at every location that poses danger to children, so mind them at all times.

Health   Icelanders are blessed with a very healthy environment. The use of geothermal and hydroelectric power has made pollution almost negligible. Some say Iceland has the purest tap water in the world, and even surface water is generally potable.

The incidence of insect-, water-, or food-borne infection is extremely low.

Sun/Elements The sun can be strong even at this northern latitude. Bring sunblock and lip balm and use sunglasses to protect from the glare. Iceland's extreme variations in daylight hours may also wreak havoc with your body clock, so bring an eye mask to help you sleep in summer. In the short days of winter, Icelanders combat depression by downing a shot of vitamin D–rich cod liver oil each morning.

Insects Iceland has a few bees and wasps, so bring a remedy if you have an allergy.

Motion Sickness Bring motion sickness pills if you plan on boating, long ferry rides, or bumpy road trips.

Holidays Icelanders celebrate 13 public holidays each year, and many shops, banks, and other businesses are closed on those days. It's best to check to make sure your destination will be open before setting out.

Holidays include New Year's Day (January 1); Easter weekend (including Maundy Thursday, Good Friday, and Easter Monday); the First Day of Summer (late April); Labour Day (May 1); Ascension Day (40 days after Easter); Whitmonday (7th Monday after Easter); Independence Day (June 17); Commerce Day (1st Monday in August); Christmas Eve and Christmas Day (Dec 24 and 25); and St. Stephens Day (Dec 26).

See "Calendar of Events" (p. 28) for other celebrations.

Insurance Even insured U.S. citizens may have to pay all medical costs upfront and be reimbursed later. Before leaving home, find out what your health insurance covers. To protect yourself, consider buying medical travel insurance.

Internet Access Most places to stay do not provide Internet terminals for guests, so your best and least expensive resource is often the public library, which usually charges around 200kr per hour. But Iceland is a good place to bring your laptop or tablet: Free Wi-Fi is widely available, and the crime rate is low. In Reykjavík and Akureyri you won't have trouble finding a cafe with free Wi-Fi, but in the rest of the country you'll have to ask around. You can usually find a creative solution, from sitting in a hotel lobby (you're unlikely to be thrown out) or loitering outside a library door when it's closed. Reykjavík's airport offers free unlimited Wi-Fi.

LGBT Travelers Iceland was much more homophobic in 1978, when the country's first gay organization was founded in Reykjavík. The small population and close-knit family networks made it difficult for gay men and lesbians to escape the disapproval of older generations. Today, same-sex marriages are legal, several prominent cultural figures are openly gay,

and the former Icelandic Prime Minister Jóhanna Sigurðardóttir made history in June 2010 by becoming the first head of state to marry her same-sex partner legally. Outside Reykjavík there isn't any gay scene to speak of, but the worst any gay couple is likely to encounter is a frown.

The main gay and lesbian group in Iceland is **Samtökin '78,** Laugavegur 3, 4th floor, Reykjavík (www.samtokin78.is; ✆ 552-7878), open Monday to Friday 1 to 5pm. The group holds open-house social gatherings at the **Rainbow Cafe** Mondays and Thursdays 8 to 11:30pm and Saturdays 9pm to 1am. **Q-Félag Stúdenta,** in the same office (www.queer.is; ✆ 848-5271), is the gay and lesbian student group at the University of Iceland. It welcomes e-mails from young visitors.

The best online schedule of gay events is found at **www.gayice.is**. The **Reykjavík Gay Pride Festival** (www.hinsegindagar.is/en) usually takes place the first week of August. For the gay and lesbian scene in Reykjavík, see "Nightlife," in chapter 4.

Money & Costs Iceland's monetary unit is the **krona** (sometimes abbreviated as "ISK," but written as "kr" in this book), plural **kronur.** Coins come in 1, 5, 10, 50, and 100 kronur denominations; bank notes are in denominations of 500kr, 1,000kr, 2,000kr, and 5,000kr. Frommer's lists exact prices in the local currency. However, rates fluctuate, so before departing consult a currency exchange website such as www.xe.com/ucc to check up-to-the-minute rates.

Passports & Visas All visitors to Iceland must carry a passport, valid at least 3 months beyond the return date. If your trip to Iceland is under 90 days, no visa is required for U.S. or Canadian passport holders.

Senior Travel Iceland is often thought of as a travel destination for rugged outdoorsy types, but age simply shouldn't factor into whether Iceland is the right destination. Senior tourists are anything but a rare sight throughout the country. When deciding whether to rent a car, though, know that driving in Iceland is hazardous and requires very good reflexes, coordination, and vigilance. Unless you are fully confident in your driving abilities, an arranged tour is the safer bet.

Senior discounts are usually available at museums and other tourist attractions. Note that the retirement age for Icelanders is 67. Visitors aged 65 or 66 are not normally entitled to discounts, though gatekeepers at various attractions may not be inclined to argue.

Many reliable agencies and associations target the 50-plus market. **Road Scholar** (formerly **Elderhostel;** www.roadscholar.org; ✆ **800/454-5768**), a not-for-profit company, arranges worldwide study and adventure for those age 55 and

over, with a few "intergenerational" trips. Road Scholar has eight first-rate tours to Iceland, from 9 to 24 days long. **ElderTreks** (www.eldertreks.com; ✆ **800/741-7956** or 416/558-5000 outside North America) offers an 11-day small-group Iceland tour, restricted to visitors ages 50 and older.

Smoking In 2007, smoking was banned in all bars, restaurants, cafes, hotels, and other accommodations. Smokers huddle outside, swathed in blankets under heat lamps.

Staying Connected

Telephone Calls to Iceland from overseas require the **country code prefix,** which is 354. All phone numbers within Iceland are seven digits. Numbers beginning with 6, 7, and 8 are reserved for cellphones. No calls are "long distance" within Iceland, and you don't need to dial the prefix.

Calling Iceland: Dial the international access code (011 from the U.S.; 00 from the U.K., Ireland, or New Zealand; or 0011 from Australia), then **354** and the seven-digit number.

International calls from Iceland: Dial 00, then the country code (U.S. or Canada 1), then the area code and number. Rates do not vary by time of day.

Directory assistance within Iceland: For numbers inside Iceland, dial ✆ **118; Icelandic phone books** are found beside public phones and list residents by their first name and profession.

Toll-free numbers: Icelandic numbers beginning with 800 are toll-free, but calling a U.S. 1-800 number from Iceland counts as an overseas call.

Public phones: Coin- and card-operated public phones are increasingly hard to find, but post offices are a good bet. Using a public phone for local calls is usually cheaper than calling from a hotel. Charges for calls within Iceland vary according to time of day. Phone cards are easily found at post offices, gas stations, and markets. The smallest denomination is 500kr. More and more public phones also accept credit cards. **International calling cards** are widely available at fuel stations and convenience stores across Iceland. These cards usually provide better rates than calls made from hotels or directly from public phones.

Rechargeable online phone cards: Ekit (www.ekit.com) offers rechargeable phone cards with good rates and a toll-free access number in Iceland (✆ **800-8700**). Rates to the U.S. and Canada are currently 28¢ per minute, plus a 59¢ service charge per successful call. Rates to the U.K. are 48p per minute depending where you call, plus a 38p service fee per successful call.

Mobile Phones Iceland has one of the world's highest per capita number of cellphones, and coverage is reliable in most populated areas. The "Ring Road" circling Iceland is entirely covered.

The three letters that define much of the world's wireless capabilities are GSM. GSM phones function with a removable plastic SIM card.

In the U.S., T-Mobile and AT&T Wireless use this quasi-universal system; in Canada, Rogers customers are GSM. Many phones, especially in the U.S., are not "multiband" (synonymous with "tri-band" or "quad-band") and will not work in Iceland. For U.S./Canadian visitors, even if your phone uses GSM, and you have a multiband phone (such as many Sony Ericsson or Samsung models), the company you're contracted to has probably "locked" your phone. In this case, you cannot simply buy an Icelandic SIM card, insert it into your phone, and start making calls.

Those with **multiband phones** can call their wireless operator and ask for **"international roaming"** to be activated on their existing account. This option is usually expensive. If you plan on using a cellphone in Iceland, you may well want to buy a **prepaid GSM** plan after you arrive.

Prepaid **GSM phone cards** are available from 2,000kr with four main Icelandic phone companies, **Vodafone** (www.vodafone. is; ☏ **1414** or 1800; outside Iceland ☏ **599-9000**), and **Nova** (www.nova.is; ☏ **519-1919**). All companies also offer GPRS and services for Internet access through your phone; almost all areas in Iceland with GSM also have GPRS. Branches of **Vodafone** (all locations: ☏ **599-9000**) in Reykjavík are at Kringlan Mall, Smáralind Mall, and Skútuvogur 2, which is a little closer to downtown but harder to get to by bus. **Nova** has branches in the major shopping malls.

When you sign up for a prepaid GSM plan in Iceland, the SIM card is typically free, and the lowest starting credit is 1,000kr. Typical rates within Iceland are 21kr per minute for the first minute, then 25% less after that, and 15kr for a text message, no matter what time of day or week. For the other companies, the price of a call drops as much as 50% within Iceland if you are calling another cellphone operated by the same company. There is also a "friends" option where you can choose a few numbers to call for free. Calls are all free between users of Nova SIM cards. GPRS costs are typically 20kr per 5 megabyte from Nova and slightly higher with other companies.

Tip: Be sure to ask for your voicemail and other prompts to be in English.

In Iceland, only the caller pays for the call, even for calls from overseas. This makes cellphones a great way for people from home to keep in touch with you. Currently the Nova rate for international calls from Iceland per minute to the U.S. is 32kr.

Your phone account can be continually restocked by buying prepaid cards called *Frelsi* (Freedom) at fuel stations and convenience stores around the country. To make sure you buy the right card, specify whether your cellphone uses Síminn or Vodafone, Nova, etc.

Satellite Phones "Satphones" can be helpful in the more remote parts of Iceland. Two providers serve the country: **Iridium** satellite phones get the best coverage, whereas **GlobalStar** phones get only marginal coverage with a weaker signal. Iceland has no satellite phone agency, but products can be rented or purchased from two companies.

You can rent satphones from **RoadPost** (www. roadpost.com; ☏ **888/290-1606**). Phone rental costs $8 per day.

Voice-Over Internet Protocol (VoIP) A broadband-based telephone service such as **Skype** (www.skype. com) allows you to make free international calls from your laptop or in an Internet cafe. The people you're calling may also need to be signed up, or there will be a small fee. Check the sites for details.

Student Travel Iceland is tough for students on a tight budget, but youth hostels and "sleeping-bag accommodation" at guesthouses and farms can be lifesavers.

For visitors ages 12 to 26, the **"Youth Restricted Fare" on Air Iceland** offers big savings if you're willing to fly standby and take your chances on availability. Multi-trip **bus passports** from **Sterna** also have student discounts. The **International Student Travel Confederation (ISTC)** website (www.isic.org) offers the **International Student Identity Card (ISIC)** and lists companies, attractions, and places to stay in Iceland that offer student discounts.

The card, which also provides students with basic health and life insurance and a 24-hour helpline, is valid for up to 18 months. You can apply for the card online or in person at **STA Travel** (www.statravel.com; ✆ **800/781-4040** in North America). If you're no longer a student but still under 26, STA's **International Youth Travel Card (IYTC)** entitles

you to some discounts. **Travel CUTS** (www.travel cuts.com; ✆ **800/592-2887**) offers similar services for both Canadians and U.S. residents.

Taxes Visitors are entitled to a refund on the **value-added tax (VAT,** or sales tax) for purchases of eligible goods. See p. 82 for more information.

Index

344

Photo Credits

Map List

Frommer's Iceland, 3rd Edition

Published by
FROMMER MEDIA LLC

ISBN 978-1-62887-442-6 (paper), 978-1-62887-443-3 (e-book)

Editorial Director: Pauline Frommer
Editor: Alexis Lipsitz Flippin
Production Editor: Kelly Dobbs Henthorne
Cartographer: Roberta Stockwell
Photo Editor: Meghan Lamb
Assistant Photo Editor: Phil Vinke

For information on our other products or services, see www.frommers.com.

Frommer Media LLC also publishes its books in a variety of electronic formats. Some content that appears in print may not be available in electronic formats.

Manufactured in United States of America

5   4   3   2   1

ABOUT THE AUTHOR

Nicholas Gill is a food and travel writer based in Brooklyn, New York, and Lima, Peru. He has spent the past decade exploring the boundaries and possibilities of cuisine in the Americas. He is a cofounder of Newworlder.com, and contributes to publications like *The New York Times*, *Wall Street Journal*, *Food Magazine*, *Bon Appétite*, *Saveur*, *New York Magazine*, and *Roads & Kingdoms*.

ABOUT THE FROMMER TRAVEL GUIDES

For most of the past 50 years, Frommer's has been the leading series of travel guides in North America, accounting for as many as 24% of all guidebooks sold. I think I know why.

Though we hope our books are entertaining, we nevertheless deal with travel in a serious fashion. Our guidebooks have never looked on such journeys as a mere recreation, but as a far more important human function, a time of learning and introspection, an essential part of a civilized life. We stress the culture, lifestyle, history, and beliefs of the destinations we cover, and urge our readers to seek out people and new ideas as the chief rewards of travel.

We have never shied from controversy. We have, from the beginning, encouraged our authors to be intensely judgmental, critical—both pro and con—in their comments, and wholly independent. Our only clients are our readers, and we have triggered the ire of countless prominent sorts, from a tourist newspaper we called "practically worthless" (it unsuccessfully sued us) to the many rip-offs we've condemned.

And because we believe that travel should be available to everyone regardless of their incomes, we have always been cost-conscious at every level of expenditure. Though we have broadened our recommendations beyond the budget category, we insist that every lodging we include be sensibly priced. We use every form of media to assist our readers, and are particularly proud of our feisty daily website, the award-winning Frommers.com.

I have high hopes for the future of Frommer's. May these guidebooks, in all the years ahead, continue to reflect the joy of travel and the freedom that travel represents. May they always pursue a cost-conscious path, so that people of all incomes can enjoy the rewards of travel. And may they create, for both the traveler and the persons among whom we travel, a community of friends, where all human beings live in harmony and peace.

Arthur Frommer